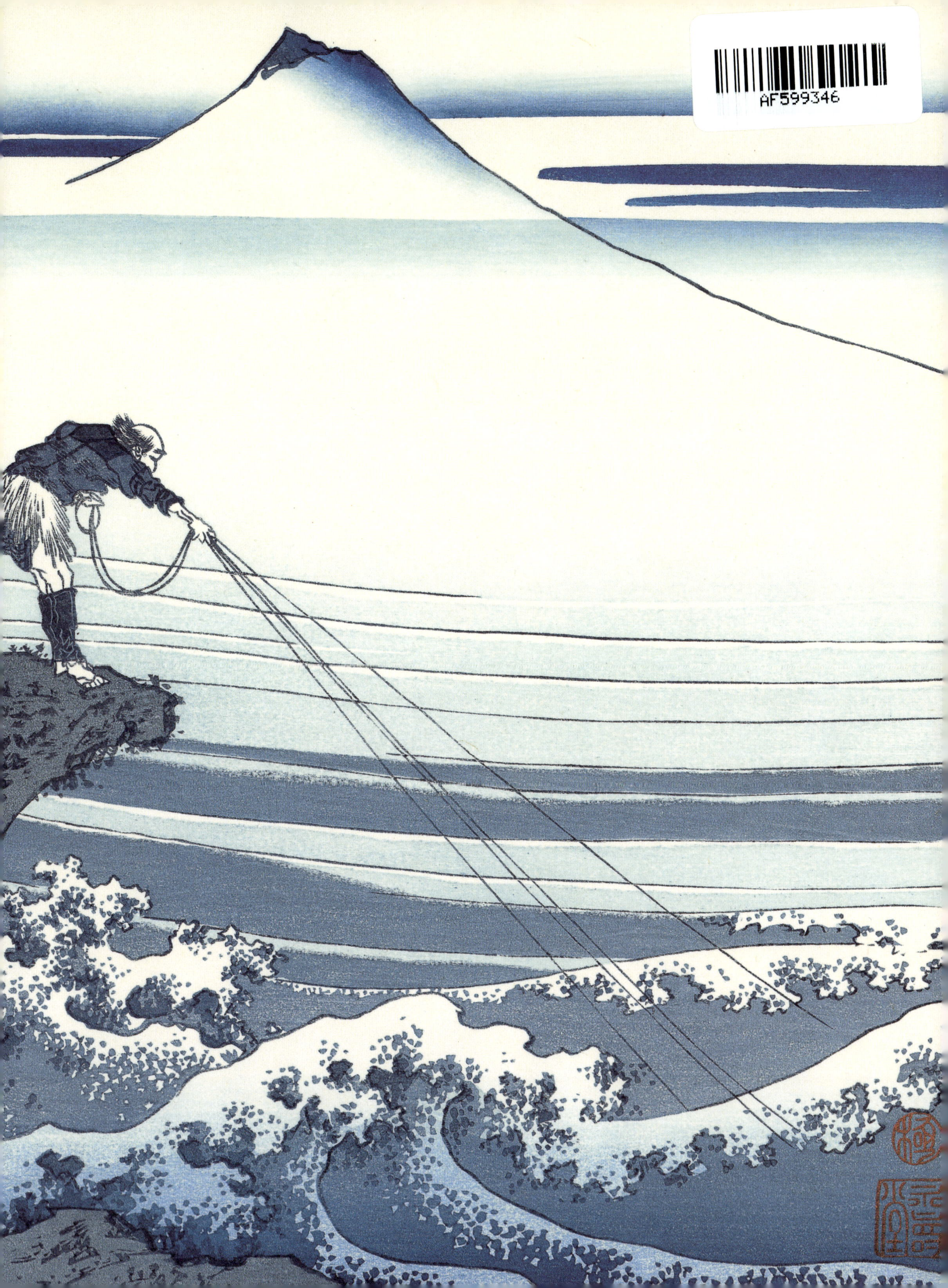

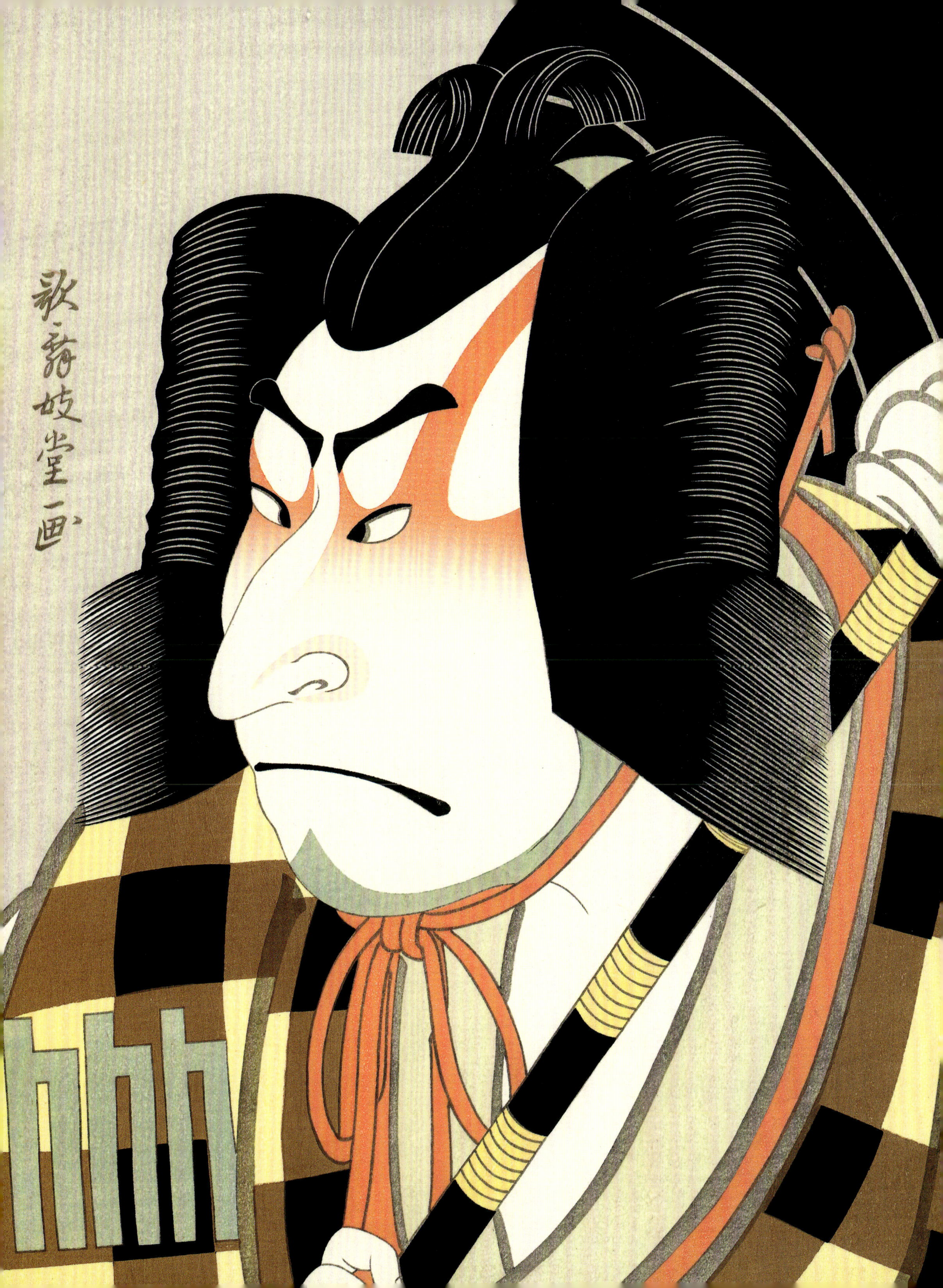
歌舞妓堂画

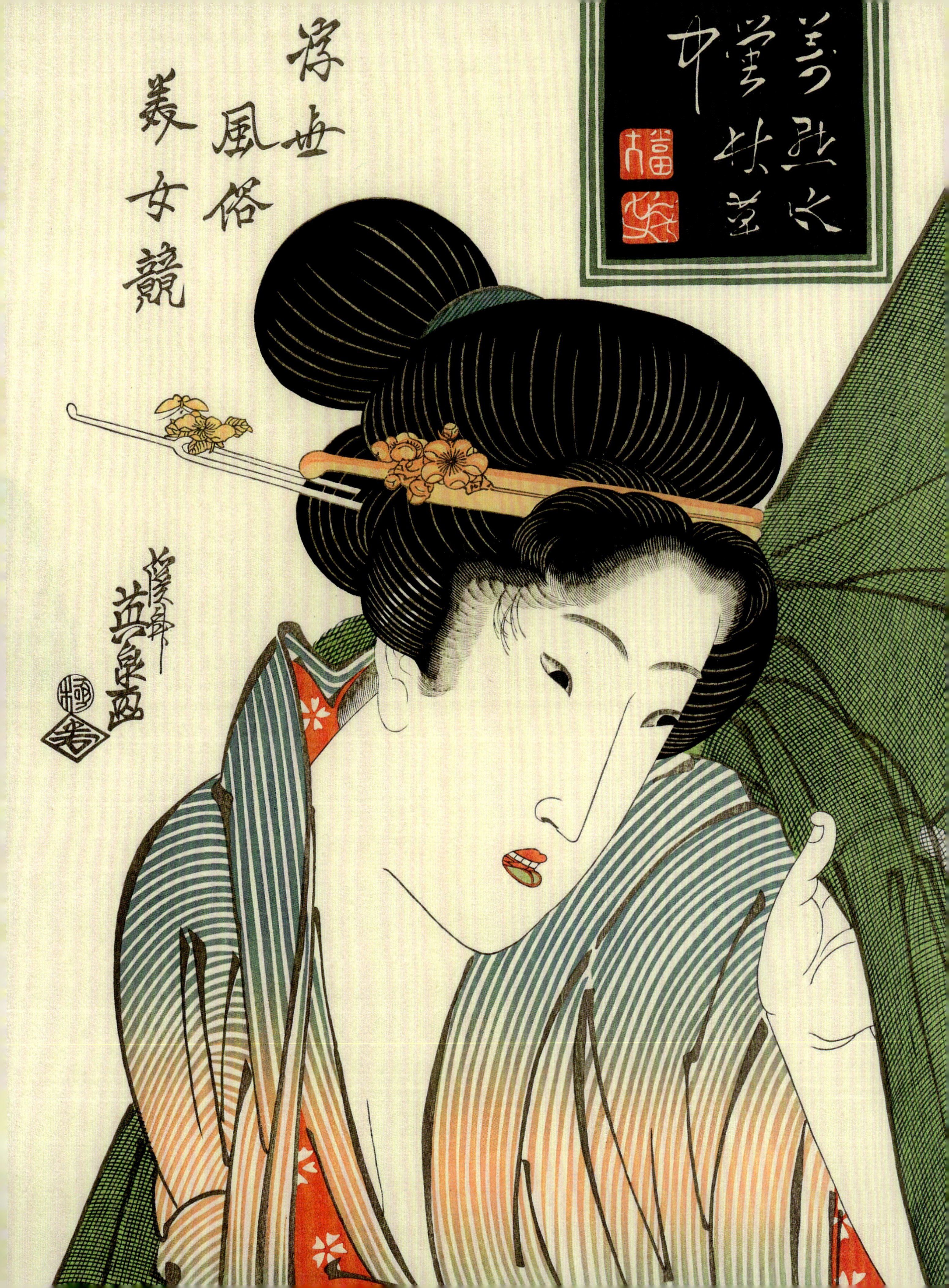
浮世風俗
美女競
渓斎
英泉画

Ukiyo-E

The Art of the Japanese Print

浮世絵

Frederick Harris

TUTTLE Publishing

Tokyo | Rutland, Vermont | Singapore

To Mun, with love forever

Published by Tuttle Publishing, an imprint of Periplus Editions (HK) Ltd.

www.tuttlepublishing.com

ISBN: 978-4-8053-1098-4
ISBN: 978-4-8053-2021-1 (for sale in Japan only)

AUTHOR'S NOTE
Names in capital letters in the captions refer to the names by which the print artists are best known, whether family names or art or professional names.

Distributed by
North America, Latin America & Europe
Tuttle Publishing
364 Innovation Drive
North Clarendon, VT 05759-9436 U.S.A.
Tel: 1 (802) 773-8930; Fax: 1 (802) 773-6993
info@tuttlepublishing.com; www.tuttlepublishing.com

Japan
Tuttle Publishing
Yaekari Building, 3rd Floor
5-4-12 Osaki, Shinagawa-ku
Tokyo 141 0032
Tel: (81) 3 5437-0171; Fax: (81) 3 5437-0755
sales@tuttle.co.jp; www.tuttle.co.jp

Asia Pacific
Berkeley Books Pte. Ltd.
3 Kallang Sector #04-01/02,
Singapore 349278
Tel: (65) 6280-1330; Fax: (65) 6280-6290
inquiries@periplus.com.sg; www.tuttlepublishing.com

GPSR representative
Matt Parsons
matt.parsons@upi2mbooks.hr
UPI-2M PLUS d.o.o., Medulićeva 20
10000 Zagreb, Croatia

28 27 26 25 10 9 8 7
Printed in China 2506CM

Front endpaper: HOKUSAI The Lone Fisherman at Kaji-kazawa (page 106).
Back endpaper: HIROSHIGE Night Snow at Kambara (page 112).
Page 1: ENKYO The Actor Nakamura Natkazo II (page 96).
Page 2: EISEN Woman Getting out of a Mosquito Net (page 80).
Pages 4–5: HOKUSAI Fishing Boats at Choshi (page 107).
Pages 6–7: KUNISADA Two Courtesans (page 58).

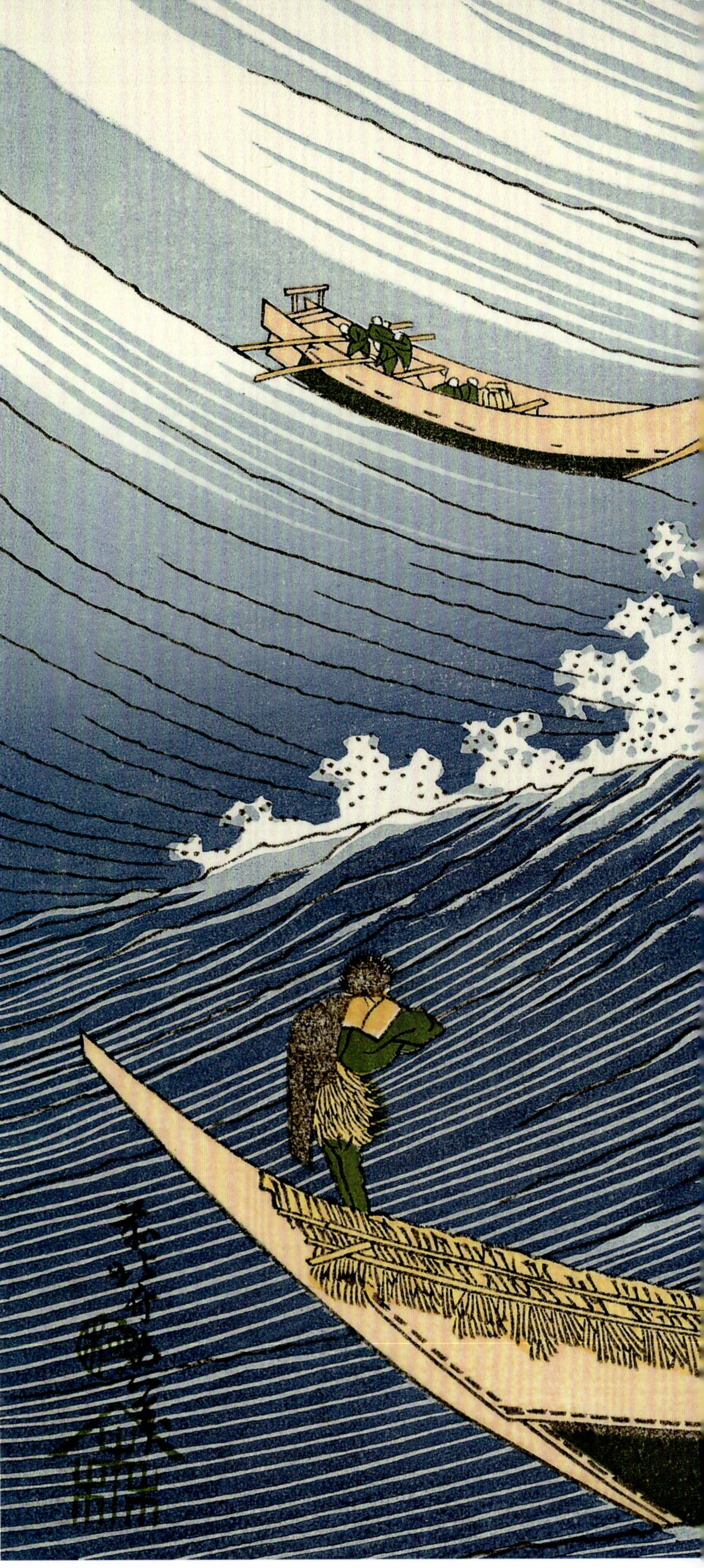

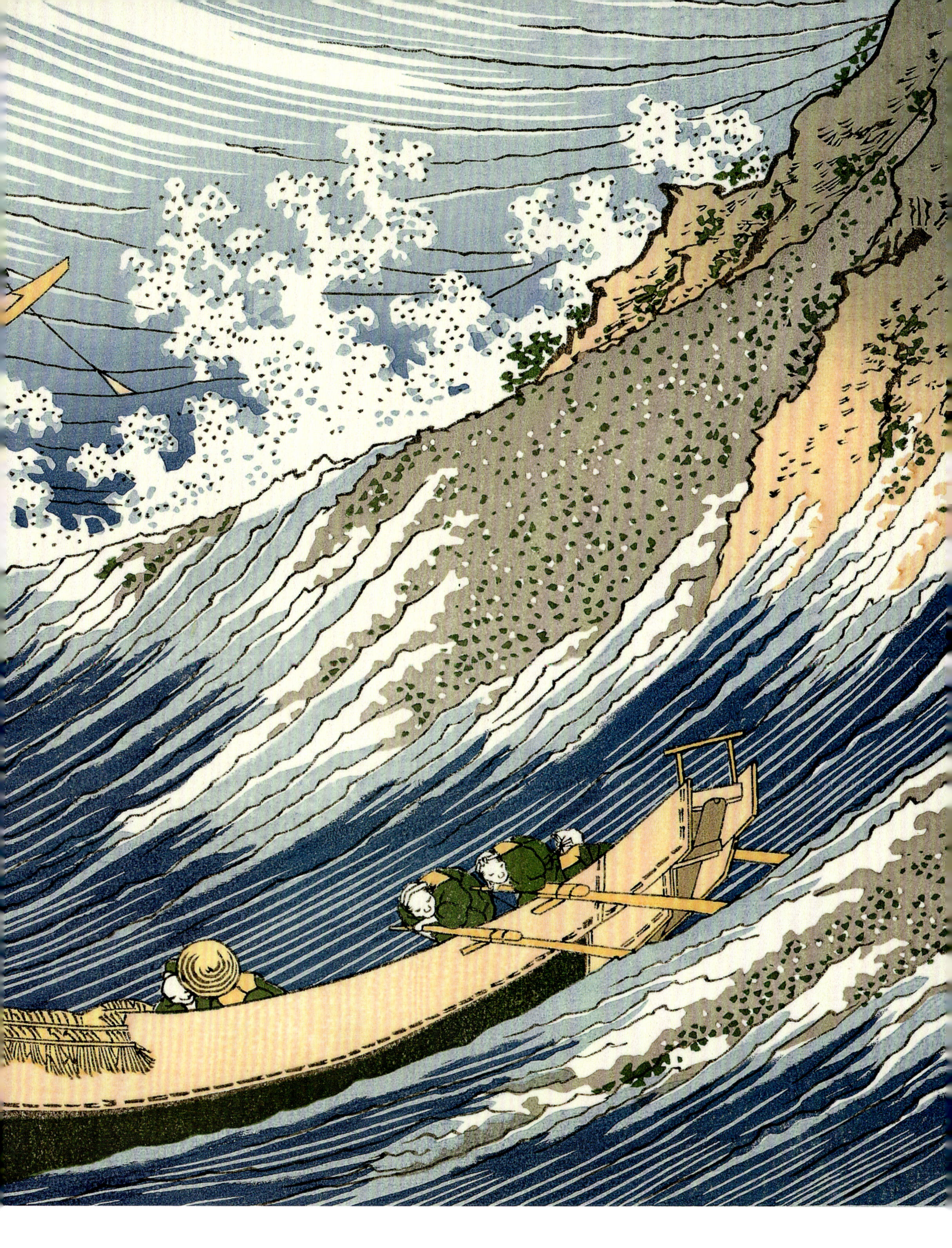

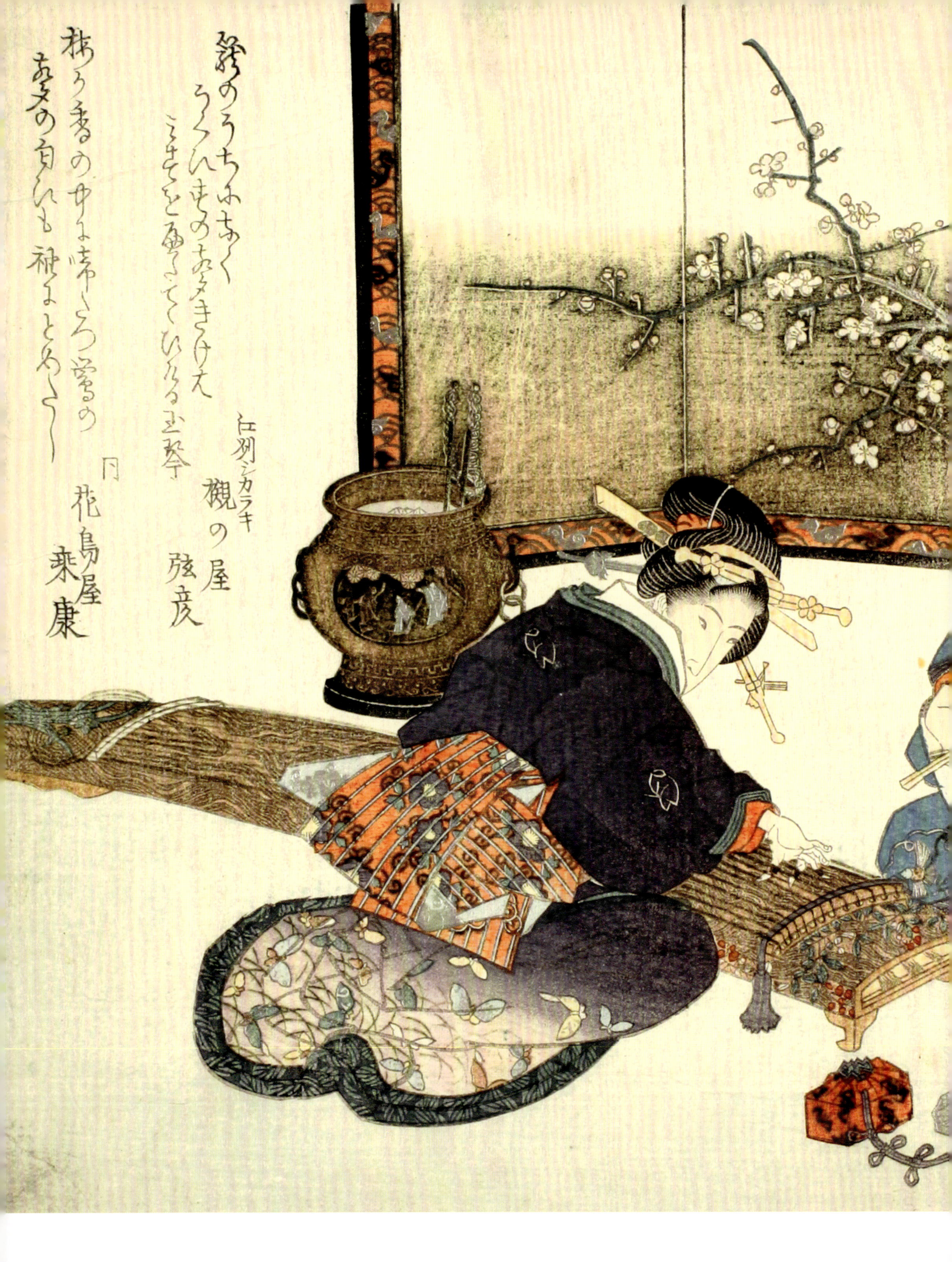

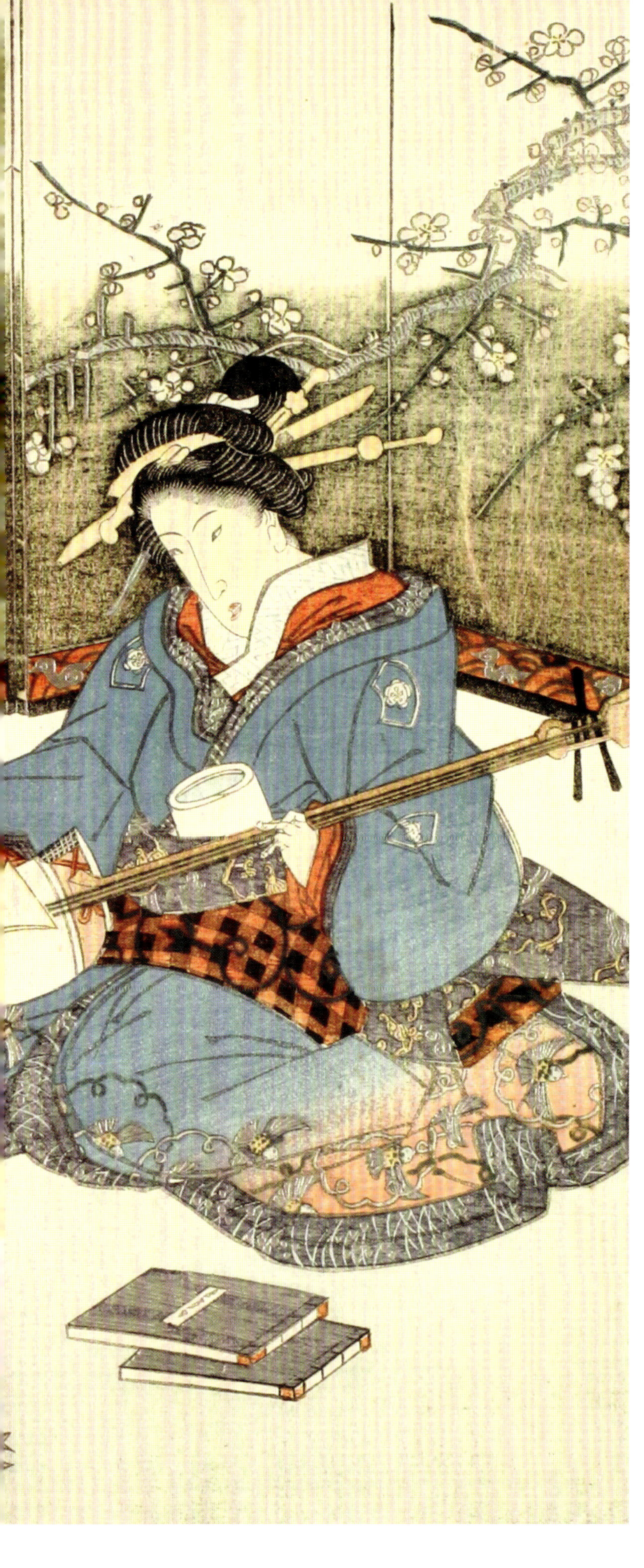

CONTENTS

Preface

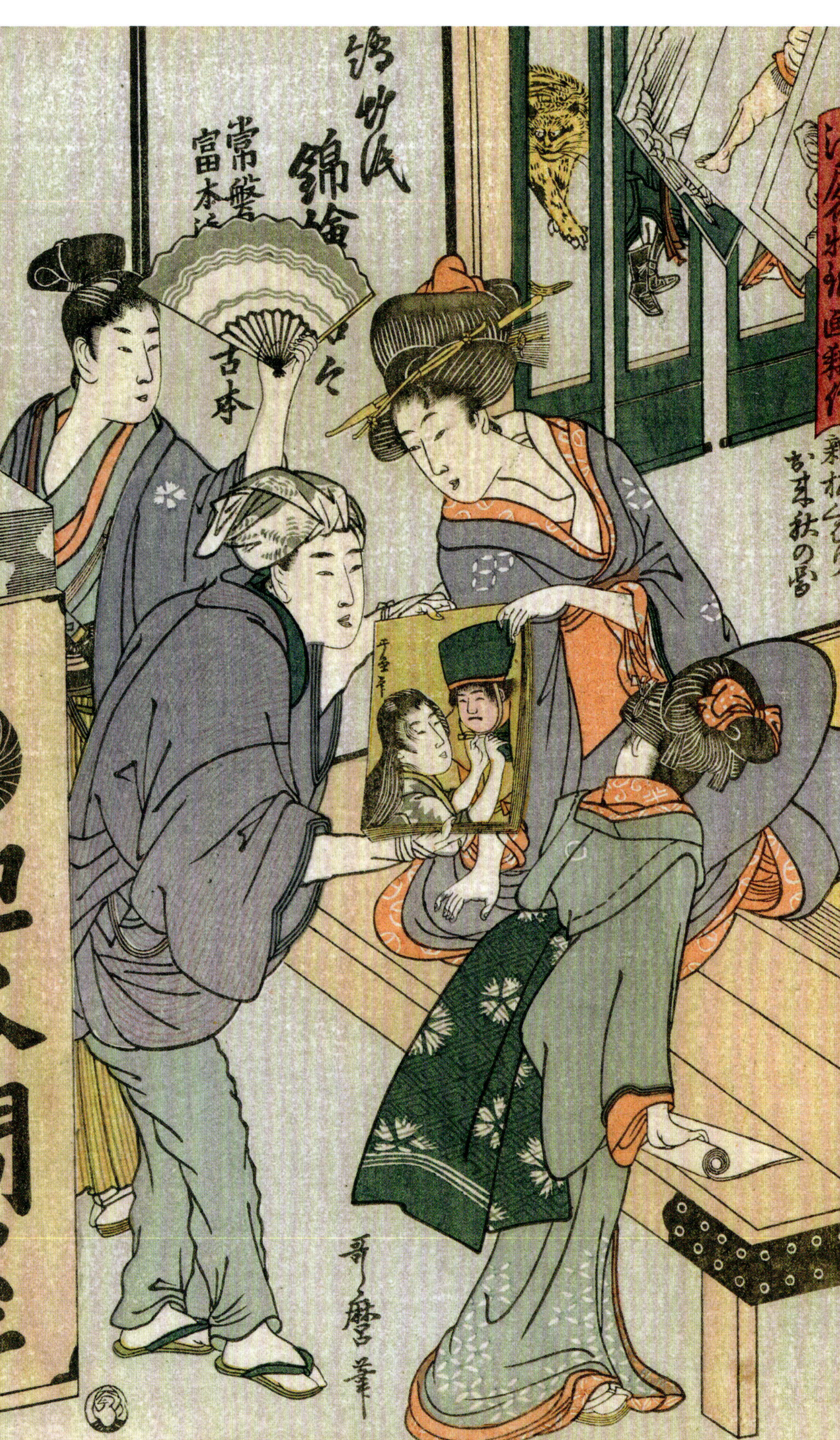

FIG. 1
Kitagawa UTAMARO
歌麿 (1754–1806)
Entrance to a Picture Dealer's Shop
江戸名物錦画耕作 (1790s)
Polychrome woodblock print (*nishiki-e*), 22 x 15 cm
Author's Collection

The focus of this print is a picture dealer showing a sheet of *ukiyo-e* to some female customers. Three scrolls hang on the wall in the rear of the shop. Other prints are suspended from the ceiling, one of which depicts a *sumo* wrestler, a popular subject at the time.

My aim in writing this book is to appeal to a new generation of art lovers and collectors in the world of *ukiyo-e* (literally "pictures of the floating world"), a genre of Japanese woodblock prints and paintings produced between the seventeenth and twentieth centuries depicting city life, in particular activities and scenes from the entertainment district of Edo, the old name for Tokyo, such as beautiful courtesans and *geisha*, popular actors and bulky *sumo* wrestlers, as well as tales from history and, later, scenes from nature.

As an artist who has lived in Japan for over fifty years, my interest in Japanese prints is primarily aesthetic. Of particular fascination to me is why and how the images and styles of the art form have changed between the mid-seventeenth century up to the early years of the twentieth century when prints by publishers came to an end and artists started to print their own work, the latter a subject beyond the scope of this book.

Another area of personal interest is the production of *ukiyo-e* and I will discuss the methods and materials employed in producing Japanese prints. Years ago I had the opportunity of working with a printmaker. These memories are still vivid and I would like to share them with the reader.

Countless volumes on Japanese prints stand on the shelves of public libraries and schools or are in the hands of private print collectors. Most of these books limit their range to the pictures of the *ukiyo-e* school of printmaking, simply because it is the largest and most complex area of print study. It is also the area of greatest interest to the majority of collectors. *Ukiyo-e* offered a wide range of subject matter that could be used as decoration for battledores or fans or, because it was mass-produced, mounted into inexpensive scrolls for the average city dweller.

Many of the numerous volumes on *ukiyo-e* approach the subject chronologically or organize it according to the different schools of picture making. This book differs somewhat in that it approaches the Japanese print by subject. By investigating particular subjects, the book offers valuable information needed for the appreciation of prints within these selected areas. It also deals with subjects that are usually not found in other books, such as the audience for Japanese prints and where and how such prints may be purchased.

After an introductory chapter on the historical background of *ukiyo-e*, including the way Buddhist prints from China influenced the development of Japanese printmaking, I will focus in Chapter 2 on how the prints are made. The unique materials used by the craftsmen have not changed over hundreds of years. These materials and their uses, combined with the high quality of craftsmanship, allow viewers to admire the prints beyond the aesthetic qualities that produce the deepest emotional responses.

It is also important for readers to realize that the making of prints was a collaborative effort between the artist, woodblock carver, printer and publisher. The artist was the creator of the picture only. His efforts were, in turn, taken over by a publisher who had workshops where woodblock cutters and printers were engaged in turning the artist's work into a multiple-image product. On occasion, calligraphers were called in to participate in the composition of prints, bestowing a professional look on the poetic text.

As will be seen in Chapter 3, woodblock printed books are a major element in the study of Japanese woodblock printing. These books can be individual picture books displaying the artist's oeuvre, illustrated novels or instruction books on how to draw. Like single-sheet prints, the books were also produced as travel guides or used to describe *kimono* or other patterns. Many collectors have dedicated their collections solely to the picture book.

Chapter 4, Poetry Prints and Picture Calendars, will allow the reader to enter the world of Japanese literature. It was the poets, either by themselves or the society they belonged to, who commissioned artists to create limited editions of poetry-related prints (*surimono*), some incorporating calendars (*egoyomi*). Because these compilations were privately financed and the number of editions limited, the quality of craftsmanship and materials of these works is far superior to the commercial productions turned out in mass quantities.

In the following chapters (5–11), I will take the reader on a journey through the favorite subjects of *ukiyo-e* print artists: graceful and stylish women from the teahouses, shops and pleasure quarters of Edo; flashy and popular *kabuki* performers, often gracing posters advertising theater performances; enormous *sumo* wrestlers; landscapes and scenes from nature depicting birds and flowers; once-censored erotic images; well-known scenes and characters from history; and how the new foreign community was viewed by the Japanese, especially their customs and dwellings in Yokohama.

Who bought these pictures and why—ranging from the earliest Buddhist pilgrims to the contemporary crowds at the annual College Women's Association charity exhibitions in Tokyo—is the theme of Chapter 12.

Throughout the book, the lives of the print artists are discussed. Some artists are well documented, others are a complete mystery, but the lives of all of them are part of a great study and I will relate the information that is available.

During the Taisho period (1912–26), a time of modernization and industrialization in Japan but also one of cultural preservation, a book was published featuring the *mon* (seal) of every publisher of Japanese prints, together with their name and location. It is fitting that one of the illustrations from that book, of which I own a first edition, should be reproduced here (**Fig. 1**). It is a woodcut copy of an Utamaro print showing a picture dealer's shop.

Frederick Harris

CHAPTER ONE

Historical Background

The history of the Japanese print follows two main trajectories. The first is the use of woodblock cutting in the eighth century as a means of producing reproductions of religious texts. The second is the development, over a number of phases, of the woodcut technique as an illustration form. The earliest bold "black ink printed pictures" (*sumizuri-e*) that developed around 1600, gave way in the period 1720–40 to delicately hand-colored "pink pictures" (*beni-e*) tinted with a pink ink produced from the safflower, and two-color hand-colored prints (*tan-e*) using red and green pigments. This led to the evolution, around 1745, of the earliest mass-produced color woodblock prints, literally "pink printed pictures" (*benizuri-e*), which initially used two color blocks, a light green and a light red, in imitation of the hand-colored *tan-e* color scheme. A third color, yellow, was added in the 1750s. The final stage of development, the mass-produced multicolored block-printed "brocade pictures" (*nishiki-e*) that we generally associate with this art form today, began in the mid-1760s in Edo (the former name for Tokyo).

In the available literature on ancient Buddhist prints, there is no consensus as to when woodblock prints were first made in Japan although most sources agree that the purpose of the print was to spread the knowledge of Buddhism in Japan. Woodblock-printed books from Chinese temples, carried by travelers, were seen in Japan as early as the eighth century. There is also agreement that the technique, and subsequent expertise of the craft, originated in China and was probably brought to Japan via Korea.

In Japan, the earliest documented examples of woodblock printing comprise small slips of paper containing prayers (*darani*), which were inserted into small hollow pagodas carved from the wood of Japanese cypress trees (**Figs. 2, 3**). These prayers, about 45.5 cm (18 inches) long and 5 cm (2 inches) wide, were part of the *Hyakumanto Darani* commissioned by Empress Shotoku (718–70), the 46th and 48th imperial ruler of Japan, as thanksgiving for the suppression of a rebellion. The small pagodas, with their prayer paper inserts, were distributed by the thousands to various temples throughout Japan in the mid-eighth century. About a hundred of them still remain at Horyu-ji Temple in Kyoto. Eventually, most were sold or given away to donors to the temple.

There is speculation as to whether the original block for the *Hyakumanto Darani* was wood or copper. Most experts think the block was wood, but 1,000,000 copies would wear the block down severely. Logistically, it is difficult to contemplate where this vast amount of printing was done, and how many printers and wood workers were employed in creating it. The printing and the production of 1,000,000 pagodas from Japanese cypress wood purportedly took six years to complete. It was a tremendous task, and all done by the hands of superb craftsmen.

Other survivors of this massive effort of dissemination are still to be found in numerous temples, museums and private collections throughout the country (**Figs. 4, 5**). Because of their antiquity, there are some concerns about the authenticity of some of the blocks carved with prayers. There is one that was supposedly carved by Kobo Daishi, the founder of Japanese Buddhism, in the seventh to eighth century. But whether it is authentic or not is irrelevant. What is important is that it dates from the time when Buddhism was gaining a foothold in Japan. Some of these blocks were used for reprinting at later dates as well as in ancient times. Indisputably, *darani* represent the earliest examples of woodblock printing in Japan.

Over the following centuries, Buddhist-related prints became available for study. Some comprised sutras or Buddhist precepts while others were printed in outline and colored by hand. Many images, small in size, were stuffed into the hollows of Buddhist statues as late as the fourteenth century. It is possible that other unknown prints are still lying inside the empty voids of statues in some of Japan's temples.

Wooden movable type was also introduced from China, where it was developed in the mid-eleventh century and used to publish Buddhist prayer books. Printed religious illustrations often accompanied the text, and in the fifteenth century a remarkable horizontal scroll with illustrations over 4.5 meters (15 feet) long printed from numerous blocks was produced.

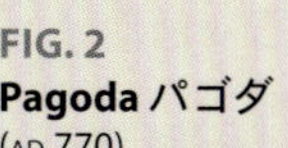

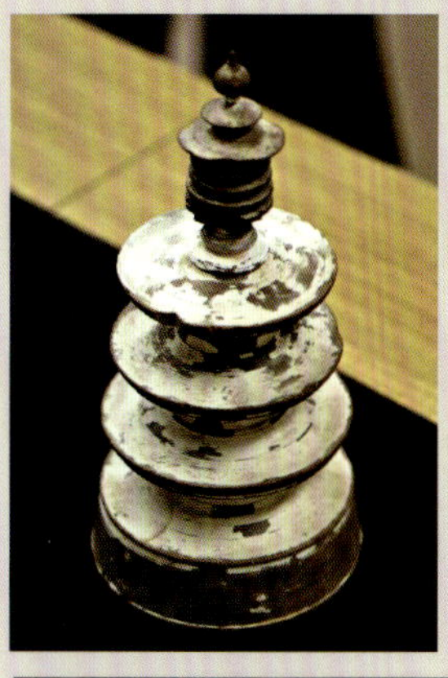

FIG. 2
Pagoda パゴダ
(AD 770)
Japanese cypress wood, 35 x 10 cm
Photo courtesy Yagi Book Store

Originally from the Horyu-ji Temple in Kyoto, this carved pagoda contained a copy of the *Hyakumanto Darani*, probably the world's oldest woodblock print.

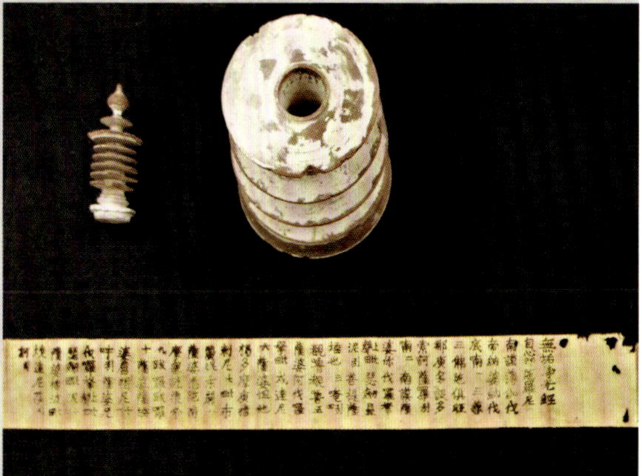

FIG. 3
Pagoda 上部をはずしたパゴダ
(AD 770)
Japanese cypress wood, 35 x 10 cm
Photo courtesy Yagi Book Store

The top of the pagoda in Fig. 2 is removed, revealing the hollow space in which the printed prayer is rolled up and inserted. The prayer is shown in its entirely on the lower portion of the photo.

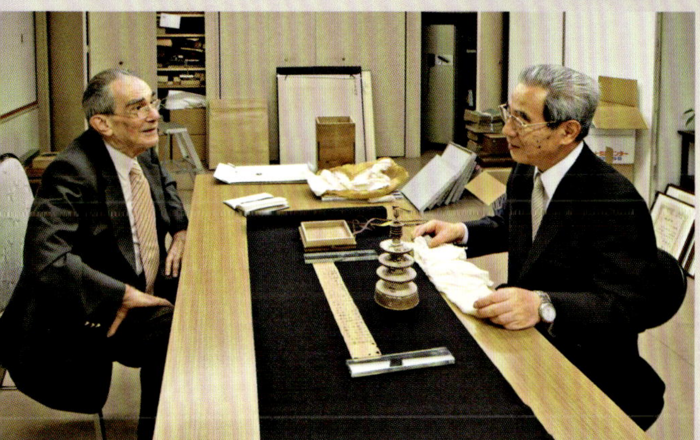

FIG. 4
Author examining the Hyakumanto Darani and its original container, a wood pagoda, with the owner of Yagi Book Store, Akira Yagi.
Photo courtesy Yagi Book Store

I was fortunate to be able to handle this ancient print, which comprises ten different *darani* (prayers), and its carved cypress wood pagoda container.

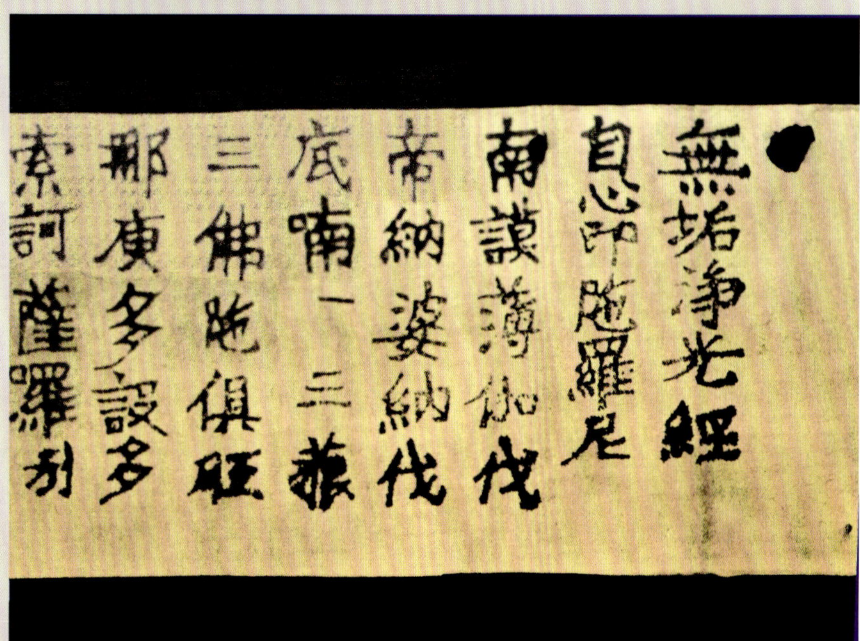

FIG. 5
Detail of a copy of the Hyakumanto Darani (AD 770).

Between the early twelfth to the late sixteenth century, Japan suffered from long periods of strife and civil war, power struggles between clans and imperial courts, and attempted invasions by the Mongols. During these times, fires gutted many of the storehouses of the nobility, the wealthy and the temples. Famous monasteries, which also functioned as publishing centers, were burnt. Kyoto, the capital, was devastated. It was not until the Edo period (1615–1867), when the Tokugawa family of *shogun* fastened their grip on the country and kept out foreign influences that change slowly occurred. The relative peace that ensued after centuries of political unrest provided an ideal environment for the development of popular culture, including art in a commercial form.

The secular development of woodblock printing, along with theater and other amusements, can be traced to the urbanization that took place in the late sixteenth century in Japan as a result of the declining influence of the warrior *samurai* class and the rise of a class of merchants and artisans (*chonin*), literally "town people," who began writing stories or novels based on urban life and culture, and painting pictures that were compiled in picture books. Although in theory the lowest social class under the Tokugawa *shogunate*, the *chonin* soon became economically the most powerful group—a thriving merchant class who lived for the moment and had the money to enjoy it. They enjoyed luxurious lives, free of the influences of the classicism of the nobility and the Confucianism of the *samurai* class. Much of their wealth and spare energy was spent in diversions available in Edo's "floating world," the realm of entertainments (courtesans, *geisha*, teahouses, *kabuki* theater, *sumo* wrestling) outside their mundane, everyday world. Certainly, the popularity of the prints showing the ordinary daily life of townsmen was in complete contrast to the works of official painters who serviced the nobility and the *samurai* class. These painters mostly

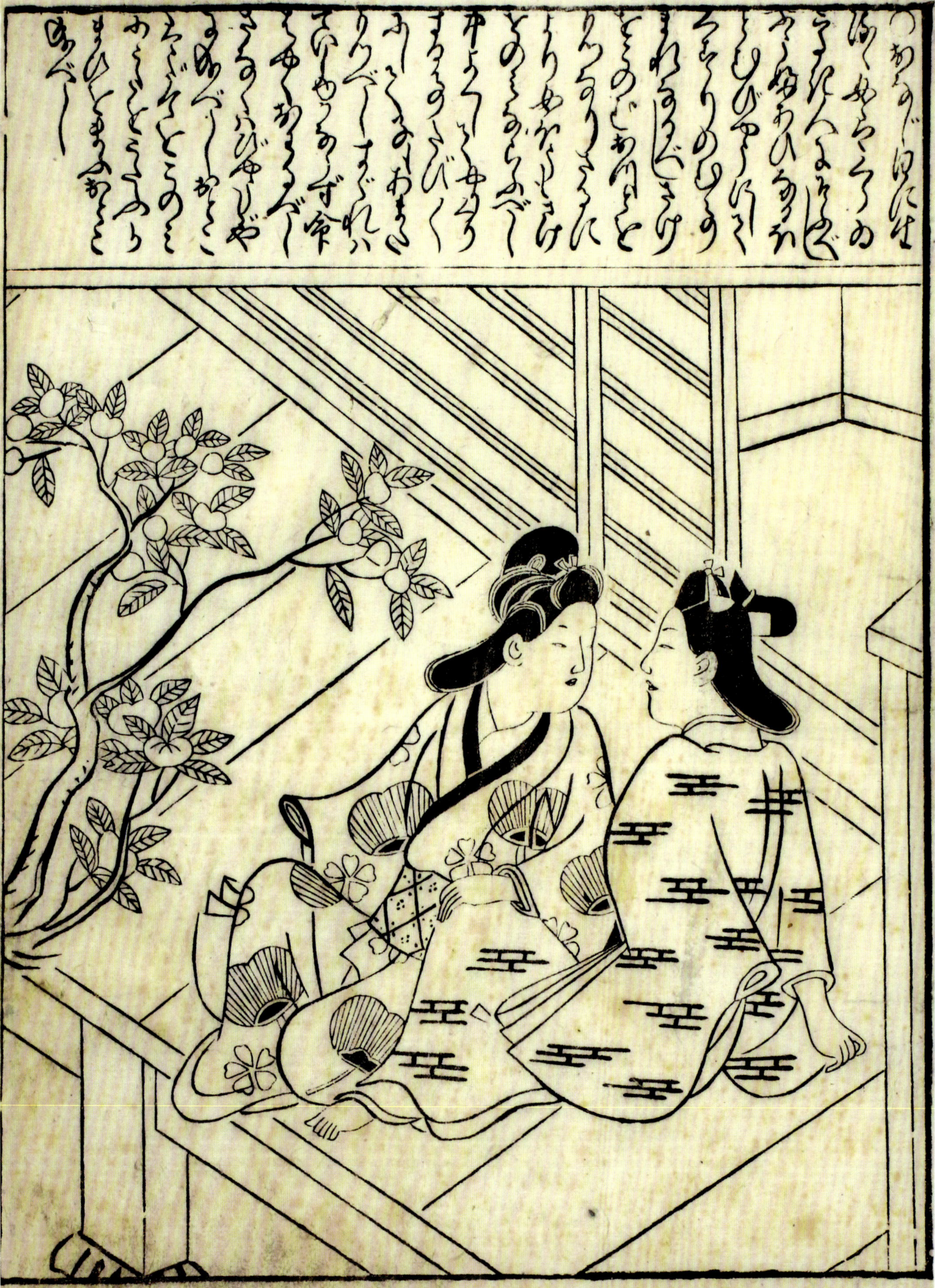

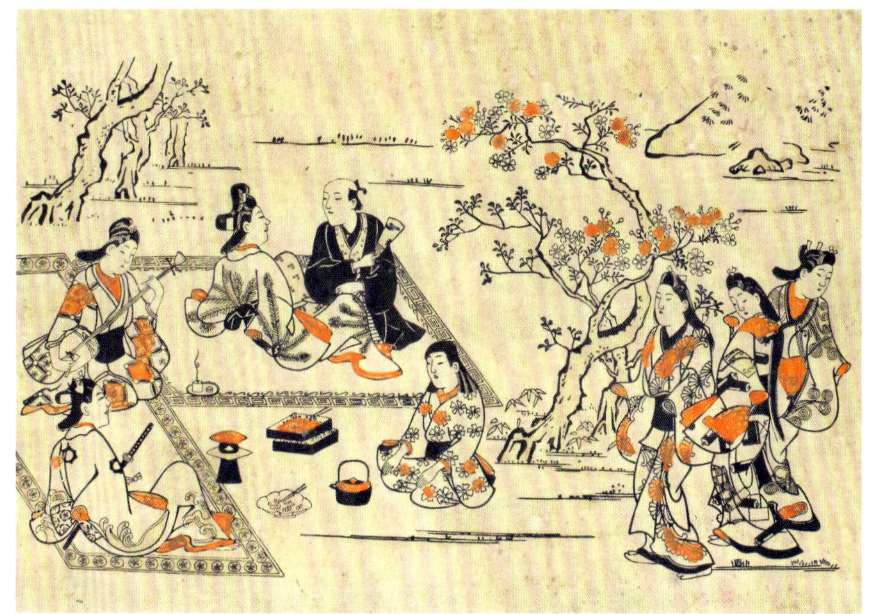

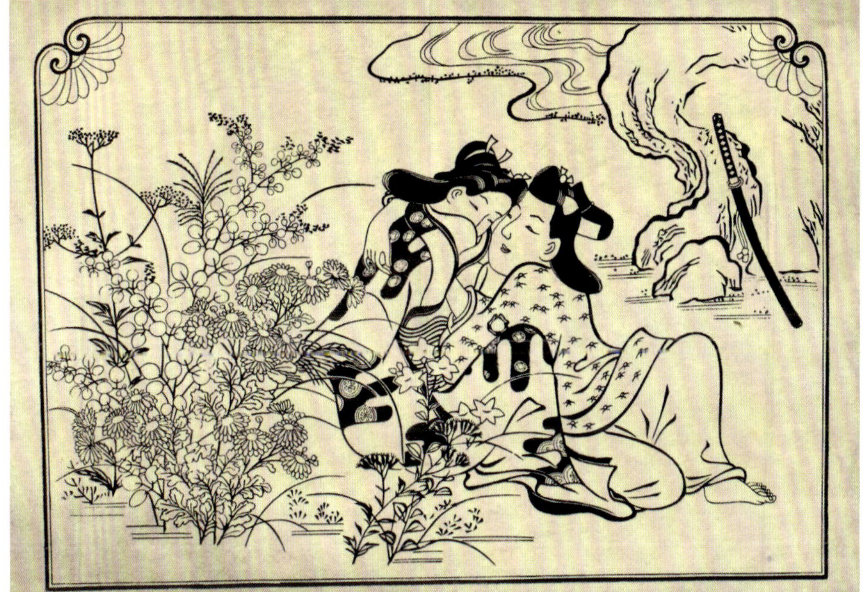

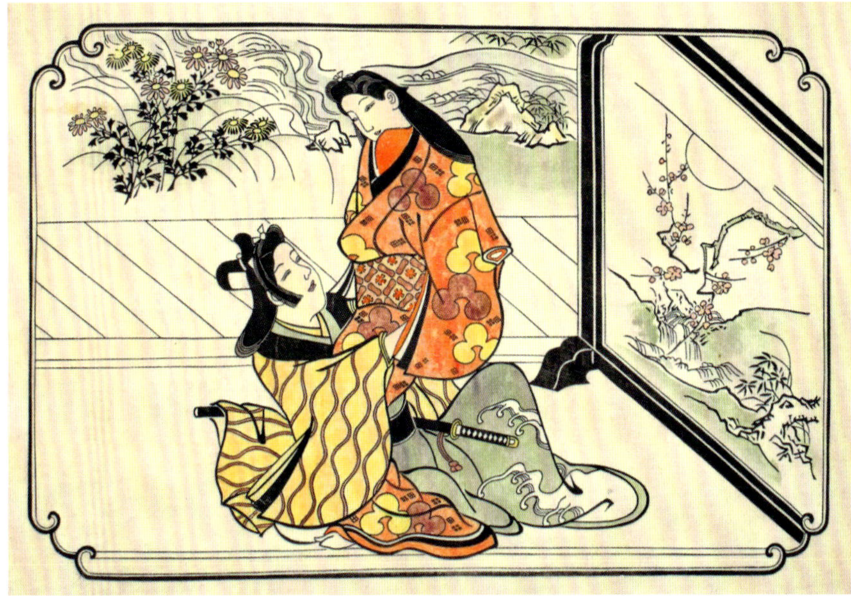

FIG. 6 (left)
Hishikawa MORONOBU
菱川 師信 (1618–94)
Lovers on the Veranda
ベランダの恋人 (1650s)
Black and white print (*sumizuri-e*), 26 x 18 cm
Author's Collection

This black ink (*sumi*) printed illustration from a novel is an example of curvilinear composition held together by the architectural elements of the interior. Only the hairstyles, created with deep black accents, and the *kimono* patterns allow us to distinguish between the man and the woman.

FIG. 7
Hishikawa MORONOBU
菱川 師信 (1618–94)
Cherry Blossom Viewing 花見 (1680s)
Hand-colored black and white print (*tan-e*), 33 x 44 cm
Author's Collection

A high-ranking official and his follower enjoy the *ohanami* (cherry viewing) while being entertained by courtesans, one of whom plays the *shamisen* while three others dance. Mats have been set on the ground, incense is burning and *saké* is being heated and served. Other than the costumes, the exact same scene takes place annually all over Japan during the cherry blossom season.

FIG. 8
Hishikawa MORONOBU
菱川 師信 (1618–94)
or Nishikawa SUKENOBU
祐信 (1671–1751)
Lovers in the Garden 庭園の恋人 (1690s)
Black and white print (*sumizuri-e*), 26 x 35 cm
Author's Collection

As most early prints are unsigned, it is uncertain who the artist was. It is a typical Moronobu composition although the scalloped curves in the upper corners was a device used extensively by Sukenobu. The print is probably the first page of a book of *shunga* (erotica). The *samurai* has his hand inside his lover's *kimono*, feeling her breast. His sword leans against the rocks. This composition is perfectly balanced between the detailed flowers on the left and the simplicity of the right side, with the two figures separating the compositional elements.

FIG. 9
Hishikawa MORONOBU
菱川 師信 (1618–94)
or Nishikawa SUKENOBU
祐信 (1671–1751)
Lovers 恋人 (1690s)
Hand-colored black and white print (*tan-e*), 23 x 34 cm
Author's Collection

A love scene in front of a garden, in which the framed painted screen in the interior repeats almost exactly the view from the veranda. The lovers are just beginning their adventure as the *samurai* has yet to remove his sword.

came from the Tosa and Kano schools of Japanese painting, founded in the fifteenth century.

It is perhaps not surprisingly that the first subject matter of *ukiyo-e*, itself an ambiguous term but most often referred to as "pictures of the floating world," should depict the hedonistic way of life in the after-hours world of Edo, even then a very large city. In the early stages, most *ukiyo-e* were created as posters advertising local entertainment such as theater performances and wrestling and services offered by teahouses, restaurants, bars and brothels. Many carried portraits of popular actors and beautiful women from the tearooms, shops and pleasure quarters of Edo. Some were specially created as souvenirs for clientele, sometimes in the form of flat fans.

The largest volume of secular woodblock printing was, however, confined to book illustration relating to poetry and other educational purposes, such as travel guides, advice manuals, art books, satirical novels, books on urban culture, play scripts for the puppet theater, and to *ukiyo-e*. Images in books were almost always in monochrome (black *sumi* ink only), and for a time art prints were also monochrome or done in only two or three colors. Although *ukiyo-e* were often used for book illustrations, they gained most popularity as single-sheet prints.

Thanks to the rapidly increasing level of literacy as well as the growing affluence of the merchant class, *ukiyo-e* became extremely popular among the middle (merchant) class. Even if these people could not yet afford an original painting, a mass-produced woodblock print was easily within their reach. They were the cheapest way to decorate homes. The prints could be pasted on walls and sliding doors (*fusuma*) or on blank folding screens. Tall, narrow prints could also be glued to the pillar dividing the room panels (*hashira-e*) or hung as scrolls (*kakemono*), especially in the alcove of a room.

The merchant class also came to influence the subject matter of *ukiyo-e*. The more or less sophisticated world of urban pleasures was also animated by the traditional Japanese love of nature. Scenes from the natural world, particularly landscapes, were particularly popular and are among the most famous *ukiyo-e* today. *Ukiyo-e* traditions were to have an enormous impact on Western art in the late nineteenth century.

For many years there has been debate over the artist responsible for starting *ukiyo-e*. Although it is likely that there was no single originator but, rather, a slow development coinciding with the creation of novels and plays compiled in book form that required picture illustrations, two names are often proposed as the originators of *ukiyo-e*—Iwasa Matabei (1578–1650) and Hishikawa Moronobu (1618–94). Matabei, however, was primarily a painter, not a printmaker, who specialized in genre scenes of historical events and illustrations of classical Chinese and Japanese literature. Moreover, he died before the Genroku era (1688–1704), generally considered to be the Golden Age of the Edo period when popular culture flourished and new art forms like *kabuki* and *ukiyo-e* became very popular, especially among the townspeople. This was also the period immediately following religious-related woodcut production.

Moronobu not only painted but also turned out hundreds of prints in the form of illustrated books. Although Chapter 3 of this book is dedicated to illustrated books, so many of Moronobu's books and albums have been dismantled and sold as separate sheets to collectors that we can also view his work as individual stand-alone prints even if they were once part of a book or album. As the most prolific artist of the seventeenth century, he deserves to be given credit as the true founder of the so-called "primitive" *ukiyo-e* printing period.

Even though Moronobu is known as an Edo artist, many of his books were published in Kyoto where he studied under Kano Tanyu, a master painter of the Tosa school of art. This links with the beginnings of *ukiyo-e* from *Tosa-e*—works produced by artists of the popular school of art who serviced the artistic needs of the upper classes of Japan.

Moronobu's prints are pure *sumi-zuri-e*, bold black and white designs (**Figs. 6–9**). An outline, consistent in size, weaves in and out of the figural compositions and is broken only by the solid black patterns of the costumes and the hair arrangements. Texture is introduced by the use of small patterns. His figures always seem to be bent at the knee, producing a dance-like stance. On occasion, one can come across a Moronobu print that is hand colored in the subtlest choice of hues.

In the traditions established by Moronobu, we next meet one of the most prolific of the Genroku artists, Nishikawa Sukenobu (1671–1751). The first dated work of his is 1699. Prior to this, he is recorded to have studied in both the Tosa and Kano schools of painting. Sukenobu brought a lifelike presence to his figures (**Fig. 10**). We sense the actual weight of the human body, not just a doll-like replica. Sukenobu was interested in women of all classes, from the nobility to the common peddlers of the day who went from house to house selling everything from food to firewood, and in all aspects of their lives. His figures twist and turn and perform movements that are natural and believable. Sukenobu's line also varies a little more than his predecessors. There is almost a calligraphic quality to his work, which becomes much more apparent with the group of artists who came after him. Another follower of Moronobu, Sugimura Jihei (active 1681–97), specialized in *shunga* or erotic prints in a flamboyant and decorative style but also portrayed beautiful women (**Fig. 11**).

There follows two early eighteenth-century groups from Edo who conclude the "primitives": the Torii school, which dominated the print world for over seventy-five years and specialized in actor and theater prints (see Chapter 6),

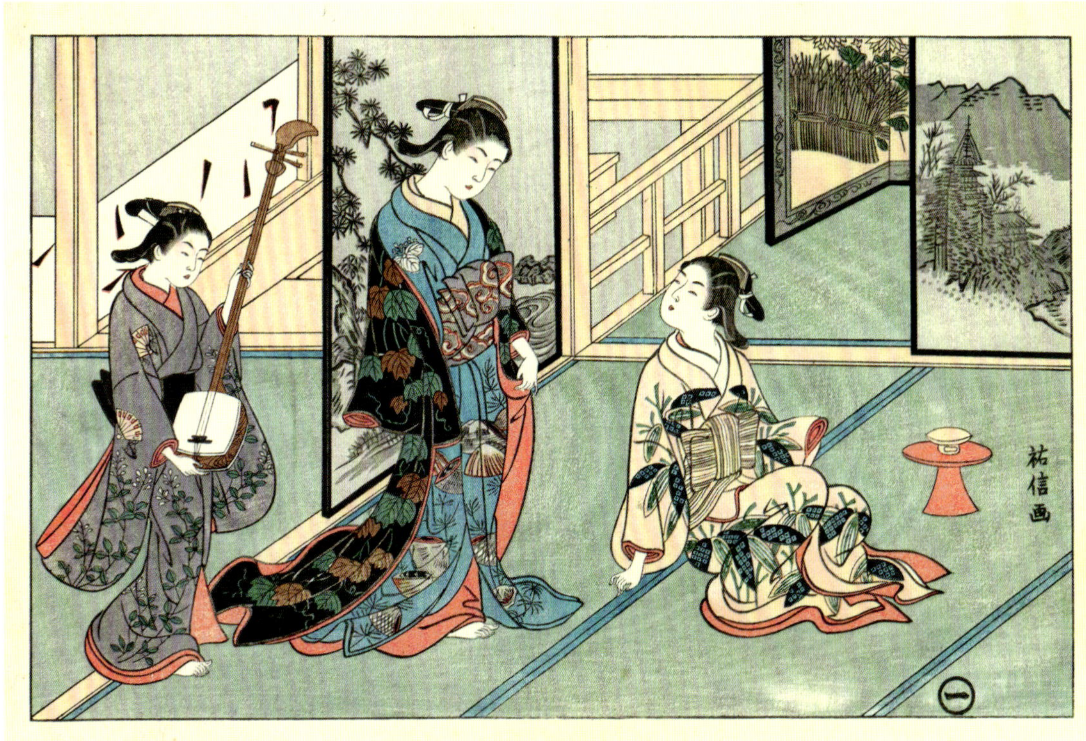

FIG. 10
Nishikawa SUKENOBU
祐信 (1671–1751)
Three Courtesans Preparing for a Party
宴に備える3人の遊女 (1710s)
Hand-colored black and white print (*tan-e*), 28 x 38 cm
Author's Collection

This is a good example of an indoor–outdoor scene. The relative importance of the three courtesans is indicated by their differing sizes.

and the Kaigetsudo school, primarily known for its prints of beautiful women dressed in elaborately patterned *kimono* (see Chapter 5).

The Torii school, founded by Torii Kiyonobu I (1664–1729) (**Fig. 12**), produced such artists as Torii Kiyomasu I (ca. 1694–1716?), who lived a short but talented life and is believed to be either the son or younger brother of Kiyonobu I (**Figs. 13, 14**), and his successors, Torii Kiyomasa II (1706–63) (**Figs. 15, 16**) and Torii Kiyotada I (1720–50) (**Fig. 17**). The early Torii school artists worked so closely together and were so intermixed by family ties and teacher–pupil relations that it takes a great deal of expertise to differentiate their work. For example, some people believe that Kiyomasu II and Kiyonobu II are one and the same person. Others say Kiyomasu II was the adopted son-in-law of Kiyonobu II.

The Kaigetsudo school, founded around 1700–14 by the painter Kaigetsudo Ando (n.d.), includes in its ranks several significant artists, among them Nishimura Shigenobu (active 1724–35) (**Fig. 18**), Okumura Masanobu (1686–1764) (**Fig. 19**) and Ishikawa Toyonobu (1711–85) (**Fig. 20**). As with the Torii school, the styles of the various Kaigetsudo artists are very similar and it is often difficult to differentiate them. However, all tended to work in larger format prints and almost all portray a single female figure, at times with an attendant. The prints swing in an uncontrolled rhythm using an exciting thick calligraphic line to define the pose. There is a wonderful contrast between the thick curvilinear outline and the very fine thin line that describes the features of the head, hands and feet. As an artist, I am interested in the fact that these Japanese prints follow a concept identical to one commonly employed by the artists in the Italian Renaissance, namely the counter spiral. The head and feet point in an opposite direction to the torso, giving the figure, even though stationary, a sense of movement. This concept came naturally to the Japanese whereas it took years for it to be understood in Europe.

All of the prints in this chapter are brightly colored by hand, a technique that will be discussed in more detail in the relevant chapters. These hand-painted prints have interesting descriptive titles, depending on what colors dominated. Most of them are referred to as *tan-e*. There is some disagreement among scholars as to whether the term *tan* refers to a deep chrome yellow or to an ochre yellow. Others call *tan-e* vermillion, with yellow and green being subordinate colors. Prints tinted in red only are referred to as *beni-e*. The word *beni* for red is still commonly used for women's lipstick, which is called *kuchi-beni* (*kuchi* meaning mouth). If lacquer was used in the hand coloring, the prints are known as *urushi-e*, *urushi* being the word for lacquer.

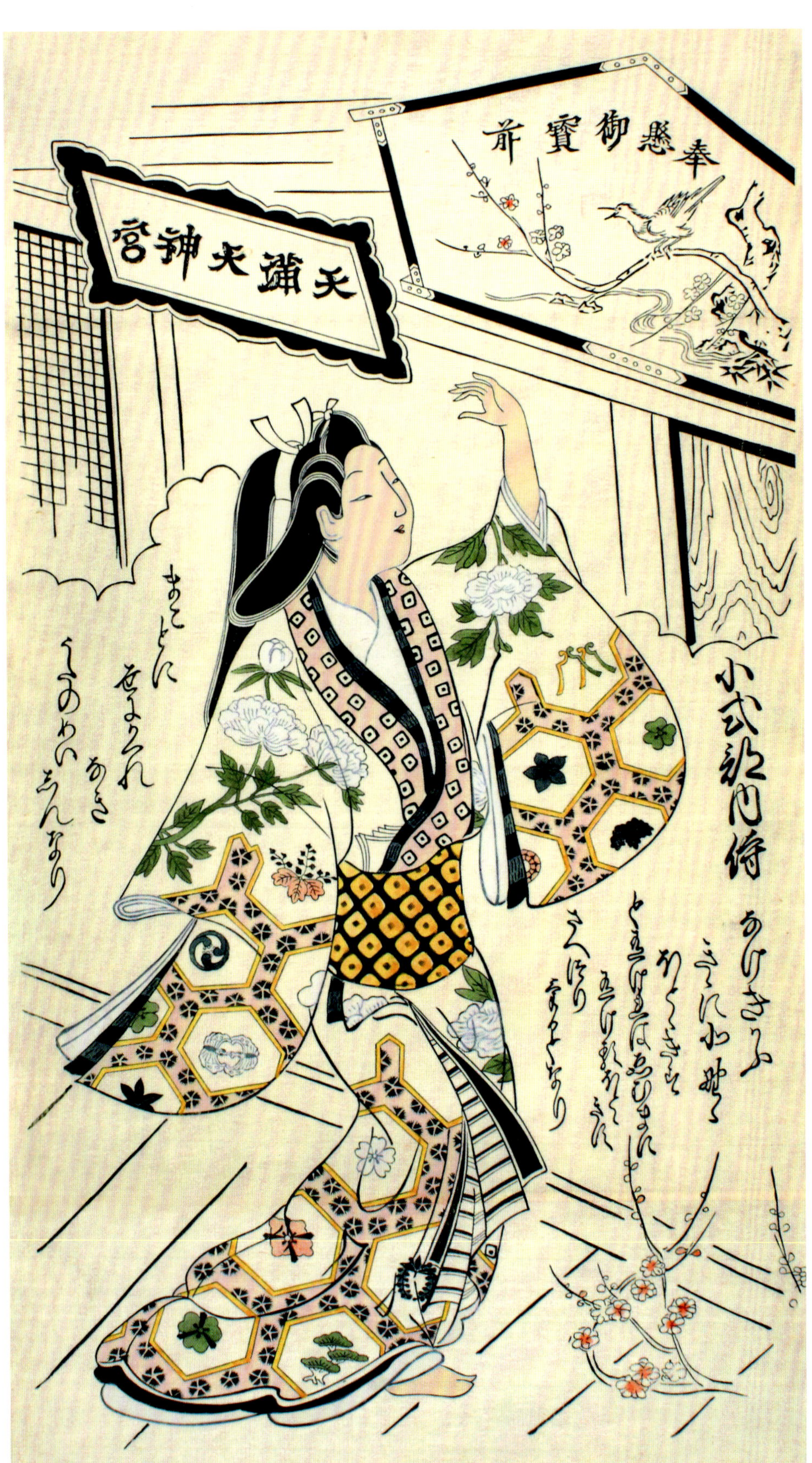

FIG. 11
Sugimura JIHEI
治兵衛 (active 1681–97)
The Court Lady Koshikibu-no-Naishi 小式部内侍
Hand-colored black and white print (*tan-e*), 59 x 33 cm
Author's Collection

The court lady Koshikibu-no-Naishi was a well-known poet in the middle of the Heian period, who went to service at the court at the age of twelve, led a rather promiscuous life, and after her second child died at the age of twenty-six. Four of her poems are included in an Imperial compiled anthology. This picture, which has a wonderful rhythm of black, shows her visiting the Kitano Shrine expecting to see and hear a cuckoo sing. Her hand points to the *ema* (votive tablet) with a painted cuckoo, which started to sing as she was composing a poem about it.

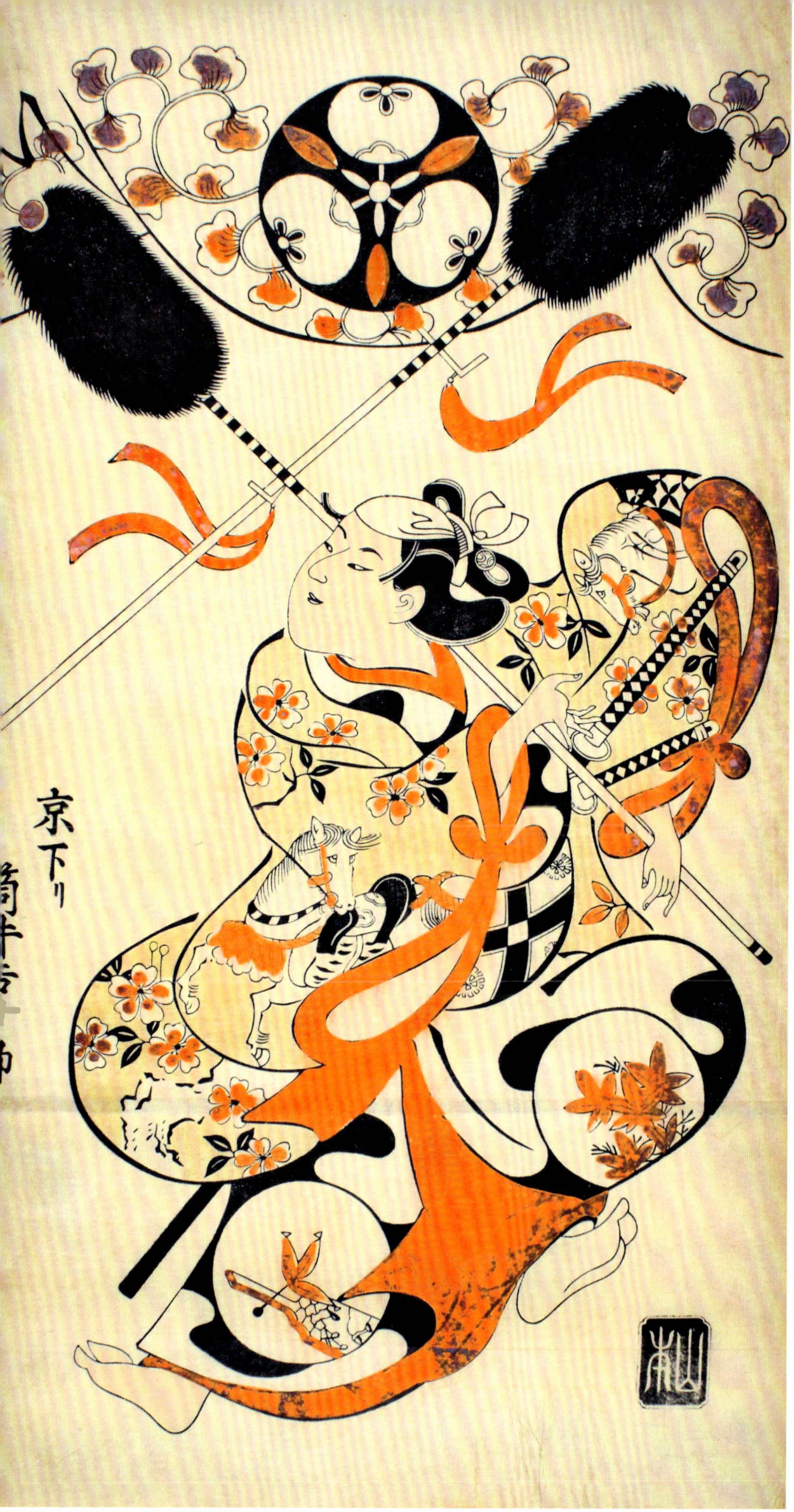

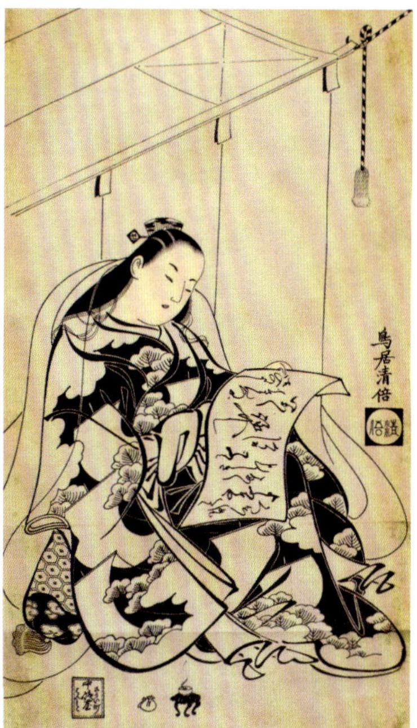

FIG. 12 (left)
Torii KIYONOBU I
清信 (1664–1729)
The Actor Tsutsui Kichijuro 筒井吉十郎の京下り (1700s)
Hand-colored black and white print (*tan-e*),
54 x 31 cm
Author's Collection

This exciting print shows an actor as a *samurai* in an animated and provocative pose brandishing two fur-covered spears. The patterns on the *kimono* are indifferent to the folds as they swirl about the figure.

FIG. 13 (above)
Torii KIYOMASU I
清倍 (ca. 1694–1716?)
Reading a Love Letter 恋文を読む
(1700s)
Black and white print (*sumizuri-e*),
53 x 31 cm
Author's Collection

In this print, a dramatic display of calligraphic brush strokes creates a sense of rhythm and counter rhythm. Some of the finer lines are not related to the specific forms but are included purely as abstract elements to hold the design together.

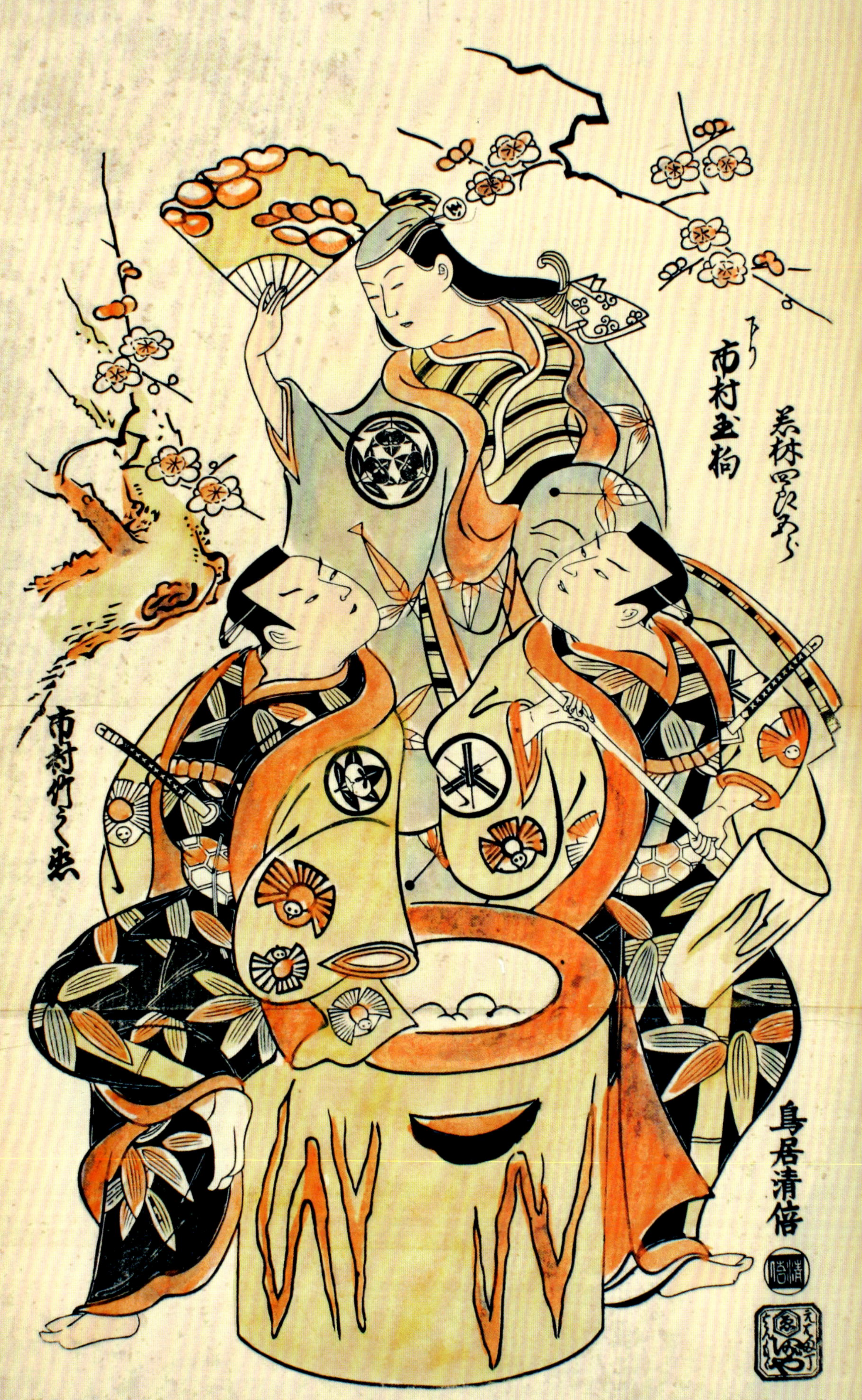

市村玉柏
若林四郎五郎
市村竹之丞
鳥居清倍

FIG. 14
Torii KIYOMASU I
清倍 (ca. 1694–1716?)
Three Kabuki Actors Pounding Rice Paste 三歌舞伎役者の餅つき
Hand-colored black and white print (*tan-e*), 58 x 31 cm
Author's Collection

Here, three actors with their family crests prominently displayed are pounding rice inside a wooden barrel into *mochi* (rice paste), a ritual usually performed during the New Year season. The figure on the right holds the wooden mallet. The rice paste is hardened and cut into small squares that are either roasted or included in a New Year soup.

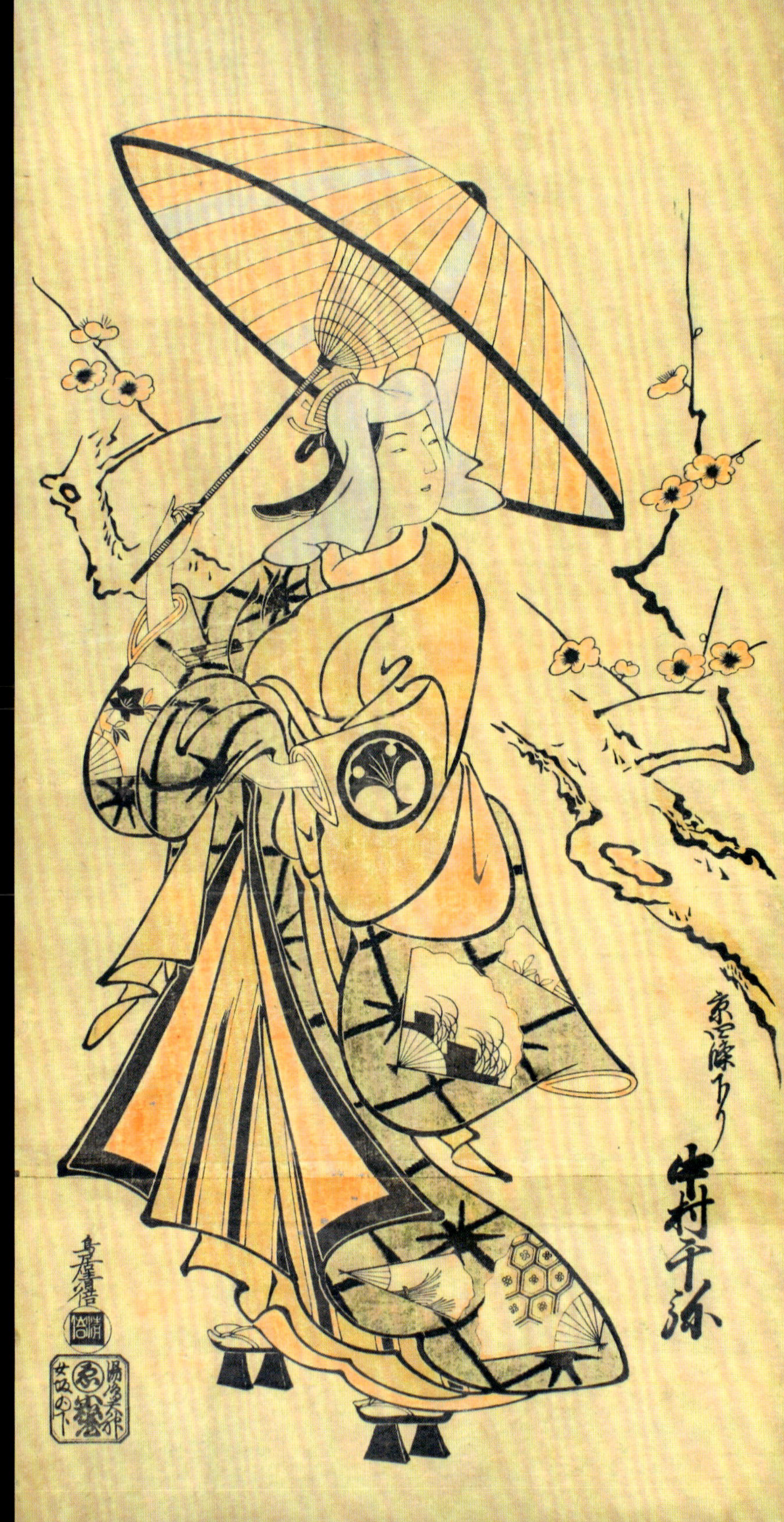

FIG. 15
Torii KIYOMASU II
二代　清倍 (1706–63)
The Actor Nakamura Senya
中村　千弥
Hand-colored black and white print (*tan-e*), 60 x 31 cm
Author's Collection

In this print, Nakamura Senya stands under a cherry tree in full bloom, with a *hi-gasa* (sunshade umbrella).

FIG. 16
Torii KIYOMASU II
二代 清倍 (1706–63)
Three Cities' Famous Courtesans 三都 大夫
Hand-colored black and white print (*tan-e*), 33 x 46 cm
Author's Collection

This print of three actors in courtesan costumes standing in front of three different houses of pleasure would have been cut into three separate sheets as the publisher's mark, Urokogataya, appears on all three subjects. This is primarily a study of eighteenth-century Edo fashion.

FIG. 17
Torii KIYOTADA I
清忠 (1720–50)
Kabuki Actor and Two Puppies
歌舞伎役者と二匹の子犬 (1750s)
Hand-colored black and white print (*tan-e*), 34 x 16.5 cm
Author's Collection

A woman is watching two little puppies play at her feet. This is a lovely print whose charm is enhanced by the addition of the animals, which is rare in early eighteenth-century Japanese prints.

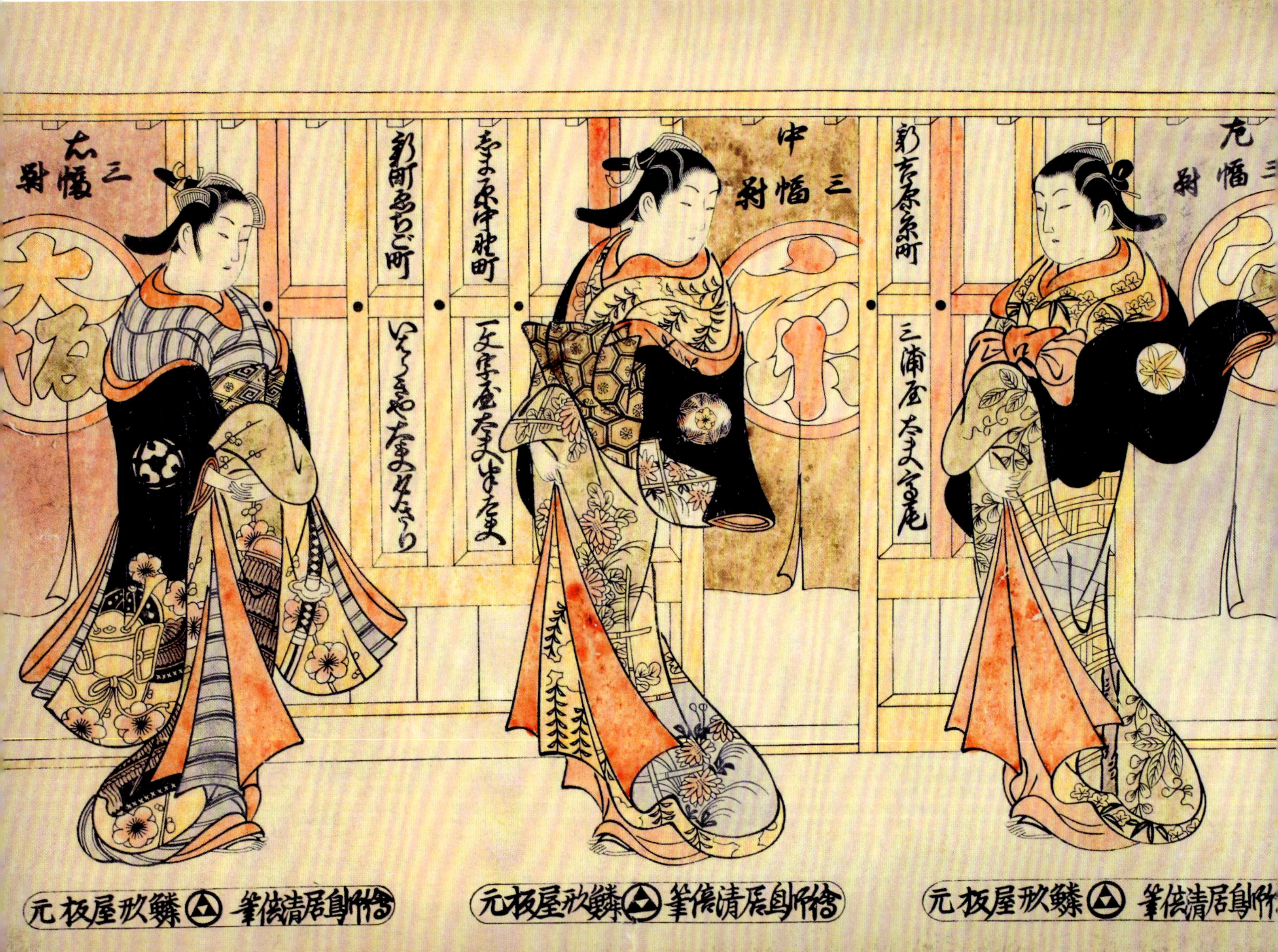

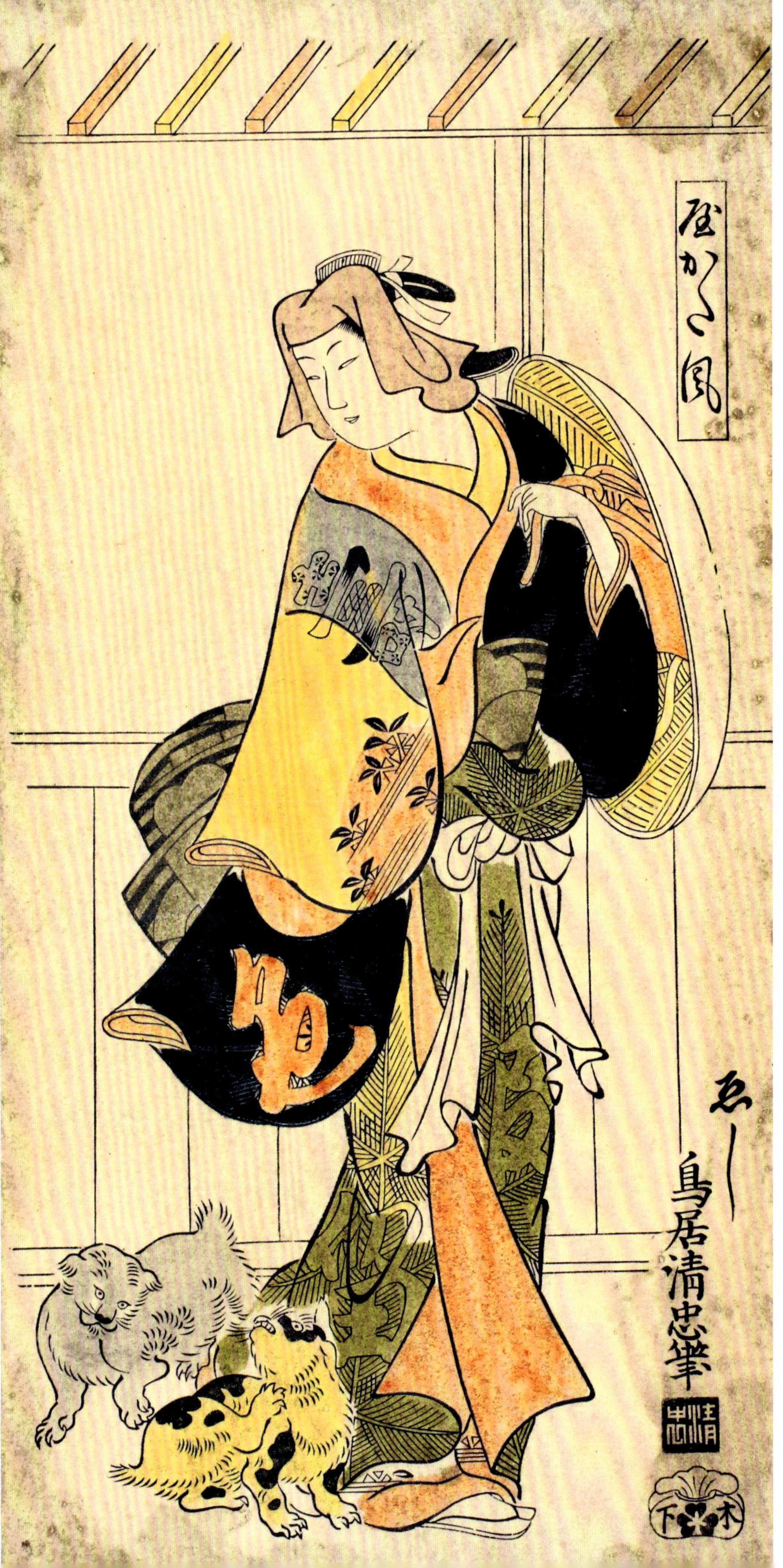
鳥居清忠筆

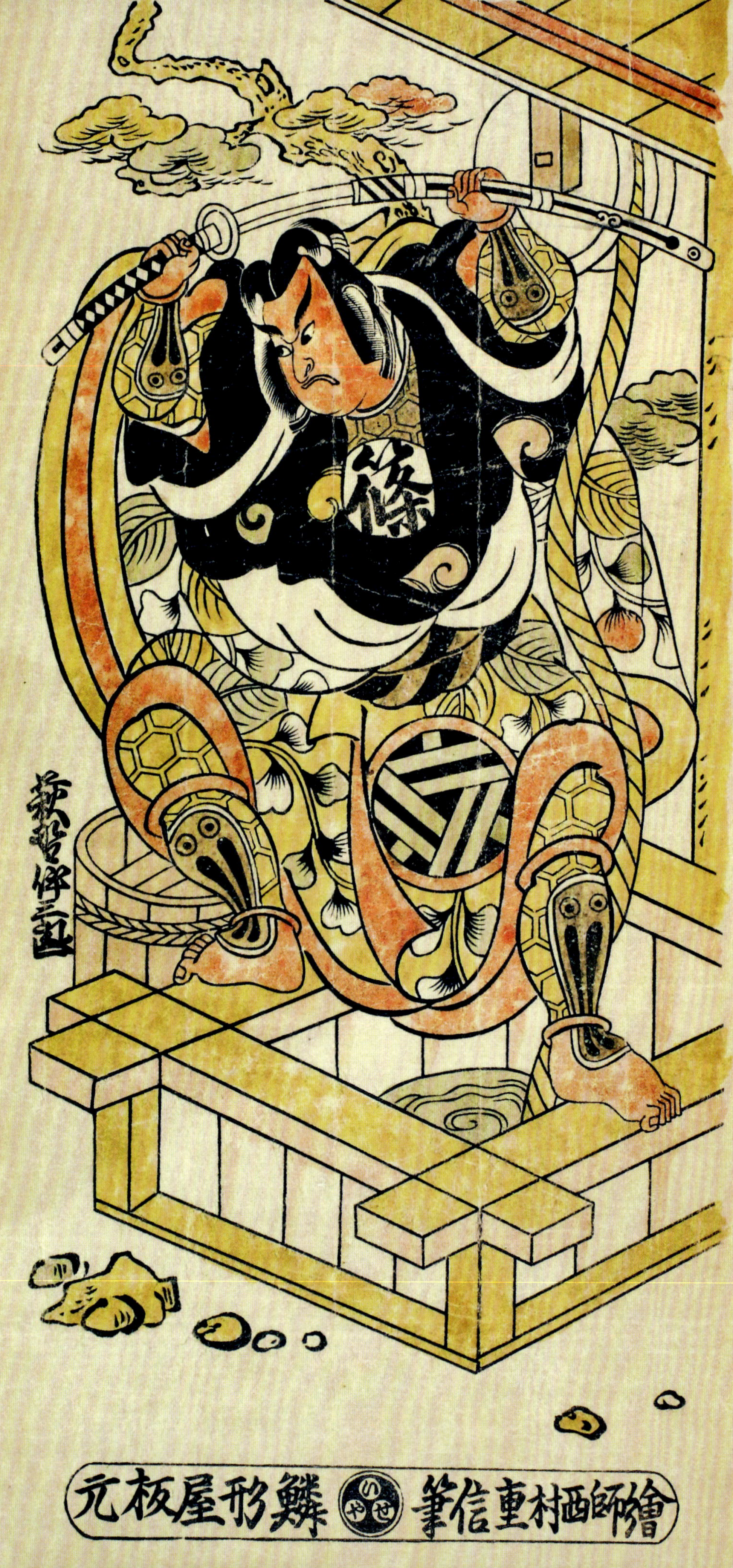

FIG. 18
Nishimura SHIGENOBU
西村　重信 (active 1724–35)
Kabuki Actor 歌舞伎役者
(1730s)
Hand-colored black and white print (*tan-e*), 33 x 15.5 cm
Author's Collection

This possibly depicts the actor Ogino Isaburo in a threatening pose on top of a well. It is almost an abstract picture as many of the enclosed elements are included for design purposes only, for example, the red and yellow hand encircling the left side of the figure. The artist Shigenobu may not have existed but could instead have been a fictitious name created by a publisher who was able to work in the Masanobu style.

FIG. 19
Okumura MASANOBU
奥村　政信 (1686–1764)
The Courtesan Chokaro
遊女張果郎 (1710s)
Hand-colored black and white print (*tan-e*), 59.5 x 31.5 cm
Author's Collection

The courtesan's *obi* (sash) is tied in a distinctive bow, which is not a style adopted by women from other walks of life. The contrast between the heavy curved lines of the *kimono* and the fine lines of the head, hands and foot make this an exquisite composition.

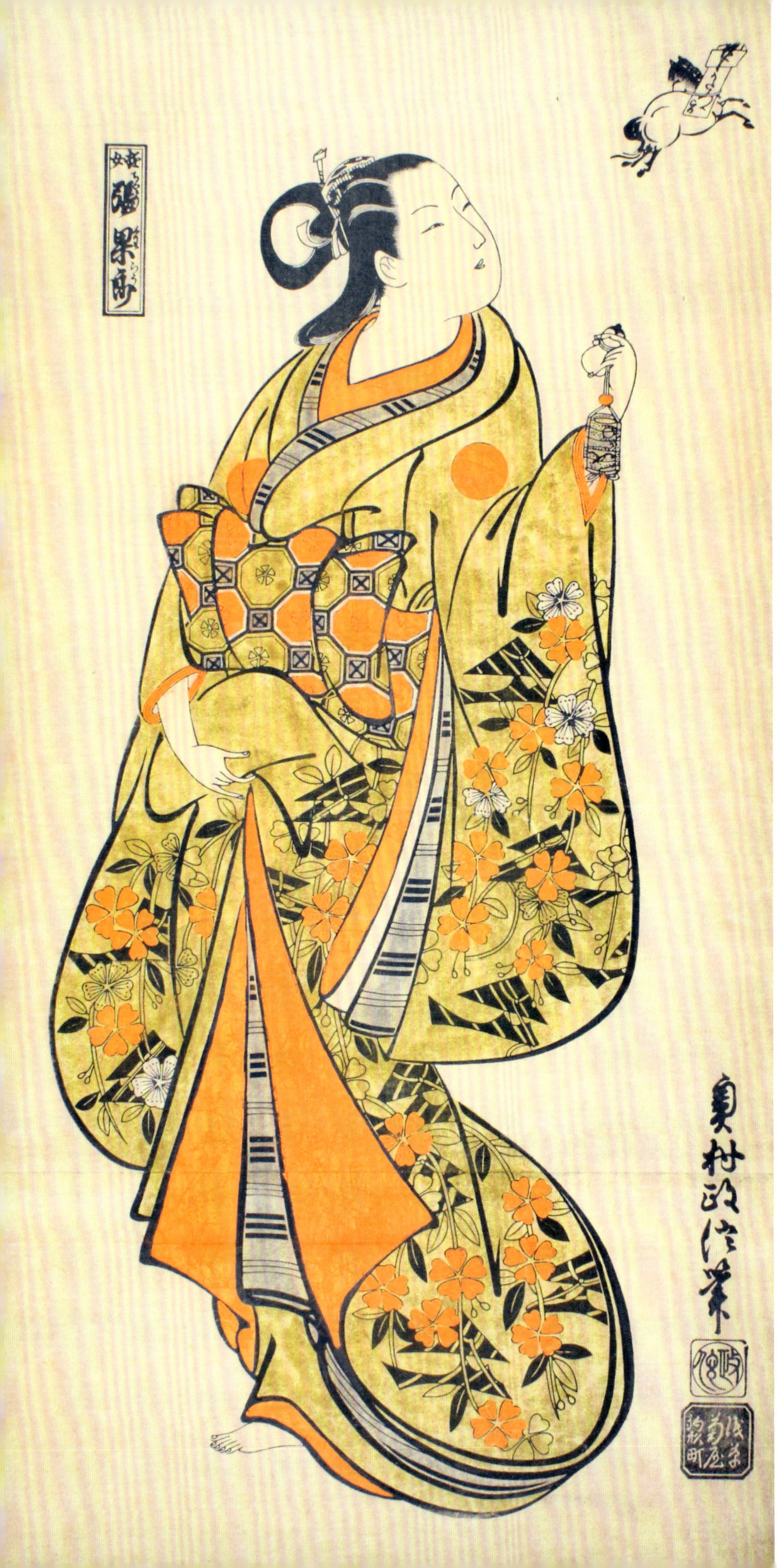

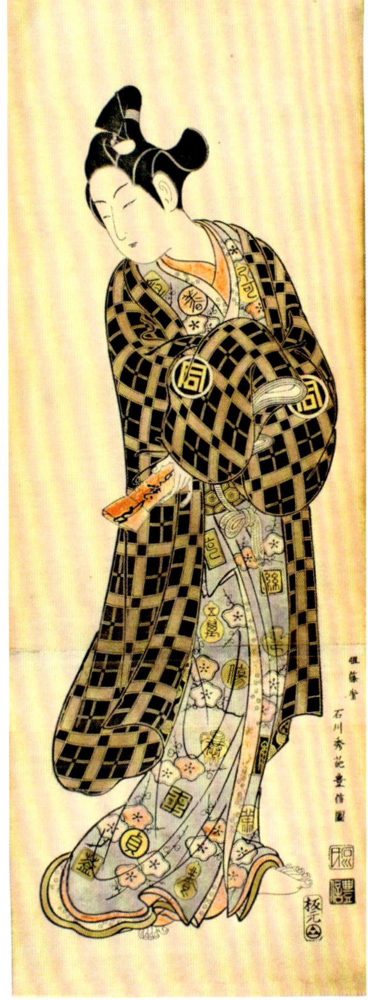

FIG. 20
Ishikawa TOYONOBU
石川 豊信 *(1711–85)*
The Actor Sanogawa Ichimatsu 佐野川市松 (1740s)
Hand-colored black and white print (*tan-e*), 68 x 25.5 cm
Author's Collection

The actor Sanogawa Ichimatsu stands in a graceful and stately pose with his head pointing in the opposite direction to his feet. He is holding a letter or poem in one hand while the other is encased in his *kimono* sleeve. The last twenty years of Toyonobu's life were spent running his family's inn and he therefore produced no prints after 1765.

CHAPTER TWO

Materials and Techniques

When I first arrived in Japan in 1953, over a half-century ago, I had the opportunity to meet and work with a group of young artists in Kobe, who showed great interest in me personally and my experiences in art schools in New York. During those years there were not many American artists living and working in Japan. I was a novelty to them, as they were to me. When I mentioned that I had studied printmaking at the Art Students League, and that my teacher had worked in Japan prior to World War II, they asked if I would be interested in doing a part-time internship with a woodblock cutter and printer. He was a true craftsman who made a living producing matchbook covers, menus, coasters, name cards, etc., which at that time was the most common and inexpensive form of reproduction. I remember everything about him except, unfortunately, his name.

My recent reading on the subject of producing prints, and my research into modern methods confirmed my vivid memories of those many years ago.

It is important for readers to realize that the Japanese prints shown in this book were not created solely by the artists whose names appear on them. A symbiotic relationship existed between artist, woodblock carver and printer and the team coordinator, the publisher. The stages of making *ukiyo-e*—the design, carving, printing and publishing—were separate activities done by different and highly specialized artisans and thus were the products of a collaborative effort. In some cases, the artist did not even choose the colors that the print contains. There are, of course, many exceptions, but in most cases the volume of printing was so great that there was not enough time for the artist to supervise each production. He may not have even had the ability to do so. The carvers and printers were skilled craftsmen employed by a publisher who also paid the artist for his original design. The final product was then sold by the publisher to the public, with the artist's signature, publisher's name and

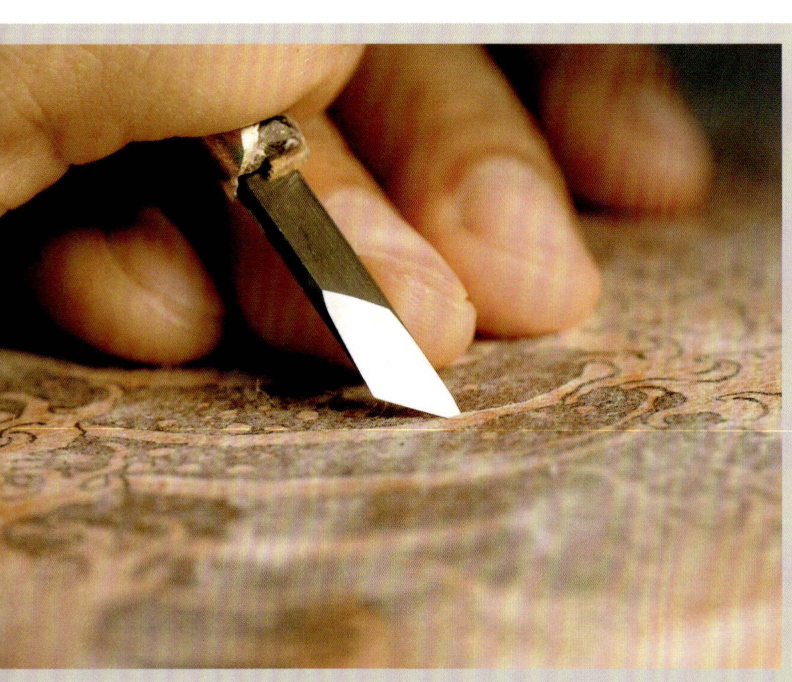

FIGS. 21, 22
Cutting with a knife
Courtesy of Adachi Institute of Woodcut Prints

FIG. 23
Using a chisel to peel away the unwanted area
Courtesy of Adachi Institute of Woodcut Prints

FIG. 24
Printing with a baren
Author's Collection

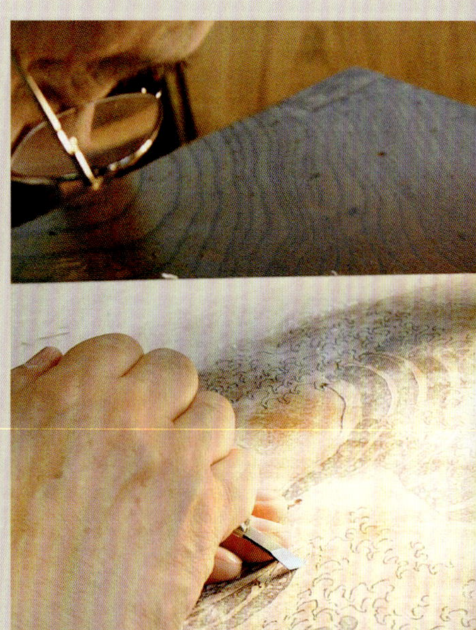

sometimes the publisher's address added to it. The woodblock carvers and the printers remained the unknown artisans of Japan. Their apprenticeship was long, sometimes up to ten years. Their devotion to their craft was absolute, but only in very rare instances did their names appear on a print.

The process of creating *ukiyo-e* started with the artist. It was his job to produce a drawing or "preparatory picture," called a *shita-e*, for the publisher in black *sumi* ink. Sometimes the artist would develop his drawing to a very high level of detail and completeness. At other times he would provide a more sketchy drawing, perhaps only showing the contours of his figures and suggestions for the background. The details were then filled in by professional block copyists (*hikko*), or even by advanced students. The *hikko* would then create a tracing or "base block picture" (*hanshita-e*) on very thin translucent paper, which was then passed to the block cutter for the next stage—transferring the design to the woodblock.

Traditional Japanese woodblock prints were made from designs carved into planks or blocks of cherry wood (*sakura*), a moderately hard, fine-textured, straight-grained wood suited to carving designs in high relief. Cherry wood was also fairly resistant to warping caused by the wet pigments and moist paper used in the printing process. The blocks, about 3.5 cm thick, were the product of years of drying and curing and creating a surface that was suitable to carve before they were cut up into workable sizes. Because the block cutter worked on both sides of the wood, care had to be taken not to damage either the top or the reverse of the block.

Traditionally, the carver sits on a cushion (*zabuton*) at a low table. The angle of his work surface is at the level of his bent arm. He first places the *hanshita-e* block design face down on the block of wood, which is covered with an even coating of glue (*nori*) made from rice flour and water. The drawing is carefully pressed onto this sticky surface. The back of the drawing is then carefully rubbed with the hand to remove the fibers from the paper so that the black *sumi* lines are visible for the cutting process to come. Basically, one is exposing the drawing from the rear. I remember from my experience at the craftsman's studio that rubbing the paper is a difficult task. The paper is so thin that the chances of making a hole in it are great. I had to practice in areas where there were no *sumi* lines. After the glued paper has dried, the block is brushed with a light coating of oil so that the *sumi* lines are clearly visible.

Next comes the cutting process, another delicate task (**Figs. 21–23**). Keeping in mind that the thin black lines and other surfaces remaining on the block comprise the printed image, the woodblock cutter cuts through the back of the paper into the wood, leaving the lines or areas of the design in high relief while cutting down into and removing the surrounding wood (**Figs. 26, 27**). The final design that is produced is called the "key block" (*dai-ban*). Carvers use as many as seven different tools—knives, gauges and chisels—for the cutting process. The most useful is the knife called *hangito*. The craftsman holds it upright and cuts the block at an angle of about 35 degrees, generally in the direction of the brush that initially inscribed the design. The tools are sharpened on stones ranging from rough to fine with oil. The sharpening of the tools itself is

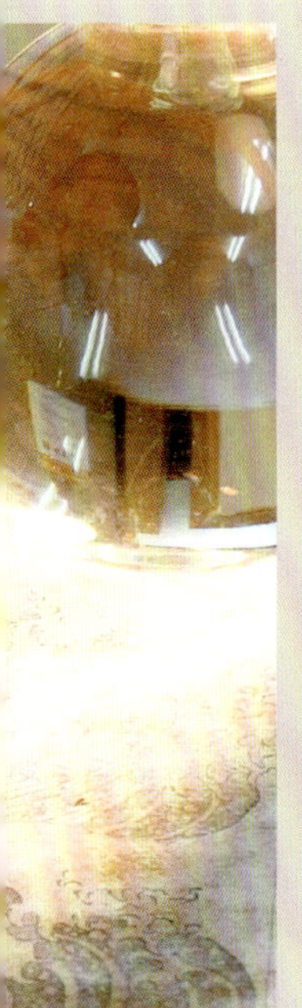

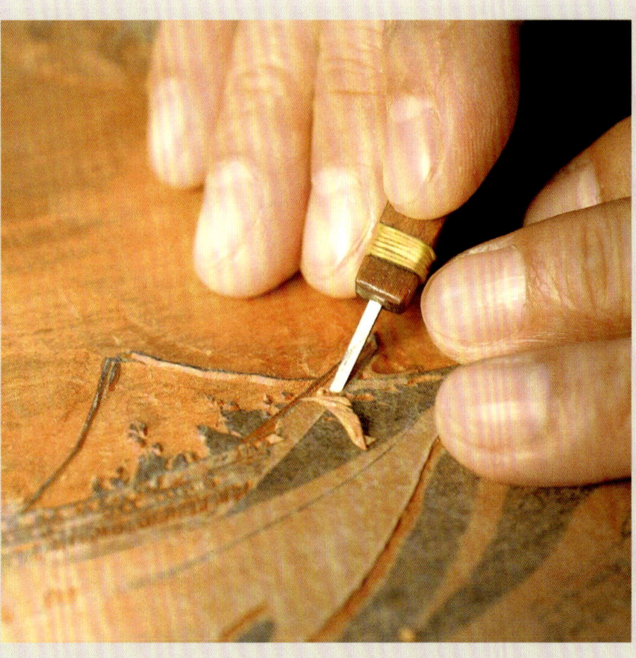

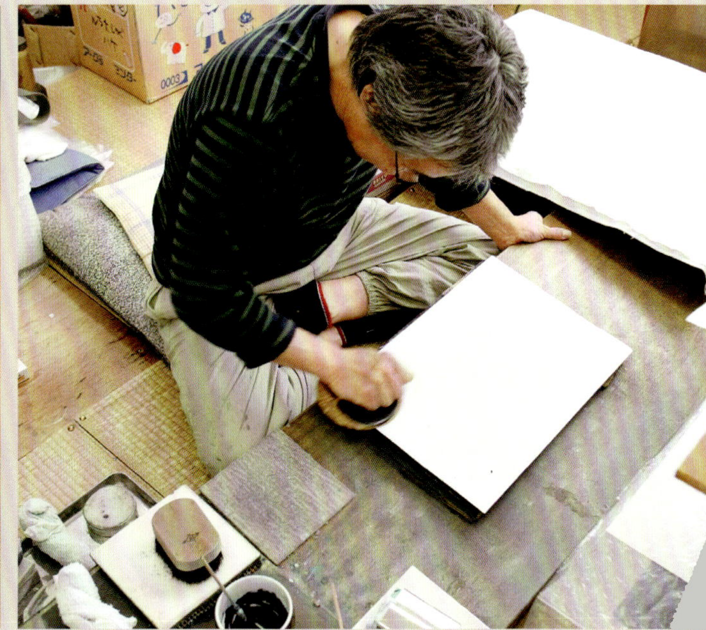

an elaborate procedure, just as taking care of the stones is.

While the earliest Japanese prints were almost always reproduced in monochrome black ink and required a single key block (**Fig. 28**), as soon as the growth of the popularity of *ukiyo-e* brought with it a demand for color, the woodblock cutter had to produce sets of blocks for each design since each color was produced from a different block. Thus, separate blocks had to be cut for each of the colors of the design in addition to the key block that was used to print the black outline. On the color blocks, all areas were cut or chiseled away except for the flat areas meant to take the colors, which were left in relief. If, however, two color areas were sufficiently separated from each other, sometimes these two colors could be printed from the same block. Altogether, block cutting was a time-consuming and demanding process that required the skilled hands of master carvers to replicate the unique and exact features in the artist's original design, while at the same time demonstrating their own woodcarving talents.

Because color prints were produced from multiple blocks, with each block in a different color and sequentially impressed onto the paper, the woodblock carvers had to employ a system to insure that the image from the key block and the colors from the different color blocks would correspond perfectly on the same sheet of paper when printing. They developed a system of guide marks (*kento*), cut with a special chisel at the same two locations into every block used to make a single design. At the lower right-hand corner of the block they carved an L-shaped corner called *kagi* and in the lower left side a small rectangular straight piece called *hikitsuke*. The sheet of paper would fit into these two slots and be perfectly positioned every time on the individual blocks. The final print would thus bear the impressions of each of the blocks in perfect registration.

Now came the job of the printers. The pigments used for printing traditional prints were always water based, made either from mineral or organic (vegetable) sources. The most important is black *sumi*. It is produced mostly from burnt pine mixed with rapeseed oil to produce soot, which is formed into a stick called *nikawa* using glue. The same *sumi* stick or a liquid version called *bokujyu* is used in traditional Japanese painting. Sometimes the *sumi* was mixed with *nikawa* to produce a glossy finish. This was effective on hair or on some *kimono* patterns. As with their European counterparts, the other colors used were all primary colors—yellow, blue and red. As in Europe also, the translucent quality of these colors could be mixed to achieve a multitude of other hues. The introduction of Prussian blue in the eighteenth century had a great impact on Japanese landscape prints, especially those of the famed print artists Utagawa Hiroshige and Katsushika Hokusai.

Each pigment was applied to the blocks by the printers with a unique Japanese brush called a *hake*. It looks much like a Western-style scrubbing brush except the hairs come from the tail of a live horse. Once inserted into the wooden handle, the hairs are shredded on the surface of a dried shark's fin. The hairs in a horse's tail are hollow and the shredding leaves about a quarter of the hairs intact. When the brush is used to apply pigment, it is first dipped in water and then inserted into the pigment. Pressing down on the brush allows the water to mix with the pigment and flow evenly on the block. The block is dampened evenly with water, taking care to avoid any pooling or puddles. The care that the printer takes in making sure there is no excess ink or color adjacent to the cutting line is most important. The moistened paper is then gently laid down upon the inked surface of the block for printing, making sure that it is aligned with the registration marks carved into the blocks.

Traditional Japanese paper used in printmaking has a very long history in Japan. Originally developed in the first century in China, it found its way into Japan directly from China and also via Korea. The qualities of Chinese paper are extremely appealing. As a painter, I have used both *kanshi* (Chinese paper) and *washi* (Japanese paper). However, the paper used for woodblock printing needs strength to resist the strong pressures applied to it. It also has to be absorbent, flexible and stable when dampened for printing. The techniques and materials developed in Japan were found to be the most suitable for the woodblock printing process.

The three main papers used are *kozo*, *gampi* and *mitsumata*. *Kozo*, a generic name for three different types of mulberry trees that are grown as farm crops, is the most widely used. Trees two years or older have qualities in their bark and leaf structure which make them most suitable for the production of paper. The fiber produced is long, flexible and strong. *Gampi* paper is generally harvested from the wild in southern parts of Japan and is therefore relatively scarce. It is strong, translucent and thin, with a silky quality. *Mitsumata*, in the same family as *gampi*, is hardier and takes longer to grow but is expensive. Paper making in Japan is a study in itself, and beyond the scope of this book. But without the correct quality of paper available to the publisher, printmaking would never have succeeded.

The printers used a special pad called a *baren* to press or burnish the paper against the inked woodblock, thus applying the designs and colors from the woodblocks onto the paper (**Figs. 24, 25**). A disk-like pad about 15 cm in diameter that fits into the palm of the hand, with a flat bottom and on the reverse side a knotted handle, the *baren* is composed of a core (*shin*) of cord twisted from straw and/or bamboo fiber and arranged in a tight spiral, placed on a backing disk (*ategawa*) and wrapped in a cover (*kawa*) formed from a tightly wound and twisted bamboo sheath. *Baren* of differing thicknesses and cord fibers are used to achieve variable pressures during printing. Today, *baren*

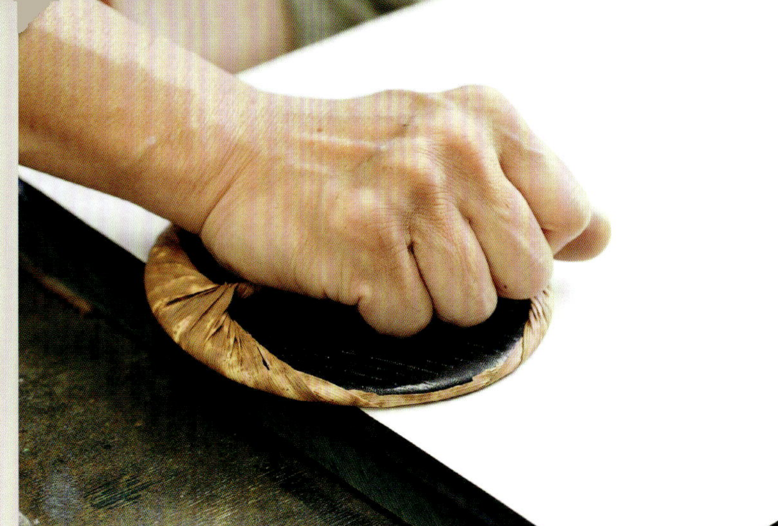

FIG. 25

Holding the baren in the proper position

Author's Collection

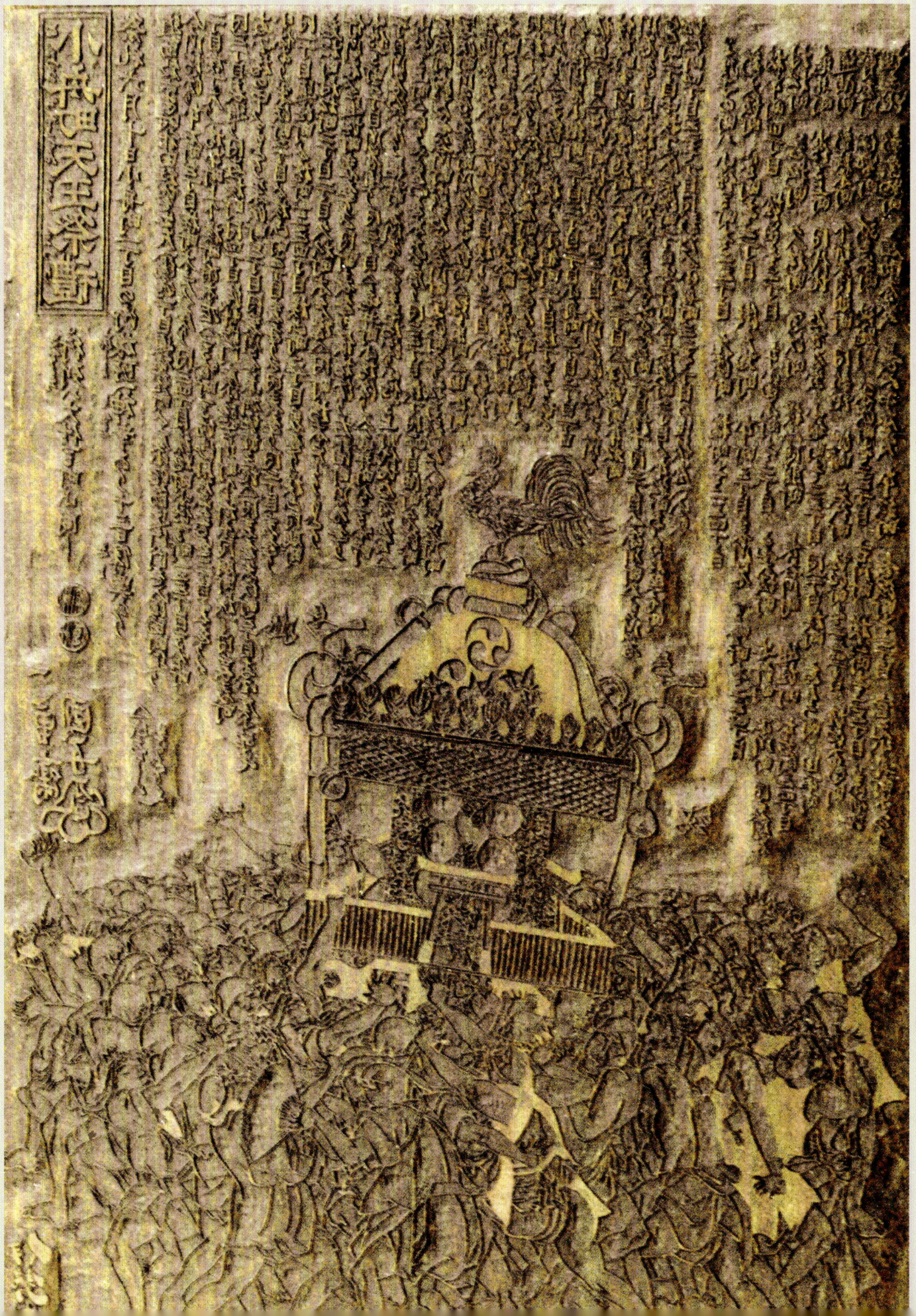

FIG. 26

An original key block (39 x 27 cm) from a drawing by Utagawa Kuniyoshi (1797–1861), which was a *kawaraban* (newsletter) inviting people to join in the festival of carrying the *mikoshi* (portable shrine). The amount of work that went into the carving is remarkable. It is a wonderful example of the carver's craft.

Courtesy of Adachi Institute of Woodcut Prints

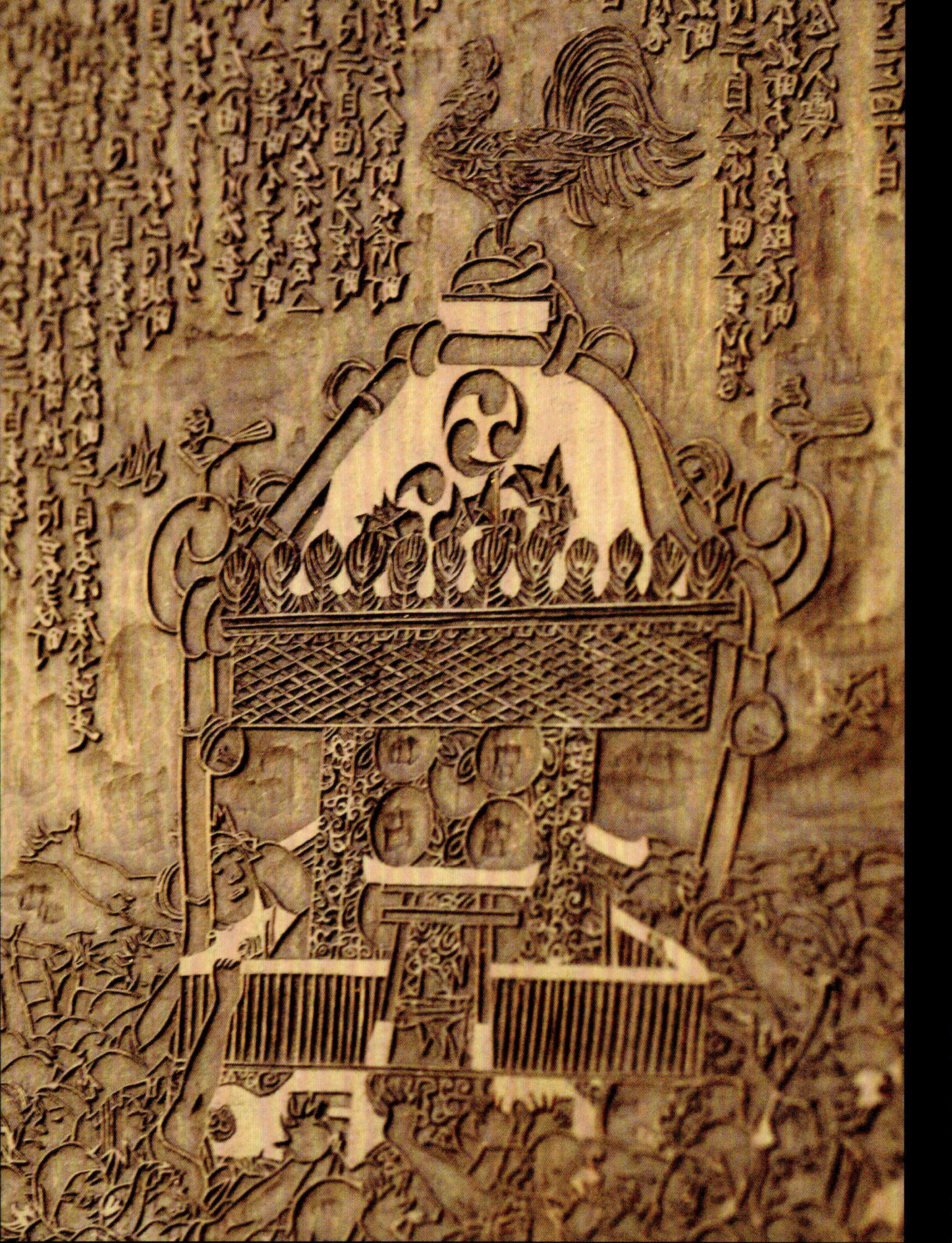

FIG. 27
Close-up of the same block
Courtesy of Adachi Institute of Woodcut Prints

FIG. 28
Monochrome print pulled from the block
Author's Collection

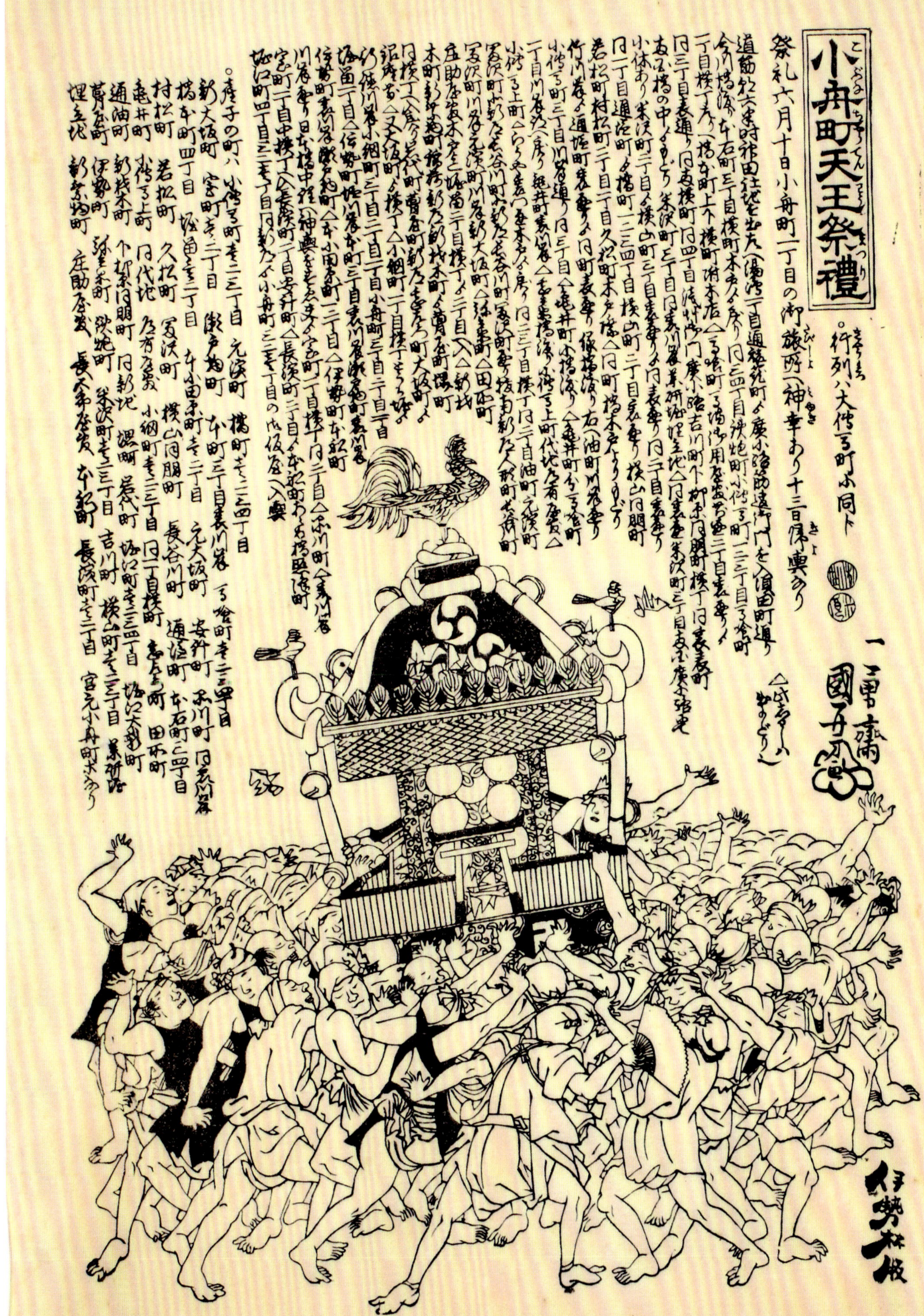

小舟町天王祭禮
祭礼六月十日小舟町二丁目の御旅所へ神幸あり十三日帰輿あり

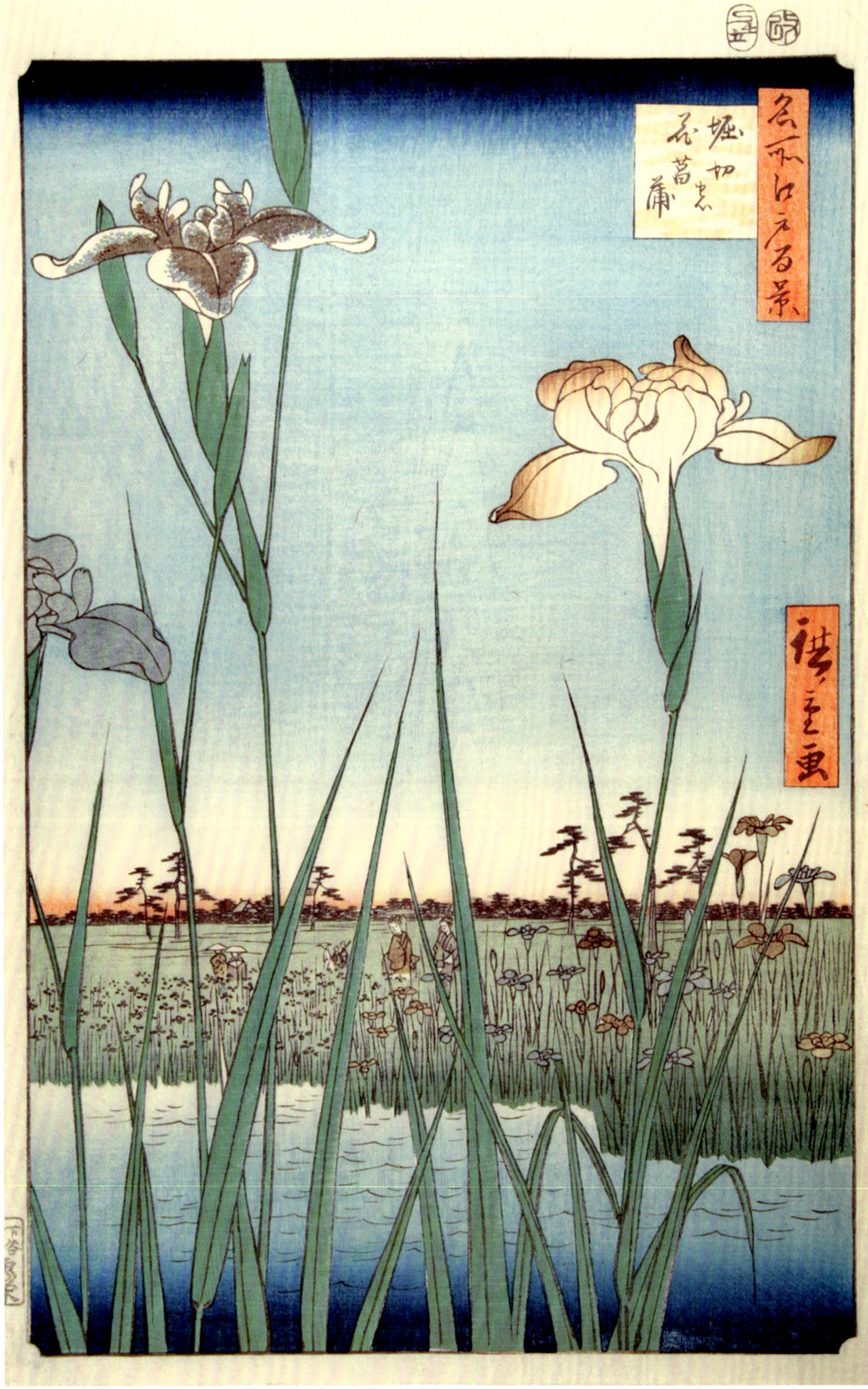
名所江戸百景
廣重画

FIG. 29
Utagawa HIROSHIGE
広重 (1797–1858)
Horikiri Iris Garden, from *One Hundred Famous Views of Edo* **堀切の花菖蒲** (1857)
Bokashi gradation technique, 39 x 27 cm
Courtesy of Mita Arts Gallery

In this series, Hiroshige showed his mastery of space by clearly distinguishing the foreground, middle ground and background. The flowers in the foreground are the main focus. The iris to the left is so close it becomes cropped. A closer examination of the print reveals young women in the middle ground and other figures further back. The design is simply marvelous, and is enhanced by the printer's talent in the *bokashi* technique, as exemplified by the gradation of pink to white in the main iris, and the treatment of the sky. The light blue sky fades into a pink horizon, which is reflected in the water, before eventually turning dark blue along the upper border.

can be purchased. Like anything else, the finest quality is very expensive, but once bought and properly cared for can last a lifetime. The craftsman I worked with made his own *baren* using age-old methods. For example, he made the *ategawa* by gluing a sheet of *minogami* paper every day for 100 days onto a cylindrical block of wood. The grain of the paper was reversed every day. After the pad was completely dry, he covered it with a thin sheet of gauze brushed with black lacquer and then trimmed around the edges.

Apart from skill with the *baren*, printers developed other techniques for enhancing the color quality of prints. One such technique is *bokashi*, the shading or gradation in the depth of a color that is accomplished by careful applications of pigment and water mixed on the block with the *hake* brush (**Figs. 29, 30, 32**). The *baren* is carefully applied to allow one or two colors to fade into each other. This is most apparent in the landscapes of Hiroshige and Hokusai, but can also be observed in the soft pinks seen on the cheeks of beauties and in the softness around the folds of the eyes, especially in the prints of the later part of the eighteenth century (**Fig. 31**).

Print sizes are always created to the specific woodblocks cut for the purposes of printing the pictures. The most common print sizes are, however, *aiban*, *chuban* and *o-ban*. Many print dealers refer to the sizes of their prints by name rather than by precise measurements.

Aiban, 34.5 x 22.5 cm. Half of the paper size called *kobosho* (see *Bai-oban* below) has been called *ainishiki*.

Bai-oban, 45.7 x 34.5 cm. Full size *kobosho*. Quite a few "primitives" are this size.

Chuban, 25.5 x 19 cm. One quarter of an *o-bosho*. Often used by Harunobu, Kiyonaga, Eishi, etc.

Chu-tanzaku, 38 x 12.7 cm. Half of an *o-ban*, cut lengthwise.

Hashira-e, 73 x 12 cm. Pillar prints, a narrow, upright format usually on two sheets pasted together either before or after printing.

Hosoban, 33 x 14.3 cm. Also called *hose-e*. Most of the Katsukawa actor prints are this size.

Hoso-e, see *Hosoban*.

Kaku-surimono, 21.3 x 18 cm. Used for square *surimono*. This size is sometimes called *shikishiban*.

Kakemono-e. Tall and wide prints, much wider than a *hashira-e*.

Koban, 22.8 x 17.2 cm. Half of an *aiban*, on which two designs were usually printed at a time.

Ko-tanzaku, 34.5 x 7.6 cm. One-third of an *aiban* upright.

Mameban. Any print smaller than a *ko-yotsugiri*. They vary considerably in size.

Mitsugiri, 25.5 x 12.8 cm. One-third of an *o-ban* but divided horizontally the other way from *tanzaku*.

Naga-oban, 60.5 x 30.2 cm. Some primitives by Kiyonobu and others are this size.

Naga-ban, 51.5 x 23 cm. Broader and shorter than a *hashira-e*. Hokusai's *Imagery of the Poets* and some Utamaro and Toyokuni prints are this size.

O-ban, 38.2 x 23 cm. The most common sheet size, both vertical and horizontal. It is half of a sheet called *o-bosho* or *masa*.

O-bosho, 51.2 x 23 cm. Kitao Masanobu's celebrated book, *Beauties of the Green Houses*, is this size.

Ogata chuban, 28.3 x 21.7 cm. One quarter of a paper called *obiro-bosho*. Many Harunobu prints are of this size.

O-hosoban, 38 x 17 cm. Formerly sometimes called large *hose-e*. Some hand-colored prints are this size.

O-tanzaku, 38 x 17 cm. The same size as an *o-hosoban* but this term is used for large Hiroshige flower and bird prints, etc.

Sho-tanzaku, 25.5 x 9.5 cm. One quarter of an *o-ban* divided vertically.

Tanzaku, see *Chu-tanzaku*, *Ko-tanzaku*, *O-tanzaku*, *Sho-tanzaku*.

Yotsugiri, 19 x 12.5 cm. One quarter of an *o-ban*. Usually four prints were printed at a time.

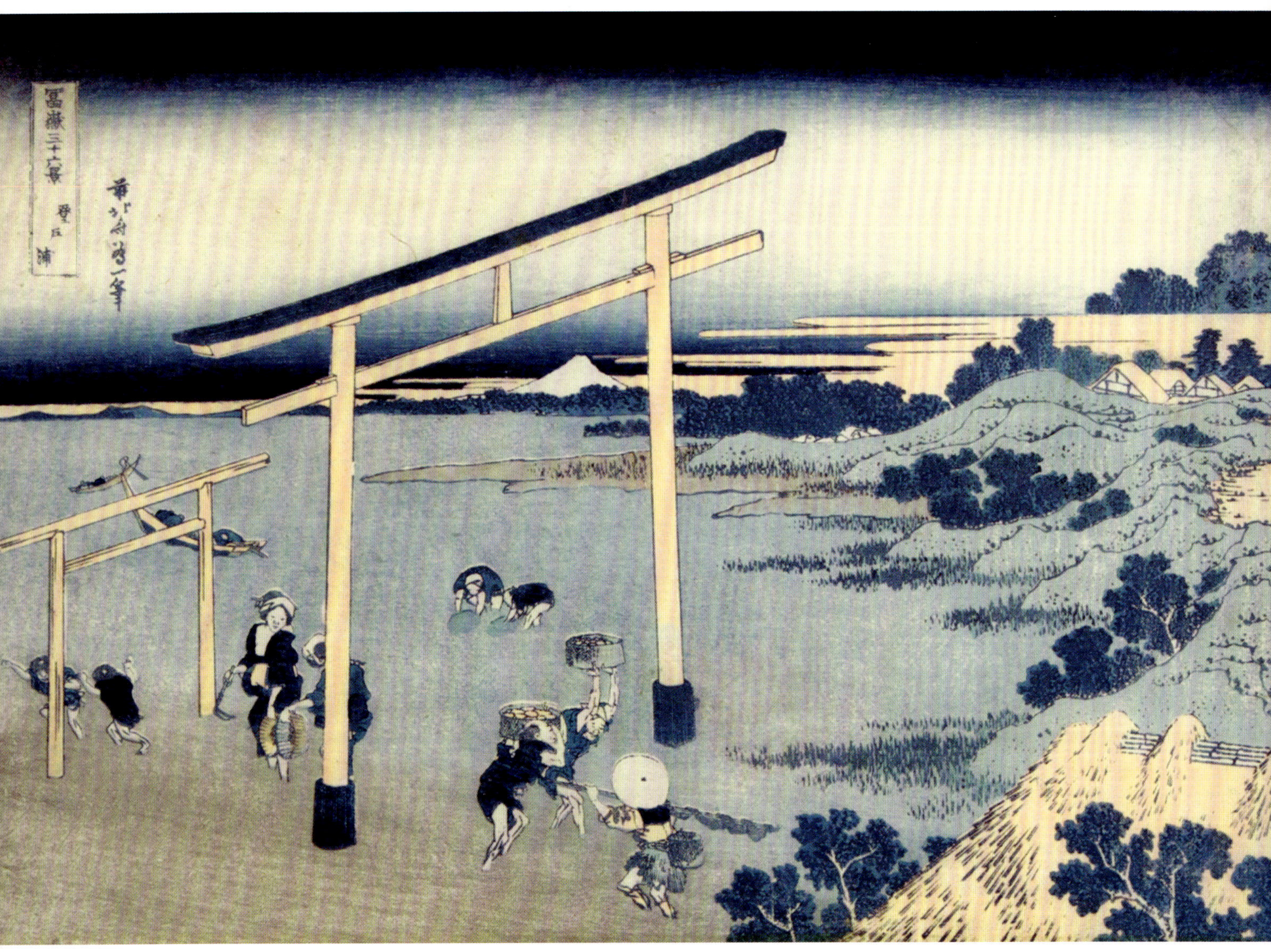

FIG. 30
Katsushika HOKUSAI
北斎 (1760–1849)
The Bay of Noboto, from *Thirty-Six Views of Mount Fuji* 登戸浦 (1830s)
Bokashi gradation technique, 39 x 27 cm
Courtesy of Mita Arts Gallery

This print of people gathering clams along the shore barely exposes Mount Fuji in the distance as a white silhouette. The *bokashi* in the blue sky is very effective, but the printer's real talent is demonstrated in the foreground as the brown dry land gently turns into grayish blue water. This is a good example of misunderstood perspective, but the overall design deserves to be appreciated without the correct perspective.

FIG. 31
Hamada JOSEN
濱田 如洗 (1875–?)
December, Clear Sky After Snow
十二月雪晴れ (1924)
Bokashi gradation technique, 34.5 x 19 cm
Author's Collection

Hamada Josen is a relatively unknown artist. He studied with the illustrator Tomioka Eisen, but apart from his contribution to the collection *New Ukiyo-e Beauties* in 1924 almost nothing is known about him. I have never seen any other example of his work. It is quite remarkable as his portrait of this beauty exemplifies the essence of Japanese femininity. She stares not at the viewer but to the right. She is bundled up in a heavy coat and decorative black shawl with a peek of bright red *kimono* underneath. The cold weather has forced her to tuck her hands into the *kimono* sleeve. The *bokashi* printing on the girl's face is the subtlest imaginable. The pink flush on her cheeks and the way it creates the form of the nose and rosebud lips and the soft shadow under the eyelid is as fine as was ever printed.

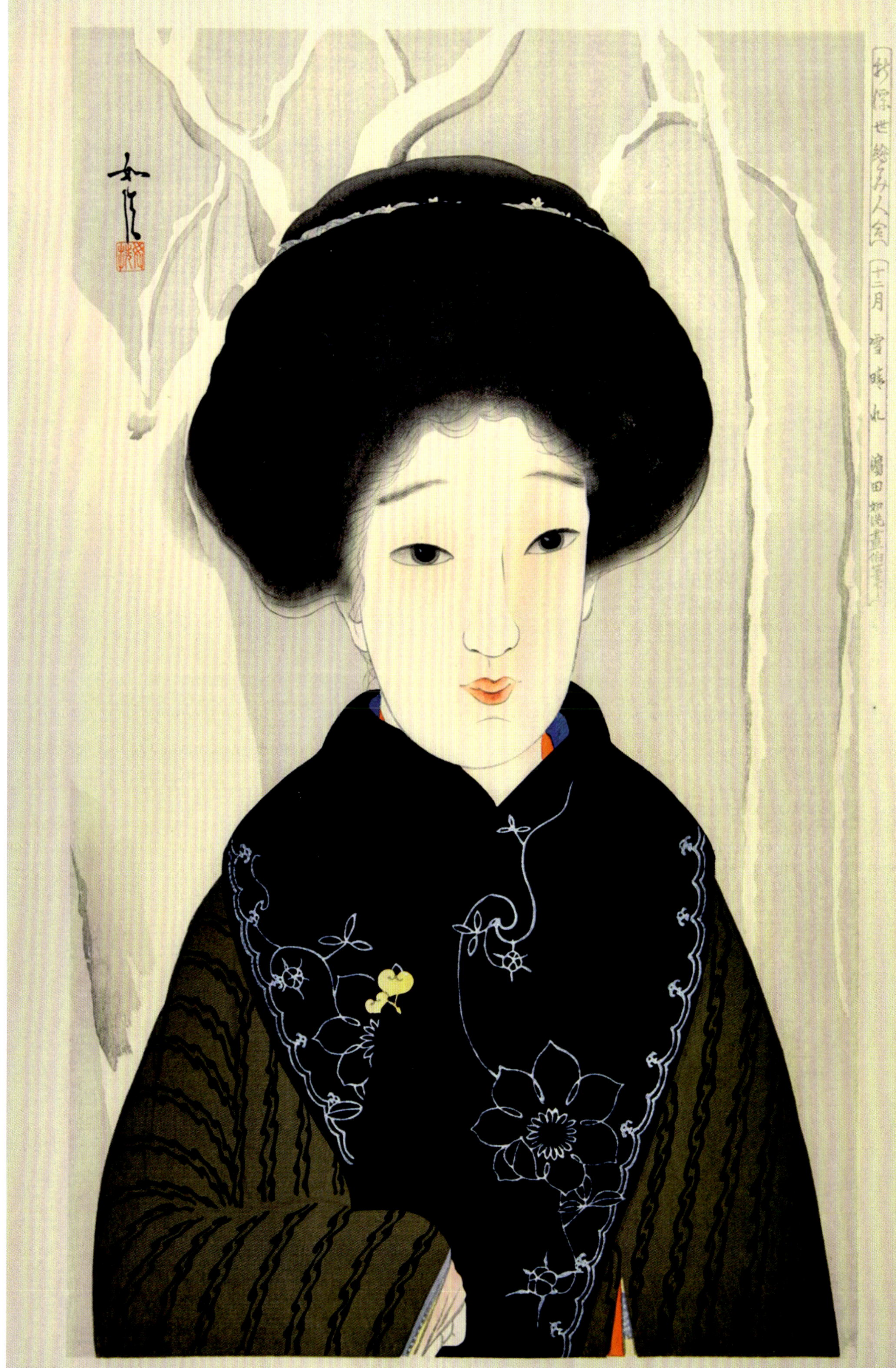
新浮世絵美人合
十二月 雪晴れ

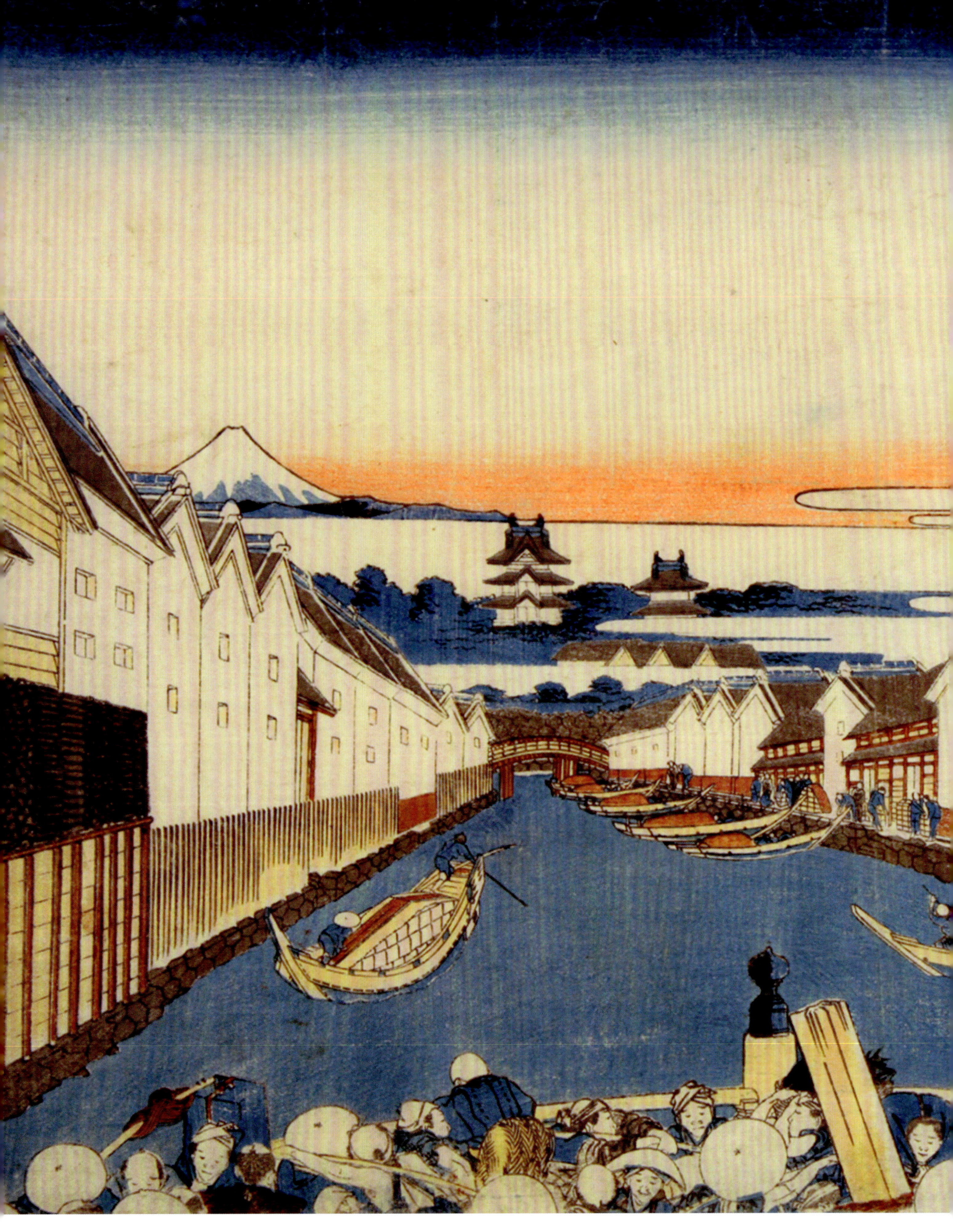

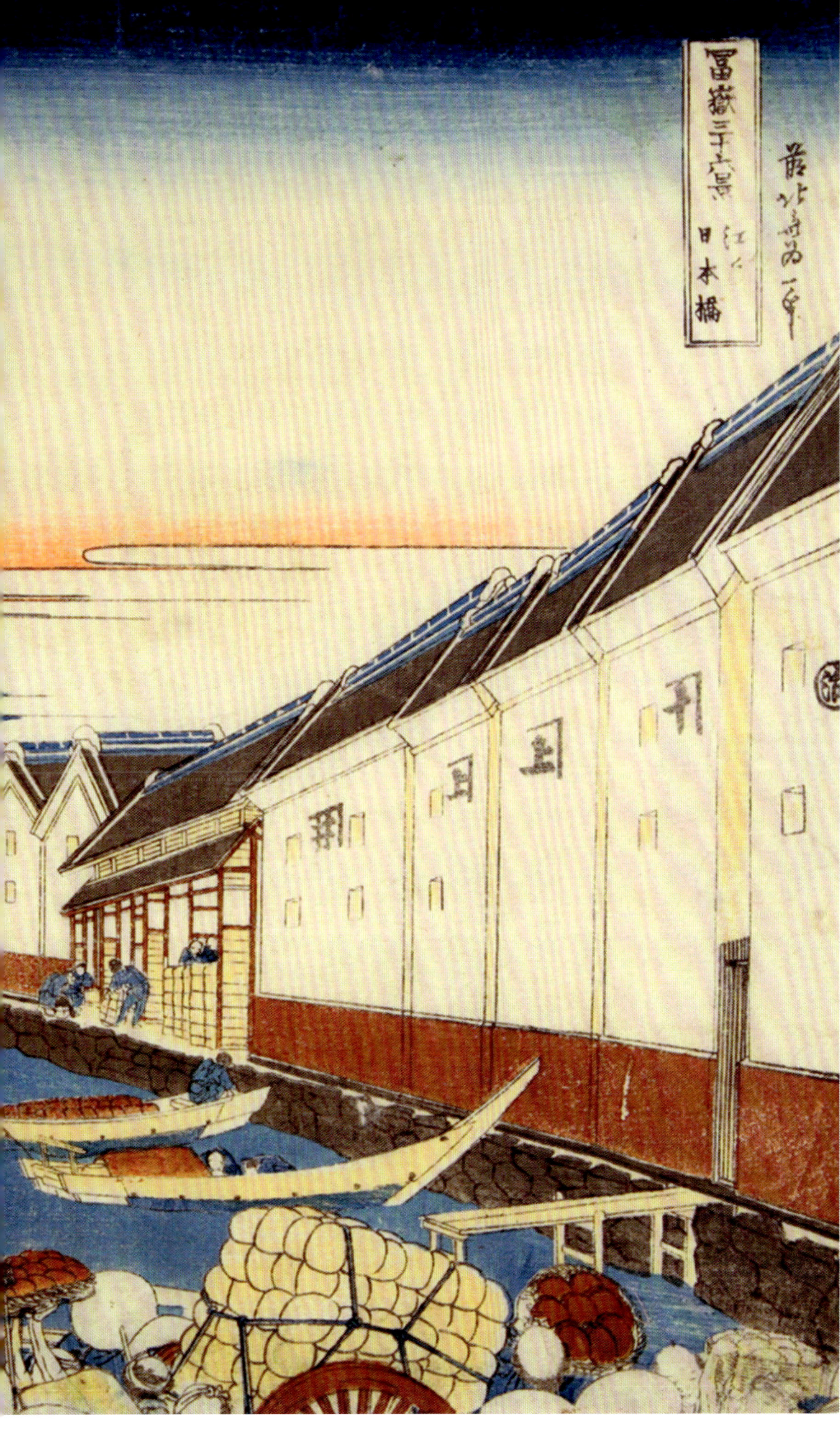

FIG. 32
Katsushika HOKUSAI
北斎 (1760–1849)
Nihonbashi, Edo, from *Thirty-Six Views of Mount Fuji* 江戸日本橋 (1830s)
Uki-e, bokashi gradation technique, 39 x 27 cm
Courtesy of Mita Arts Gallery

This is a perfect example of a *uki-e* (perspective print or "floating picture") showing the influence of the perspective technique in the European engravings that were becoming available through the Dutch port of Deshima. In the foreground, crowds of people, some bearing merchandise, push and shove as they cross the bridge in both directions. Nihonbashi was the gateway in Edo that led to Kyoto. This view is a subject featured often by *ukiyo-e* artists. It is included here as an example of the fine use of *bokashi* printing in the blue and orange bands of the sky, which highlight Mount Fuji in the distance.

CHAPTER THREE

Book Illustrations

FIG. 33a Travelers with baggage climbing a slope.

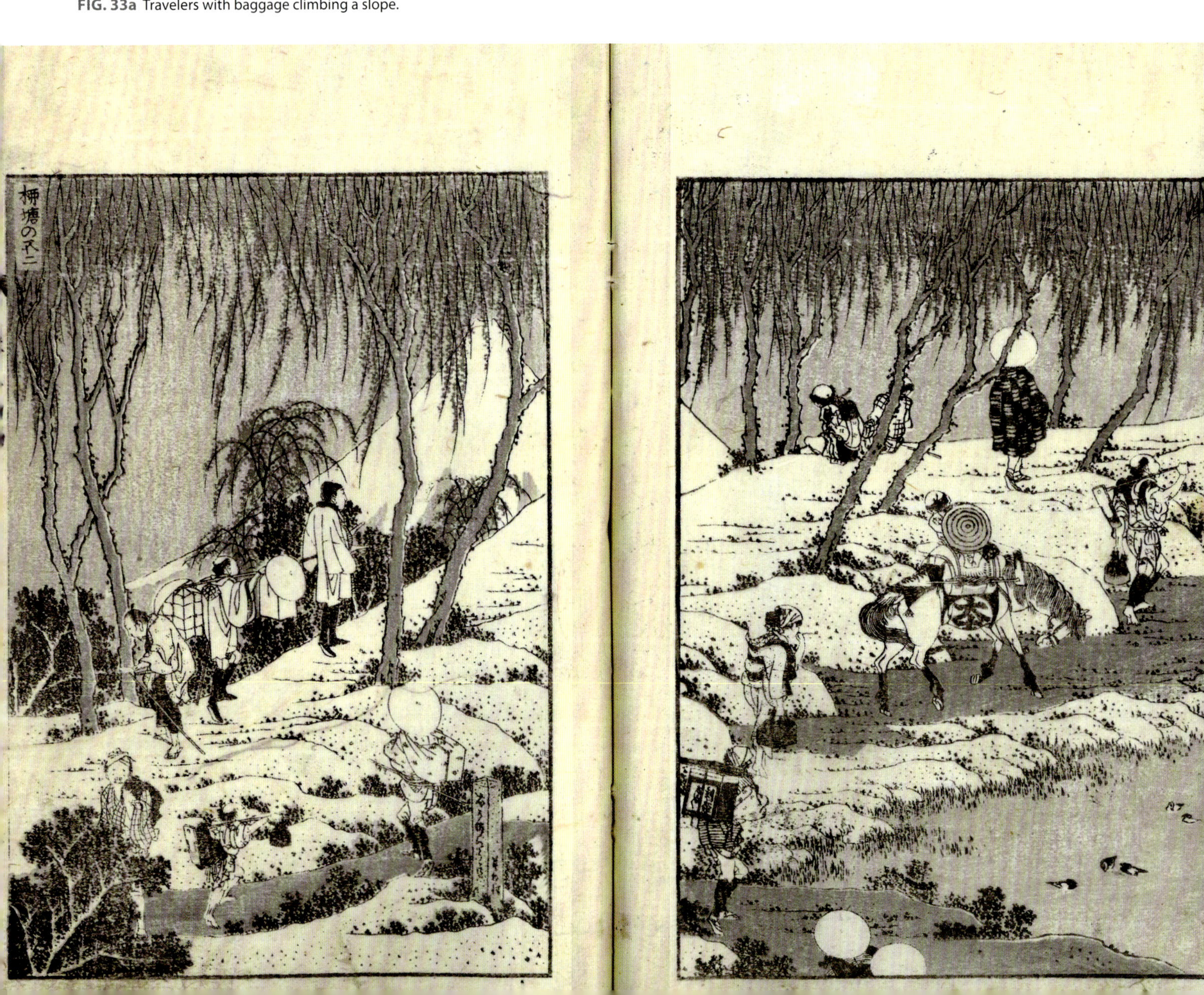

Although the technique of printing from woodblocks had been known in Japan since the eighth century, the first Japanese illustrated woodblock-printed book did not appear until the early years of the seventeenth century. By the eleventh century, as Buddhism from China took hold in Japan, Buddhist temples were producing their own woodblock-printed books of sutras, mandalas and other Buddhist scriptures and images. Temples also distributed images to pilgrims as votive prints, amulets or in exchange for monetary offerings. Buddhists believed that creating numerous images of the Buddha would help to prepare one's path toward salvation. One way of doing this was to stamp hundreds of block-carved images. Sheets of stamped images were also used as offerings for the dead and, as we have seen in Chapter 1, printed sheets of sutras were placed inside religious icons or statues as a form of thanksgiving. For centuries, printing was the virtual monopoly of Buddhists as it was too expensive for mass production. Moreover, outside the religious sphere, it did not have a receptive, literate public.

In about 1600, the first Japanese movable type, using some 100,000 wooden type pieces, was created under the direction of Tokugawa Ieyasu and was used to print a number of political and historical texts. But it soon became clear that the running script style of Japanese writings was more effectively reproduced using woodblocks and so these were again adopted and by the mid-1600s were used for nearly all printing. The images continued to be cut. The woodblock medium, although time-consuming and expensive, was far less so than the traditional method of copying books by hand. It rapidly gained popularity among artists and calligraphers and was used to produce small, cheap art prints as well as books. At a small studio in Saga, Honami Koetsu (1558–1637) and Suminokura Soan (1570–1632) created woodblocks of both the texts and images of several Japanese classics, among them the *Ise monogatari (The Tales of Ise)* in 1608, for a small circle of literary connoisseurs. Other printers in Kyoto quickly adapted the technique to producing cheaper books in large numbers for a wider, more general audience. These books included travel guides, novels, play scripts, art books and books on urban culture. Yet other publishers produced both books and single-sheet pictures. At the time, of course, the images in these books as well as the art prints were almost always monochrome, although occasionally colors were painted in by hand. The illustrations were often crude and subordinate to the text. There is also a general uniformity to the books and in almost all cases the identity of the artist is unknown. Soon, however, the illustrations became more and important and provided the masses with an affordable form of art. Even the illiterate, who wanted to be entertained although they could not read, bought books purely for the enjoyment of the pictures, including erotic picture books and fashion books of *kimono* patterns. Many of the illustrations in these books came to be contributed by well-known artists in contrast to the anonymous craftsmen of the past.

As mentioned in the introduction to this book, the so-called "primitive" *ukiyo-e* printing period began with the bold black and white designs of Hishikawa Moronobu (1618–94), who turned out hundreds of prints for illustrated books (*e-hon*), many of which were later unbound and sold as individual pictures. For this reason, it is impossible to separate the illustrated book in Japanese woodblock printing from single-sheet pictures. The only major difference is the purpose of the art form. Thus, the subject matter of a book became the main determining factor in the artist's approach to the pictures he created.

In response to the demands of the merchant commoner class during the seventeenth century for images of contemporary urban life in a new style, *ukiyo-e* artists began to blend elements from the traditional styles of painting in which they had been trained, such as the Tosa, Nanga, Maruyama-Shijo and Kano schools, with fashionable modern approaches to develop a hybrid form of popular art. The artists were not totally dedicated to the rules and traditions of these schools and deviated quite liberally according to the texts they were illustrating and the artistic trends of the time. Eventually, book illustrations would encompass all these aesthetic approaches to picture making, leading to an eclecticism of several styles that became typical of *ukiyo-e*.

At the beginning of the seventeenth century, however, the Tosa school of painting, founded in the fifteenth century, was the dominant influence on *ukiyo-e*. Exponents of the Tosa school painted mostly for the court and for aristocratic patrons who favored classic scenes as well as Chinese-inspired themes and styles, such as bird and flower paintings. Their painting style was distinguished by flat decorative compositions with fine, detailed line work and brilliant colors. Although the new breed of *ukiyo-e* artists adopted some Tosa elements, one of the major differences between the evolving *ukiyo-e* and the classic Tosa illustrations was the treatment of the figure. Whereas in the early Tosa illustrations the figure was an incidental part of a large scene, in *ukiyo-e* the figure became the main focus of attention. Indeed, figures become so large as to take up the entire space, reducing the background to an accommodating sub-factor.

As the seventeenth century drew to a close, there was a gradual transformation from Tosa-inspired illustrations to the more commonly accepted *ukiyo-e* tradition. This new era of pictorial illustration did not entirely abandon classical subjects, such as scenes of nature, but it focused on subjects that were more specific, more relevant to the everyday life of the patrons of *ukiyo-e*, especially in the major cities of Edo, Osaka and Kyoto, experiences that were distinct from the ostensibly more refined tastes of the ruling élite. It was a slow evolution but the enormity of it without doubt signaled a complete shake-up of the Japanese art world. It was at this time that we start to witness the Japanese culture that the West associates with Japan. The subject matter described the pleasures of living in the big cities—*kabuki* theater, *sumo* wrestling and, above all, the amorous adventures that awaited young men at the pleasure quarter.

At this time, too, there were two distinct regional styles of *ukiyo-e*, the dominant Edo school, centered in the city of the same name, and the Kamigata style, from an area encompassing Kyoto and nearby Osaka, the former cultural and economic heart of Japan. Apart from the fact that the volume of Edo prints far outnumbered those published by the Kamigata artists, the main difference lay in the range of subject matter. Whereas Kamigata prints almost exclusively depicted *kabuki* actors, those from Edo portrayed the whole gamut of contemporary urban subject matter. Aesthetically, there was not much difference at this time between the two worlds. Moreover, lots of artists moved back and forth between the cities since they were all major publishing centers. It was only at the end of the eighteenth century that the distinct appearance of the Kamigata prints is more noticeable, especially in those featuring large heads of *kabuki* actors.

Several big names are associated with *ukiyo-e* book illustrations. An important Kyoto illustrator at the beginning of the eighteenth century was Omori Yoshikiyo (active 1702–17). Even though little is known about his life, he produced some of the most remarkable images of the courtesan in the Shimabara district of Kyoto, the equivalent of the pleasure quarter in the more famous Yoshiwara of Edo.

For much of the eighteenth century, the Torii *samurai* clan in Edo, initially producers of *kabuki* theater billboards, posters and other promotional materials, were highly influential in the *ukiyo-e* depiction of actors and *kabuki* scenes. Led by Torii Kiyonobu I (1664–1729), who moved from Osaka to Edo in 1687 where he studied under Moronobu Hishikawa, among others, a greater emphasis on the energetic action and dramatic poses that one would see on the *kabuki* stage was introduced in full-size independent paintings and prints characterized by bold, thick lines. As the Torii school expanded, series of picture books with little text but very fanciful in spirit were produced. The books became known by the colors of their covers—red, black or blue. Paintings and prints of courtesans, erotic scenes and *sumo* in more graceful, delicate mainstream *ukiyo-e* styles also became a part of the Torii repertoire. Torii Kiyonaga (1752–1815), the last of the great Torii artists and one of the greatest of all *ukiyo-e* artists, retained much of the drama, energy and theatrical sensibility of the core Torii style, but he also introduced a previously unseen level of realism in his depictions of the urban culture of Edo, including its beautiful women.

The most important of the picture book artists is without a doubt Katsushika Hokusai (1760–1849), the former name referring to the part of Edo where he was born, whom we shall meet again in later chapters, so broad was his repertoire. He is the most prolific artist the world has ever seen. His prints number in the tens of thousands. He had a long life, dying at eighty-nine. It was also a complicated life. Either for monetary reasons or to make a new start, he changed his name some thirty times, sometimes even setting his name so that another poor artist could profit from his reputation.

Of the countless books Hokusai illustrated, two in particular stand out. The first is *One Hundred Views of Mount (Fugaku Hyakkei)*, a three-volume work published in 1834 and 1835 (**Fig. 33a–i**). Considered the masterpiece among his landscape picture books, the series was printed three times during his lifetime and countless times since. Although the illustrations lack the glamor of some of his most famous pictures, such as "The Great Wave Off Kanagawa" and "Red Fuji" from his

FIG. 33a–i
Katsushika HOKUSAI
北斎 (1760–1849)
Fugaku Hyakkei (One Hundred Views of Mount Fuji) 富嶽百景より (1834, 1835)
Book, 3 volumes, 22.5 x 16 cm
Author's Collection

Hokusai had a personal obsession with Mount Fuji. The views in both his Fuji books depict not only the whole mountain but also include imaginative treatments of it as a mere background detail—seen through a window, reflected in water, viewed as a silhouette or just a shadow. It is beyond comprehension how Hokusai could conceive the inventive composition on each page using only black lines and gray tones.

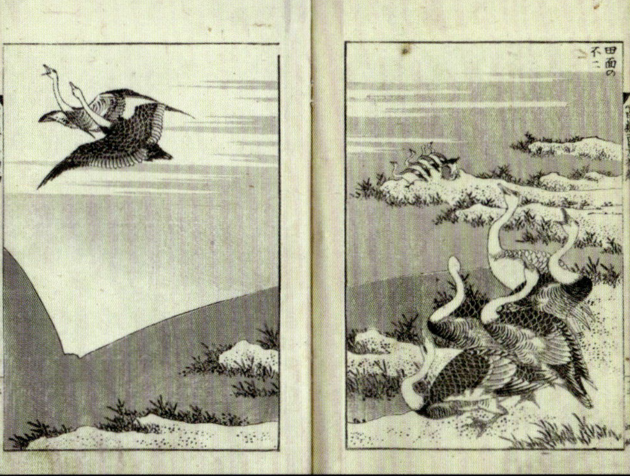

FIG. 33b Geese flying over a lake with Mount Fuji reflected in the water.

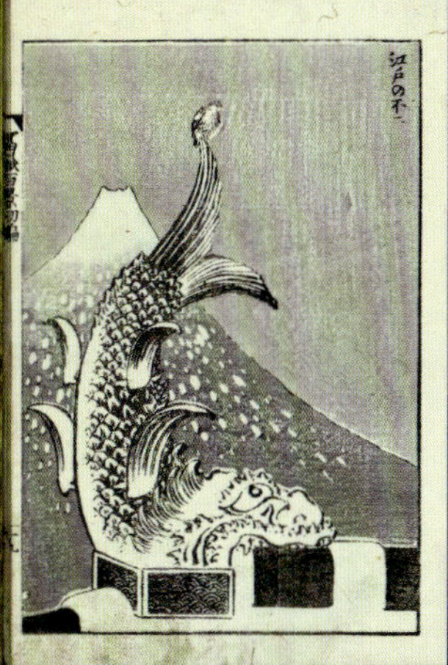

FIG. 33c Decorative sculpture of a mythological fish with a bird perched on top.

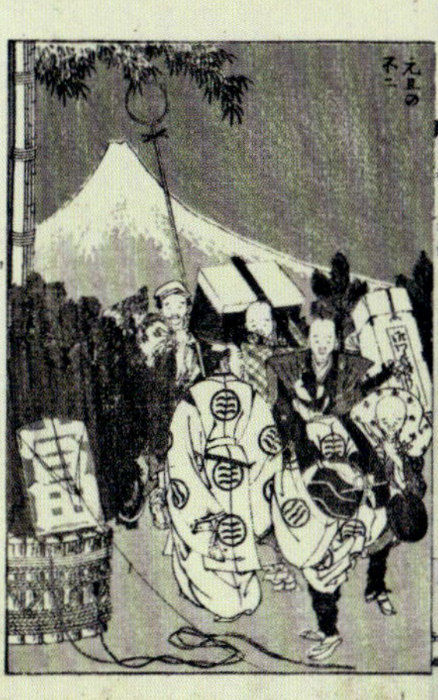

FIG. 36d Travelers coming and going toward Mount Fuji with a kite in the foreground.

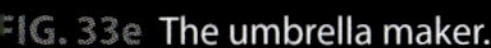

FIG. 33e The umbrella maker.

FIG. 33f Travelers passing under a religious ornament tied to a tree in the foreground.

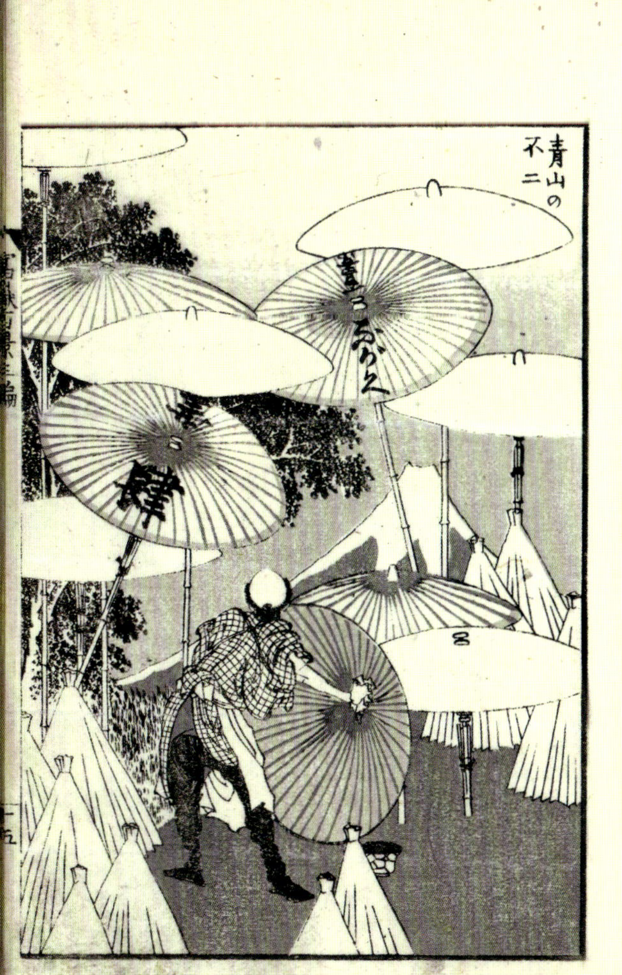

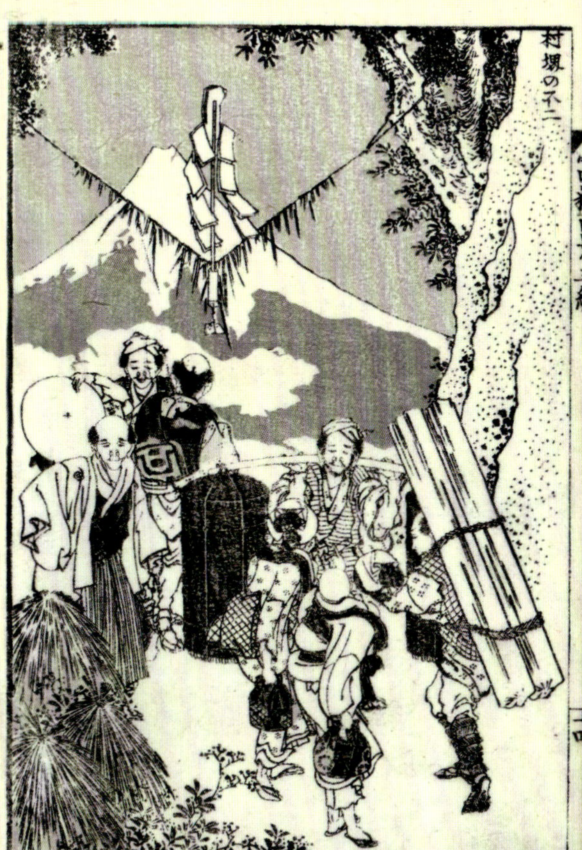

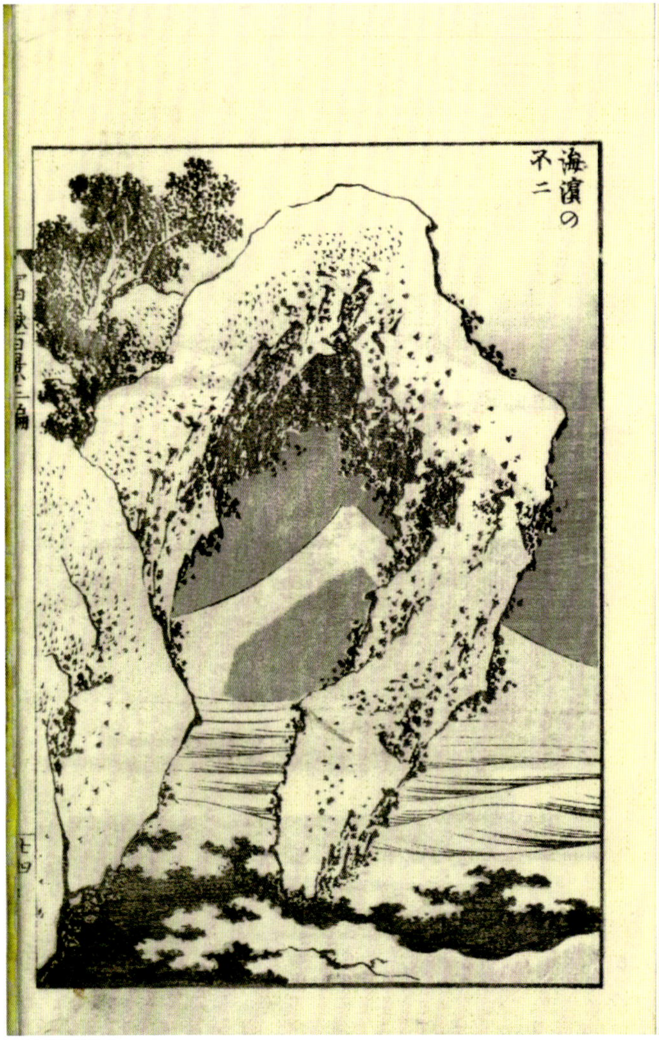

FIG. 33g Fuji seen through a natural rock formation.

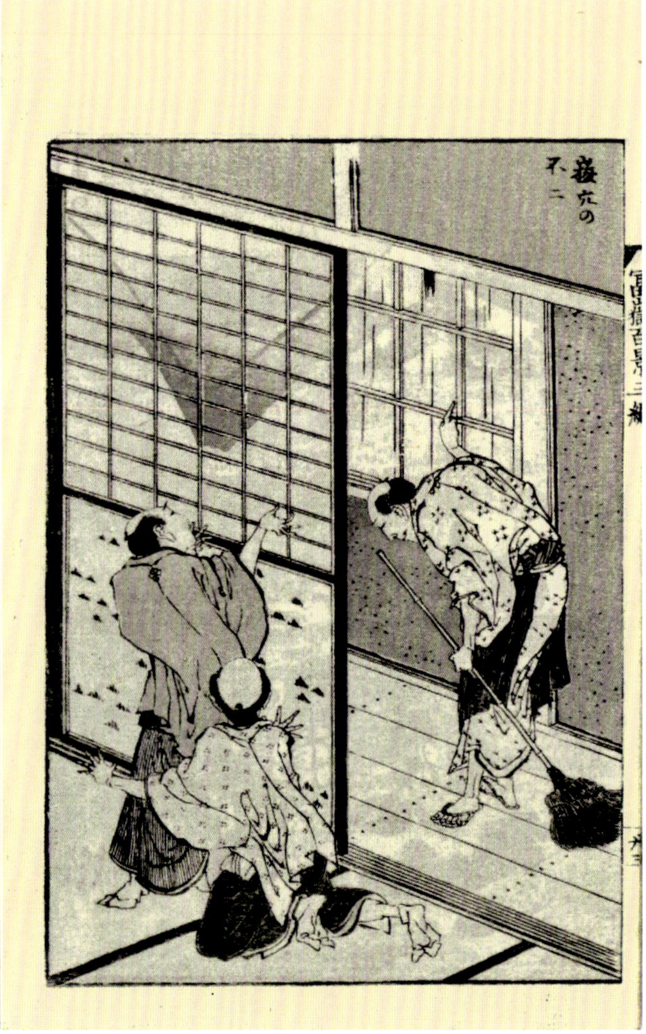

FIG. 33h An optical illusion when Mount Fuji appears upside down through two glass surfaces.

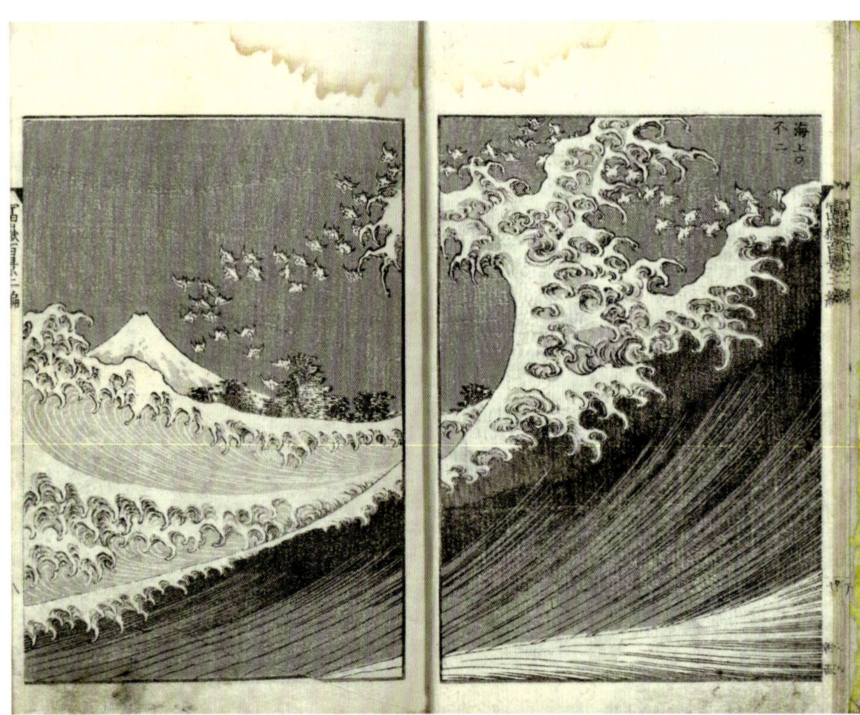

FIG. 33i Pure Hokusai "great wave" theme where waves mingle with water birds.

earlier series, *Fugaku Sanjuroku-kei (Thirty-six Views of Mount Fuji)*, published in 1831, they embody something far more significant. They show what a creative spirit can impart on a single and simple theme—a mountain venerated by generations of Japanese as the source of the secret of immortality. Even today, climbing Mount Fuji is a cherished task by Japanese and foreigners alike. The two Fuji series started a whole new style of landscape *ukiyo-e*. Not only did they secure Hokusai fame at home and abroad, they were also to leave a lasting impression on the art world, including leading artists in nineteenth-century Europe.

In the postscript to *Fugaku Hyakkei*, Hokusai wrote what I believe epitomizes his life: "From the age of six I had a mania for drawing the forms of things. By the time I was fifty I had published an infinity of designs; but all I produced before the age of seventy is not worth taking into account. At seventy-three I learned a little about the real structure of nature, of animals, plants, trees, birds, fishes and insects. In consequence when I am eighty I shall have made more progress; at ninety I shall penetrate the mystery of things; at a hundred I shall certainly have reached a marvelous stage; and when I am a hundred and ten everything I do, be it a dot or a line, will be alive. I beg those who live as long as I to see if I do not keep my word."

Hokusai's second great achievement was the hugely successful fifteen-volume *Hokusai Manga* published between 1814 and 1834 (**Fig. 34a–j**). Crammed with nearly 4,000 sketches, the books constitute a veritable encyclopedia of Japanese life. By covering every topic imaginable, from flora and fauna to everyday life and the supernatural, Hokusai transformed *ukiyo-e* from portraiture focused on courtesans and actors into a much broader genre. Although drawn in three art styles—Tosa, Kano and *ukiyo-e*—the *ukiyo-e* style dominates the entire set. The best prints depict the different occupations of the common people as well as *samurai*. Hokusai's people are drawn with a humor and wit never seen before. They also reveal his remarkable knowledge and understanding of the human body. For this reason, I consider Hokusai, together with Rembrandt, the two greatest draftsmen who ever lived. Both men are noteworthy for the quick, decisive way they could put complicated forms and actions on paper without unnecessary detail. The *Hokusai Manga* continues to be reprinted regularly, with new blocks being cut. Meiji period copies done in the late nineteenth century are expensive, even as copies.

Picture books during the Hokusai years flourished and most artists were happy to enter the world of publishing. It was good business and many artists, especially in Edo, were able to make a comfortable living. Subject matter ranged from pure comics to travel guides, the theater and, naturally, the gay quarter. These were the subjects the *ukiyo-e* masters thrived on, that offered unlimited aesthetic possibilities, providing them with a good livelihood and helping to establish their reputations. One such artist was Katsushika Taito II (active 1810–53), a pupil of Taito I, the name Katsushika Hokusai used between 1811 and 1820. Taito II was one of Katsushika Hokusai's best pupils and collaborated with his mentor on early volumes of the *Hokusai Manga* and other illustrated books. Hokusai gave Taito II his name in 1820. Unsurprisingly, Taito II worked in much the style of his great master (**Fig. 37a–c**).

At the same time, artists from other schools of art ventured into the illustrated book world. Among them were descendants of the hereditary secular painters of the Kano school of painting. Their interests lay less in illustrating novels than in keeping alive the traditions of Kano Tanyu (1602–74), the most successful member of the Kano school in the Edo period and the principal decorator of the massive castles and sumptuous homes of the *samurai* class. For these he created a number of large-scale works for screens and wall panels depicting natural subjects in bright colors and with extensive use of gold leaf. Tanyu's later return to the restrained designs and subdued tones of the early Kano painters, and a renewed interest in ink monochrome, set the standards for the later Kano artists who ventured into book illustration but were keen to transmit the Kano school style. Many of their illustrations were copies of well-known paintings by past Kano masters in which detailed realistic depictions of animals and other subjects in the foreground were juxtaposed with "negative space" implying mist, clouds, sea or sky in the background or to indicate distance. They also produced instruction manuals on how to paint in the traditional manner.

Other painting schools influenced the development of *ukiyo-e*. One was the Nanga ("Southern painting") or Literati school in Kyoto, named after the Chinese Southern school of painting. Nanga artists considered themselves intellectuals or literati and shared an admiration for Chinese culture. Their paintings, usually rendered in black ink, sometimes with soft colors, almost always depicted traditional Chinese subjects such as landscapes and birds and flowers. One of the most important painters and book illustrators of the Nanga or Literati school of artists was Tani Buncho (1763–1840) (**Fig. 35a, b**). Although he studied the painting techniques of the Kano school in his youth and worked with masters of other schools to develop a wide stylistic range, he is best known for his Chinese-inspired landscapes in the literati style. He illustrated almost thirty books, mostly with landscapes.

Another Kyoto painting school was the Maruyama, founded by the realist painter Maruyama Okyo (1733–95), who advocated tranquil Western naturalism mixed with the Eastern decorative style of the Kano school. An offshoot of the Maruyama, the Shijo school, named after the street in Kyoto where many major artists were based, was started by one of Okyo's former students, Matsumura Goshun (1752–1811). The Shijo style was a synthesis of the rival Nanga and Maruyama schools,

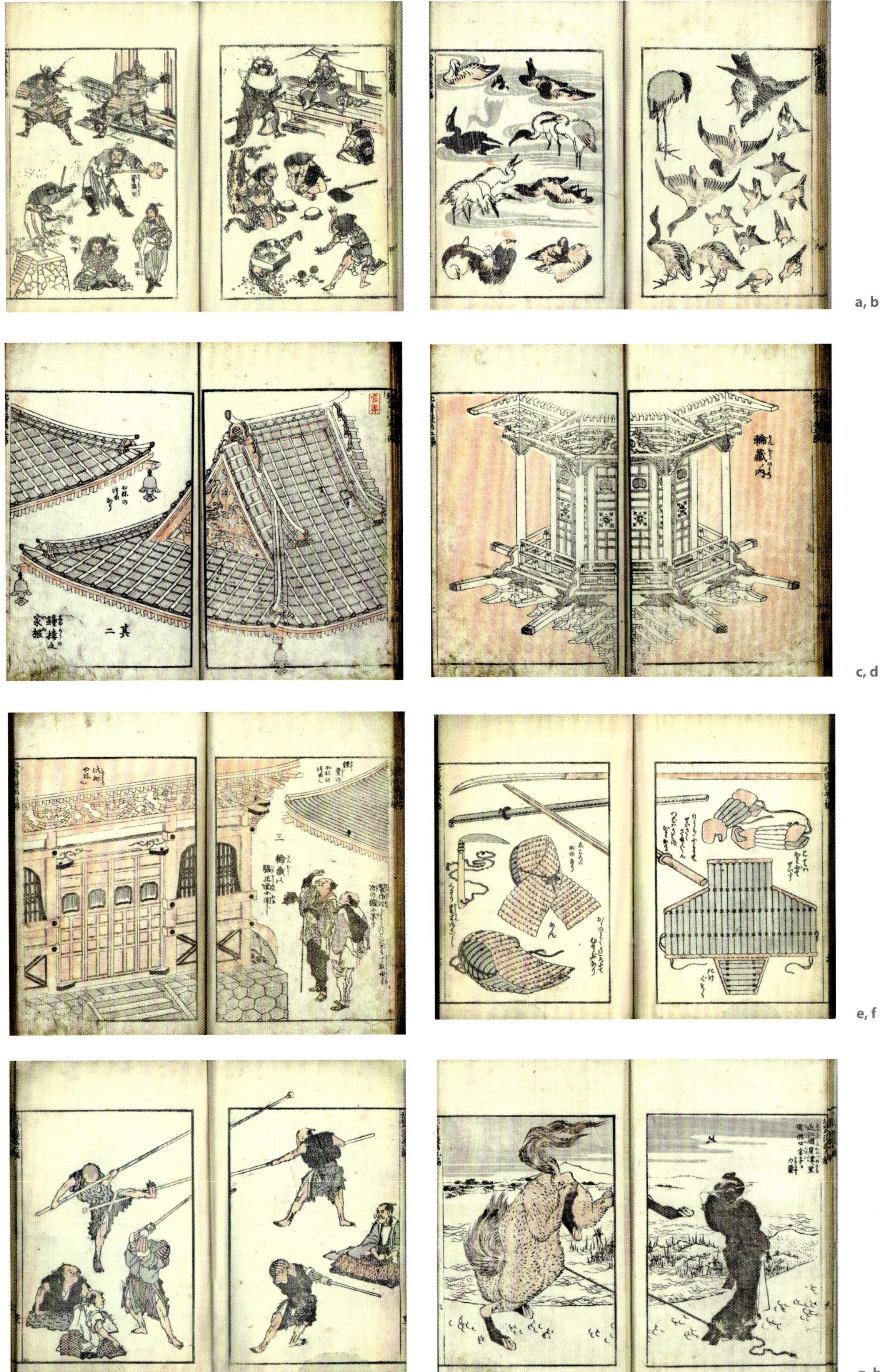

a, b

c, d

e, f

g, h

FIG. 34a–j
Katsushika HOKUSAI
北斎 (1760–1849)
***Hokusai Manga* 北斎漫画より** (1814–34)
Book, 15 volumes, 22.5 x 16 cm
Courtesy of Hara Shobo

Hokusai's fifteen-volume *Manga*, a compilation of over 4,000 drawings of everyday people, animals, religious figures, etc. is an amazing feat of conceptual ideas. Although the series does not have the aesthetic appeal of the *Fugaku Hyakkei (One Hundred Views of Mount Fuji)*, it is astonishing for the breadth of its subject matter and is at once humorous, scientific and beautiful. The later volumes do not have the verve and liveliness of the early volumes but are still remarkable. The examples shown are taken from four of the original volumes.

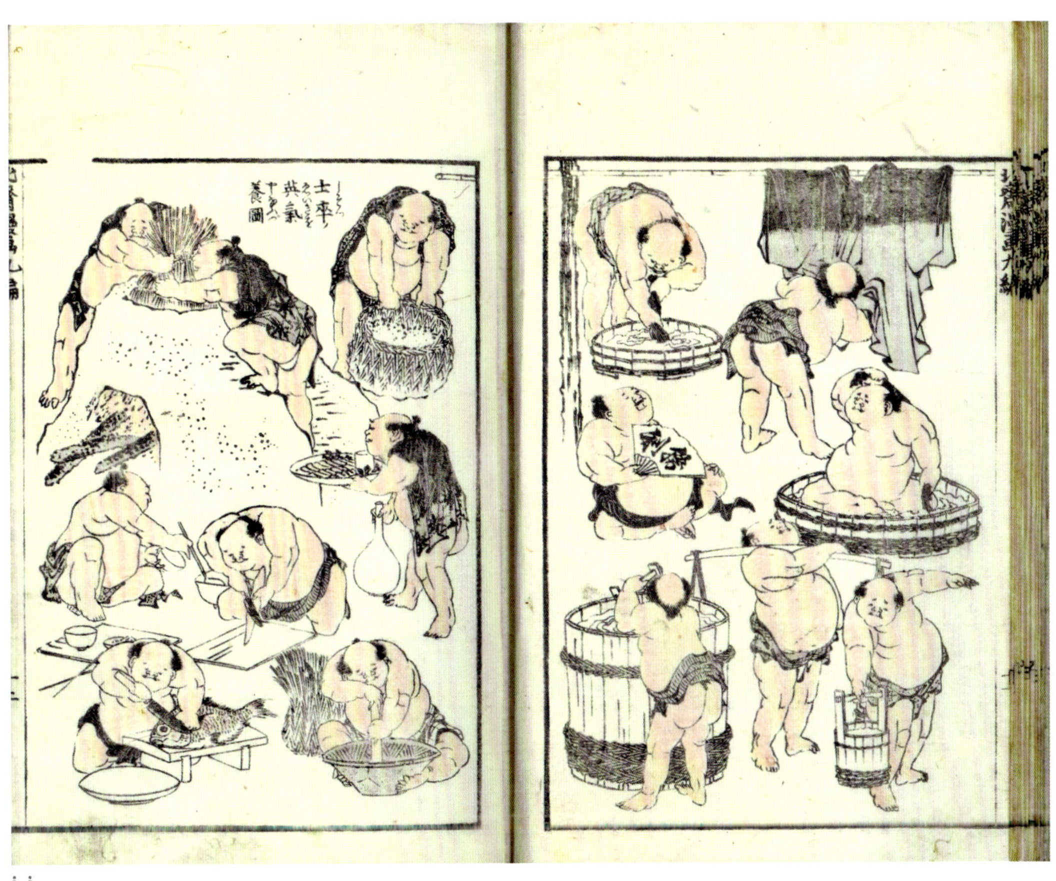

i, j

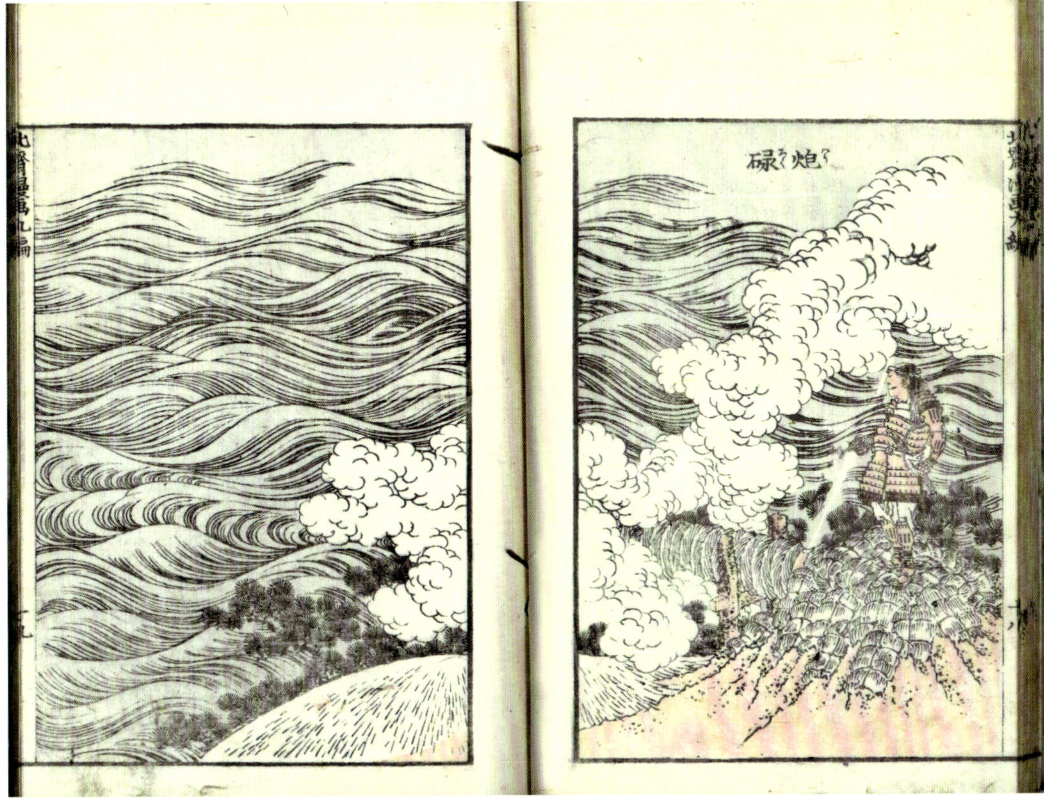

FIG. 34a
Samurai and mythological characters (Vol. 4).

FIG. 34b
Birds, some of which are in flight. (We must remember the careful observation necessary to draw from memory as there was no photography) (Vol. 4).

FIG. 34c–e
Architectural roof details (Vol. 5).

FIG. 34f
Samurai armor and weapons (Vol. 6).

FIG. 34g
Positions of fighting with a spear (Vol. 6).

FIG. 34h
An angry horse being controlled by a woman (Vol. 9).

FIG. 34i
A fat man washing and preparing food (Vol. 9).

FIG. 34j
A *samurai* contemplating a turbulent sea (Vol. 9).

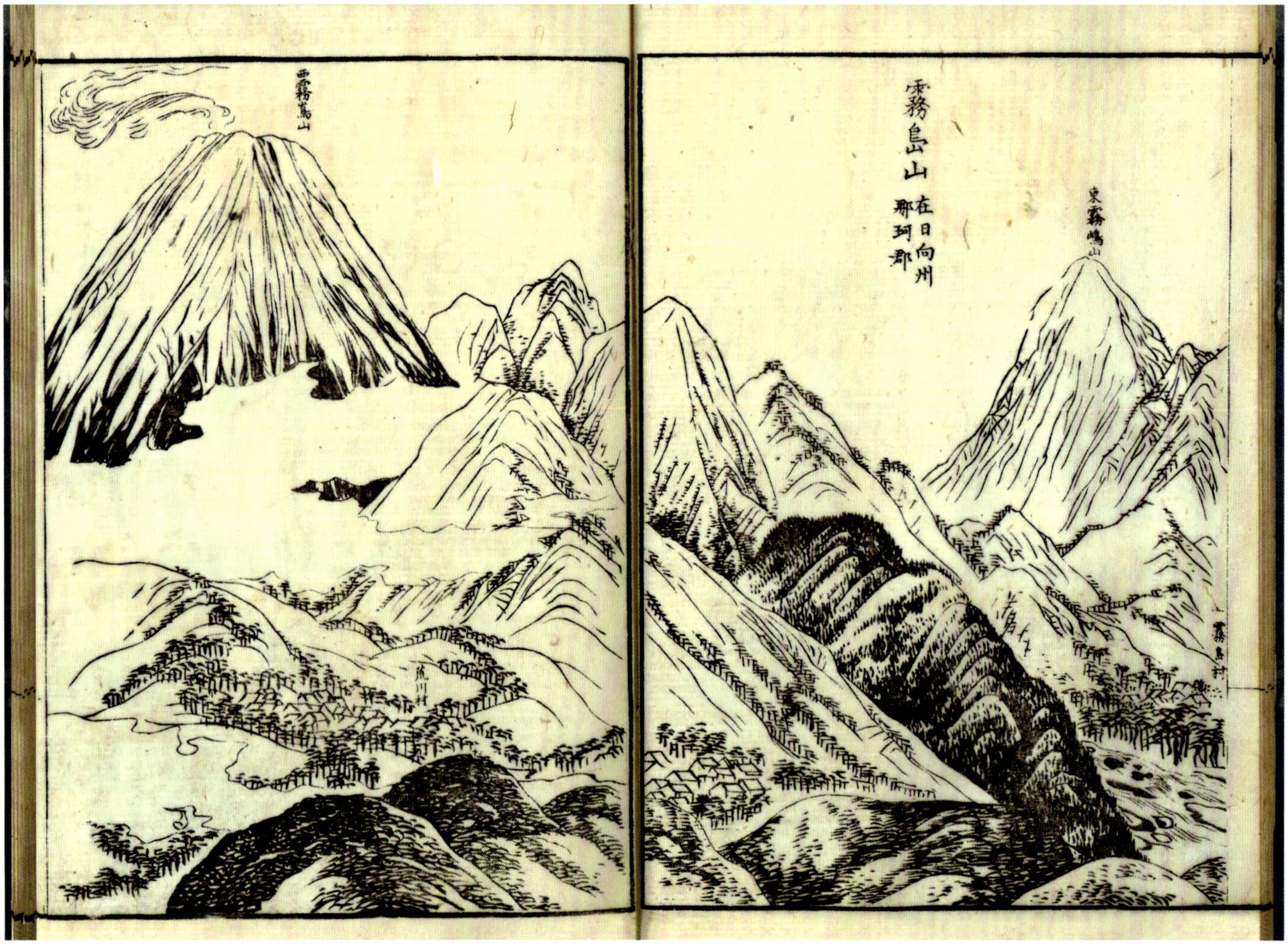

FIG. 35a, b
Tani BUNCHO
谷 文晁 (1763–1840)
Nihon Meisan Zue (Mountains of Japan) **日本名山図絵** (1804)
Book, 3 volumes, 25 x 35 cm
Author's Collection

Considered one of Buncho's masterpieces of book illustration, the pictures in this book are painted in the typical Northern Chinese literal style of rendering volume. Mountains assume shapes that are articulated with nothing but thin lines of *sumi* ink. The darker tones are groupings of trees growing around the contours of the large masses. A closer look reveals the villages at the base of the mountains. The implied scale of human habitants to the grandeur of the mountains creates a contrast so great that it leaves us in awe.

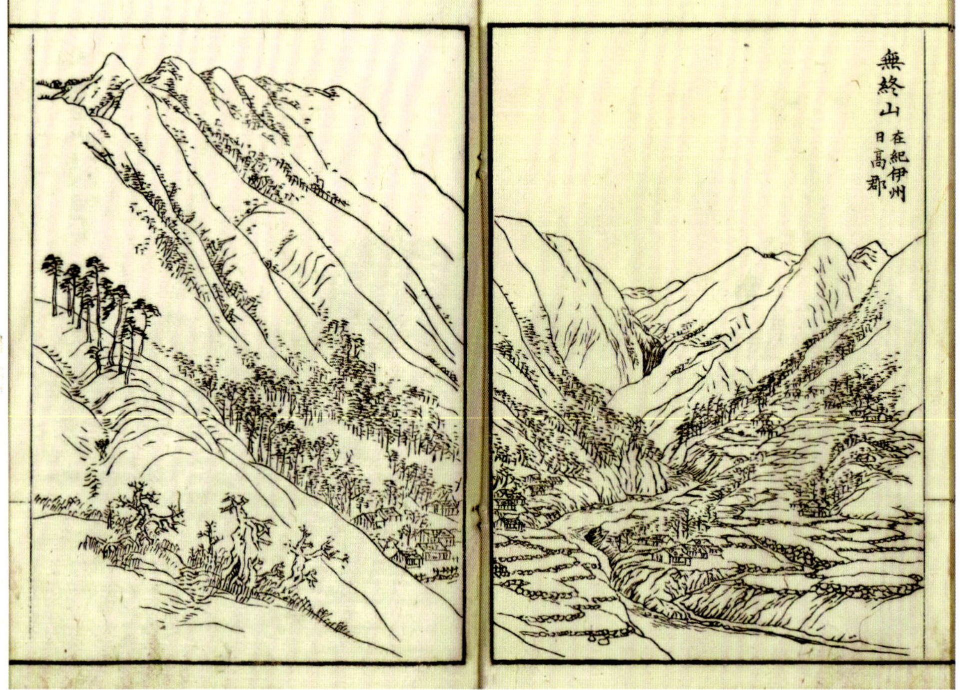

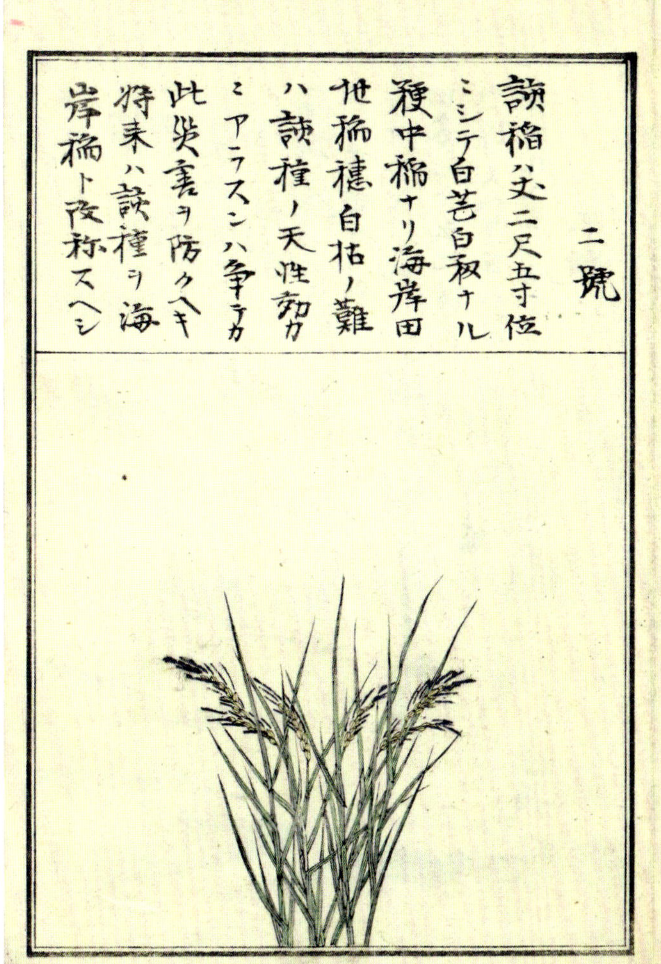

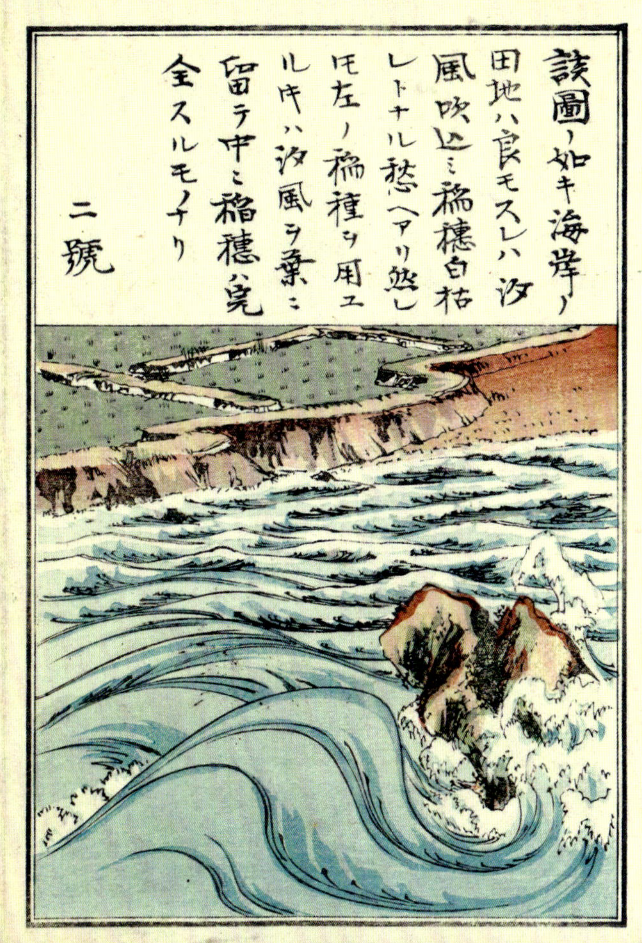

FIG. 36a, b
ANONYMOUS
Land Suitable for Rice Cultivation
稲作 (1896)
Book, 20 x 13.5 cm
Author's Collection

Occasionally, books of scientific interest or those aligned with the particular interests of publishers were produced. The illustrations for this book, published in Kyoto in 1896, are exceptional. Examples of the sketches of rice and the environments in which rice grows would have been of great interest to a specialized agricultural-minded audience. They are included here to give the reader an idea of the broad scope of subject matter covered in nineteenth-century book publishing.

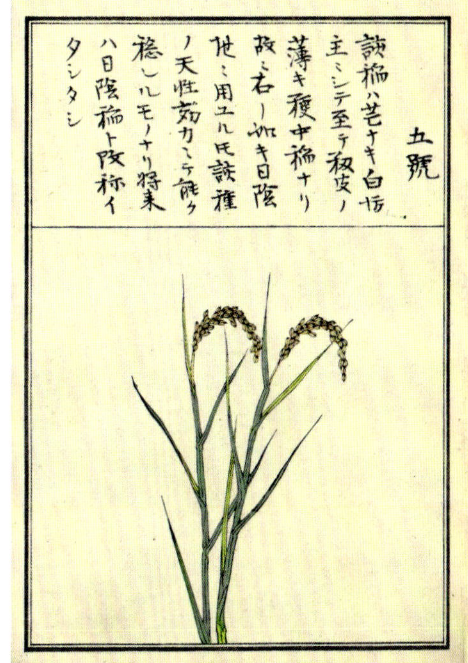

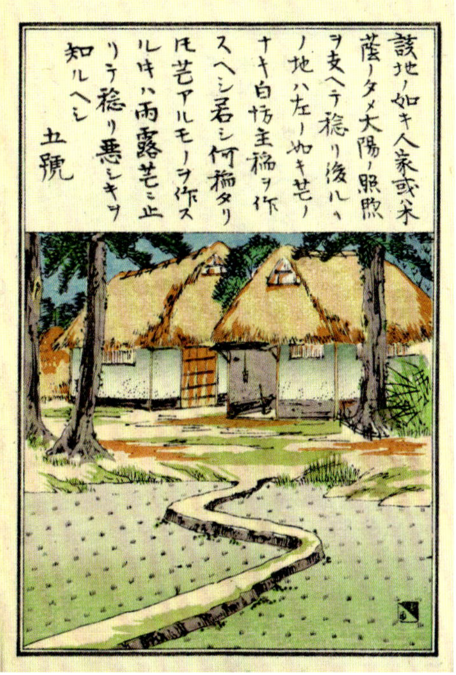

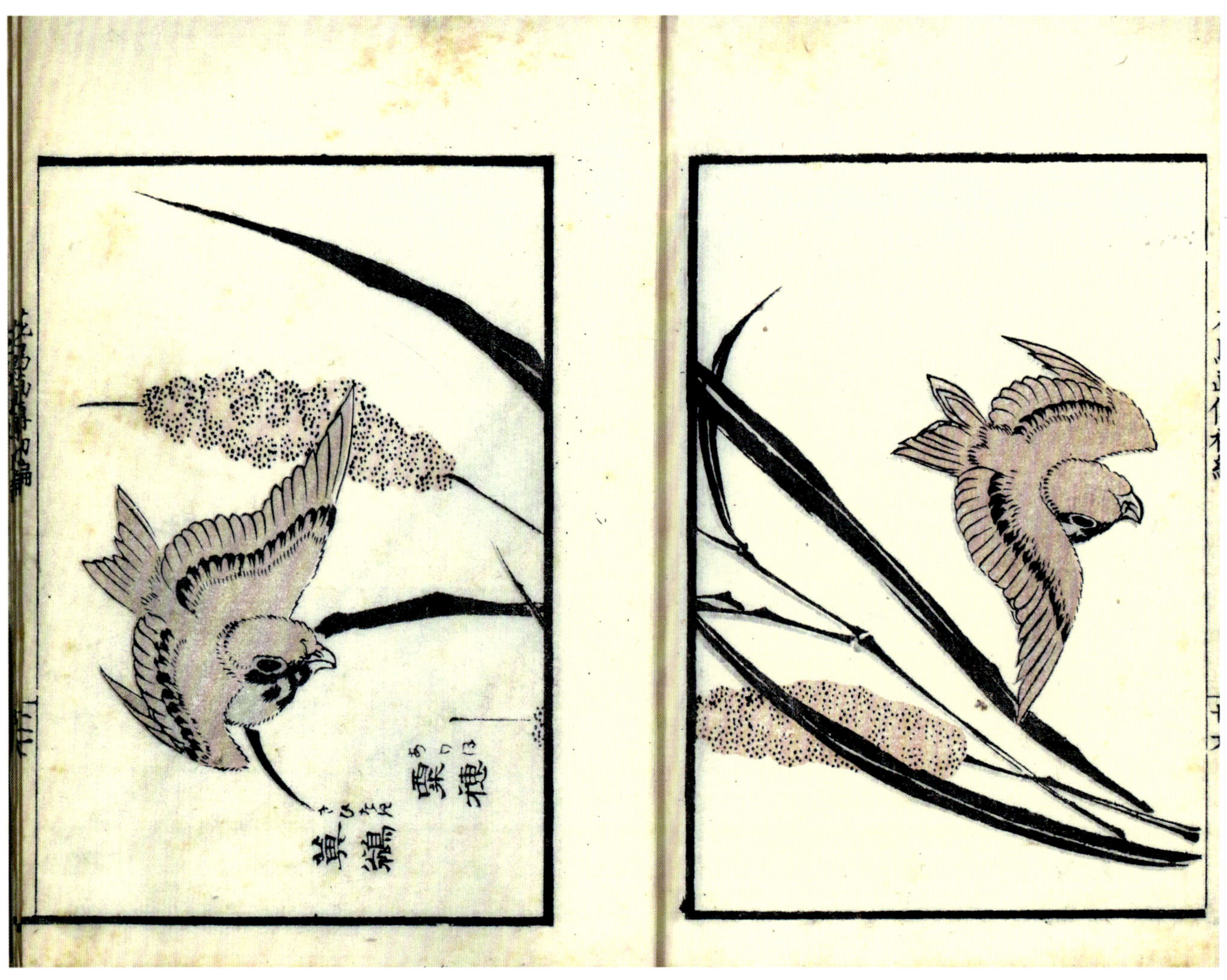

focusing on Western-influenced objective realism but achieved with traditional Japanese painting techniques.

One such illustrated book deserves particular mention, the three-volume *Seitei Kacho Gafu (Seitei's Album of Birds and Flowers)* published in the Meiji period (1868–1912). The artist, Watanabe Seitei (1851–1918), was primarily a painter who also illustrated some beautiful books, most of which concentrated on flowers and birds (**Fig. 38a–d**). In these he blended Western realism with the delicate colors and washes of the Maruyama-Shijo school, thereby introducing a new approach to bird and flower painting (*kacho-e*). Japanese artists devoted a great amount of time studying the anatomy and flying patterns of birds. When we think there was no photography at the time, it is uncanny to imagine an artist so well versed in the characteristics of birds that he can picture them in such natural states as Seitei does in his book. It is absolutely beautiful, with each page more stunning than the last. The printing makes extensive use of the *bokashi* gradation technique. Many of the illustrations approach the appearance of watercolors. They epitomize the essence of Japanese taste.

Artists from the powerful and prolific Utagawa school worked in all genres of *ukiyo-e*, including book illustrations. One of the finest exponents was Utagawa Sadahide Gyokuransai (1807–73), who illustrated many books relating to warriors (**Fig. 39a–g**).

The artists mentioned above, among many, many others, contributed to some of the most beautiful books of the late eighteenth and nineteenth centuries. The illustrations in these books developed into a pure Japanese aesthetic sensitivity in composition and understanding of form. They were no longer dependent on a black outline and achieved what seemed impossible in the medium of book illustration through woodblock printing.

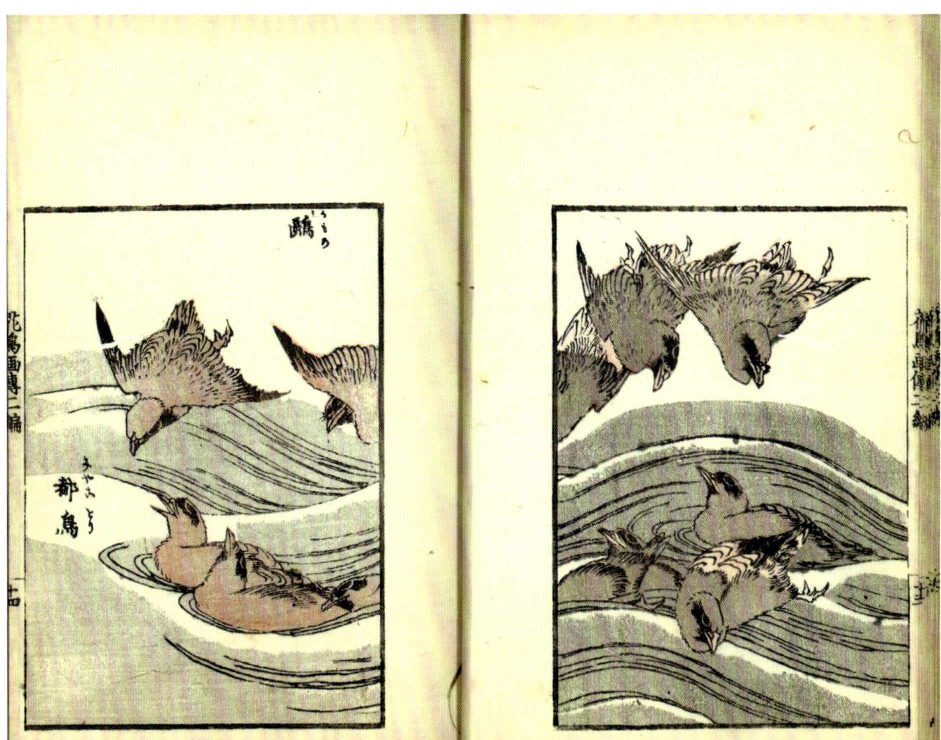

FIG. 37a–c
Katsushika TAITO II
二代載斗 (active 1810–53)
Kacho Gaden (Picture Book of Flowers and Birds) 花鳥畫田
Book, 2 volumes, 22 x 13.5 cm
Author's Collection

We can see Hokusai's mastery of space and design in his student's work. The birds in all three examples are full of life, playfully flying around flowers or diving into the rapidly flowing river. Apart from the green at the foot of the geese, the book is printed in black, gray and pink.

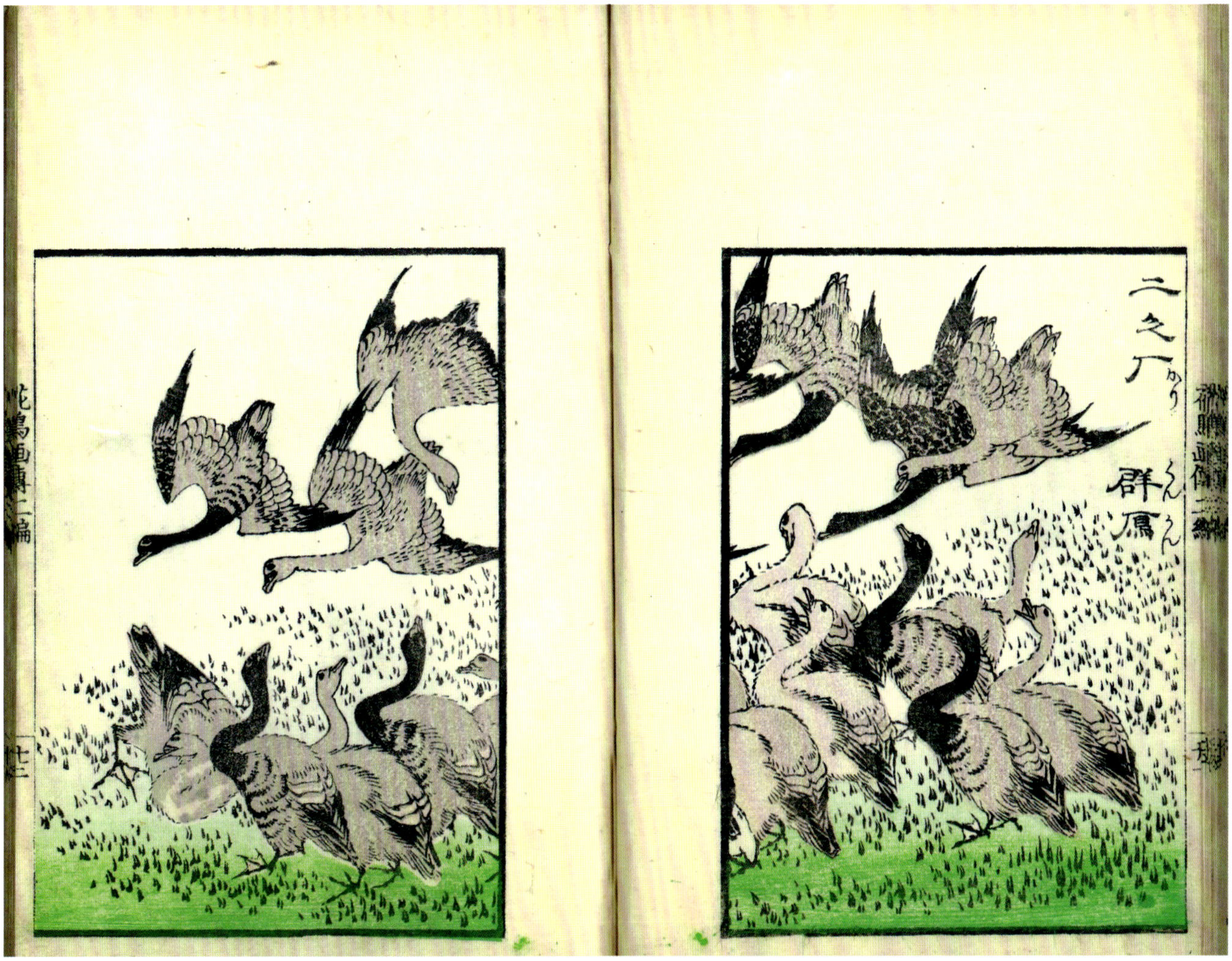

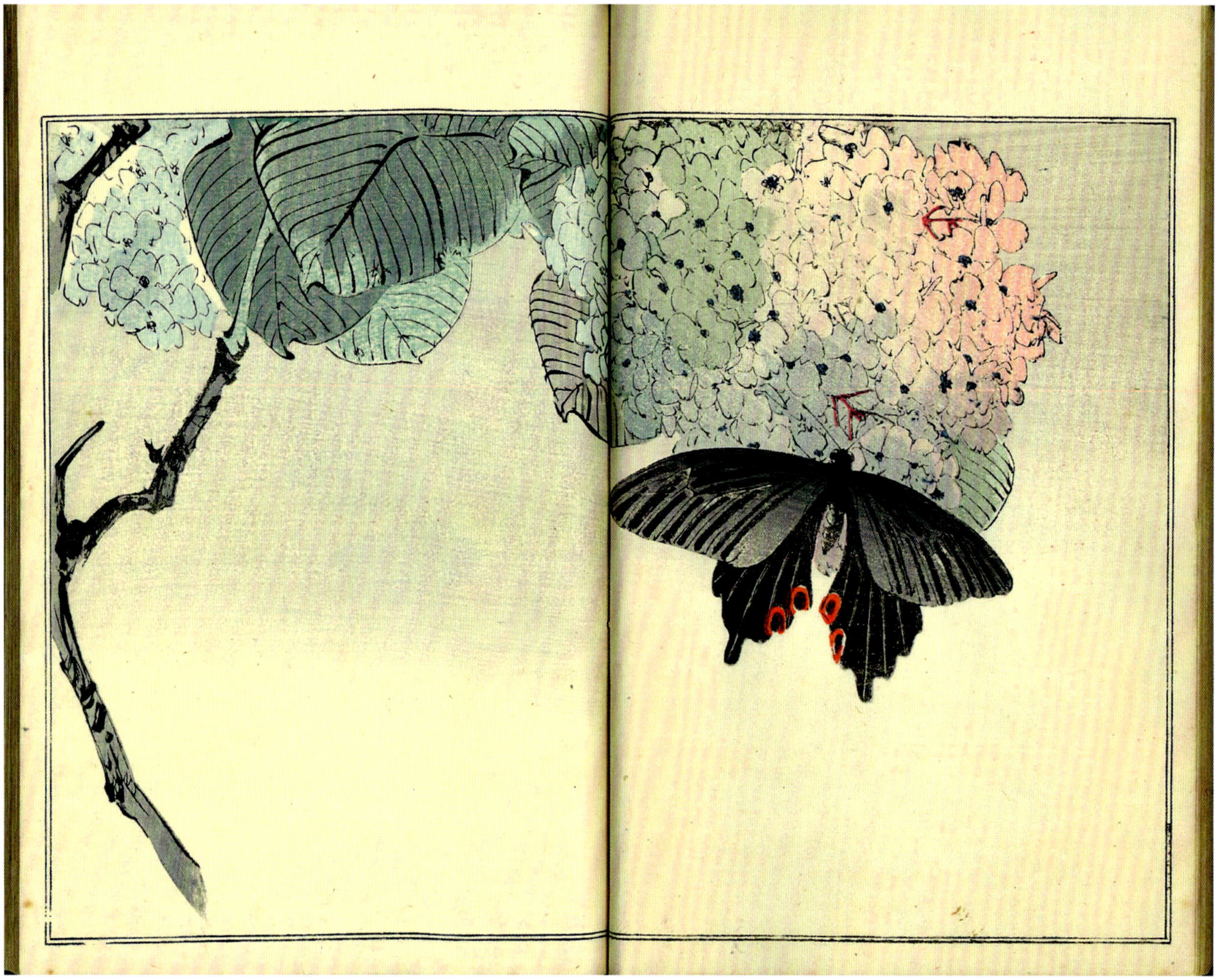

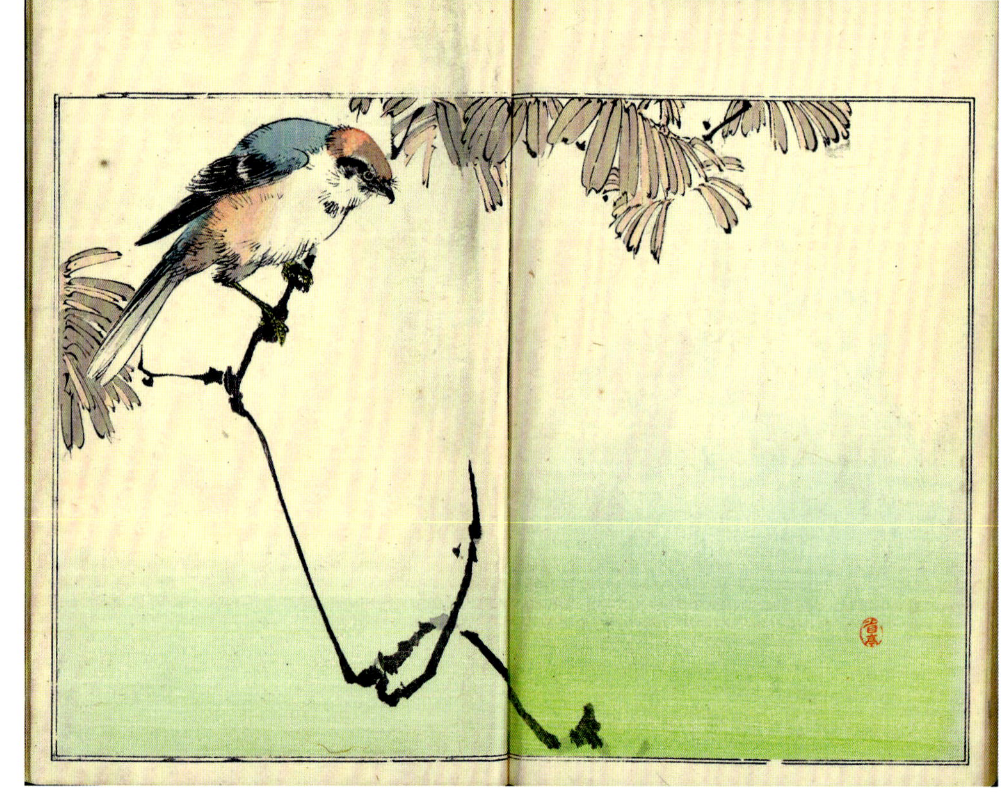

FIG. 38a–d
Watanabe SEITEI
渡邊省亭 (1851–1918)
Seitei Kacho Gafu (Seitei's Bird and Flower Album)
省亭花鳥画譜 (1916)
Book, 3 volumes, 24.5 x 16.5 cm
Author's Collection

Seitei's simple, asymmetrical compositions combine graceful calligraphic lines with delicate details and shading. In almost all of them, the subject is positioned in the corner of the design, leaving the rest of the page as negative space. His work was influenced by contemporary European paintings, which utilized light and shadow and perspective to give the impression of dimensionality.

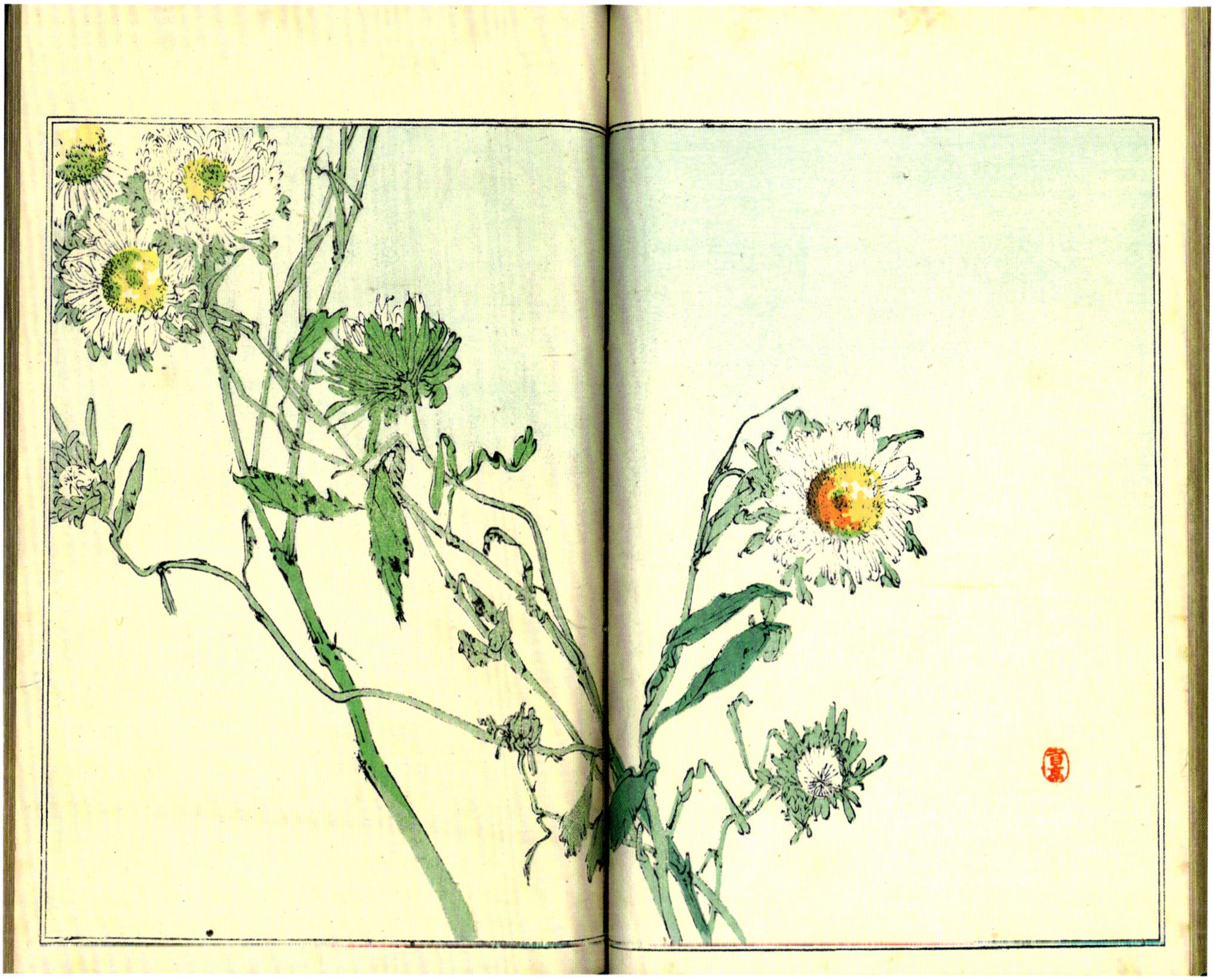

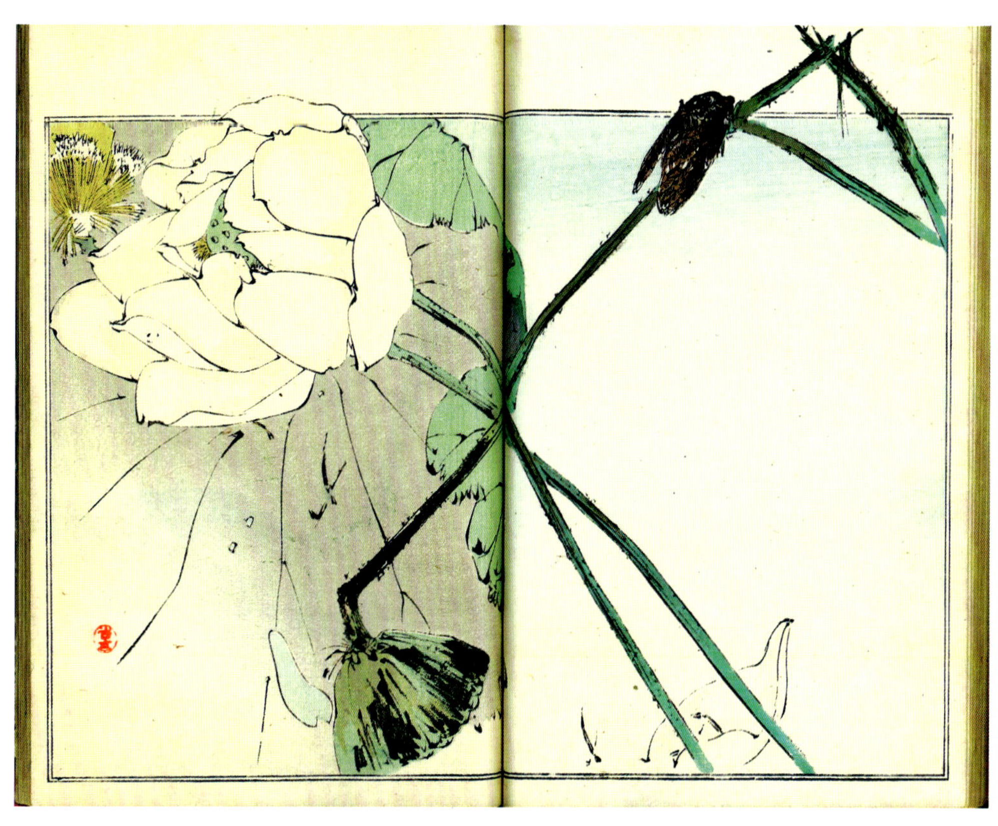

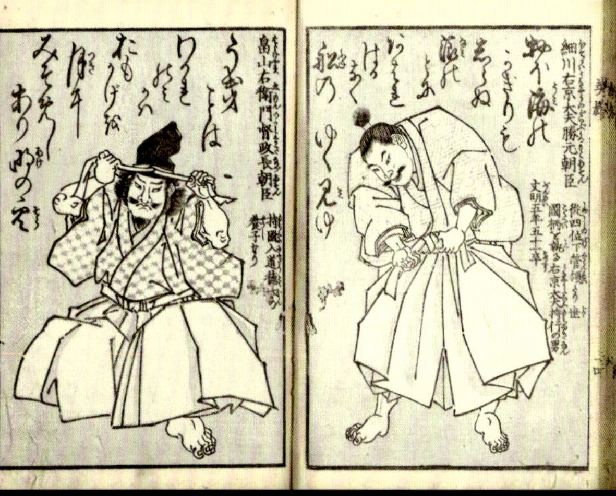

FIG. 39a The *samurai* in his undergarments.

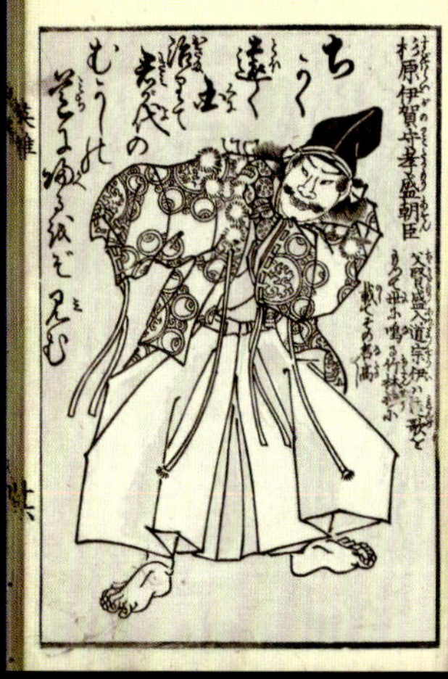

FIG. 39b Putting on gloves and donning his outer garment.

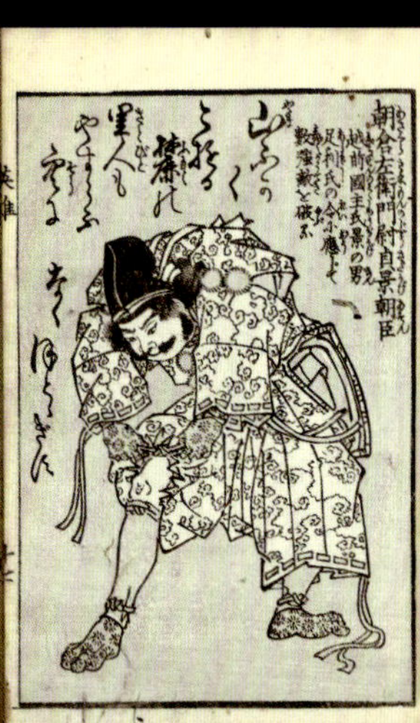

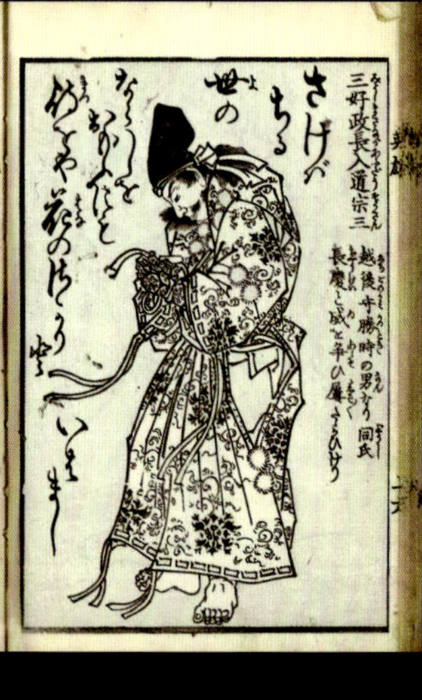

FIG. 39c Lacing his socks.

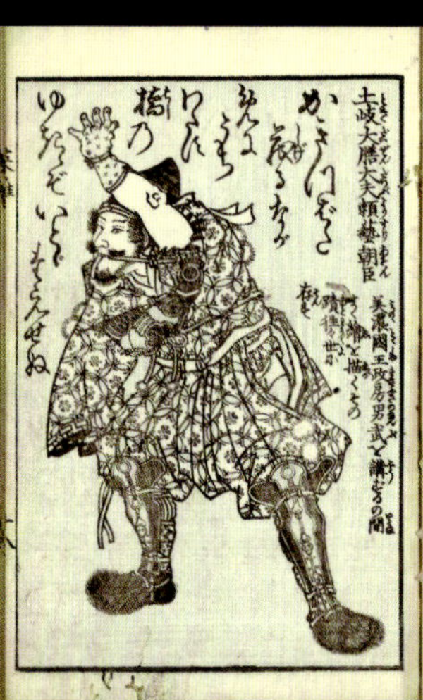

FIG. 39d Tying his fur-lined boots.

FIG. 39e The back of the samurai as he secures his armor.

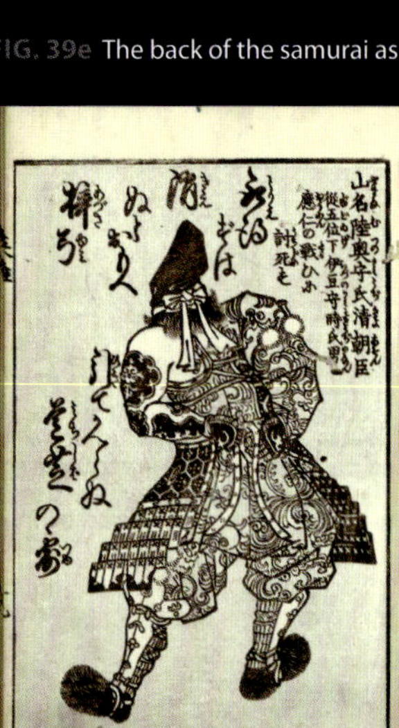

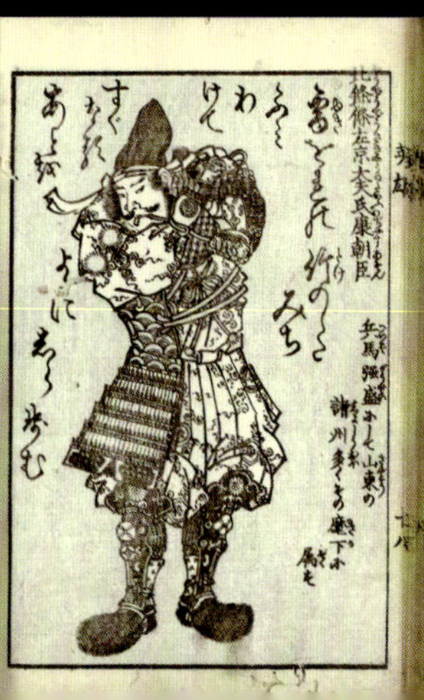

FIG. 39f His armor in place as well as his elaborate sword.

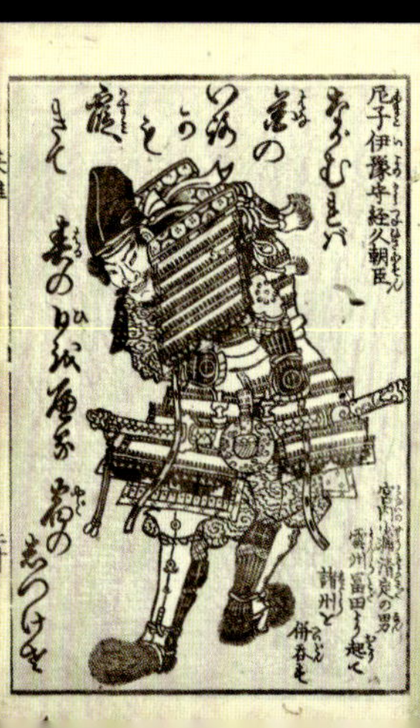

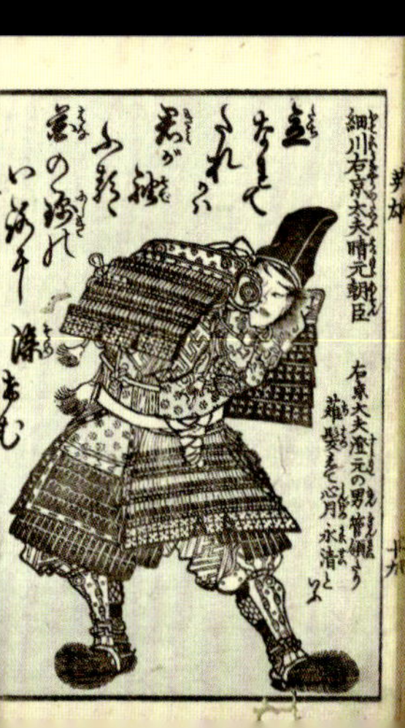

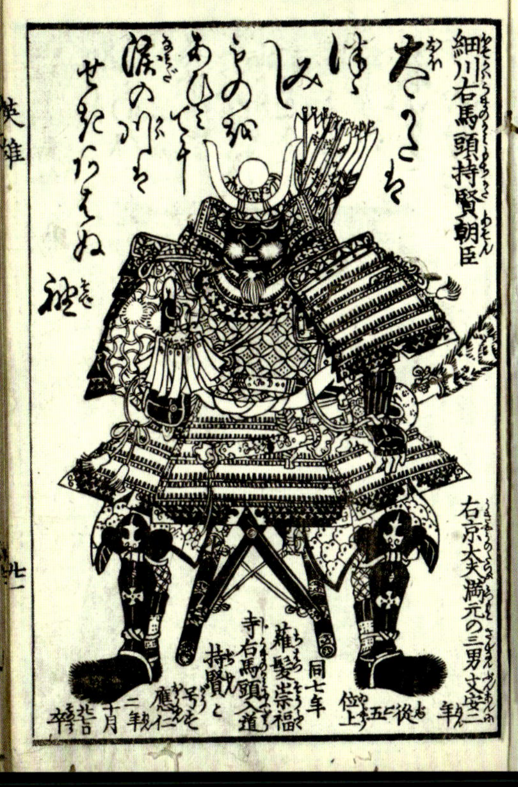

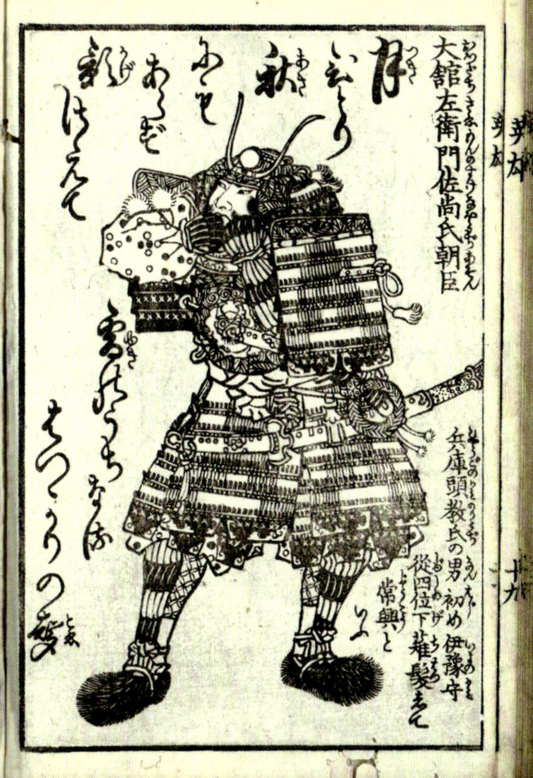

FIG. 39a–h
Utagawa SADAHIDE Gyokuransai
玉蘭斉　貞秀 (1807–73)
From *Eyu Sanjyu Rokkasen Gafu*
英雄三十六歌仙より
(1847)
Book, 18 x 12.5 cm
Author's Collection

Although Sadahide was a leading exponent of the panoramic view, painting bird's-eye views of Japan's main cities, he also illustrated many books related to warriors. This unusual book, published in 1847 by the Toto Book Store in Osaka, describes a *samurai* preparing for battle. Even though the *samurai* wears a sword, as we can see the battle is mostly conducted with bow and arrows.

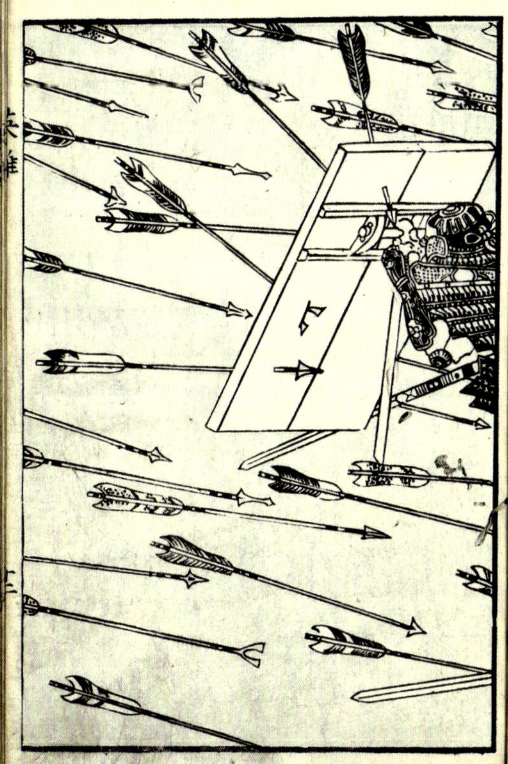

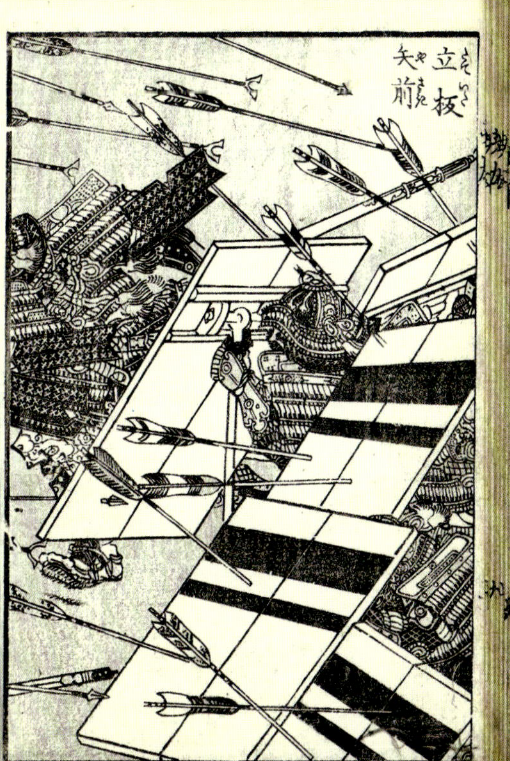

FIG. 39g
His helmet and arrows in their quiver, giving him the fierce look of a high-ranking *samurai*.

FIG. 39h
The battle begins with an onslaught of arrows.

CHAPTER FOUR

Poetry Prints and Picture Calendars

Toward the end of the eighteenth century, a renaissance of sorts occurred in Japanese intellectual circles. It comprised an energetic reawakening in pursuit of a form of poetry called *kyoka*, literally "mad verse" or "crazy verse." Unlike the more popular *haiku*, poems composed of three lines of seventeen syllables (5–7–5), *kyoka* were written in the classical five-line *tanka* or *waka* form with thirty-one syllables (5–7–5–7–7). *Kyoka* were not "mad" or " crazy" in the sense of wild expression and ideas. Rather, they were "playful" in that they did not conform to traditional rules about language and content, and the humor they contained was set in word play such as puns or in the gentle mocking of classical poetry. This meant that any educated person could compose and appreciate *kyoka*, unlike *waka* that required a deep knowledge of archaic language and intricate poetic rules. Although *kyoka* were present as early as the eighth century and appear in the classic *waka* poetry anthology, the *Man'yoshu*, the first collection of *kyoka*, *Hyakushu Kyoka (Kyoka on One Hundred Brands of Drinks)*, is attributed to a priest named Gyogetsubo (1265–1328). It features *kyoka* parodies of famous literature as different kinds of drinks.

By the early eighteenth century, *kyoka* were popular in the Kamigata region of Japan, encompassing Kyoto and Osaka, but by mid-century the center of activity had shifted to Tokyo (Edo). There, *kyoka* asserted itself as an independent poetic form with a variety of schools led by masters who would judge the quality of *kyoka* contributed by participants at their gatherings. It was such a popular movement that it bridged all levels of Japan's stratified society. *Daimyo*, *samurai* and merchants, as well as actors, writers, courtesans and other inhabitants of the "floating world," joined together to produce an art form that crossed all boundaries. Toward the end of the century, however, the ruling *shogun*'s government took steps to reinstate the once strict code of ethics of the warrior *samurai* class, including a ban on the writing of poetry, and to curb what they regarded as the excessive lifestyle of the *chonin* (townspeople). This effectively put paid to the widespread popularity of *kyoka*. In the mid-nineteenth century, there was a slight revival, but compared to the days of glory of the century before it was negligible.

FIG. 40
Totoya HOKKEI 北渓 (1780–1850)
Kintaro Subduing a Devil
鬼を成敗する金太郎 (1845)
39 x 27 cm
Courtesy of Mita Arts Gallery

Kintaro was the son of a legendary character in Japanese mythology called Yamauba, who resided in the mountains in what is today the Kanagawa area. She had an affair with a red dragon, hence the bright red skin color of her son Kintaro, a child of supernatural strength. This *surimono* is illustrating a Japanese traditional festival called Setsubun, where everyone throws soya beans from their houses as well as inside shouting "Out with the devil and in with good luck." Here, we see Kintaro stepping on the devil while tossing beans. He is holding a sword instead of the battleaxe he is best known for.

The legacy of *kyoka* lies in its role as a catalyst for a highly imaginative fusion of the arts in Edo—its poetry, fiction, calligraphy, *ukiyo-e* and theater. Many *kyoka* appeared in illustrated woodblock-printed verse books and *e-hon* picture books as well as on single-sheet prints. The blend of poetic calligraphy and pictorial design formed highly desirable commercial products. But they also began to appear in a new woodblock-printed form—*surimono*. Translated literally as "printed thing,"

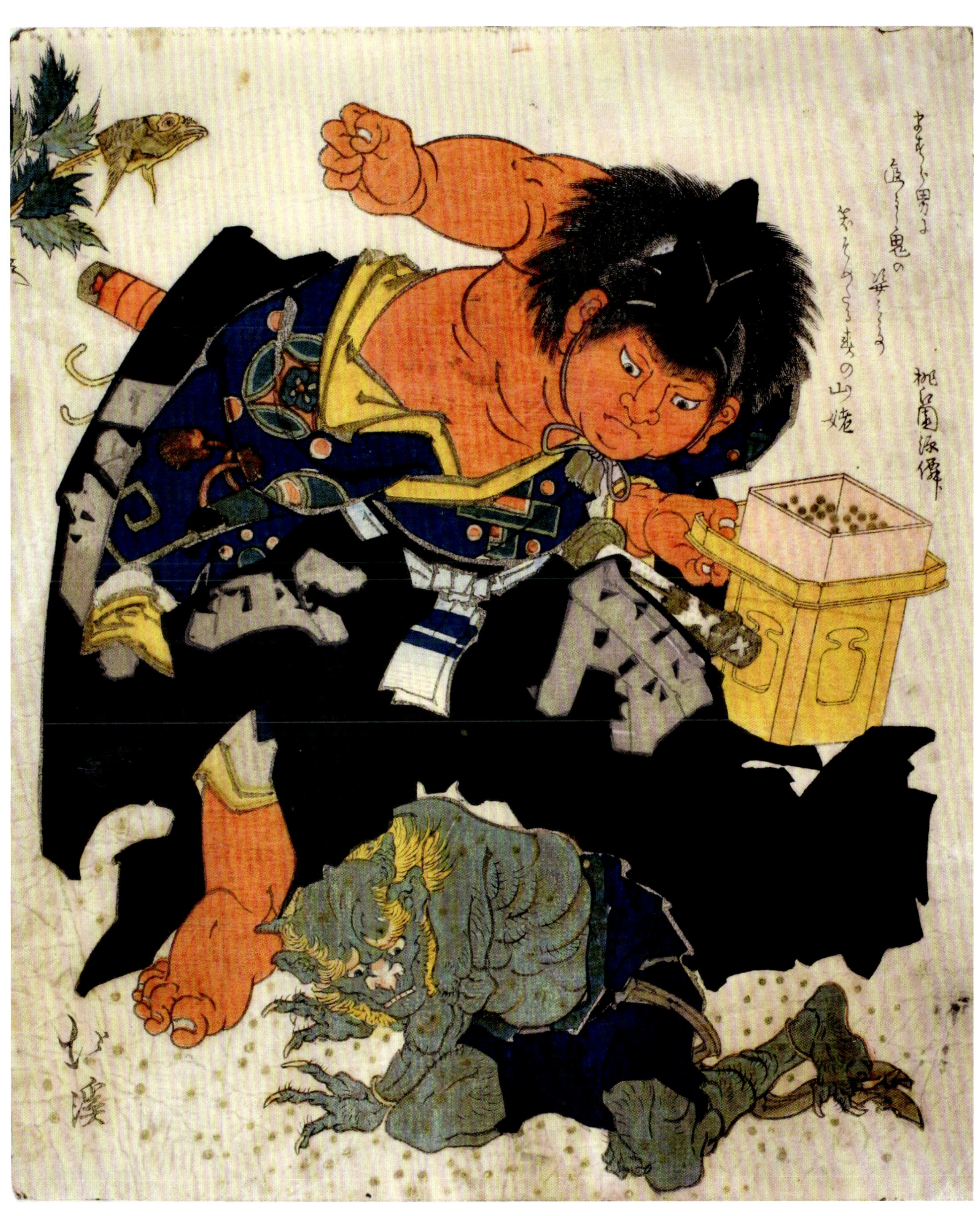

FIG. 41
Totoya HOKKEI
北渓 (1780–1850)
Morning Sun 朝日
26.5 x 39 cm
Courtesy of Mita Arts Gallery

Some may argue that this is not a true *surimono* as it lacks a poem, but the composition and general quality of the printing suggest that for some reason the negative space to the left, suitable for a *kyoka*, was not completed. The subject is a hermit smoking while boiling water for tea at his mountainside home. Even though he is wearing sandals, what looks like another pair is draped over a tree trunk. His fan is torn, possibly from constant beating in the effort to get the charcoal to burn brighter. He turns to the left, contemplating the morning sun as it rises over the horizon. The subdued gray and green are in sharp contrast to the bright red sun.

the word *surimono* in theory refers to all woodblock prints, but in the vocabulary of the Japanese print world it typically indicates commissioned or privately issued prints that were distributed in limited editions and not placed on sale. *Surimono* were created with pictures only, poetry only or pictures accompanied by poetry, each for a specific purpose. Part of their fascination for me is that they were not the result of either commercial or religious motivation, unlike virtually every other print art form in world history. Another is that they were the product of a unique collaboration between a print artist and a *kyoka* poet.

A forerunner to *surimono* were *egoyomi* or "picture calendars." Originating as privately produced and (often) amateur prints for the New Year, and printed on single sheets, *egoyomi* conveyed in pictorial form the sequence of long and short months of the Japanese calendar in a particular year. Sometimes only a reference to the zodiac year was given via images of a tiger, monkey, rabbit, etc. in the print's design. *Egoyomi* were popular among both literate commoners and *samurai* for gift exchanges at the New Year, and were commissioned by the wealthiest among them. Afterwards, poems became the driving force in the production of prints for the New Year and thus *surimono* containing *kyoka* poems overtook *egoyomi* in popularity.

Many *surimono* were commissioned by poets who were members of poetry clubs or groups, who would distribute

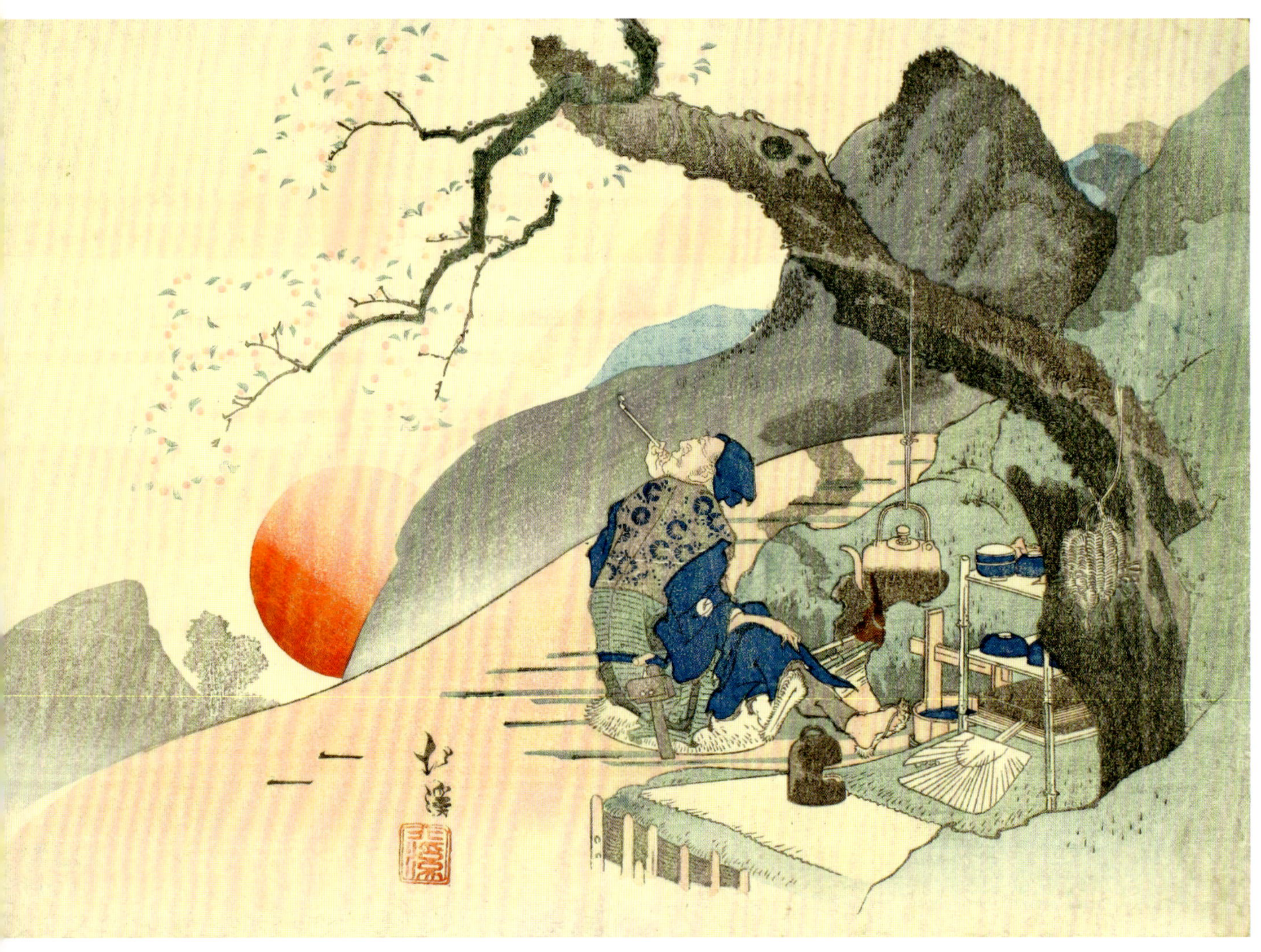

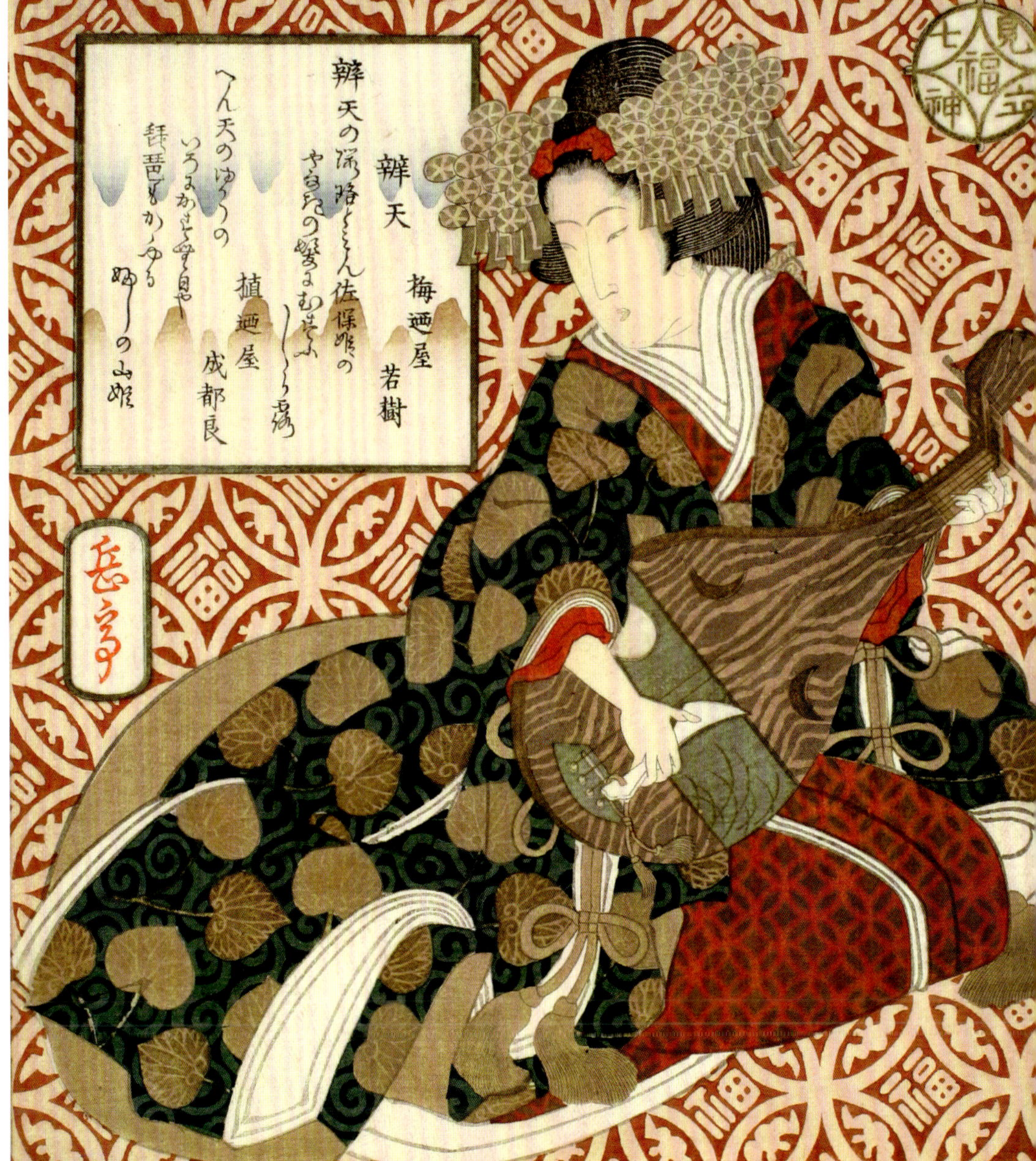

FIG. 42
Sadaoka GAKUTEI
定岡岳亭 (1786–1868)
From *Mitate Shichi-Fukujin (Women Representing The Seven Gods of Good Fortune)* みたて七福神より (1860s)
26 x 19.5 cm
Courtesy of Mita Arts Gallery

Here, a woman plays a *biwa*. Some of the prints in this series relate to a New Year theme, and from the woman's elaborate headpiece we can assume this is one of them. The entire series uses the circular pattern as the background for the female figure.

them to fellow members, friends and colleagues to promote their own or the club's poetry, announce poetry gatherings as well as the winning poems in poetry competitions, commemorate anniversaries or offer greetings on special occasions, such as the New Year or the cherry blossom season. Other *surimono* were distributed to announce important public performances, such as musical performances or plays, or for personal occasions or reasons. *Kabuki* actors would commission *surimono* prints to promote their plays or to commemorate important events in their careers, such as a change of stage name and even the stage debuts of their sons. Courtesans would use *surimono* to advertise themselves.

Kyoka poetry was a key element in much of *surimono* print design. The *kyoka* groups would privately commission artists to design compositions reflecting the themes of their short poems. Since the *kyoka* were written first, often in very stylized calligraphy, the print artists generally used the poems as a source of inspiration for the print designs. Subject matter covered almost anything, from historical and legendary subjects to bird and flower renditions, and from landscapes to beautiful women. Seasonal imagery, like pine and bamboo, was frequently incorporated into designs, as were lucky symbols and zodiacal animals. Moreover, unlike in standard *ukiyo-e* printmaking, the "still life" flourished in *surimono*. Still life subjects ranged from everyday objects such as fruit and flowers to unusual items like clocks, telescopes and other scientific objects, which in themselves became the source of inspiration for the poets.

Because of the inclusion of a poem, the production of a *surimono* was slightly different to that of a commercial print. It required an additional step. The printer sent the commissioned pictorial design to the client-poet for approval, leaving space for the poem or poems to be written. Upon the client's approval, the image was then sent to the calligrapher who wrote the verse on the proof print. This was then carved on a separate block. Needless to say, the relief carving of the *kanji* characters on the block took a great deal of technical skill. It was then up to the printer to incorporate the two blocks into the finished print.

Catering to the refined tastes of their wealthy and literati patrons, *surimono*

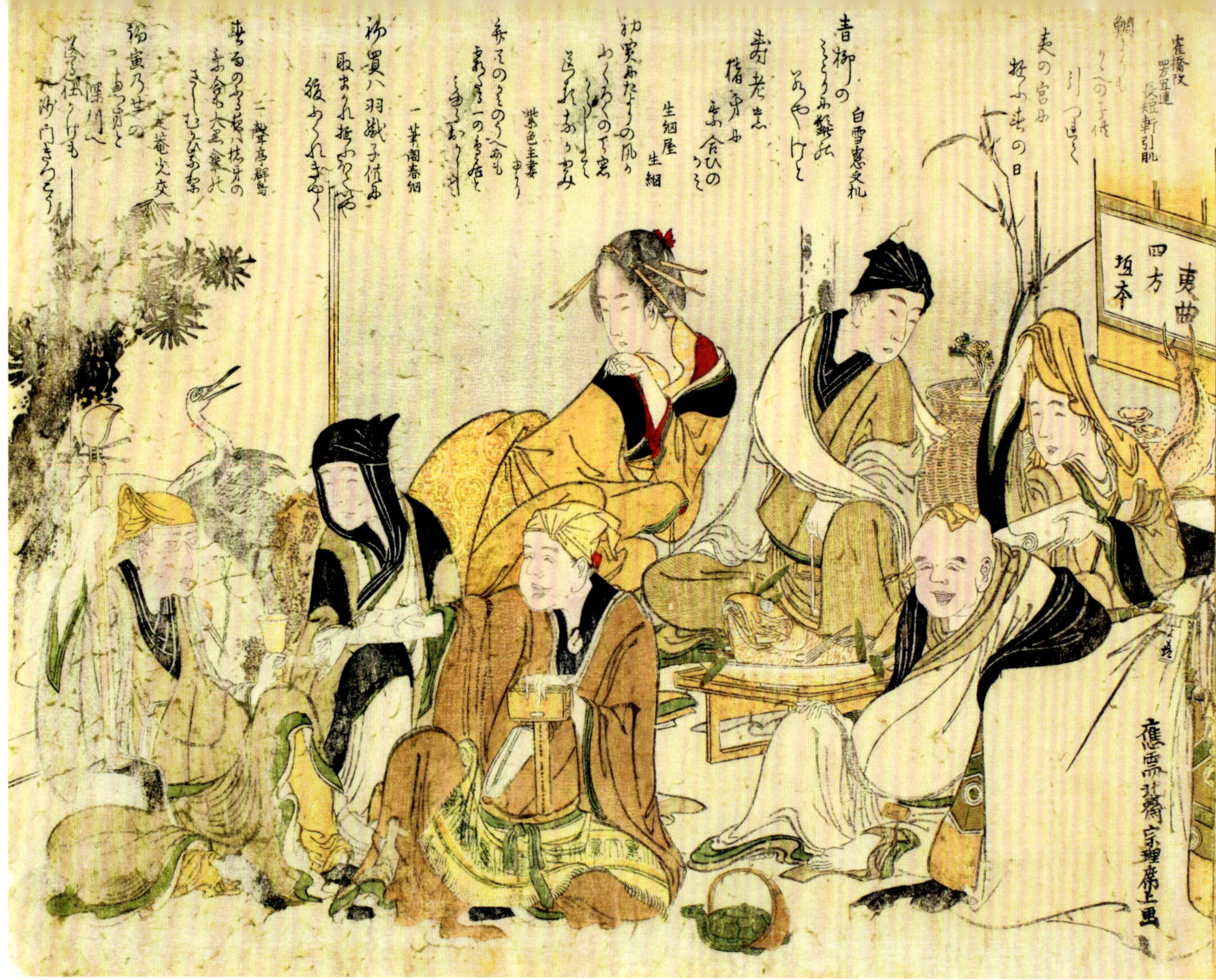

allowed for a much higher standard of production than the typical commercial print of the day. The craftsmen producing *surimono* also formed an élite community compared with their contemporaries who worked for commercial publishers. They were paid handsomely and not restricted to using cheap materials. In fact, the *hosho* paper used for *surimono* was thicker and stronger than normal in order to withstand the finest printing techniques not commonly used in most commercial prints. These included elaborate embossing and the abundant use of metallic-based pigments such as gold or silver, which needed stronger pressure to be applied to the paper to insure the metal would be correctly exposed on the surface. Mother-of-pearl and mica were also included on deluxe *surimono* commissioned by wealthy clients.

The *surimono* we typically see is a square format, roughly about 20 cm by 18 cm. It is called a *shikishi-ban*, the same size as the *shikishi* or poem card that is sold in all stationary shops throughout Japan. Initially, the *surimono* were much larger, in fact bigger than the common commercial print called an *o-ban*, which was then divided into different sizes depending on the subject. They could also accommodate large numbers of poems. After printing, they were folded into unique patterns so that the recipient of the folded *surimono* would receive a pleasant surprise upon opening them, fold by fold.

Since *surimono* were privately commissioned, they were issued in very limited editions, anything ranging from twenty to a hundred. As private works, they were also not required to list the publisher's name or seal or to show the date of printing. Unfortunately, the relatively small numbers created meant that such prints were not plentiful. With the expansion of popular taste for *surimono* in the early twentieth century, many copies started to appear in the market place. It takes a true specialist to distinguish between the originals and the forgeries. The true connoisseur wants to obtain the best, which of course is the original.

FIG. 43
Katsushika HOKUSAI
北斎 (1760–1849)
Gathering of Poets 詩人 (early 1800s)
25.7 x 32.6
Courtesy of Mita Arts Gallery

This horizontal composition, typical of Hokusai's early 1800s work, shows a gathering of six poets and a female entertainer with a startling red accent in her under *kimono*. The scene at first appears to be set outdoors, with arcane and pine tree to the left, but is actually indoors and on the left is a painted wall. The central figure is offering *saké* to the *shamisen* player on the left. The oddest member of the group is the bald man with the large stomach on the right. He is barefooted, with a towel on his head. On the upper portion are the *kyoka* poems composed by the group.

FIG. 44
Utagawa TOYOKUNI I
豊国 (1769–1825)
Courtesan 遊女 (1820)
26 x 26 cm
Courtesy of Mita Arts Gallery

This print depicts a courtesan ready to serve an unseen guest a large cup of tea or *saké* from a cast-iron vessel. We can tell the drink is very hot as she holds the cup by the rim and base to avoid burning her hand. She sits next to an oil lamp, which is lit. It is an evening scene. She is wearing her outer *kimono*. Other *kimono* are casually hung from the clothes rack behind her. It is an inviting picture full of innuendo.

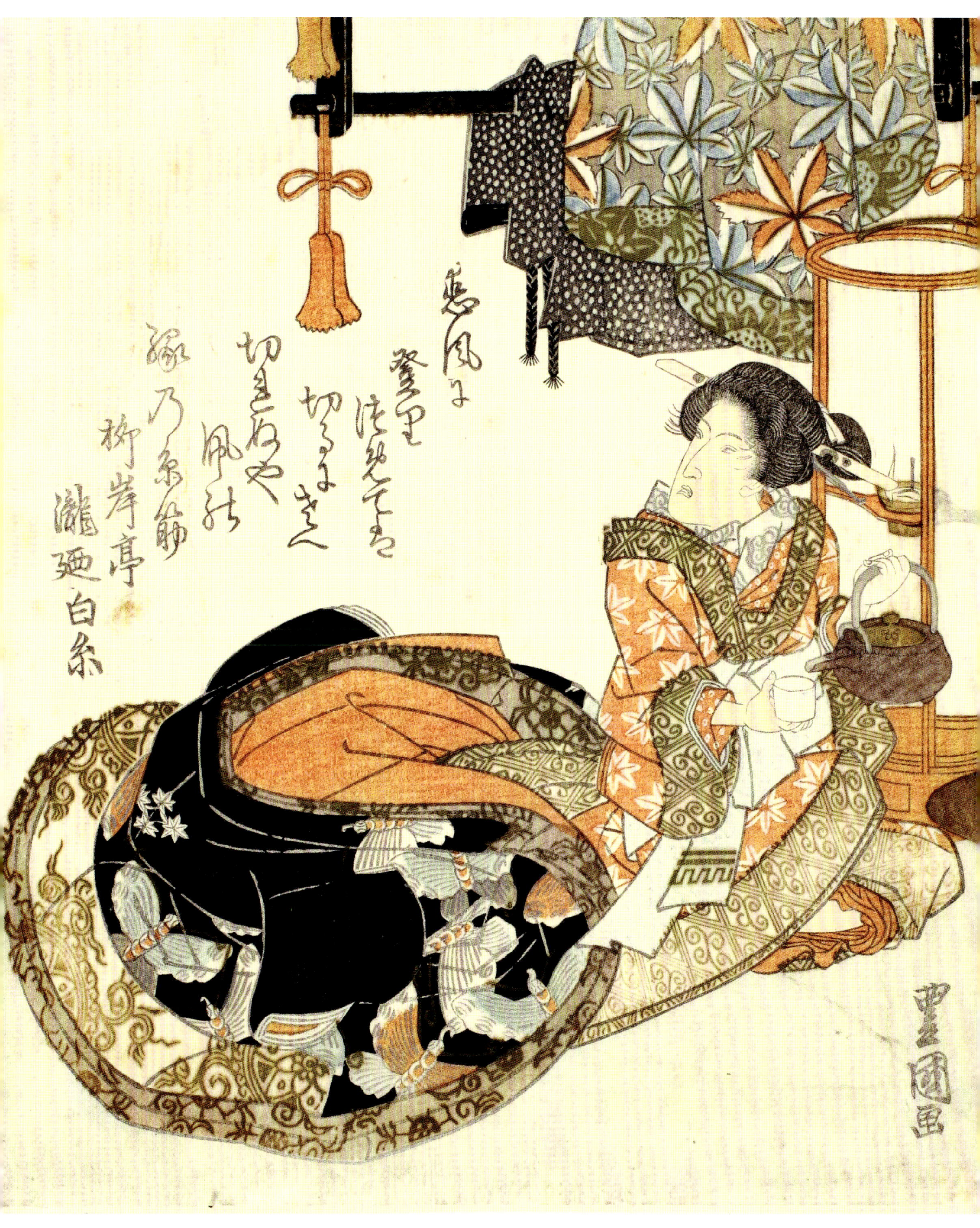
柳岸亭
瀧廼白糸
豊国画

Almost all of the most famous Japanese *ukiyo-e* artists of the Edo period produced some *surimono*. Some were more active in the genre than others and a handful are known primarily for their *surimono* prints. Among the better known exponents are the versatile Katsushika Hokusai (1760–1849) (**Fig. 43**) and his pupils Totoya Hokkei (1780–1850) (**Figs. 40, 41**), Sadaoka Gakutei (1785–1855), one of Hokusai's most creative students and one of the premier designers of *surimono* (**Fig. 42**), and Ryuryukyo Shinsai (1764–1820). Two other famous *surimono* print artists are Utagawa Toyokuni I (1769–1825) (**Fig. 44**) and his major pupil Utagawa Kunisada (1786–1865), also known as Utagawa Toyokuni III (**Figs. 45, 46**). Following the tradition of the Utagawa school, Toyokuni and Kunisada's main preoccupation was with *kabuki* and actor portraits, but they also designed some outstanding *surimono* containing other subject matter, including portraits of beautiful women. Kunisada is credited with the term "decadent" as his work changed the standards of the accepted female form from the previous half century.

FIG. 45
Utagawa KUNISADA
国定 (1786–1865)
Two Courtesans 二遊女 (1860s)
26.5 x 39 cm
Courtesy of Mita Arts Gallery

Here, two courtesans play a duet with *koto* and *shamisen* in front of a beautiful *byobu* (screen) decorated with plum blossoms. The courtesans' thick *kimono* and the plum blossom theme, together with the *hibachi* stove, indicate a winter scene. The finger positions of the hands appear to be drawn quite accurately. The *shamisen* player has a roll of tissue tucked into her *obi*, suggesting other activities.

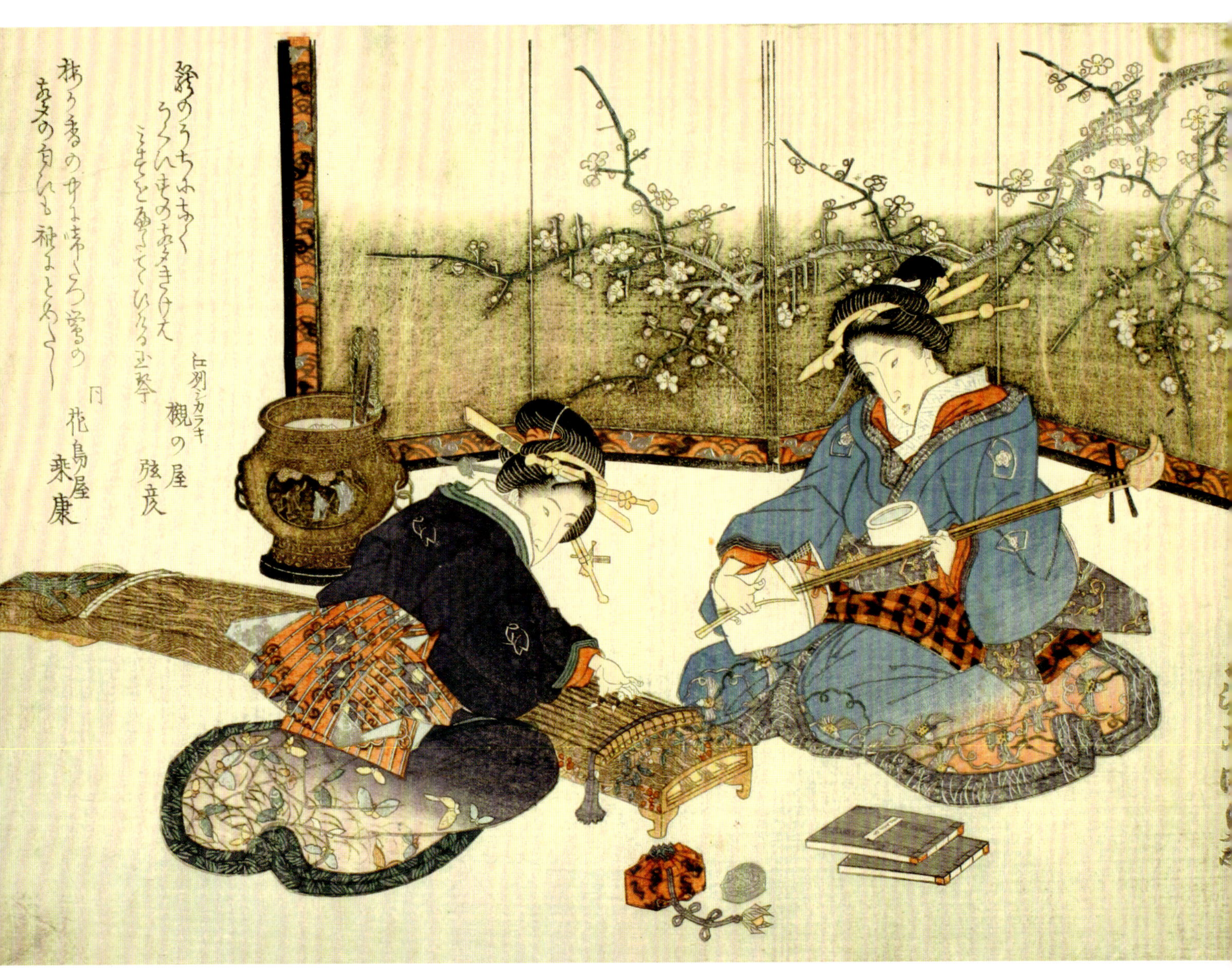

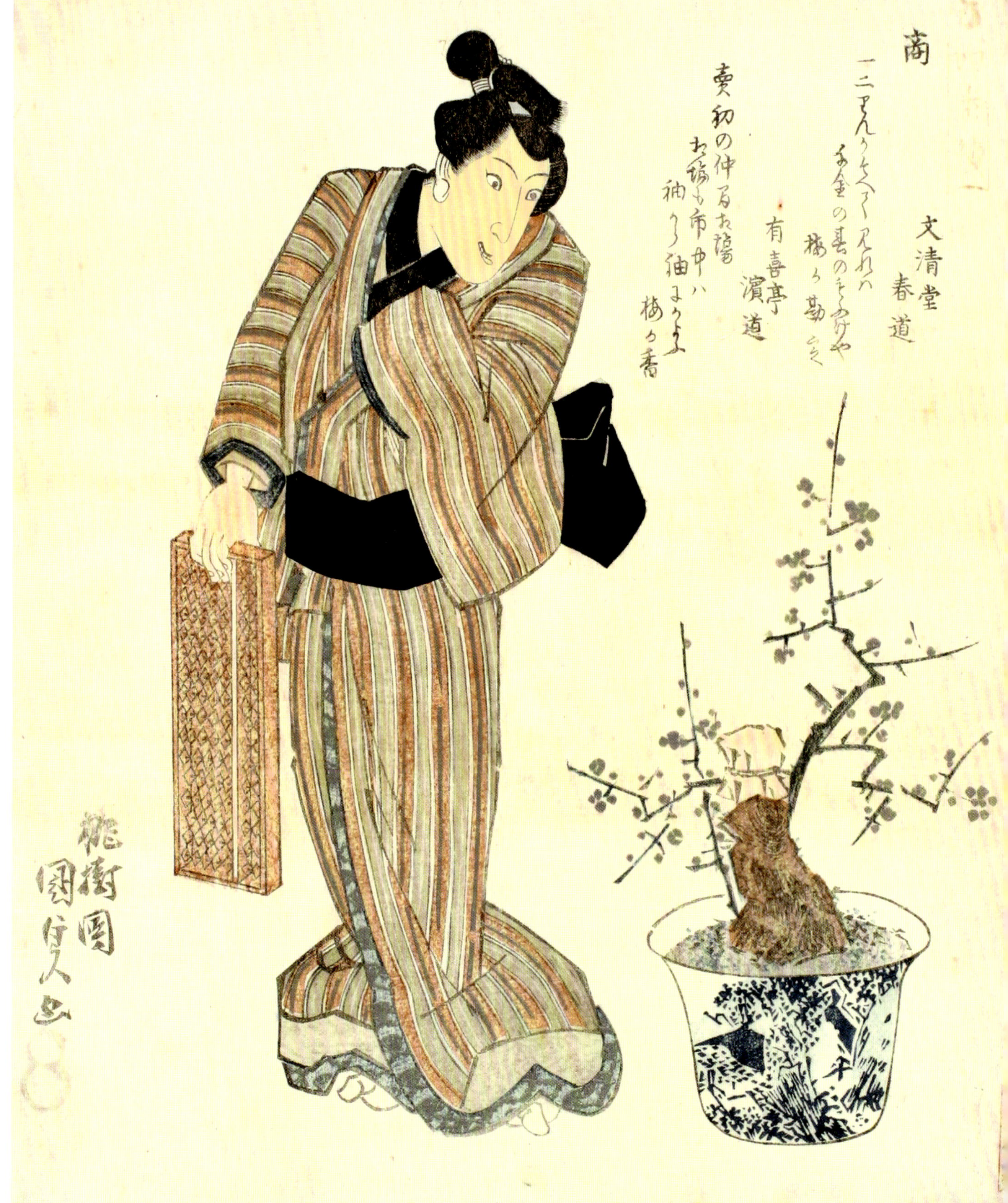

FIG. 46
Utagawa KUNISADA
国定 (1786–1865)
Scent of Plum 梅の香 (1860)
39 x 26.5 cm
Courtesy of Mita Arts Gallery

In this print, a male figure, possibly an actor playing the role of a merchant carrying a large *soroban* (abacus), admires a large *bonsai* (miniature tree) of a plum tree with blossoms. The container, a blue and white ceramic pot, could possibly be from Imari.

CHAPTER FIVE

Beautiful Women

Beautiful women (*bijin*) are one of three main themes in *ukiyo-e* woodblock prints, the other two being *kabuki* actors and landscapes. Because the costumes and make-up used in *kabuki* remained relatively static between the mid-seventeenth and nineteenth centuries, the styles in which actors are depicted in *ukiyo-e* did not change significantly. Similarly, the depiction of landscapes remained visually fixed until the introduction of Western perspective and other pictorial ideas imported from Europe altered the way Japanese viewed scenes.

In contrast, the portrayal of women changed radically during the Edo period (1600–1868) as classical Japanese aesthetics blended with contemporary urban themes in *ukiyo-e* to celebrate the hedonistic world inhabited by *geisha* and courtesans and by famous *kabuki* actors. It was a man's world, dominated by merchants, artisans, the attendants of *daimyo* who were required to spend months in Edo, and other officials. The *kabuki* theater, brothels and teahouses were where they went for relaxation and entertainment. It was where they encountered beautiful women. Publishers promoted the expensive pleasures of the Yoshiwara district by naming and advertising the courtesans and the houses employing them. Brothels also commissioned portraits of their most attractive girls. Numerous prints portray the courtesans standing in front of an establishment with their names prominently displayed on the *noren* (awning). They also commissioned fans—the flat fan shape is unique to Japan—bearing portraits of beautiful courtesans. The prints and fans were either sold or given away as mementos to satisfied clients. Companies also promoted their products, such as *saké*, by commissioning prints of beautiful women posing with the goods.

In keeping with this transient, idle world, beautiful women in *ukiyo-e* were generally depicted alone, in pairs or in groups, playing games to amuse themselves, preparing themselves for the night in the amusement quarter, or walking through the cities of Edo or Osaka with their attendants or children. There was a focus on the female form, on elaborate hairstyles and costly hair ornaments, and on lavishly decorated *kimono*. It was only later that more types of women were depicted doing a greater variety of activities.

Prior to the evolution of *ukiyo-e*, artistic representations of courtesans of the pleasure quarters were considered taboo in aristocratic and religious circles. Rather, from the eleventh through the thirteenth centuries paintings for the nobility predominantly featured scenes. The Buddhist or Shinto-related figures in these paintings wear costumes that were conceived centuries ago. They also contain symbolic elements that are ageless and constant. But in an art form catering to the merchant townsman, fashions could change drastically over night. These trends could be almost instantly captured in *ukiyo-e*. Prints of beautiful women (*bijin-ga*), most often of famous courtesans and *geisha*, were avidly

FIG. 47
Suzuki HARUNOBU
春信 (1725–70)
Couple Under an Umbrella in Snow
雪中相合傘 (1760s)
31 x 21 cm
Courtesy of Adachi Institute of Woodcut Prints

One of Harunobu's masterpieces, this is a stark, simple statement of two lovers under a *wagasa* (Japanese folding umbrella) in the snow. The man's features are not much different from the woman's; typically, in some of Harunobu's pictures it is difficult to separate the genders. The *wagasa* as we know it was not developed until the late Edo period, and is a frequent symbol in prints and as a prop for the stage.

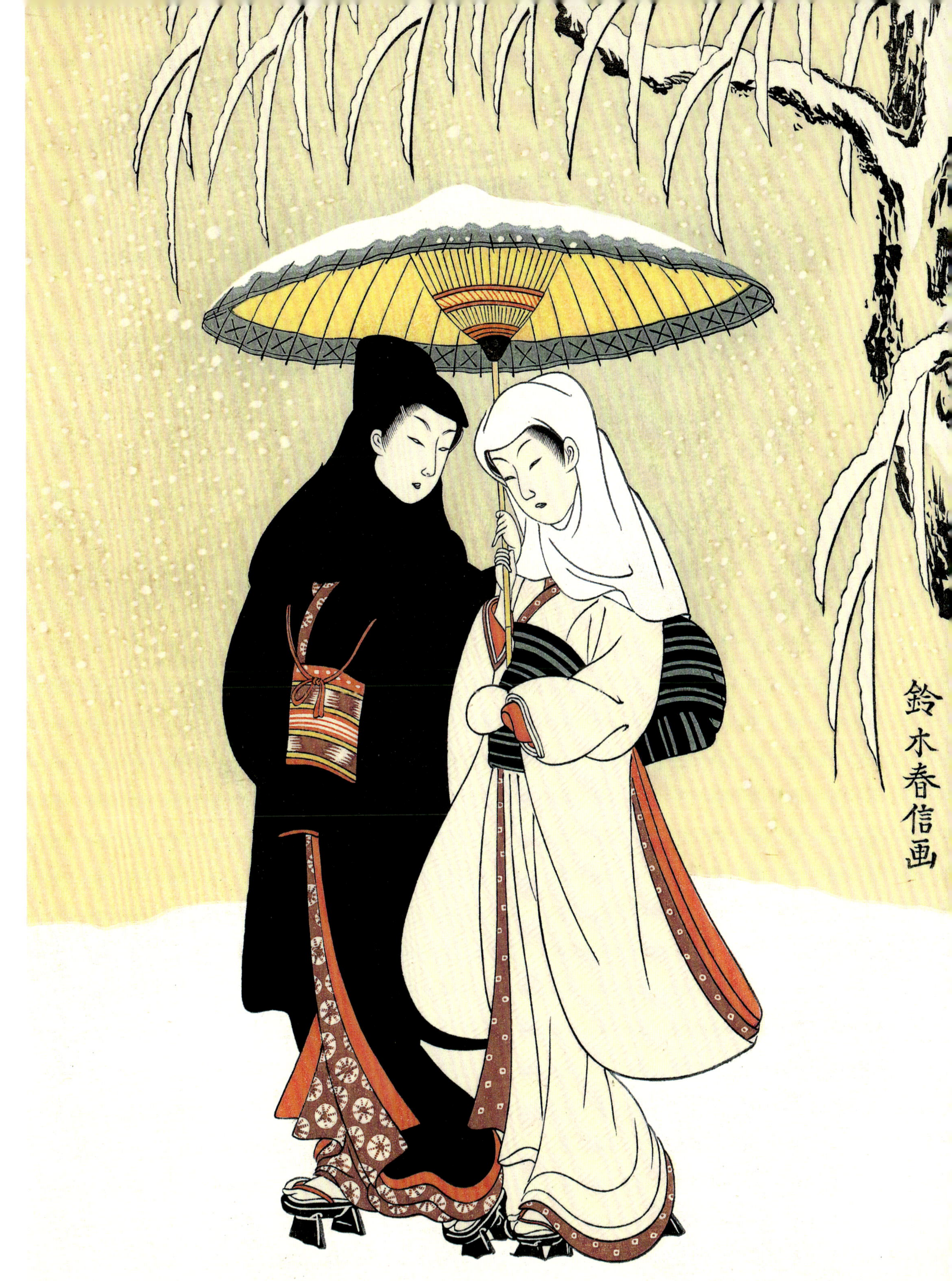
鈴木春信画

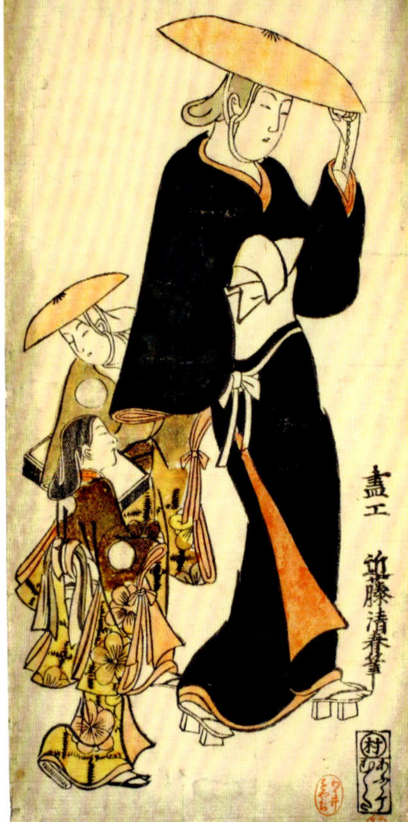

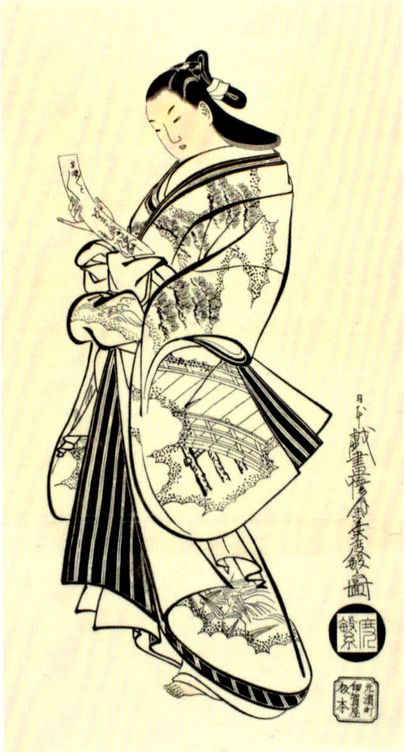

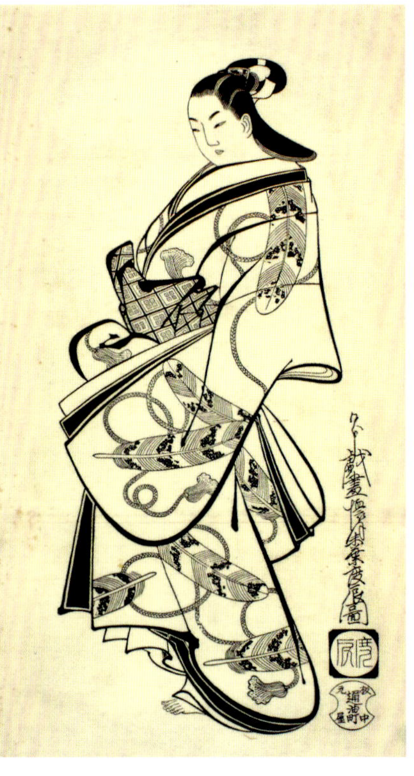

purchased by the fashion-conscious and pleasure-seeking public of the "floating world." They showed beauties modeling the latest hairstyles, accessories, cosmetics and textile designs. And because the prints were so cheap and easily accessible, they were enormously influential, in much the same way that today's technology is able to disseminate popular culture far and wide and at enormous speed. Many of the *kimono* in the courtesan portraits were, in fact, designed by the print artist. As such, textile designers would purchase the prints to glean ideas for fabrication.

The publishers of *ukiyo-e*, besides being the source of production of the prints with the collaboration of a stable of artists, woodblock cutters and printers, were also responsible for the distribution of the pictures. In the early eighteenth century, prints were sold by hawkers in the streets of Edo. Later, the publishers' distribution system included traveling salesmen and retailers who promoted the pictures in a way similar to today's magazines of popular culture. Edo had a population exceeding one million. *Ukiyo-e* as a commercial art form had to reach a mass audience and exploit the emotions of a developing plebeian culture. The art also had to be affordable to the masses.

It is well known that art has a direct influence on what constitutes

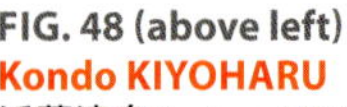

FIG. 48 (above left)
Kondo KIYOHARU
近藤清春 (active 1705–30s)
Mother and Children 母と子 (1730s)
Hand-painted lacquer picture (*urushi-e*), 33 x 15 cm
Courtesy of Mita Arts Gallery

This is a perfect example of an early attempt at *bijin-ga*. This mother and her two children is an unusual subject for the time, as it is independent of the *kabuki* theater. The mother has the bent posture of figures of the Genroku period (1688–1735), and to emphasize the black lacquer of the *kimono* her hair is tinted in a light gray tone.

FIG. 49 (above center)
Kaigetsudo DOHAN
懐月堂 度繁 (active 1710s)
Beauty 美人
Black and white print (*sumizuri-e*), 59 x 32.5 cm
Author's Collection

This print perfectly exemplifies the beautifully dressed courtesans from the Yoshiwara pleasure quarter that were a hallmark of the Kaigetsudo school. Dohan made a total of twelve full-length portraits of courtesans and this is one of only two in existence. It is from an old re-cut block, exactly like the original. The line is very calligraphic. The eye follows the rhythm from the top of the *kimono* down to the heavy hemline and back up again to the sleeve. The stripes to the left are echoed in the stripes on the sleeve. The hair is a counter movement to the entire curvilinear design.

FIG. 50 (above right)
Kaigetsudo DOSHIN
懐月堂 度辰 (active 1704–16)
Beauty 美人
Black and white print (*sumizuri-e*), 61.5 x 33 cm
Author's Collection

As in Fig. 49, the calligraphic line in this print by another member of the Kaigetsudo school, Doshin, is extremely strong. Noteworthy are the staccato strokes of the upper border of the *obi* and the rope and feather pattern following the line of the beauty's body. Dark strokes thrust out only to be counterbalanced by opposing diagonals. It exemplifies a very contemporary attitude toward picture making.

FIG. 51 (opposite above)
Suzuki HARUNOBU
春信 (1725–70)
Iris 杜若 (1760s)
26 x 19.5 cm
Courtesy of Mita Arts Gallery

Harunobu, the true founder of the *nishiki-e* (full color print), typically portrayed women of doll-like proportions in an idealized environment. The woman here is thin and seems to have no weight under her *kimono*. Her face is drawn in some detail, including a semblance of a nostril. The young child seems to have fallen asleep while practicing his calligraphy; his brush has slipped from his hand and lies beside him on the *tatami* mat.

a beautiful woman. The shape of a woman's body and face, how she carries herself, her hairstyle and make-up, as well as the styles and patterns of her clothing are constantly changing. Pictures had to keep up with the fashions in vogue at the time. Initially, the ideal woman was based on the first secular female forms of the Nara and Heian periods (794–1185) depicted in the scrolls illustrating the epic stories of the time, such as the early eleventh-century *Genji monogatari (The Tale of Genji)* by Murasaki Shikibu. Women's faces were plump, with rounded cheeks, high foreheads framed by heavy eyebrows, small vermillion mouths and noses drawn cursorily with a hook-shaped line. Eventually, an attempt was made to impose individuality on the depiction of women other than by using the symbolic generic symbols that were accepted then.

In the seventeenth century, with the introduction of *ukiyo-e*, women's portraits began to be imbued with much greater realism. Women were still plump, their hair was put up so that it exposed the nape of the neck, their shoulders were pulled back and their bodies, covered in flowing *kimono*, showed the stomach thrust forward. In some respects, this pose resembles some early Buddhist statues, which were given a similar stance.

The tastes of pivotal woodblock artists and popular actors as well as changes in urban society's conception of femininity had a continuing impact on fashion. The *ukiyo-e* beauty as we know her today was developed and spearheaded by a number of artists during the first three decades of the eighteenth century. Among the earliest was an independent artist, Kondo Kiyoharu (active 1705–30s), who was either influenced by or was a pupil of Okumura Masanobu (1686–1764) (**Fig. 48**). He was the first to brush lacquer on the surface of prints.

At much the same time, several Kaigetsudo artists began to specialize in *bijin-ga*. The Kaigetsudo was a school of painters active during the Genroku

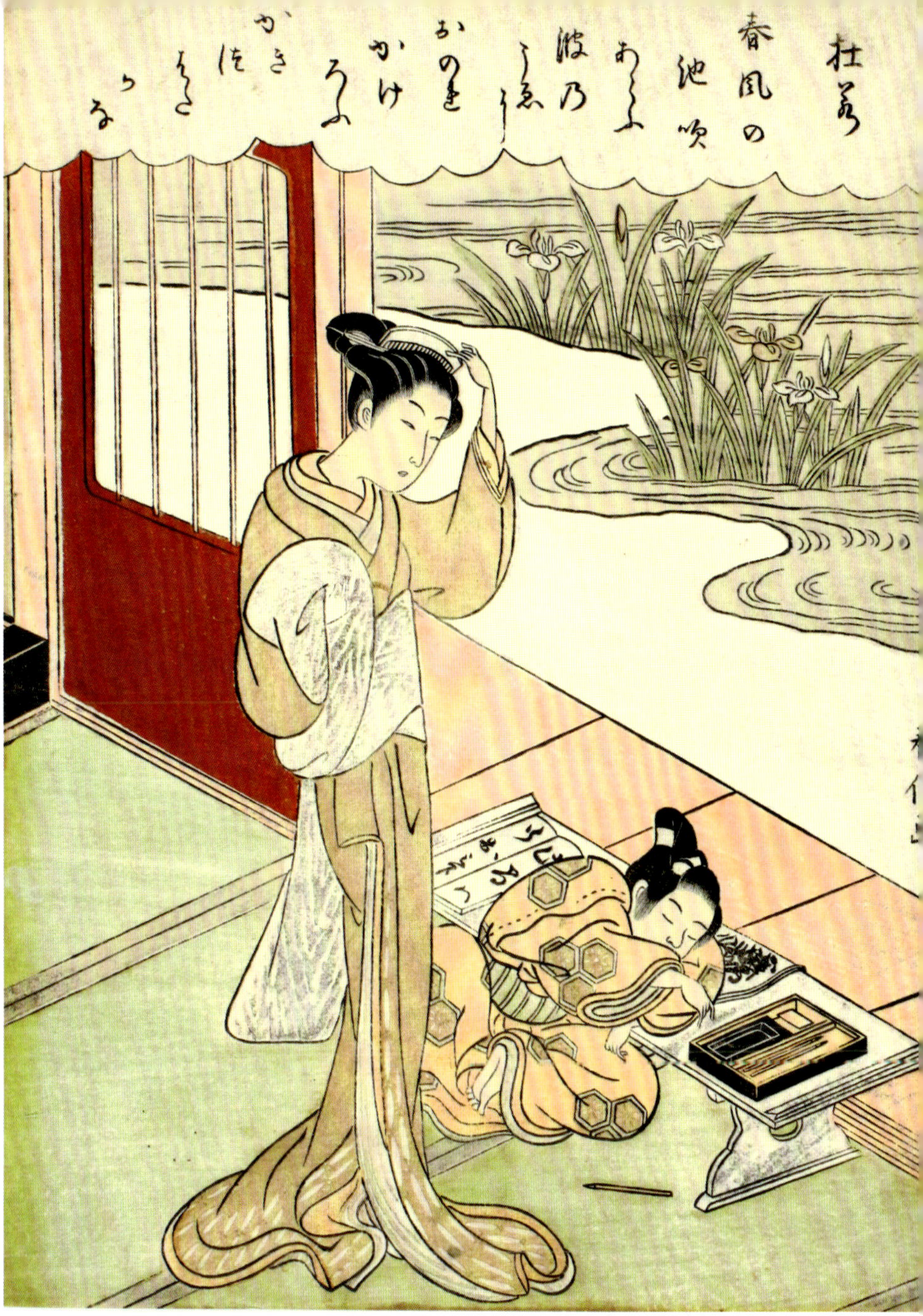

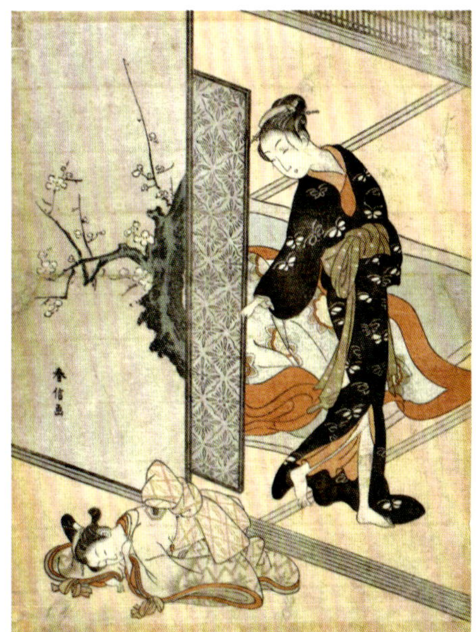

FIG. 52
Suzuki HARUNOBU
春信 (1725–70)
Taking a Nap うたた寝 (1760)
26 x 19.5 cm
Courtesy of Mita Arts Gallery

In this well-conceived composition, the young girl sleeping in the foreground forms the base of a zigzag movement in the background latticework of the door. The *tatami* borders carry our eye through the picture, even with the interruption of the vertical *fusuma byobu* screen and the standing woman. The woman appears to have just woken up; her hair is disheveled and the *futon* (bedding) is still rumpled. An interesting element in this picture is the three-dimensional sense of the *futon*. It is well drawn and the fabric pattern follows the folds realistically, unusual in prints of the early eighteenth century.

FIG. 53
Suzuki HARUNOBU
春信 (1725–70)
Osen in the Rain at Kasamori Shrine
雨中夜詣 (1760s)
31 x 21.5 cm
Courtesy of Adachi Institute of Woodcut Prints

This magnificent print depicts Osen, the daughter of the owner of the Kagiya teahouse next to Kasamori Shrine. Considered the most beautiful girl of her day, an inspiration to artists and poets alike, she was eighteen when this was painted, a year before she married a *samurai* and stopped posing as a model. The picture has a number of exciting elements: pouring rain, swaying pine trees, a swinging lantern (indicating night time), a *wagasa* which cannot be opened, and layers of undergarments exposed to the weather. The red pillar to the left is the *torii* (archway) to the Shinto shrine.

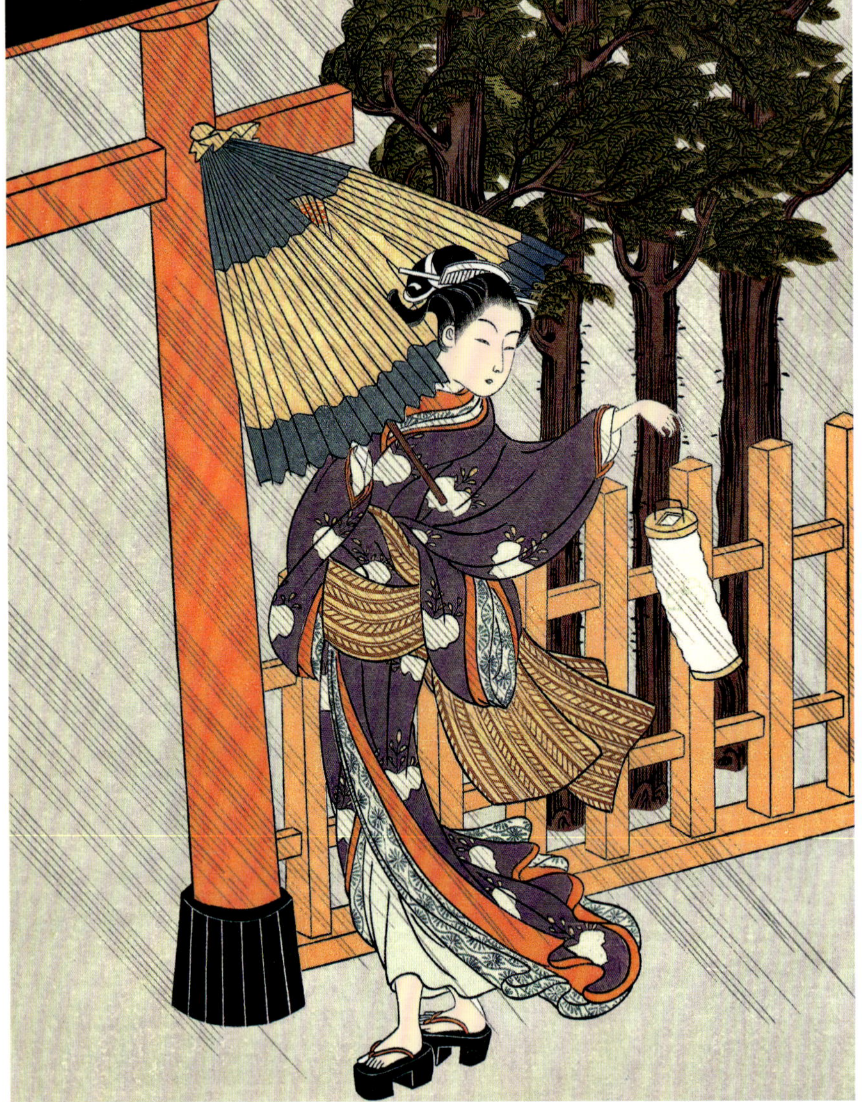

period (1688–1735) known primarily for paintings and prints of beautiful women clad in colorful and intricately patterned *kimono*. Although the women portrayed are beautiful and graceful, their poses are somewhat stereotyped. However, their *kimono* were at the vanguard of fashion of the time. Kaigetsudo Ando, the founder, was never a printmaker, only a painter, but a number of his followers, including Dohan (active 1710s) (**Fig. 49**), and Doshin (active 1704–16) (**Fig. 50**), These two artists produced large prints, what is called *kakemono-e* size, of women, in a style that employed thick lines and bright colors. Initially, the prints were probably glued down on a cheap backing to use as a hanging scroll for those unable to afford an original painting. Today, only about forty Kaigetsudo prints survive in total.

The most distinguished of the early eighteenth-century *bijin-ga* artists was undoubtedly Suzuki Harunobu (1725–70), an Edo-born artist and one of the large group of artists whose work was devoted to the portrayal of scenes from the Yoshiwara, the amusement district of Edo. He also produced a large group of *mitate-e* (classical themes with a modern twist).

All of Harunobu's *bijin-ga* display standing figures—graceful, slender beauties—dressed in colorful and fashionable *kimono* (**Figs. 51–56**). But although the figures are beautifully conceived, they lack personality. There is practically no individuality in them. They all seem childlike and very feminine. In fact, some of his male figures have the same soft feminine quality as the women. Harunobu comes closer to the *Genji* sense of beauty than any other artist in *ukiyo-e*. His work almost without exception portrays women in pairs. They include a wide range of types, from characters drawn from classic literature to prostitutes, teahouse waitresses, courtesans and young men and children. He offers us a pure, idealistic view of Edo where we never witness anything ugly or uncomfortable; all is charm and elegance. Poems inscribed in the upper portion of some prints further enhance the romantic, lyrical atmosphere.

Despite the lack of personality in his characters, Harunobu, at the age of forty, emerged as the master of the color print. He is, in fact, credited with being the creator of *nishiki-e* (multiple color prints). His initial attempts were in the form of *egoyomi* (illustrated calendars) (see Chapter 4), but his output was limited until he started making pictures of beautiful women using a full color palette. Encouraged by the enthusiastic reception of the color prints, he embarked upon a period of great artistic activity during which he produced some

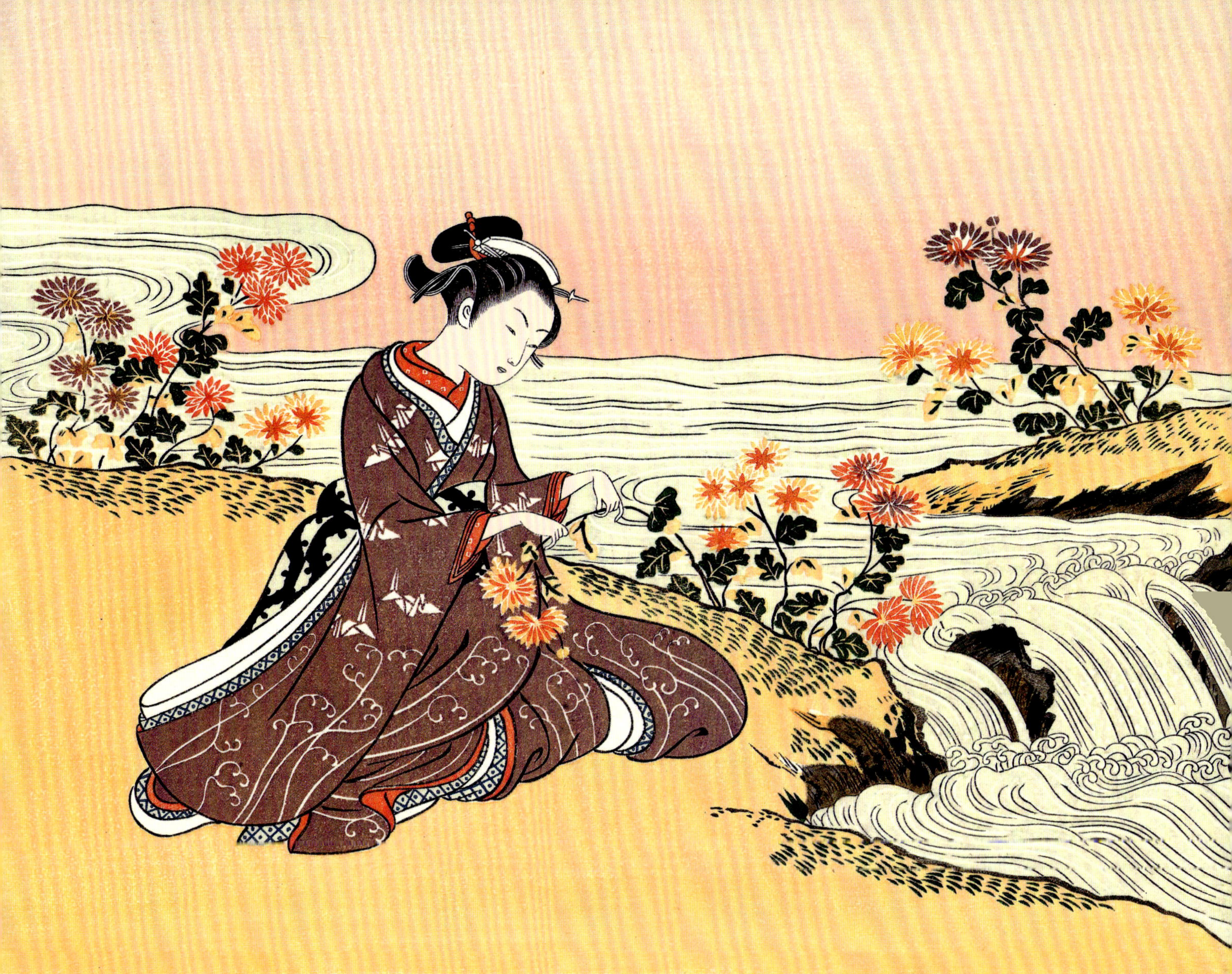

FIG. 54
Suzuki HARUNOBU
春信 (1725–70)
Collecting Chrysanthemums by a Stream
見立菊慈童 (1760s)
29 x 22 cm
Courtesy of Adachi Institute of Woodcut Prints

This is an unusual composition in the *yokoban* horizontal format because in almost all cases *yokoban* of one or two figures were *shunga* (erotica). *Yokoban* were more commonly employed for landscapes or scenes featuring large groups of people.

600 prints over a period of six years. His career was cut short when he died at the age of forty-five.

Other than his *shunga* (erotic) work, most of Harunobu's pictures are in the *chuban* size, which he felt most comfortable working with. His pictures are full of color from border to border. There is very little white space, and sometimes he will use a solid color, such as shocking pink, for the background. Even though his use of color sometimes borders on the extreme, he had great technical mastery over printmaking and many of his prints are outstanding for the beauty of their design and the superb quality of their execution.

The influence of Harunobu looms large in the work of several artists who followed in his footsteps but were nevertheless able to truly epitomize the beauty and character of Japanese women. One such artist, Isoda Koryusai (1735–90), was a pupil and friend of Harunobu, and was part of a group of artists who collaborated at the time of Harunobu's death to continue the efforts of multicolored prints. He was not as prolific as Harunobu, but what he did do was sometimes outstanding. His figures tend to be more robust than Harunobu's winsome, delicate types, and his prints have a stronger rust red coloring (**Fig. 57**). His beauties command center stage and more completely fill the pictorial space.

Koryusai also enjoyed working in the unusually long, narrow format of the pillar print, as did his contemporary Torii Kiyotsune (active 1750s–70s). Pillar prints (*hashira-e*) were produced specifically to allow the average homeowner the possibility of decorating the slim wooden pillar separating the modular wall panels of a home. As they were glued directly to the wood, many do not survive. A pupil of Torii Kiyomitsu (1734–85), Torii Kiyotsune's work represents something of a departure from the theatrical and energetic core style of the Torii school and his women are more delicate and graceful, less bold, and more in the mainstream style of *ukiyo-e* (**Figs. 58, 59**).

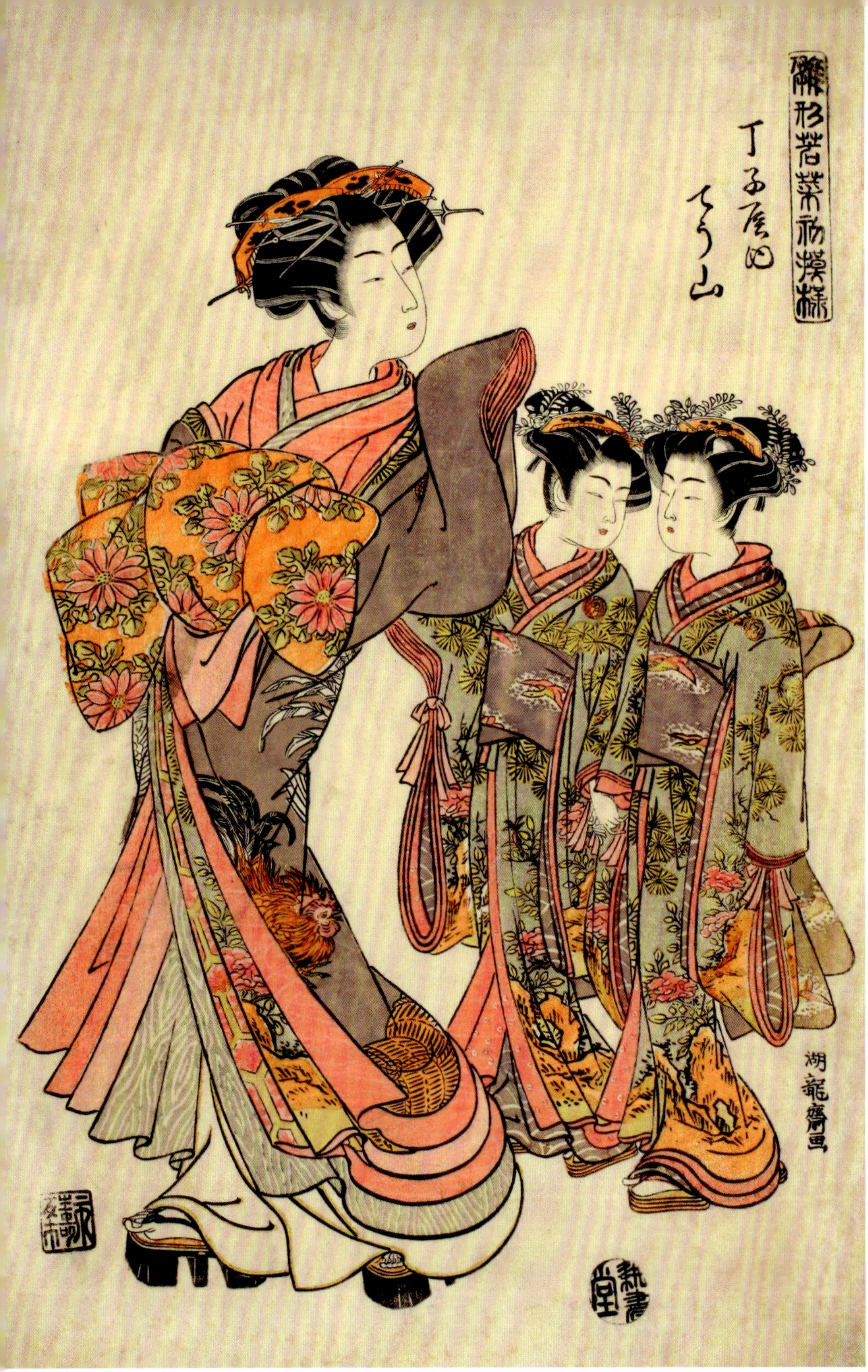

Kitagawa Utamaro (1754–1806), more than any other artist, personifies the essence of Japanese womanhood in his prints. He dedicated his entire artistic life to exploring female beauty and his sensitive portrayals are generally regarded as the finest and most evocative *bijin-ga* in all of *ukiyo-e* (**Figs. 60, 61**). In his prints, he was able to capture subtle aspects of the personalities and moods of women of all classes, ages and circumstances. Like Hokusai and Hiroshige, Utamaro is an icon in Japanese culture and, alone among his contemporaries, he achieved a national reputation during his lifetime. His work is purely Japanese. There are no outside influences. Unfortunately, to those who

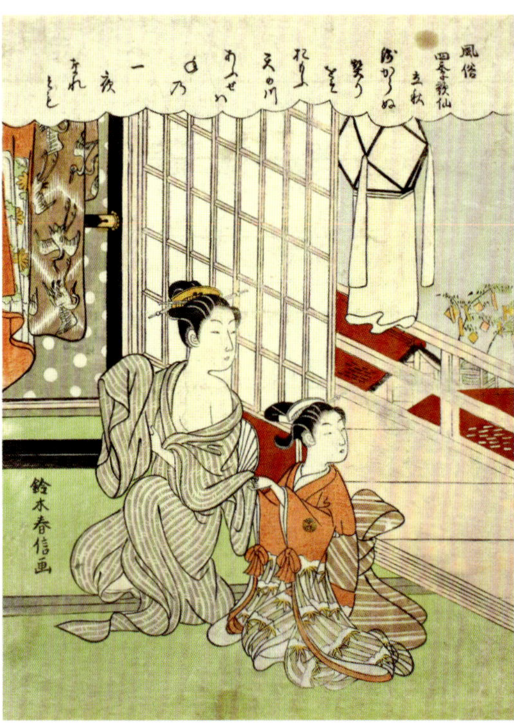

FIG. 55 (left)
Isoda KORYUSAI
湖竜斉 (1735–90)
Courtesan Chozan of the Choshiya
丁子屋ちょう山 (1770s)
26 x 19.5 cm
Courtesy of Mita Arts Gallery

Portraits of courtesans and the names of the houses (*Choshiya*) they worked for were a popular form of advertising and a lucrative source of income for artists. Here, two *kamuro*, employed to serve the courtesan, wear identical *kimono* supplied by the *Choshiya*. Even during the Edo period *kimono* were expensive and young teenage girls could not afford to buy their own. The courtesan's elaborately tied *obi* and seductive pose, which allows the layers of her undergarments to be seen, are enticing.

FIG. 56 (above)
Suzuki HARUNOBU
春信 (1725–70)
The First Day of Autumn 立秋 (1765–70)
26 x 19.5 cm
Courtesy of Mita Arts Gallery

In this beautiful interior scene, a young assistant (*kamuro*) is helping a courtesan to put on her sleeping *kimono*. Her left breast is exposed. The drawing of the arm as it struggles to slip through the sleeve of the *kimono* is very well articulated. A more elaborate day *kimono* hangs on the hanger behind. Paper decorations for the Tanabata festival, which falls on the seventh day of the seventh month, hang on the trees in the background. This festival celebrates the yearly reunion of two star lovers based on a Chinese legend that says a bridge of birds spans the Milky Way, allowing time for the lovers to be together.

have never stepped foot in Japan the nuances of eroticism and sensuality are only superficially realized in Utamaro's pictures.

Although Utamaro's subject matter was varied and included actor and warrior prints as well as pictures for poetry and nature books, in about 1791 he started to concentrate on making single portraits of women rather than prints of women in groups that were favored by the majority of *ukiyo-e* artists. In them he focused on the woman's face and upper half of the body, creating a radically distorted female using exaggerated proportions, large heads set upon long slim necks and coiffures bulging out to the edge of the prints. These "large head" views were called *okubi-e*. Whether he was the first to venture into *okubi-e* is uncertain as a few other artists at this time were creating prints portraying large *kabuki* heads. What we do know is that Utamaro became the undisputed master of the genre of *bijin-ga okubi* (large heads of beautiful women).

Utamaro is known not only for the quality of his portraits but for the sheer number of prints he produced. He lived for a while with his publisher, Tsutaya Juzaburo, and possibly this offered the unique opportunity to be as productive as he was. The 1790s is known as the Golden Age in printmaking and remained so until forty years later with the advent of Hokusai and Hiroshige in landscape art. This Golden Age, largely because of the influence of Utamaro, is centered on the life of beautiful woman. Tsutaya, his publisher, died in 1796 at the age of forty-eight. This was a serious blow to Utamaro and other artists as well. He subsequently was to work for more than forty different publishers. Unfortunately, this prolific activity—over 2,000 single-sheet print designs during his working career—produced a number of works of unquestionable mediocrity.

What are the elements that give this special quality to Utamaro's *ukiyo-e* beauties? The most obvious is the jet-black color of the hair. Japanese women's hair is, in fact, composed of different shades of black and dark brown. But in the prints the pure *sumi* black is startling. The shape of the hairstyle in exposing a long curved neckline is a striking contrast to the edge of the *kimono*. The three-quarter profile was the most popular view of the face. Full profiles were not attempted until the early twentieth-century *shin hanga* (new print) portraits. A straight full face is almost never attempted because of the difficulty in drawing the nose in a full frontal position. Some portraits show women with their eyebrows shaved, which was the custom for married women. The eyes are usually half closed, and the lips, if not

FIG. 57
Suzuki HARUNOBU
春信 (1725–70)
Getting Fresh Air on the Veranda
縁先美人 (1765–70)
22 x 29.5 cm
Courtesy of Adachi Institute of Woodcut Prints

In this intimate portrait of a courtesan party silhouetted behind the sliding doors of a teahouse, one of the courtesans is playing a *shamisen* while another is about to pour *saké* for a customer. The main subject looks a little tipsy as she steps out to the veranda to get some fresh air. Her white *kimono* contrasts vividly with her red *obi* and violet and red undergarments. Her loosely tied *obi* indicates that it can be easily untied. Unlike most of Harunobu's slim, flat-chested women, the courtesan is well built, with obvious breasts and hips.

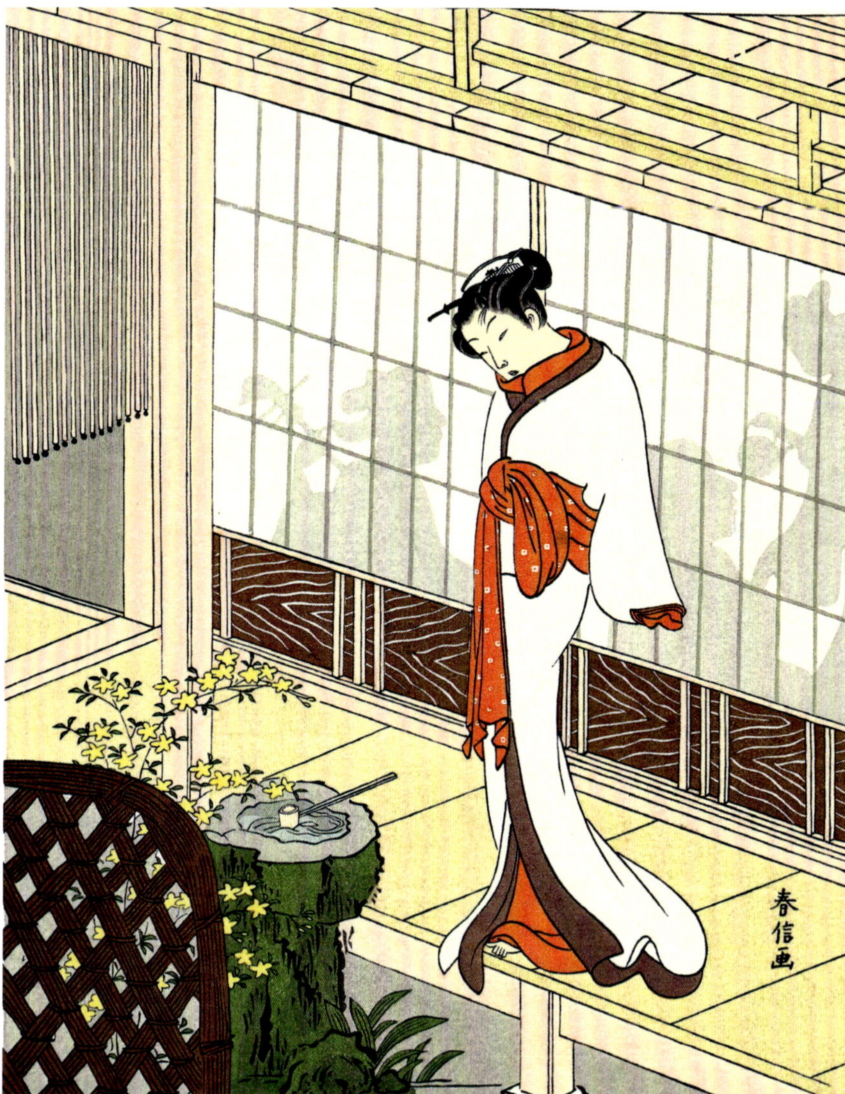

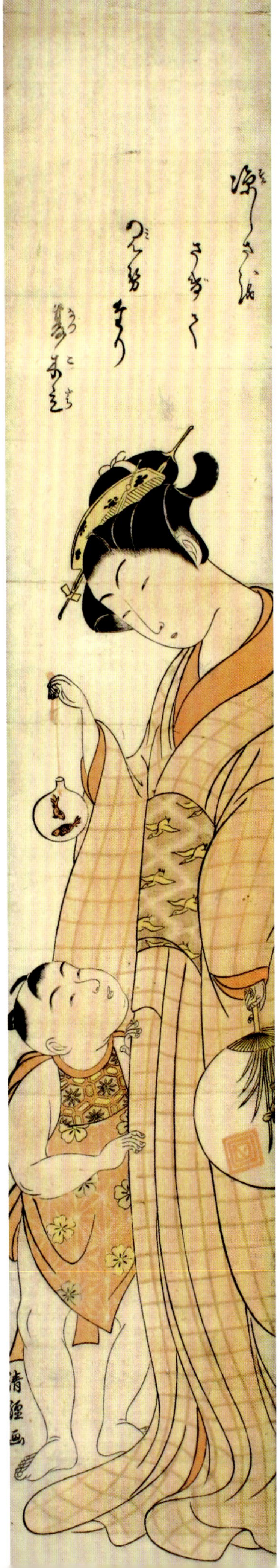

closed, show some indication of teeth. A person's emotional reaction to any given situation is indicated by the artist altering ever so slightly the sizes and shapes of the eyes and lips. Utamaro also employed blind printing (embossing) to create softness to the skin. This technique, called *musen-zuri*, was one that was also employed by Harunobu in his *kimono* textile patterns.

Ernest Fenollosa (1853–1908), the great American art critic, claimed that Torii Kiyonaga (1752–1815), the son of an Edo bookseller, captured the perfect proportions of Japanese woman in his prints (**Figs. 62–64**). Fenollosa used the Western proportions of Greek statues as his benchmark and stated that Kiyonaga came closer to these ideals than any other *ukiyo-e* artist. Known as *hatto-shin*, the proportion of head to body in Kiyonaga's work is one-eighth. He was also a great master of color, employing both deep and light tones with great taste. Compared with his predecessor Harunobu, the female figures in Kiyonaga's prints seem fuller and more mature. This may, in part be explained by his use of larger sheets of paper (*o-ban* rather than *chuban*) as well as a preference for the diptych (two-part) or triptych (three-part) form, which make his prints seem larger and more impressive; they could also be mounted into hanging scrolls. Kiyonaga was initially a Torii artist specializing in *kabuki* themes. His early work was not exceptional until the 1780s when he had a miraculous outburst of energy and started to produce women of simple grandeur usually in a procession format. He was a master of *kimono* fashion and created a statuesque beauty, but lacked an emotional response to the activities of the environment in which the figures participated.

Several other distinguished *bijin-ga* artists were active in the Utamaro tradition. Choki Eishosai (active 1780–early 1800s) was not as prolific as some of his contemporaries and for the most part not as creative, but he developed his own style of tall, slender figure clad in colorful *kimono*, often set against an

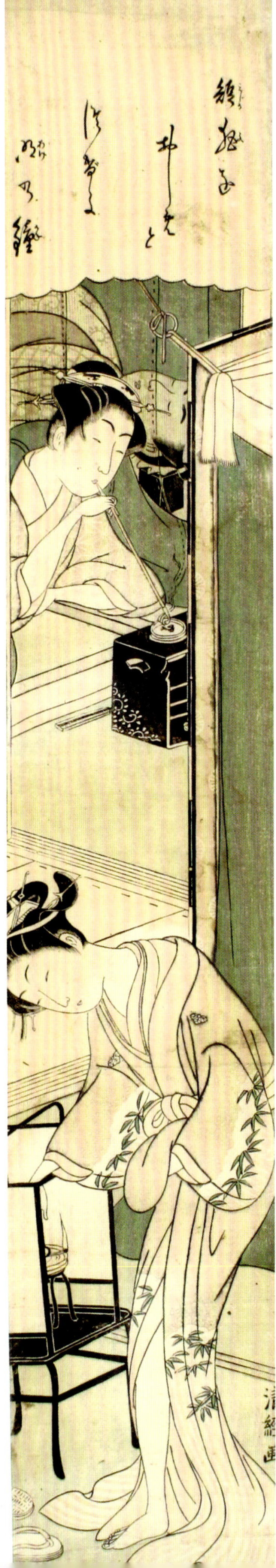

atmospheric background (**Fig. 65**). He was particularly skilled at the half-length figure in which the subject is placed upright near the margin of the composition. His printing techniques are often outstanding.

The eldest son of a *samurai* family and a former household official and court painter who resigned his position to satisfy his obsession for making *ukiyo-e* depicting the Yoshiwara pleasure quarter, Chobunsai Eishi (1756–1829) found artistic expression in full-length prints of women (**Fig. 66**). Eishi and Utamaro influenced each other, but Utamaro was not able to achieve the elegance and aristocratic noblesse of Eishi's *bijin-ga*. Perhaps influenced by his concept of *samurai* women, Eishi's women tend to appear quiet, motionless and expressionless.

Utagawa Toyokuni (Toyokuni I) (1769–1825) was one of the great masters of *ukiyo-e* of the late eighteenth century. As one of the renowned heads of the Utagawa school, he was to influence a whole new generation of *ukiyo-e* designers. Although he started out mostly portraying *kabuki* actors, under the influence of Torii Kiyonaga he designed some wonderful pictures of beautiful women (**Fig. 67**). He seems to have studied those print artists who came before him, especially Utamaro, for a time producing a synthesis of their styles, before creating his own. He captured the world around him with great clarity, including the world of *bijin* (**Fig. 68**). One of his more talented pupils, Utagawa Kunimasa (1773–1810) died young, at thirty-seven, and his talent was never fully realized. But it is said that his pictures of beautiful women exemplify the decorate pageantry of his master (**Fig. 69**).

About fifty years after the Golden Age of classical *ukiyo-e*, toward the end of the Edo period, an extraordinary change occurred in the *ukiyo-e* artists' attitude regarding the portrayal of female beauty. There was no longer an escape into portrayals of idealized beauty. Rather, this new era, called the Bunsei era (1818–30), demanded art

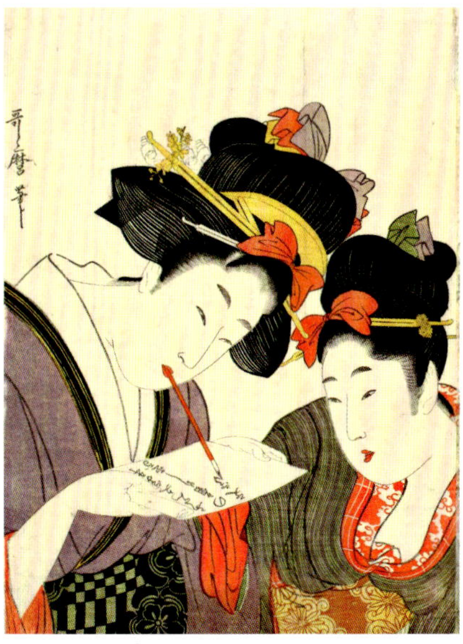

FIG. 58 (opposite left)
Torii KIYOTSUNE
鳥居清経 (active 1750s–70s)
Summer Festival 夏祭り (1770s)
Pillar print, 69.6 x 11.8 cm
Courtesy of Mita Arts Gallery

In this pillar print, a young woman in a light summer *kimono* dangles two gold fish in a container in front of a child. Other than the costumes, this same scene can be seen throughout Japan today in neighborhood festivals.

FIG. 59 (opposite right)
Torii KIYOTSUNE
鳥居清経 (active 1750s–70s)
Two Beauties 二美人 (1770s)
Pillar print, 68.3 x 11.6 cm
Courtesy of Mita Arts Gallery

In this pillar print, two young courtesans prepare for bed. The woman in the rear has a customer in bed sound asleep. She takes one last puff on her tobacco holder before her companion extinguishes the oil lamp (*andon*). It is a wonderful composition, allowing the eye to travel from the courtesan's exposed leg in the foreground zigzagging back to the sleeping man.

FIG. 60 (above)
Kitagawa UTAMARO
歌麿 (1754–1806)
Two Beauties 二美人 (1800s)
39 x 27 cm
Courtesy of Mita Arts Gallery

There is a nice contrast between the longer-faced woman and her plump companion in this "large-head" portrait, which is beautifully highlighted with touches of red. The courtesans probably worked for the same house as indicated by the similar style of their hair ribbons. One is trying her hand at writing with a brush held between her teeth, not an easy task as it required great dexterity.

FIG. 61 (below)
Kitagawa UTAMARO
歌麿 (1754–1806)
Portrait of a Courtesan, from a series called *Six Jewel Rivers* 六玉川シリーズから遊女のポートレイト (1790s)
39 x 27 cm
Courtesy of Mita Arts Gallery

Utamaro used the theme of the mythological rivers as an excuse to create a magnificent portrait of a sensual woman with her lips parted and teeth slightly exposed. The extremely fine line of her long neck and face is the work of a master craftsman, as is the execution of her hair. I have never seen a similar coiffure in any other print. The woman's hair, as it winds around the *kanzashi* (hair pin), is beautifully drawn, especially the fine white lines in front. The softness of the skin is sensed by the very fine outline as it contrasts with the bolder lines forming the *kimono*.

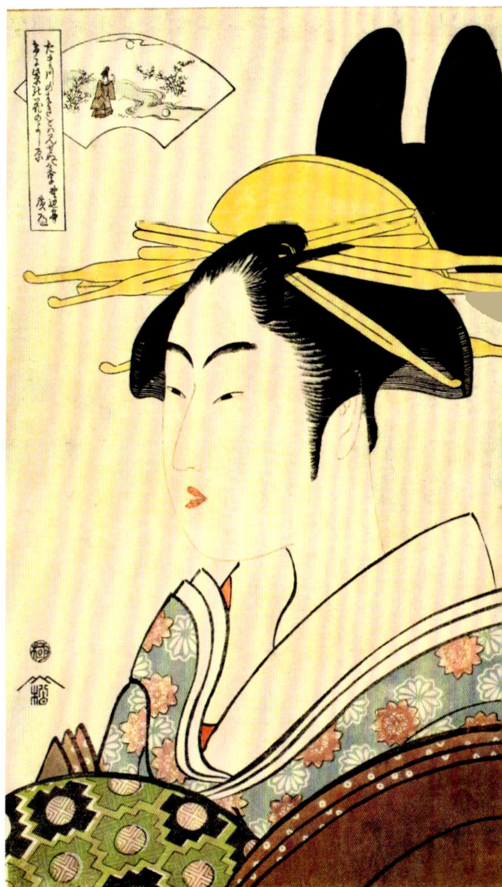

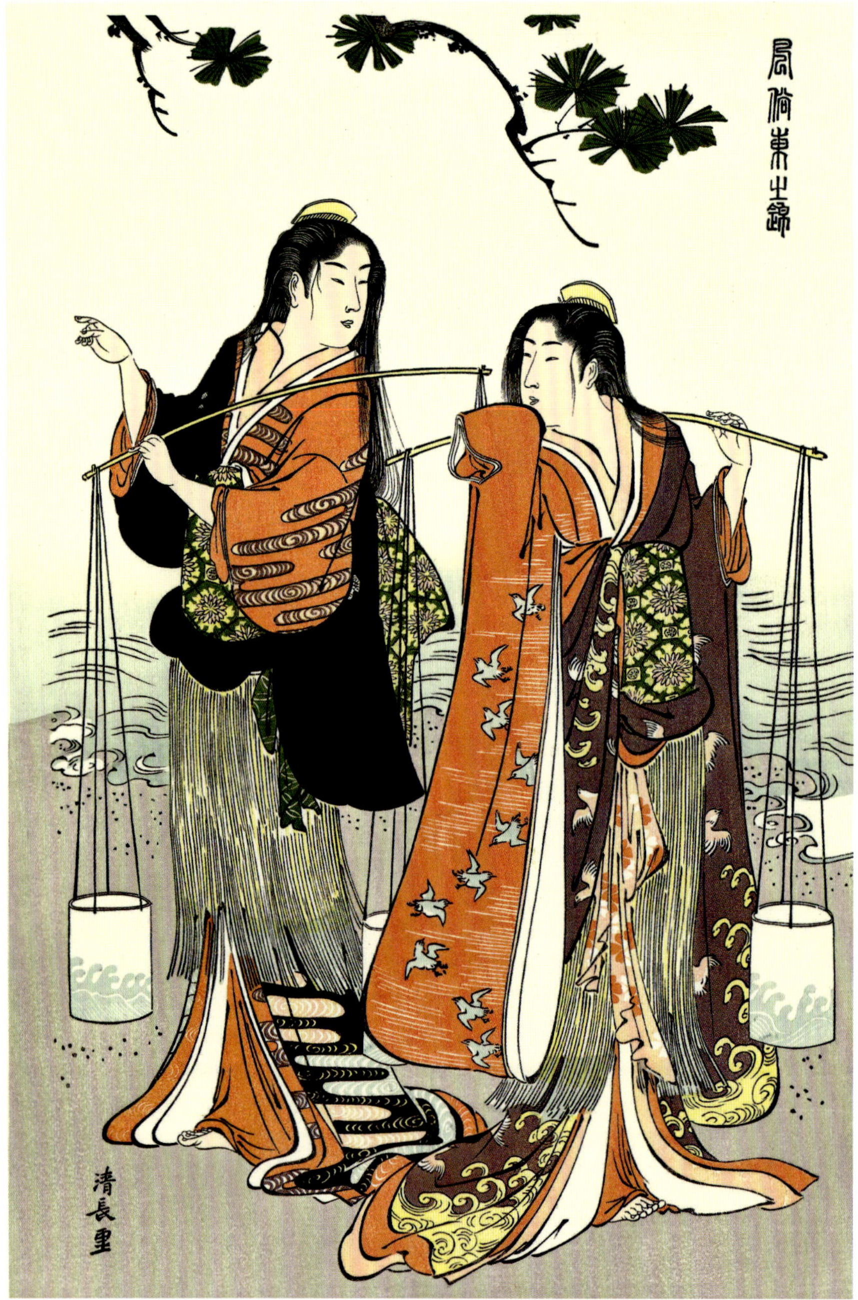

FIG. 62
Torii KIYONAGA
鳥居 清長 (1752–1815)
Shiokumi Dance 汐汲み (1780s)
39.5 x 27 cm
Courtesy of Adachi Institute of Woodcut Prints

This is a story about two women who were occupied with gathering salt from the sea. They suffered tragic love affairs, and in this print are performing a dance dedicated to that story. Kiyonaga generates a simple grandeur and dignity. His body proportions, known as *hatto-shin* (proportion of head to body is one-eighth), are the epitome of perfection. Some critics compared them to Western standards. Kiyonaga was also a great master of color, employing both deep and light tones with great taste.

FIG. 63
Torii KIYONAGA
鳥居 清長 (1752–1815)
Returning from the Bath in the Rain
雨中湯帰り (1780s)
39.5 x 27 cm
Courtesy of Adachi Institute of Woodcut Prints

Kiyonaga's delicate line was instrumental in his depiction of graceful and appealing women. There is a great deal of dignity and charm in this print of three young women on their way back from the communal bathhouse. Two of them have their cotton *kimono* draped over their arm. The girl on the right has her *obi* loosely knotted, whereas the other two have the *obi* tightly tied. We can almost hear their conversation.

that confronted life directly and without illusion. It was an era that has been labeled by some Japanese and Western critics as "decadent," and the three artists who were most active at that time—Utagawa Kunisada, Utagawa Kuniyoshi and Keisai Eisen—were called "The Decadents." These same critics believed that *ukiyo-e* ended with Hokusai and Hiroshige, dismissing outright the artists of the 1820s. Beginning in the 1930s, there has been a re-evaluation of their work and they are now regarded as being among the "giants" of the Japanese print.

Utagawa Kunisada (1786–1865) was an apprentice in the workshop of Toyokuni I and was old enough to witness the Golden Age of *ukiyo-e* when Utamaro was at his best. In keeping with a tradition of Japanese master–apprentice relations, he was given the official artist name of Kunisada, the first character deriving from the second character of his master's name. Initially an illustrator of woodblock printed picture books (*e-hon*), following the tradition of the Utagawa school his main output (about 60 percent) from around 1809 was *kabuki* and actor prints. He was also active at this time with a series of *bijin-ga* (about 15 percent of his output) and from 1820 to 1860 portraits of *sumo* wrestlers. Regarded as a trendsetter, Kunisada was in tune with the tastes of urban society and he continuously developed his style. He was also extraordinarily productive, creating a staggering 35,000–40,000 designs for individual woodblock prints during his lifetime.

Kunisada's women assumed postures and an appearance different from his predecessors (**Fig. 70**). The sources of his models were the same courtesans, teahouse waitresses and daughters of merchants, but they are shorter, more rounded, and generally far from the elegant women depicted by Utamaro or Kiyonaga. They are often posed with slightly bent backs and knees, giving them a bunched up, stumpy look. But details on their faces appear for the first time, such as eyelashes and soft

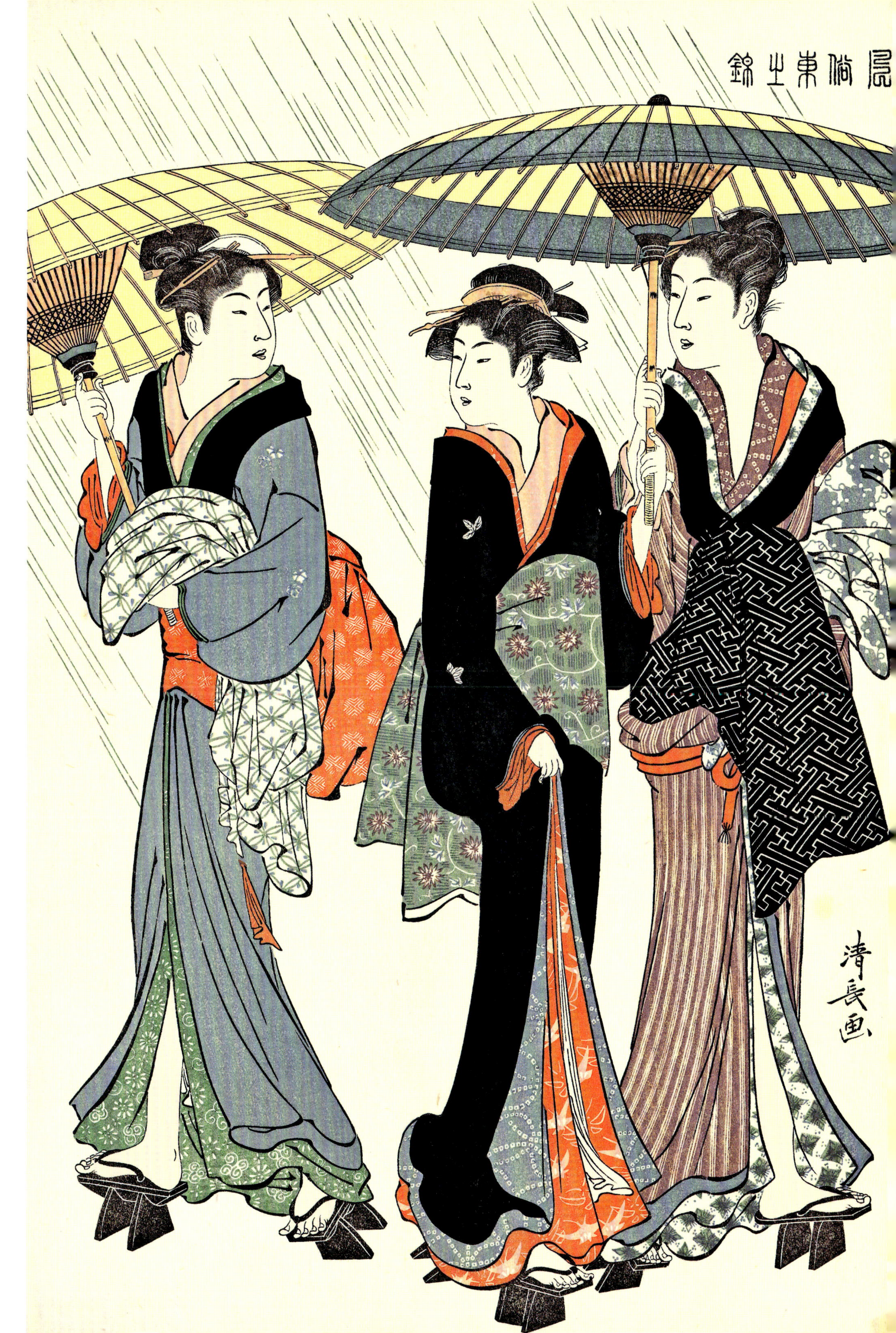
風俗東之錦
清長画

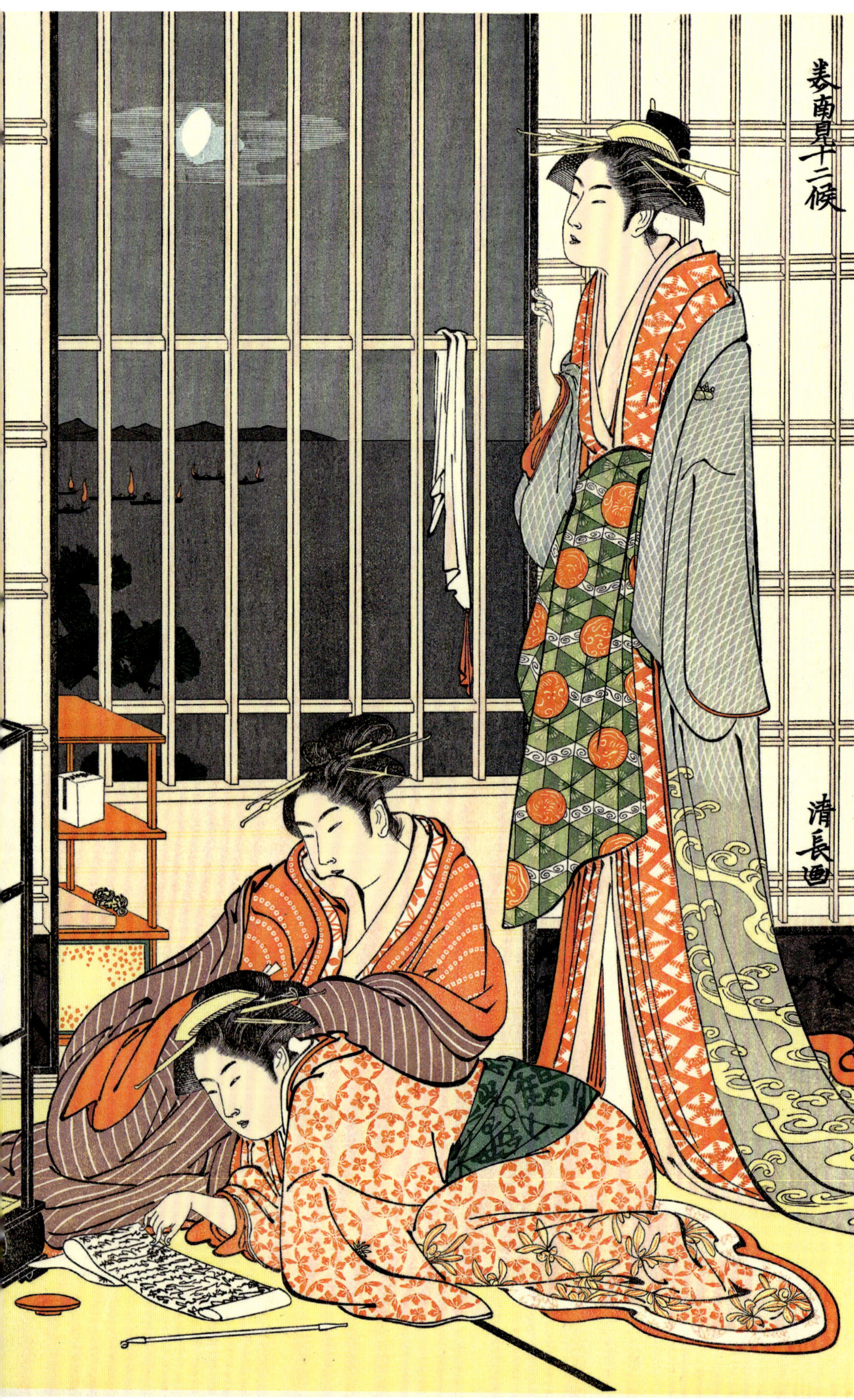

FIG. 64
Torii KIYONAGA
鳥居 清長 (1752–1815)
Courtesans in a Moment of Leisure 九月 (1780s)
39 x 26 cm
Courtesy of Adachi Institute of Woodcut Prints

The women in this pleasure house near the Shinagawa River are dressed casually as they wait for their next customers to appear. Outside, torch-lit boats move on the water. The women have been smoking and drinking to pass the time. The girl in the foreground is reading a love letter to her friends. We can sense the heat of summer and, with the windows wide open, the expectation of a breeze.

FIG. 65 (opposite)
Choki EISHOSAI
栄松斉 長喜 (active 1780–early 1800s)
Sunrise at New Year
初日の出 (1790s)
39.5 x 26.5 cm
Courtesy of Adachi Institute of Woodcut Prints

In this print, one of the most outstanding *bijin-ga* created by any *ukiyo-e* artist, a woman outside her residence in Fukagawa greets the New Year sun. In the morning chill, she pulls her *kimono* more tightly around her neck. Symbolic of the New Year is the blooming *fukujuso* plant on the water basin. As in many of Eishosai's compositions, the woman is placed upright to one side of the print.

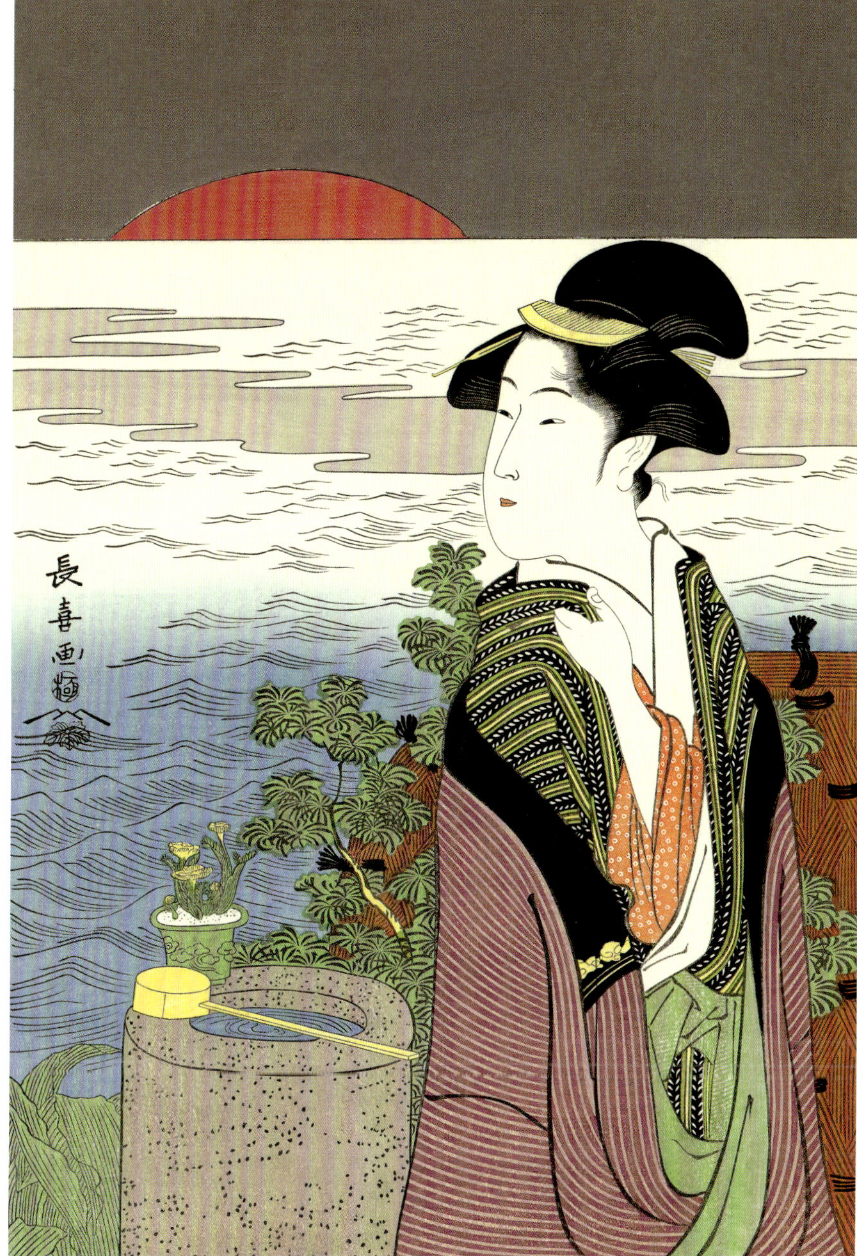

red rouge on the cheeks by a careful *bokashi* printing. The exotic symbolism in the prints is more overt. Basically, we reach a greater realism; the women assume poses that are more theatrical, without being true theater. Kunisada eventually took the name of Toyokuni III. Most of the prints done under his new name were *kabuki* related and if they were *bijin-ga* they became a more mass-produced industry. Colors became gaudy and ostentatious. He, among others, used the triptych to enlarge his designs to a more impressive size, as a single cured woodblock could never handle such a large picture.

Utagawa Kuniyoshi (1797–1861), the son of a silk dyer and the second of the so-called "decadent" print artists, fits into several different categories of the *ukiyo-e* world and is discussed in later chapters on animals, historical subjects and warrior themes and legends. He did, however, do some remarkable pictures of beautiful women in the decade 1818–27 after he had set himself up as an independent artist (like Utagawa Kunisada, he was initially an apprentice in the workshop of Toyokuni I and became one of his chief pupils) (**Figs. 71–73**). He also experimented with large textile patterns and light-and-shadow effects found in Western art. Like Kunisada, Kuniyoshi's women had large heads in relationship to their bodies. Their proportions immediately separate them from the elegance of Utamaro or Kiyonaga.

In the 1840s, strict regulations were put into place in Japan that banned subject matter of the *ukiyo-e* artist that the authorities deemed to be risqué. Among them were pictures of courtesans, *geisha* and actors. To circumvent these restrictions, Kuniyoshi created several series of beautiful women in the guise of famous characters of Japanese legend or as the illustration to a poem; if one were sophisticated enough, it was possible to find hidden meanings in the picture that would entice the imagination. He also did a series, in 1852, featuring the products, mostly sea life, from different provinces, which he used as a background picture within a picture of a beautiful woman. On occasion, he worked with a second artist to create a single composition. Fan prints (*uchiwa-e*) were another source of income for Kuniyoshi, who had the reputation of being unreliable with money and not very responsible.

Keisai Eisen (1790–1848), the son of a noted calligrapher and poet and the third of the "decadent" artists, specialized largely in *bijin-ga*. He produced an incredible number of large head and close-up bust portraits and standing studies of women depicting the fashions of the time (**Fig. 74**). Like his contemporaries, he worked in a variety of genres and, like them, suffered from overproduction as pressures to produce new works led to a large but uneven output. But his finest pieces are striking and highly original works. He was also a prolific writer.

Eisen was immersed in Yoshiwara, the gay quarter, and thus the women in his prints are mostly courtesans. Eisen's women are far removed from the idealism of early Edo artists. Instead of the usual grace and elegance, they display a certain voluptuousness and ripe sensuality. In his full-figure pictures, the poses are always adjusted to allow the courtesans' red undergarments to be revealed. His women's *kimono* are often loosely fitted, allowing an abundance of flesh to be seen, and on occasion a woman's breast is exposed. The accessories in the scene have overt symbolism, which to the knowledgeable participant in the gay world would be easily understood. Eisen's proportions are also more in

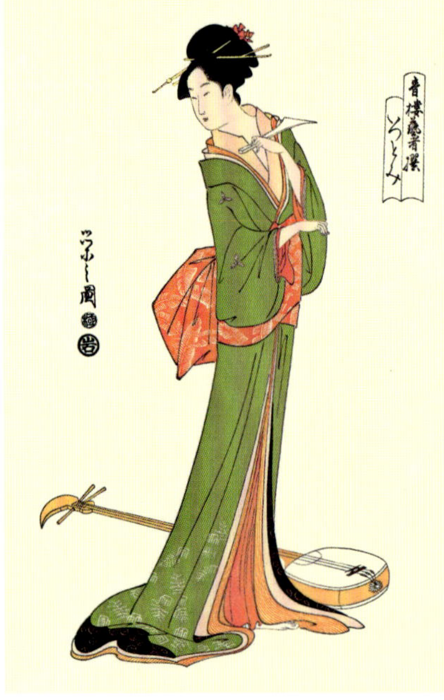

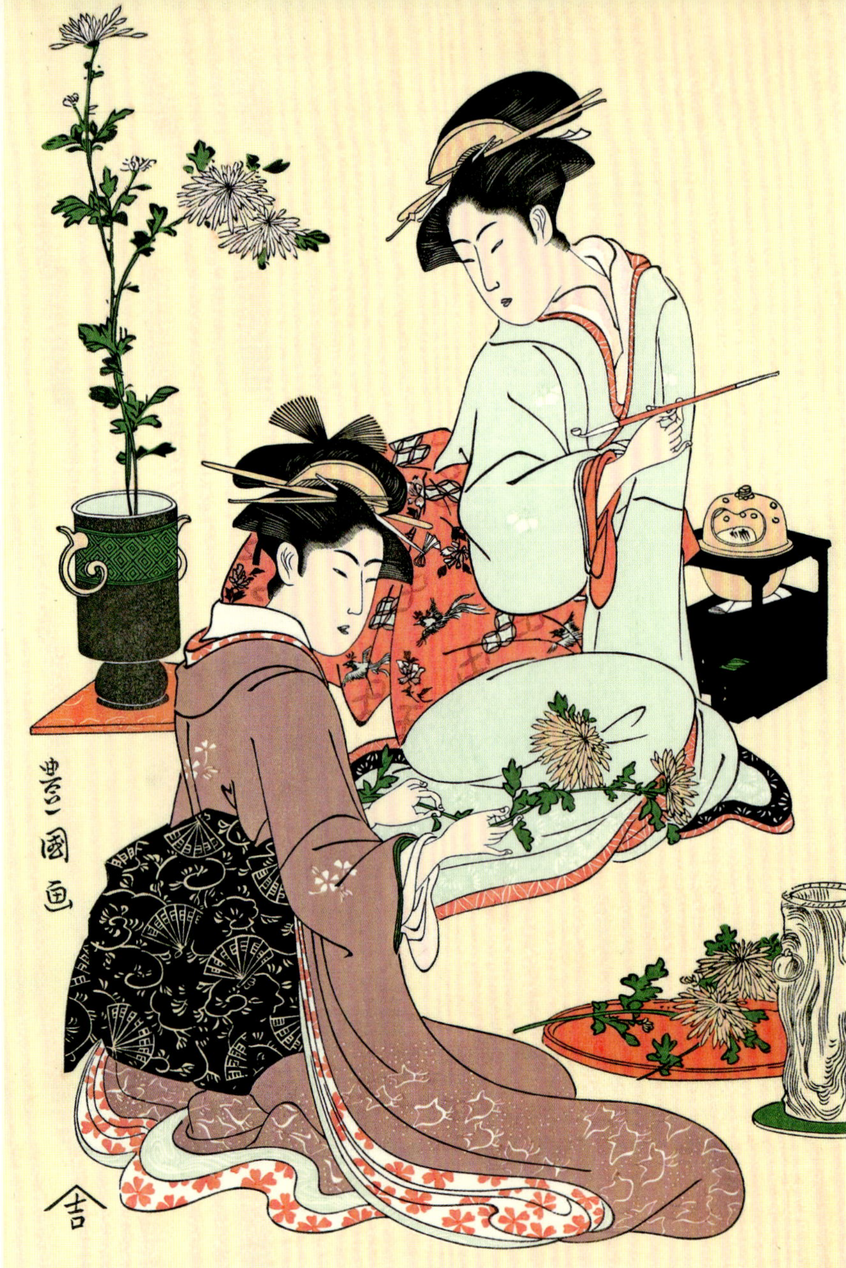

FIG. 66
Chobunsai EISHI
鳥文斉 英之 (1756–1829)
The Courtesan Itsutomi いつとみ (1790s)
40 x 26 cm
Courtesy of Adachi Institute of Woodcut Prints

This depiction of Itsutomi, one of the most famous courtesans of mid-nineteenth century Edo, epitomizes the Golden Age of *ukiyo-e*. Her graceful and refined features and motionless stance characterize Eishi's creations. Itsutomi stands in front of her *shamisen*, holding the plectrum in her hand. She glances toward her right while her full figure faces left. This "contrapasto" pose was very popular in *ukiyo-e* art. This print, a copy of which is in the Tokyo National Museum, is registered as an "Important Cultural Property."

FIG. 67
Utagawa TOYOKUNI I
豊国 (1769–1825)
Flower Arrangement 生け花を生ける娘
38.5 x 25.5 cm
Courtesy of Adachi Institute of Woodcut Prints

This is a wonderful composition showing two women creating a flower arrangement of chrysanthemum branches. The strong curve of the hips of the girl holding a smoking pipe frames the branches of the flowers in the other woman's arms. This is a delightful scene of fashionably dressed women of the upper class in a warm home environment.

keeping with the late eighteenth century. His figures are not as dumpy as those of Kuniyoshi or Kunisada. They are more sensual, more alive.

Born and raised a practicing *samurai*, Yoshu Chikanobu (c. 1838–1912) is probably the last of the true *ukiyo-e* artists. He trained with the "decadents," Kunisada, Kuniyoshi and Eisen, whose work eventually gave birth to new art forms in the Meiji and Taisho periods. Chikanobu saw the possibilities of fusing traditional designs with foreign ideas, which were entering Japan in profusion. He became particularly well known for his prints illuminating the great cultural transition from the era of the *samurai* to the modernity of the Meiji. A perfect example is his print of five different women during the plum blossom season, which shows the changes in women's fashion, hairstyles and make-up (**Fig. 75**). He is best known for his triptychs of single topics and series.

With the deaths of the artists above and with the nineteenth century drawing to a close, a drastic change occurred in the world of printmaking as well as in the approach of drawing the female form as a print subject. Following the Meiji Restoration in 1868, Japan opened its doors to imports from the West, including photography. The commercial value of *nishiki-e* dropped considerably as *ukiyo-e* began to fall out of fashion. The time-consuming method of the woodblock had to compete with modern methods of printmaking, such as lithography and photography, which could be reproduced by mechanical means.

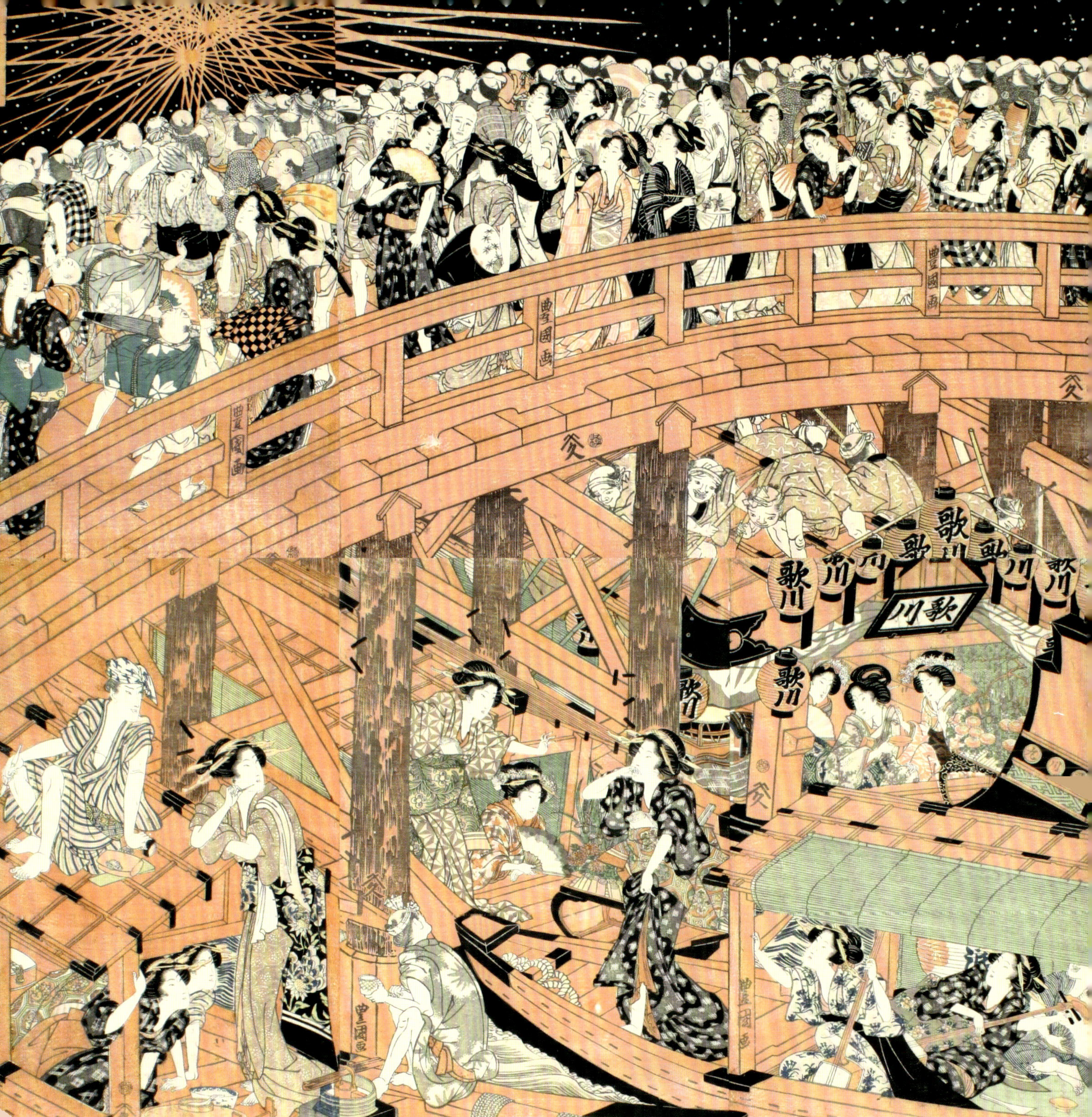

FIG. 68
Utagawa TOYOKUNI I
豊国 (1769–1825)
Fireworks at Ryogoku 両国花火の図 (1820s)
6-panel print, 78 x 79.5 cm
Author's Collection

This is a fascinating and very rare print composed of six sheets forming one composition. It is also a remarkable feat of printing to have kept the register intact on all six sheets. The people on the far side of the bridge—an assortment of characters, including parents with children and older folk—are watching fireworks. In the center distance, people seem to be watching each other. On the near side of the bridge, they are absorbed in observing the gay life and partying going on in small boats tied up under the bridge. Courtesans are playing *shamisen* while some are dancing. Everyone is having a great time under the eyes of a curious crowd of pleasure seekers themselves. The boatmen are an intriguing part of the scene.

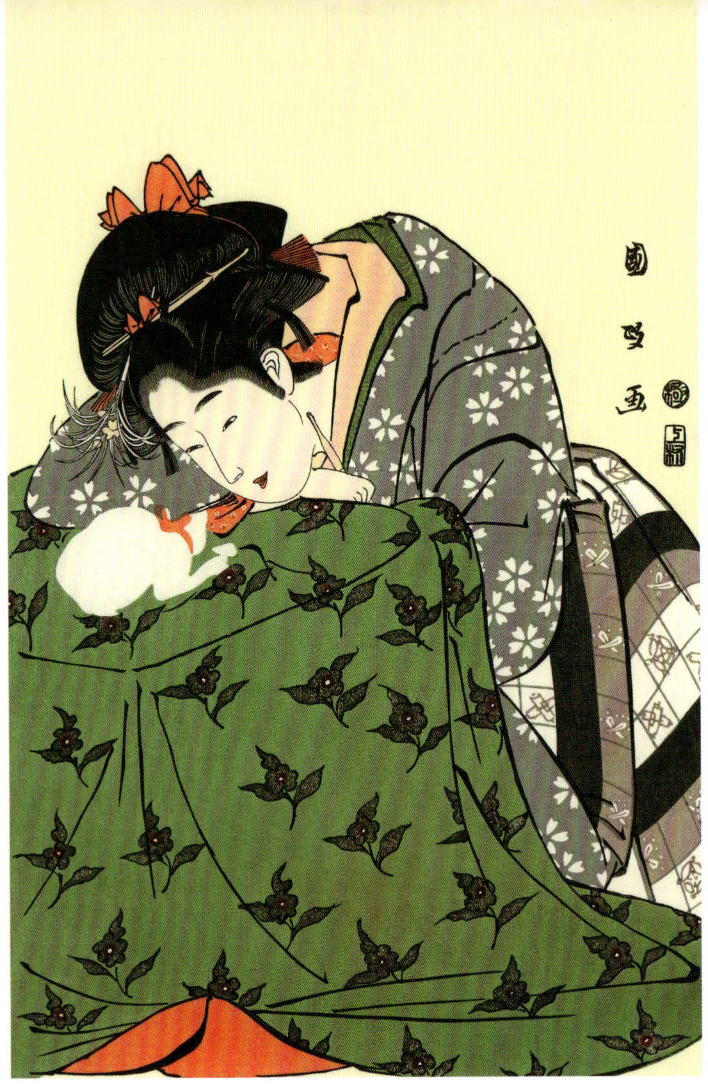

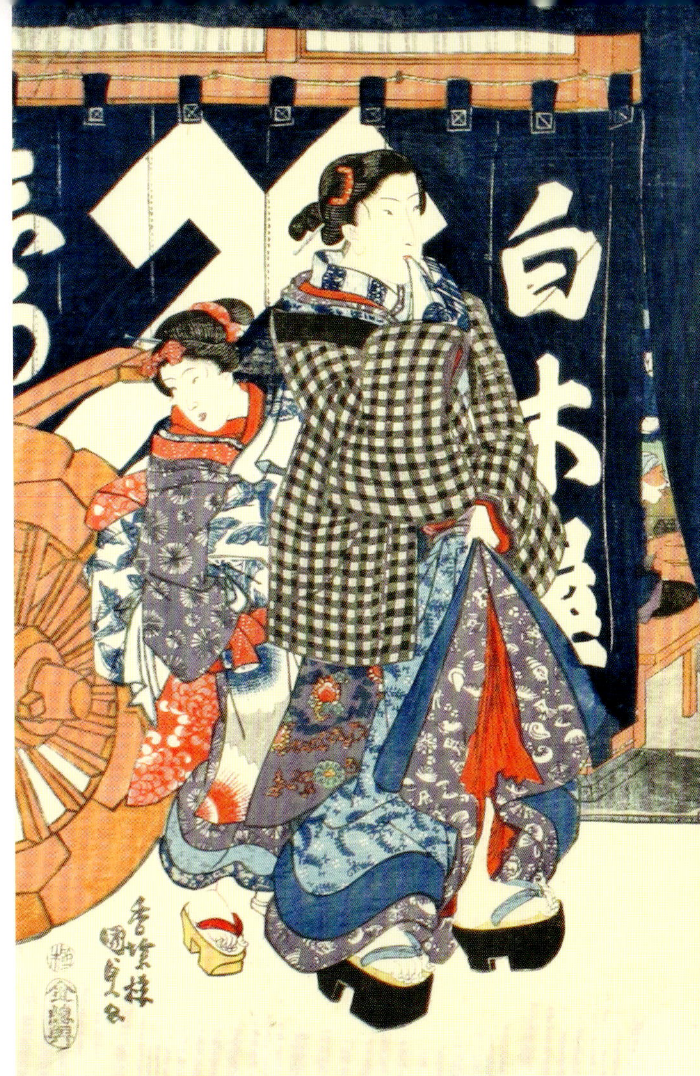

Many woodblock craftsmen became redundant. The few who continued to ply their craft were compelled to turn to new print forms. Some were employed by a small number of publishers operating in Edo who had begun creating individual prints from the work of the painters. Initially, the woodblocks were meant as reproductions of paintings, but would eventually evolve into the production of specific prints made from woodblocks.

Other artists were forced to find employment as magazine illustrators or turn their hand to painting as an outlet for their creativity. Yet others found an employment opportunity in the need for *kuchi-e*, attractive frontispieces for novels, designed to attract sales. These were almost always produced by woodblock and folded either once in the middle or twice to fit into the book behind the cover.

The attitude toward the picture was also now influenced by Western prints and photography, which resulted in a more realistic depiction of the subject. Inspired by European impressionism, the artists incorporated Western elements such as the effects of light and shadow and the expression of individual moods, at the same time focusing on strictly traditional Japanese themes.

One of the obvious changes that occurred can be seen in the patterning of *kimono*, as exemplified by Yoshu Chikanobu (see Fig. 75). In *ukiyo-e* the fabric pattern—bright flowers or any other design—runs across the figure without concern for the folds in the material, including at the sleeves. With the new way of drawing, the pattern related to the folds and was either cropped or shifted to follow the movement of the body.

Another innovation was the use of shading to illustrate the turning of the form. The figure was no longer absolutely flat but would approximate three-dimensional shapes by a subtle use of *bokashi* printing. Shading also came to be used in drawing faces. Soft shadows under the lower lips, over the eyelids and around the nose created the illusion of solid forms. Eyelashes were drawn to give expression and were no longer depicted as thin lines. The drawing of the hands became an important feature. Fingers actually took on positions of bone articulation.

Kajita Hanko (1870–1919) was among the late nineteenth-century transitional artists who earned his living mainly from illustrations and *kuchi-e*. The illustrations were added as supplements to serial novels of the soap opera kind avidly read by women. Although Hanko achieved some small fame as a painter in the Japanese style, it was his outstanding woodcuts of beautiful women during the Meiji period that attracted attention (**Fig. 76**). He used his wife Usui Takako, a novelist, as his model; she unfortunately died of tuberculosis at the age of twenty-four, as did he at the age of forty-seven.

Another transitional artist was Hashiguchi Goyo (1880–1921) who, in his short life, produced no more than fourteen prints, eight of them of beautiful women (**Figs. 77, 78**). Originally an

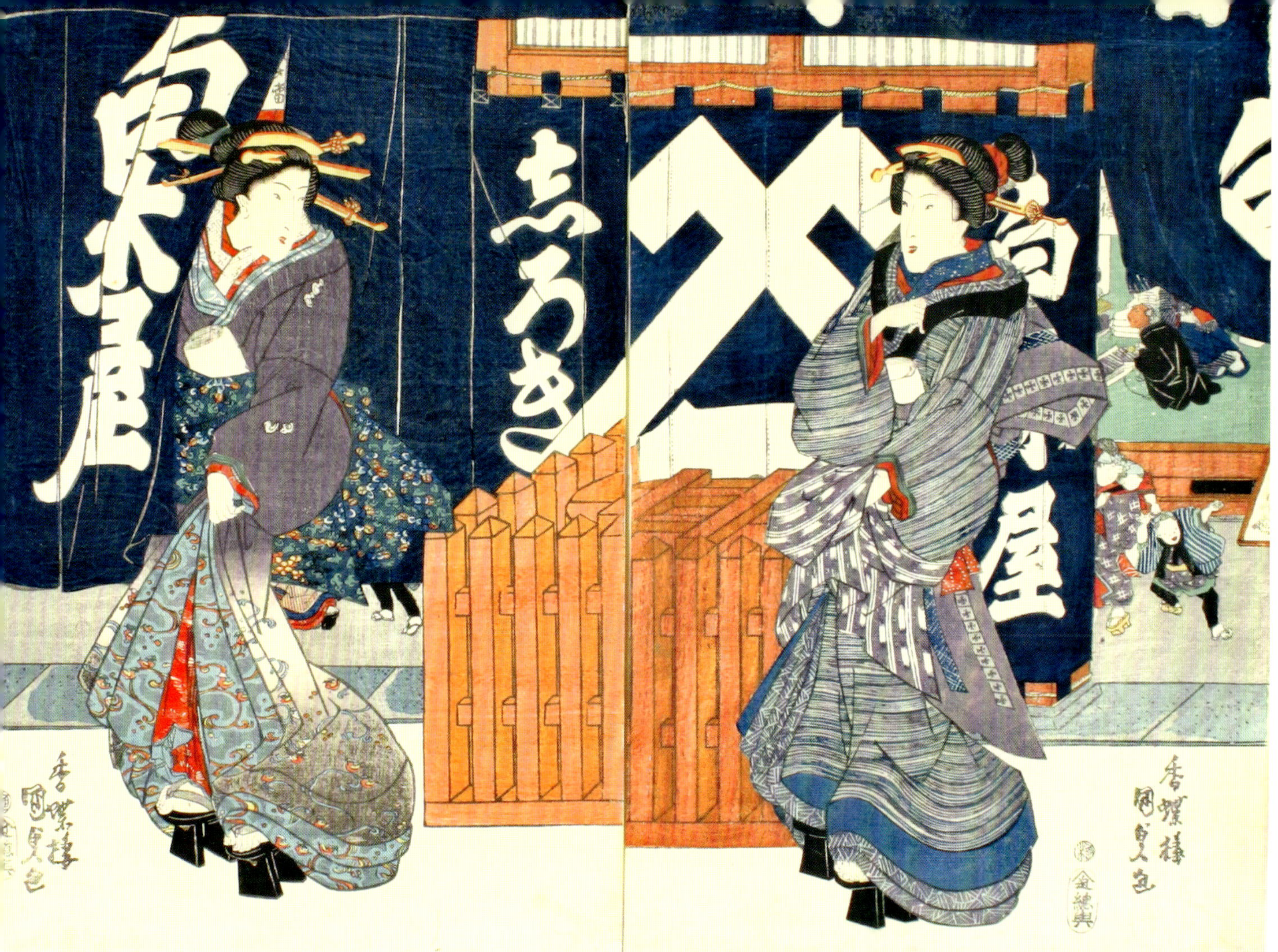

oil painter, Goyo combined Western art principles with a study of *ukiyo-e* to create a realistic approach to the drawing of women. He drew from live models. His portraits reveal subtle nuances in the features of his subjects—the eyes, noses, and especially the lips. All his prints were superbly crafted and lavishly printed, often with pearly mica backgrounds, and except for one were published in his studio under his direct supervision in order to meet his exacting standards. I have seen numerous pencil drawings of Goyo and they are as delicate as any produced anywhere in the world. For the printer and carver to capture his drawings in *ukiyo-e* is to truly create a masterpiece.

Woodblock prints produced after 1915 are generally referred to as *shin hanga* ("New Prints") and were created by Watanabe Shozaburo, who started an export woodblock print business (see Chapter 7). Watanabe had many skilled carvers and printers working for him but lacked talented artists to make print designs appealing to Western audiences. Goyo published one print with him but was not satisfied with Watanabe's printmaking standards. Because of the decline in demand for traditional *ukiyo-e* with the advent of photography, many artists had little choice but to enter into a business liaison with the innovative publisher.

Several *shin hanga* artists were recruited by Watanabe Shozaburo from a painting group led by Kaburagi Kiyokata (1878–1972), a leading revivalist and master of the *bijin-ga* genre in the Taisho and Showa periods (**Figs. 83–85**). Kiyokata initially made a living as an illustrator of popular books, especially frontispieces (*kuchi-e*), although his foremost interest was in painting and he became an official court painter. He was on the committee of the Imperial Household and Japan Art Academy. Many of his prints have a painterly quality.

One of Kiyokata's pupils, whom he introduced to Watanabe, was Ito Shinsui (1898–1972), whose long life was dedicated to portraying the beauty

FIG. 69 (above far left)
Utagawa KUNIMASA
国政 (1773–1810)
Beauty and Cat 猫に美人 (1790–1800)
39 x 26 cm
Courtesy of Adachi Institute of Woodcut Prints

This intimate scene in winter is of a young woman seated by a heated table (*kotatsu*) playing with a cat who is enjoying the warmth of the table and the attention of the woman. The careful placement of the reds in the composition—the ribbon in the woman's hair, her undergarments and the ribbon around the cat's neck—are anchored by the red heavy wool covering at the base of the *kotatsu*.

FIG. 70
Utagawa KUNISADA
国貞 (1786–1865)
Beauties in Front of Shirokiya
白木屋前の美人 (1820s)
Triptych, 39 x 79.5 cm
Courtesy of Mita Arts Gallery

In this composition, three very beautiful women in elaborate *kimono* are outside one of Japan's most famous department stores, Shirokiya, which still existed up to the later part of the twentieth century but has since closed. The woman in the center has just come out of the shop. It is a cold winter day and the three women have some difficulty in keeping their multilayered *kimono* from opening.

FIG. 71
Utagawa KUNIYOSHI
国芳 (1797–1861)
Mackerel, Tanba, from *Famous Products of the Provinces With Beauty* 山海愛度図會どこぞへいきたい 丹波 鯖釣 (1852)
39 x 26 cm
Author's Collection

In this and the following two prints, Kuniyoshi illustrates several distinctive characteristics of his portrayal of women: they are robust, with large heads, and wear *kimono* with striking textile patterns. Western shading and perspective are apparent in the small landscape pictures in the background advertising provincial products.

FIG. 72
Utagawa KUNIYOSHI
国芳 (1797–1861)
Duck, Josyu, from *Famous Products of the Provinces With Beauty*
山海目出たい図會 よい夢でも見たい 上州霞網鳥 (1852)
39 x 26 cm
Author's Collection

FIG. 73 (opposite)
Utagawa KUNIYOSHI
国芳 (1797–1861)
Casting Fishing Nets, Joshu, from *Famous Products of the Provinces With Beauty*
山海愛度図會 おもたい 伊勢海老網 (1852)
39 x 26 cm
Author's Collection

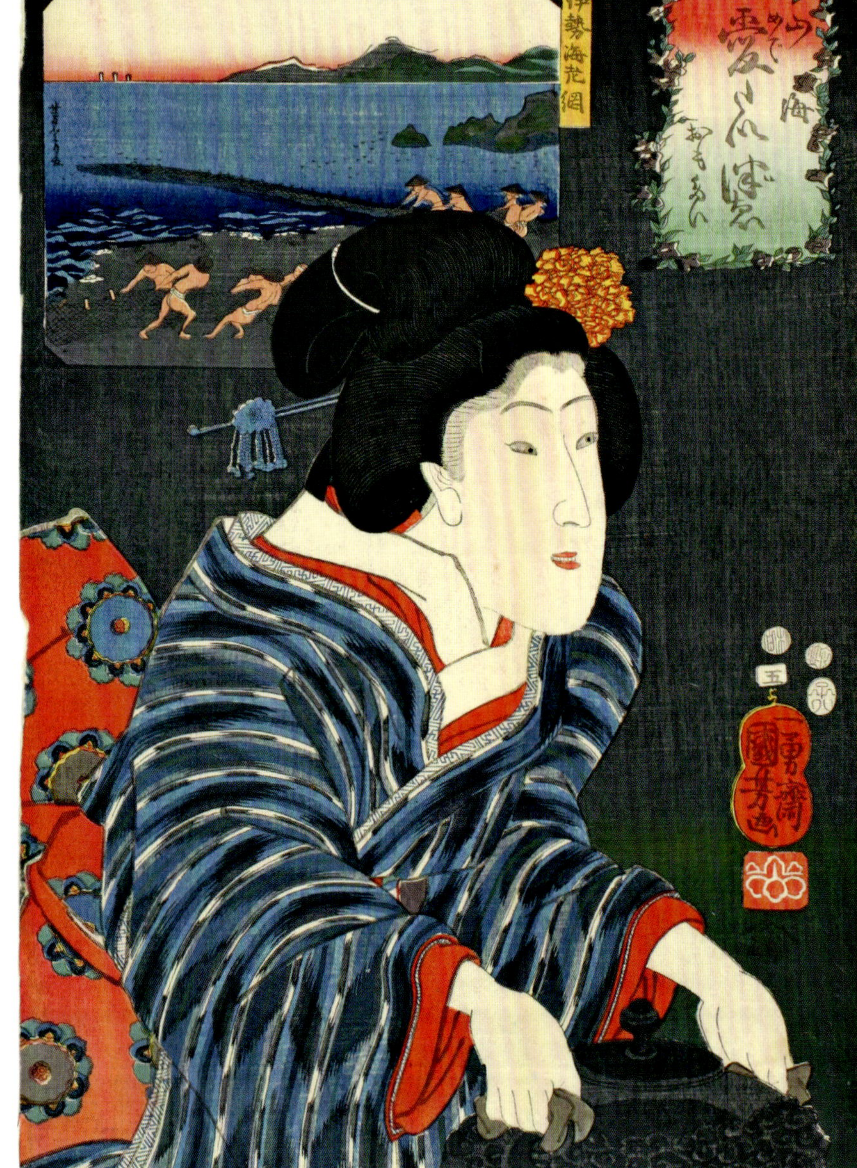

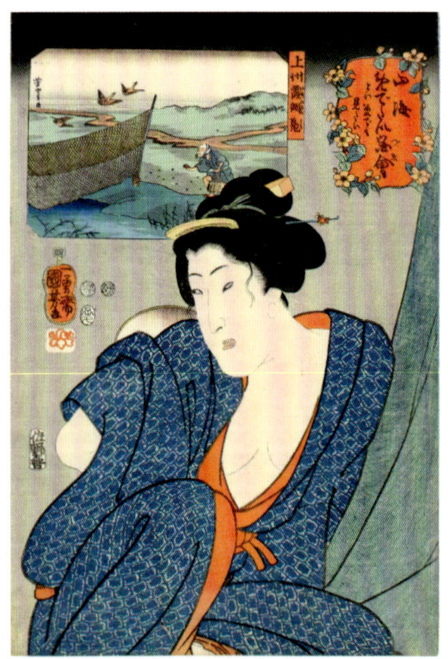

of Japanese women although he also occasionally painted landscapes (**Figs. 79, 80**). Ito started his career as an illustrator for novels and *kuchi-e* but slowly developed his personal style under the guidance of his teacher. He also developed his own technique, revolutionary at the time, of creating a "master painting" in watercolors from which Watanabe's craftsmen made the actual prints.

Of all the *shin hanga* artists, the one who stands above the rest is Torii Kotondo (1900–76) (**Figs. 81, 82**). Kotondo is a direct aesthetic descendant of two of the great Torii school artists. He studied with Torii Kiyotada II (1875–1941), where he was taught the Torii school style of *kabuki* theater billboard painting, before settling into the studio of Kaburagi Kiyokata. For some unknown reason, he did not publish his works with Watanabe. When I first came to Japan in 1952, Kotondo prints were widely available and inexpensive. Because they were so "pretty," people distanced themselves from them. They have a glamorous look and compared to *ukiyo-e* were not at all distinguished. Today, Kotondo prints sell as high as any of the great *ukiyo-e* artists. They are difficult to find and have appreciated in value at a speed incomparable to other woodblock prints. The artist only produced twenty-three prints, all of them of beautiful women except for one *kabuki* subject and all before 1934. Some were printed in several color variations. The rest of Kotondo's life was spent painting.

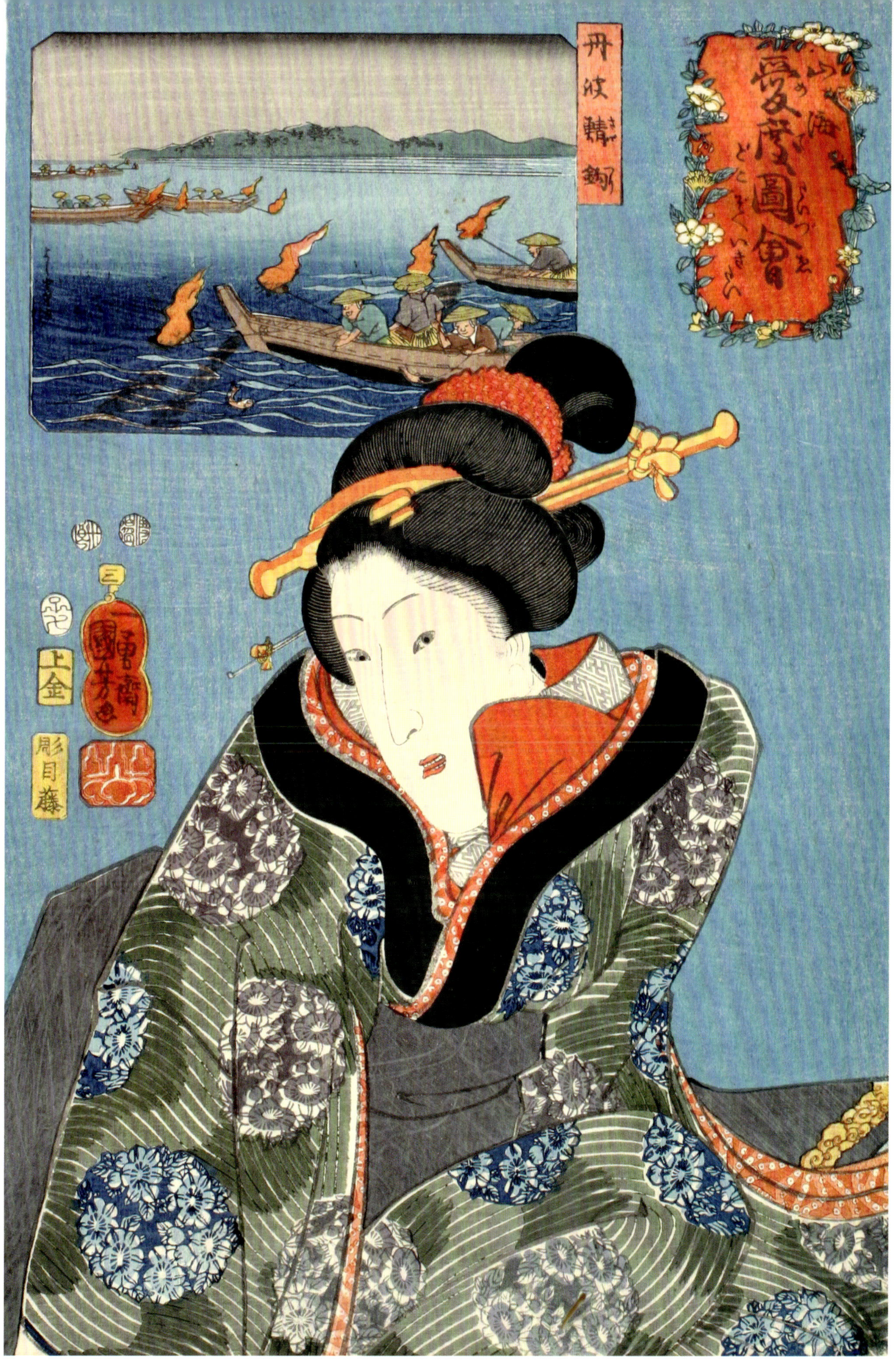

山海愛度圖會
丹波
一勇斎國芳画
三
上金
彫目藤

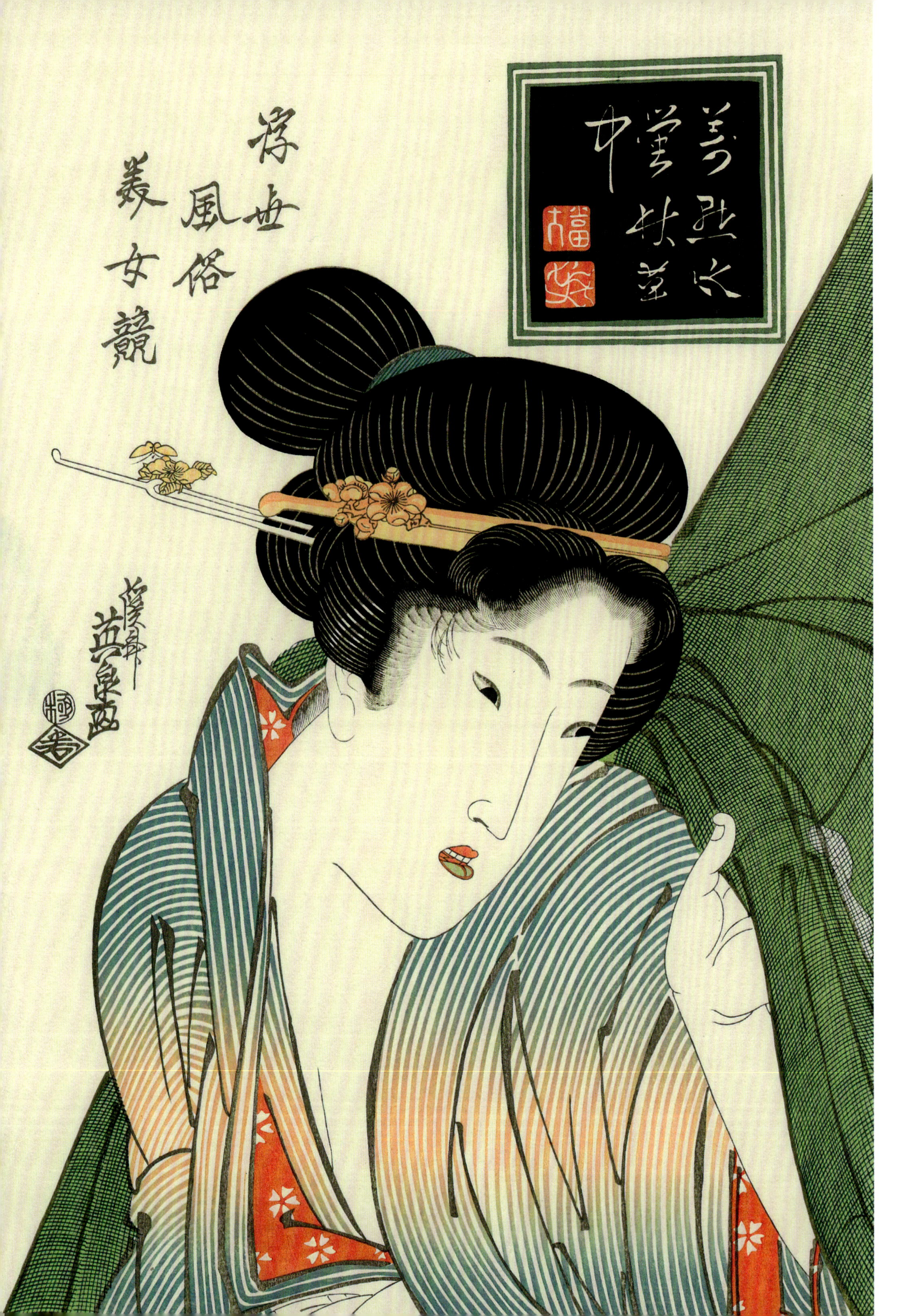
浮世風俗
美女競
渓斎英泉画

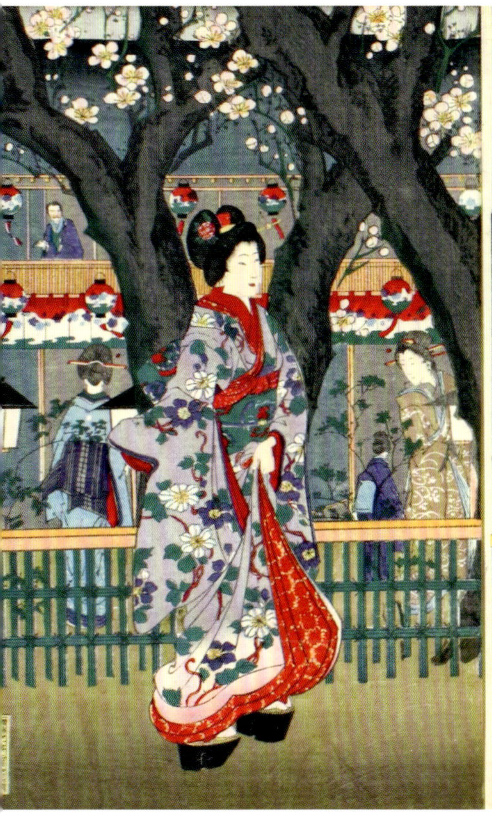
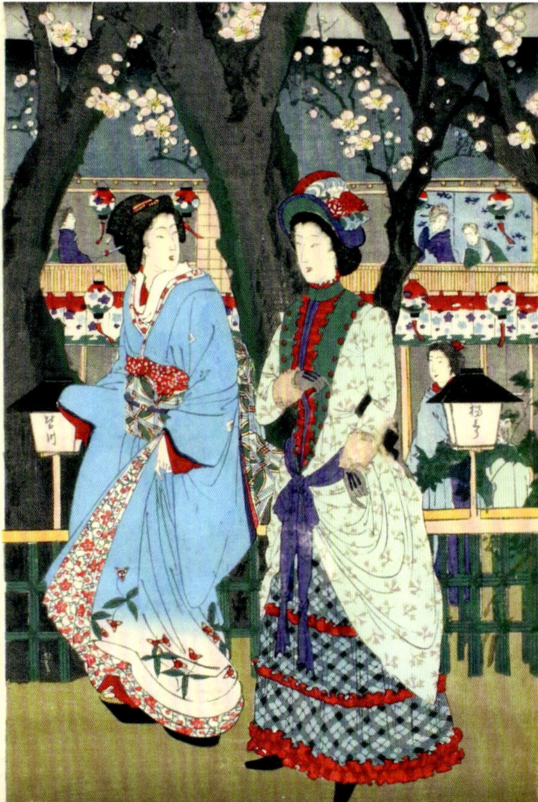
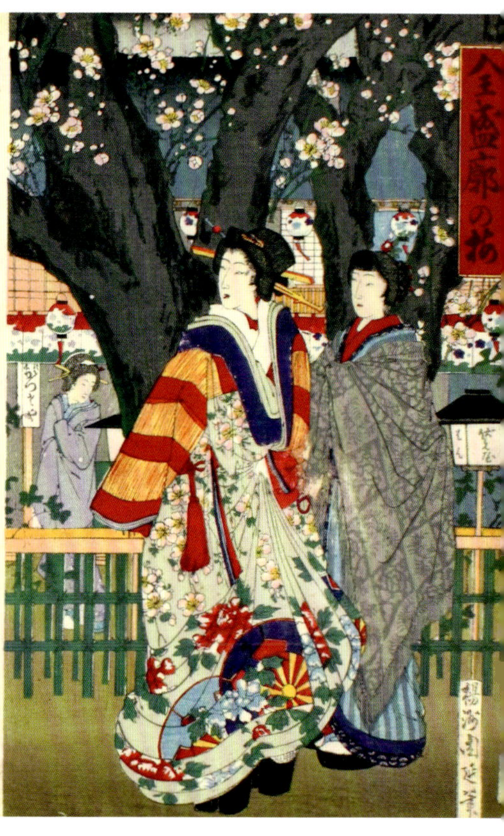

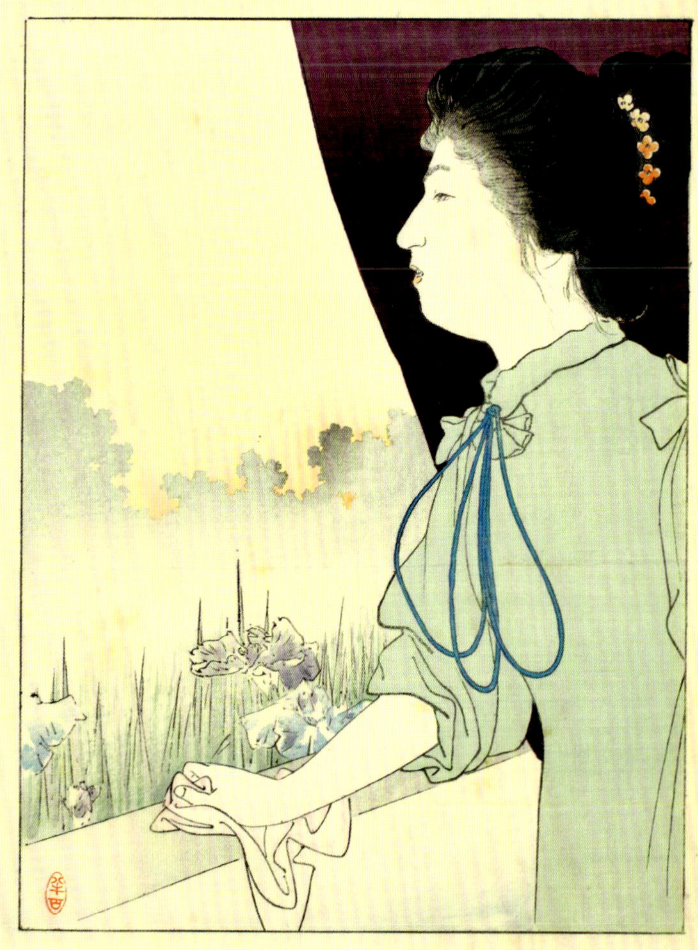

FIG. 74 (opposite)
Kajita HANKO
梶田 半古 (1870–1919)
Waiting for Her Lover
恋人を待つ女 (1915)
21 x 28 cm
Author's Collection

Hanko drew beautifully as can he seen by the profile of this young woman as she stares into the distance waiting for someone. We can feel the bone structure of her face, especially the nose and subtle drawing of the mouth, with lips slightly parted as if she were about to say something. The simple contour displays the roundness of form as if there were shading, although there is none.

FIG. 75 (left)
Keisai EISEN
渓斉 英泉 (1790–1848)
Woman Getting out of a Mosquito Net
万点水蛍 (1822)
39 x 26.5 cm
Courtesy of Adachi Institute of Woodcut Prints

In this picture, a woman has just got up from sleeping or lovemaking. Her *kimono* is loose, exposing the fullness of her breast. She also has a crumpled piece of tissue paper in her right hand, suggestive of the sexual act. The *bokashi* in the stripes of her *kimono*, the transparent quality of the mosquito net and the treatment of her hair exemplify the highest level of printmaking. Nor is her face symbolic of a generic woman. The drawing of the eyes and eyelashes, teeth and tongue make her very much her own person.

FIG. 76 (above)
Yoshu CHIKANOBU
楊州 周延 (1838–1912)
Fashionable Ladies Taking an Evening Stroll 全盛楼の梅 (1900)
Triptych, 72 x 35 cm
Author's Collection

This print illustrates perfectly the fusion of traditional designs and foreign ideas that came to characterize many prints at the end of the nineteenth century. Set against a background of restaurants and pleasure houses during the plum blossom season, four of the women wear *kimono* of contrasting styles with extremely high *geta* (wooden clogs), while the fifth is in Western dress with flat shoes. They all appear equally tall.

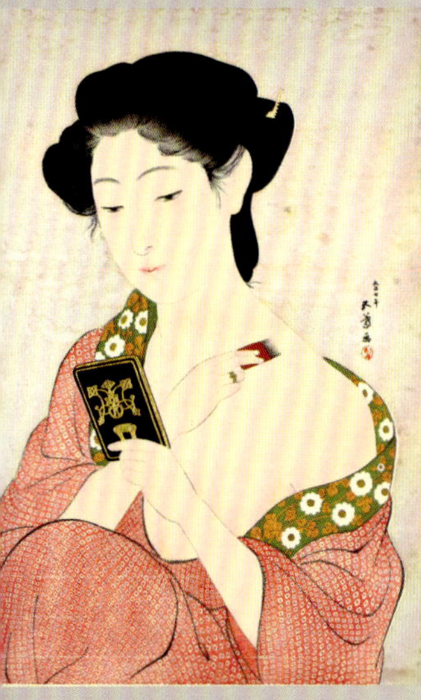

FIG. 77
Hashiguchi GOYO
橋口 五葉 (1880–1921)
Woman Applying Make-up 化粧の女 (1918)
51 x 36.1 cm
Courtesy of Mita Arts Gallery

This is a much larger print than the standard 38 to 39 cm. Like other of Goyo's women, she is superbly crafted. The forms of her eyes and lids and the delicacy of her mouth are beyond the normal expressions in drawing or printing. There is a slight *bokashi* on the contour to give a sense of roundness to the body. The fullness of the hair, and its transparency near the forehead, show the artist, block carver and printer at their best.

FIG. 78
Hashiguchi GOYO
橋口 五葉 (1880–1921)
Woman Combing Her Hair 髪梳ける女 (1920)
43.8 x 32.5 cm
Author's Collection

The girl's lips in this print are formed by the use of soft pink *bokashi* printing, with only the crease of the two lips defining the delicate form. The execution of the girl's luxuriant hair as it falls down the front of her *nemaki* (sleeping *kimono*) is of the highest standard. This is one of the great masterpieces of twentieth-century printmaking.

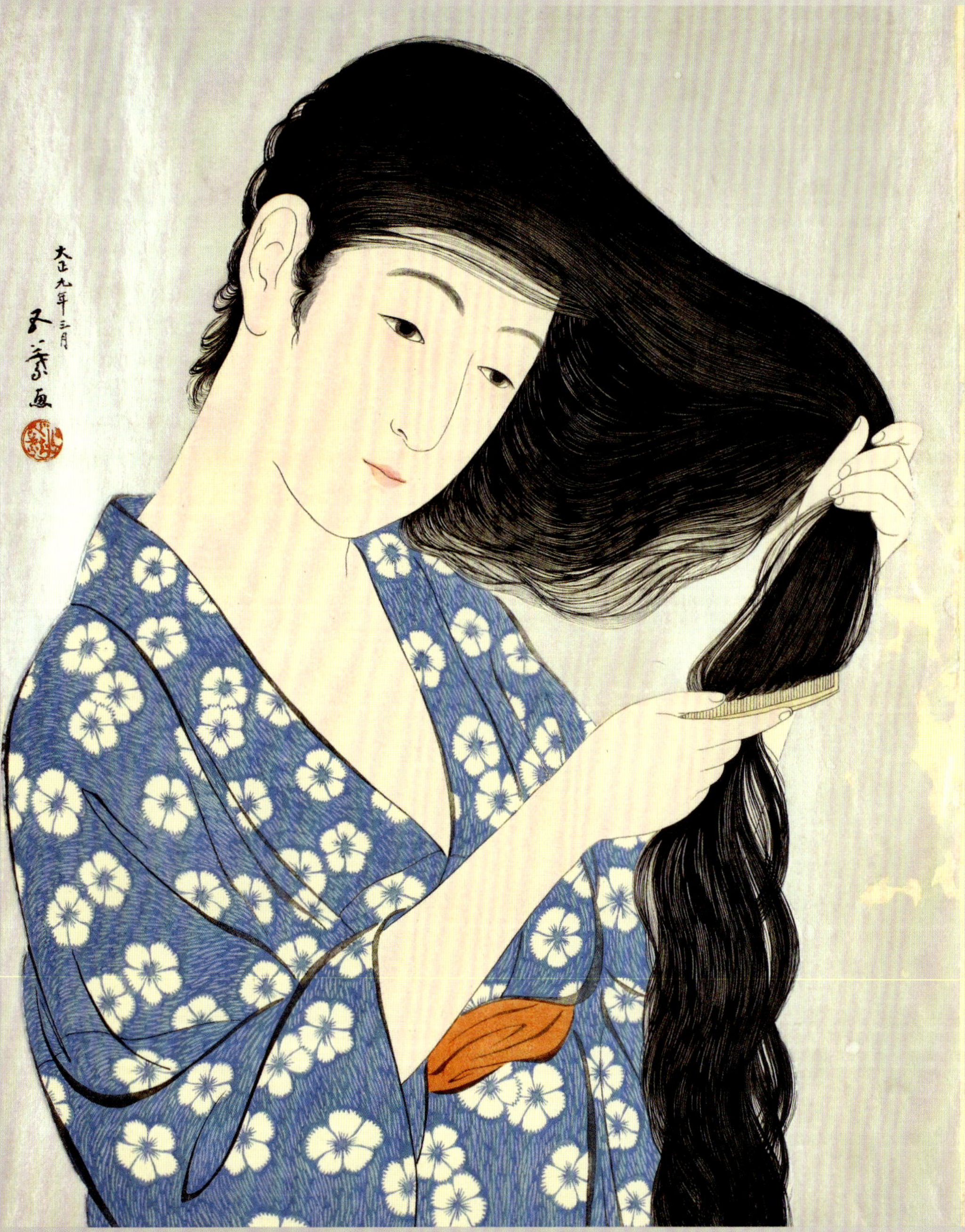

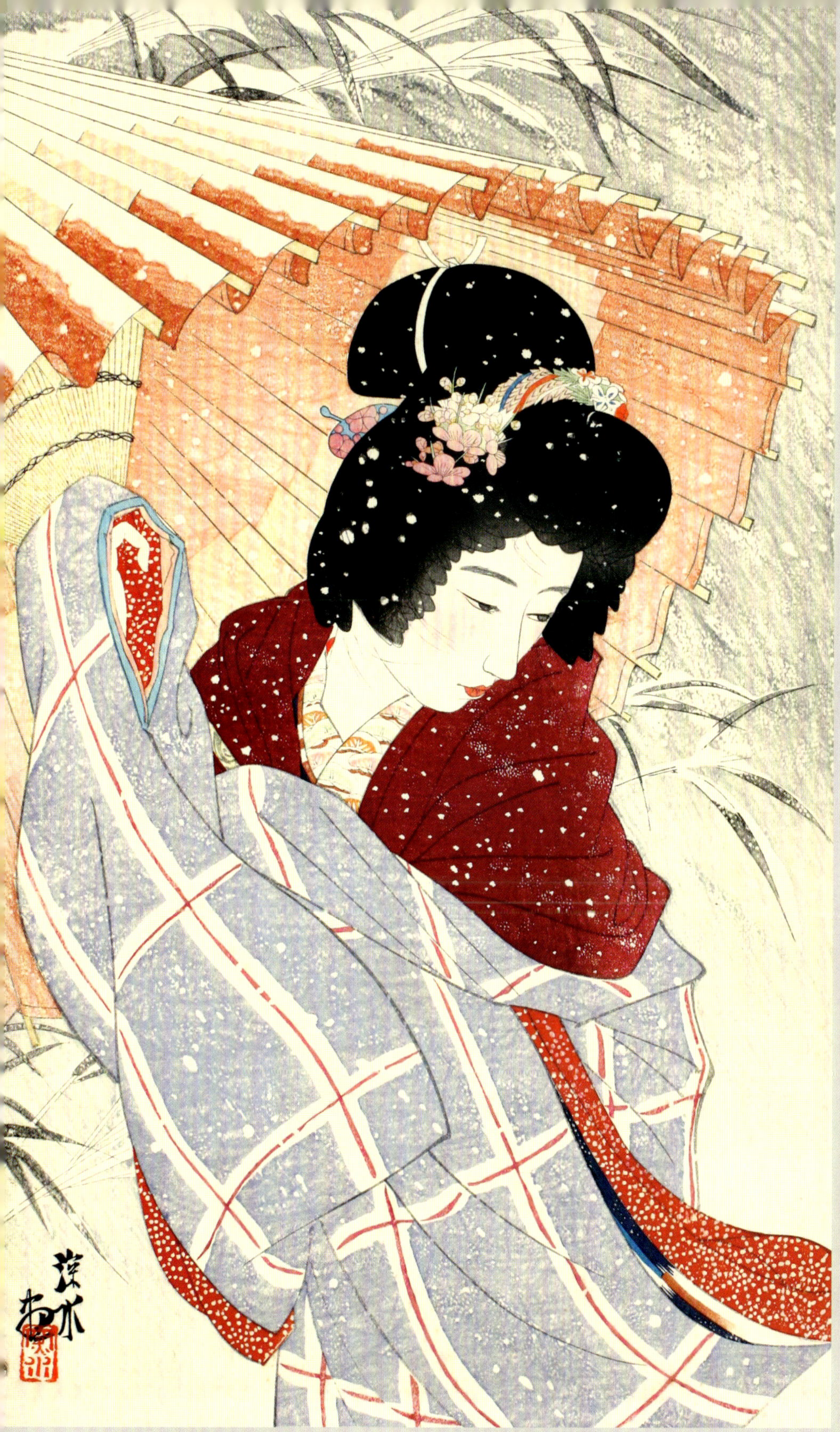

FIG. 79
ITO Shinsui
伊東　深水 (1898–1972)
Caught in a Snowstorm 吹雪 (1932)
41.6 x 25.5 cm
Courtesy of Mita Arts Gallery

The execution of this young girl's face is as good as can be found anywhere in printmaking. We sense the fullness of the lips, especially as they turn into the chin. The shape of her eyes, cast downward, makes her seem oblivious to the raging snowstorm around her *bangasa* (umbrella). Drawing *bangasa*, especially half-opened, was a challenge that Ito accomplished with ease. The pattern on her coat follows the folds in a highly realistic way.

FIG. 80
ITO Shinsui
伊東　深水 (1898–1972)
After a Bath 浴後 (1917)
42.7 x 28.5 cm
Courtesy of Mita Arts Gallery

The simplicity of this print is masterful. The girl's face is hidden by her heavy hair, which, upon careful inspection, shows the subtle manner in which it is drawn. The outline of her body is printed in soft black on a pink line, enhancing the soft quality of her skin. The drawing of the hands, especially the curve of the wrist of her right hand as she squeezes out the washrag, is exceptional. The background texture is created by the *baren* marks in the printing process, but is so carefully done that it does not blemish the white skin. The *bokashi* printing on her breast is so very delicate as to entice the viewer to want to touch it.

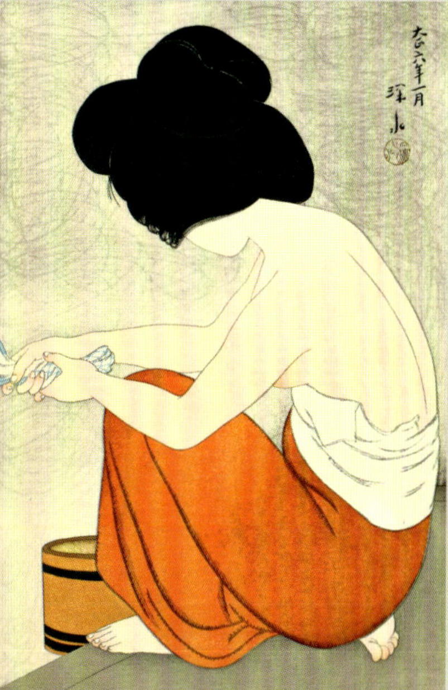

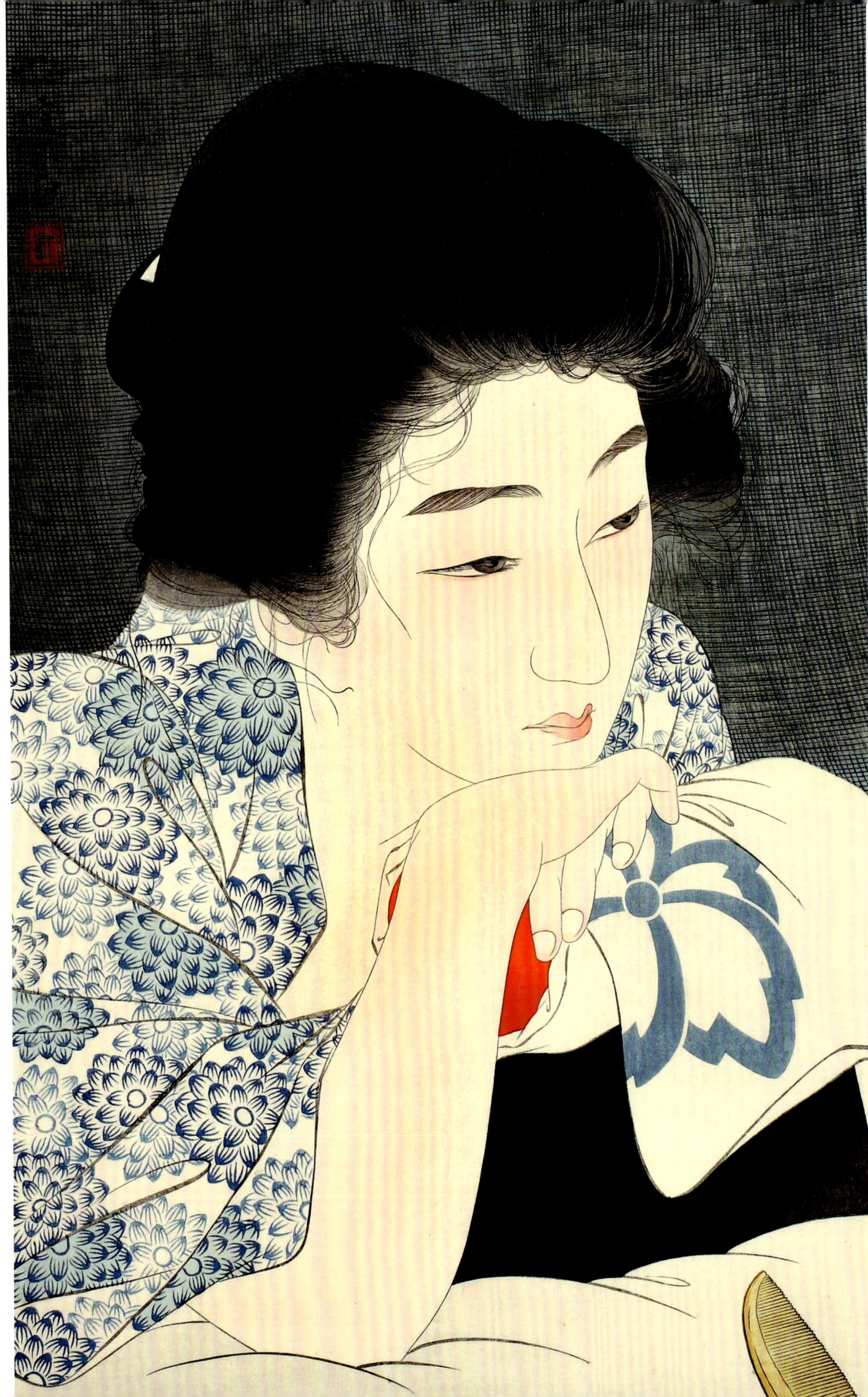

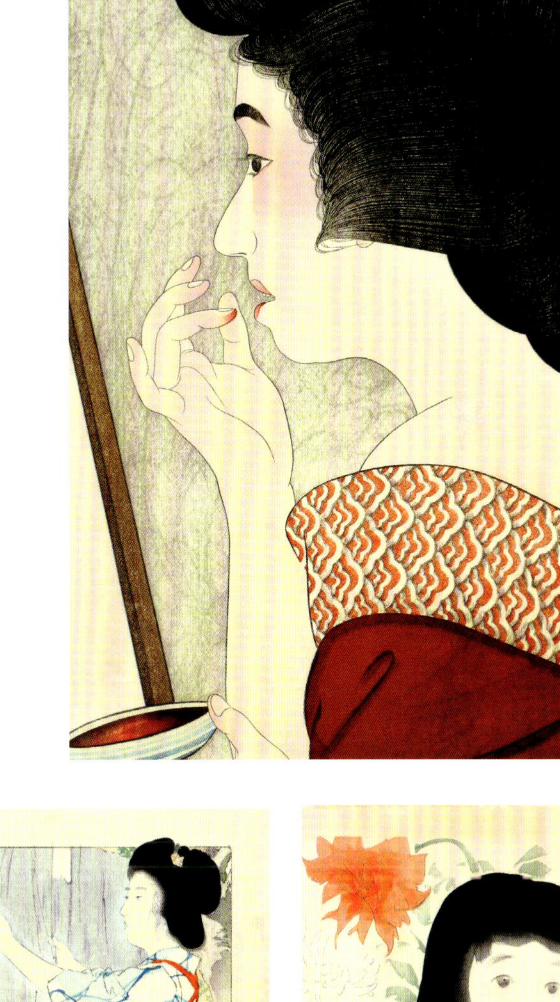

FIG. 81 (left)
Torii KOTONDO
鳥居 言人 (1900–76)
Morning Hair 朝寝髪 (1930)
40.7 x 25.6 cm
Courtesy of Mita Arts Gallery

This particular print was, for some inexplicable reason, considered provocative during the 1930s. It was banned from further publication after the first seventy prints were sold and the remaining thirty were destroyed. As in Ito Shinsui's pictures, the woman has a specific personality. She is provocative behind her mosquito net. It is obvious she has just woken up. Her hair comb lies on the bedding in front of her.

FIG. 82
Torii KOTONDO
鳥居 言人 (1900–76)
Rouge くち紅 (1930)
40.7 x 25.5 cm
Courtesy of Mita Arts Gallery

Here, as in Fig. 81, Kotondo displays his mastery of drawing. The woman's profile is very individualized. Her hand is superbly drawn, especially the articulation of the bones. The pattern on her *kimono*, as in the previous print, is masterful.

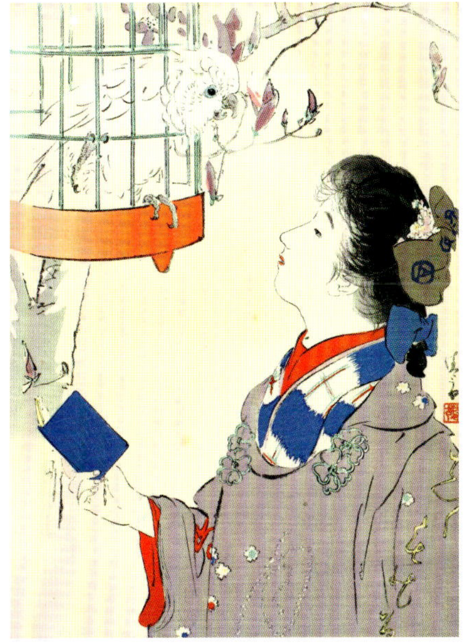

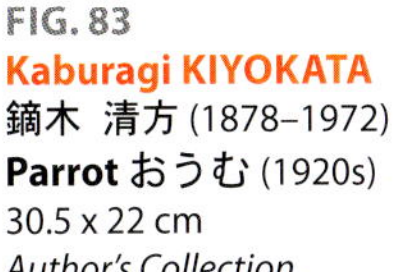

FIG. 83
Kaburagi KIYOKATA
鏑木 清方 (1878–1972)
Parrot おうむ (1920s)
30.5 x 22 cm
Author's Collection

This delightful picture, beautifully drawn, depicts a young woman teaching a parrot to talk. She is wearing a Western-style overcoat, with a scarf tucked into the collar.

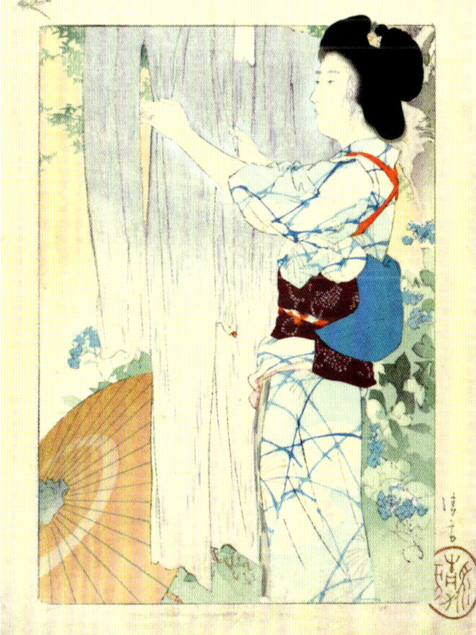

FIG. 84
Kaburagi KIYOKATA
鏑木 清方 (1878–1972)
Drying 洗濯物干し (1920s)
32 x 22.5 cm
Author's Collection

Taking advantage of bright sunshine after rain, as indicated by the umbrella, a woman with her *kimono* sleeves tied by a bright support enchants us with her beauty.

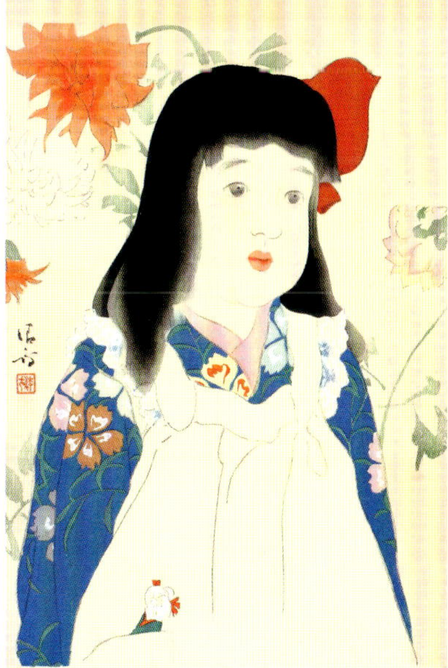

FIG. 85
Kaburagi KIYOKATA
鏑木 清方 (1878–1972)
Portrait of a Young Teenager 若いティーンエイジャーのポートレイト (1920s)
32 x 22 cm
Author's Collection

This rare print of a teenager is unusual in Japanese art, especially her large, round eyes, which captivate the viewer. One wonders what she is staring at. Her prominent red hair ribbon repeats the color of the large flower in the background.

CHAPTER SIX

Actors and Wrestlers

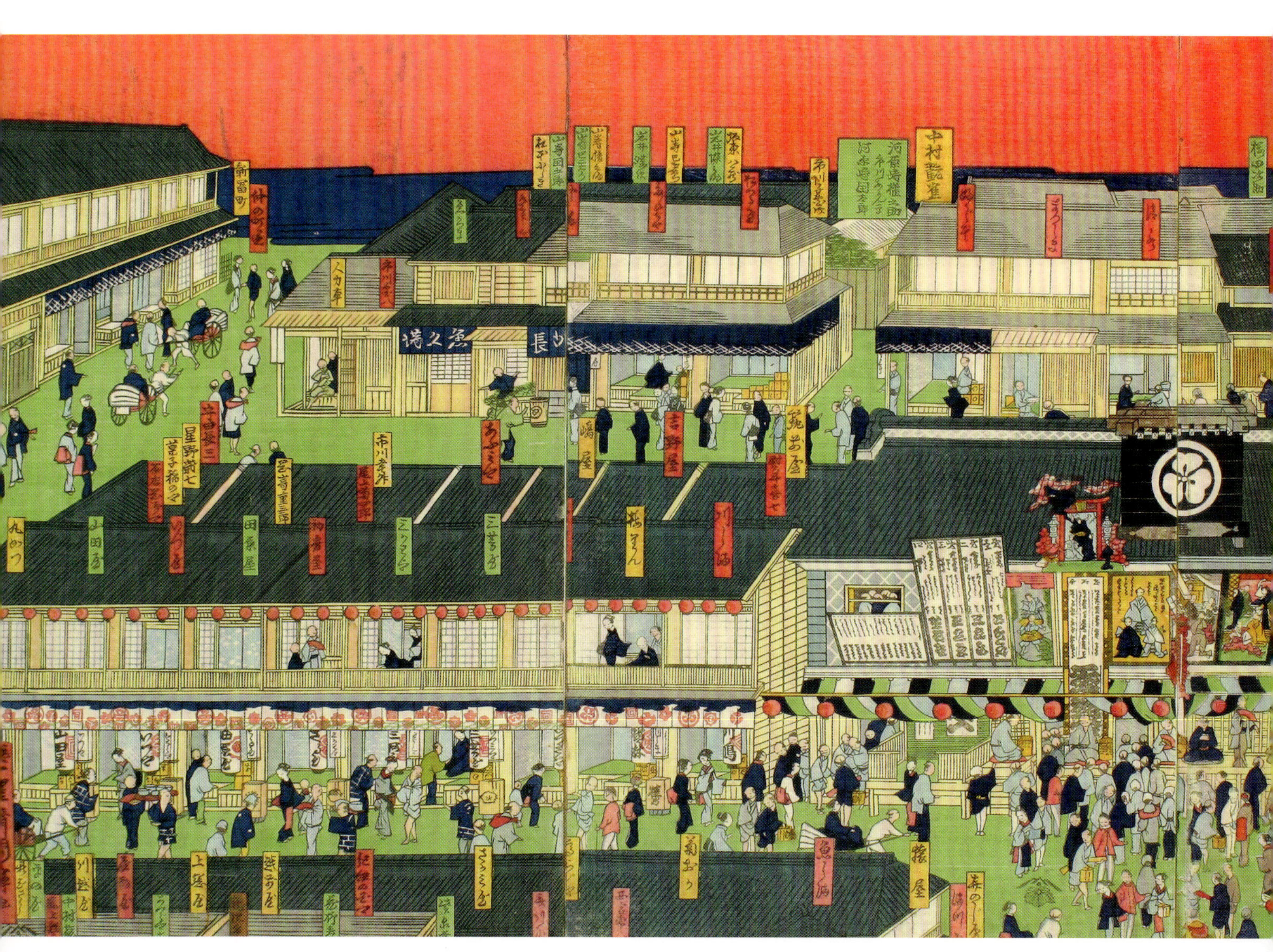

By the early eighteenth century, Edo (Tokyo) was the largest city in the world with over one million inhabitants. It was a magnet for artists, craftsmen, literati, entertainers and others tending to the needs of the thriving merchant class. In the sophisticated Edo culture and lifestyle, the largely literate population had the time and the money to spend on the more pleasurable aspects of middle-class life, whether their increasingly powerless *samurai* rulers liked it or not. Professional female entertainers (*geisha*), music, popular stories, *kabuki* theater and *bunraku* puppet theater, *sumo* wrestling, poetry, a rich literature and art were all part of this flowering of culture. Of these, the two most popular forms of mass public entertainment were without a doubt *kabuki* theater and *sumo* wrestling.

With the emergence of woodblock prints depicting images of the "floating world," it is not surprising that *kabuki* became one of the primary sources of subject material for woodblock artists. Indeed, the Japanese theater form *kabuki* is virtually synonymous with *ukiyo-e* woodblock prints. Both started at about the same time—in the mid-seventeenth century during the Genroku era (1688–1704)—and both flourished in tandem until the middle of the nineteenth century.

Kabuki originally was an all-female theatrical group featuring dancing and comedy. The term *kabuki* meant "unusual" or "shocking," and in the early seventeenth century *kabuki* did indeed have a dubious reputation as a raucous and somewhat shady entertainment. Moreover, as it gained popularity throughout the Kanto (Edo) and Kansai (Kyoto–Osaka) areas, it became associated with prostitution. As a result, the Tokugawa government censored the performances and prohibited women from performing. *Kabuki* groups started using young men to perform the same type of theater, which was called *wakashu kabuki*. As these youngsters were mostly teenagers, it did not stop the problem of prostitution, only this time it was male prostitution, which alienated the government even further. Under official pressure, *kabuki* was forced to utilize elements from the *noh* theater called *kyogen* and to develop the quality of the acting. All performers had to be of legal age and were prohibited from engaging in prostitution.

By the late seventeenth century, *kabuki* had matured into one of the most popular dramatic forms in Japan, with major stages in Edo, Kyoto and Osaka. Each venue had its own styles of performance, with the Kyoto–Osaka *kabuki* style, called *kamigata*, developing along different lines from that in Edo. The Edo stage, however, remained the dominant arena. The government permitted permanent *kabuki* playhouses to be built in these cities, enabling *kabuki* to be performed all year round. The theaters were typically adorned with posters advertising performers and were surrounded by shops and restaurants. There was a constant bustle of activity, which is beautifully captured in a print by an Edo artist, Utagawa Kuniteru (1808–76) **(Fig. 86)**.

The interior of the *kabuki* theater was developed along the lines that are familiar to us today, including the *hanamichi*, the broad platform that extends into the center of the audience seating area, and a drop curtain that allows scenes to be changed while acts on stage are still being performed. At the same time, the role of the *onnagata* (female impersonator) was developed, requiring years of discipline and training. It was also during this time that the plots of the plays became more involved and matured into the sophisticated art form we know as *kabuki* literature. During the eighteenth century, narrative music called *nagauta* was introduced. The different schools of acting and musical accompaniment reached their peak in the mid-nineteenth century, paralleling the 200-year development of woodblock prints portraying popular *kabuki* theater.

Kabuki literature as we know it today was created in the Genroku period by two main authors—the brilliant actor Ichikawa Danjuro (1660–1704), who wrote plays under the name Mimasuya Hyogo, and the most famous of all, Chikamatsu Monzaemon (1653–

FIG. 86
Utagawa KUNITERU
国輝 (1808–76)
Kabuki Theater and Surrounding Shops
歌舞伎座 (1872)
39 x 81 cm
Courtesy of Mita Arts Gallery

This image is significant for its depiction of the bustling activity in front of the *kabuki* theater in Edo (Tokyo). Large Torii school painted posters, which can still be seen today, are displayed everywhere. Surrounding the theater are restaurants and stalls where customers can still buy box lunches as well as woodblock prints of their favorite actors. Today, a shop sells photo postcards as an alternative to prints.

1724). The major plots of the plays fall into three main categories: *jidai-mono* (historical plays), *sewa-mono* (domestic drama) and *shosagoto* (dance pieces). Over the years, the *jidai-mono* and *sewa-mono* became more closely associated with current events. Political happenings were rewritten in a form acceptable to the authorities before being performed. These often contained subtle references to anti-government doctrine, which were easily understood by the general townspeople who were quick witted and sophisticated. Scandals such as suicides, illicit love affairs and other well-known issues of the contemporary scene were quickly adapted to fit into the standard drama.

For the *kabuki* audience and buyers of *ukiyo-e*, the main focus was on the actors. The prints depicting *kabuki* actors (*yakusha-e*) in full make-up, sometimes on stage, promoted not only theater productions but also the actors themselves. Crests (*mon*), strategically placed on costumes, clearly identified the actors and the roles they were playing. The theater-going public was literate in historic tales told through *kabuki* and knew all the characters and plots in the way that many people now know contemporary soap operas. There were very strong fan clubs that followed the careers and performances of the actors and their ability to interpret commonly known stories. In the Kansai district, the fan club members would attend performances *en masse*, sometimes dressed in outlandish costumes to give the theater a festive atmosphere, and would try to occupy the front rows.

Fan clubs were also sponsors of prints of their favorite actor in a role he made famous. Publishers catered to this select group by printing better quality prints on heavier paper. These prints very often came in the form of triptychs, with the central sheet portraying the principal character. The prints were much sought after by these fans and sold either in the lobby of the theater where the performances were held or in stores nearby. The plots were not as important as watching an actor

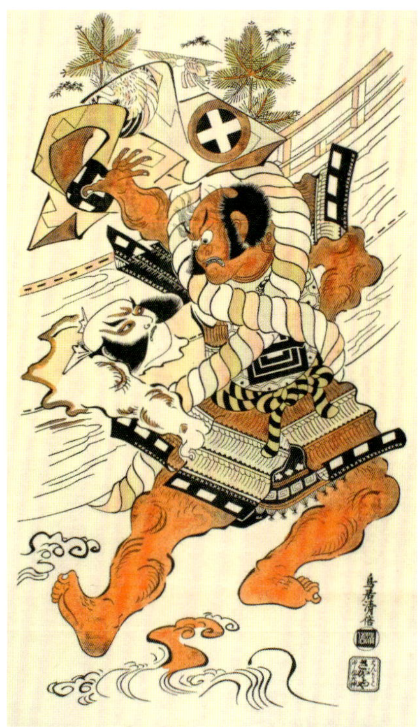

FIG. 87
Torii KIYOMASU I
鳥居清倍 (active 1690s–1720s)
Kabuki Actors Performing in *Keisei Fuji-no-Takane* けいせい富士高根を演ずる歌舞伎役者 (early 1700s)
Hand-colored black and white print (*tan-e*), 54 x 32 cm
Author's Collection

In this scene from the play *Keisei Fuji-no-Takane*, a famous story in Japanese history of revenge and filial piety, the actors Ichikawa Danzo and Otani Hiroji take the roles of the Soga Brothers. The play was performed in Edo in 1717. This is a re-cut of the original print. Only one other copy is known and it is in the British Museum. The original block is in the Tokyo National Museum.

assume a famous pose (*mie*) on the stage. He was critically judged as to how well he performed the special pose. It is these *mie* that found their way into *ukiyo-e* portraits, which were popular with the actors' fan clubs. When a popular actor died, a portrait would be issued of him dressed in a light blue robe and with a shaven head, and with his new name for his passage to heaven written on it.

The acting families handed down their roles and names from one generation to the next. Despite the popular appeal of *kabuki* and the veneration afforded the actors by the public, up until the Meiji Restoration actors were regarded as social outcasts by the authorities and were closely scrutinized. But we have come a long way. Today, some actors are regarded with such esteem that they have been designated "National Treasures."

Thousands of prints depicting famous *kabuki* actors of the eighteenth and nineteenth centuries survive. Unlike Edo, which saw actor prints flourish from the seventeenth century, the Osaka and Kyoto areas did not produce single-sheet actor prints until 1790. These Kansai prints (*kamigata-e*) have a slightly different style than their Edo counterparts. The artists strove for a closer likeness to specific actors compared to the more generic drawings of the heads that we see in Edo printmaking. The poses, even in portraits, are more animated than just offering an example of make-up techniques. The Kansai pride in production and quality of drawing and printing is often superior to the more popular prints produced in Edo.

Although many *ukiyo-e* exponents produced prints on a wide variety of subjects, others, especially those from the Torii school of painters, specialized in *kabuki* billboards, advertisements, portraits of actors and other theatrical works. Under Torii Kiyonobu I (1664–1729), considered to be the founder of the Torii school, who came to Edo from Osaka with his *kabuki* actor father, the Toriis became "hereditary artists" attached to *kabuki* theaters, developing a distinctive dramatic, some say bombastic, style. In addition to his advertising paintings, Kiyonobu left several masterpieces of actor portraits (*yakusha-e*), some in monochrome and others with color applied by hand, but all characterized by the typical bold, thick, curving Torii lines.

Several of Kiyonobu's successors focused more on the types of aesthetics and poses one would see on the *kabuki* stage rather than on dramatic and

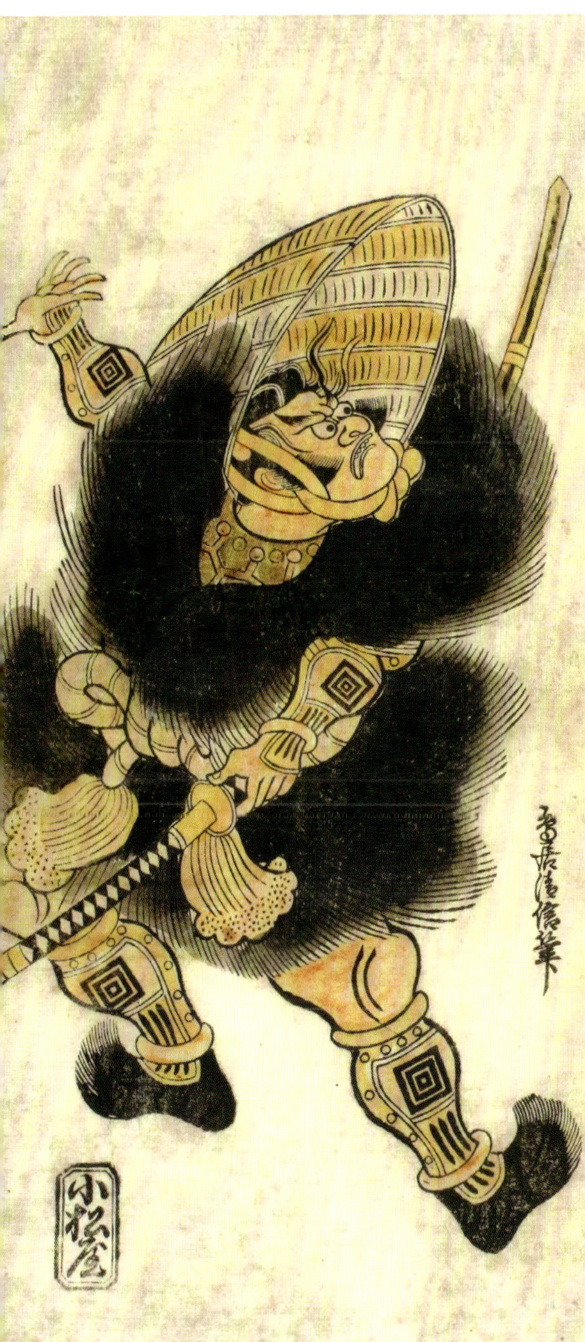

FIG. 88
Torii KIYONOBU II
二代清信 (1706–63)
The Actor Ichikawa Danjuro II
二代目市川団十郎 (1740s)
Hand-colored lacquer and ink (*urushi-e*), 33 x 15 cm
Courtesy of Mita Arts Gallery

Here, the actor Ichikawa Danjuro II plays the role of a fierce *samurai*, his character reinforced by the dramatic pose. Thick, burly legs, one of the hallmarks of Kiyonobu II's drawing style, emerge from a black bearskin robe. The actor's crest is prominently displayed on his arm and leg armor.

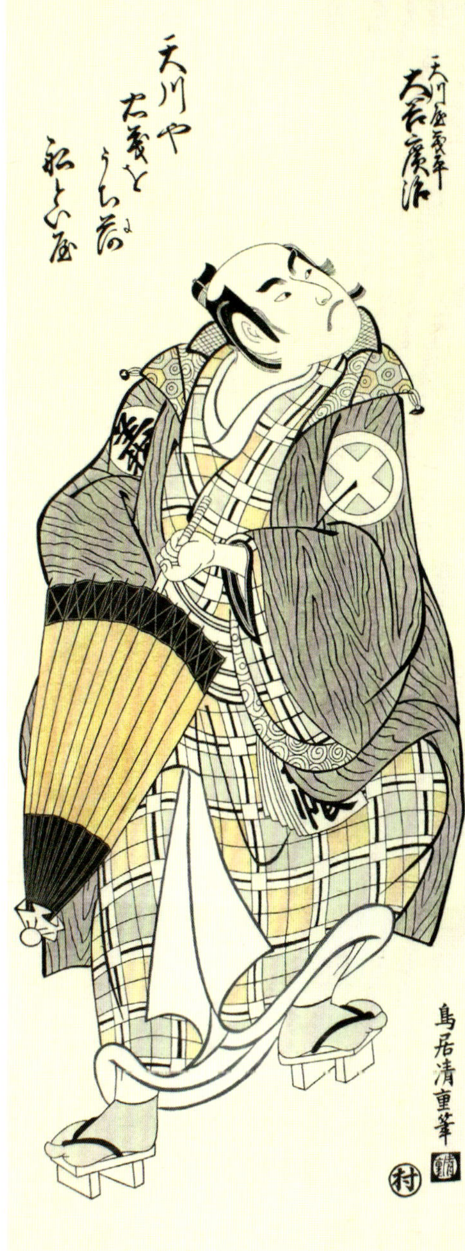

FIG. 89
Torii KIYOSHIGE
清重 (active 1724–64)
The Actor Otani Hiroji as Gihei
大谷広次のぎへい (1749)
Hand-colored print (*beni-e*), 70 x 26 cm
Author's Collection

In this print, the actor Otani Hiroji plays the role of Gihei, a merchant who supplied the forty-seven *samurai* with weapons and armor to stage their revenge attack on the mansion of the evil Lord Kira. Gihei was only trusted after a long period of trial. He is shown with an accounts book under his arm instead of a sword to indicate that he is a merchant, not a *samurai*. In typical Kiyoshige fashion, the upper portion of the print is filled with a poetic inscription.

FIG. 90
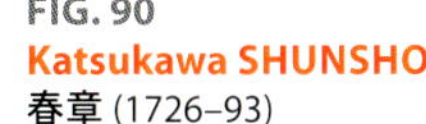
Katsukawa SHUNSHO
春章 (1726–93)
Unknown Actor 役者絵 (1770s)
Black with two colors, 33 x 15 cm
Courtesy of Mita Arts Gallery

The unidentified actor here demonstrates the restrained athleticism and deliberate posturing that characterize many of Shunso's portraits. Feet close together, arm outstretched, the actor appears to lose his balance, but does not topple. It is uncertain what the red strokes in the background signify.

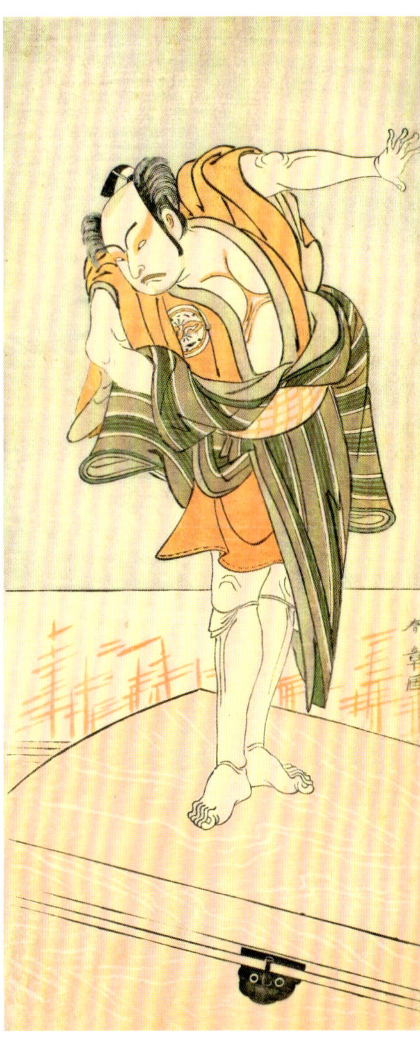

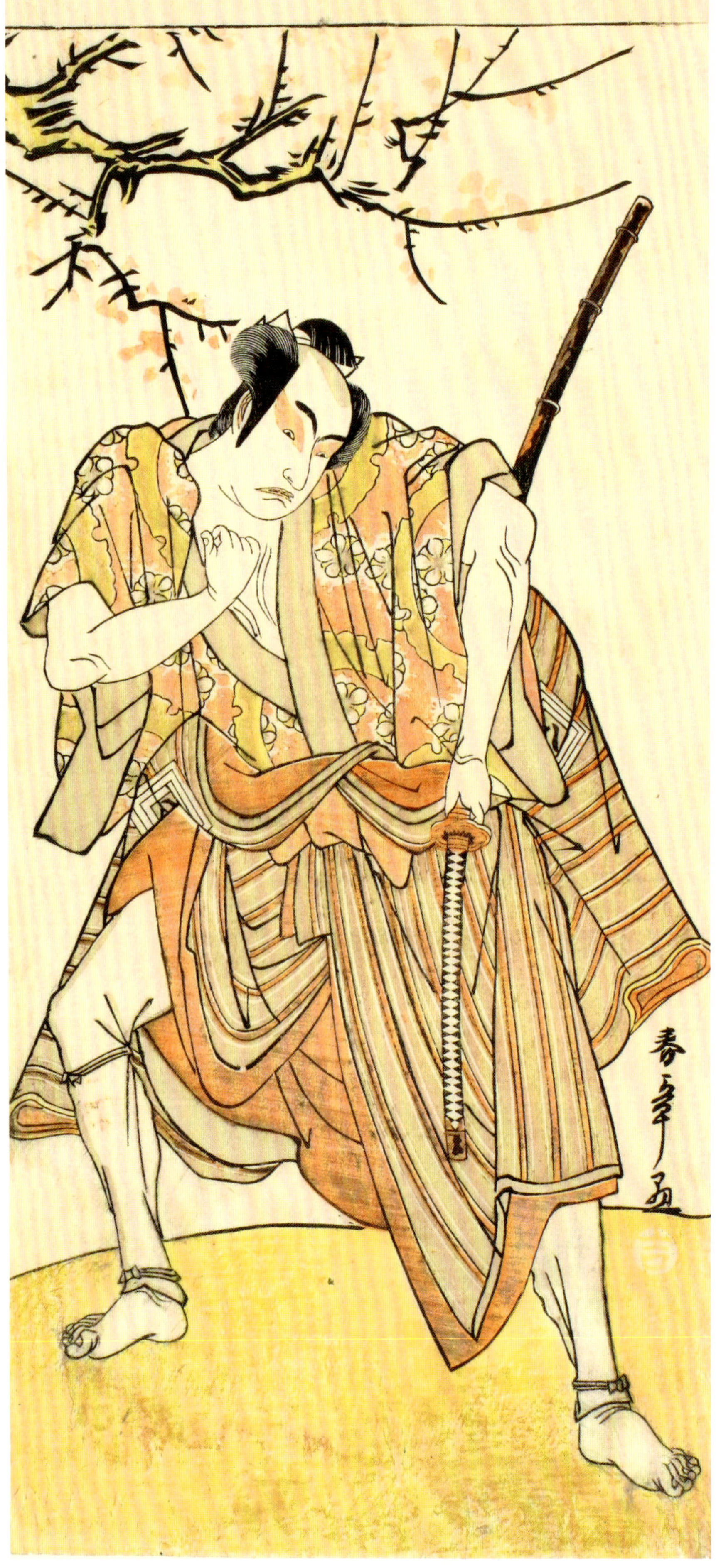

energetic depictions. For example, Kiyomasu I (active 1690s–1720s), believed to be either the younger brother or the son of Kiyonobu I, while excelling at boldly designed "masculine" prints also produced *yakusha-e* that are softer, more delicate and more graceful (**Fig. 87**). But like his father before him, Kiyonobu II (1706–63) perpetuated the strong fluid lines and colorful exuberance of the Torii style in his *kabuki* prints (**Fig. 88**). One of Kiyonobu I's pupils, Kiyoshige (active 1724–64) produced works that have finer, more angular lines, yet his early prints still exude a feeling of great strength and integrity. In his compositions, a single figure usually fills three-quarters of the space while a poetic inscription occupies the rest (**Fig. 89**). All these early Torii prints were hand colored before eventually being printed in two colors.

The development of multi-block printing in the 1760s gave birth to a new level of sophistication in *kabuki* prints. At the same time, other schools and styles of *yakusha-e* emerged. The Katsukawa school artists, for instance, sought to portray a much greater degree of realism and individuality in their depictions of actors. The leading artist of the Katsukawa school, Katsukawa Shunsho (1726–93) is best known for revitalizing *kabuki* portraiture in the 1760s after the weakening of the once dominant Torii school, and for pioneering stylized but accurate facial likenesses of actors. He is also famous for his pupils, whose names begin with "Shun." In his prints, Shunsho tried to distinguish each actor by their role, whether they were on stage or in their dressing room (**Figs. 90, 91**). Many of his prints were made in the small, narrow *hoso-ban* format.

Katsukawa Shunko (1743–1812), a gifted pupil of Shunsho and the eventual leader of the Katsukawa school, is credited with creating the first "large head" actor portraits (*okubi-e*), which reached their zenith in the prints of the great Toshusai Sharaku around 1794/5, as well as "large face" pictures (*ogao-e*),

FIG. 91 (opposite)
Katsukawa SHUNSHO
春章 (1726–93)
The Actor Ichikawa Yaezo II
二代目市川八百蔵 (1770s)
Black and two colors, 33 x 15 cm
Courtesy of Mita Arts Gallery

In this print, the actor Ichikawa Yaozo II, a long sword behind him, stands under plum blossoms as he strikes a *mie*, a tense pose or "display" at a specific point in the action of a play, deliberately struck for the audience's appreciation.

FIG. 92
Katsukawa SHUNKO
春好 (1743–1812)
The Actor Bando Mitsugoro II
二代目坂東三津五郎
33 x 15 cm
Courtesy of Mita Arts Gallery

This portrait, composed inside a fan shape, is one of many that the gifted Shunko created in this format. His bold, fluid lines echo the shape of the fan.

FIG. 93
Katsukawa SHUNEI
勝川春英 (1762–1819)
The Actor Ichikawa Danjuro
市川団十郎 (1790s)
33 x 15 cm
Courtesy of Mita Arts Gallery

Shunei's prints allow us to view some of the greatest, and most notorious, performers of his day, including the lineage of the Ichikawa Danjuro family. Here, the atmosphere of *kabuki* is captured in the striking pose, facial expression and gorgeous costuming of the actor and the evocative background.

FIG. 94
Katsukawa SHUNEI
勝川春英 (1762–1819)
The Actor Sawamura Sojuro
澤村宋十郎 (1790s)
33 x 15 cm
Courtesy of Mita Arts Gallery

In this dramatic print, the actor appears to be performing a dance movement. His moving head and long white twirling hair contribute to the action in the scene. What is also fascinating is the extreme foreshortening of his right hand, drawing the viewer into the background.

in which an actor's face fills the entire picture (**Fig. 92**). He also produced prints depicting actors and accompanists on stage. Katsukawa Shunei (1762–1819), initially a pupil of Shunsho, was a painter, printmaker and musician deeply immersed in the world of *kabuki* although his main strength lay in warrior prints (**Figs. 93, 94**). He became a leading figure of the Katsukawa school. His finest work was done after 1790, and was a major influence on Toshusai Sharaku.

Toshusai Sharaku (ca. 1770–ca. 1825) was one of the most mysterious artists in the history of Japanese art. In a period of less than a year during 1794–5, he designed over 140 woodblock prints of *kabuki* actors and *sumo* wrestlers before disappearing completely from the art scene, some say because the radical and often undesirable nature of his art aroused the hostility of the Edo art world. Others believe he was the *noh* dancer Saito Jurobei, but that has never been proven. His works, typically *okubi-e*, with caricature-like heads against a dark or mica-dusted background, were purportedly sponsored and printed by Tsutaya Juzaburo, the most successful publisher at the time. Sharaku's prints are exceptional for the revolutionary way in which they depict the individual features of an actor and the characteristics of his role (**Figs. 97–100**). A little-known *ukiyo-e* designer, Kabukido Enkyo (1749–1803) was possibly one of Sharaku's students, or else heavily influenced by the master. He was active as a printmaker for only one year, 1796, during which he made seven known prints in the style of Sharaku, with vigorous, exaggerated faces (**Fig. 101**).

For the remainder of the nineteenth century, the Utagawa school under Utagawa Toyokuni (Toyokuni I) (1769–1825) became the most powerful and famous woodblock print school in Japan. Toyokuni took prints related to the *kabuki* theater, especially his actor prints, to new heights, and was the most influential man on the next generation of *yakusha-e* designers. His prints portray what he saw, with none of the exaggeration of Sharaku. They are not mere pictures of actors; they show actors acting (**Fig. 95**).

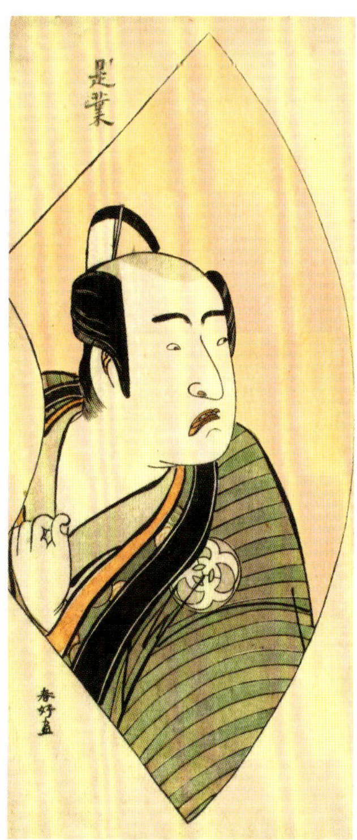

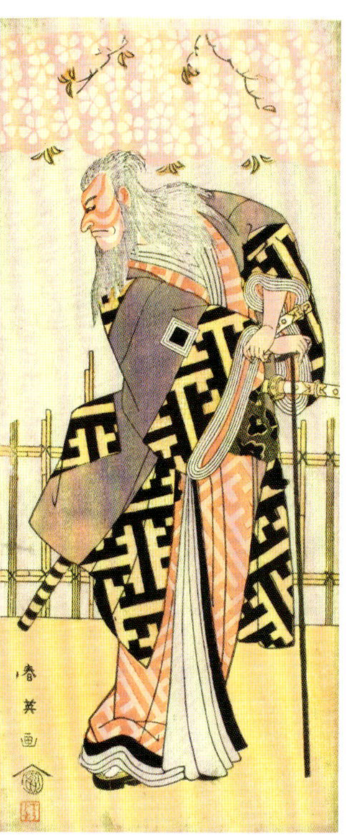

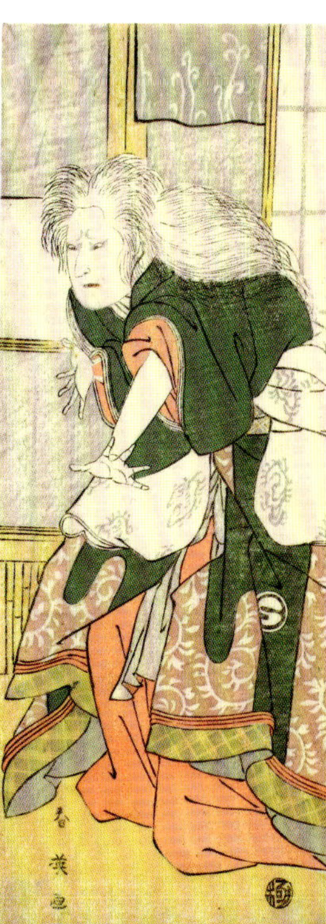

FIG. 95 (below)
Utagawa TOYOKUNI I
豊国 (1769–1825)
Unknown Actor 役者大首絵 (1790s)
39.5 x 27 cm
Courtesy of Mita Arts Gallery

This "large head" portrait (*okubi-e*) of an unknown actor, one of Toyokuni's masterpieces, is typical of the realistic way in which he depicted his subjects. Here, the actor's penetrating stare and severe mouth (the upper lip slightly overlaps the lower) evoke a difficult personality.

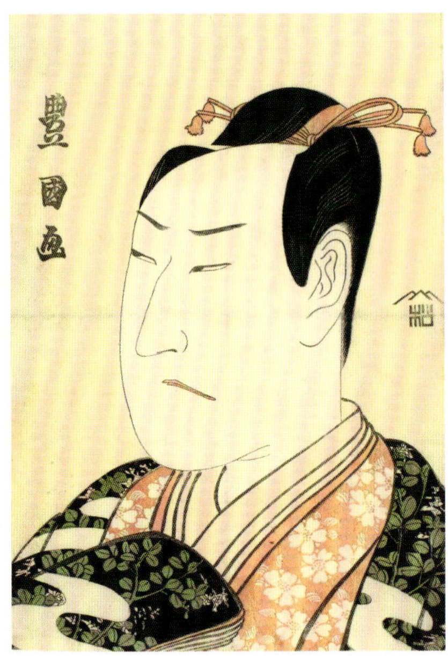

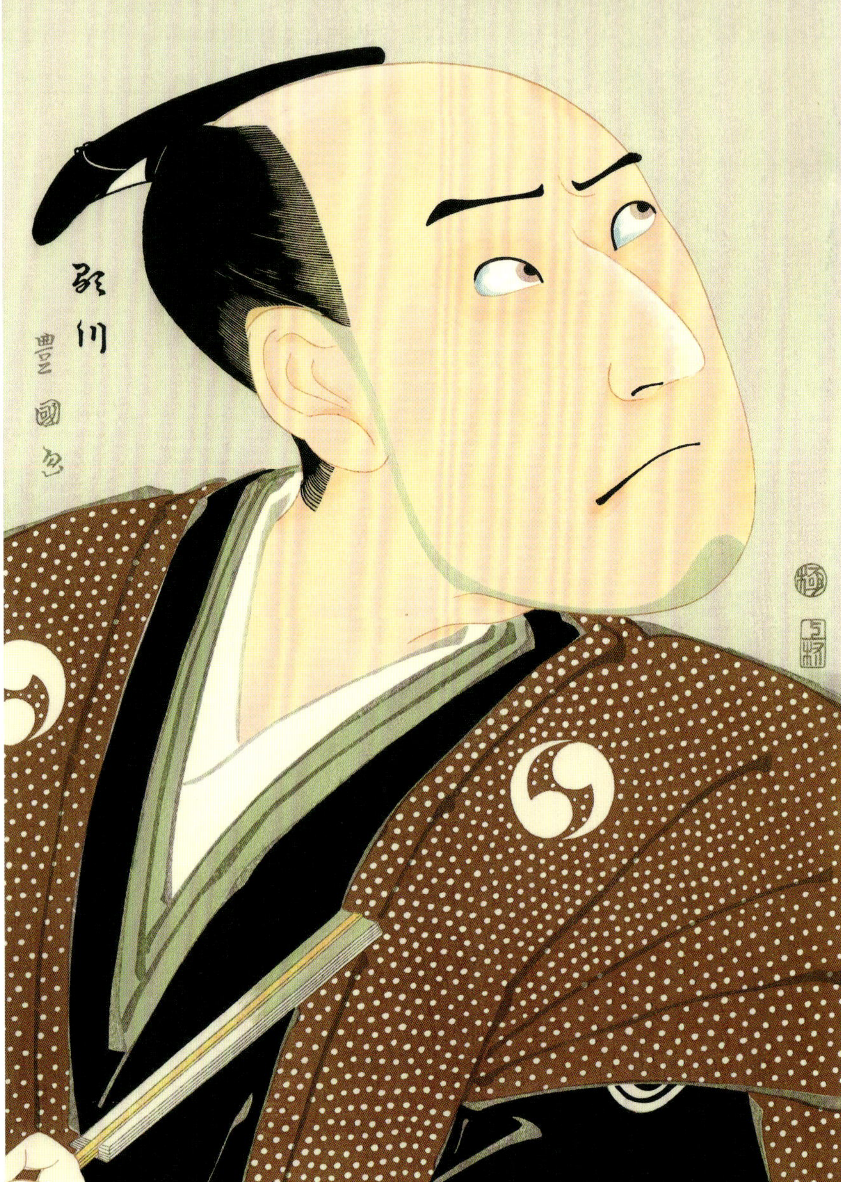

Of Toyokuni's twenty-nine pupils, Utagawa Kunisada (1786–1865) was one of the star attractions of the Utagawa school and Toyokuni's successor. Known as Toyokuni III later in his career (Toyokuni II being Toyoshige), Kunisada followed the traditional pattern of the Utagawa school in being mainly preoccupied with *kabuki* and actor prints although he also dabbled in other subject matter. A trendsetter of the *ukiyo-e* print, he eschewed the stylistic constraints set by his contemporaries and continuously developed his style (**Fig. 102**). His striking images of performers and the performances of classic plays show the vitality of *kabuki* theater during his time. From the mid-1840s, Kunisada produced works under the name of Toyokuni III, especially "big head" actor portraits (**Figs. 103, 106**). Another Utagawa school artist, Utagawa Yoshitora (active ca. 1840–80), a pupil of Kuniyoshi, also carried on the school's tradition of *kabuki* portraits although his primarily interest was *Yokohama-e* (prints depicting Westerners from the enclave of Yokohama). His "large head" actor portraits are very much in the mold of Toyokuni III (**Figs. 104, 105**).

Apart from the Torii and Utagawa schools, the Osaka school of printmakers also specialized in *kabuki* prints, many of them specially commissioned for *kabuki* theaters, although their output was only a fraction of that produced in Edo. Hasegawa Sadanobu I (1809–79), who came from a long line of *ukiyo-e* artists, was one of the more prominent printmakers of the Osaka school specializing in *kabuki*, but turned to landscape in his later years. His expressive faces and poses and bold lines

FIG. 96 (above)
Toshusai SHARAKU
写楽 (ca. 1770–ca. 1825)
The Actor Sawamura Sojuro III as Ohoshi Yuranosuke 三代目澤村荘十郎 (1794–5)
38 x 26 cm
Courtesy of Adachi Institute of Woodcut Prints

This dynamic "big head" portrait (*okubi-e*), with its exaggerated, caricature-like features, is enhanced by a masterful display of printing techniques, especially in the nose, eyes and ear. There is also a wonderful contrast between the detail and colors of the actor's *kimono* and the pale background.

FIG. 97
Toshusai SHARAKU
写楽 (ca. 1770–ca. 1825)
The Actor Ichikawa Ebizo as Takemura Sadanoshin 市川海老蔵 (1794–5)
39.5 x 26.5 cm
Courtesy of Adachi Institute of Woodcut Prints

In this print, black has been used to full effect in the hair, eyebrows, eyelids and snarling mouth. The rest of the outlines are printed in gray. This is one of Sharaku's most famous prints, and has been reproduced commercially in almost every manner, including a postage stamp.

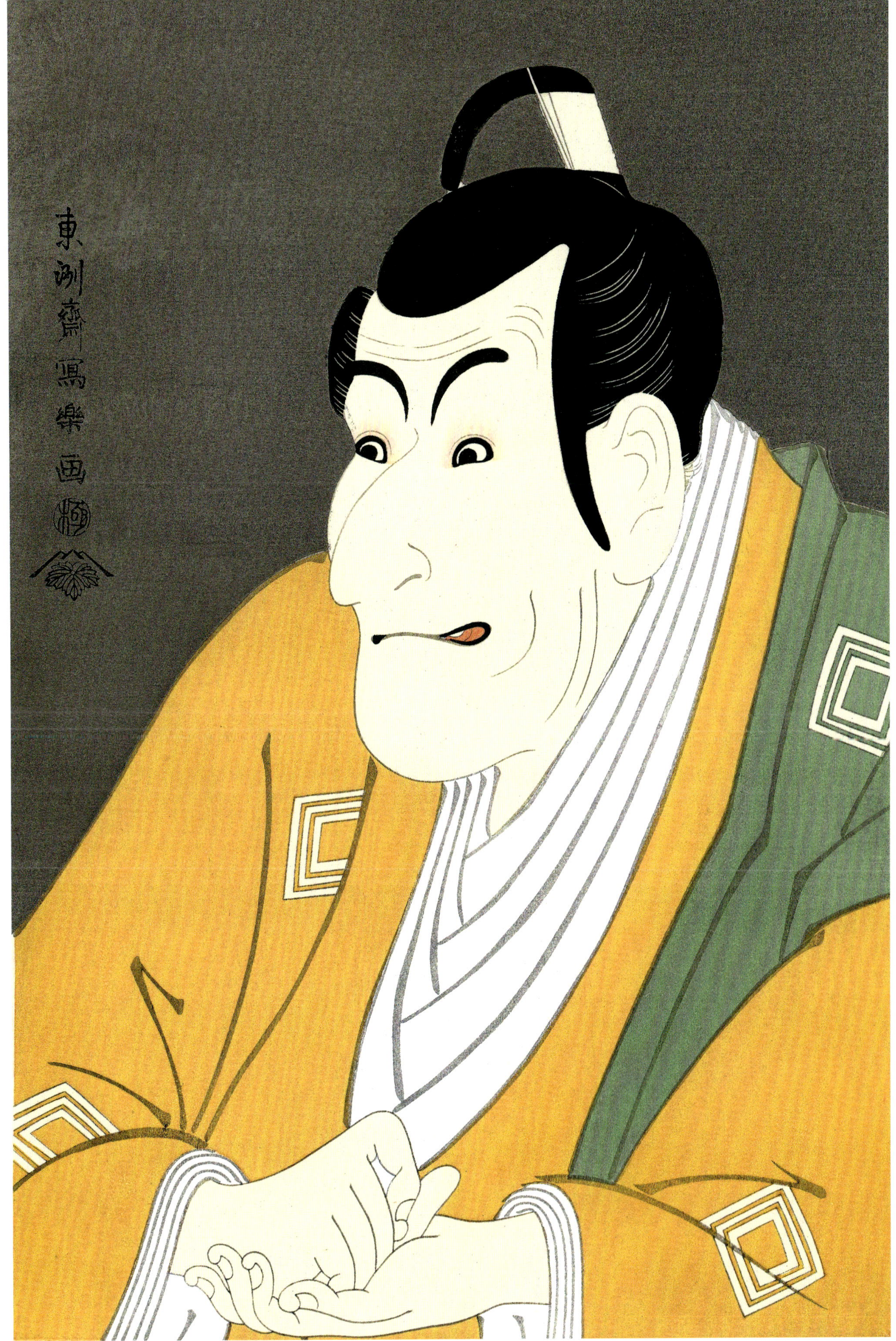
東洲齋寫樂画

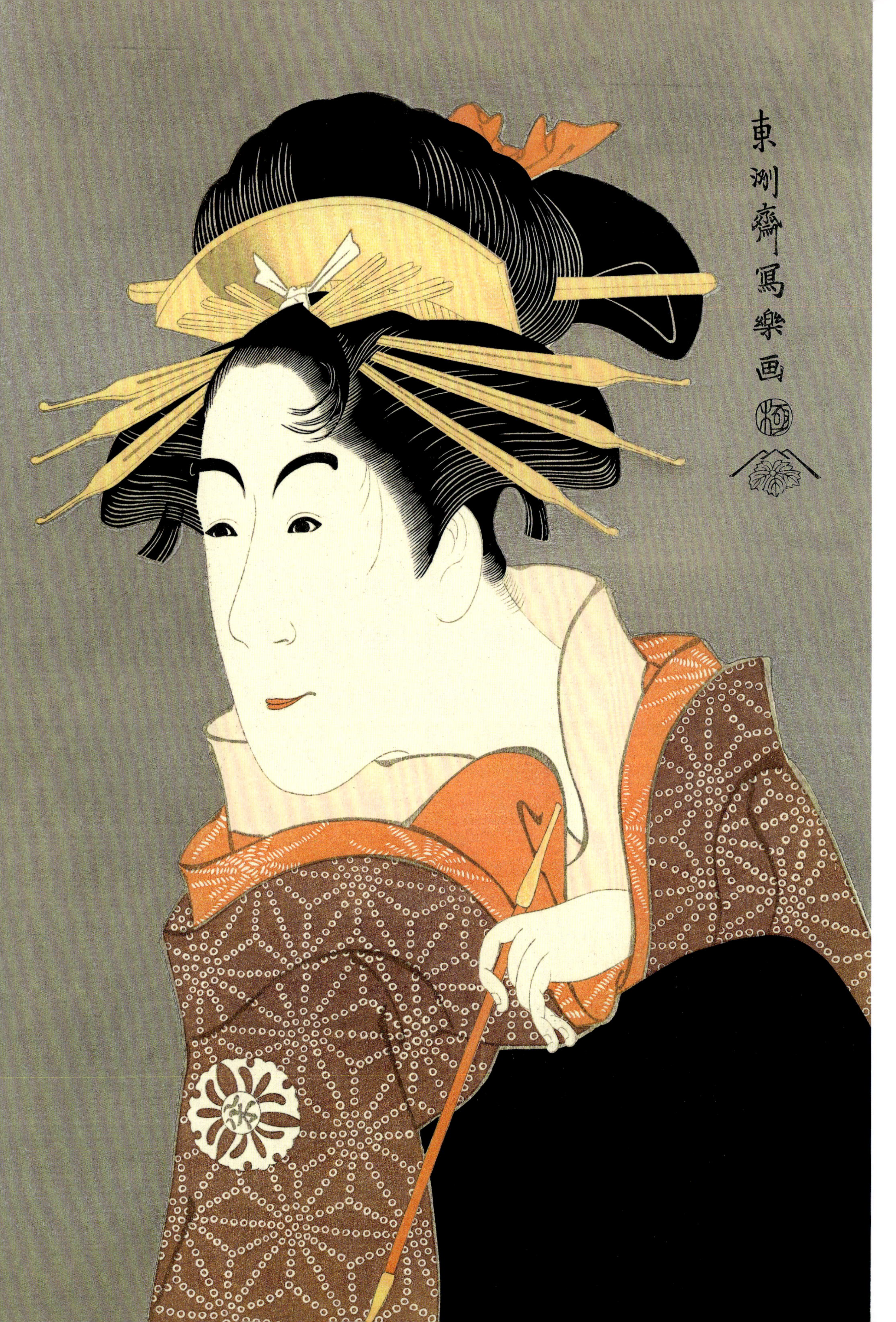
東洲齋寫樂画

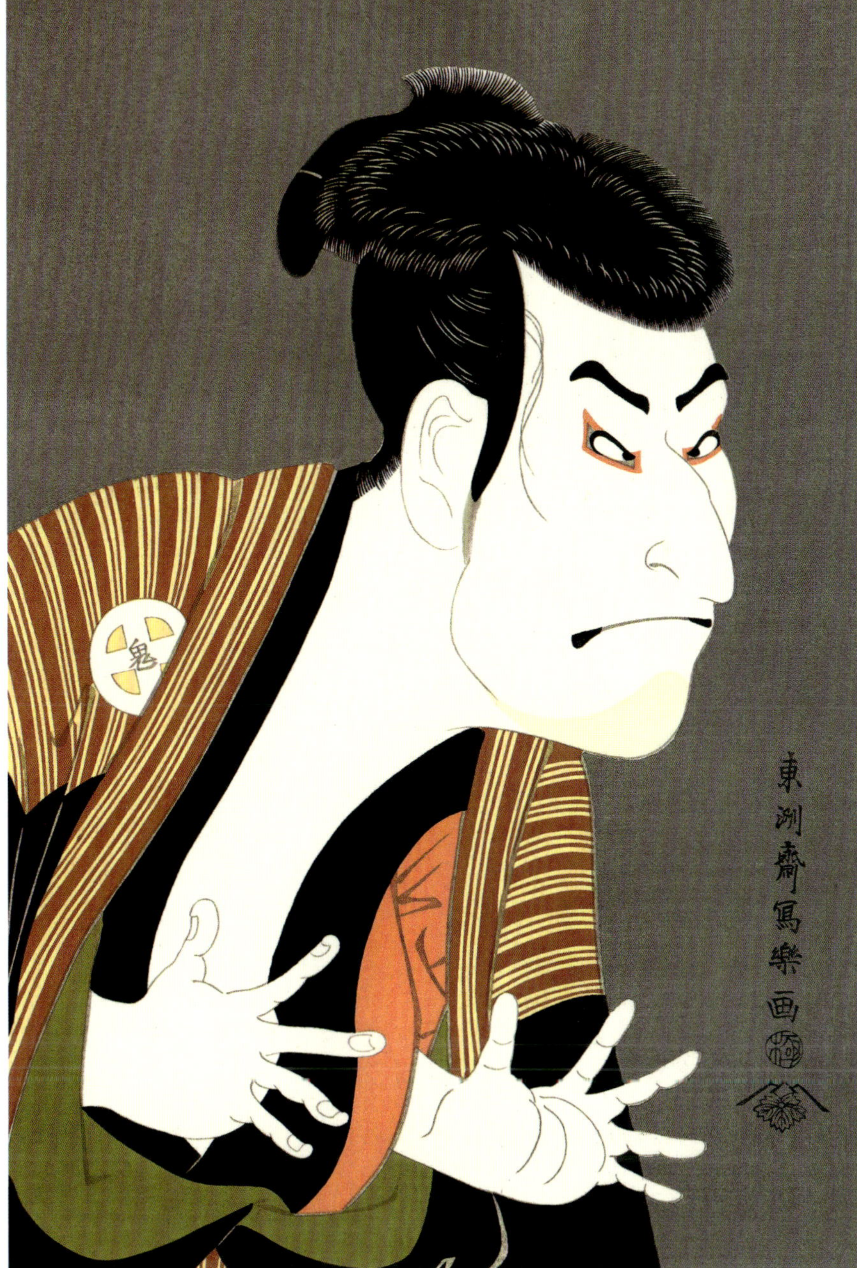

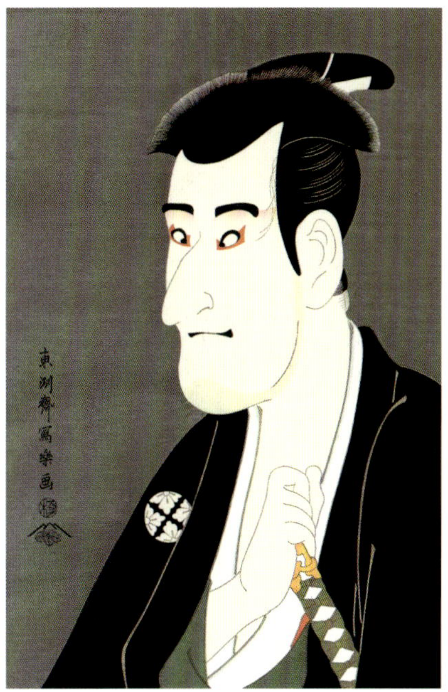

and the comparatively busy background have a surprisingly modern look. The bright, garish hues of the new aniline dyes that are used, as opposed to the more muted tones of traditional vegetable dyes, also enhance the impact (**Figs. 107, 108**). His contemporary, Konishi Hirosada (ca. 1810–64), was particularly skilled in depicting actors on the Osaka *kabuki* stage. Like Sharaku, he boldly captured the character, mood and momentary emotions of his actors, although his figures are often drawn in exaggerated, distorted ways. A hallmark of his work is the imaginative and interactive arrangement and placement of the figures in diptychs and polytychs (**Fig. 109**).

As noted earlier, *sumo* wrestling, along with the *kabuki* theater, was one of the most popular forms of entertainment for the masses in the Edo period although its history goes back much further than that, around 1500 years. *Sumo* has its roots in the Shinto religion. The matches were dedicated to the gods in prayers for a good harvest. During the early Edo period, professional *sumo* groups were formed to entertain the rapidly expanding middle class. Sponsored by "promoters" and sometimes the wrestlers themselves, matches and tournaments were initially held as fund-raising events in the grounds of temples and shrines, where there was less likelihood of disturbances and fights breaking out among the audience. Eventually, dedicated venues with special *sumo* rings were set up, and about 300 years ago *sumo* officially became the national sport of Japan.

FIG. 98 (opposite)
Toshusai SHARAKU
写楽 (ca. 1770–ca. 1825)
The Actor Matsumoto Yonesaburo as Shinobu Posing as Keiwaizaka-no-Shosho
松本米三郎のしのぶ (1794–5)
39.5 x 27 cm
Courtesy of Adachi Institute of Woodcut Prints

The character shown in this print is one of two sisters who became courtesans to enable them to seek revenge for their father's murder. As in many of Sharaku's pictures, the background is printed with mica dust to produce a subdued sparkling effect. The technical virtuosity of the print is astonishing. Matsumoto Yonesaburo was one of the most accomplished *onnagata* (performers of female roles in the all-male *kabuki* theater).

FIG. 99 (left)
Toshusai SHARAKU
写楽 (ca. 1770–ca. 1825)
The Actor Otani Oniji as Edobei the Manservant 二代目大谷鬼次の奴江戸兵衛
(1794–5)
39 x 26.5 cm
Courtesy of Adachi Institute of Woodcut Prints

This strong face, with its curved contours, looks as though it is ready to burst out of the picture. The nervous drawing of the hands, even though somewhat odd, suggests anxiety. When one views historical dramas on television or at the movies in Japan, it is common to see actors imitating the poses and facial expressions shown in Sharaku's pictures.

FIG. 100 (above)
Toshusai SHARAKU
写楽 (ca. 1770–ca. 1825)
The Actor Ichikawa Komazo II as Shiga Daishichi 市川高麗蔵の志賀大七 (1794–5)
38 x 25.5 cm
Courtesy of Adachi Institute of Woodcut Prints

This print of one of the villains in *kabuki* drama is almost monochromatic with the exception of the touch of red in the eye make-up and a sliver of exposed undergarment. The green and gold in the sword and *kimono* at the bottom are the only relief from the startling black *kimono* and hair. The blacks convey a threatening appearance to this character's role.

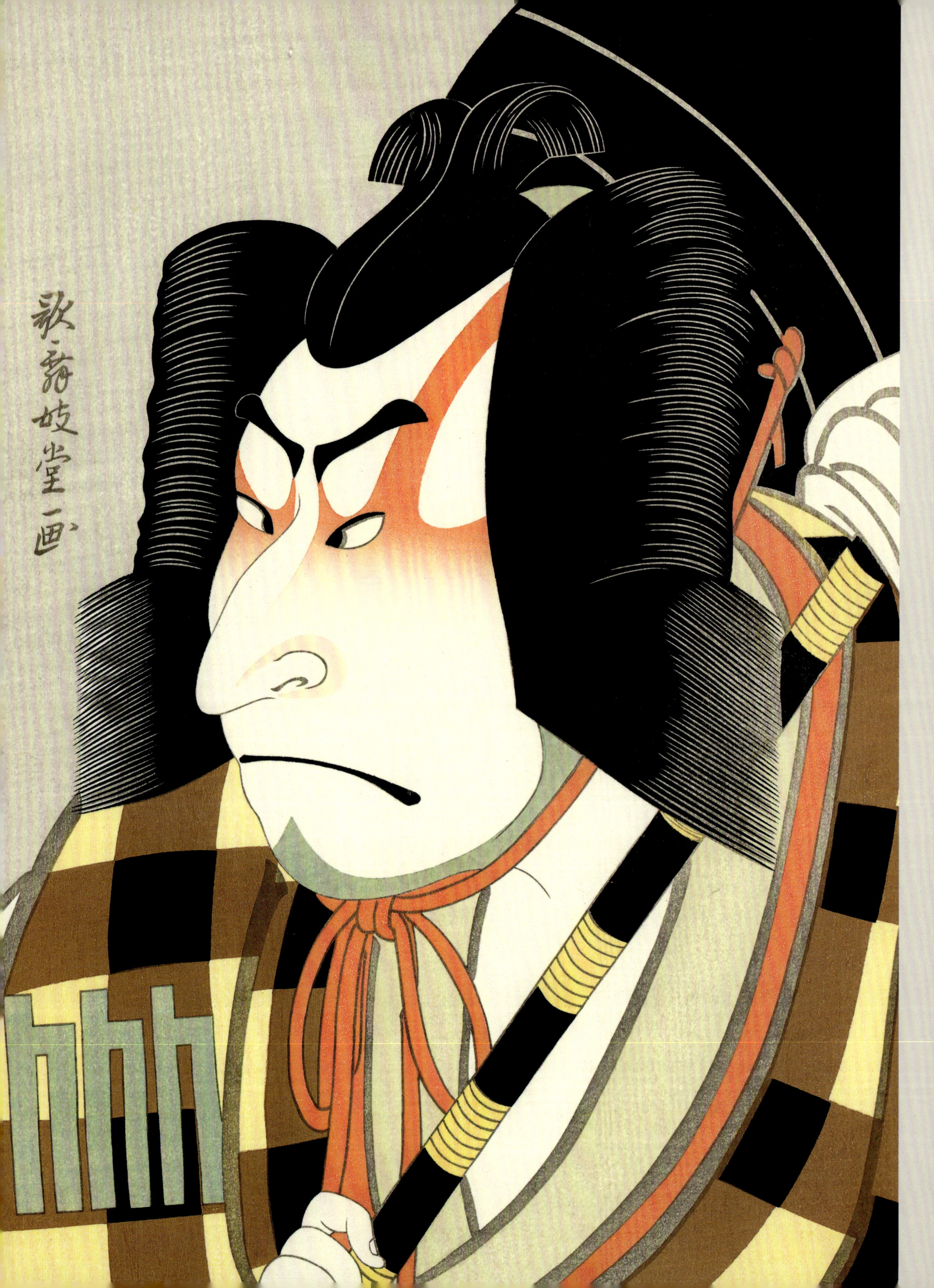
歌舞妓堂画

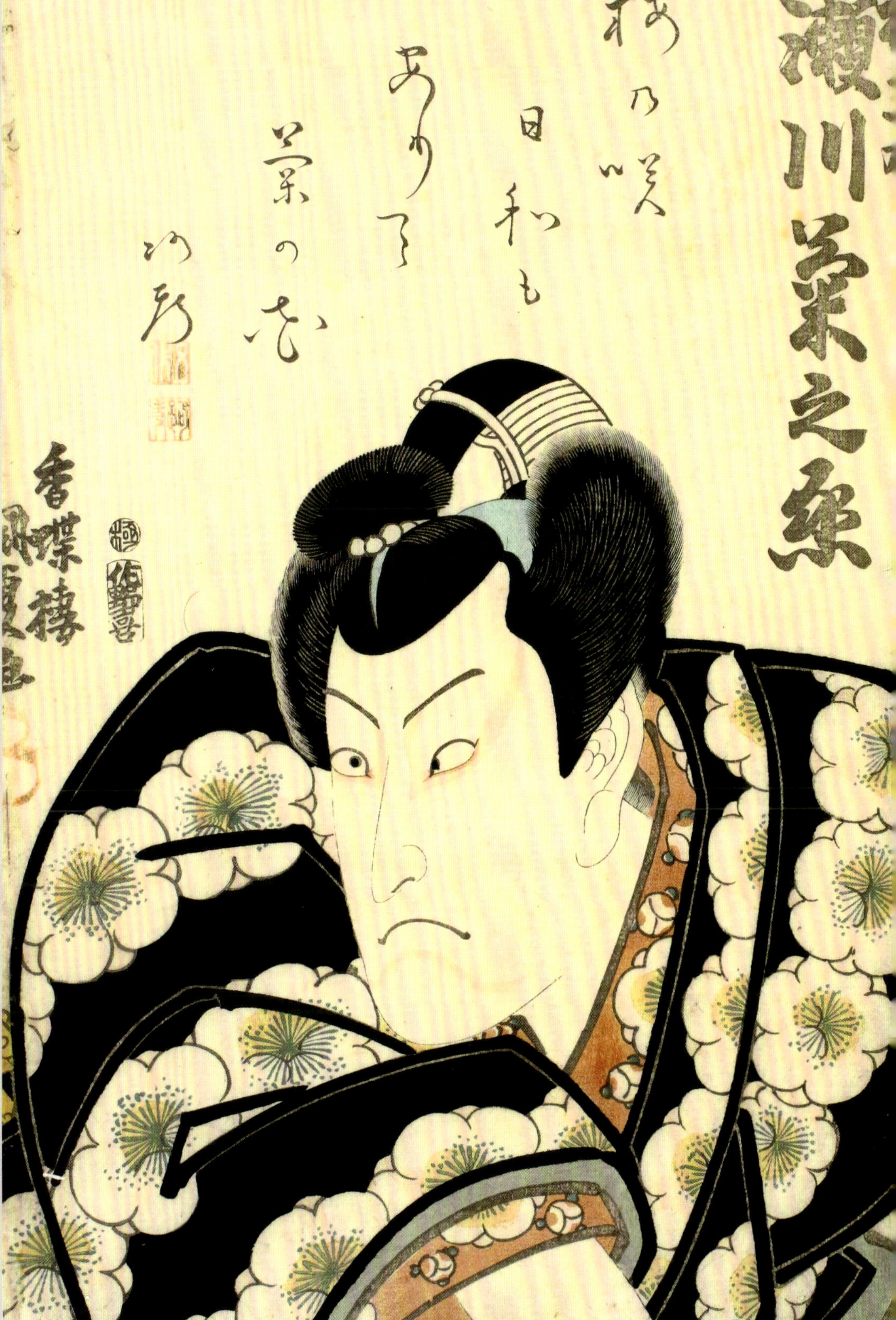

FIG. 101
Kabukido ENKYO
歌舞伎堂　艶鏡 (1749–1803)
The Actor Nakamura Nakazo II as Matsuomaru in *Sugawara Denju Tenarai Kagami* 菅原伝授手習鑑より (1796)
37 x 27 cm
Courtesy of Adachi Institute of Woodcut Prints

The vigorous, exaggerated face of this actor echoes the style employed by Sharaku in his close-up images of the "big heads" of *kabuki* actors. Enkyo boldly captures the character, mood and emotion of the actor.

FIG. 102
Utagawa KUNISADA (Toyokuni III)
国定（三代豊国）(1786–1865)
The Actor Segawa Kikunojo
瀬川　菊之丞 (1840s)
25 x 35 cm
Author's Collection

This exciting portrait, even though unfortunately trimmed slightly on the left side, is a fine example of Sharaku's influence in the art of "big head" portraits. The left and right sides of the *kimono* come together at the bottom center. The abstract pattern of the black is perfectly balanced.

The early Edo period also coincided with the birth of *ukiyo-e*, and as *sumo*'s popularity began to spread many *sumo* prints (*sumo-e*) were produced. Like other genre prints of actors and beautiful women, the images of famous *sumo* wrestlers were extremely popular with the public and were sold at *sumo* stadiums. As with *kabuki*, the fan clubs of popular wrestlers demanded pictures of their idols whose careers they followed avidly. This subject became a lucrative business for the publishers who created the prints to meet the demand. It also meant that ordinary attendees could also purchase something to take home after a match.

The sport of *sumo* is rich in tradition, pageantry and color. *Ukiyo-e* artists recorded the rituals that preceded matches, the ring-entering ceremonies, the actions of two wrestlers during a bout, the preoccupation of audiences with food and betting, the temples and shrines where tournaments were held, and the leisure activities of wrestlers in teahouses and among courtesans. But above all, they concentrated on portraits of the great stars of the ring. The spectacle of *sumo* wrestling was a challenge to *ukiyo-e* artists. Not only was it difficult to capture lightning fast action on paper, but the wrestlers' nearly naked bodies also posed a problem, especially as the artist was expected to make the faces of both contestants equally visible. The artists' preoccupation with single figures was therefore not surprising. In these, the wrestlers' finely delineated forms are achieved with bold lines and often-exaggerated features, emphasizing their physical prowess. Their topknots and aprons (*mawashi*) reflect a long, un-changed history.

During the fifty-year period 1775–1825, *sumo-e* were almost always designed by Katsukawa school artists, but for the rest of the Edo period and during the Meiji they were made exclusively by artists of the Utagawa school. The powerful drawing style of Katsukawa Shunko (1743–1812) was particularly well suited to *sumo-e*. In his prints, the massive physiognomies of his wrestlers, clad in beautifully ornamented *mawashi*, dominate the space (**Fig. 110**). Likewise with his contemporary, Katsukawa Shunei (1762–1819) (**Fig. 111**), whose *sumo-e* and warrior prints are noteworthy for their commanding style.

Utagawa Kuniyoshi (1797–1861), the leading artist of the warrior print in *ukiyo-e*, was equally at home portraying tough, lively and spirited *sumo* wrestlers (**Fig. 112**), but it was his contemporary, Utagawa Kunisada (Toyokuni III) (1786–1865), who was the most productive *sumo-e* artist of all (**Fig. 113**). From 1820 to 1860, he dominated the market for portraits of *sumo* wrestlers. Around 300 *sumo* prints by him are known.

The production of *sumo* prints was barely affected by the Tenpo Reforms of 1841–3, when governmental authorities strictly regulated the content of *ukiyo-e*, but in the late nineteenth century *sumo* became a political issue. Meiji period Japan wanted to catch up with the West and become a world leader. The ruling parties of Japan feared that wrestlers with their loincloths and topknots conveyed an uncivilized image of Japan. Fortunately, many Japanese questioned the wholesale Westernization of the country and remained loyal to their culture and traditions. The status of *sumo* wrestling was reinstated by the Meiji Emperor in 1885, but by that time of course *ukiyo-e* was on a slow decline and the output of *sumo* prints had diminished.

FIG. 103
TOYOKUNI III (Utagawa Kunisada)
三代豊国 (1786–1865)
The Actor Sawamura Tossho 沢村訥升 (1863)
26 x 19.5 cm
Courtesy of Mita Arts Gallery

This is a good example of how an artist's work can be adjusted to suit popular taste. Toyokuni III's "big head" prints, like the one here, have stronger, more garish colors and a completely different aesthetic concept compared to the work of earlier *kabuki* artists. The portraits are less sophisticated but still have a charm of their own.

FIG. 104
TOYOKUNI III (Utagawa Kunisada)
三代豊国 (1786–1865)
The Actor Kawarazaki Gonjuro
河原崎権十郎 (1860)
39.5 x 27 cm
Courtesy of Mita Arts Gallery

Even though this is a late period print, it still has the majesty of the early works by Toyokuni III. Some of this can be attributed to the *bokashi* printing in the background and costume. The actor's personality comes through in his role as he stares down an obvious unseen opponent.

FIG. 105
Utagawa YOSHITORA
芳虎 (active ca. 1840–80)
The Actor Ichikawa Fukutaro
市川福太郎 (1862)
26 x 19.5 cm
Courtesy of Mita Arts Gallery

Although Yoshitora is best known for his prints depicting Westerners from the foreign settlement of Yokohama (*Yokohama-e*), the majority of his designs cover the whole spectrum of *ukiyo-e* subject matter, including actors. He was also adept at mimicking the styles of other artists of the Utagawa school, as this portrait reveals.

FIG. 106
Utagawa YOSHITORA
芳虎 (active ca. 1840–80)
The Actor Onoe Tamizo
尾上多見蔵 (1862)
39.5 x 27 cm
Courtesy of Mita Arts Gallery

This Yoshitora portrait is almost as good as the work of his famous mentor, Utagawa Kuniyoshi. The manner in which the face and torso occupy the picture plane right up to the very edges without having to crop is masterful. We can sense the excitement in the actor's role. His make-up demonstrates an ecstatic stage experience.

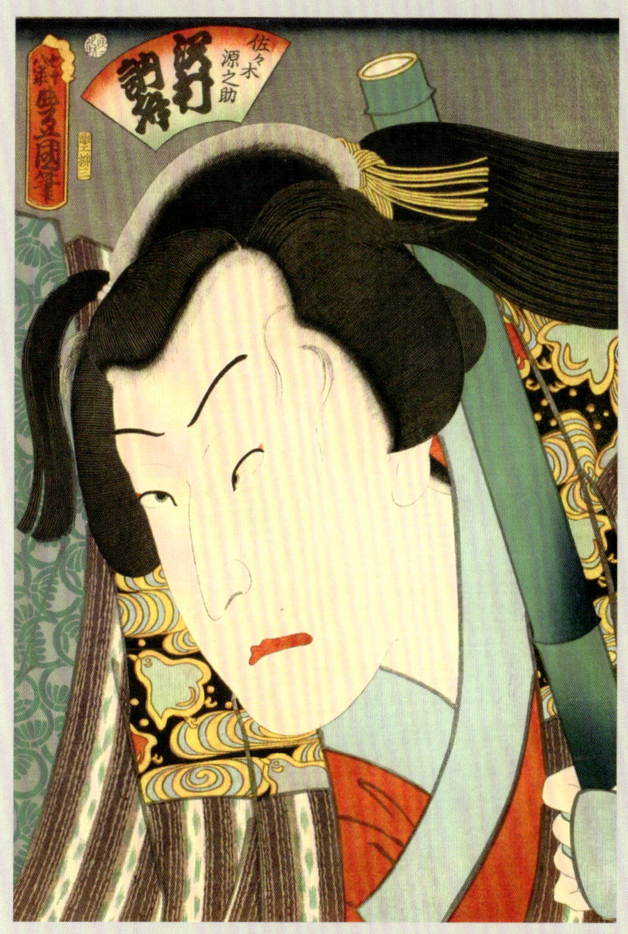
佐々木
源之助

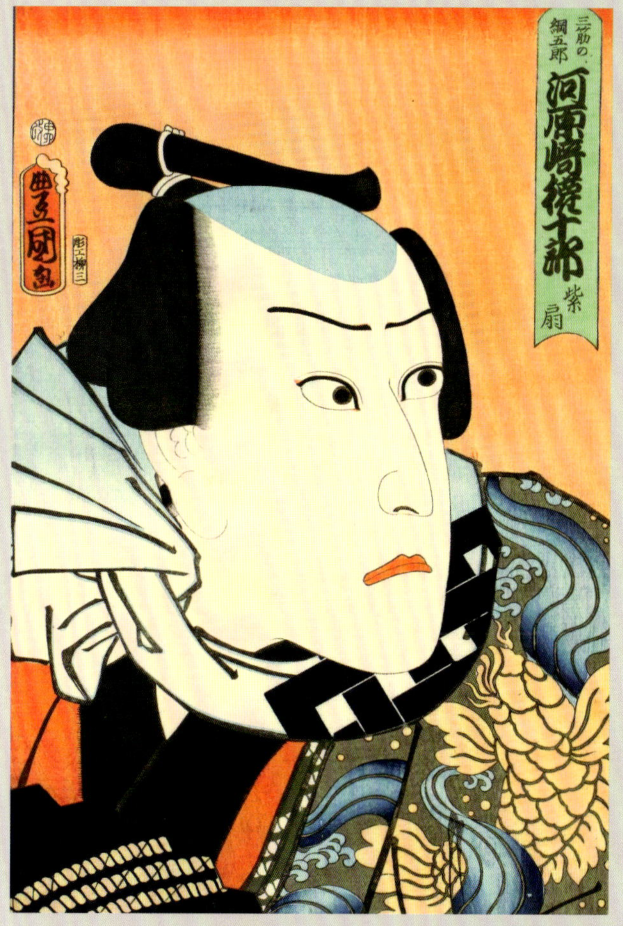
三升の
綱五郎
河原崎権十郎
紫扇

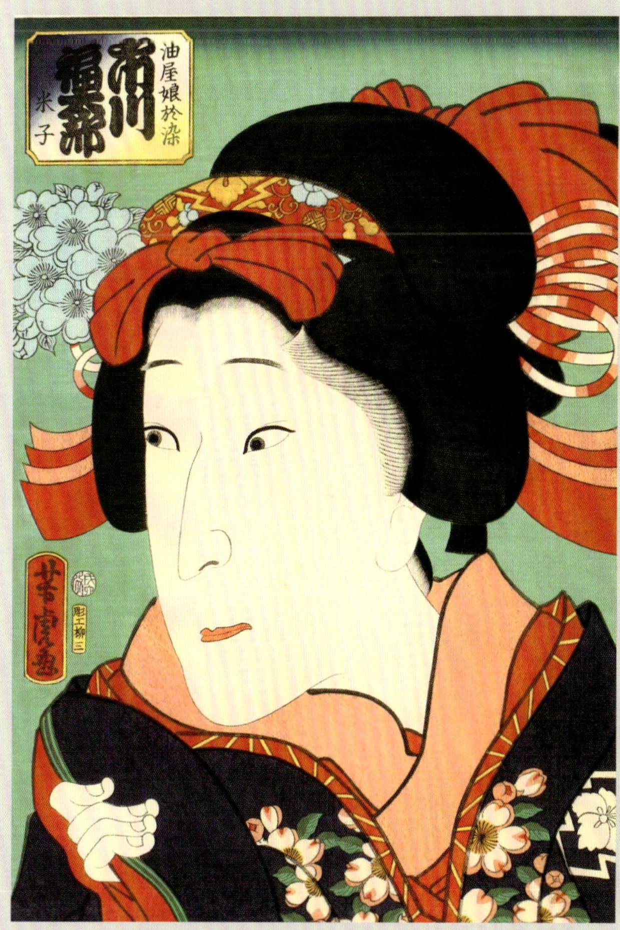
油屋娘於染
米子

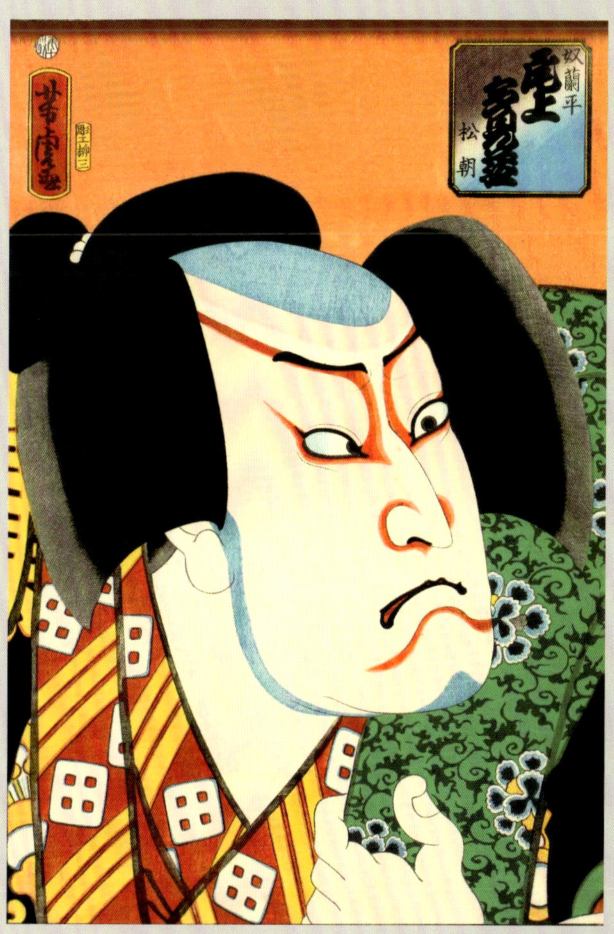
奴蘭平
松朝

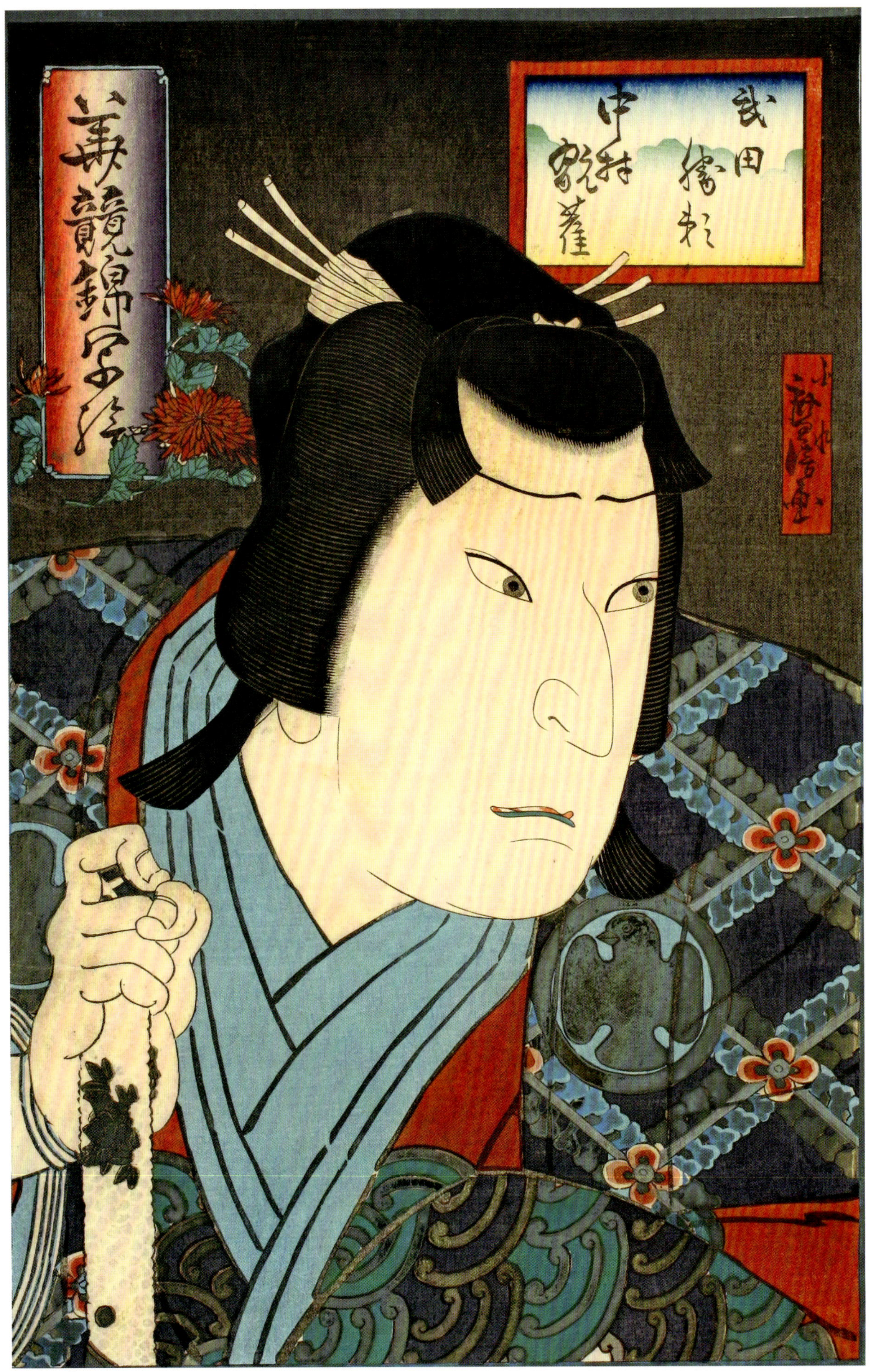

FIG. 107 (left)
Hasegawa SADANOBU I
貞信 (1809–79)
Portrait of Nakamura Kanjoku 中村翫雀 (1850s)
39.5 x 27 cm
Courtesy of Mita Arts Gallery

A hunched posture, allowing a greater view of the back of the actor's attractive *kimono*, is a feature of Sadanobu's portraits, as is the symbolic detail (here chrysanthemums) surrounding the cartouche in the background. The actor's hand is closely, if not naturally, defined. The overall boldness of line and color contribute to a modern, harmonious effect, no doubt popular at the time.

FIG. 108
Hasegawa SADANOBU I
貞信 (1809–79)
Portrait of Arashi Tokusaburo 嵐　徳三郎 (1850s)
39.5 x 27 cm
Courtesy of Mita Arts Gallery

This portrait, even busier than the one in Fig. 107, is in the distinctive Sadanobu style. An iris bloom and lotus pods decorate the background.

FIG. 109
Utagawa HIROSADA
広貞 (ca. 1810–64)
Unknown Osaka Actors 大阪役者絵 (1850s)
Diptych, 26 x 39 cm
Courtesy of Mita Arts Gallery

The portraits shown in the diptych here are separate pictures but it is obvious the artist intended them to be seen together. Even though the emphasis is on the head, there is still a great deal of action revealed in the upper part of the torso.

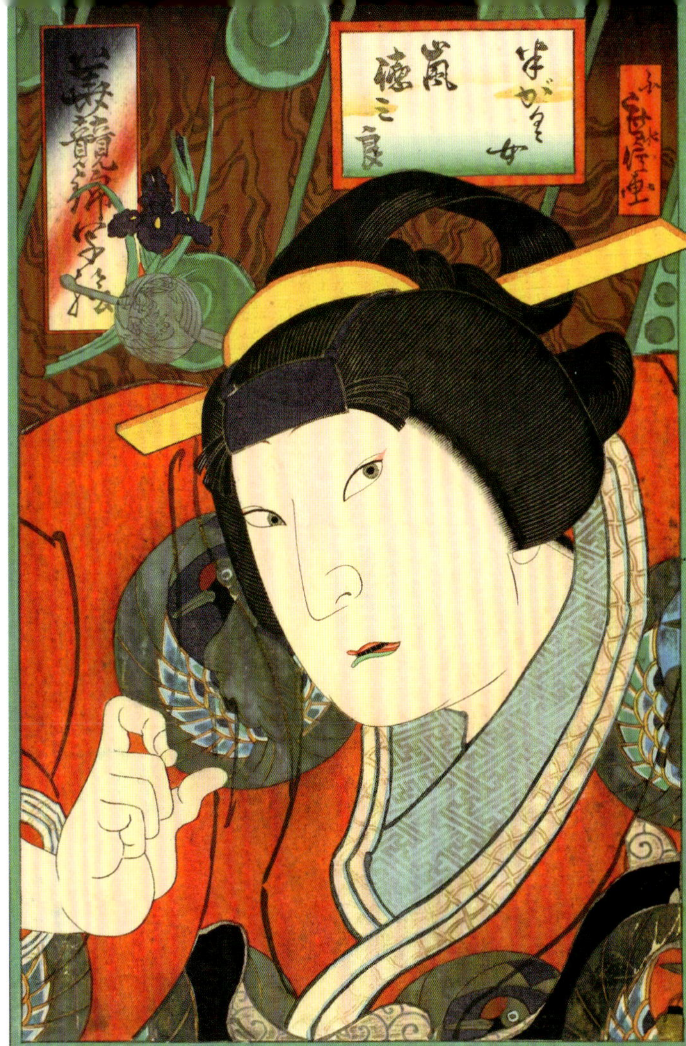

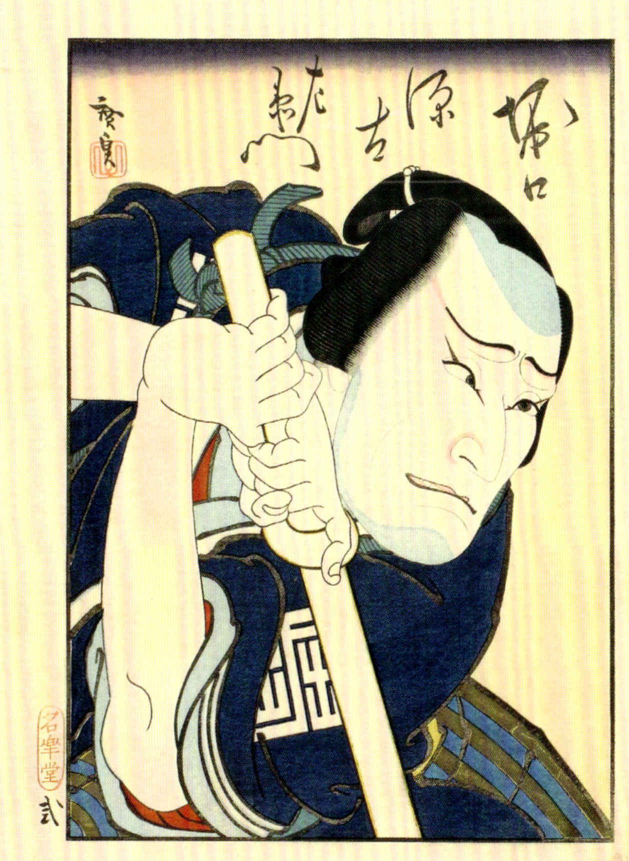

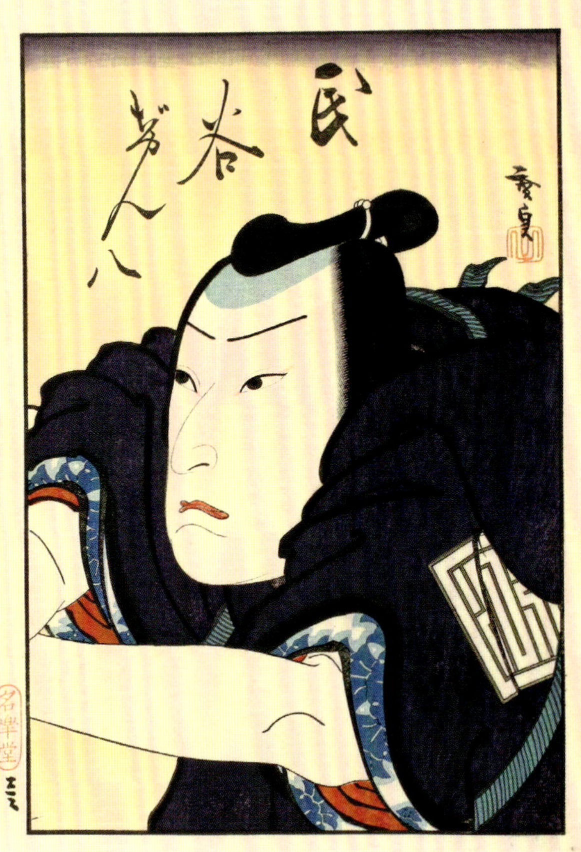

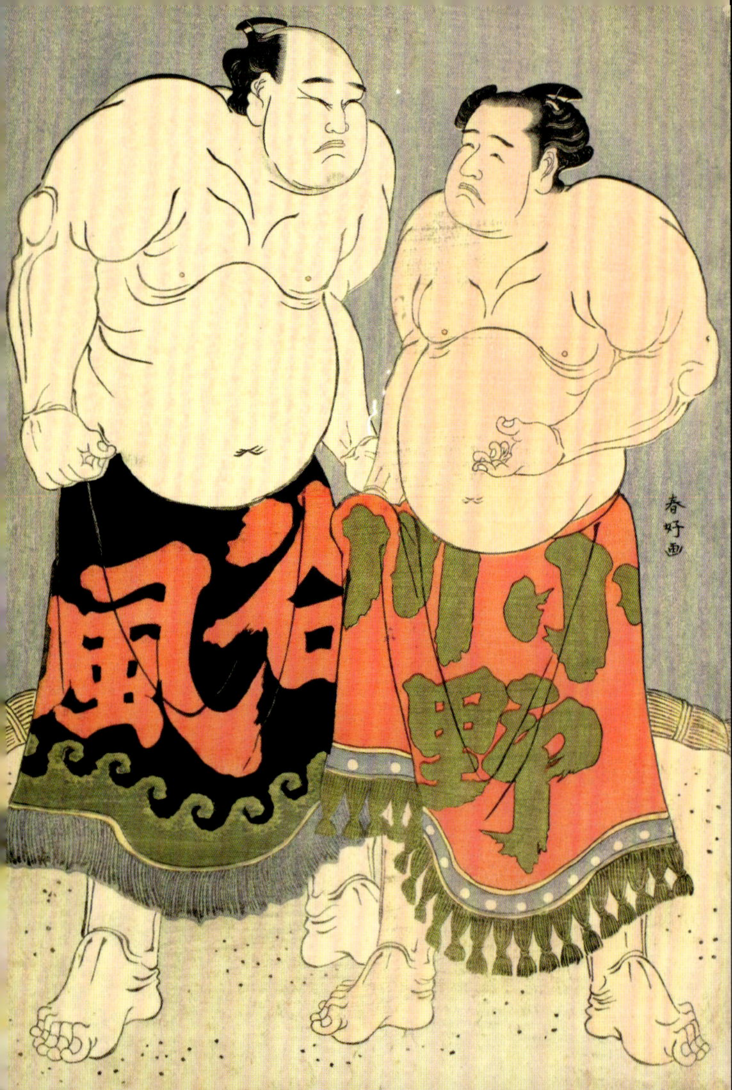

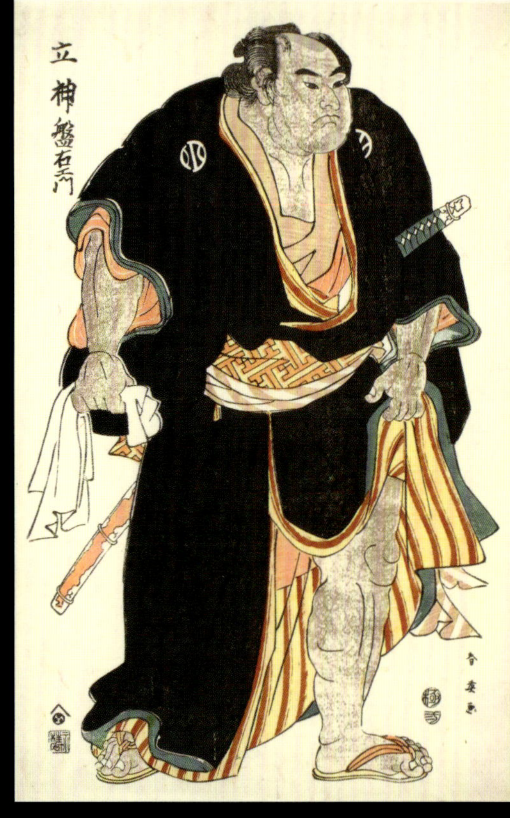

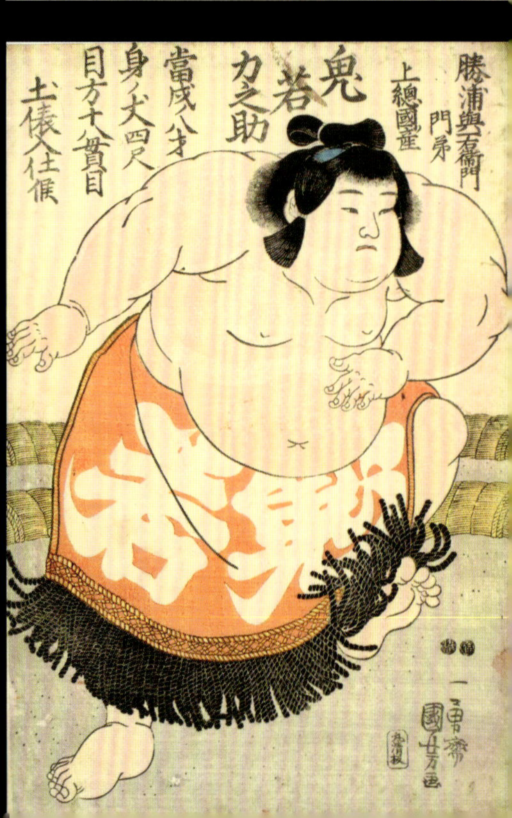

IG. 110
atsukawa SHUNKO
春好 (1743–1812)
he Sumo Wrestlers Onogawa and anikaze 相撲絵 小野川と谷風 (1810)
9 x 27 cm
ourtesy of Mita Arts Gallery

n this print, two famous early nineteenth-entury wrestlers are portrayed in the ring *dohyo*) facing one other, each trying to nnerve his opponent. The edge of the *ohyo* is indicated by bunches of straw. he wrestlers are wearing beautifully rnamented silk aprons (*mawashi*) em-lazoned with their names. There is an xciting contrast in colors between the vrestlers' *mawashi* and their skin tones.

IG. 111 (above right)
atsukawa SHUNEI
春英 (1762–1819)
umo Wrestler 立神盤右エ門 (1810)
9 x 27 cm
ourtesy of Mita Arts Gallery

his imposing wrestler is dressed in formal ttire, a luxurious black *kimono* with striped ilk lining. The print, while in perfect con-dition, shows some oxidation on the skin. he printer probably used an ink to create rough skin texture, which over 200 years as not stood up to time and environment.

FIG. 112 (right)
Utagawa KUNIYOSHI
国芳 (1797–1861)
Sumo Wrestler on the Dohyo (Ring)
土俵上の鬼若力之助 (1850s)
39 x 27 cm
Courtesy of Mita Arts Gallery

The *mawashi* on this wrestler is similar in design to the Shunko print above even though the print was created some fifty years later. The wrestler has braided side locks, which is unusual. His stance depicts the initial face-off between two wrestlers when the feet are placed in a solid bal-anced position next to each other.

FIG. 113 (opposite)
TOYOKUNI III (Utagawa Kunisada)
三代豊国 (1786–1865)
The Wrestlers Arauma and Koyanagi Fighting 相撲力士 荒馬と小柳 (1840s)
39 x 27 cm
Courtesy of Mita Arts Gallery

This is one of the few prints showing a wrestling bout in action. The wrestler with his hands on his opponent's belt has the advantage, as it is easier to throw an opponent off balance from this position or carry him out of the ring.

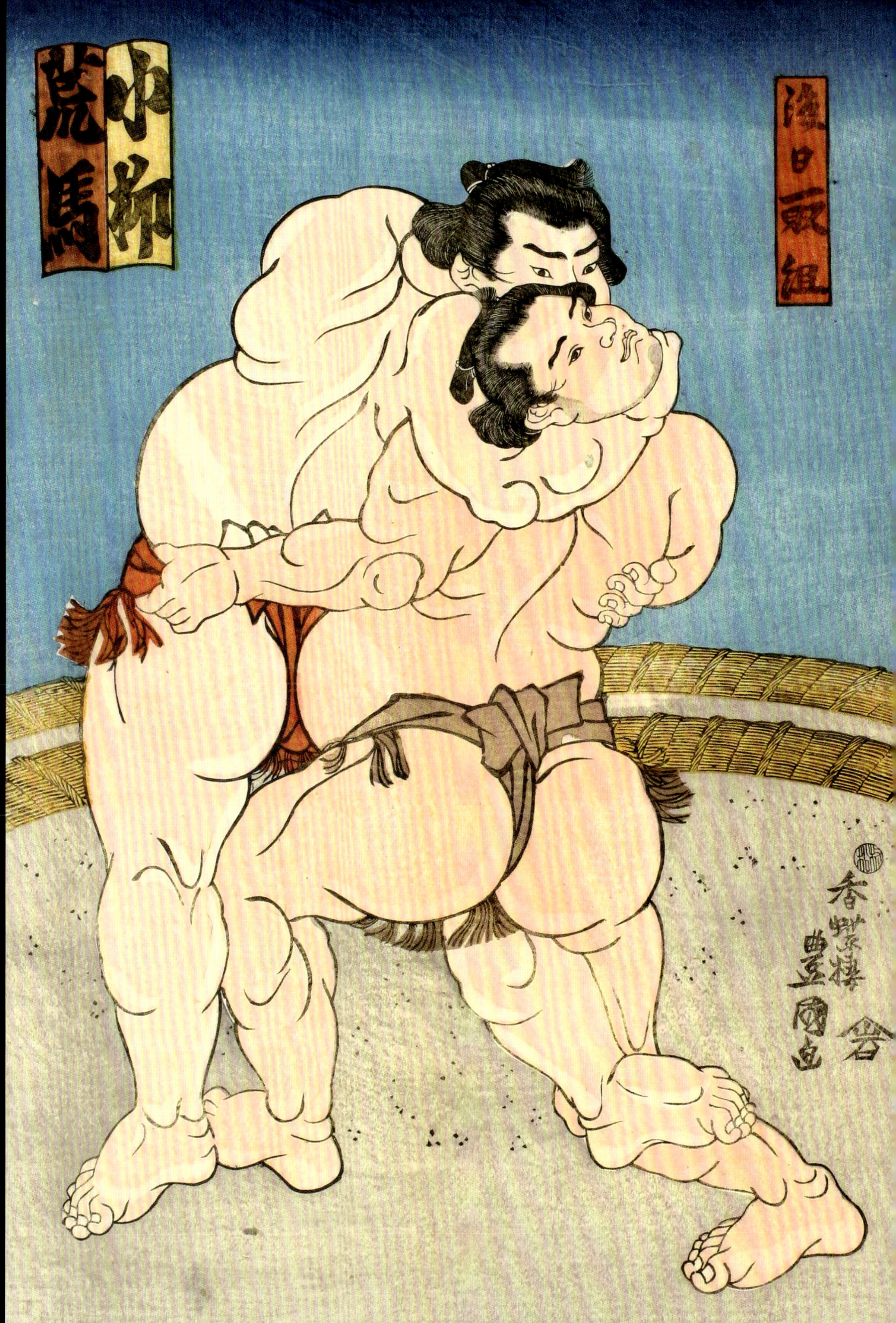
小柳
荒馬
當日取組
香蝶楼豊国画

CHAPTER SEVEN

Landscapes

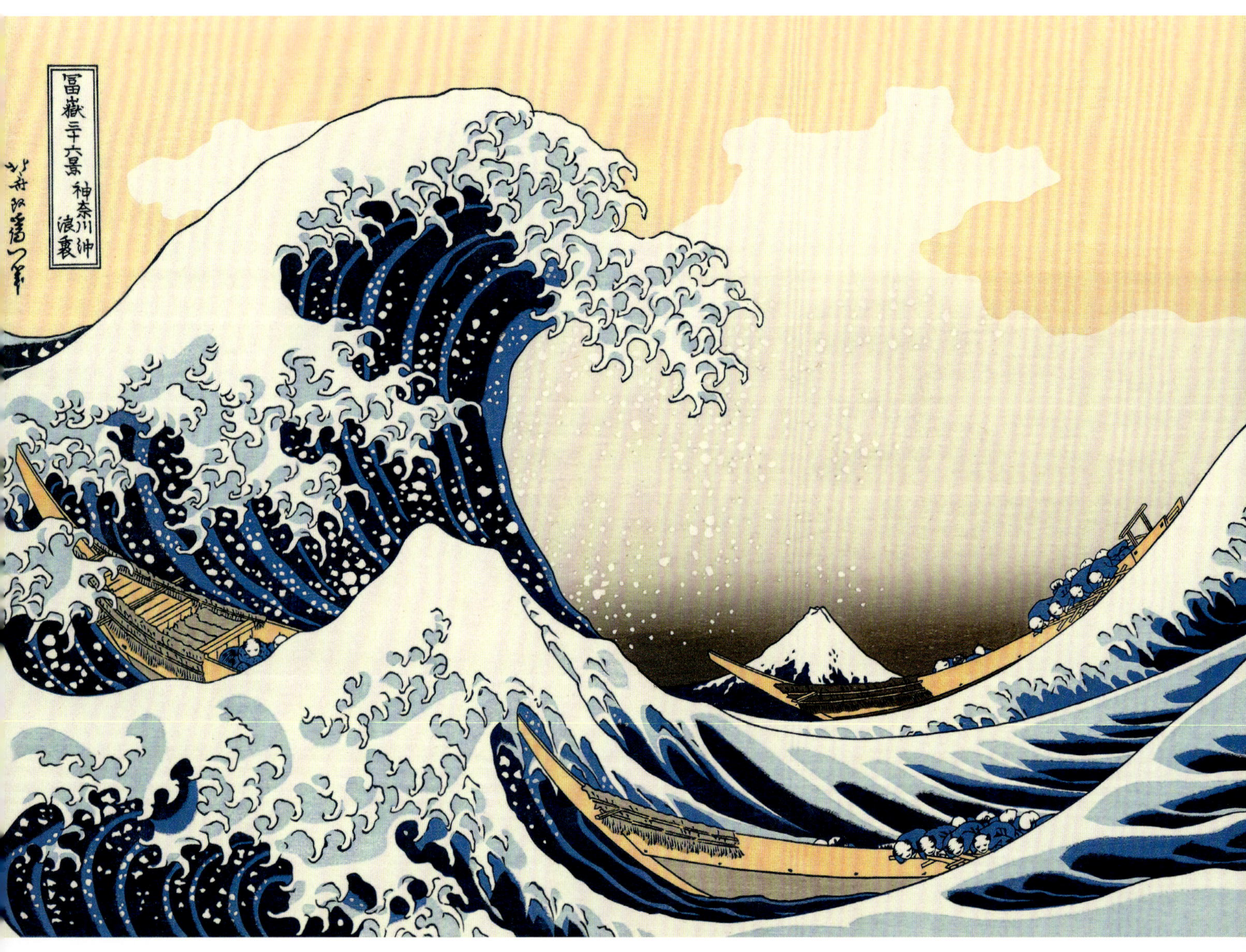

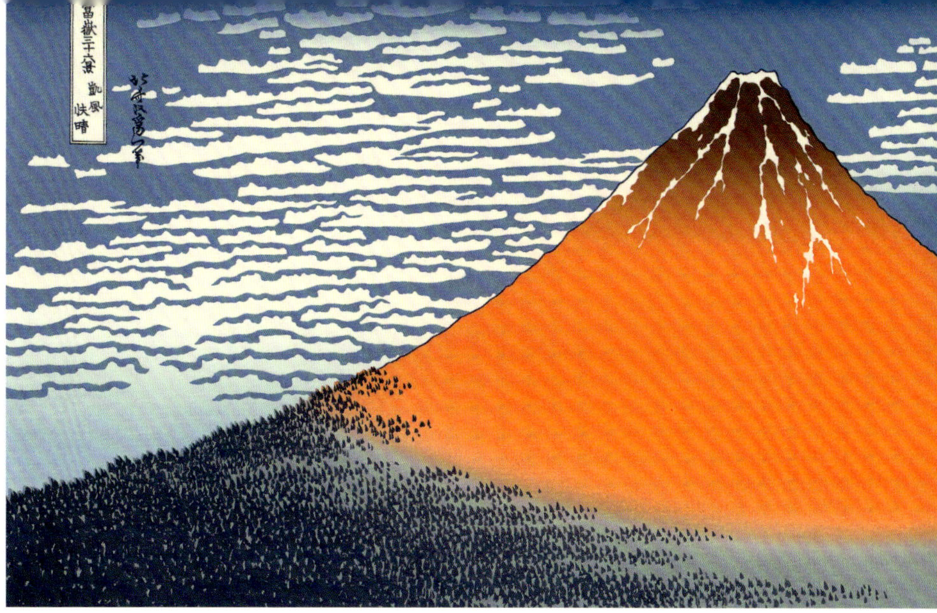

FIG. 115
Katsushika HOKUSAI
北斎 (1760–1849)
Red Fuji, from *Thirty-six Views of Mount Fuji*
凱風快晴 (1826–31)
28.5 x 38.8 cm
Courtesy of Adachi Institute of Woodcut Prints

In this print, Hokusai achieved the ultimate statement of Japan's most revered natural wonder. Mount Fuji is the highest mountain in Japan, and with its almost perfect symmetry has been worshipped in art and literature since the Nara period (719–84). Countless pilgrims climb the mountain annually, and to see the sun rise from its peak is an unforgettable emotional experience. The "Red Fuji" is an extremely simple composition with a limited palette of blue, green and red and a skilled use of *bokashi* printing.

Traditional landscape painting in Japan has its roots in China. Likewise, the Chinese produced color prints about three-quarters of a century before the Japanese. There are basic differences between Chinese and Japanese landscape painting and their European counterpart, the most important being the European use of the sun to define form and create shadows. Very seldom are there any shadows in Chinese and Japanese landscape painting. The second basic difference is the position of the viewer. In traditional Chinese painting, the viewer moves into the landscape, his viewpoint changing as he proceeds. It is virtually impossible to see the tops of mountains or trees from the foreground. Instead, one has to view the scene in sections from the foreground to the middle ground and eventually the background. This explains why houses and people in the distance are not smaller as they recede into the background. Moreover, the position of the eye level changes so that one can have a worm's-eye view in one area and a bird's-eye view in another. In the last half of the eighteenth century, the landscape served mainly as a backdrop for a figural composition. It was not until the nineteenth century that the landscape itself became a worthy subject of woodblock prints.

Traditional Japanese landscape painting was not meant to describe a particular location. If names of mountains or vistas were indicated on a picture, it was purely the imagination of the artist at work. Many Japanese scenes were placed in China and painted by artists who had never set foot there. The traditional artist used the sun and moon only as a decorative device. The same applied to changes in the weather, which usually offered the four seasons as a traditional change of cosmic time. These basic principles were understood by *ukiyo-e* artists and, in some cases, incorporated in their works, but by and large they chose to ignore them. The townspeople—shopkeepers, workers, entertainers and others—did not have the artistic training to appreciate such an esoteric art form. They were practical people who liked to travel and to purchase pictures of the local shrines and temples and beauty spots they visited, perhaps afterwards mounting them in albums, much as the modern-day traveler takes photographs or buys postcards. Sometimes they would purchase fans bearing the same scenes. It was not important that the scenes shown were not a photographic likeness. To the buyers, the imaginative concept of a place was more important than a realistic image.

While many woodblock print artists attempted landscapes, it was the creative and innovative genius of two artists in particular—Katsushika Hokusai and Utagawa Hiroshige—that conclusively shifted the emphasis in *ukiyo-e* from a style of personal portraiture focused on courtesans and actors into a broader style of art focused on landscapes, plants and animals. The landscape prints they produced are in a category of their own in the world of art. They are not abstractions of imaginary places but are easily acceptable to our pictorial vocabulary. They are of specific places. They are also colorful and composed in such a way that the viewer is made to feel that he is part of the scene.

Katsushika Hokusai (1760–1849) was the greater designer of the two, an eccentric genius whose imagination knew no bounds (**Figs. 114–120**). He was drawn to diverse artistic influences, among them Chinese and Western art, which helped to make him a universal artist. Some of his famous series, such as *Thirty-six Views of Mount Fuji* (1826–31) and *One Hundred Views of Mount Fuji* (1834), have become icons in Japanese art. His waterfall series shows his imagination reaching heights never before attained by any other artist. Hokusai lived to be eighty-nine years old. His life went through many stages, and with each stage he adopted a new name, but as the 1830s drew

FIG. 114
Katsushika HOKUSAI
北斎 (1760–1849)
The Great Wave off Kanagawa, from *Thirty-six Views of Mount Fuji*
神奈川沖浪凱 (1826–31)
26 x 38 cm
Courtesy of Adachi Institute of Woodcut Prints

This print has to be the most commonly recognized image of Japanese art. It is indeed a masterpiece, and probably one of the great masterpieces of the world. To quote a friend, the late Charles Mitchell, when describing this print: "Hokusai claimed that all things in the universe were basically triangular or round. A careful study of this design will reveal that it is composed mostly of triangles and circles. It is extremely interesting to analyze the intricate structure and relationships. It is also worth noting that the complicated geometrical pattern did not result in a static design but in one that is the very epitome of dynamic movement and actions."

near, his vision and single-minded passion saw the creation of his majestic Fuji series and the series of waterfalls. Hokusai started the Fuji series when he was seventy years old.

At this time also, he attempted to revolutionize the palette of *ukiyo-e* by creating a masterful monochromatic use of Prussian blue, also known in Japan as Berlin blue (*bero*). A synthetic color imported from Europe to Japan in 1829, and the first of the synthetic colors to be used, the dark opaque blue revolutionized landscape prints because it allowed for many tones and also could be mixed with other colors. In Japan, prints in Prussian blue are known as *aizome-e*. About ten of the original printings of the *Thirty-six Views of Mount Fuji* were done entirely in tones of Prussian blue, making them monochromatic prints. They aroused a great deal of controversy at the time of publication, primarily because of the use of Berlin blue. Yet, the first series of five prints feature water and it seems entirely fitting to use blue. No other color could possibly have accomplished the same result.

Prior to 1830, other blues were available, in particular indigo blue (*aibo*), but natural vegetable or mineral dyes were generally expensive to produce and were more light sensitive than aniline colors distilled from coal tar, and thus faded easily. Other synthetic colors were eventually introduced, such as the red in Hokusai's famous "Red Fuji," but the *hanshita-e* (key block) for the entire series was printed in blue, not black, as was the norm.

Aizome-e became very fashionable and was utilized by numerous artists other than Hokusai. The first artist to exploit the color was, in fact, Eisen in 1829, but in the 1830s its popularity soared and we have examples of Kunisada and Sadahide also creating monochrome prints in Berlin blue. Many of these prints were in the format of *uchiwa-e* (fan prints). Unfortunately, because of persistent usage many fans eventually became torn and were discarded. A fine example is the Hiroshige fan print of fishing boats reproduced from my own collection (see Fig. 126).

The set of eight prints of Hokusai's waterfalls, although not recognized as Japanese print icons in the same way as the "Great Wave off Kanagawa" or the "Red Fuji," are to me his masterpieces. They are the most contemporary of all his compositions, embracing abstract qualities that do not appear in world art until the twentieth century. The variations constructed around a simple theme of descending water, either in a gushing column or undulating over the sides of a mountain, are remarkable. The compositions also contain figures that initially go unnoticed against the power of the falling water, but on closer examination reveal all sorts of human activity.

Hokusai had a prodigious energy. It is estimated that he drew over 70,000 different designs in his long life. His working period spanned over seventy years, which meant he had to produce three or more designs daily. It is hard to imagine a man working so tirelessly every day to accomplish this body of work—and, moreover, to create his best work during his golden years. Hokusai stands apart from all the other *ukiyo-e* artists. His imagination, power of conception and mastery of design were not equaled by any who came after him. Although he had students who could produce bird and flower books and other illustrated material, no one could ever match the power, versatility and creativity of the single-sheet prints that Hokusai made.

Utagawa Hiroshige (1797–1858) took the landscape to new heights, consolidating it as an independent subject and adapting it to the tastes of the public (**Figs. 121–126**). Although in the early years he confined himself to common *ukiyo-e* themes such as beautiful women, *kabuki* actors and warriors, he was inspired by the success of the landscape prints of his near-contemporary Hokusai to make a dramatic turnabout around 1830 and focus on landscapes. He did not have the imagination nor did he create the revolutionary composition of Hokusai, but he did have an attribute that Hokusai lacked—he was able to imbue his landscapes with a sense of poetry. Particular moods of the seasons, weather and time of day lend his landscapes a convincing closeness to nature. One can smell the grass, feel

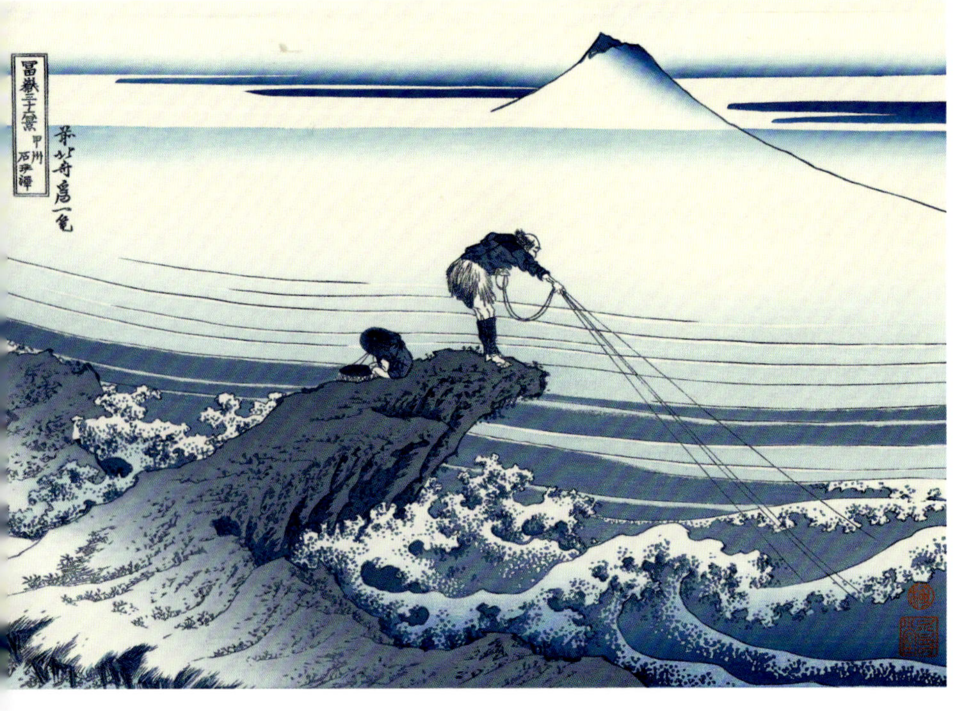

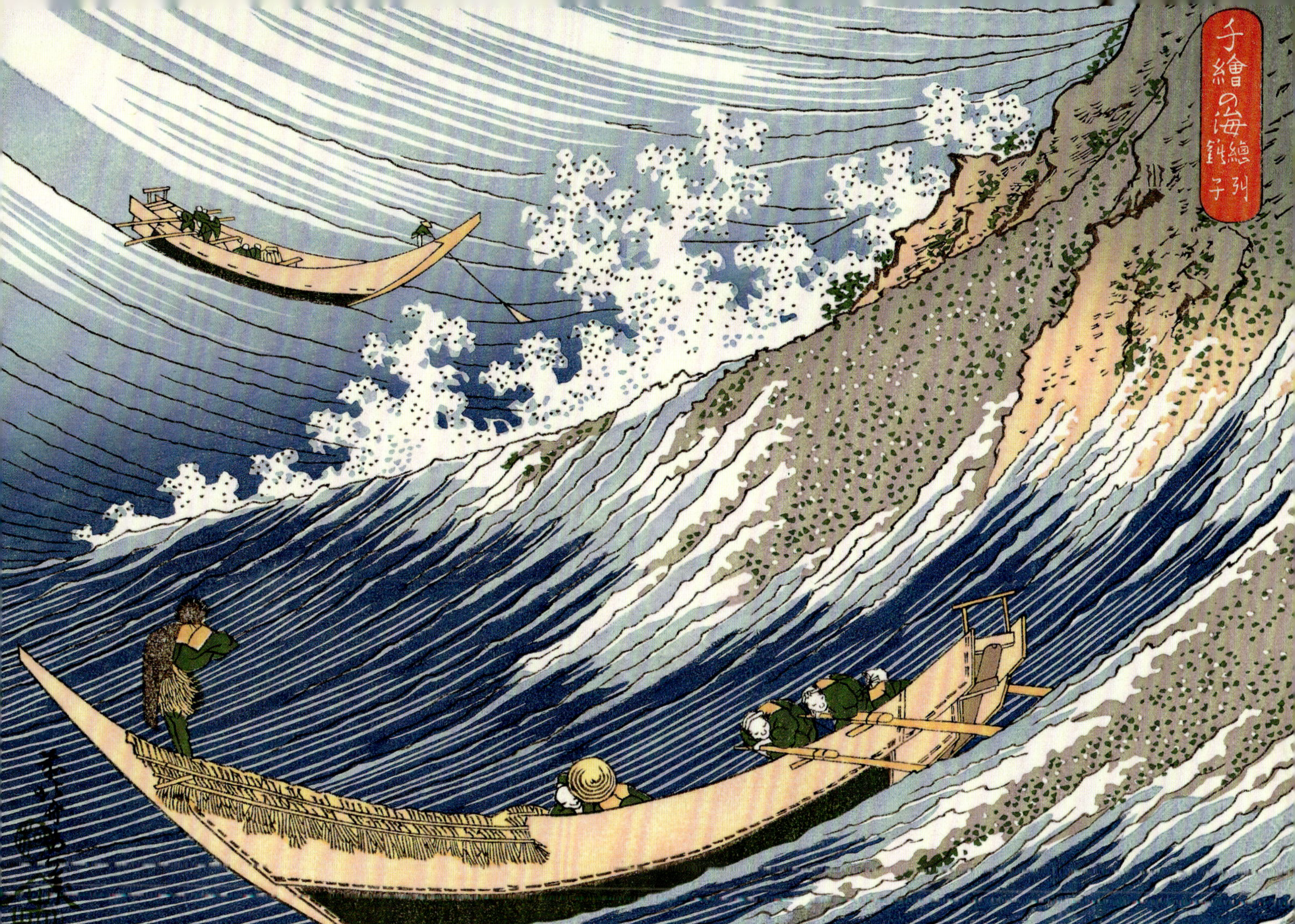

FIG. 116 (opposite)
Katsushika HOKUSAI
北斎 (1760–1849)
The Lone Fisherman at Kajikazawa, from *Thirty-six Views of Mount Fuji*
甲州石班沢 (1826–31)
25.5 x 38.5 cm
Courtesy of Adachi Institute of Woodcut Prints

The composition of the fisherman pulling in his net echoes the shape of Mount Fuji in the background. The lines of the net held by the fisherman form a circle. The triangle and the circle were keys to Hokusai's compositions. Unlike his contemporary Hiroshige, Hokusai does not gradually progress from the foreground to the background. There is an abrupt transition. In this picture, Tosa school-style mist separates the distance with a typical Japanese conventional device.

FIG. 117
Katsushika HOKUSAI
北斎 (1760–1849)
Fishing Boats at Choshi, from *One Thousand Pictures of the Ocean*
総州銚子 (ca. 1833–4)
19.5 x 27.5 cm
Courtesy of Adachi Institute of Woodcut Prints

The theme of men using all their energy to combat the forces of nature is brought to life in this imaginative picture of fishermen in small craft battling the waves to haul in their daily catch.

the mud, be warmed by the sun, blown by the wind, drenched by the rain or frozen by the snow simply by absorbing the atmosphere in his pictures. He also managed to achieve a sense of realistic depth by adapting Western principles of perspective and receding space to his own works. As much as I admire Hokusai and wish to emulate him, I love Hiroshige and know his art is intuitive and far beyond my capabilities.

Hiroshige was born into a family of minor officials who were responsible for fire control in the city. Even though his position was relatively unimportant, it did allow him to freely travel the roads he loved to sketch and absorb the scenery that became famous from his journeys. Sent on a shogunal delegation to the imperial court in Kyoto in 1832, Hiroshige traveled along the 500-kilometer (300 mile)-long Tokaido Road, a coastal highway linking the metropolis of Edo with the capital of Kyoto. In his *Fifty-three Stations of the Tokaido* that resulted (1833–4), he revived the familiar territory of travel guides, portraying the starting and finishing points and the overnight stops along the way by means of fifty-five painterly single-sheet woodblock prints. Each of the stops was a way station or inn where the traveler could spend the night or rest for a few days before continuing his journey. Some of the inns were very elaborate as feudal lords or other important dignitaries would also stop to change or care for their horses, and expect accommodation for the attendants who accompanied them.

This large series was a resounding commercial success—the popular equivalent to Hokusai's Fuji series—and encouraged Hiroshige to become a full-time artist working extensively within the realm of *meisho-e* (pictures of famous places). For the next twenty years he concentrated his efforts on landscape prints, although he excelled at *kacho-e* (bird and flower prints) at the same time. He created numerous other large series, as opposed to the small sets of eight or ten prints that he and other artists previously made,

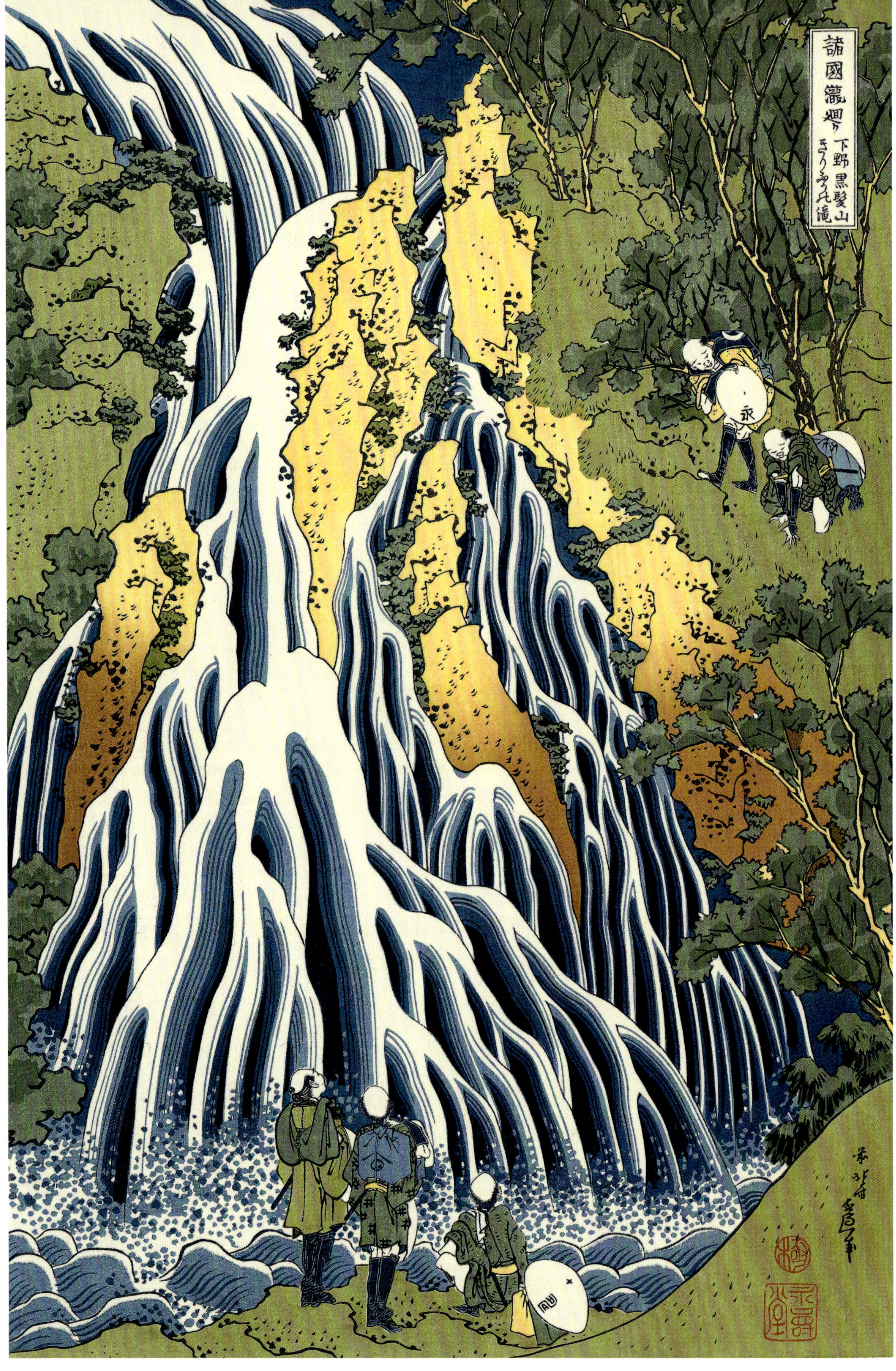
諸國瀧廻り
下野黒髪山
きりふりの滝

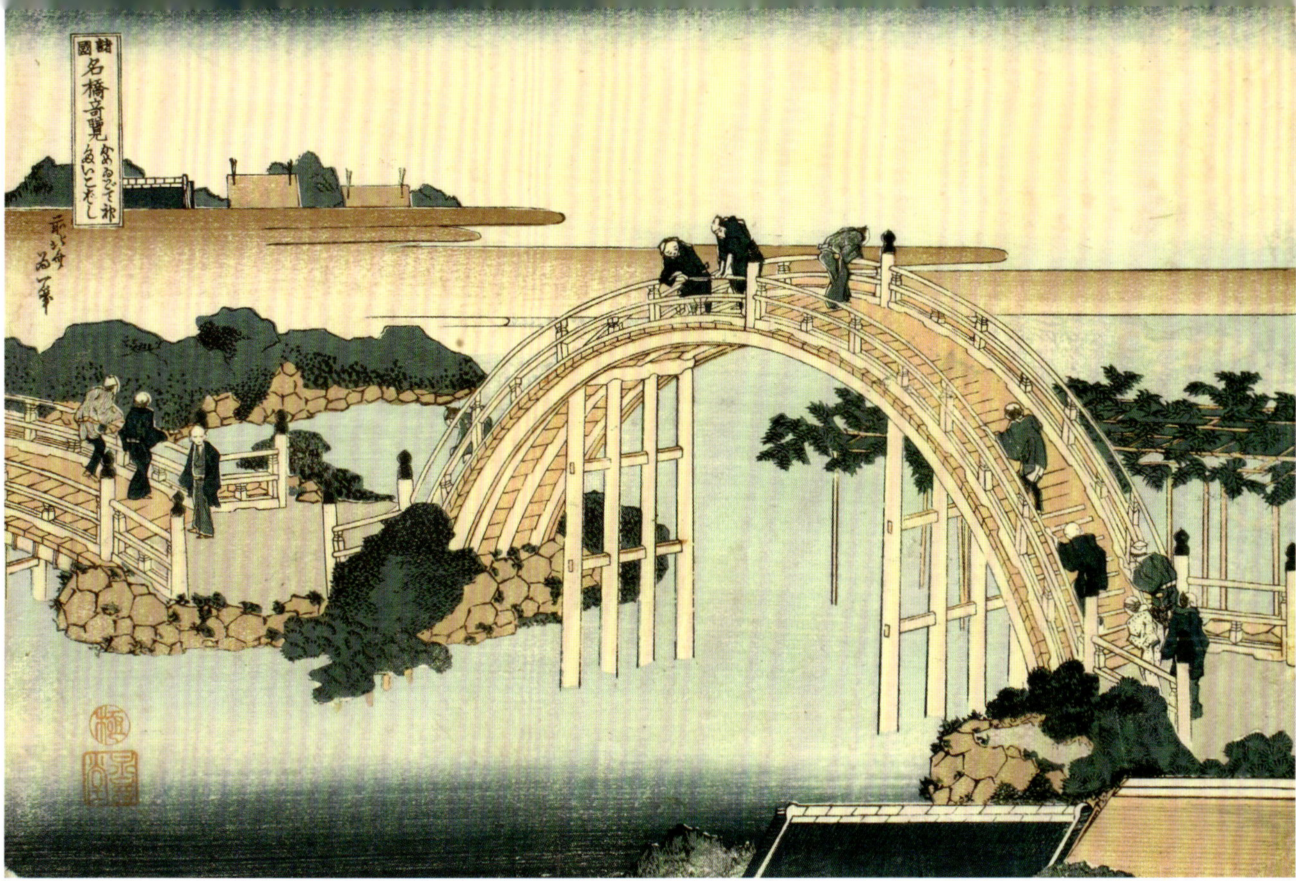

FIG. 118 (left)
Katsushika HOKUSAI
北斎 (1760–1849)
Kirifuri Waterfall at Mount Kurokami In Shimotsuke Province 下野黒髪山きりふりの滝 (ca. 1832)
38.5 x 26.5 cm
Courtesy of Adachi Institute of Woodcut Prints

This print of a waterfall near Nikko was published to encourage city dwellers to venture on trips to the countryside. The modernity of the composition is remarkable. Also noteworthy is the scale of the falls compared to the figures in the foreground and the climbers on the slope to the right of the falls. The use of dots in this print as well as in other Hokusai pictures may have had an influence on the painting techniques of his European contemporaries, especially the French Impressionists.

FIG. 119
Katsushika HOKUSAI
北斎 (1760–1849)
Drum Bridge at the Kameido Tenjin Shrine, from *Rare Views of Famous Bridges in All Provinces* 亀戸天神たいこ橋 (ca. 1834)
38.5 x 23.5 cm
Courtesy of Mita Arts Gallery

Hokusai's bridges are not as exciting as his Fuji and waterfall series but do offer some marvelous compositions. To quote the late Hokusai expert, J. Hillier: "The greater topographical accuracy, the less the chance of evaluating a design completely satisfying in itself. In this set Hokusai was obviously bent on portraying the particular bridge, instead of the typical bridge. There is a greater attention to the identifying detail, to the picturesque effect." The Drum Bridge startles us with so arduous an ascent. As in other Hokusai prints, the middle ground is obliterated by Tosa school-style bands of mist.

including *Sixty-nine Stations of the Kisokaido* (ca. 1839) and *One Hundred Famous Views of Edo* (1856–8).

The intimate, almost small-scale works within his various series are especially noteworthy for their unusual vantage points, seasonal allusions and striking colors as well as the people portrayed in them. In all his compositions we witness the characters and travelers he met on his journey. They are completely human and show us their experiences of life on the road. Almost always they are people of his own social class, and offer us in their actions and attitudes a sense of humor. To quote Yone Noguchi, the first critic of Japanese prints in English in the early twentieth century: "He is, in truth, the only native and national artist of Japan." Hiroshige was, however, more interested in catering to his audience than in accurately depicting scenes that appeared before him. Many were inventions of his imagination. Although he certainly did travel to those destinations, the liberty he took to alter the scene was part of his artistic license. His independence of vision was, to him, more important than a factual representation of the place.

Altogether, Hiroshige published sixteen different series of the *Tokaido* by different publishers and in various sizes. Three other series were published in collaboration with other artists. He never repeated himself and continuously found excitement and inspiration from this one source of material. He kept diaries of his travels, some of which have been translated. They allow us to experience his daily activities as he wanders his trails. Hiroshige's popularity and the reprinting of his works gave birth to a whole corpus of writing on the subject. But it also led to a lowering of printing standards. When the blocks were overused, the outlines became blurred, or the registration of the color blocks lost their alignment. Sometimes new blocks were cut, especially by other publishers, or old blocks were bought and new pieces plugged into them. Variations on the blocks or colors caused series of prints to be erroneously labeled second edition, third edition, etc. Prints from the original blocks sometimes contained variations in the colors or the *bokashi* where the sky or ground faded in different directions. Collecting Hiroshige is thus a test in connoisseurship of Japanese prints. A unique element in his prints is the border around the edges, which has indented rounded corners. But there are thousands of Hiroshige prints on the market without borders as these were cut off when prints were removed

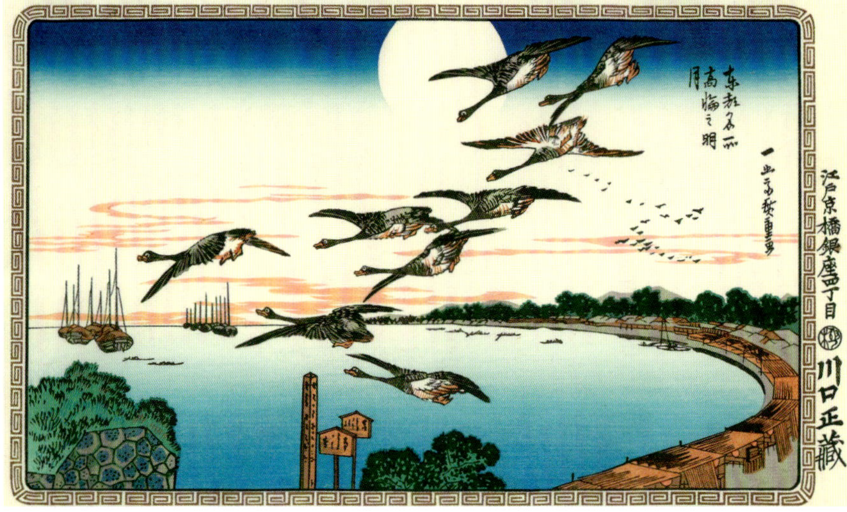

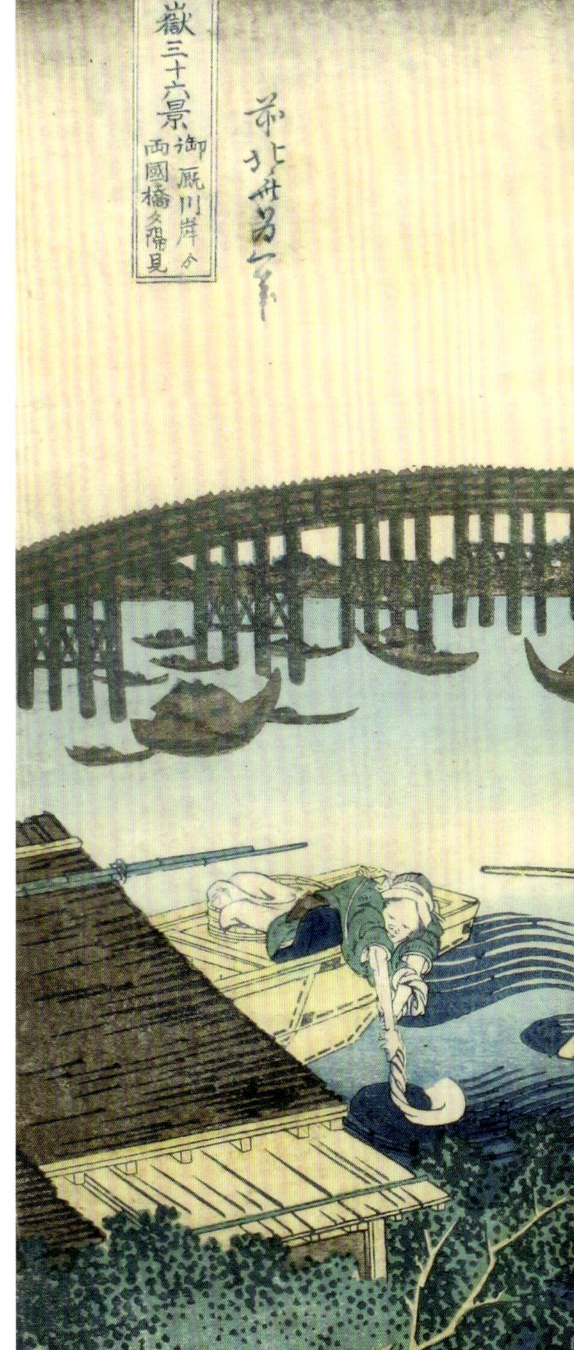

from albums to be sold individually. Japanese collectors often pasted the prints into albums as a collection of memories of a trip taken.

Despite the problem of overproduction and the toll it took on artistic quality, Hiroshige's landscapes series were enormously popular both at home and abroad. They greatly influenced European artists, especially French Impressionists, from the 1870s onwards. Elements of his style were copied in oils by Van Gogh and were included in the compositions of Whistler and Degas. His prints were collected enthusiastically by Monet.

Hiroshige died of cholera in 1858 at the age of sixty-two. He had lived his entire life in Edo. A daughter born from his second marriage married a print artist who Hiroshige adopted and on whom he bestowed the name Hiroshige II; her second husband, another pupil of Hiroshige, is today known as Hiroshige III. Hiroshige II tried to carry the torch of his father-in-law, but never achieved the same level of success and recognition.

With the death of Hiroshige, landscape in the form of single-sheet prints came to an end. Although he had followers, the poetry was gone even though the scenery remained. Woodblock landscape continued in the form of illustrated books (see page 36) until the advent of a single individual who resurrected that pictorial reality in the early twentieth century. This individual was Watanabe Shozaburo (1885–1957), art dealer, publisher and businessman extraordinaire, who started his working life in an export company that also dealt in prints. After learning the export business and gathering connections to foreign importers, he set up his own company in 1906. Sensing a market for Japanese prints in North America and Europe, Watanabe began to export reproductions of famous and popular prints by *ukiyo-e* masters that he commissioned from trained artisans.

Not content with dealing in reproductions alone, Watanabe soon turned his sights on developing and selling new woodblock prints targeted at art lovers rather than the mass consumer market. Thus the *shin hanga*, literally "new woodblock prints," movement was born. In Watanabe's view, the European and American market wanted woodblock prints that featured an idealized, exotic Japan that had ceased to exist at the end of the Edo period in 1868. Instead of following the *ukiyo-e* tradition of black outline and flat patterns of color, the prints would re-create through the print medium an aesthetic expression based on Western concepts of landscape painting. They would be prints without outlines and in appearance resemble Western watercolors.

Watanabe's exposure to the Western market coincided with his patronage of many painters and print artists who were approaching the landscape medium in the Western mode. After 1868, all kinds of cultural imports came to Japan from the West, including photography and printing techniques, which were greeted with great enthusiasm. The art of *ukiyo-e* could not compete and went into decline in Japan. At the beginning of the twentieth century, many artists and artisans trained in traditional *ukiyo-e* printmaking were forced to make a living as illustrators for newspapers and by designing *kuchi-e* (frontispiece illustrations) distributed with novels and magazines. A parallel change in artistic taste and direction also relegated images of the "floating world" to the annals of history. The time was ripe for a new print genre. The themes would comprise somewhat romantic and idyllic renditions of famous temples, landscapes and other images thought to appeal primarily to Westerners but also to many Japanese. They would be finely crafted.

Among the collaborating *shin hanga* artists in Watanabe's circle were Kawase Hasui (1883–1957), who worked exclusively on exquisite landscape prints, including seasonal themes such as spring blossoms, summer rains,

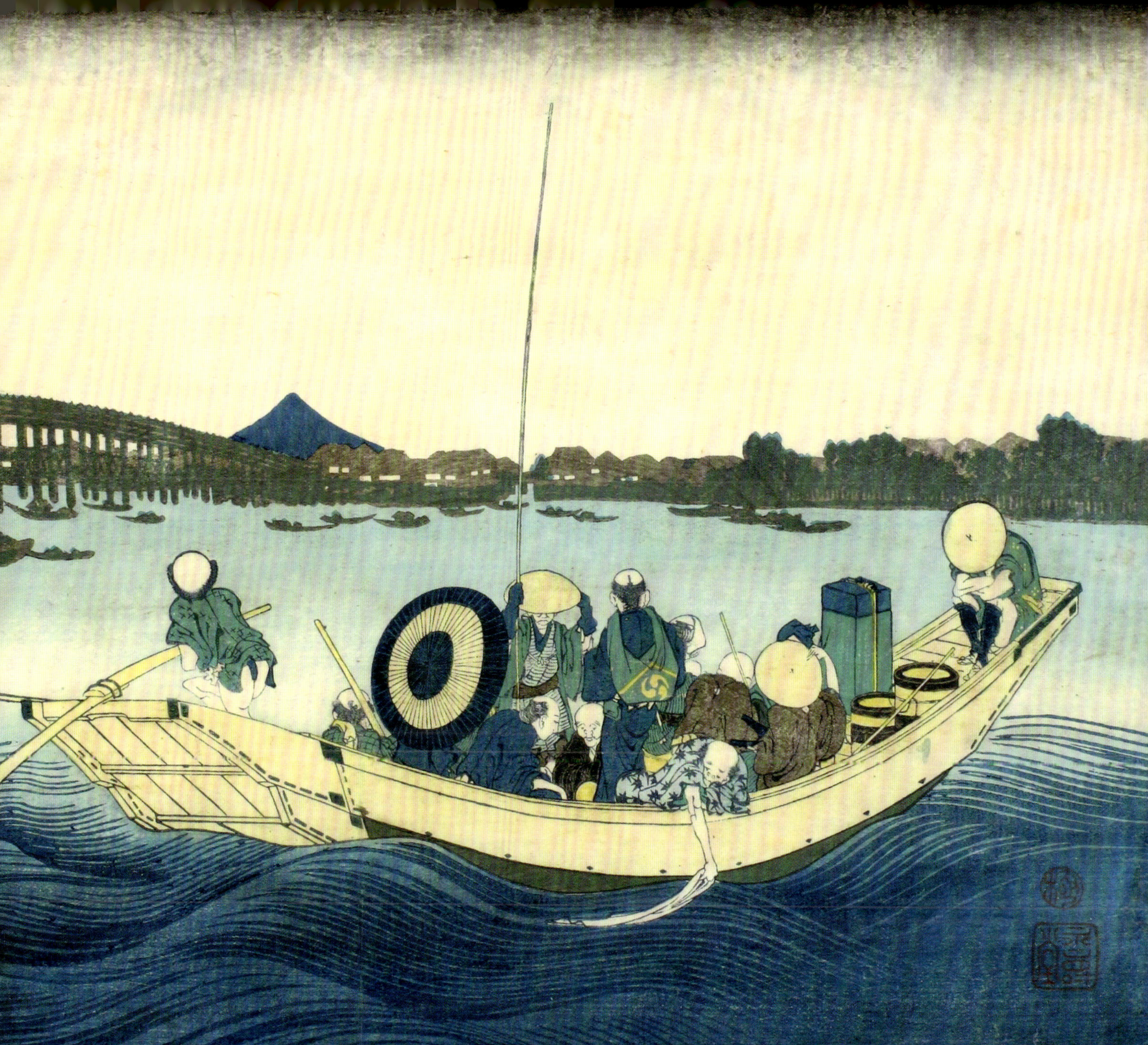

autumn foliage and gentle snowfalls as well as night-time scenes (**Figs. 127–129**); Hiroshi Yoshida (1876–1950), noted for his day and night scenes or images at different times of the day or in different weather conditions; and Ito Shinsui (1898–1972), a painter best known for his images of beautiful women who produced a set of eight scenes of Lake Biwa. *Shin hanga* covered the entire spectrum of Japanese subject matter, but it was in the areas of landscape and beautiful women where they excelled in creating prints of exceptional beauty, reaching a level of craftsmanship in print production never before imagined.

FIG. 120 (above)
Katsushika HOKUSAI
北斎 (1760–1849)
Viewing Sunset Over the Ryogoku Bridge from the Ommaya Embankment, from *Thirty-six Views of Mount Fuji* 富嶽三十六景 御厩川岸より両国橋夕日見 (1826–31)
38.5 x 25 cm
Courtesy of Mita Arts Gallery

Even though the title of this fascinating print is about viewing sunset, only about half of the travelers are actually looking at Mount Fuji in the distance. The man on the right is asleep. Others are washing their laundry or engaging in conversation. What is also amazing is the length of the bridge. The perspective view suggests an unbelievable engineering feat. This print is included as an example of Hokusai utilizing the middle ground. There are no bands of mist separating the foreground from the background.

FIG. 121 (opposite above)
Utagawa HIROSHIGE
広重 (1797–1858)
Full Moon at Takanawa, from *Famous Places in the Eastern Capital*
高輪の明月 (ca. 1831)
38.5 x 23.8 cm
Courtesy of Adachi Institute of Woodcut Prints

This print is pure poetry and shows Hiroshige at his best. The perspective is almost Western in concept. The formation of the flying geese against the circular white moon in front of a Berlin blue sky raises questions as to where the viewer would be standing. In the distance are boats in the harbor. Takanawa was a way station where travelers presented their documents before leaving or entering the city of Edo.

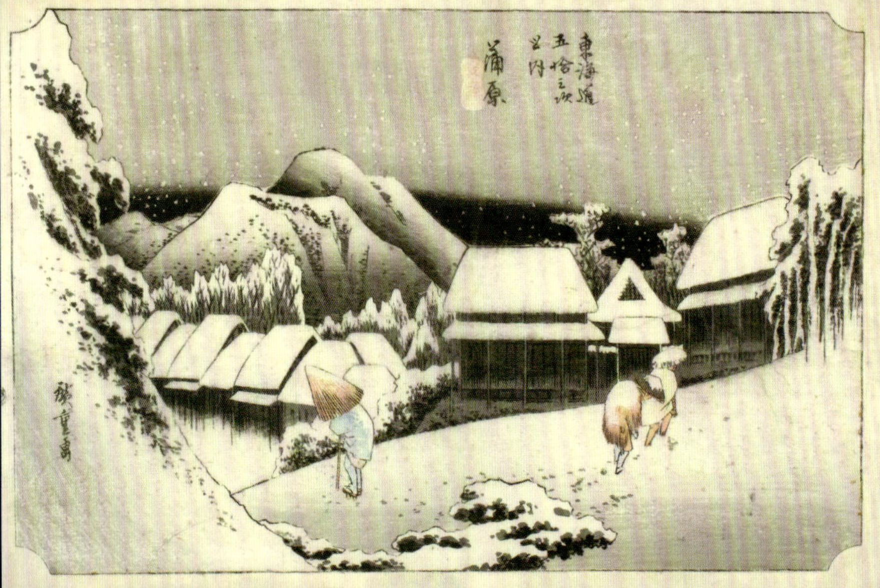

FIG. 122
Utagawa HIROSHIGE
広重 (1797–1858)
Night Snow at Kambara, from *Fifty-three Stations of the Tokaido* 蒲原夜の雪 (1833–4)
27 x 39 cm
Courtesy of Mita Arts Gallery

This masterpiece went through two major versions, one showing the sky becoming almost black at the horizon, the other showing the sky darkening from top down in a *bokashi* technique. The version here, with the darkened horizon, has more drama and emphasizes the cold white snow, especially on the roofs and treetops. This is basically a monochrome print with the addition of yellow, red and blue on the people out in the fierce snowfall. In this very effective composition, the figure on the left leans to the left, the figures on the right lean to the right, while the center is left open with a great deal of graded black detail under the central house. One's eye is led through the snow-covered rocks in the exact center of the composition.

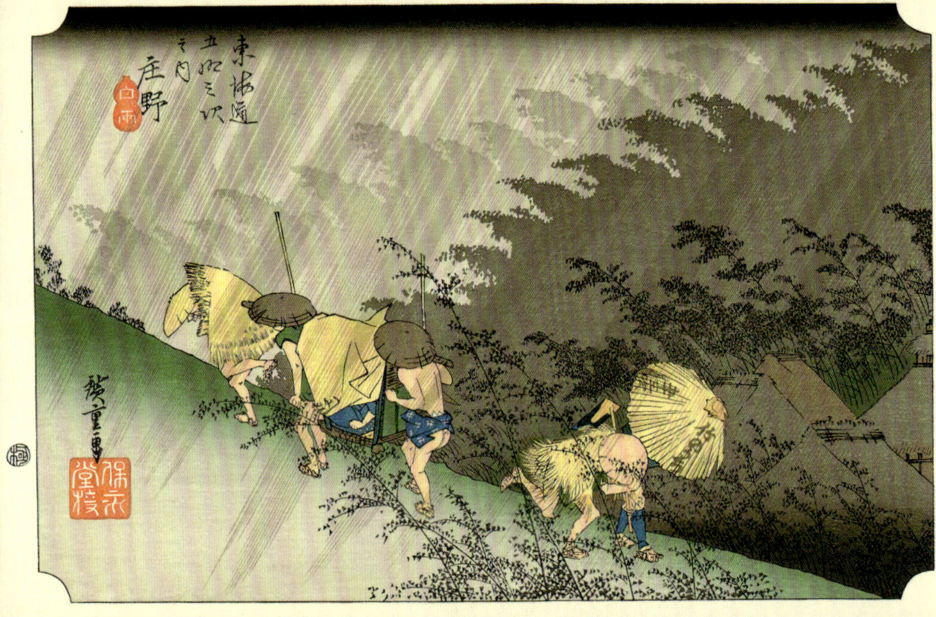

FIG. 123
Utagawa HIROSHIGE
広重 (1797–1858)
White Rain at Shono, from *Fifty-three Stations of the Tokaido* 庄野　白雨 (1833–4)
38 x 25.5 cm
Courtesy of Adachi Institute of Woodcut Prints

Along with the Kambara print (Fig. 122), the Shono print rates as among the finest, if not the finest, design in the series. It is a remarkable example of the skill of the printers in controlling the multitude of grays that depict the pouring rain as it drenches the travelers who move in both directions to escape it. The popularity of this picture also caused many revisions. There is a whole body of literature devoted to the Shono print, including a long article by the great scholar D. Richard Lane on the variations in the details of the Shono, especially on the umbrella at lower right, which bears the characters Takenouchi, the name of the owner of the publishing house. The two *kago* bearers have covered their vehicle with a yellow oilcloth and we can just see the occupant's hand just peeking out from underneath.

FIG. 124 (right)
Utagawa HIROSHIGE
広重 (1797–1858)
Sudden Shower over Shin-Ohashi Bridge and Atake, from *One Hundred Famous Views of Edo*
おお橋あたけの夕立ち (1856–8)
39 x 27 cm
Courtesy of Mita Arts Gallery

When we look at the Shin-Ohashi Bridge and the Shono we can understand why the Japanese say Hiroshige is "wet" compared to Hokusai being "dry." As in other compositions, the figures are running out of the picture plane. The red underskirts of the two women on the left provide a pleasant color accent next to Hiroshige's signature block. Compositionally, Hiroshige creates a fantastic element of visual movement back into the exact center of the picture with the boatman's lumber barge.

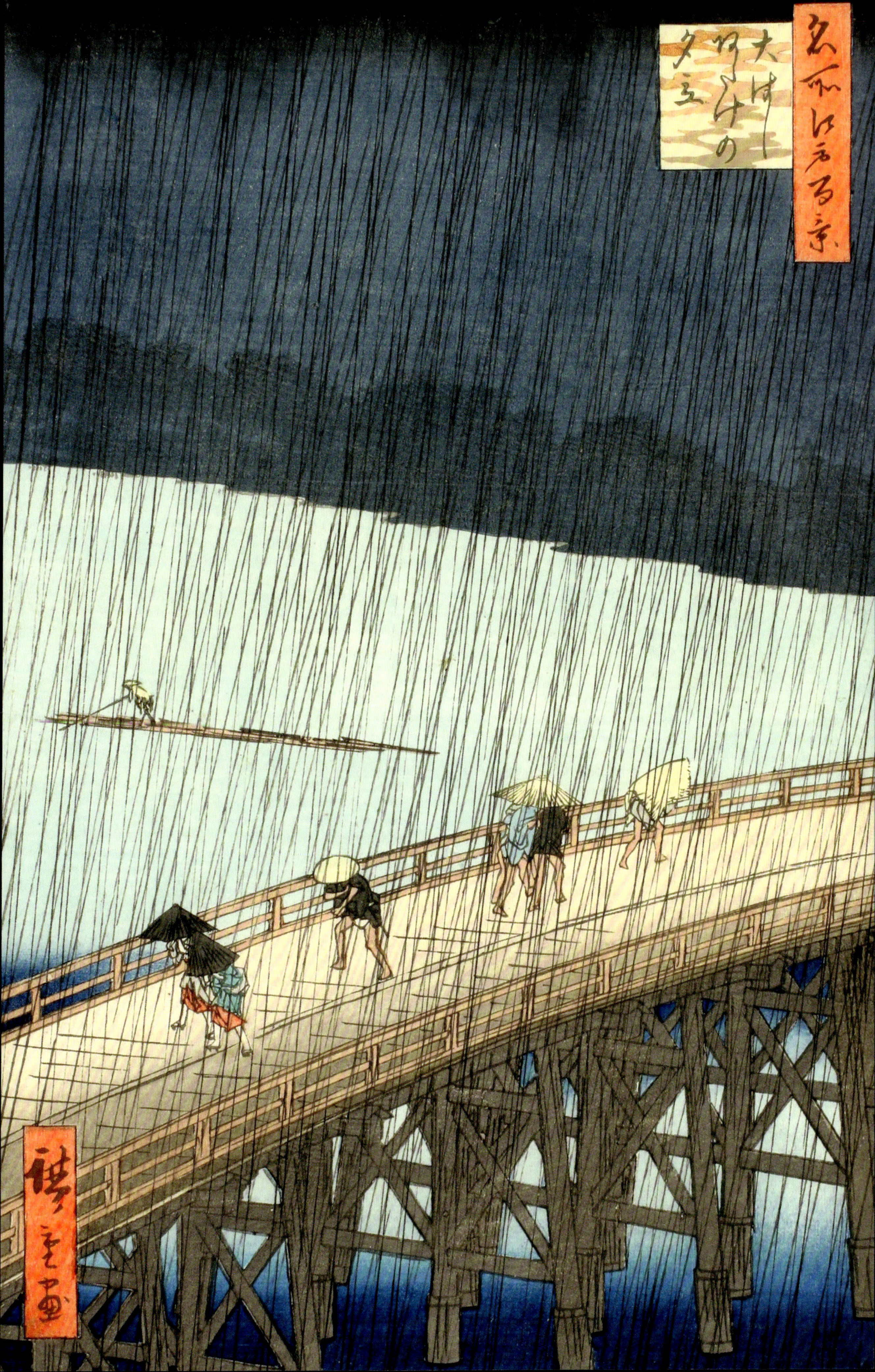
名所江戸百景
大はしあたけの夕立
廣重画

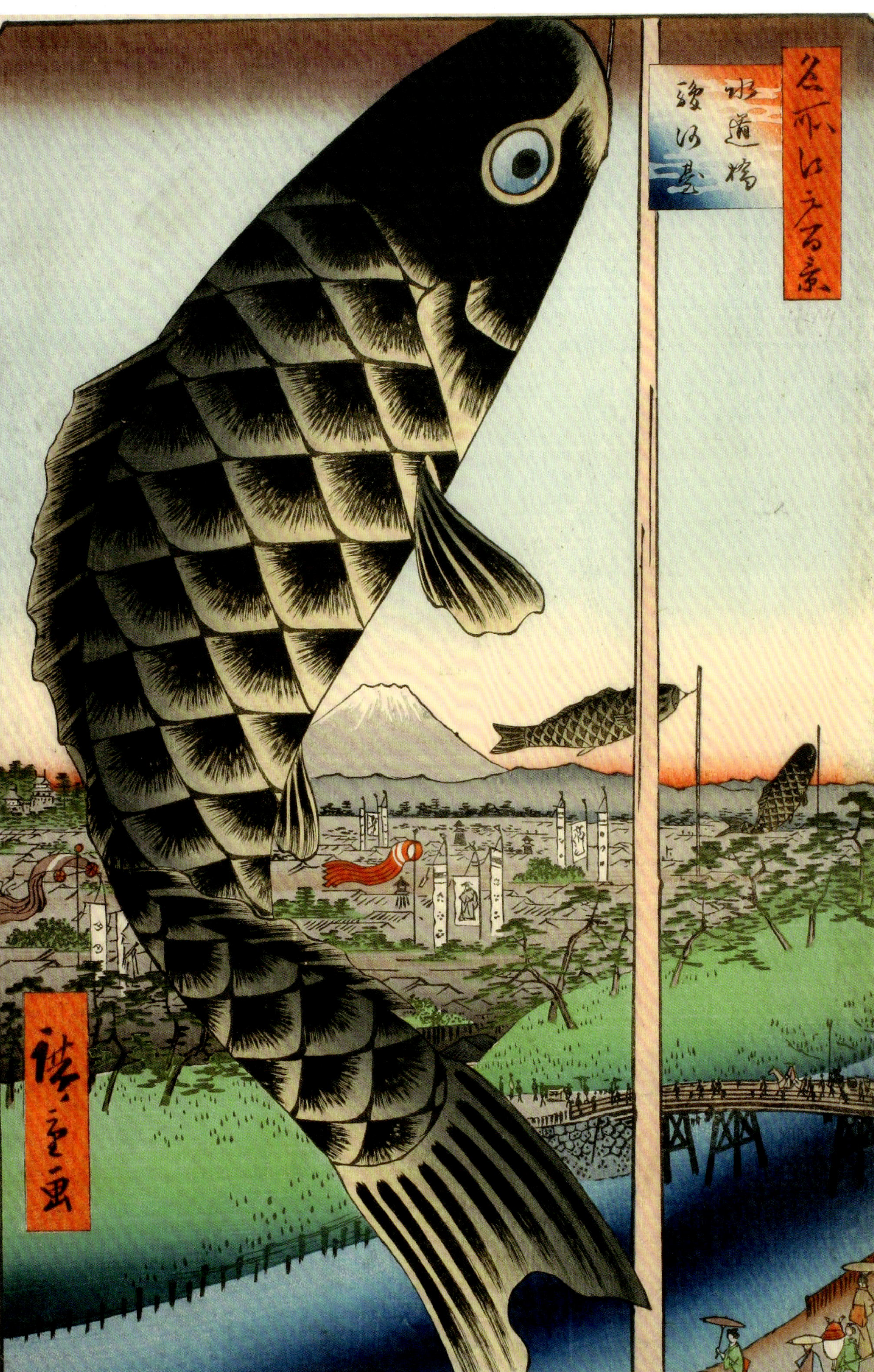
名所江戸百景
水道橋
駿河臺
廣重画

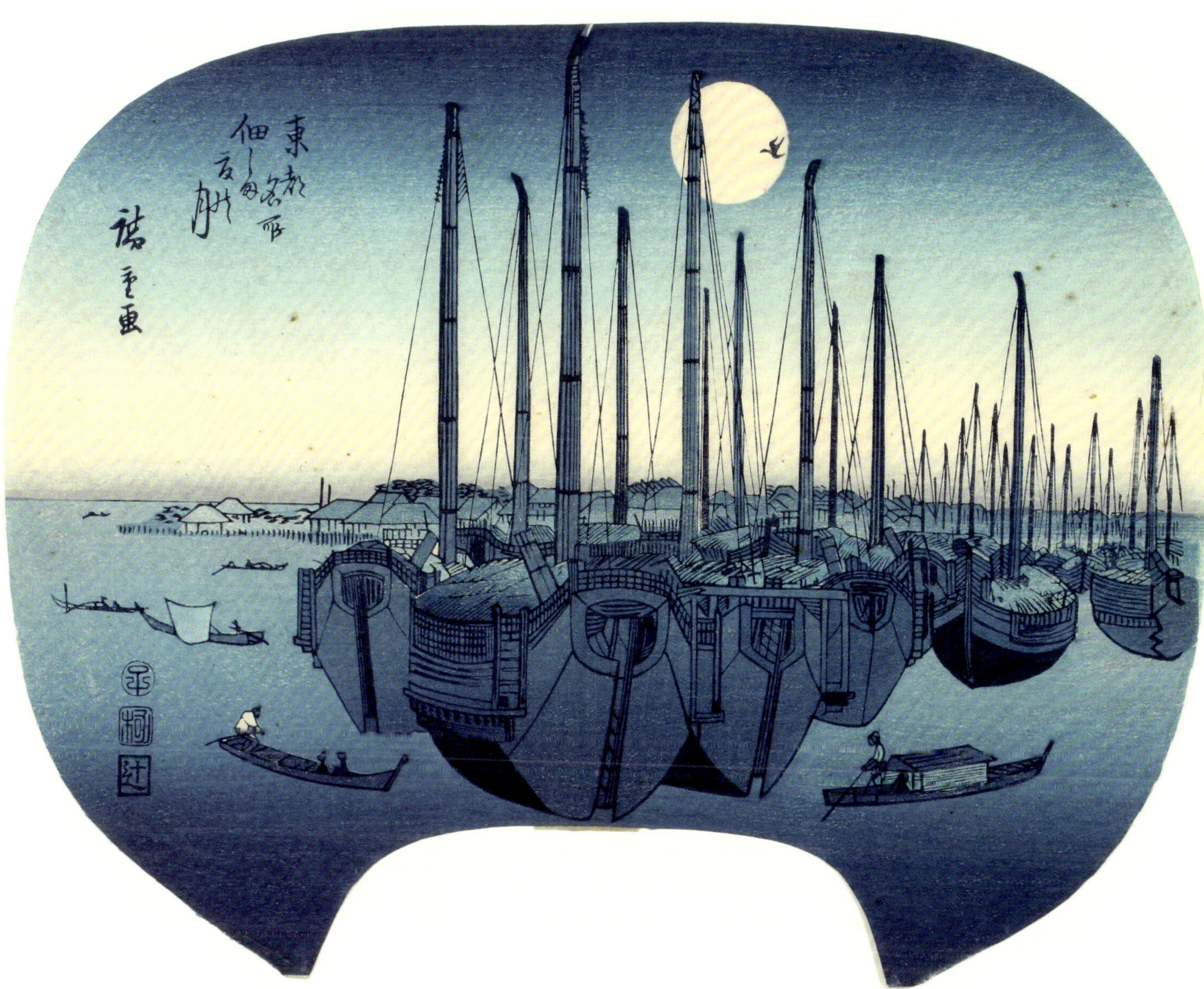

FIG. 125 (left)
Utagawa HIROSHIGE
広重 (1797–1858)
Suido Bridge and Surugadai, from *One Hundred Famous Views of Edo* 名所江戸百景 水道橋駿河台 (1856–8)
22.2 x 50.8 cm
Courtesy of Mita Arts Gallery

There is a wonderful *tour de force* in this composition. The title of the print comprises only a minor element in the middle foreground and our eye wanders back to Mount Fuji. But it is the use of *bokashi* by the printer in the scales of the carp streamers, which are flown annually on Boy's Day, that imparts a sense of drama and mystery to what is a common subject. Other streamers and banners take us into the distance. The central streamer is especially dynamic when we see the small figures at lower right and realize the difference in scale. What adds to the mystery is where the viewer is standing to be able to see such a view.

FIG. 126
Utagawa HIROSHIGE
広重 (1797–1858)
Full Moon at Tsukuda Island, from *Sixty-nine Stations of the Kisokaido* 佃しま夜の月 (1852)
27 x 39 cm
Author's Collection

This *uchiwa-e* (fan print) is a wonderful example of *aizome-e*. The luxuriousness of the Berlin blue in all its multitude of tones is completely captivating. Fan prints were a very popular art form but, of course, were subject to wear and tear when they were waved back and forth in the heat of summer. Thousands were printed but only a fraction survived.

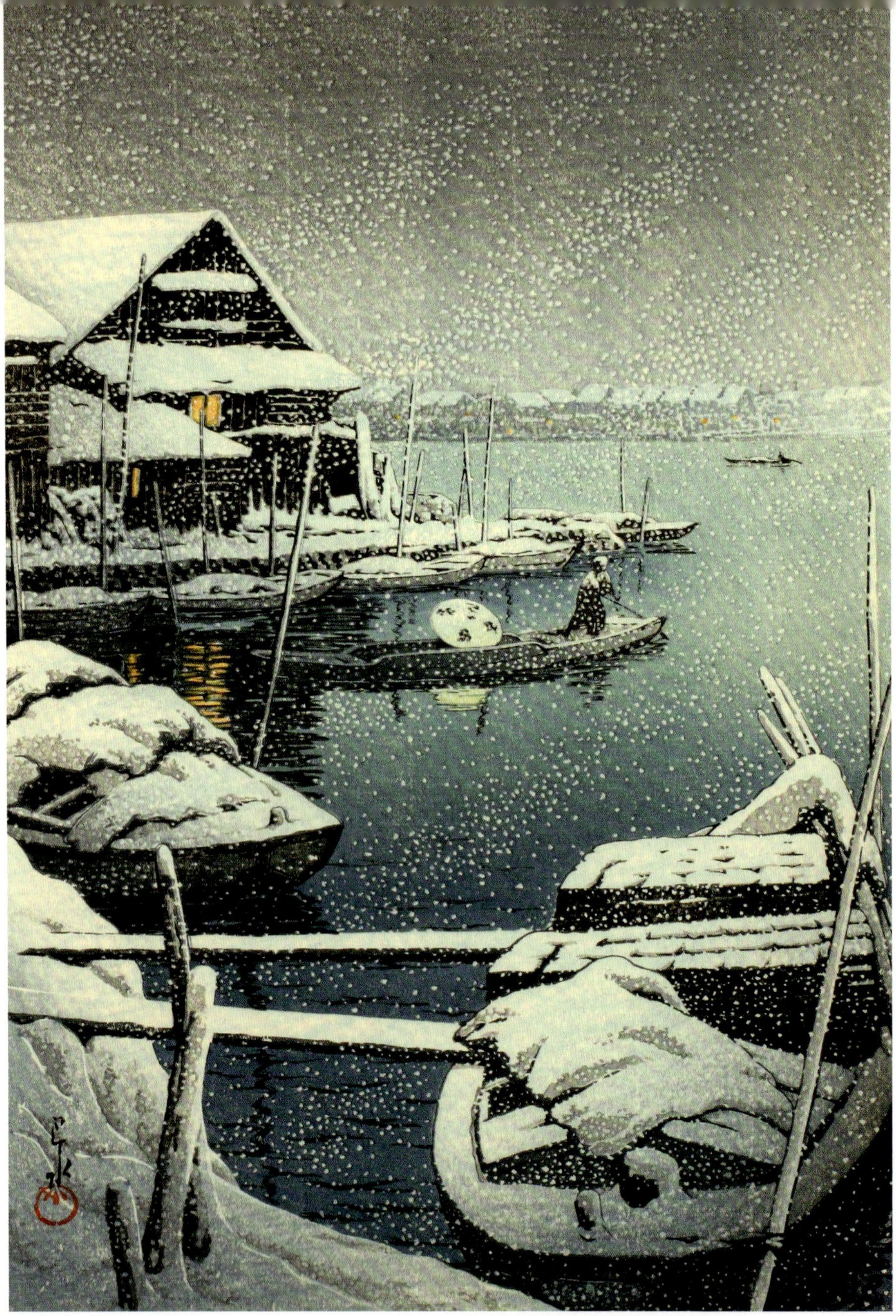

FIG. 127
Kawase HASUI
川瀬 巴水 (1883–1957)
Snow at Mukojima 雪の向島 (1931)
36.1 x 24.1 cm
Courtesy of Mita Arts Gallery

Hasui, one of the most prominent of the early twentieth-century woodblock print artists and the first to be named a Living National Treasure in Japan, continued the poetic aesthetic of Hiroshige, with numerous delicate gradations of color. There is a clear separation of space between the foreground, middle ground and background. The human element is there in the boat in the center, giving us a sense of scale. The lights in the windows indicate human occupation. We shiver as we feel the heavy falling snow.

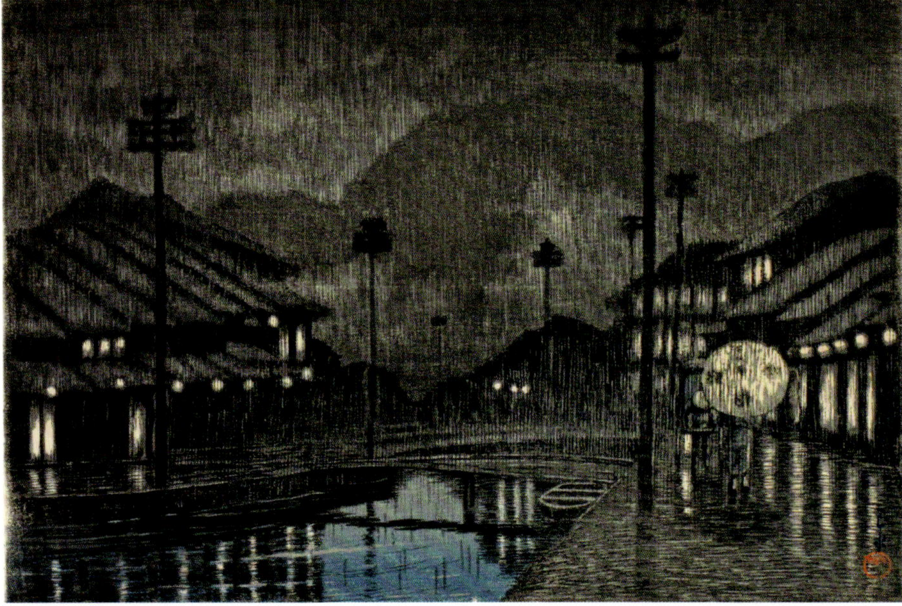

FIG. 128
Kawase HASUI
川瀬 巴水 (1883–1957)
Kinosaki Tajima 但馬城崎 (1924)
23.9 x 36.2 cm
Courtesy of Mita Arts Gallery

Like no other artist, Hasui was capable of creating moods with his designs. Unlike in the prints of Hokusai and Hiroshige, here the rain is real, wet and lonely, a night when we would rather stay at home. The landscape is pure reality.

FIG. 129 (right)
Kawase HASUI
川瀬 巴水 (1883–1957)
Zojo Temple, Shiba 芝増上寺 (1925)
36.4 x 24 cm
Courtesy of Mita Arts Gallery

This print truly recalls Hiroshige in showing how humanity resists the forces of nature. The woman can barely cope with the snow and the wind that is blowing her kimono as she struggles toward the temple. Hasui spent a large part of his life traveling in order to catch views like this "live."

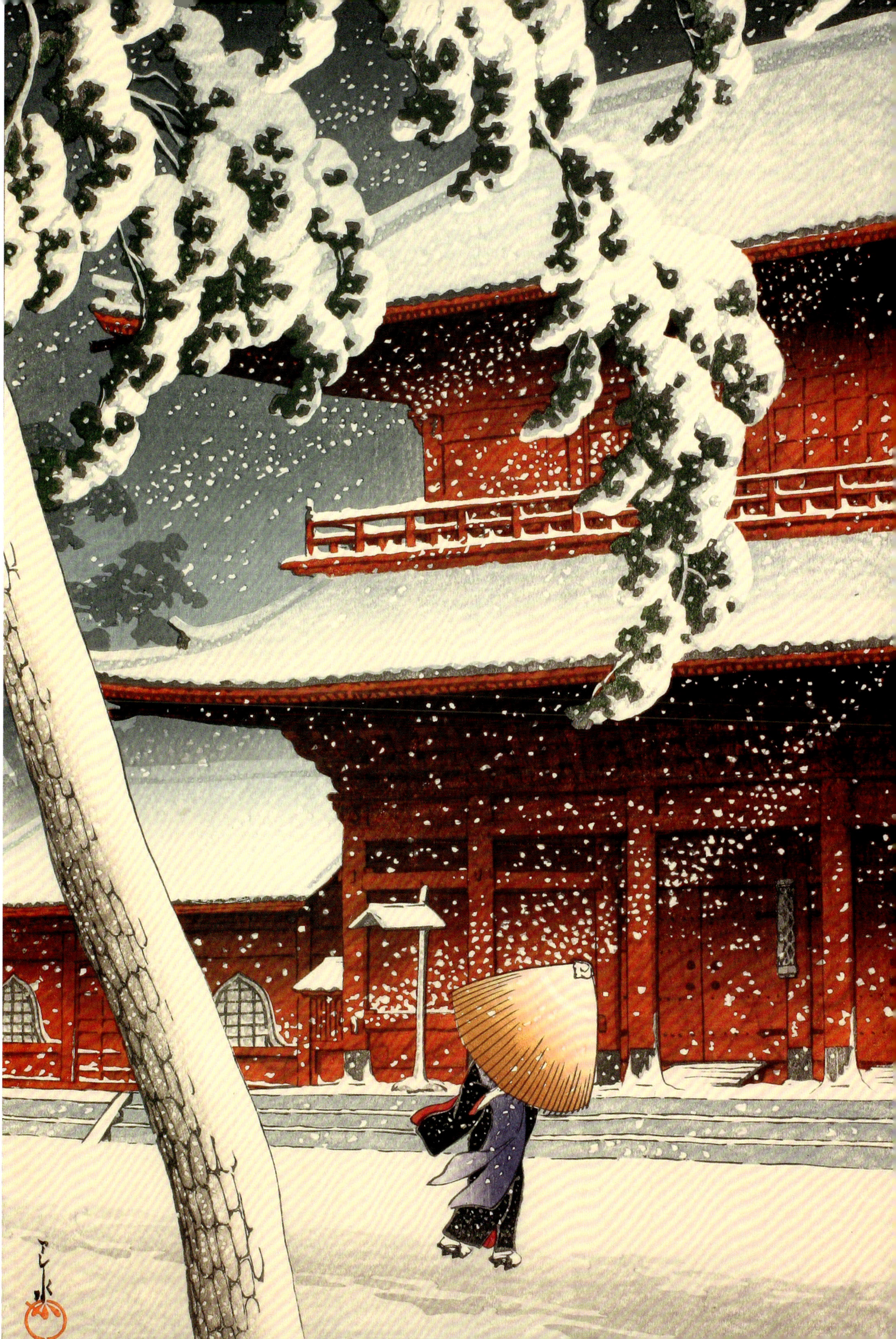

CHAPTER EIGHT

Sensual Pleasures

FIG. 130
Suzuki HARUNOBU
春信 (1725–70)
Shunga 春画 (1770s)
39 x 27 cm
Courtesy of Mita Arts Gallery

Voyeurism was a common theme in *shunga* prints. Houses had simple sliding doors made of paper. Sound was easily carried from one space to another, and the curious were tempted to watch what they might have heard in the corridor or room next door. This print depicts a maidservant watching the beginning of the sex act as the woman gently inserts the man's penis into her vagina. The maid is masturbating as she watches what is going on. We can see her exposed right knee as her left hand plays with herself. The couple are not on the bedding yet, as it is still neatly folded in the back of the room. The space is beautifully designed. The eye travels from the foreground diagonal pattern to the center, then back to the right and again to the left with the repeat of the diagonal. Harunobu was a master of composition. His erotic subjects are treated with the same refinement and sophistication as his other subjects.

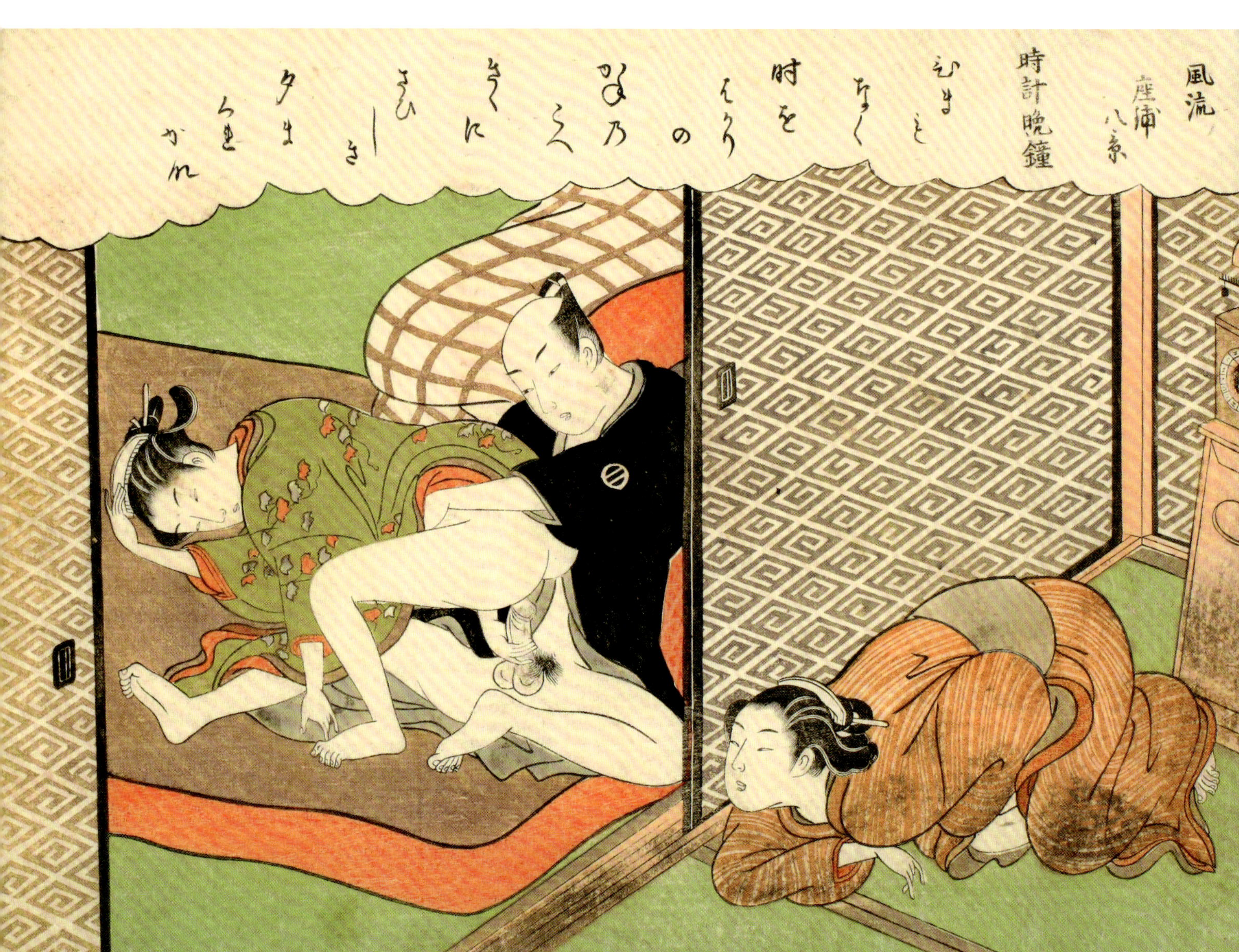

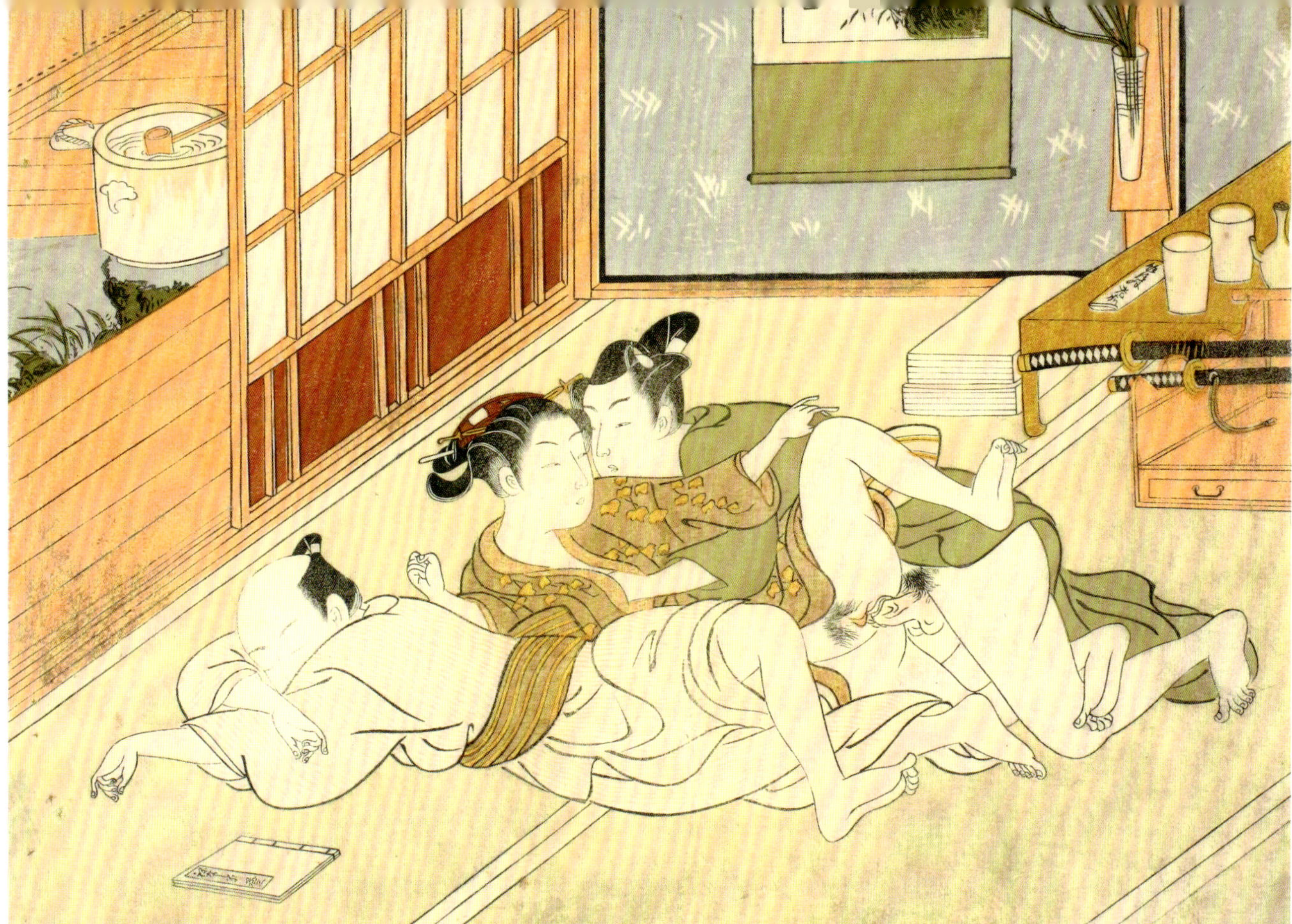

FIG. 131
Suzuki HARUNOBU
春信 (1725–70)
Shunga 春画 (1770s)
19.5 x 26 cm
Courtesy of Mita Arts Gallery

Another common theme in *shunga* involves an amorous couple making love with an intruder, an onlooker or an unaware third person present. Here, the husband is sound asleep after reading while a young lover engages the man's wife in foreplay. This is a domestic interior, not a brothel, evidenced by the presence of the two swords in a special stand. The two large drinking vessels on the table, probably glasses as they have no surface design, suggest they have been drinking some type of Western beverage. This is a detail that Harunobu would not miss. The visitor has left one *zori* (shoe) on the veranda. One is left wondering about the story behind the print.

Shunga, literally "springtime picture," "spring" being a typical euphemism for erotica, is the generic Japanese term for erotic prints, paintings, scrolls and books. Erotic art has been produced in China, Japan, India and other Asian cultures for centuries, long before it became prevalent in the Western world. In Japan, the tradition of *shunga* began in the seventh or eighth century, mostly in the form of painted hand scrolls depicting sexual scandals from the Imperial courts and monasteries. But it was the genre of *ukiyo-e* woodblock prints produced during the Edo period (1603–1868) depicting the full range of sensual pleasures that reached the creative peak of erotic art. By the beginning of the twentieth century, however, much of the production of *shunga* had been driven underground by repeated governmental attempts to suppress it. The introduction of Western technologies at the beginning of the Meiji era (1868–1912), in particular mass reproduction methods like photography and lithography, had further serious consequences for *shunga*, which could not compete with erotic photography. Today, a resurgence of interest in *shunga*, both in Japan and abroad, has led to a reassessment of *shunga* as being among the finest of all calligraphic art.

Happily, attitudes in Japan regarding *shunga* have also changed over the years, resulting in the publication of large numbers of books containing uncensored material. Twenty years ago, this chapter could not have been illustrated in the way it is. The Japanese government took a very long time to come to terms with one of the finest art forms in its cultural history.

When I first came to Japan, books about *shunga* had the genitals either blocked out with squares of blank paper or cropped out of the picture. This, of course, only drew more attention to what was known, but not seen, and reinforced the view that erotica was bad, wicked, vile, wrong or corrupt. It was only with the awareness of European acceptance of *shunga* in public exhibitions and the accompanying catalogs that reached Japan, as well as the publication of a number of *shunga* studies in Japan and the West from the mid-1970s, that the government slowly relaxed its censorship of sex-related illustrations. *Shunga* was no longer regarded as a kind of medieval pornography but considered an equal partner with other, more acceptable

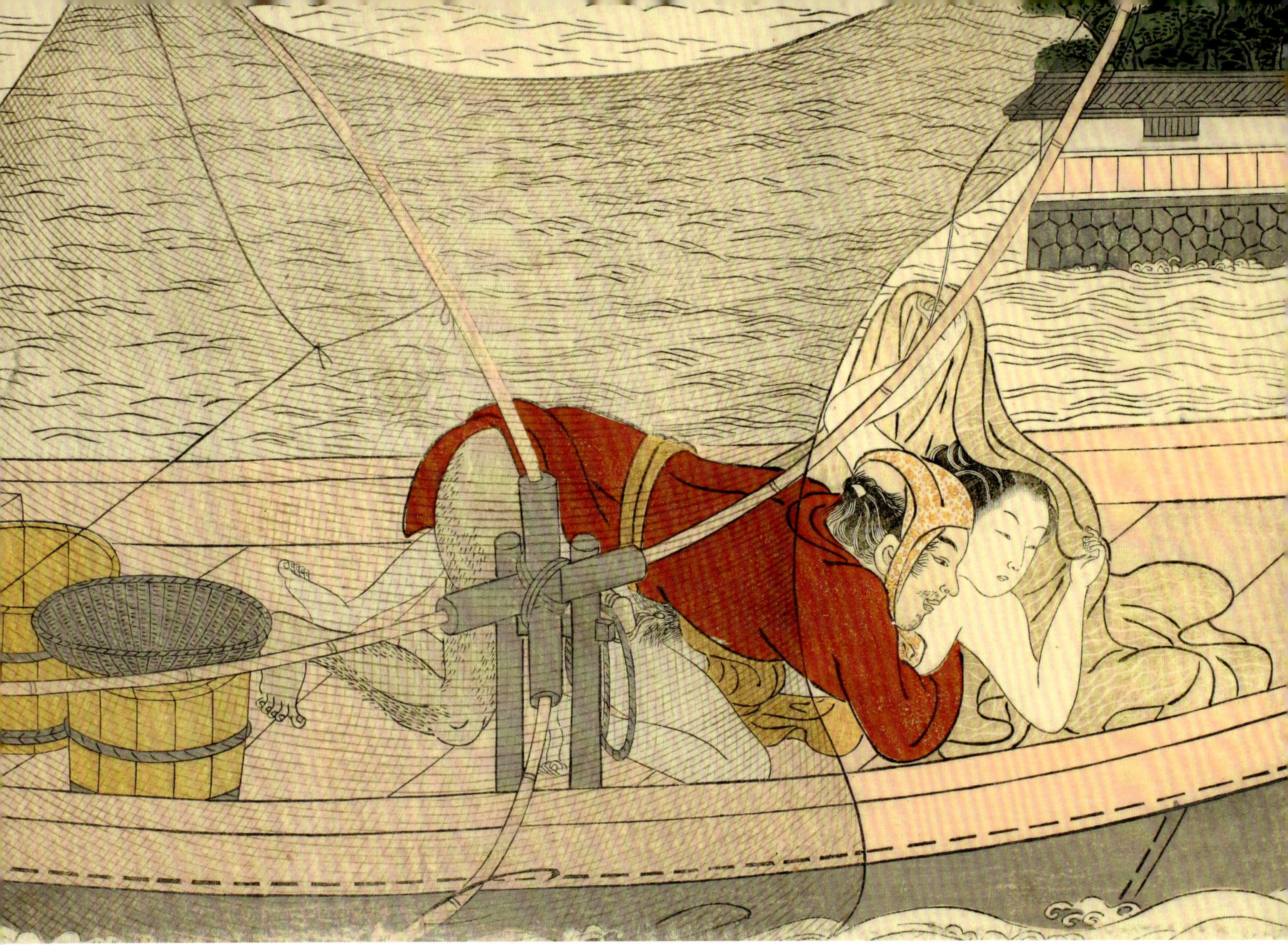

themes in the world of Japanese printmaking. Technically and historically, *shunga* prints have, of course, always been an integral part of *ukiyo-e*.

The *shunga* print was both the natural outgrowth and the fullest expression of urban culture and entertainment during the Edo and early Meiji periods in Japan. As noted in earlier chapters, the "floating world" of the major cities was transient and hedonistic, advocating decadent Bacchanalian goals. It was also a male-dominated arena where men, in the seventeenth century, outnumbered women by almost two to one. With many *daimyo* and *samurai* obliged to spend half the year in Edo (today's Tokyo), removed from their families in the provinces, as well as the newly rich townspeople (*chonin*) looking for pleasure, the market for prostitution was enormous. To control and police the burgeoning sex industry in Edo, the brothel district of Yoshiwara was set up and licensed by the government.

Enclosed by a wall and with its entrance through one gate, Yoshiwara had its own culture and ethical codes, and provided every possible service. Life for the courtesans at Yoshiwara imitated the social structures outside its wall. Living in a world within a world, they were ranked and given privileges accordingly. Although the women represented in *ukiyo-e* epitomize female beauty, the reality of their everyday existence was harsh, and their professional life was usually over by the time they were in their mid-twenties.

Whereas the *ukiyo-e* movement as a whole sought to express an idealization of contemporary urban life, *shunga* sought to express the sexual relations of the ordinary townspeople—husbands and wives, courtesans, merchants, artisans, farmers, *kabuki* actors, gigolos, etc.—but in a humorous and lighthearted way. Old and young alike are shown engaging in a great variety of mostly heterosexual but also homosexual lovemaking techniques, situations,

FIG. 132
Suzuki HARUNOBU
春信 (1725–70)
Shunga 春画 (1770s)
19.5 x 26 cm
Courtesy of Mita Arts Gallery

In this print, a fisherman takes time off from his work to enjoy a little fun with a young woman. Who could she be? Her *kimono* is rather plain and there are no adornments in her hair. She is not a courtesan, perhaps a young person from the docks. They are lying behind a large fishing net designed to catch very small fish, judging from the basket and relatively small wood containers. The man is hairy, a feature almost never present on a *samurai* or nobleman. Only fishermen, carpenters or other tradesmen would be given hair on their arms and legs.

FIG. 133
Suzuki HARUNOBU
春信 (1725–70)
Shunga 春画 (1770s)
19.5 x 26 cm
Courtesy of Mita Arts Gallery

A number of elements make this picture, which shows love on a veranda near a stream with a white bird, interesting. The area around the genitals has been rubbed away so that the color and details are not visible. This commonly occurs when a print is used as a stimulus for masturbation. The oxidation on the ink on the wooden veranda is a much sought-after effect by Japanese collectors. Behind the woman, whose toes are curled in sexual bliss, is an ashtray and container for a pipe and tobacco. Tobacco was introduced by the Portuguese and smoking became a popular pastime during the Edo period.

positions and possibilities, including a wide range of fetishes. Couples are often shown in unrealistic contorted positions with exaggerated genitalia (enlarged for greater visibility given the small scale of most *shunga*) and wearing expressions of sexual ecstasy. They are almost always fully clothed or covered with a blanket. Nudity was not inherently erotic in Edo-period Japan, where people were used to seeing the opposite sex naked in communal baths. Clothing in *shunga* helped to identify the occupations of the people in the pictures and draw attention to parts of the body that were exposed.

Symbolism also features widely in the intimate scenes depicted in *shunga*. Objects abound with sexual innuendo. Plum blossoms represent virginity; bonsai trees take on the suggestion of the male's erect penis; tissues indicate impending or past ejaculation; silk robes symbolize the curves and undulations of the female vagina. Any accompanying text, such as poetry or dialog, in a picture further enhances the sexual message. *Shunga* tests the knowledge of the viewer to find hidden values and elements, which, once understood, make viewing the pictures so much more enjoyable.

In spite of its explicit sexual content, *shunga* carried very little stigma. The perception of sexuality in Edo-period Japan differed from that of the modern Western world. Sex was regarded as a natural enjoyable event. The body was a spirit, just as the earth or any other natural aspect of creation was. There

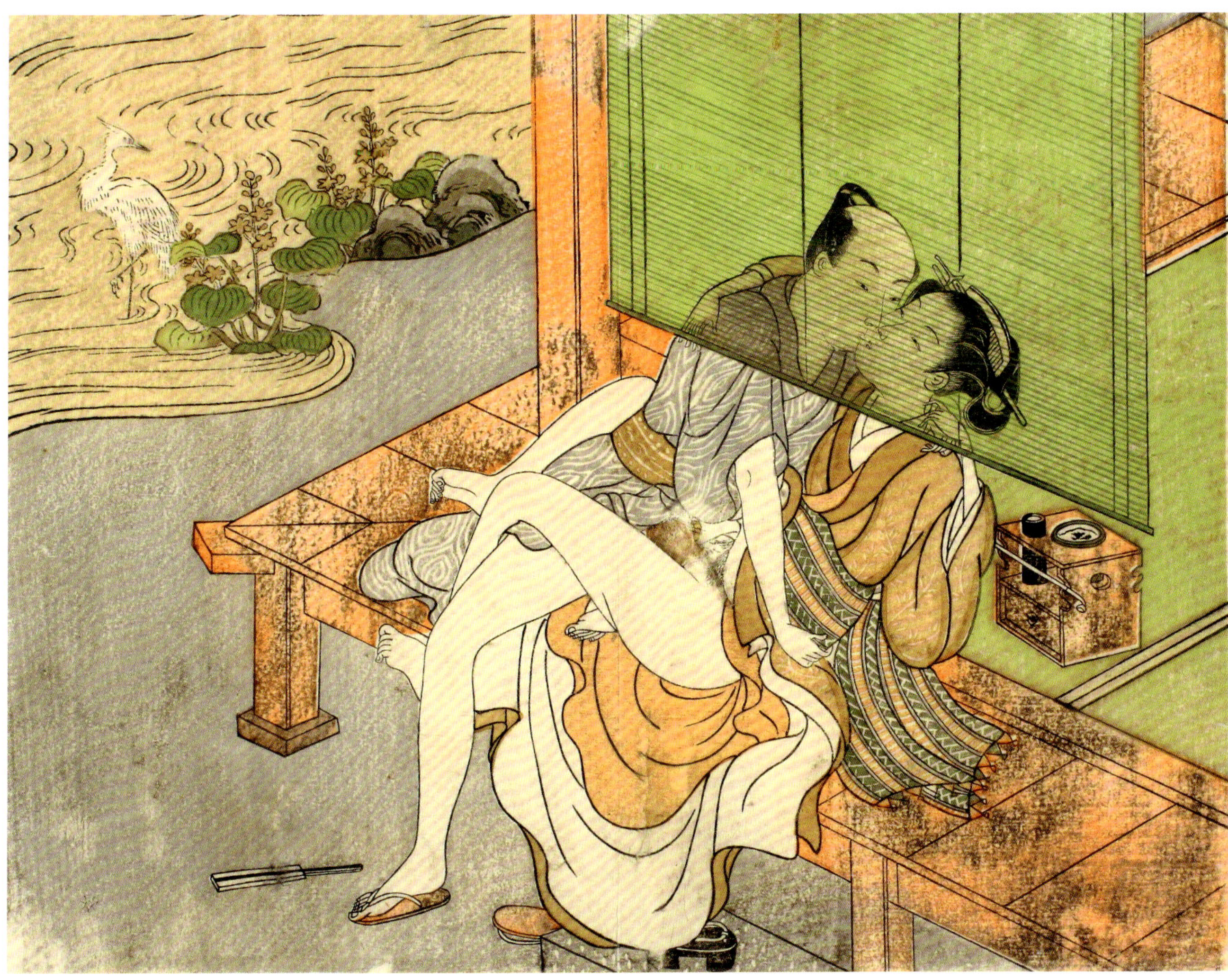

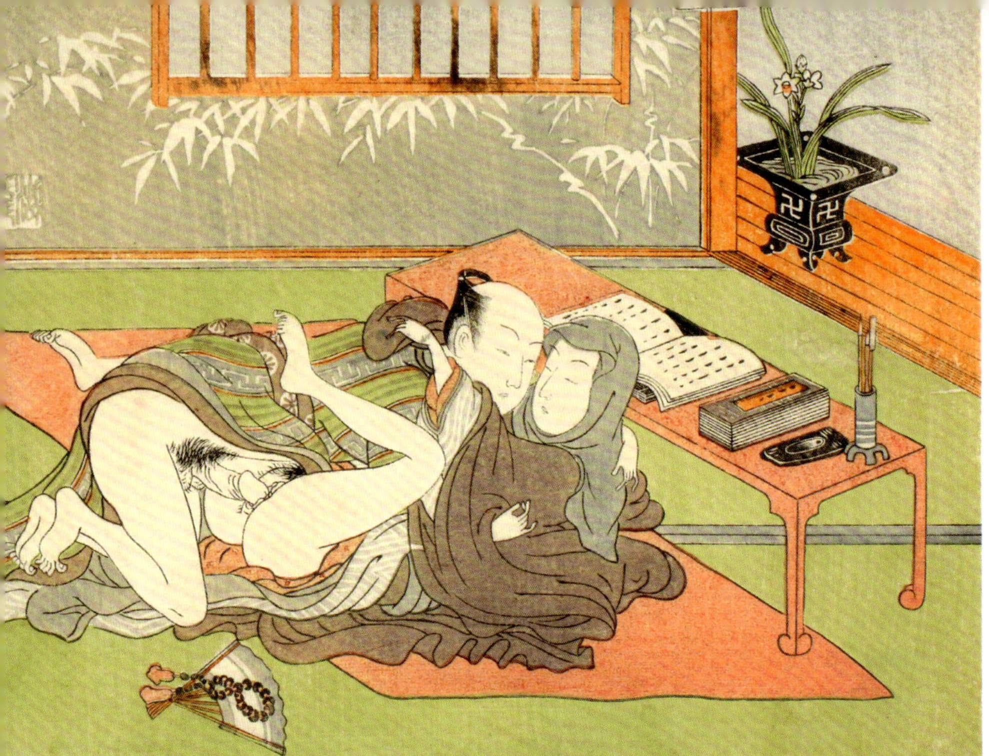

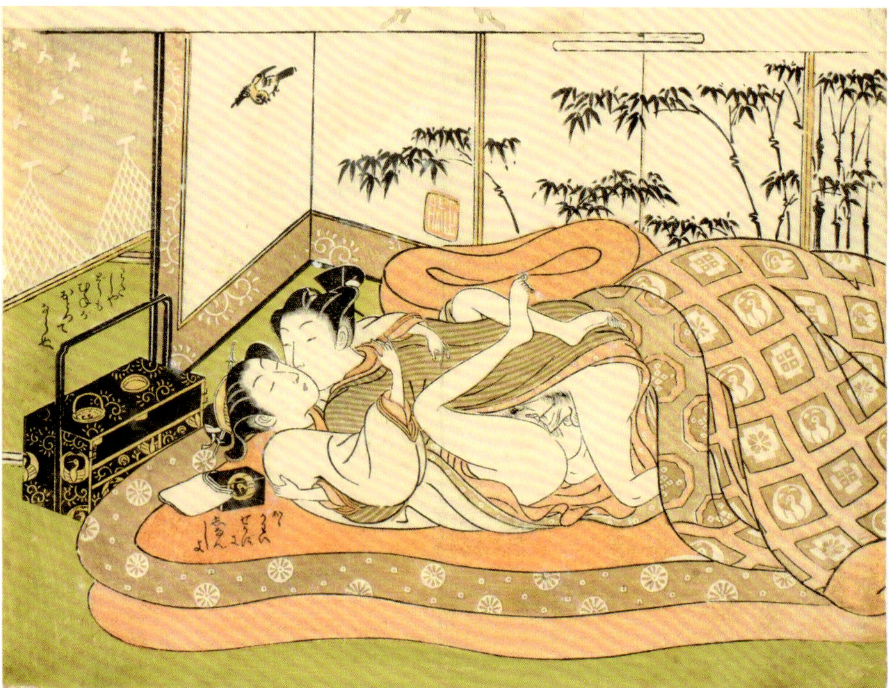

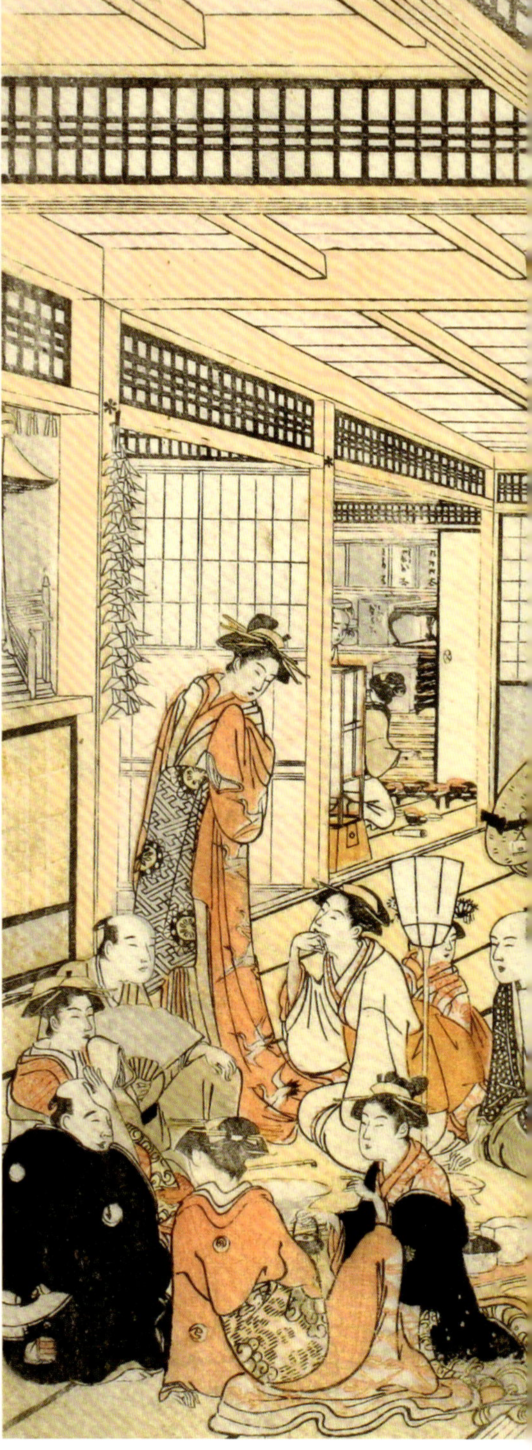

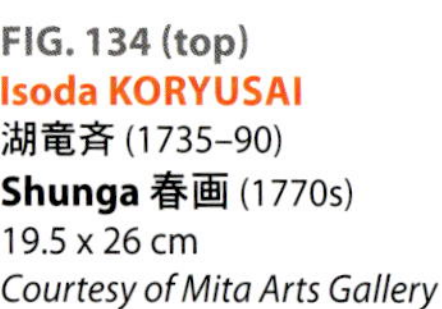

FIG. 134 (top)
Isoda KORYUSAI
湖竜斉 (1735–90)
Shunga 春画 (1770s)
19.5 x 26 cm
Courtesy of Mita Arts Gallery

Koryusai was a prolific artist of *shunga*, with over 500 extant designs in this field, typically issued in sets of twelve. Here, we witness an intruder making love to a nun in the middle of her prayers. It is a very intimate setting. Her prayer beads are lying next to her. On the writing table is a book of prayers, brushes and an ink stone. Also on the table is another book, narrower than the prayer book. This is a copybook where one would write a poem or, in this case, copy one of the sutras from the prayer book. This is an interesting detail that would be missed by most people. There is no sign of a struggle, which means that the visitor is welcome. Sex obviously did not conflict with the nun's religious beliefs.

FIG. 135 (below left)
Isoda KORYUSAI
湖竜斉 (1735–90)
Shunga 春画 (1770s)
19.5 x 26 cm
Courtesy of Mita Arts Gallery

This is obviously a brothel scene. At the head of the *futon* (bedding) is an elaborate lacquer tobacco case, which would not be seen in an ordinary home. The courtesan has also prepared folded tissue paper and placed it next to her head. Tissue is a typical symbol of *shunga*. Neatly folded paper means the sex act has just begun, while crumpled paper strewn around indicates it is over. The bamboo folding screen creates a lovely framework for the figures. This is a charming quiet, intimate scene, very comfortable to look at. We feel we are not disturbing the lovers by watching them enjoy themselves.

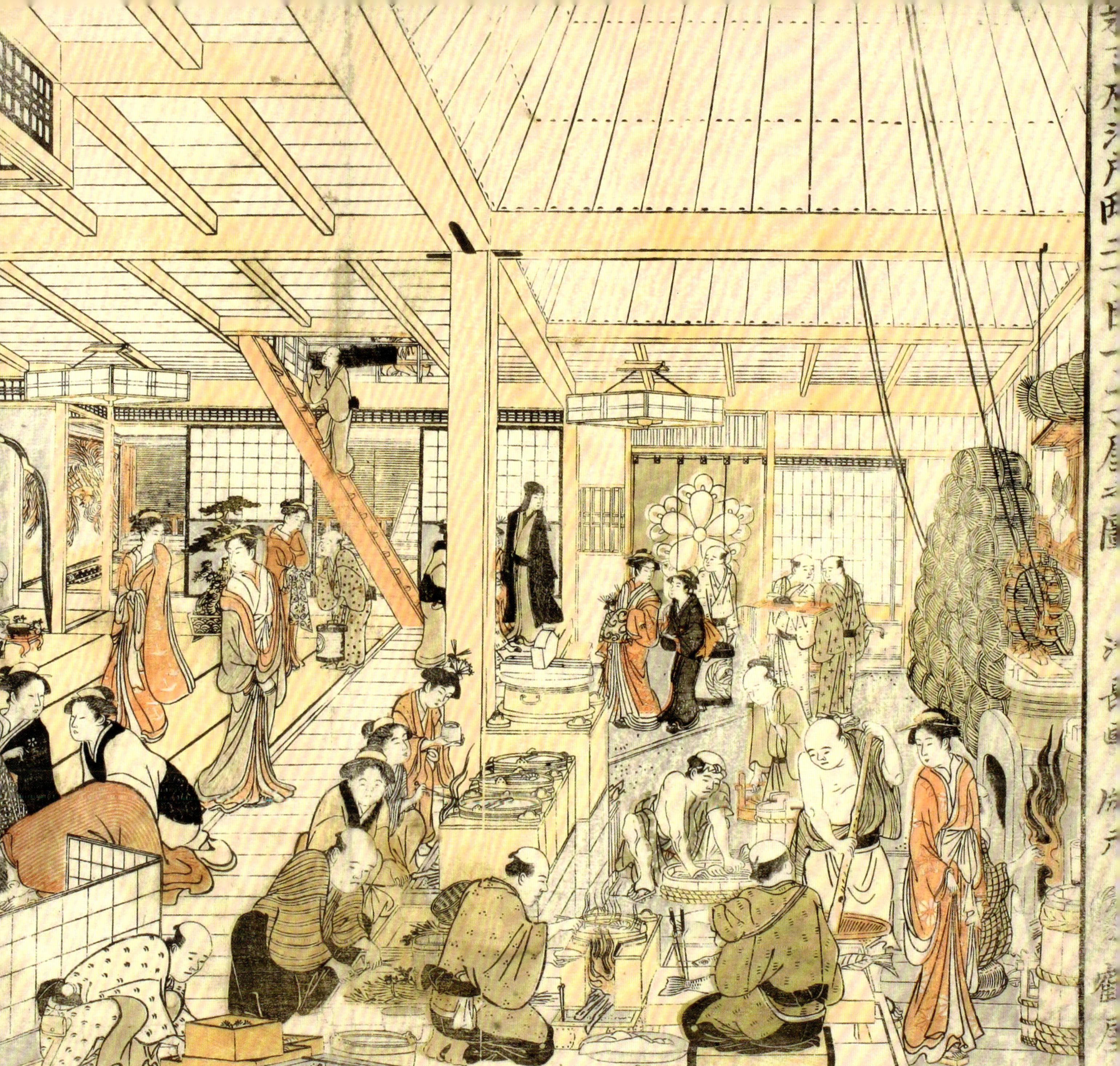

FIG. 136
Torii KIYONAGA
清長 (1752–1815)
Courtesans' House Choshiya in Shin-Yoshiwara
新吉原丁子屋の図 (1780s)
29.9 x 43.7 cm
Courtesy of Mita Arts Gallery

After Yoshiwara burnt down in 1657, it was rebuilt further out of central Edo with government support, and became known as Shin-Yoshiwara (New Yoshiwara). This fascinating print shows typical activities inside a brothel. Kiyonaga took artistic license to remove the walls separating the kitchen from the guest area, allowing us to see bales of rice stacked up on the right and cooking activities in front. Rice is cooking in the largest cauldron in the center. The other three cauldrons hold soup. The man with his *kimono* off his shoulders is grating sesame in a mortar with a large pestle. The man in the foreground with his back to us is cutting up a large fish for *sashimi*. The guests to the left are enjoying lively conversation with the courtesan. To their left is a *kami-dana* (household altar) and a row of folded paper cranes. At center back someone is going upstairs to where the private rooms are situated. No swords are to be seen, as it was obligatory for those wearing them to leave them at the entrance.

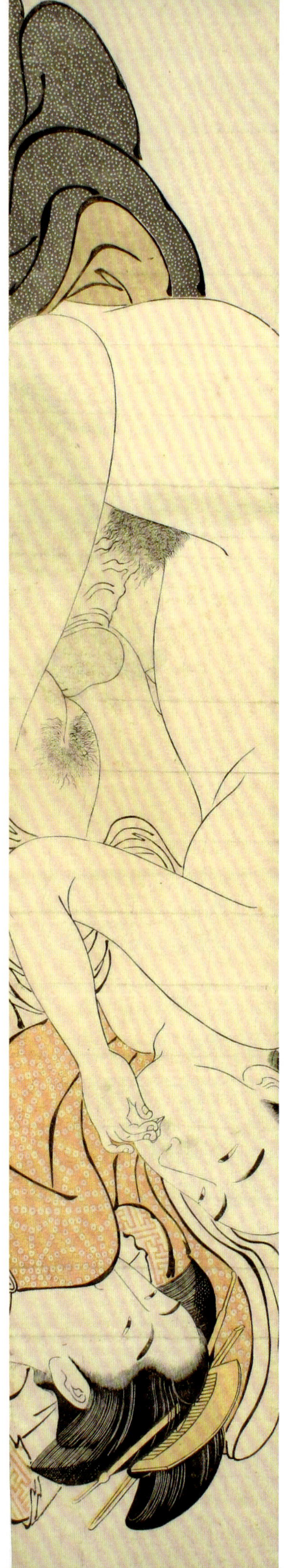

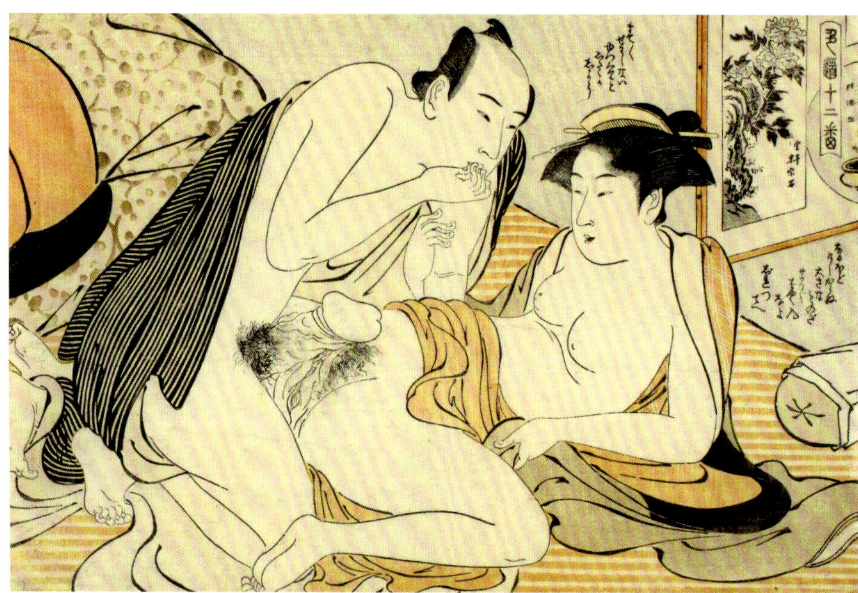

FIG. 137 (left)
Torii KIYONAGA
清長 (1752–1815)
Volumes of a Sleeve 袖の巻 (1780s)
11.8 x 68.3 cm
Courtesy of Mita Arts Gallery

This is an extremely rare work in the typically tall, narrow format of the pillar print (*hashira-e*). Such prints were designed for affixing to the thin vertical pillar separating the interior paneling of a home. Unusually, this print, titled *Sode no maki*, comes from a well-known set of twelve prints made especially for private viewing, not for a pillar. It takes an exceptionally fine artist to compose in this format. It is very seldom, if ever, that a complete set is seen.

FIG. 138 (above)
Torii KIYONAGA
清長 (1752–1815)
Shunga 色道十二番 (1780s)
27 x 39 cm
Courtesy of Mita Arts Gallery

Reflecting the larger format of this print, the figures are bigger, occupying almost the entire space. The genitals are also disproportionately large. It is a skillfully conceived composition. The stripes on the man's *kimono* and the flooring create an abstract framework around the nude figures. The man is putting his fingers to his mouth to taste the woman's excretions during foreplay.

FIG. 139 (opposite)
Kitagawa UTAMARO
歌麿 (1754–1806)
Shunga 春画 (1800s)
27 x 39 cm
Courtesy of Mita Arts Gallery

In keeping with the large print format, the man's genitals assume a comical size. Compared with many *shunga*, there is a lot of personality in the faces. The woman is truly enjoying the moment. She has a look of complete satisfaction on her face. The positioning of the figures is quite unrealistic though. The man's toe in the woman's face is an amusing touch and would provide enjoyment to the viewer.

was no equivalent to the Western concept of pornography as moral corruption or sense of personal sin. Indeed, the concept of sin in the Japanese Shinto religion does not exist as it does in the Judeo-Christian world. In Japan, order and social obedience play a greater role than the right or wrong in the way a person uses his body.

Accepting *shunga* pictures was a natural extension of this attitude toward sex. In rural communities, fertility rites relating to the soil and other aspects of agricultural created a phallic worship, which can still be observed in some shrines and during festivals, where the phallic symbol is venerated. Superstitions and customs also surrounded *shunga*. It was considered lucky, for example, for a *samurai* to carry *shunga* into battle as protection against harm. Similarly, *shunga* placed in warehouses and homes was believed to provide protection against fire.

Shunga prints were initially made in the form of painted horizontal hand scrolls (*emakimono*) or small, folded illustrated "pillow books" (*enpon*). Only later did they appear in separate broad sheets. In both the scrolls and *enpon*, the pictures are presented in an unrelated sequence of sexual tableaux rather than a structured narrative, which partly explains why it was easy to later dismount and sell many of them as separate sheets. The pictures created were almost always horizontal, primarily because the subject demanded this format. Single sheets mounted as albums were often made into *oribon*, an accordion-type fold-out format. This allowed the viewer to enjoy all the pictures at a glance. Sets of *shunga* usually appear in twelve sheets, which may relate to the twelve months of the year. These can be broken into four sets of three pictures relating to the four seasons.

Shunga prints produced in Edo tended to be more richly colored than those made in Kyoto and Osaka, reflecting the Edo taste for novelty, luxury and greater detail, especially in the background, compared with the *kamigata* preference for a more muted, understated style. Because of government censorship, most *shunga* were not signed and therefore the names of the artists are always attributed. After regulations became more relaxed in the mid-1800s, artists often concealed their names in a small section of the picture, for example, amongst the calligraphy on a fan.

While it is agreed that the Yoshiwara pleasure quarter was the main source of inspiration for *shunga*, there has been much speculation over the last few years as to the main audience for them. Some people believe that *shunga* were originally published as erotic manuals to train inexperienced courtesans, while others refute this, maintaining that courtesans seldom saw *shunga* books or albums even though they might have been the inspiration behind them. Yet others point out that courtesans would have considered the involved entwined positions of the arms and legs vulgar and outlandish; some have been quoted as saying they would probably break a bone trying to assume such positions. Indeed, if we consider that the forty-eight positions pictured or referred to in *shunga* are related to the forty-eight holds or throws of *sumo* wrestlers in the ring, this may well be true.

In reality, most of the *shunga* pillow books and prints were sold outside the gay quarter and outside Edo. Although shops inside Yoshiwara sold *shunga*

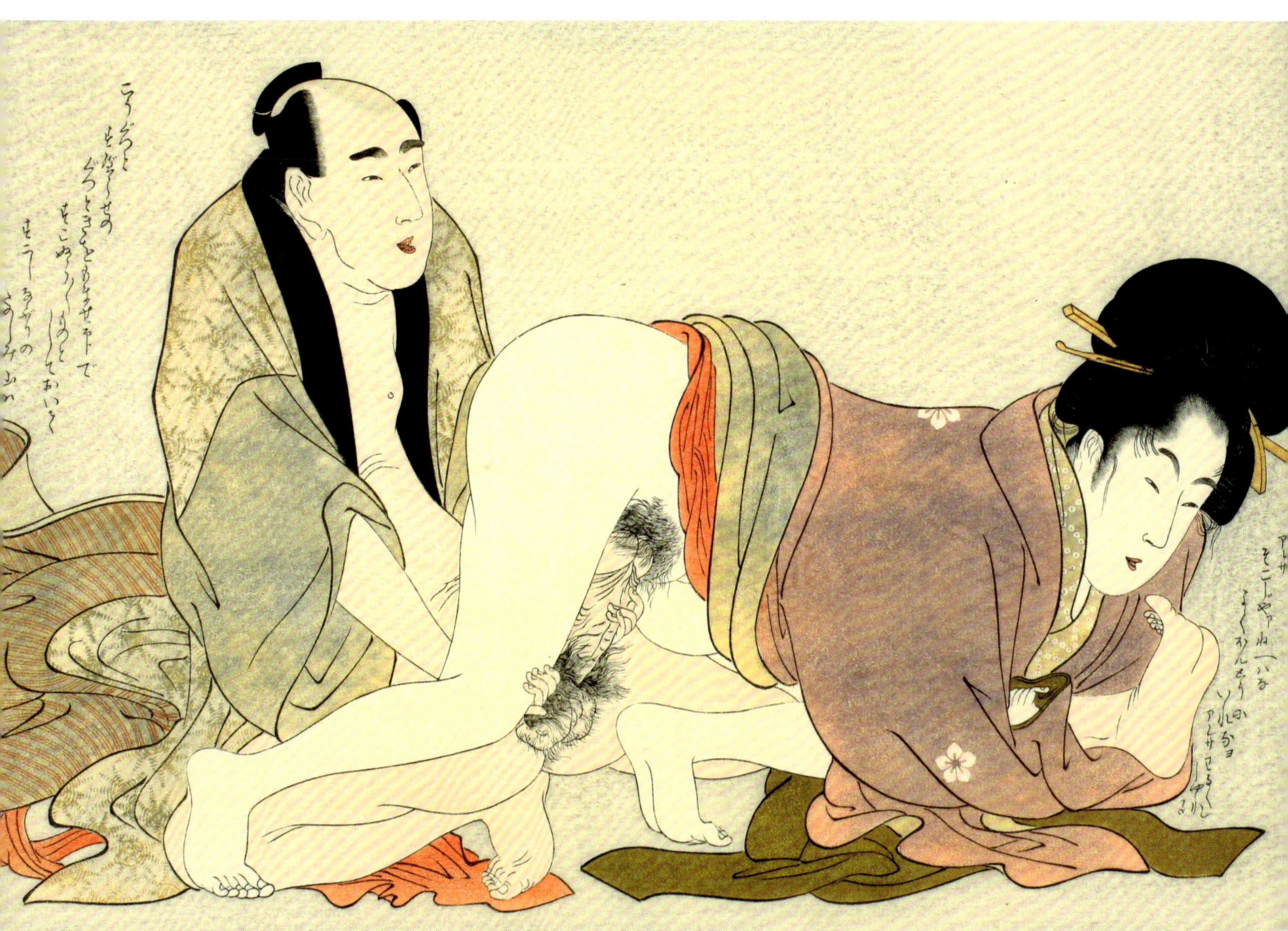

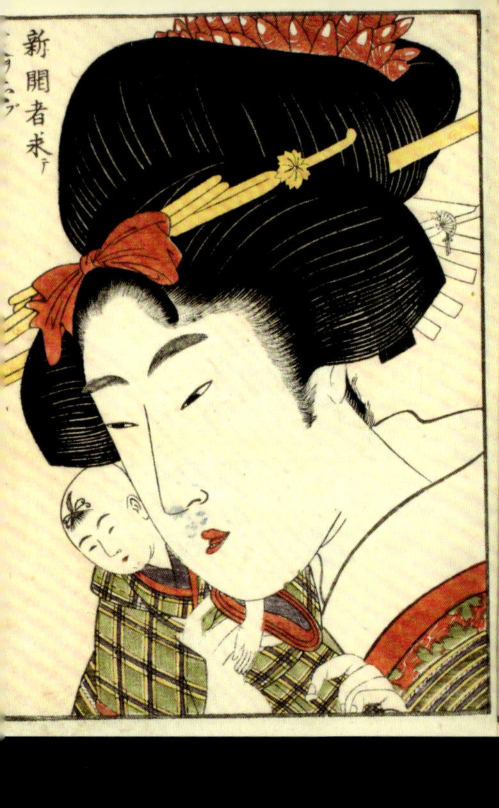
新開者來テ

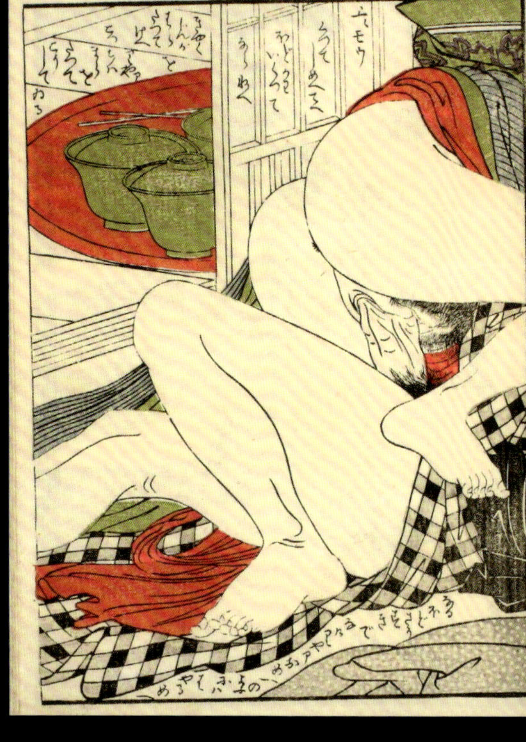

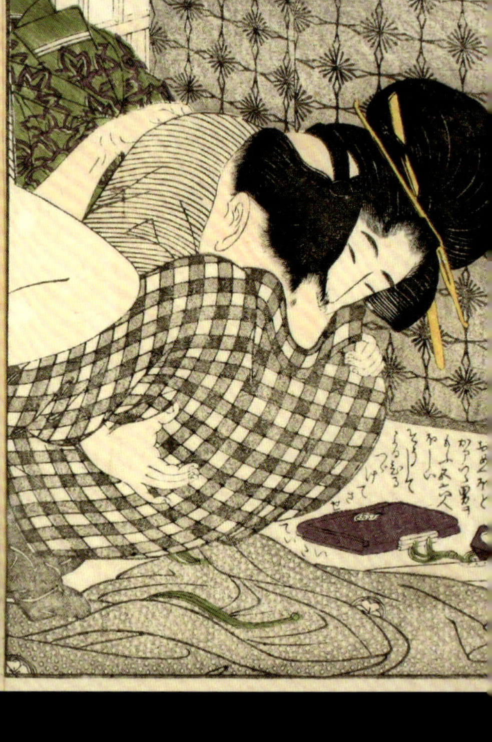

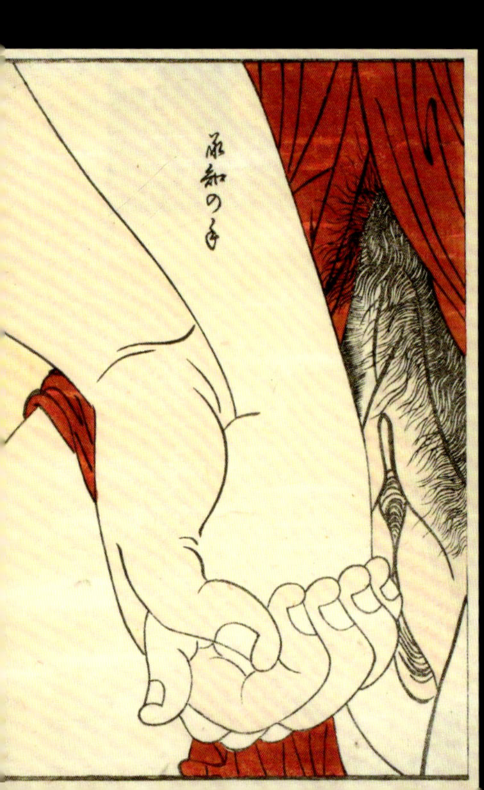
承知の手

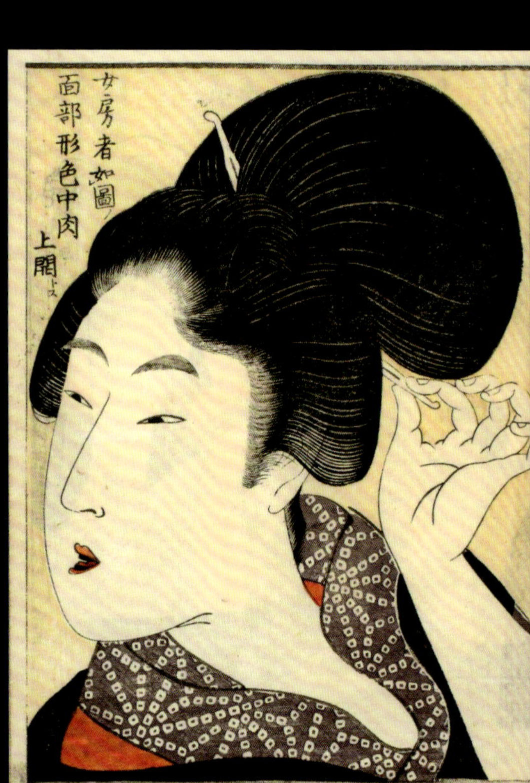
女房者如圖
面部形色中肉
上開トス

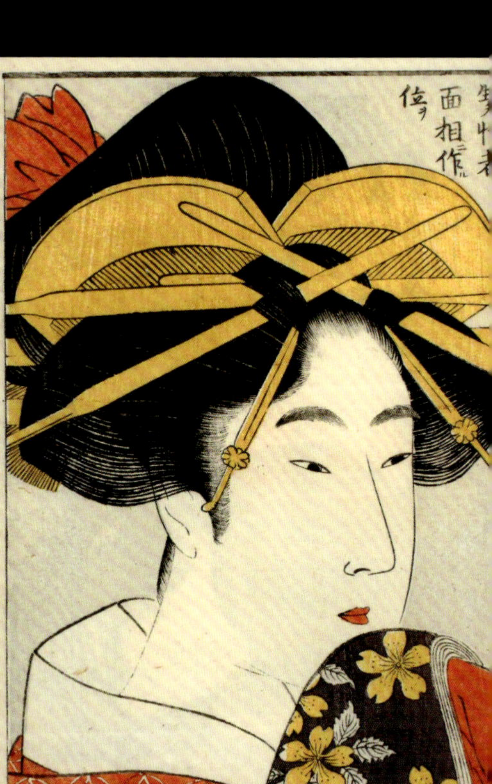
面相作ル
位ヲ

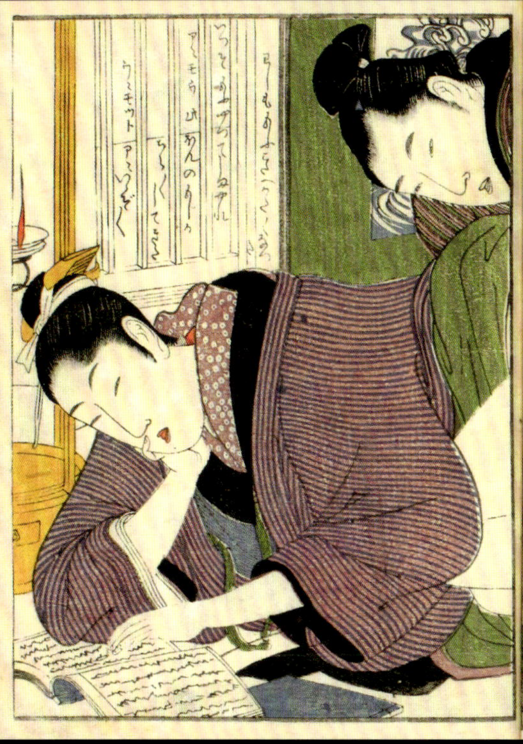

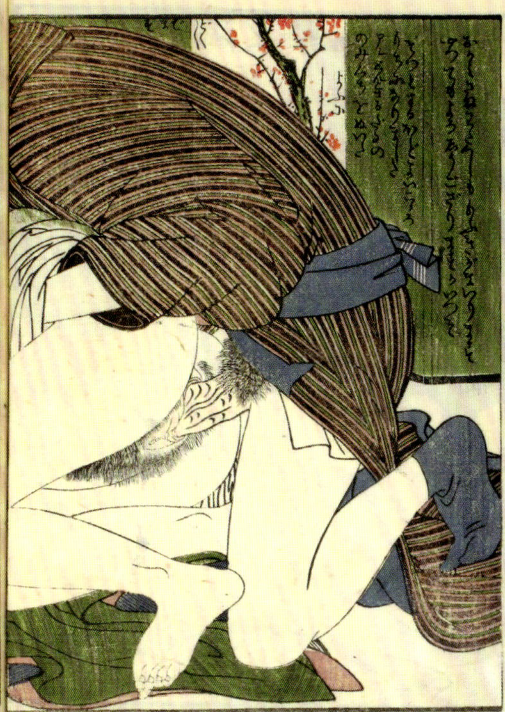

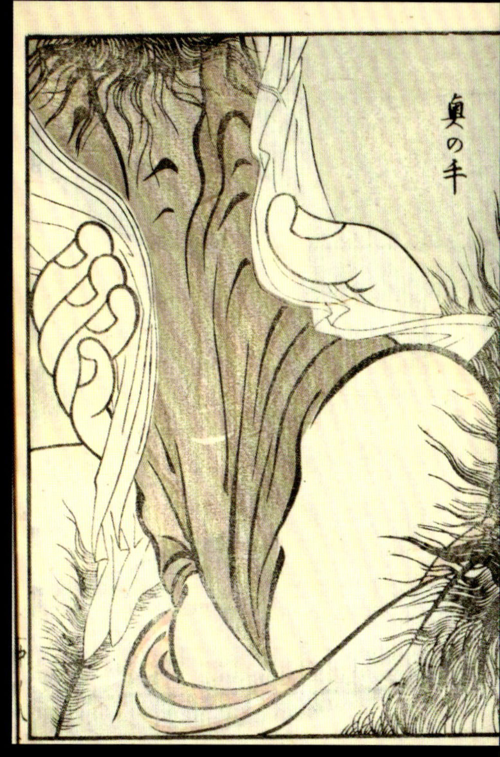

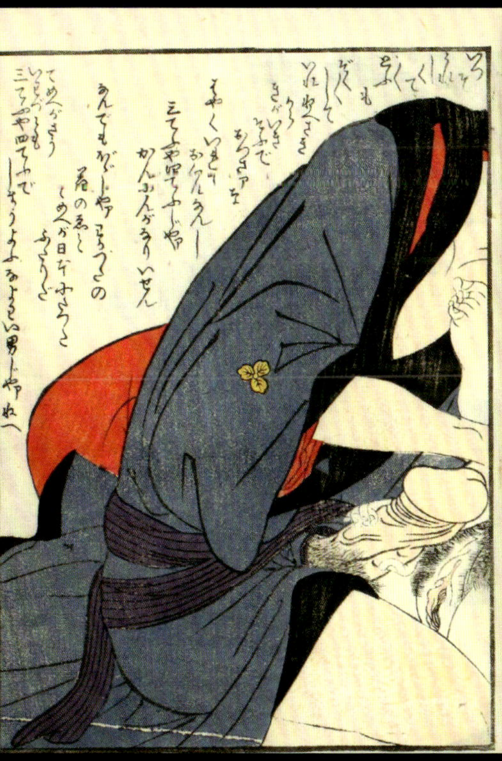

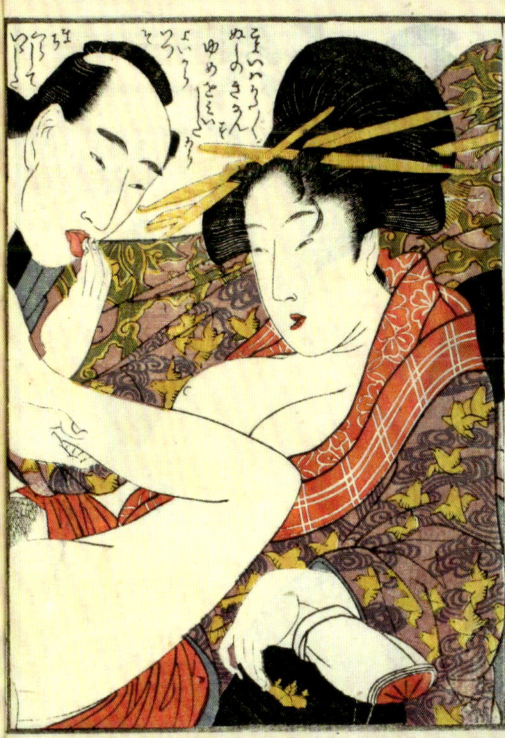

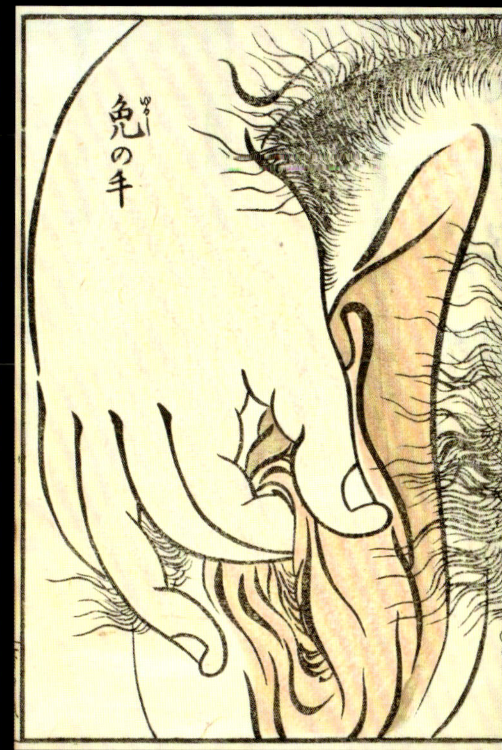

FIG. 140
Kitagawa UTAMARO
歌麿 (1754–1806)
SHUNGA 春画 (1800s)
6 single pages and 3 double pages from a three-volume set, 19.5 x 26 cm
Courtesy of Mita Arts Gallery

Utamaro produced over thirty *shunga* books, albums and related publications with titles like *Twelve Hours in the Pleasure Quarters* and *An Array of Passionate Lovers*. The books were published in sets of three. His draftsmanship and humor are admirable in the examples shown here from three picture albums (*enpon*). Each accordion-type, freestanding album contains twelve pictures glued to the pages: two pages of text; at the front a full-page portrait of a beautiful courtesan with a stylish robe and elegant hairstyle; in the center four double-page spreads illustrating the activities of the couple; and at the back a full-page close-up of genitalia. The drawing, especially of the genitals, is imaginatively done.

books as souvenirs to those who patronized the brothels, salesmen took their stock to the rural areas, and often found customers in the castles where the women were left alone while their husbands were serving the *daimyo* in Edo. More than half of the purchasers of *shunga* were women. People in rural areas could also obtain *shunga* from someone operating a *kashihonya* (lending library), who would also take his collection outside the main urban areas to more remote places.

Although *shunga* prints and books were probably bought and enjoyed by both men and women of all classes of society for the fun of viewing sexually stimulating exotic images, they served also for the sexual education of young men and women. In many families it was the custom to give brides *shunga* albums that were treasured and passed down from mother to daughter. Aside from their practical usefulness, these albums were valued for their beauty.

Almost all *ukiyo-e* artists, with the exception of Sharaku, tried their hand at *shunga* at some point in their careers. It did not detract from their reputation as artists. Conversely, nearly all the great masters of *ukiyo-e* believed that designing competent *shunga* was vital to their artistic standing and considered their creations to be on par with the rest of their work. *Shunga* also sold more easily and at higher prices than other subject matter—beautiful women, *kabuki* actors, landscapes and the like—and experienced, first-rate artists found they could earn a very good, and stable, living from it. In fact, the production of *shunga* represented about 30 percent of their output. The quality of *shunga* art, of course, varied, as did the price. Some

FIG. 141
Katsushika HOKUSAI
北斎 (1760–1849)
Shunga 春画 (1820s)
27 x 39 cm
Courtesy of Mita Arts Gallery

Hokusai takes us much further into the enlarged image compared to Harunobu, Koryusai and even Utamaro. Fifty years have passed since Harunobu, and the aesthetics have changed with the times. The robust figures are now often completely nude. The genitals are enlarged and the backgrounds are simple color patterns based on fabrics and other textures. The colors are carefully placed to emphasize the whiteness of the figures. In this print, the couple is having intercourse for the second time as the crumpled tissues in the foreground indicate.

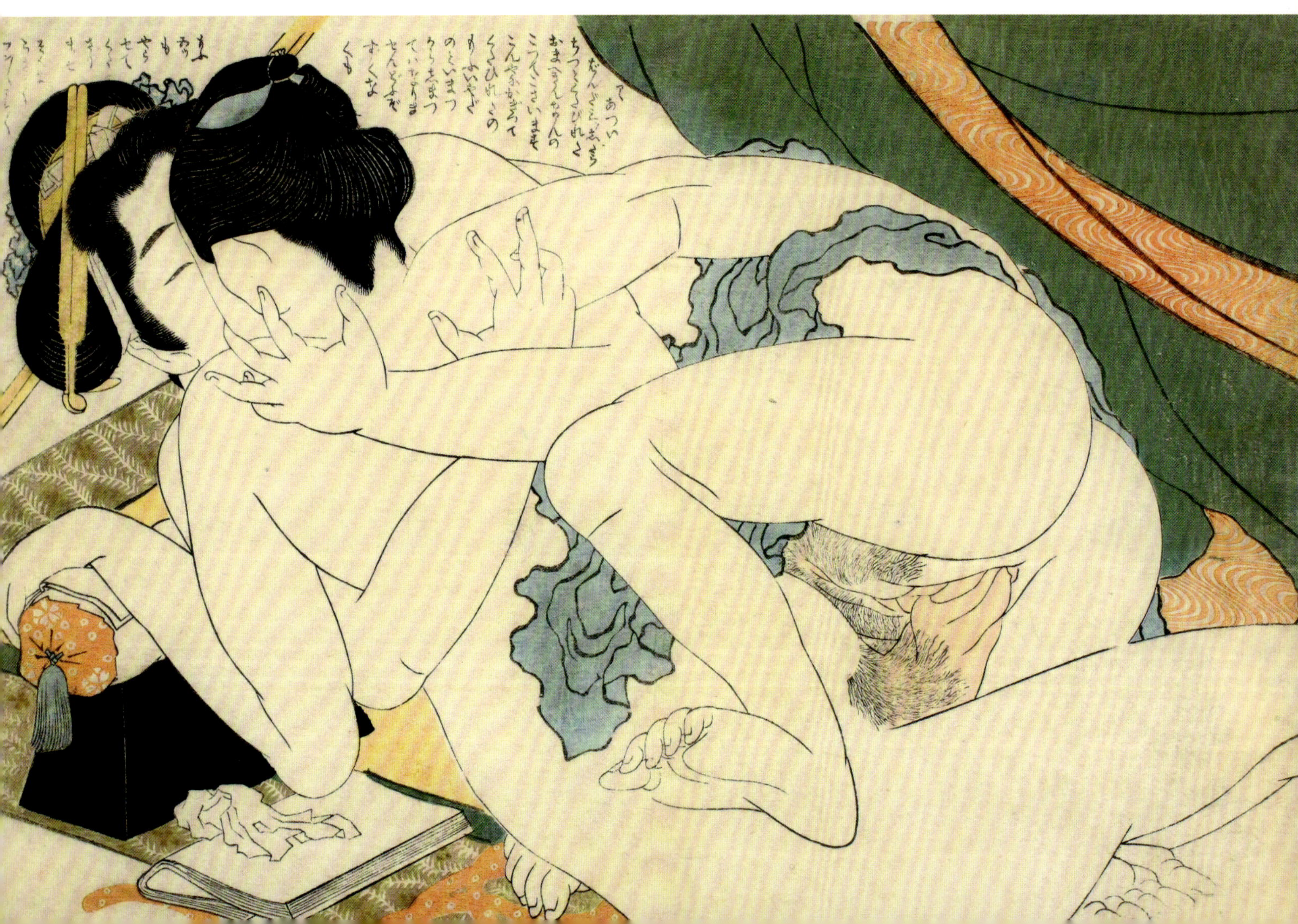

FIG. 142
Katsushika HOKUSAI
北斎 (1760–1849)
Shunga 春画 (1820s)
27 x 39 cm
Courtesy of Mita Arts Gallery

Hokusai's total output of prints runs into the thousands. The number of *shunga* is relatively small in comparison, but his imagination and the effort he took to create a composition different from his contemporaries is apparent. The eyes of this couple are closed in ecstasy.

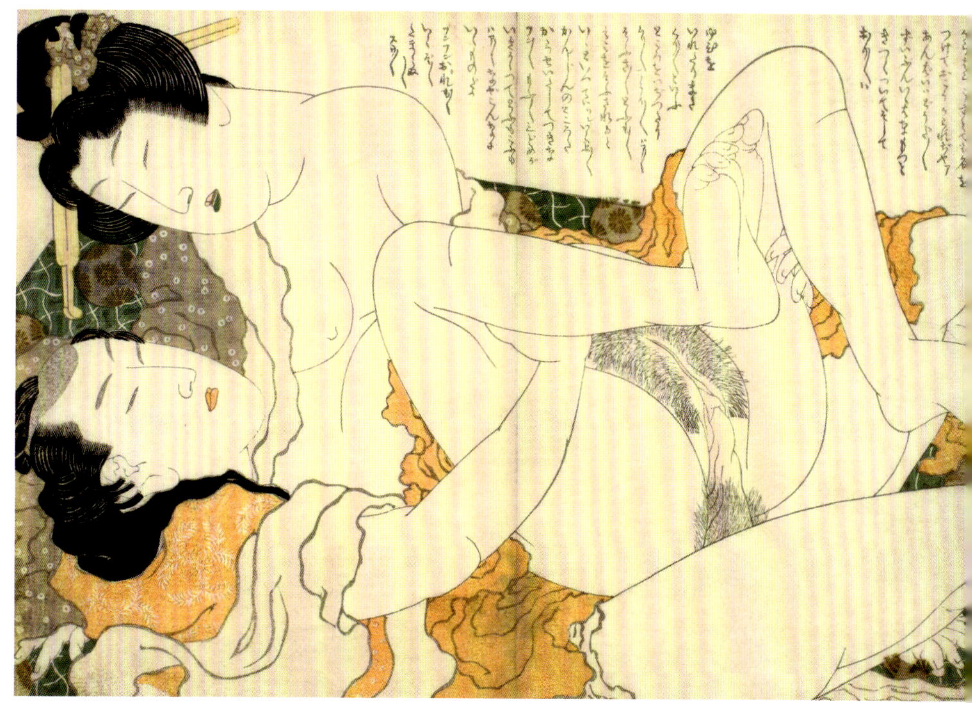

FIG. 143
Kikugawa EIZAN
英山 (1797–1867)
Shunga 春画 (1820s)
27 x 39 cm
Courtesy of Mita Arts Gallery

Eizan's prints are largely limited to beautiful women, including some *shunga*, with his own figural style. This print is obviously not set in a brothel, nor is the woman a professional, but in all probability the man is not her husband. The cup of tea, writing box, fan and general atmosphere suggest a domestic scene of sorts. The whiteness of the couple's skin is sensitively portrayed against a background of fabric and the outdoor garden.

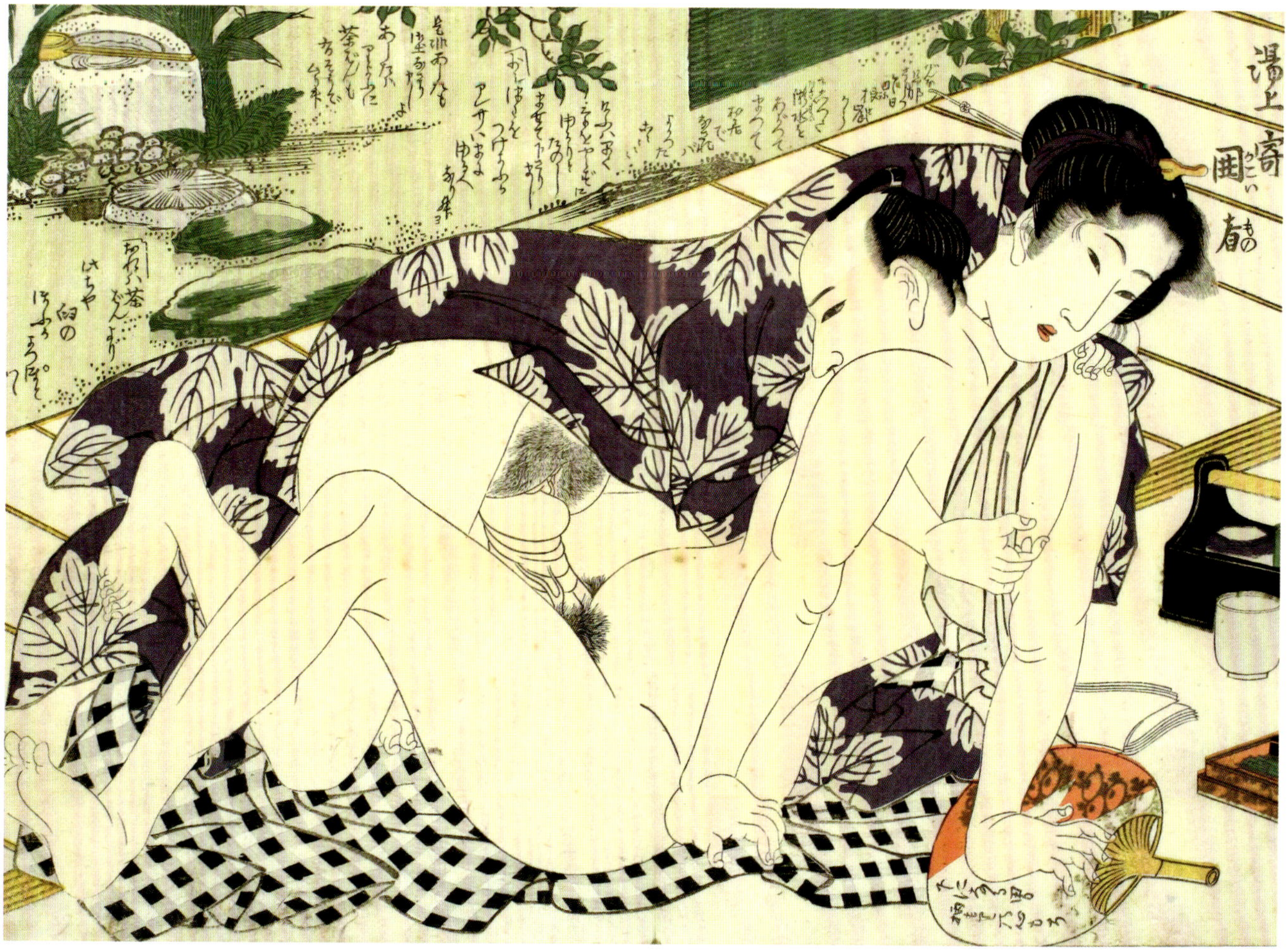

of it, especially that commissioned by wealthy merchants and *daimyo*, was elaborate and detailed. Some of it was limited in color, widely circulated and cost little more than a simple meal.

The aesthetic quality of *shunga* compositions follows a different path from other genre. The early masters were Suzuki Harunobu (1725–70) (**Figs. 130–133**) and Isoda Koryusai (1735–90) (**Figs. 134, 135**), who produced pictures in the small *chuban* size. The figures were small in relation to their surroundings, which included detailed interiors. The interior established the location—a person's house, a brothel, some place outdoors or another location. If it was a set of twelve pictures, the first print set the mood, and is referred to as *abunai-e* (risqué). The genitalia in the rest of the set, although enlarged, were not as exaggerated as they eventually became with the prints of Torii Kiyonaga (1752–1815) (**Figs. 136–138**), Kitagawa Utamaro (1754–1806) (**Figs. 139, 140**) and Katsushika Hokusai (1760–1849) (**Figs. 141, 142**) and the artists who followed these two masters, such as Kikugawa Eizan (1797–1867) (**Figs. 143, 144**). Kiyonaga, Utamaro and Hokusai in their larger *o-ban* size prints had a tendency to enlarge the genitals to preposterous proportions. Their figures also filled the entire picture surface, leaving little or no room for any background detail.

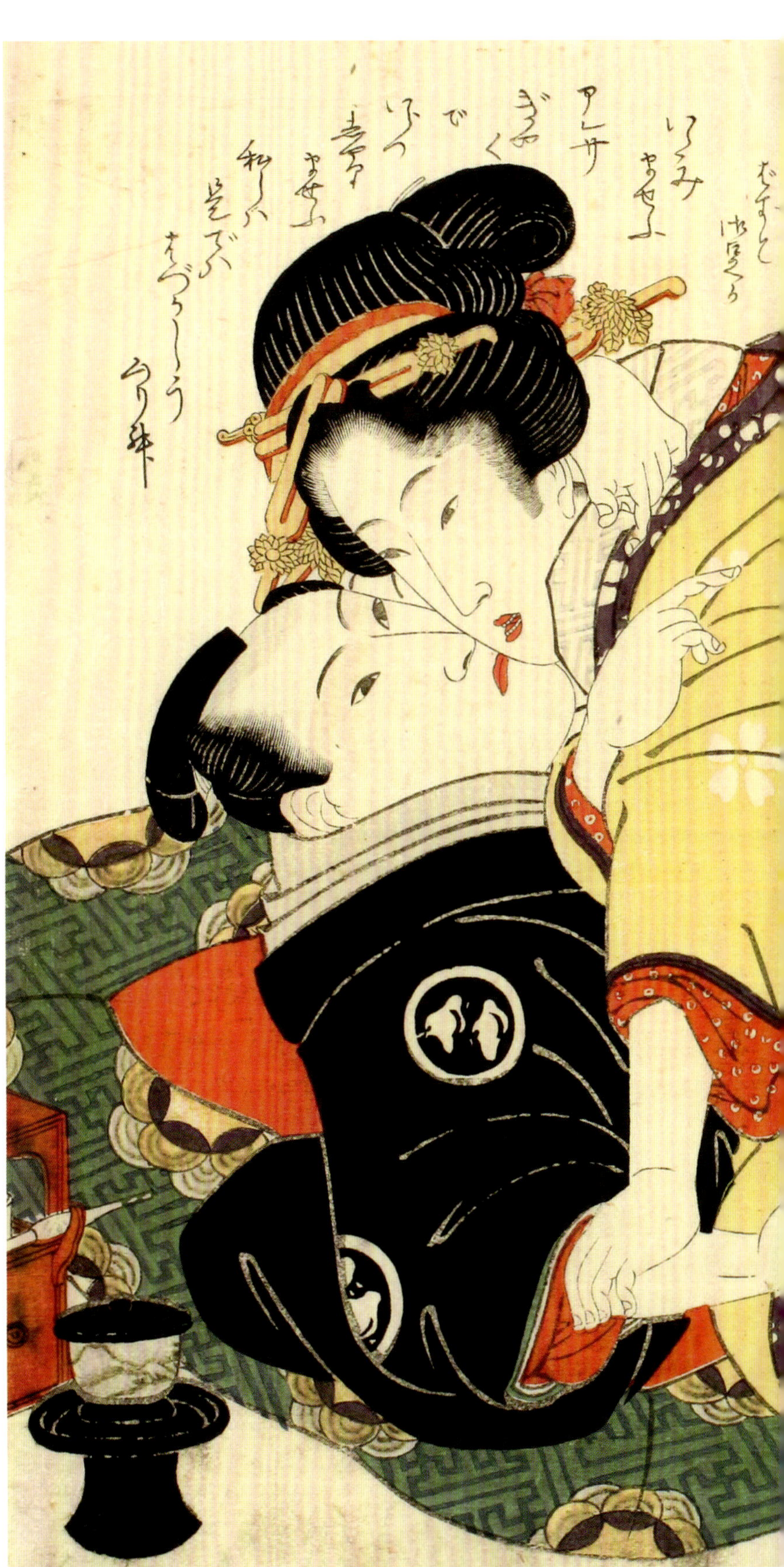

FIG. 144
Kikugawa EIZAN
英山 (1797–1867)
Shunga 春画 (1820s)
27 x 39 cm
Courtesy of Mita Arts Gallery

This is probably the first sheet in a series of twelve. The elaborate *kimono* and *kanzashi* (hair ornaments) suggest a courtesan. She and her client are just beginning to engage each other. She has not yet removed her *tabi* (socks). Other than their hands and faces, the only bare skin visible is a corner of her knee peering out from her undergarment. Interestingly, the man's undergarment is also red. The strong, diagonal composition of the print is reinforced by the clothing box on the right, which repeats the angles of the figures.

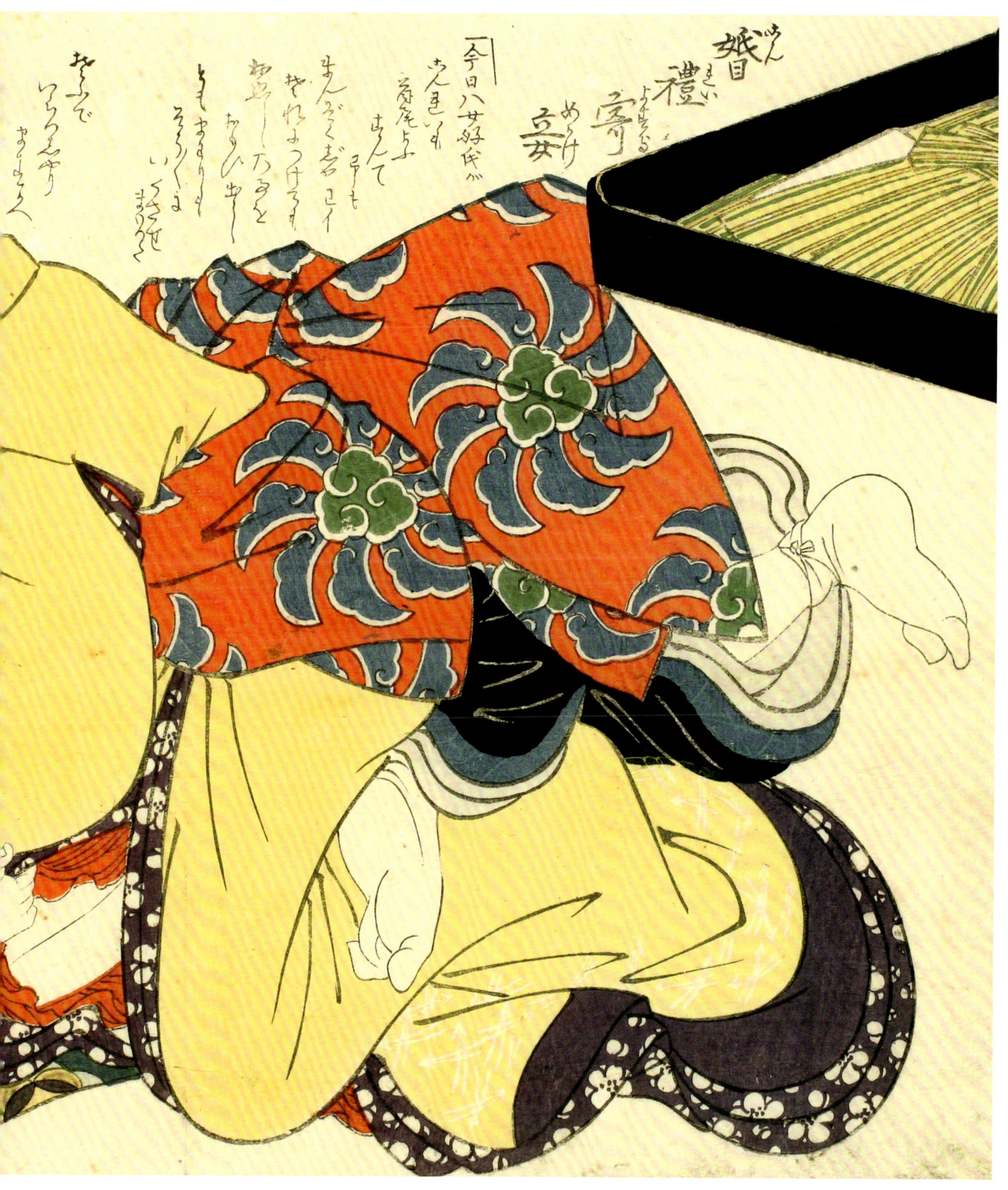

CHAPTER NINE

Birds and Flowers

For thousands of years, Asian artists, including Japanese, have shown a deep respect for and understanding of the natural world, of the beauty of the land and its myriad life forms. It is probably for this reason that nature has been more central to Chinese and Japanese paintings, prints and decorative arts than any other subject. Certainly, fascination with animals, birds, insects and fishes, combined with a love of the land, has even a longer history in Asian art than studies of the figure. The figure prior to popular literature was almost always of a religious nature, either in the form of statues to be worshipped or paintings describing the life of Buddha or the deities involved with Buddhism or the Shinto religion. For non-religious, decorative purposes, the artist concentrated on other forms of plant and animal life. Many of these plants and animals took on symbolic meanings, which have close associations with aspects of Japanese culture. Often animals or fishes were combined with fabled characters.

Unlike the study of the human figure, the aesthetic changes that have occurred in the depiction of animals and plants over the centuries have been relatively minor. The decorative style of portraying these subjects is the result of long years of detailed study on how the anatomy of animals or the structure of plants is formed. There are numerous illustrated books going back centuries showing scientific analyses of a huge range of animals and flowers, with detailed drawings and descriptions of shape, color, size, etc.

During the decade leading up the Tenpo Reforms of 1841–3, which were aimed at alleviating economic crisis by controlling public displays of luxury and wealth, the illustration of courtesans and actors in *ukiyo-e* was officially banned. As a result, many artists turned to producing landscape prints (see Chapter 7) as well as works of purely natural subject matter. These themes were not only outside the bounds of censorship but also catered to the rising popularity of travel in late Edo Japan. Particularly popular were *kacho-e*, woodblock prints of birds and flowers. Despite the name "bird and flower" print, birds and flowers were not always depicted together. Birds often interacted with their natural habitat, and other creatures came within the parameter of the genre. Generally, printmakers produced animals, birds, insects and fishes that mimicked traditional Japanese and Chinese painting, which has a long history.

FIG. 145
Tsukioka YOSHITOSHI
芳年 (1839–92)
Kintaro Catches a Giant Carp
金太郎捕鯉魚 (1880s)
Vertical diptych, 78 x 27 cm
Courtesy of Mita Arts Gallery

Here, Kintaro, the boy Hercules of Japanese mythology, who performed prodigious feats of strength, subdues a giant carp, his enemy. Kintaro and a large carp frequently appear in body tattoos. The carp descending rapids is also commonly seen. The carp, which symbolizes perseverance and the will to win, is a symbol of the male in the Children's Day festival celebrated on May 5 each year.

It was not until the *shin hanga* (new prints) movement in the early part of the twentieth century, influenced by the pre-eminent *shin hanga* publisher Watanabe Shozaburo, that *kacho-e* "bird and flower" prints along with other nature subjects progressed to a new level (see page 138). Not only did Watanabe recruit several of Japan's most accomplished artists, he also imposed stylistic changes on their output, such as a brighter palette, and injected new printing techniques to make the products more appealing to Westerners, his main customers.

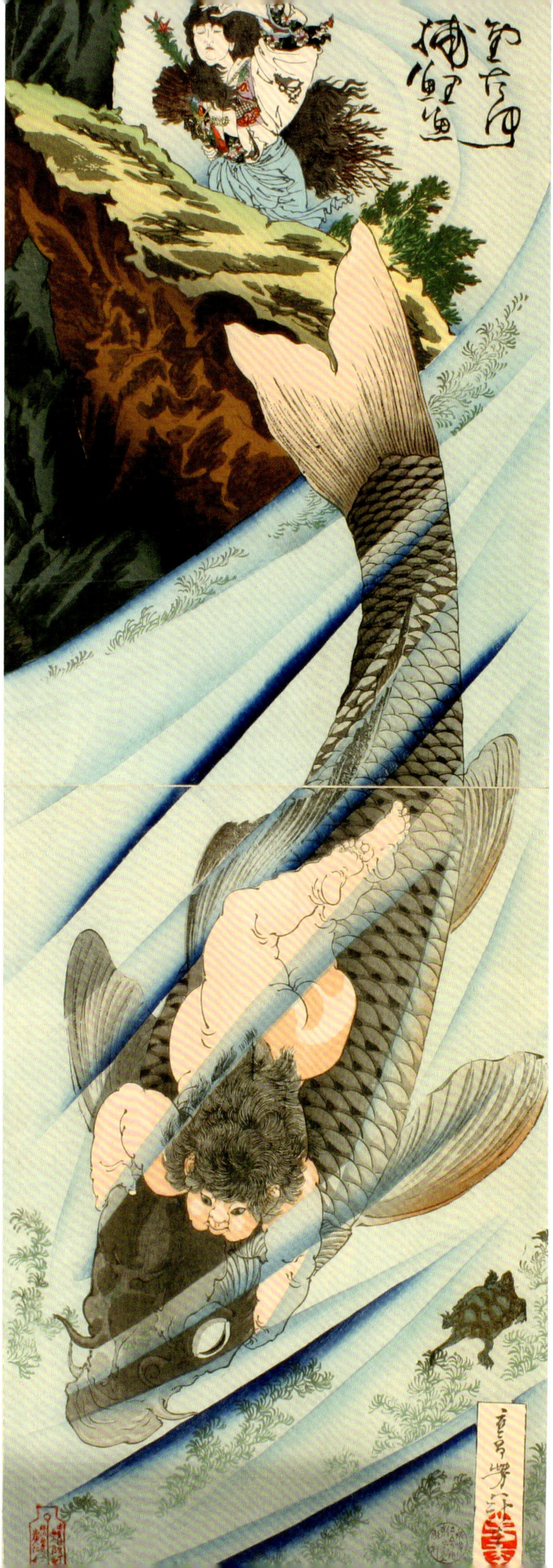

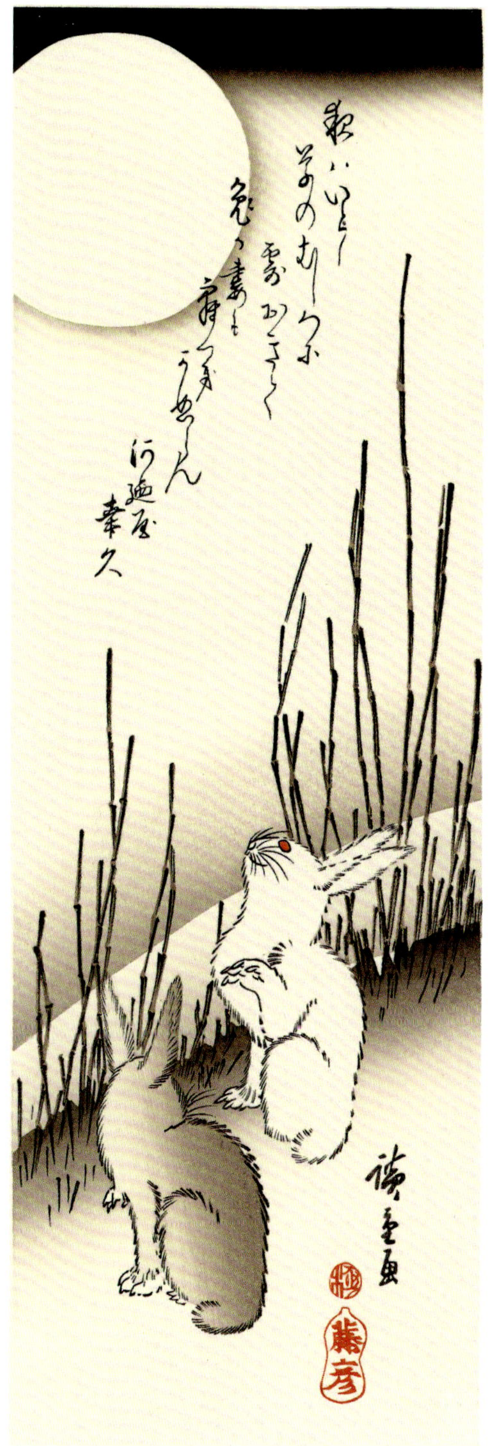

FIG. 146
Utagawa HIROSHIGE
広重 (1797–1858)
Rabbits and Reeds in Moonlight
月夜木賊に兎 (1780s)
Vertical diptych, 38.5 x 13 cm
Courtesy of Adachi Institute of Woodcut Prints

Largely a monochromatic print but for the red color accent on the rabbit's eye and the publisher's mark, this is a rather good example of the rabbit, one of the twelve signs of the zodiac, and is used throughout Japan as a symbol of the moon. The poem reads: "The night is amorous, dew covers the bed of grass, probably the rabbit's wife cannot sleep until late."

Woodblock prints started to take on the appearance of watercolors. There was an absence of the black outline to be filled in with flat or gradated colors (*bokashi*). The prints literally looked like paintings. Large numbers were exported to the United States and Europe for an eager clientele.

Although only a few print designers specialized in *kacho-e*, many others contributed to the genre. Isoda Koryusai (1735–90), somewhat of an anomaly among printmakers because he was born into the élite *samurai* class, was a prolific designer of single-sheet prints, mostly of beautiful women and erotica, but he also created numerous *kacho-e*, especially of falcons. He was heavily influenced stylistically by the great *ukiyo-e* master Suzuki Harunobu (1725–70). Particularly noteworthy is his attention to animals as subjects unto themselves (**Fig. 147**). In his sets of the animals of the zodiac and others, he went beyond the typical bird and flower subjects.

While Katsushika Hokusai (1760–1849) is best known for his ability to create magnificent landscape prints that are full of "movement" (see page 104), he was also one of the first artists to transfer bird and flower motifs from illustrations in books to an independent sub-genre of *ukiyo-e* prints. Inspired by European scientific illustrations, and always striving to show perfection, his plants and birds are precise, realistic and extremely detailed (**Figs. 152–155**). Like many of his landscapes featuring water, such as "The Great Wave off Kanagawa," some of his *kacho-e* subject matter is painted in a flowing, circular manner, such as his depiction of a flock of roosters nestled together (**Fig. 156**). When he was seventy-five, Hokusai wrote in the preface to *One Hundred Views of Mount Fuji*: "At the age of seventy-two I finally apprehended something of the true quality of birds, animals, insects, fish and of the vital nature of grasses and trees."

Following Hokusai, Utagawa Hiroshige (1797–1858) was the foremost artist of his day specializing

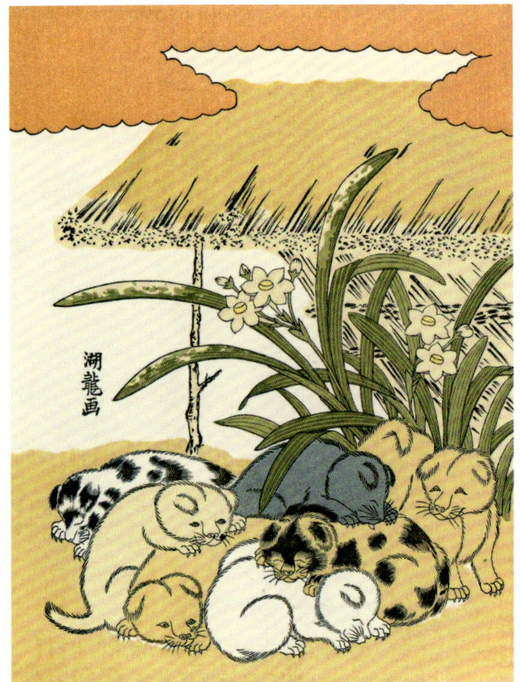

FIG. 147 (above left)
Isoda KORYUSAI
磯田 湖竜斉 (1735–90)
Puppies and Narcissus in the Snow 水仙に子犬 (1780s)
29 x 21 cm
Courtesy of Adachi Institute of Woodcut Prints

Dogs are another of the twelve signs of the zodiac and as such have a unique place in Japanese history. Sometimes they were used as a talisman to keep in childbirth. Here, the small puppies, some asleep, are enjoying the heat of the sun under the shed roof. The narcissus, forced into bloom in late winter, is considered an emblem of good fortune and is used for indoor decoration during the New Year.

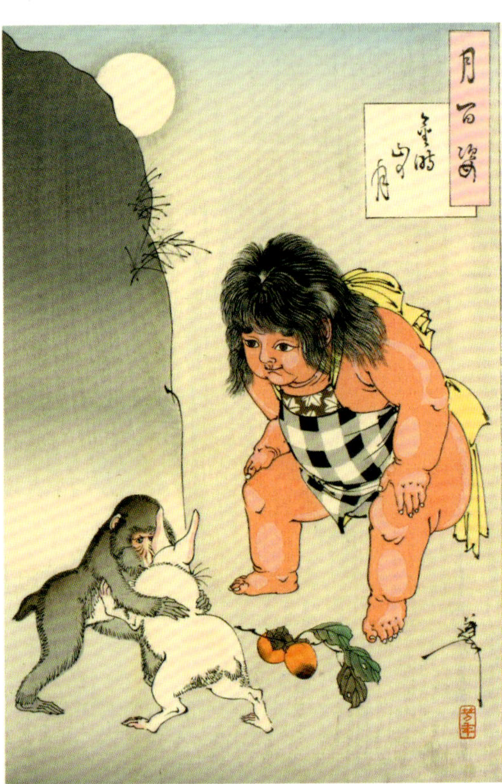

FIG. 148 (below left)
Tsukioka YOSHITOSHI
芳年 (1839–92)
Kintaro the Mountain Boy Watching a Rabbit and Monkey Fighting Over a Persimmon, from *One Hundred Aspects of the Moon* 月百姿 金時山の月 (1885–92)
39 x 27 cm
Courtesy of Mita Arts Gallery

The monkey, another zodiac sign, is considered a symbol of good fortune, and is often paired with a rabbit as being two companions of Kintaro.

FIG. 149 (above right)
Utagawa HIROSHIGE
広重 (1797–1858)
Mackerel, Crab and Morning Glory, from the Second Untitled Fish Series 魚づくし 鯖かざみがに朝顔 (1840s)
27 x 39 cm
Courtesy of Mita Arts Gallery

Hiroshige did two series of fish and other sea life, both untitled, the first in the mid-1830s and the second in the early 1840s. The studies are extremely accurate and beautifully executed, as this print and the two following show. Poems appear in the upper section of the prints. The Japanese word for crab is *kani*, and can be interpreted as a symbol of court rank and bravery. In the battle of Dannoura between the Heike and Genji clans, the crabs eaten were called Heike crabs, symbolic of the lost heroes of that famous battle.

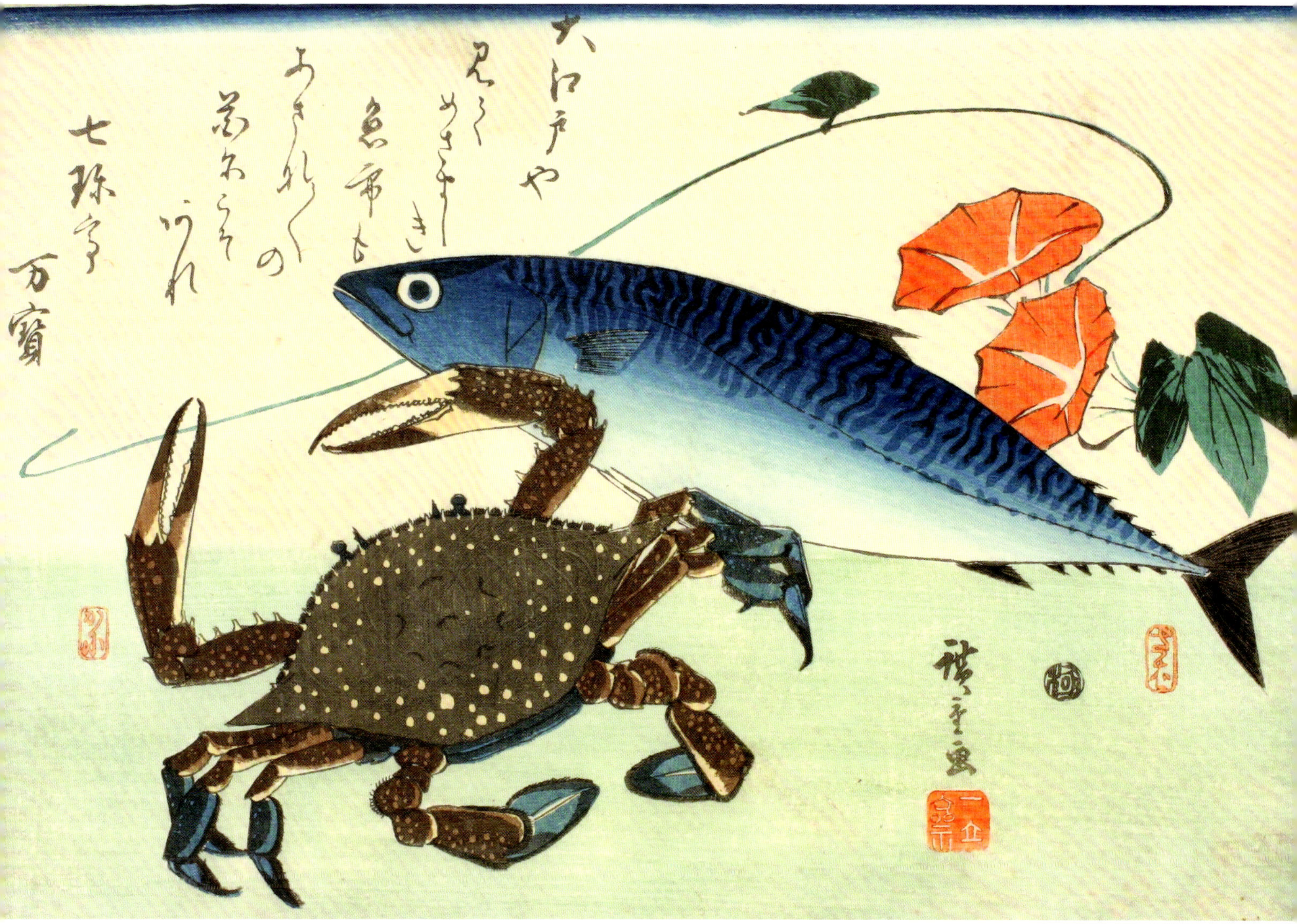

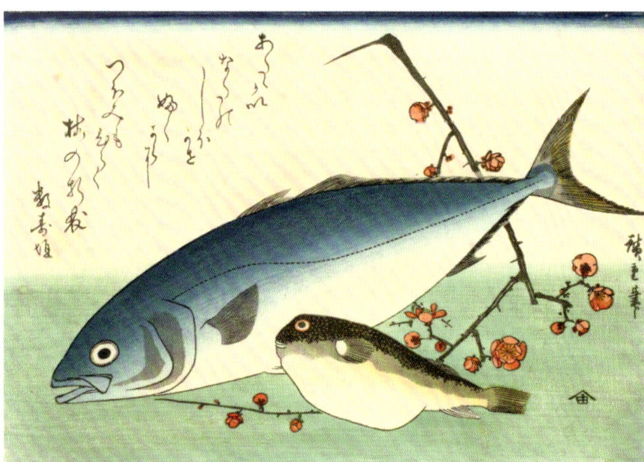

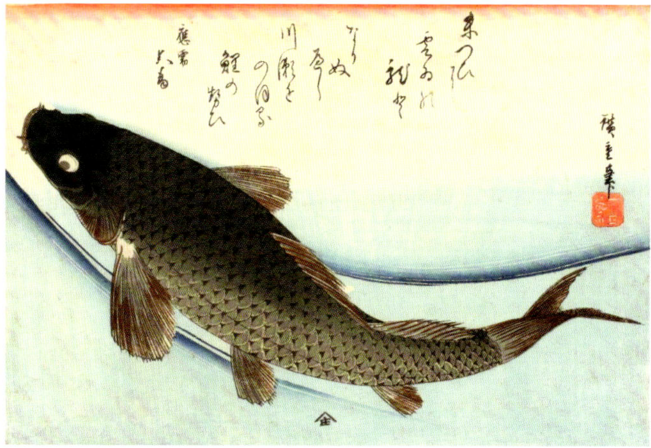

FIG. 150
Utagawa HIROSHIGE
広重 (1797–1858)
Yellowtail, Blowfish and Plum Branch, from the Second Untitled Fish Series
魚づくし いなだ河豚梅 (1840s)
27 x 39 cm
Courtesy of Mita Arts Gallery

The blowfish or pufferfish (*fugu*) contains lethal amounts of poison in the organs and skin. For this reason, *fugu* has become one of the most celebrated and notorious dishes in Japanese cuisine, and only specially licensed chefs can prepare and sell it to the public. It is sometimes caught and prepared by amateur cooks, often with fatal results.

FIG. 151
Utagawa HIROSHIGE
広重 (1797–1858)
Carp, from the Second Untitled Fish Series 鯉 (1840s)
27 x 39 cm
Courtesy of Mita Arts Gallery

The carp or *koi* was a central image of the rigid code of the *samurai* and was revered because of its courage, hence its inclusion in warrior tattoos. The rendering of the scales on this carp print are exemplary.

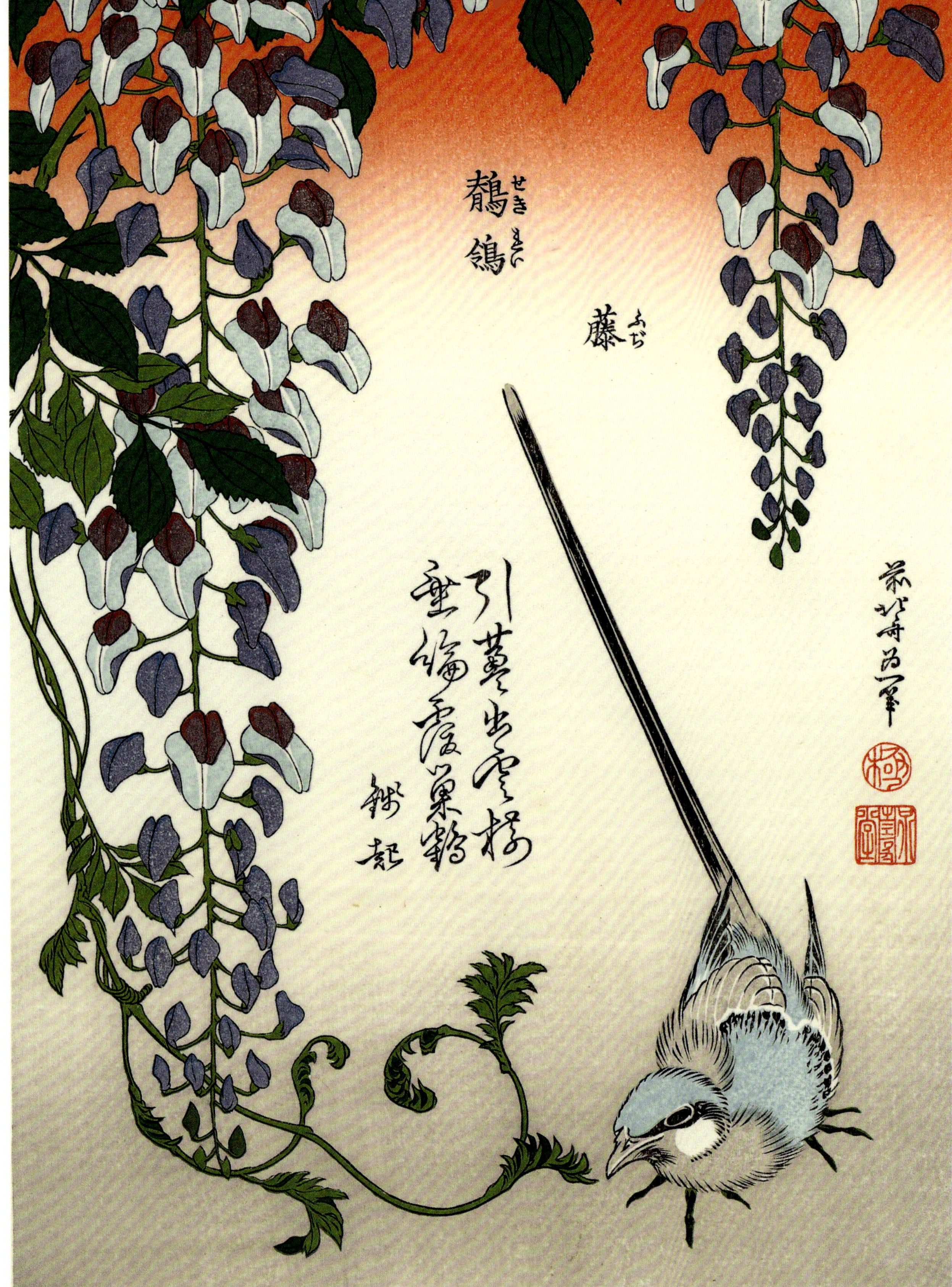

FIG. 152
Katsushika HOKUSAI
北斎 (1760–1849)
Wisteria and Wagtail 藤に鶺鴒 (1850s)
25.5 x 19 cm
Courtesy of Adachi Institute of Woodcut Prints

This is one of the small size prints (*chuban*) that Hokusai signed at the age of seventy. The composition is masterful in contrasting the wagtail's vertical line with the drooping wisteria, which is the symbol for April in the Japanese card game *hanafuda*.

in scenes of birds and flowers. He created an unprecedented 5,000 *kacho-e* designs. Many of his works were done in a style that is obviously Chinese in origin, which highlighted his refined color sense, economy of composition and delicate rendering. They are often in a long compositional format. Many include short descriptive poems (*haiku* or *kyoka*) by well-known collaborating poets. His prints feature several different sea creatures, such as carp, mackerel, yellowtails, blowfish and crabs (**Figs. 149–151**) as well as a variety of birds—eagles, geese, herons, sparrows, wagtails and swallows (**Figs. 157–161**). In contrast to Hokusai, he did not aim for perfection in his *kacho-e* and was not averse to showing the realities of nature, including its defects and oddities. Hiroshige published his *kacho-e* in several different series, including *Artistic Flowers and Birds* (ca. 1859), *Thirty-six Flowers* (1866) and two series of untitled fish prints in the mid-1830s and early 1840s, which included a variety of sea life and plants.

Utagawa Kuniyoshi's two most important students, Tsukioka Yoshitoshi (1839–92) and Kawanabe Kyosai (1831–89), dominated the era after Hokusai and Hiroshige and before the modernization of Japan eclipsed the woodblock print as an art form. Yoshitoshi was noted for his superior composition, draftsmanship and passion for his subject matter even while he suffered recurring bouts of depression and produced some disturbing images. His *One Hundred Aspects of the Moon* (1885–92) is regarded as his finest achievement. The subjects range from Japanese history and mythology—creatures included (**Figs. 145, 148**)—to scenes from Japanese historical and contemporary life and Chinese mythology, all unified by the moon motif in the background. Kyosai, a gifted sketch artist and illustrator, is primarily known for his busy but brilliant prints of the macabre and the supernatural. But he also created simpler, more naturalistic and witty pictures of domestic and wild animals—

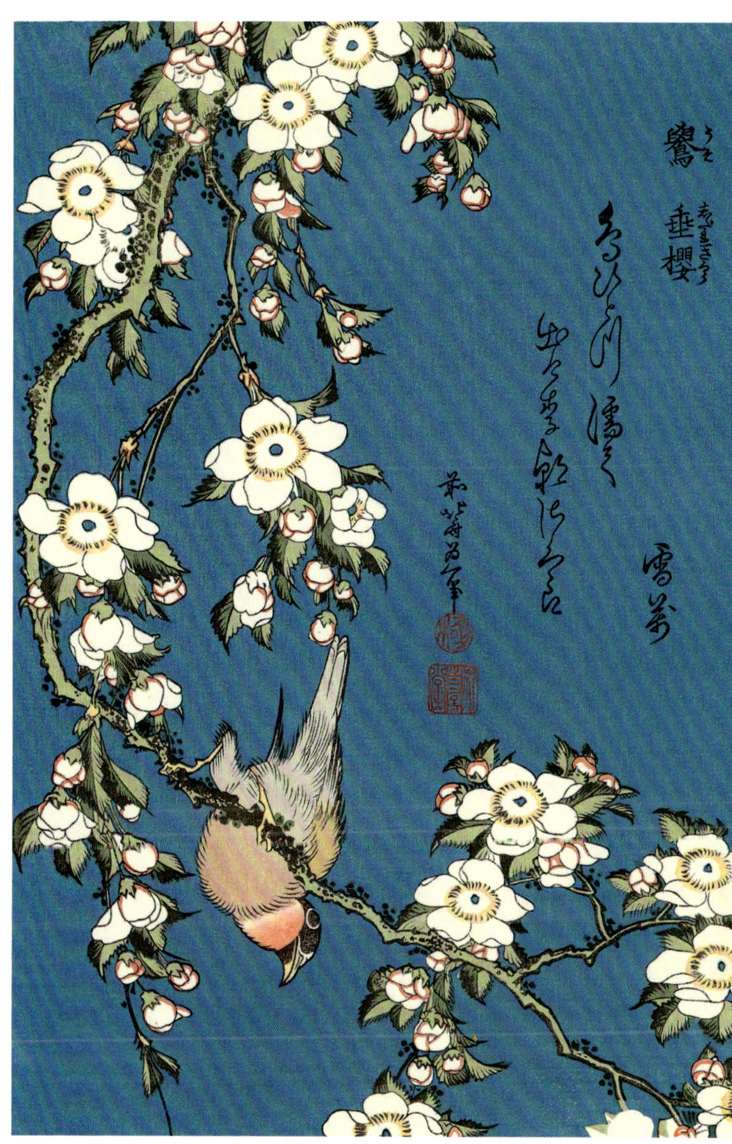

FIG. 153
Katsushika HOKUSAI
北斎 (1760–1849)
Bullfinch and Dropping Cherry Blossoms 鷽に垂桜
(1850s)
26.5 x 19.5
Courtesy of Adachi Institute of Woodcut Prints

This is another of Hokusai's small prints, which he did when he was seventy years of age. The cherry blossom is, of course, the symbol of the *samurai* or warrior because his life is so short, but beautiful when in full bloom.

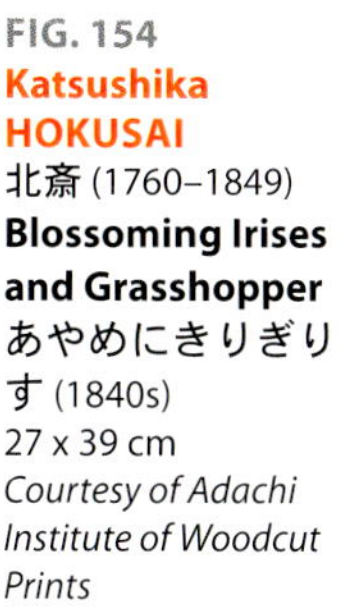

FIG. 154
Katsushika HOKUSAI
北斎 (1760–1849)
Blossoming Irises and Grasshopper
あやめにきりぎりす (1840s)
27 x 39 cm
Courtesy of Adachi Institute of Woodcut Prints

This is one of Hokusai's masterpieces among his flower prints. The veins of the leaves in parallel lines are a tribute to the master carver, as is the detail of the grasshopper, right down to the hairs on its legs. There are numerous variations of iris grown in Japan, which has been used as a motif as far back as the fourth century.

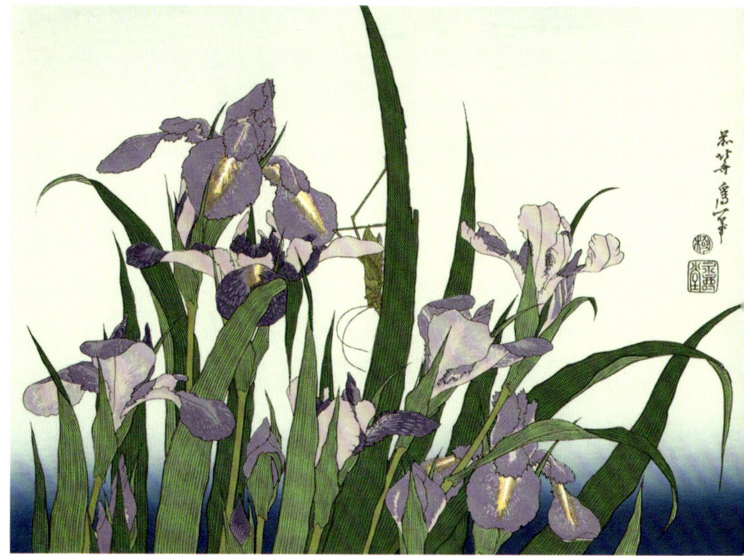

cats, rats, crows, insects, elephants and tigers (**Fig. 164**). Frogs purportedly make up the largest number of any creatures in his work.

Ohara Koson (later Shoson) (1877–1945), painter, printmaker and teacher at the Tokyo School of Fine Arts, is considered by many to be the foremost twentieth-century designer of animal and botanical portraiture in the *shin hanga* tradition, especially of bird prints. Encouraged by an American colleague, Ernest Fenollosa, to make *kacho-e* in traditional *ukiyo-e* style for the American market, Koson had several paintings made into woodblock prints. These early 1900s works are noted for their muted colors and long, narrow formats. Following a lengthy hiatus from printmaking, Koson was recruited by the *shin hanga* publisher Watanabe Shozaburo in the mid-1920s to create *kacho-e*, again primarily for a Western market. He built on the traditional style and composition of Meiji *kacho-e* but incorporated a new Western perspective and depth. His numerous designs, which became brighter, with abundant *bokashi* (graduated) printing, range from haunting realism (**Figs. 165–167**) to humorous depictions of animals at play.

Although Shibata Zeshin (1807–91) is primarily known for his work with lacquer-based inks—he invented the art form of *urushi-e*, painting with black lacquer on specially treated paper—he balanced the new with the old, focusing on traditional, conservative subjects drawn from nature (birds and flowers, insects and waterfalls) or from Japanese legends and history. His unique style, very powerful in its use of contrasting colors and values, was enormously popular and became a kind of showcase of Japan for the outside world. His depiction of crows here (**Fig. 168**) illustrates his chic, sophisticated style.

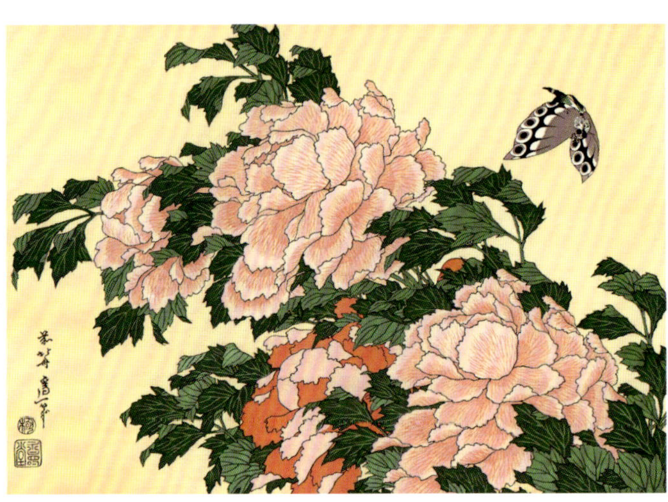

FIG. 155 (right)
Katsushika HOKUSAI
北斎 (1760–1849)
Tree Peony and Butterfly
牡丹に蝶 (1850s)
26.5 x 37.5
Courtesy of Adachi Institute of Woodcut Prints

The peony was introduced from China in the Heian period. It is considered the king of flowers and has been used extensively in textile designs as well as painted subject matter. Here, Hokusai shows us his awesome skill in depicting the butterfly in flight just as it is about to land on the blossom.

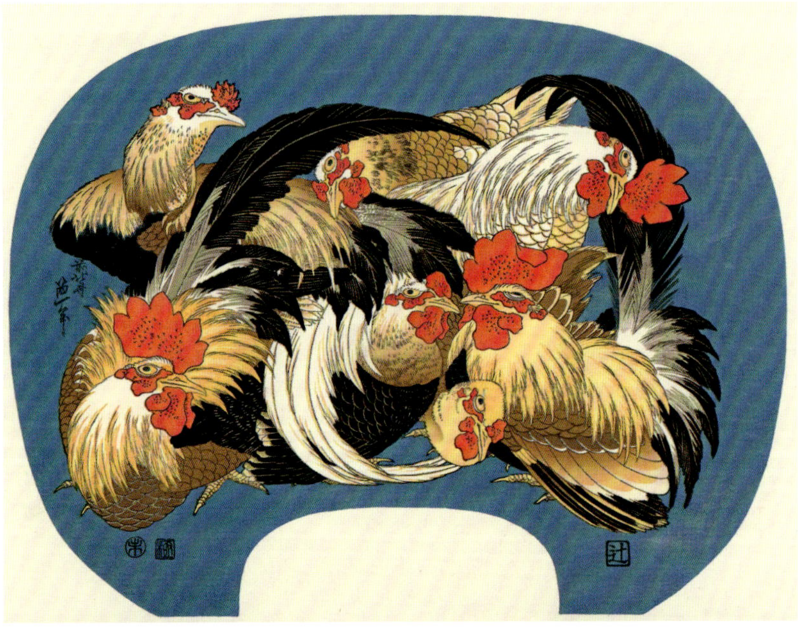

FIG. 156 (below)
Katsushika HOKUSAI
北斎 (1760–1849)
Flock of Chickens 群鶏 (1840s)
Fan print, 25 x 33 cm
Courtesy of Adachi Institute of Woodcut Prints

One of Hokusai's great prints, very rare and exceptionally beautiful, this shows seven fowls realistically gathered together to complement the round shape of the fan. The birds are carefully drawn and individualized, their facial expressions portraying a mixture of contentment and bewilderment. Their feathers swirl with movement. The cock is one of the twelve zodiac signs and in Japan represents martial spirit and courage. In ancient lore, the crying of the cock was said to lure the sun goddess out of her cave to restore light.

FIG. 157
Utagawa HIROSHIGE
広重 (1797–1858)
Jumantsubo Plain at Susaki, from *One Hundred Famous Views of Edo* 深川洲崎十万坪
(1857)
37 x 24 cm
Courtesy of Adachi Institute of Woodcut Prints

Strictly speaking, this print should be placed in the chapter on landscapes, but the eagle is so powerfully drawn and commands so much attention that it is equally appropriate to include it here. The body of the bird, twisted in movement as if ready to swoop on its prey, provides a startling contrast to the snow-covered plains below, seen from a true bird's-eye view. In first editions of this print, the claws on the eagle are highlighted in lacquer, creating a startling effect.

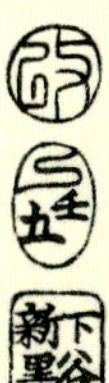

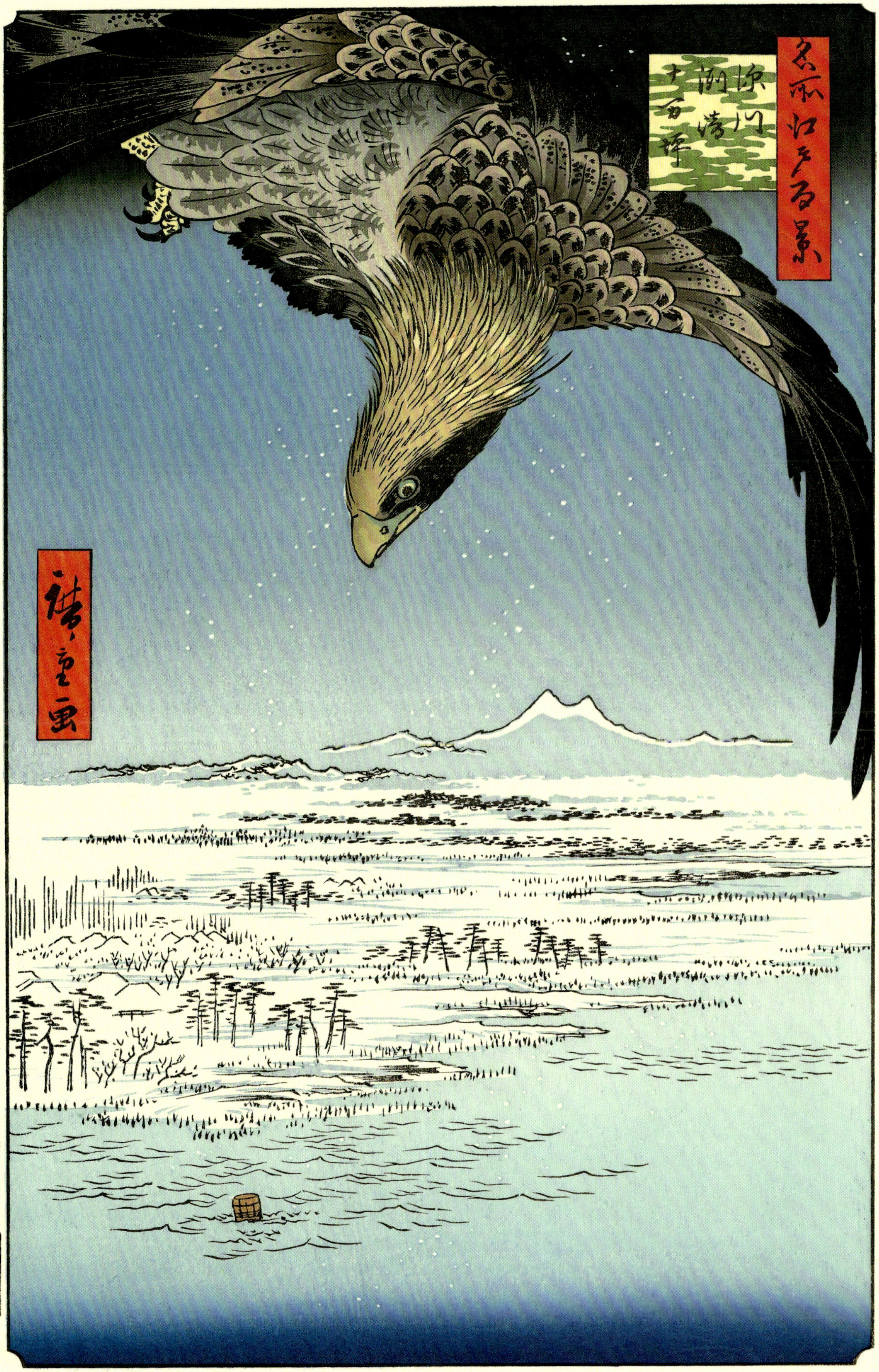

名所江戸百景
深川洲崎十万坪
廣重画
下谷新黒
魚栄

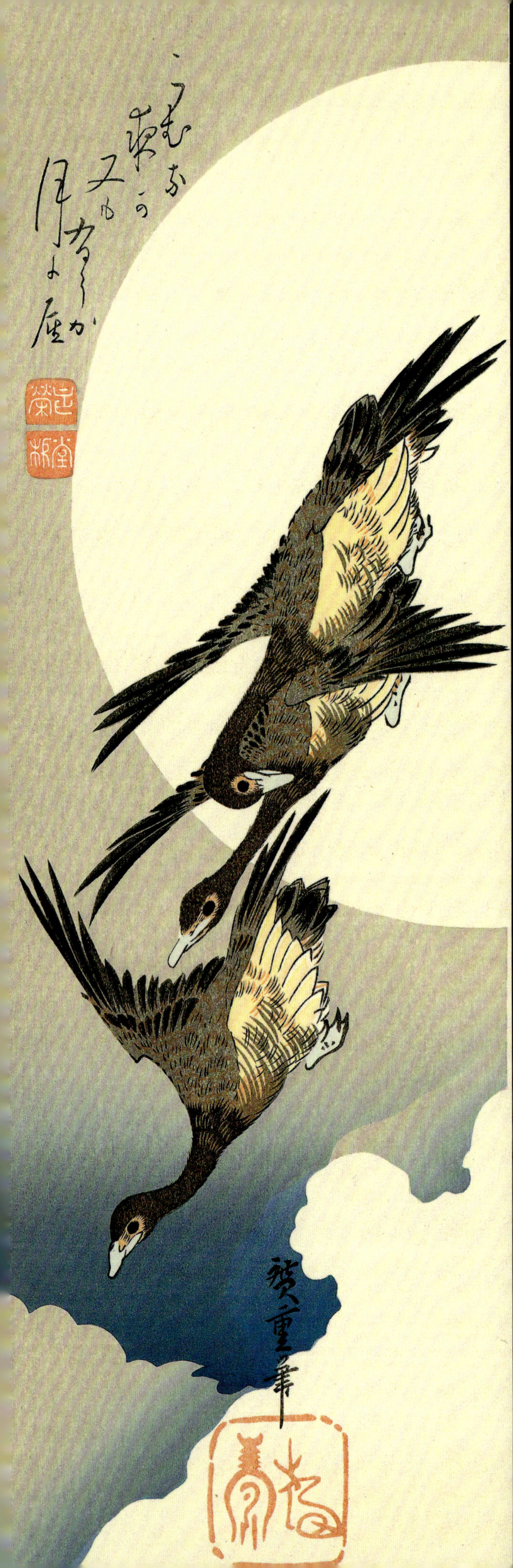

FIG. 158
Utagawa HIROSHIGE
広重 (1797–1858)
Wild Geese and Full Moon
月に雁 (1830s)
38 x 13 cm
Courtesy of Adachi Institute of Woodcut Prints

This print displays remarkable skill with the *bokashi* printing technique, used to highlight the white moon and clouds behind the dramatic blue graded sky. The return of wild geese (*kari*) in autumn was so anticipated in Japan that the eighth month was known as Kariigetsu. Wild geese have been used as a design motif since the eleventh century, and have become a symbol of long-lasting marital love.

FIG. 159
Utagawa HIROSHIGE
広重 (1797–1858)
White Heron and Blooming Irises 菖蒲に白鷺 (1830s)
38.5 x 17.5 cm
Courtesy of Adachi Institute of Woodcut Prints

This print introduces another printing technique called *karazuri* or blind embossing. The block for the feathers was cut but not inked, and the *baren* pushed the paper into the block. This technique was often used for white on white *kimono* patterns. In China, the heron is considered a symbol of longevity, but in Japan its name, *sagi*, has a double meaning for cheating, and is thus not commonly used for decorative motifs despite its beauty.

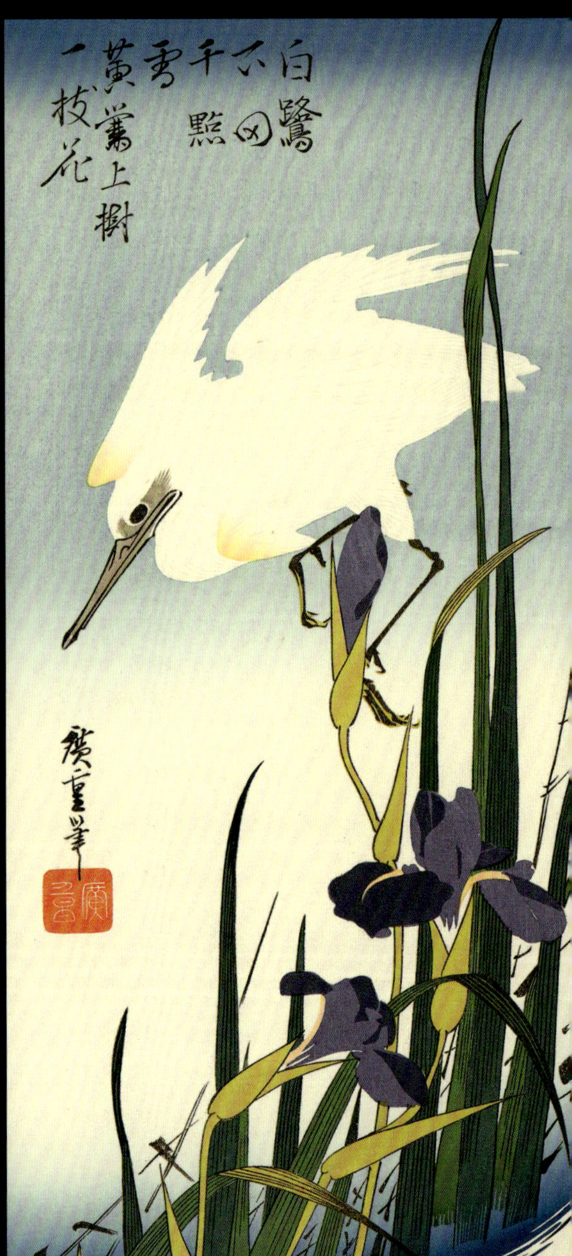

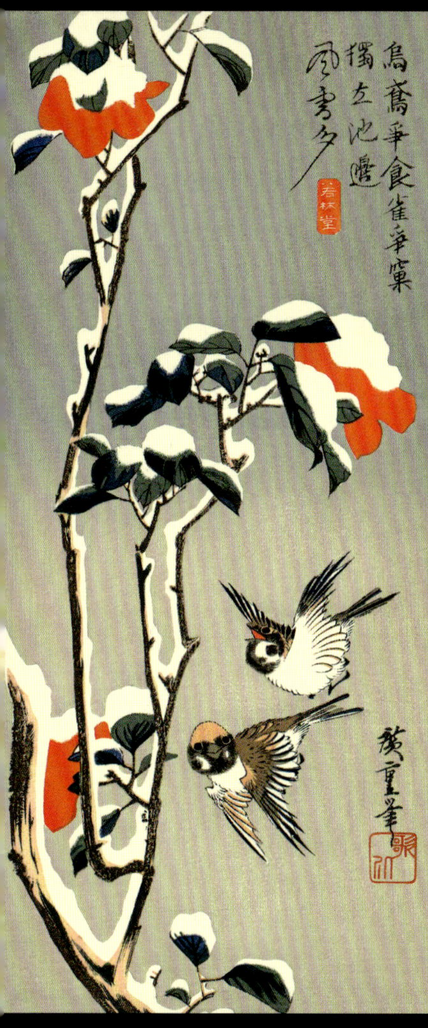

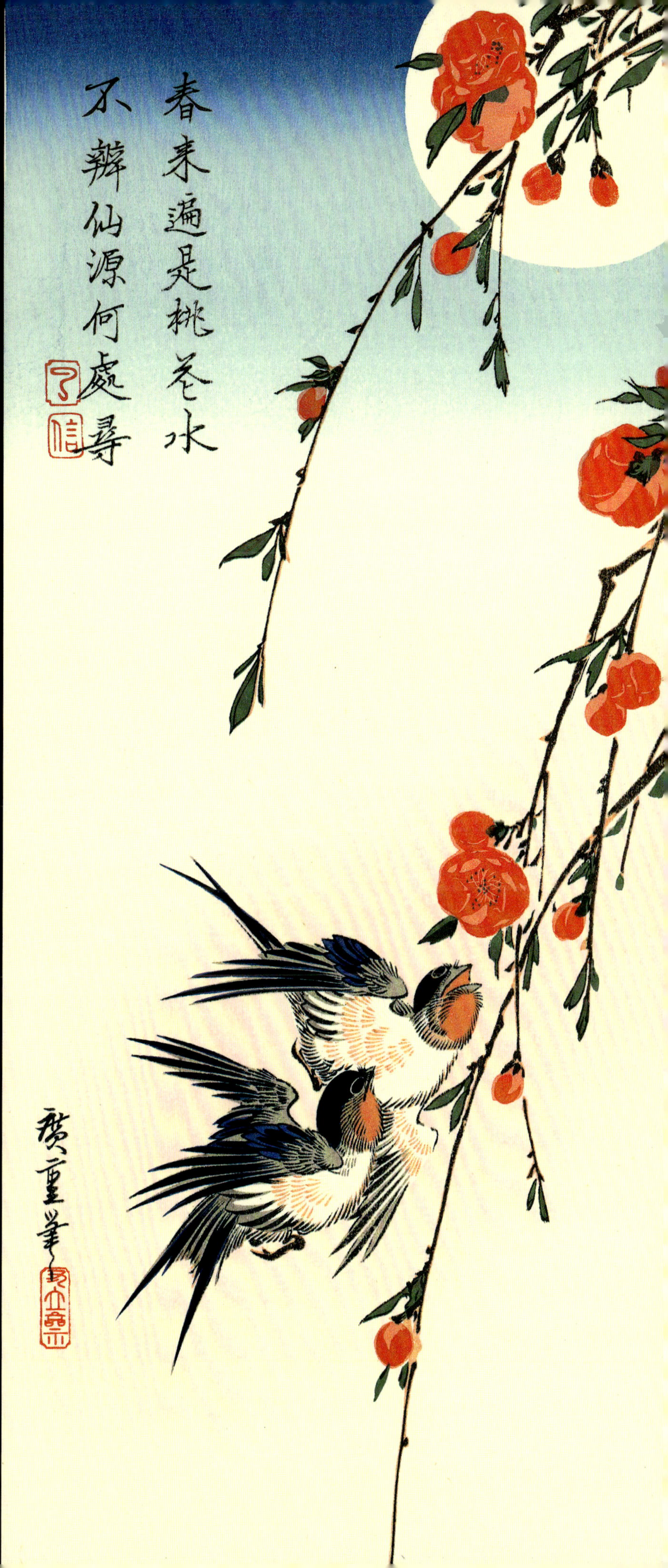

IG. 160
Jtagawa HIROSHIGE
広重 (1797–1858)
amellias and Sparrows in Snow 雪中椿に雀
1830s)
39.5 x 18 cm
Courtesy of Adachi Institute of Woodcut Prints

he sparrows appear alive in this print as they flap heir wings and look for a nest in the heavy snow-covered branch of the camellia tree. Sparrows *suzume*) are a very common theme in Japanese printing and poetry and design motifs. The bird s associated with honor, and even though very ommon throughout Japan is highly regarded.

IG. 161
Jtagawa HIROSHIGE
広重 (1797–1858)
Peach Blossoms and Swallows in Moonlight
月夜桃に燕 (1830s)
8.5 x 17.5 cm
Courtesy of Adachi Institute of Woodcut Prints

n this print, the *bokashi* technique highlights the bright white moon as the swallows look for food o feed their young. The peach is a sign of longevity while the blossoms are used for medicinal purposes. Both flower and fruit are very auspicious n Japanese culture.

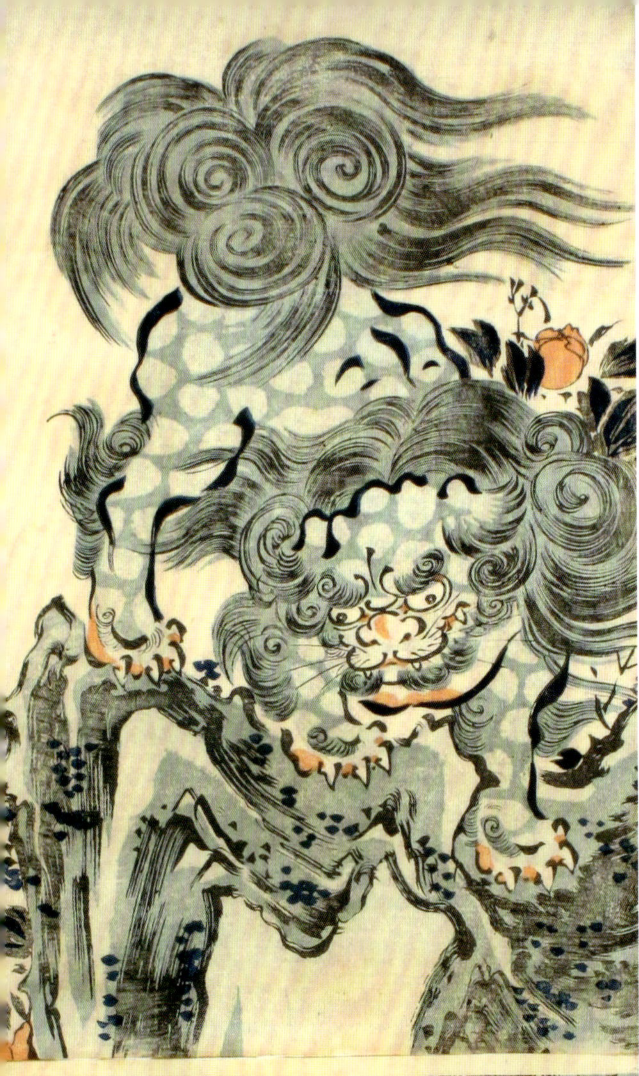

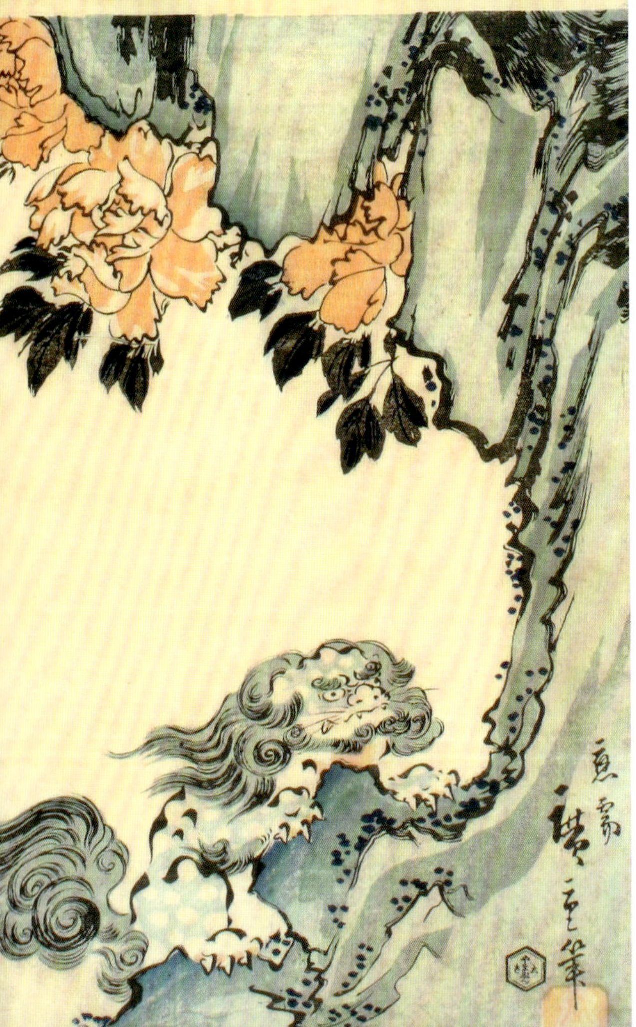

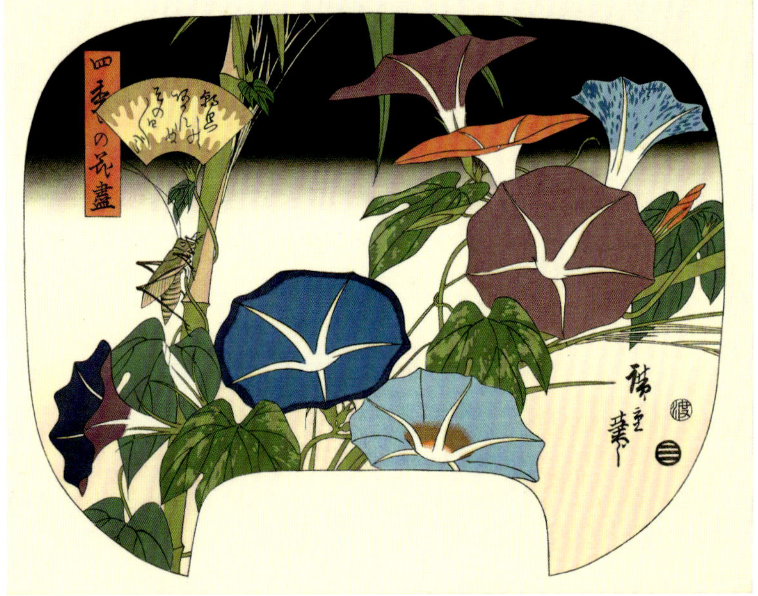

FIG. 162 (above)
Utagawa HIROSHIGE
広重 (1797–1858)
Morning Glories 朝顔 (1830s)
Fan print, 24 x 32 cm
Courtesy of Adachi Institute of Woodcut Prints

Morning glories and grasshoppers are an appropriate subject for a fan, which is traditionally discarded after one season, since they also have a short lifespan. The simplified design of the flowers displays an underlying understanding of their structure.

FIG. 163 (left)
Utagawa HIROSHIGE
広重 (1797–1858)
Shishi and Cub 獅子 (1850s)
Vertical diptych, 78 x 27 cm
Courtesy of Mita Arts Gallery

With a limited palette of grays and pinks, Hiroshige created this dynamic composition of a legendary Chinese lion, which was adopted into Japanese culture from China and Korea. It is used extensively in Okinawa as a decorative element in home architecture. It is also known as Komainu, and is found at the entrance of Shinto shrines.

FIG. 164
Kawanabe KYOSAI
暁斉 (1831–89)
Wild Tiger 猛虎 (1861)
39 x 27 cm
Courtesy of Mita Arts Gallery

This exciting print shows a wild tiger devouring a fox. Tigers have been known in Japan for centuries through Chinese art and the skins imported from Asia. The anatomy is very stylized but draws attention to the tiger's courage and fierce attributes.

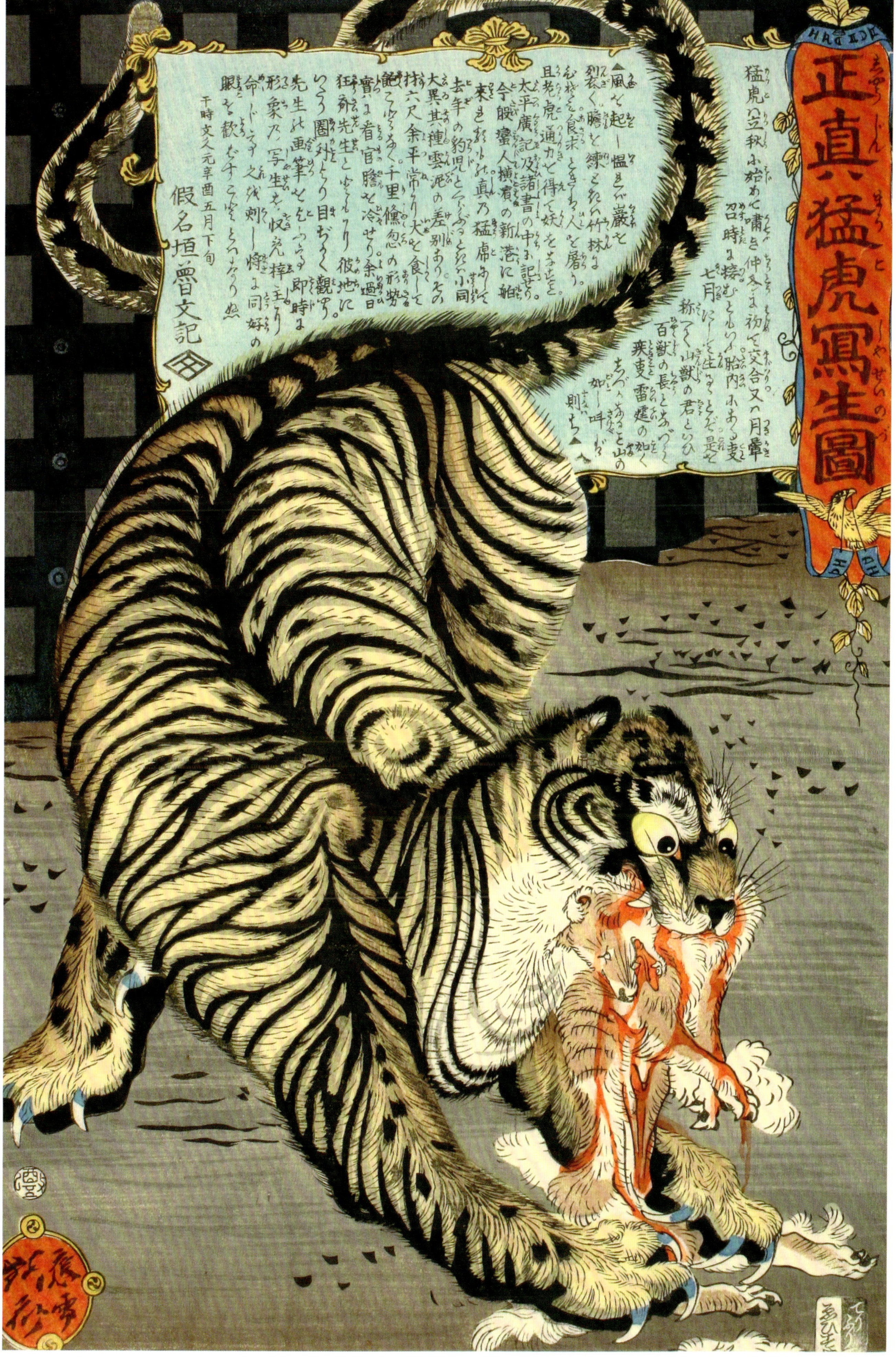
正真猛虎寫生圖
假名垣魯文記

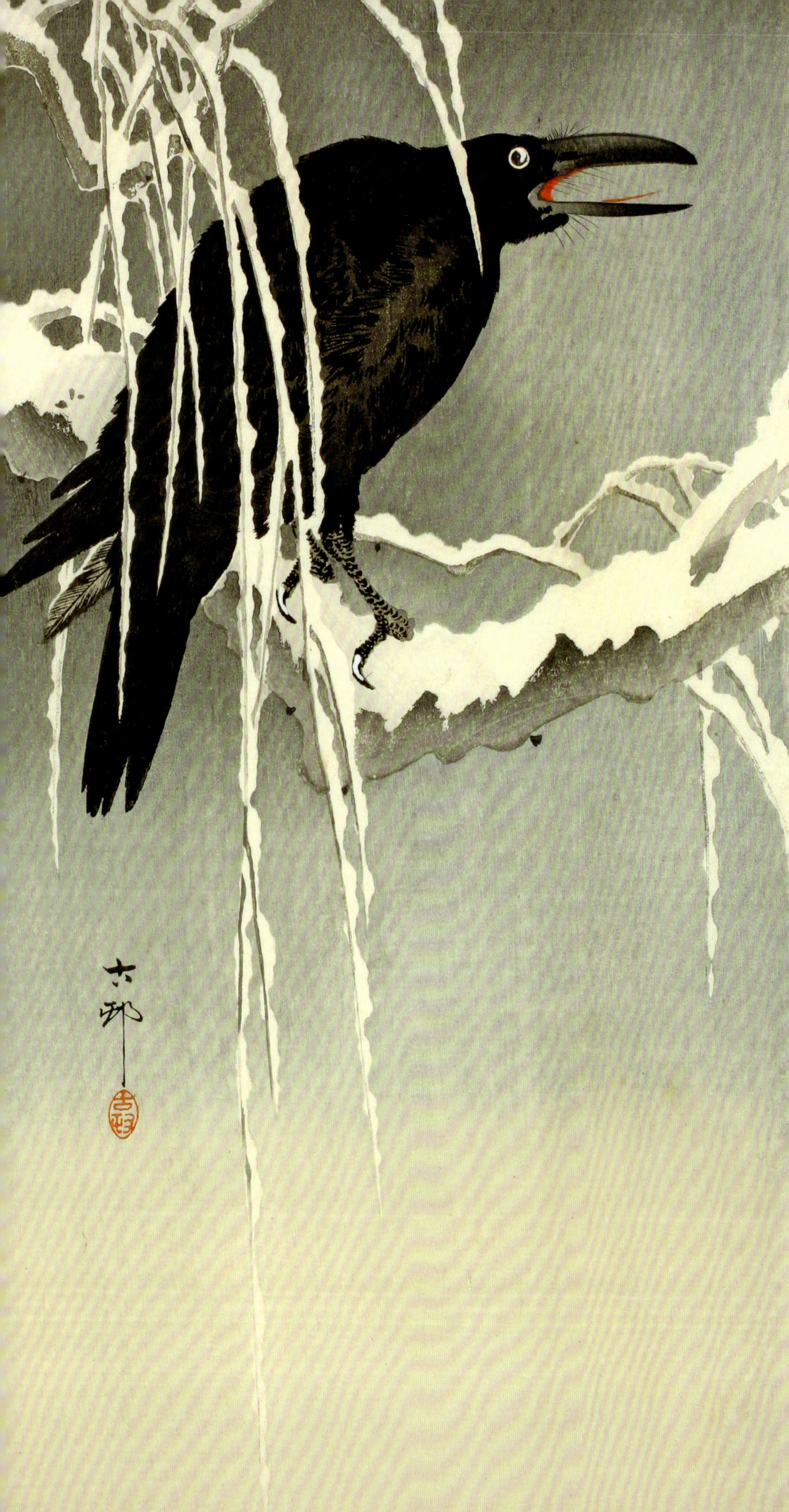

FIG. 165 (left)
Ohara KOSON
小原　古邨 (1877–1945)
Crow on a Snowy Bough
雪中の烏 (1920s)
35.7 x 18.8 cm
Courtesy of Mita Arts Gallery

The crow was one of Koson's favorite birds. In this print, a solitary crow perches on the snow-covered bough of a tree, calling out into the wilderness. We can sense the crow's intelligence, persistence and power. The touch of red visible in its open mouth provides a dramatic contrast to the largely monochromatic print.

FIG. 166
Ohara KOSON
小原　古邨 (1877–1945)
Autumn Grasses, Flowers and Moon 月下の秋草 (1920s)
37.4 x 19 cm
Courtesy of Mita Arts Gallery

Koson's reverence for the natural world is apparent in the meticulous way he has rendered the pampas grass with white flowers, yellow maiden-flowers and blue Chinese bellflowers against the soft colors of the hazy moon.

FIG. 167
Ohara KOSON
小原　古邨 (1877–1945)
Nuthatch Atop Persimmon
柿に小鳥 (1920s)
34.7 x 19.1
Courtesy of Mita Arts Gallery

Koson's skill as a painter is evident in the watercolor effect of his prints. Likewise, the skills of the woodblock carver and printer are reflected in the carefully delineated detail, such as the veins of the leaves and the claws of the bird splayed across the top of the dark red fruit.

FIG. 168
Shibata ZESHIN
柴田　是真 (1807–91)
Crows 烏 (1888)
24.6 x 25.9 cm
Courtesy of Mita Arts Gallery

In this fine print, energized crows appear to chase each other across the sky. The contrast of the black crows silhouetted against an orange sky is striking. Zeshin created another somewhat similar print entitled "Crows in Flight at Sunrise."

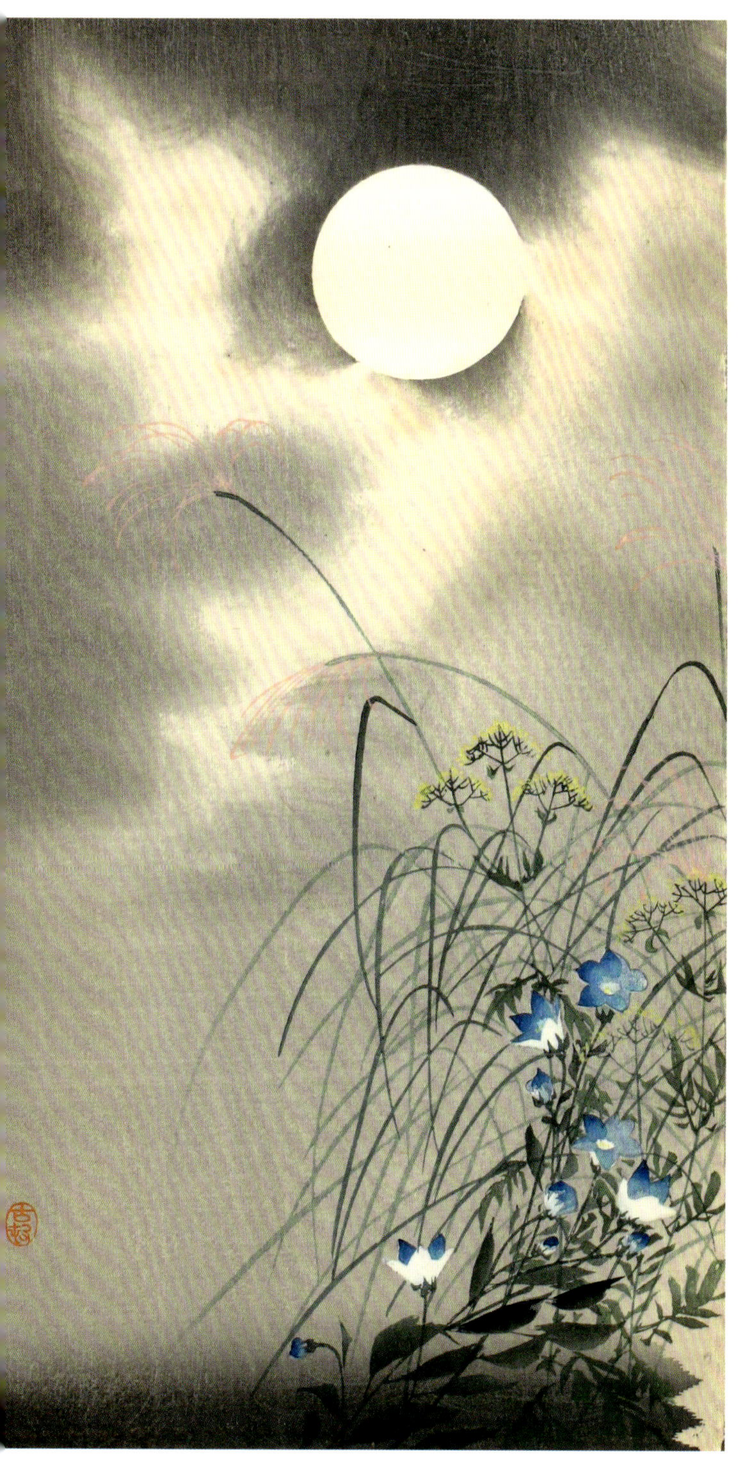

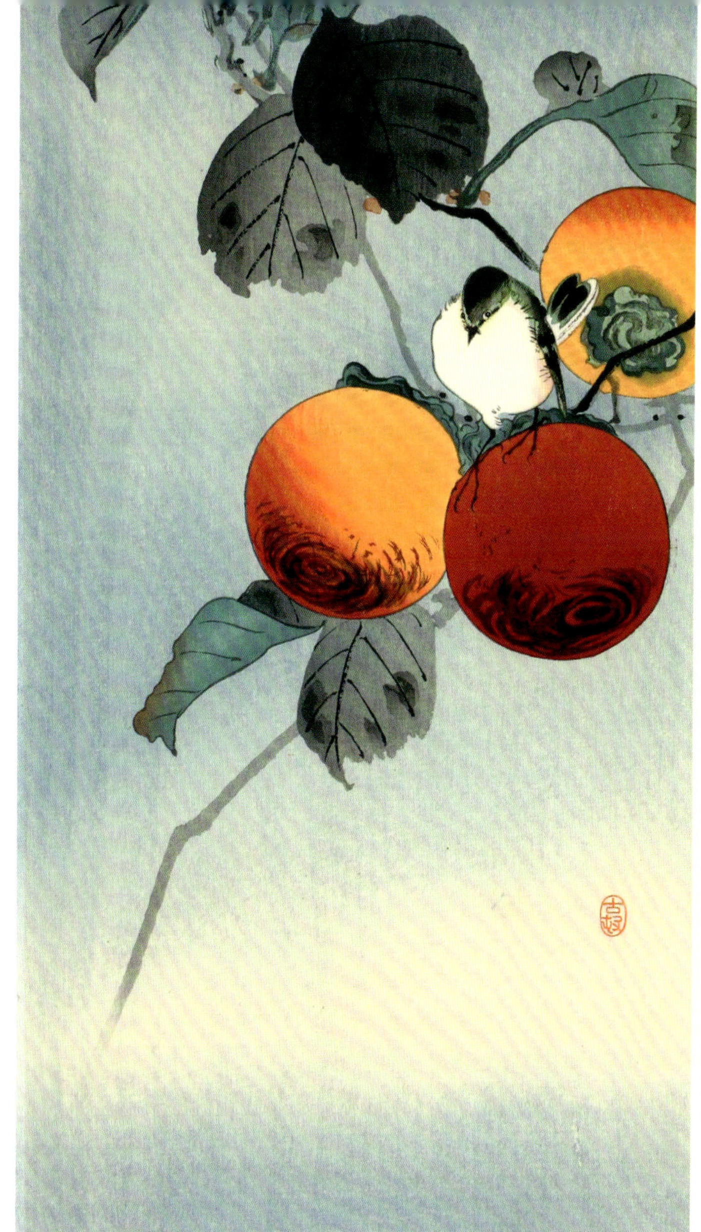

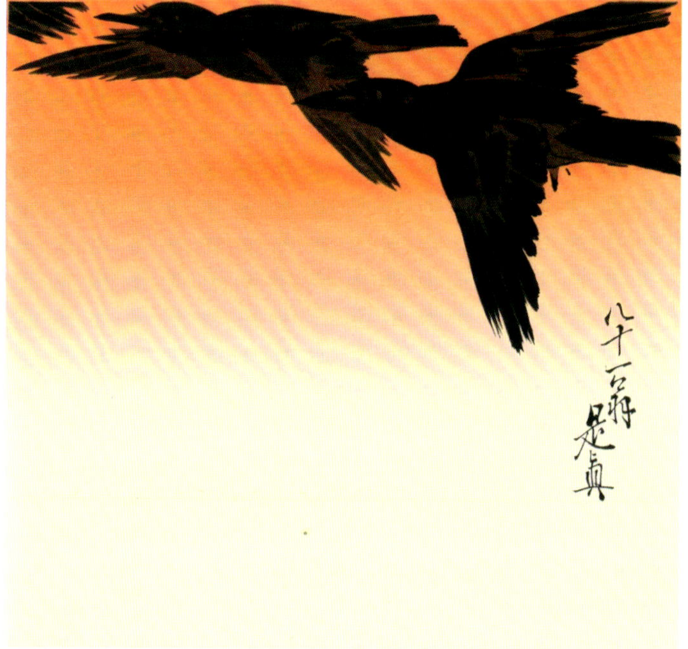
八十一翁
是真

CHAPTER TEN

Heroes and Ghosts

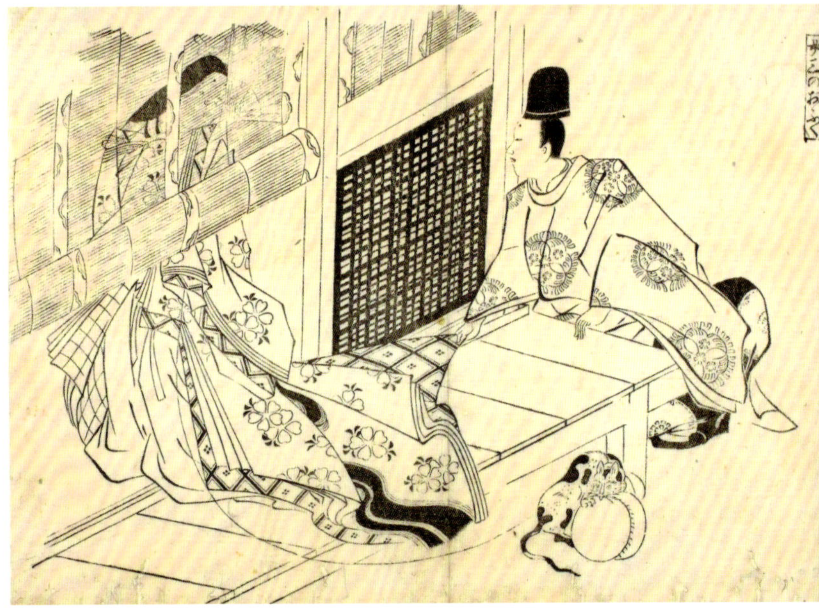

From the mid-seventeenth century, when woodblock prints depicting fully developed *ukiyo-e* subjects first took root in the metropolitan culture of Edo (Tokyo), both the subject matter and pictorial style of *ukiyo-e* underwent changes in accordance with the prevailing political climate in the country, the social and cultural context of the times and changing censorship regulations. Political and military power during the Edo period was in the hands of the *shogun* and the country was virtually isolated from the rest of the world. From the beginning of Edo *ukiyo-e*, it was illegal to depict current events with political ramifications or to comment on ruling families and their predecessors. In 1804, censorship was tightened to include a ban on the depiction of warriors who lived later than 1573.

In 1842, during the intensified censorship regulations of the Tenpo Reforms, prints of courtesans, *geisha* entertainers and *kabuki* actors were also banned. Prints with historical themes were, however, allowed, and so pictures depicting warriors, scenes of historical figures and events and legends became the main output and source of livelihood for many print artists.

In a country that remained relatively static for hundreds of years, the historical subjects of *ukiyo-e* were usually scenes from classic works of Japanese literature or imaginative impressions of legends. The numerous wars that caused so much upheaval in Japan prior to the unification by the Tokugawa *shogun* were another source of inspiration for illustrations, as were the conflicts between the Kamakura military governments and the battles between two major clans, the Minamoto (Genji) and the Taira (Heike). Another major influence in *ukiyo-e* art was the poetry-illustrated novels of the mid-seventeenth century Tosa school. These novels were romanticized versions of famous battles of previous centuries. Religion, especially Buddhism, also provided important subject material, especially in depicting the lives of famous monks, priests, and deities.

The most famous and inspirational of the literary sources was the early eleventh-century epic-length novel *Genji monogatari (The Tale of Genji)*, attributed to the Japanese noblewoman Murasaki Shikibu (**Fig. 169**). Written chapter by chapter in three parts to entertain women of the aristocracy, it details the lengthy and complex love

FIG. 169
Artist Unknown
作者不詳
From *The Tale of Genji* 源氏物語より (mid-17th century)
Black and white print (*sumizuri-e*), 25 x 36 cm
Author's Collection

The Tale of Genji, the world's first great novel, offers a peek into the political, psychological and romantic workings of the aristocracy of mid-Heian Japan, a society quite different from the merchant class that sponsored the world of *ukiyo-e*. In this print, one of the nobles is calling on a lady who is half hidden behind a *sudare* (rolled screen) while a cat plays under the veranda. The black patches on the cat's tail lead the eye up to the lady's hair. The strong latticework in the center dominates the print.

FIG. 170
Utagawa KUNISADA (Toyokuni III)
国定 (三代豊国) (1786–1865)
Tokonatsu, from *The Tale of Genji* 床夏 源氏物語より
26 x 19.5 cm
Courtesy of Mita Arts Gallery

In this scene, called Tokonatsu, Prince Genji holds a *bangasa* (umbrella) over a princess named Tamakazura, who is engaged to the prince from the Rokujo Palace. The umbrella provides a beautiful "cover" to the composition, and the flower patterns on the *kimono* blend beautifully with the garden.

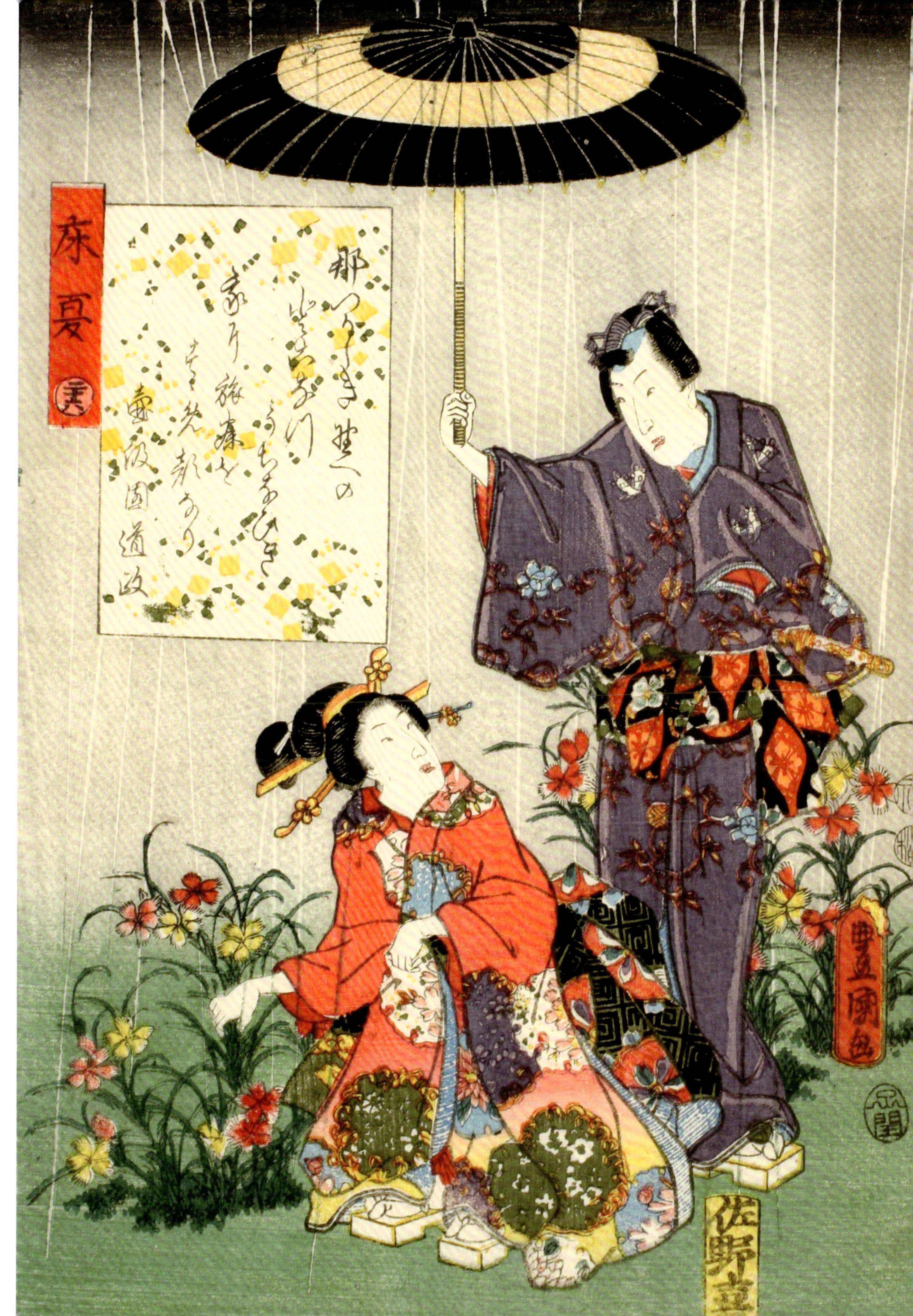
床夏
豊国画
佐野喜

adventures of a son of a Japanese emperor, Prince Genji, who is relegated to commoner status, and the early lives of two of his prominent descendants. Despite the appearance of some 400 major and minor characters, a complex web of human and spiritual relations and a complicated sequence of events revolving around Genji's romantic escapades, it is a remarkable literary work noteworthy for its internal consistency, well-developed characterization of all the major players, psychological insights and the light it throws on court life of the mid-Heian period.

Scenes from this epic, considered to be the world's oldest novel, wove their way into pictorial art in one form or another. In *ukiyo-e* printmaking, characters and episodes from *The Tale of Genji* were depicted in both single-sheet prints and triptychs. One of the greatest print exponents was Utagawa Kunisada (1786–1865), known as Utagawa Toyokuni III later in his career, who monopolized the genre of *Genji* prints for fifteen years (1835–50) (**Figs. 170–172**). It was only after 1850 that other print artists, such as Utagawa Kuniyoshi (1797–1861) and Utagawa Sadahide Gyokuransai (1807–73), the latter one of Kunisada's more accomplished students, began to produce similar designs.

A favorite subject of historical warrior print triptychs was the Japanese *samurai* Miyamoto Musashi (1584–1645), who became renowned through stories of his excellent swordsmanship in numerous duels (**Figs. 173, 174**). He created and perfected a two-handed style of swordsmanship (*nitoryu*). He is reputed to have fought over sixty duels in the service of various clans, during which he was never defeated. In his later years, he created recognized masterpieces of calligraphy and classic ink painting (*sumi-e*).

Stories and characters from Japan's rich heritage of legends abound in *ukiyo-e*. Likewise, visual representations of myths and the spirit world became a part of the historical *ukiyo-e* repertoire. Especially well known for

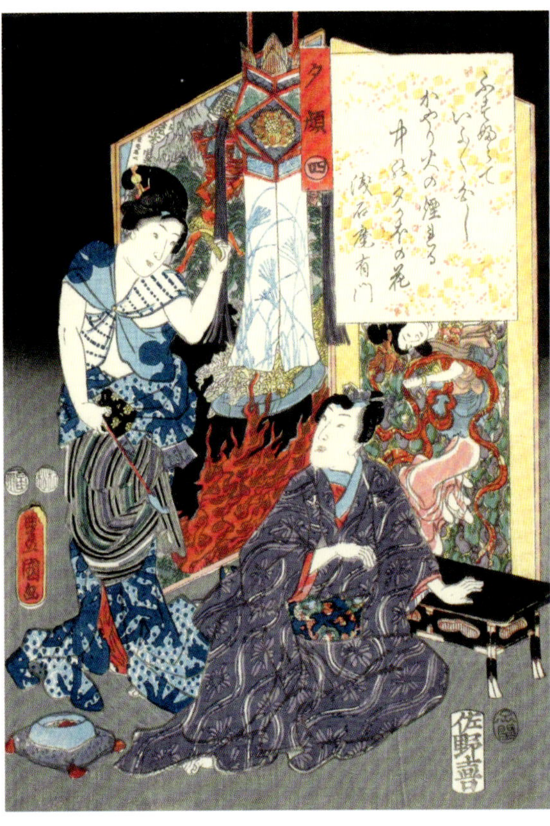

FIG. 171
Utagawa KUNISADA (Toyokuni III)
国定 (三代豊国) (1786–1865)
From *The Tale of Genji* 源氏物語より
26 x 19.5 cm
Courtesy of Mita Arts Gallery

While using *The Tale of Genji* as a source of inspiration, artists modified the cultural milieu of the Heian period to suit the contemporary scene. Here, the characters are dressed in modern Edo costumes relating to the poetry in the cartouche. In *The Tale of Genji*, poetry is frequently used in conversation, often serving to communicate thinly veiled allusions.

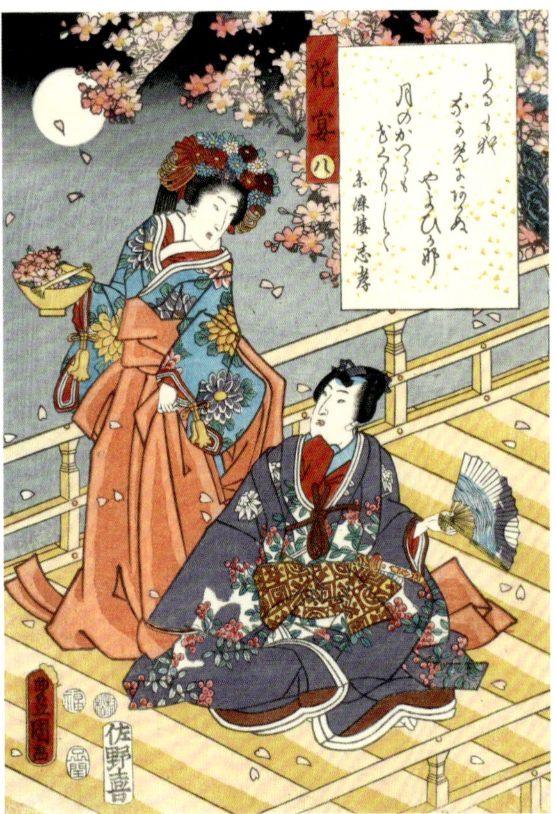

FIG. 172
Utagawa KUNISADA (Toyokuni III)
国定 (三代豊国) (1786–1865)
From *The Tale of Genji* 源氏物語より
26 x 19.5 cm
Courtesy of Mita Arts Gallery

This lovely scene under the cherry blossoms shows Prince Genji at a flower viewing party with the princess of the Rokujo Palace. Her hair covering, made of flowers, is very striking. The pattern on Genji's *kimono* is also in keeping with the event. In *The Tale of Genji*, much is made of Genji's good looks. He is also portrayed as a master of speech, poetry, music, manners and dress.

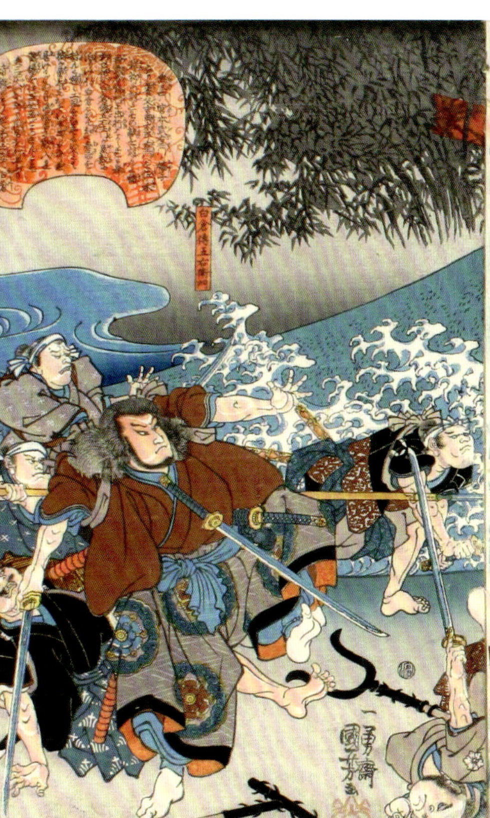

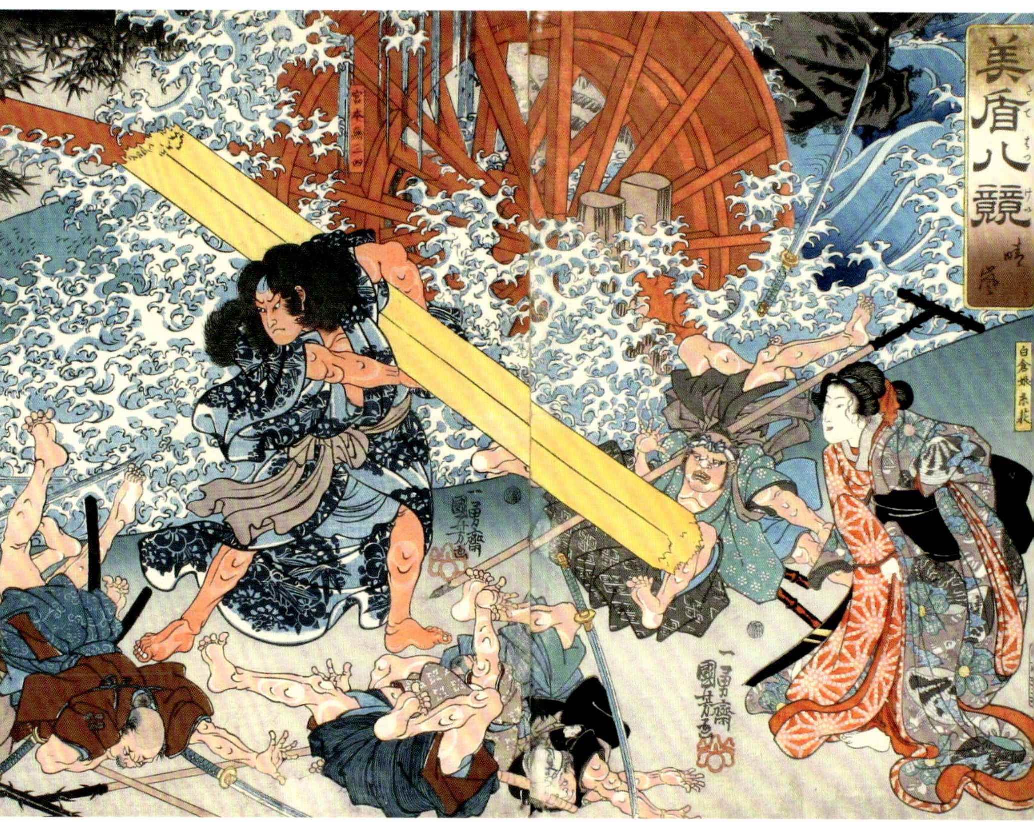

FIG.173

Utagawa KUNIYOSHI

国芳 (1797–1861)

Miyamoto Musashi 宮本 武蔵 (1840s)

Triptych, 39 x 81 cm

Courtesy of Mita Arts Gallery

This scene shows Miyamoto Musashi, probably the most famous swordsman in Japanese history, brandishing a huge wooden pillar in a duel near a large water wheel. The woman at right often appears in pictures of Musashi. She was deeply in love with him and followed him throughout his adventures, much like a modern-day "groupie."

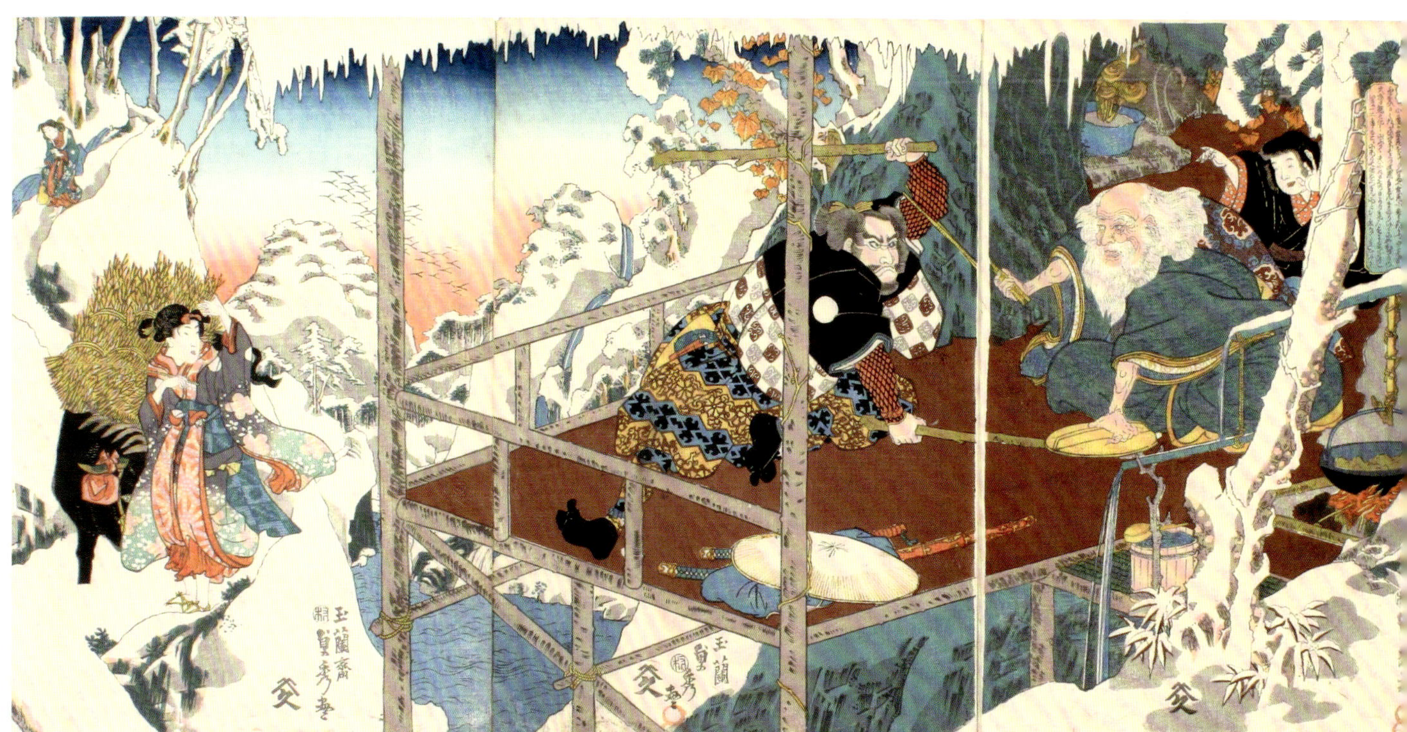

FIG. 174

Utagawa SADAHIDE Gyokuransai

貞秀 (1807–1873)

Miyamoto Musashi 宮本 武蔵 (1850s)

Triptych, 39 x 81 cm

Courtesy of Mita Arts Gallery

In this scene, Musashi is honing his two-handed style of swordsmanship, using a large sword and a companion sword at the same time, under the tutelage of his teacher, an old man named Kasahara Zuioken. To the left is his famous female admirer, who followed him wherever he went.

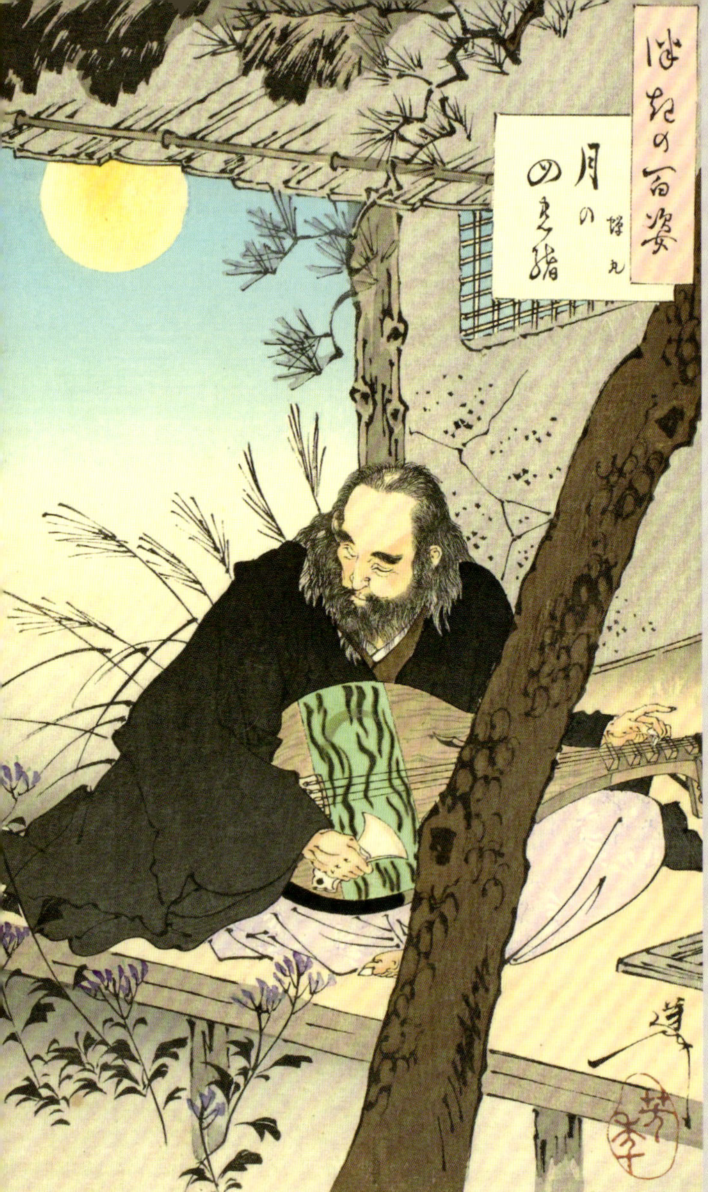

FIG. 175 (above)
Tsukioka YOSHITOSHI
芳年 (1839–92)
Semimaru, from *One Hundred Aspects of the Moon* 月百姿 せいにまる (1891)
36 x 24 cm
Author's Collection

In traditional Japan, the moon was a beloved object of beauty and a part of daily life. In *One Hundred Aspects of the Moon*, each subject—drawn from Japanese and Chinese legends, heroes of classic novels and plays, famous musicians and poets—is captured at a moment in time while suspended in a poetic dialog with the moon, sometimes a barely detectable sliver peeking through trees or a main element of the design. Here, Semimaru, the blind tenth-century poet and musician and attendant to the Emperor Uda, is tuning a string on his *biwa*, a lute-type instrument from China. The drawing of the face, hands and foot is remarkably realistic.

FIG. 176 (below)
Tsukioka YOSHITOSHI
芳年 (1839–92)
Daruma, from *One Hundred Aspects of the Moon* 月百姿　達磨 (1886)
39 x 27 cm
Courtesy of Mita Arts Gallery

Originally an Indian priest named Bodhidharma, Daruma crossed over China to introduce Buddhism in Japan in the tenth century. He is mostly shown in meditation. Here, wearing a beautifully oxidized robe, Daruma is depicted seated next to the walls of the cave that crumbled after nine years of meditating next to them. He is said to have lost the use of his arms and legs during his long meditation. His large eyes are the result of his cutting off his eyelids so that he would not fall asleep while meditating.

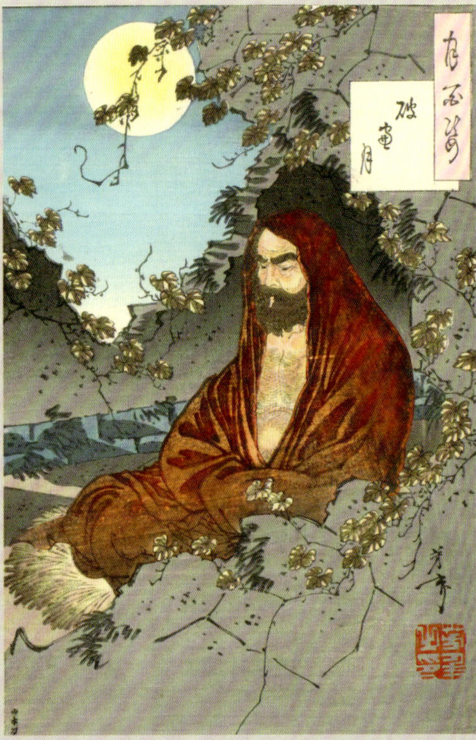

FIG. 177
Tsukioka YOSHITOSHI
芳年 (1839–92)
Kannon, from *One Hundred Aspects of the Moon* 観音 (1888)
39 x 27 cm
Courtesy of Mita Arts Gallery

Kannon was originally one of the Chinese Buddhist deities, who over the years was transformed into a female form. Today in Japan she is considered by many to be the goddess of mercy and there are numerous temples dedicated to her. She takes many forms, some of which have numerous arms each holding a different offering. She is always in white and often pictured seated on a rocky island. Here, she wears an assortment of ornaments.

FIG. 178
Utagawa KUNIYOSHI
国芳 (1797–1861)
The Hero Byokwansaku Rescuing a Woman from a Villain, from *One Hundred and Eight Heroes of the Popular Suikoden All Told* 悪党から女を助ける豪傑　病開索楊雄 (1827–30)
39 x 27 cm
Courtesy of Mita Arts Gallery

In *One Hundred and Eight Heroes of the Popular Suikoden All Told*, seventy-five fierce, tattooed heroes appear on the seventy-four known *oban*-size sheets. The series is noted for its colors, detail and surprisingly modern appearance. Here, Byokwansaku, with a sword between his teeth and his right hand gripping the throat of the villain, attempts to rescue a woman.

FIG. 179
Utagawa KUNIYOSHI
国芳 (1797–1861)
Soshiko Raio, from *One Hundred and Eight Heroes of the Popular Suikoden All Told* 挿翅虎雷横 (1827–30)
39 x 27 cm
Courtesy of Mita Arts Gallery

In this disturbing picture, Soshiko Raio is trying to kill the woman, a singer, who murdered his mother. The banana leaf appears to be used as a weapon.

FIG. 180
Utagawa KUNIYOSHI
国芳 (1797–1861)
Oni Wakamaru, from *One Hundred and Eight Heroes of the Popular Suikoden All Told* 鬼若丸 (1827–30)
39 x 27 cm
Courtesy of Mita Arts Gallery

Oni Wakamaru was the boyhood name of the legendary swordsman and warrior monk Musashibo Benkei, who became Minamoto Yoshitsune's trusted assistant. The third hand under the hero's robe could belong to a third person partially hidden behind the hero.

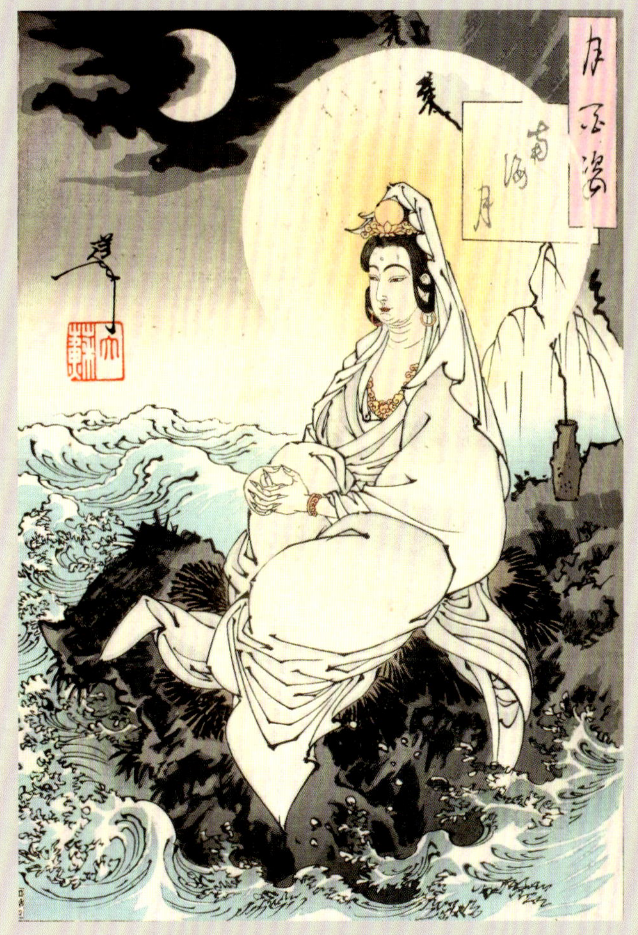

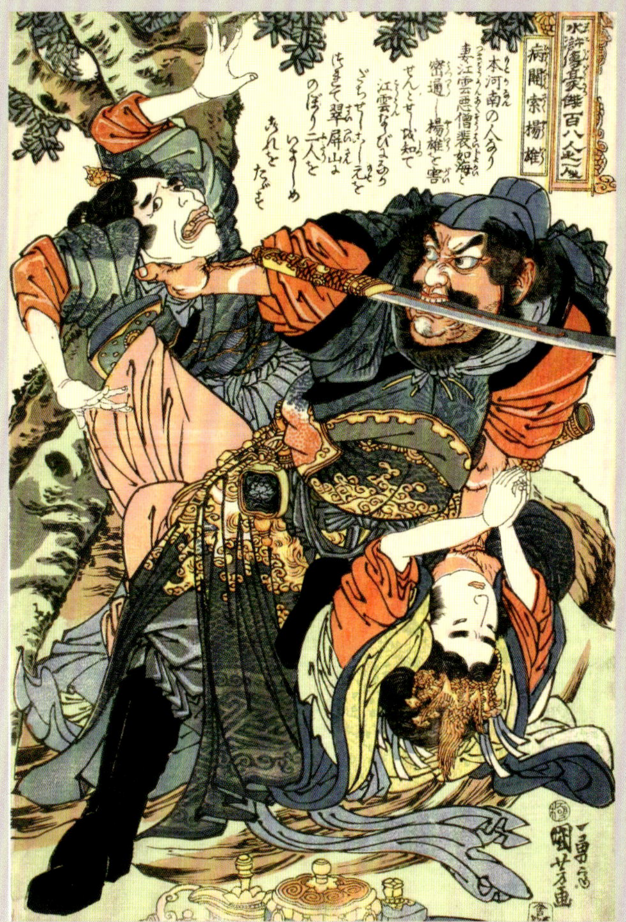

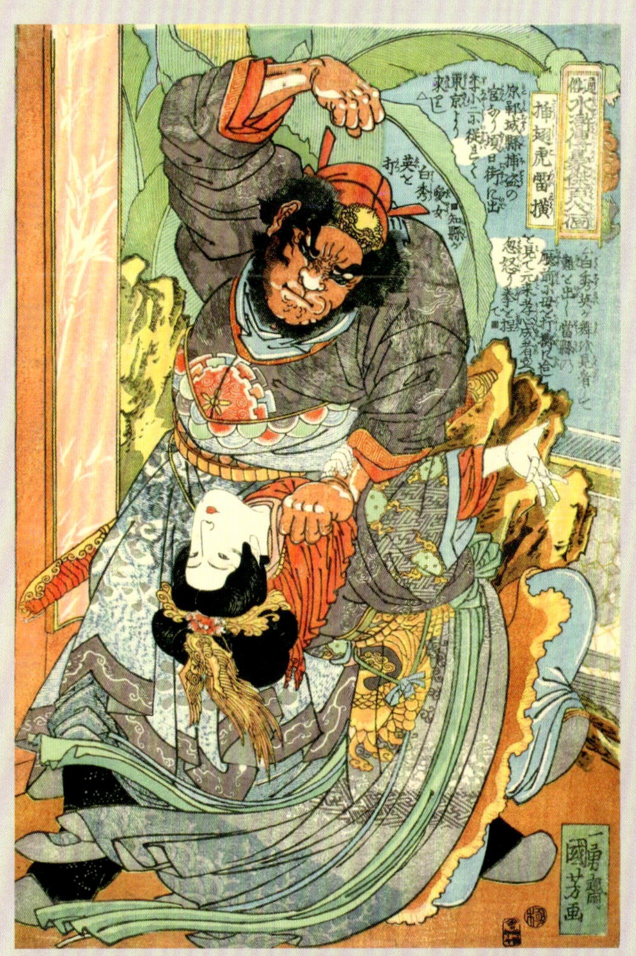

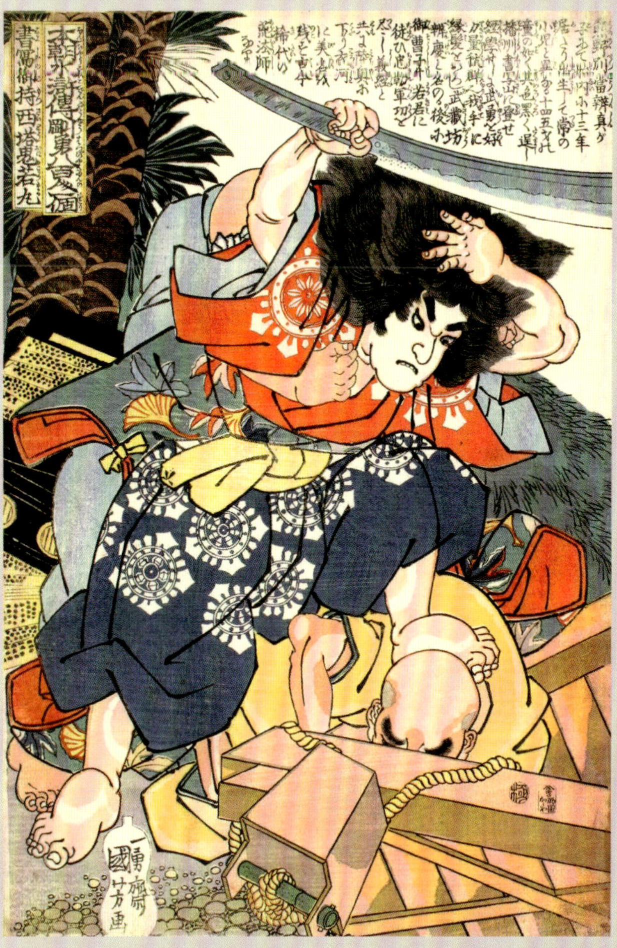

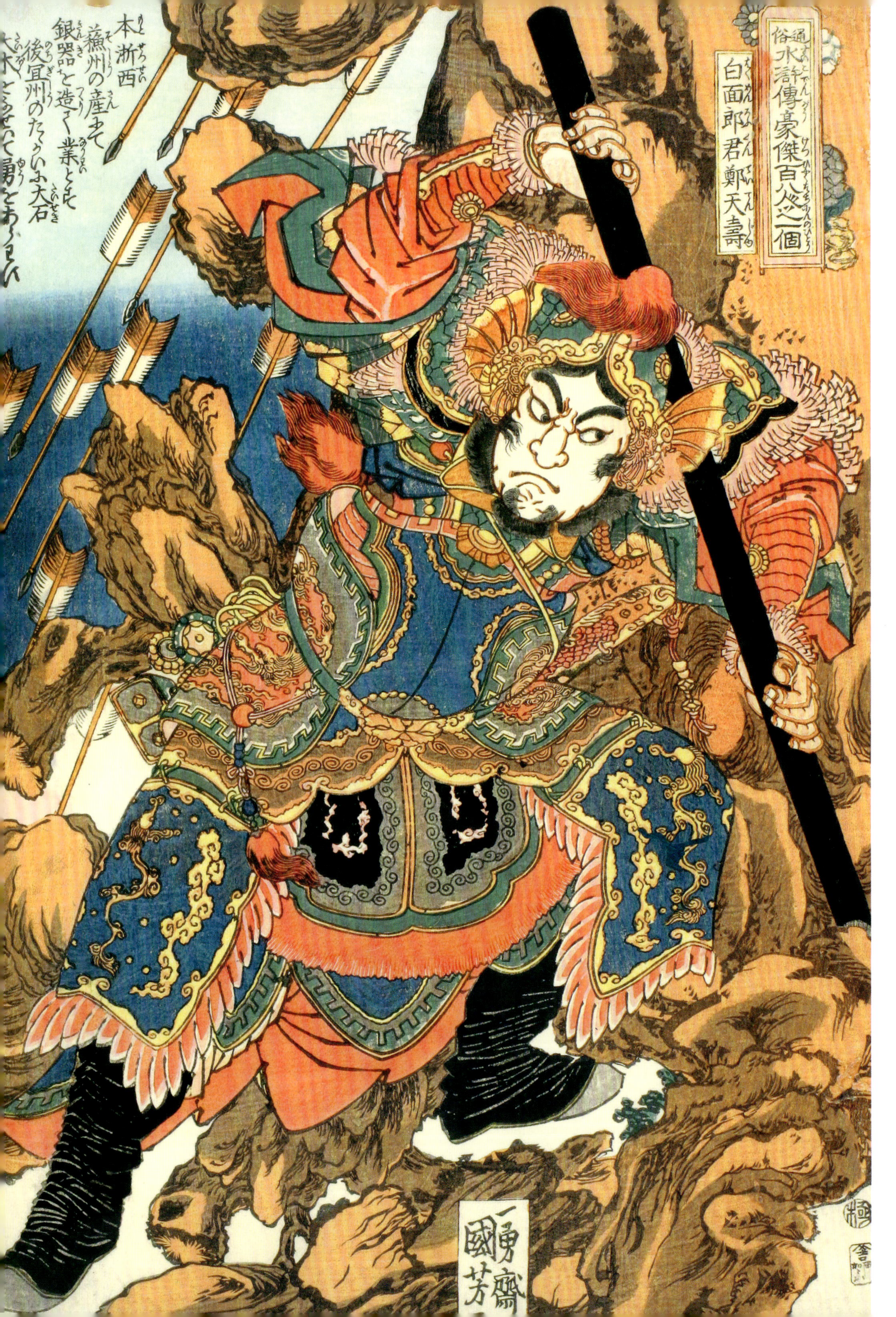

通俗水滸傳豪傑百八人之一個
白面郎君鄭天壽
本浙西
蘇州の產にて
銀器を造る業として
後宜州のたゝかひ大石
一勇齋國芳

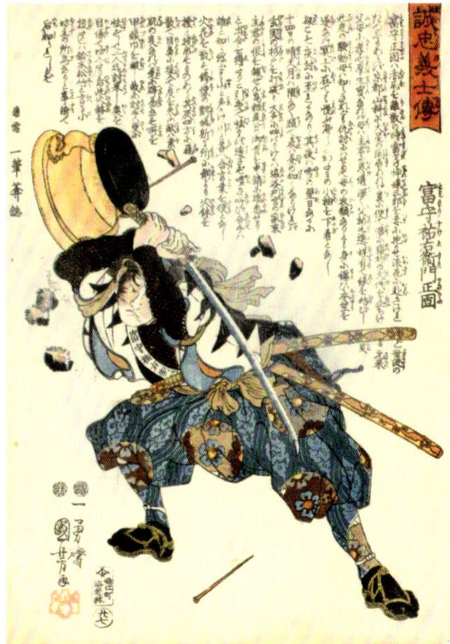

FIG. 182
Utagawa KUNIYOSHI
国芳 (1797–1861)
Tominori Masakata, from *Kanadehon Chushingura (The Revenge of the Forty-seven Ronin)* 冨森正因 (1847)
39 x 27 cm
Courtesy of Mita Arts Gallery

Kuniyoshi's biographical *Chushingura* series is a study of figures in action: the heroes bend, crouch, duck, twist, charge, slash, thrust, lean forward, fall back, pose triumphantly, etc. at the scene of an attack. Each *ronin* portrait is isolated against a blank background on which is written his biography. A unifying motif is the striking black and white dog's tooth pattern on the *ronin* costume. Here, the warrior Tominori Masakata ducks as a metal brazier is thrown at him, covering him with coals and ash. The metal tong on the ground leads the eye of the viewer into the total composition.

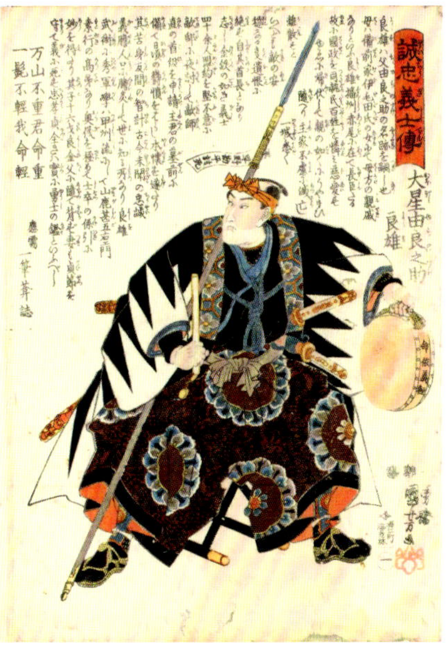

FIG. 183
Utagawa KUNIYOSHI
国芳 (1797–1861)
Ohoshi Yuranosuke, leader of the Loyal Samurai, from *Kanadehon Chushingura (The Revenge of the Forty-seven Ronin)* 大星由良之介 (1847)
39 x 27 cm
Courtesy of Mita Arts Gallery

Better known as Oishi Yoshio, Ohoshi Yuranosuke, Lord Asano Naganori's senior retainer, was forty-five years old when he led a raid on Lord Kira Yoshinaka's mansion in 1702 and beheaded the enemy of their dead master. Here, he strikes a war drum signaling the *ronin* to attack. The revenge on Lord Kira violated the strict law of loyalty to the *shogun* and the *ronin* were ordered to commit ritual suicide, which they did at the same time.

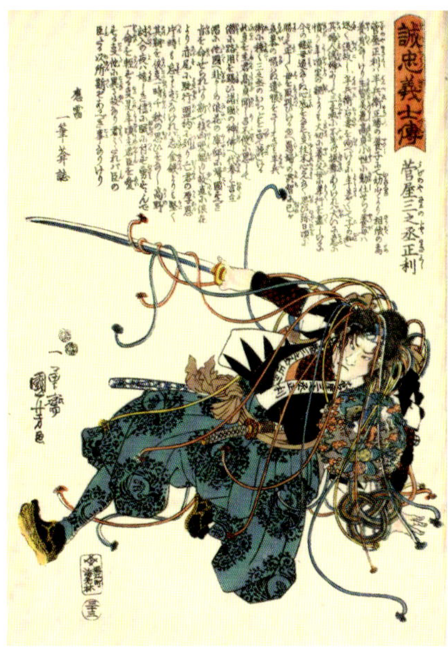

FIG. 184
Utagawa KUNIYOSHI
国芳 (1797–1861)
Sugenoya Masatoshi, from *Kanadehon Chushingura (The Revenge of the Forty-seven Ronin)* 菅谷政利 (1847)
39 x 27 cm
Courtesy of Mita Arts Gallery

Sugenoya Masatoshi is trapped in the loose strands of a scented ball (*kusudama*) while pointing his sword at the enemy. This is an exciting composition full of movement, and a tribute to Kuniyoshi's imagination.

FIG. 181 (left)
Utagawa KUNIYOSHI
国芳 (1797–1861)
Hakumenrokun Teitenja, from *One Hundred and Eight Heroes of the Popular Suikoden All Told* 白面郎君鄭天壽
39 x 27 cm
Courtesy of Mita Arts Gallery

Teitenja wields his long spear ready for combat. He was killed by an onslaught of arrows and a large stone hurled at him as he was attacking a castle.

his prints of historical warriors and battle scenes, some depicting extreme violence, the versatile artist Tsukioka Yoshitoshi (1839–92) also produced series focusing on supernatural events, ghosts, monsters and animal transformations. His many series on military and historical subjects include *One Hundred Stories of Japan and China* (1865–6), *One Hundred Warriors* (1868–9) and *Famous Generals of Japan* (1876–82), which all contain many fine prints. A later series, and perhaps the most popular of all, is *One Hundred Aspects of the Moon* (1885–92). It features subjects from Japanese history and mythology, historical and contemporary Japanese life and Chinese mythology (**Figs. 175–180**). The prints are elegantly spare, with simple backgrounds that focus on the human figure. The moon provides a unifying motif in almost all the pictures. Yoshitoshi introduced some radical technical changes in this series: a heavy use of rough brush strokes, which are expertly reproduced in the woodblock medium; a realistic portrayal of faces, which are shown from all angles; and more fully developed Western-style perspective techniques.

Utagawa Kuniyoshi (1797–1861) was another master of legendary and historical prints. He portrayed nearly 1,000 different characters depicting warriors and figures from Japan's past and from Chinese literature. Many of them are drawn from war stories such as *The Tale of the Heike* and *The Rise and Fall of the Minamoto and the Taira*. Many are also associated with superhuman feats, ghostly apparitions, dreams and omens. His prodigious output also included more than 370 warrior diptychs and triptychs between 1818 and 1861.

One of his most imaginative series is *One Hundred and Eight Heroes of the Popular Suikoden All Told*, issued over the period 1827–30. Commonly known in English as *The Water Margin*, it is the Japanese adaptation of the

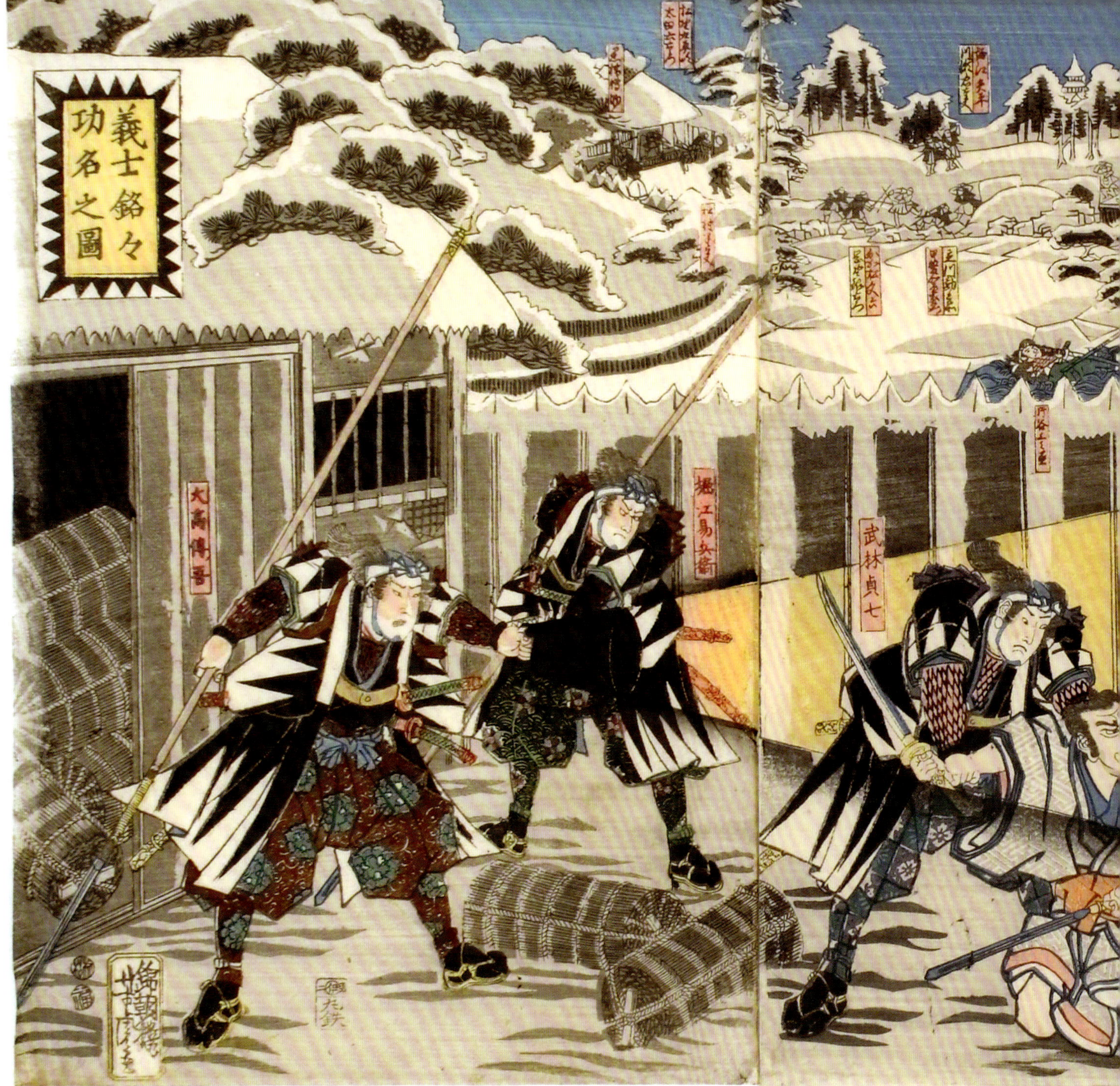

extremely popular fourteenth-century Chinese vernacular novel *Shuizu zhuan*, which recounts the exploits of a group of rebels on Mount Liang under the leadership of the brave and righteous Song Jiang. The series features single-sheet prints of individual heroes (**Figs. 179–181**). They are fierce, grimacing, muscled, tattooed Robin Hood types who, after doing battle with other brigands, became identified with Japanese warrior heroes over the tumultuous years prior to the unification of Japan. The pictures are so full of exotic detail, gore and drama, and the tattoos such a novelty, that it is no surprise that they established Kuniyoshi as a leader in the field of warrior prints.

The dramatizations of historical, military, legendary and contemporary tales on the *kabuki* stage added to the storehouse of topics for printmakers. Stories of warfare and revenge, punctuated by the heroic acts of the protagonists, were particularly popular. One of Kuniyoshi's most sought after series is *Kanadehon Chushingura*, popularly known as *The Revenge of the Forty-seven Ronin* (**Figs. 182–184**). First written for the puppet theater in 1748, and adapted soon after for actors, it has formed a staple for the *kabuki* theater down to the present day. Chronicling the famous revenge of the forty-seven masterless *samurai* (*ronin*) against the *shogun*'s master of ceremonies, Lord Kira Yoshinaka, who forced their master Asano Naganori to commit ritual suicide in 1701, the play's themes of revenge, loyalty, sacrifice, dedication and honor were enthusiastically supported by both the theater-going and print-buying public.

The play remained one of the major themes of *ukiyo-e* until the demise of the print art at the beginning of the twentieth century. Artists drew seemingly endless variations and nuances

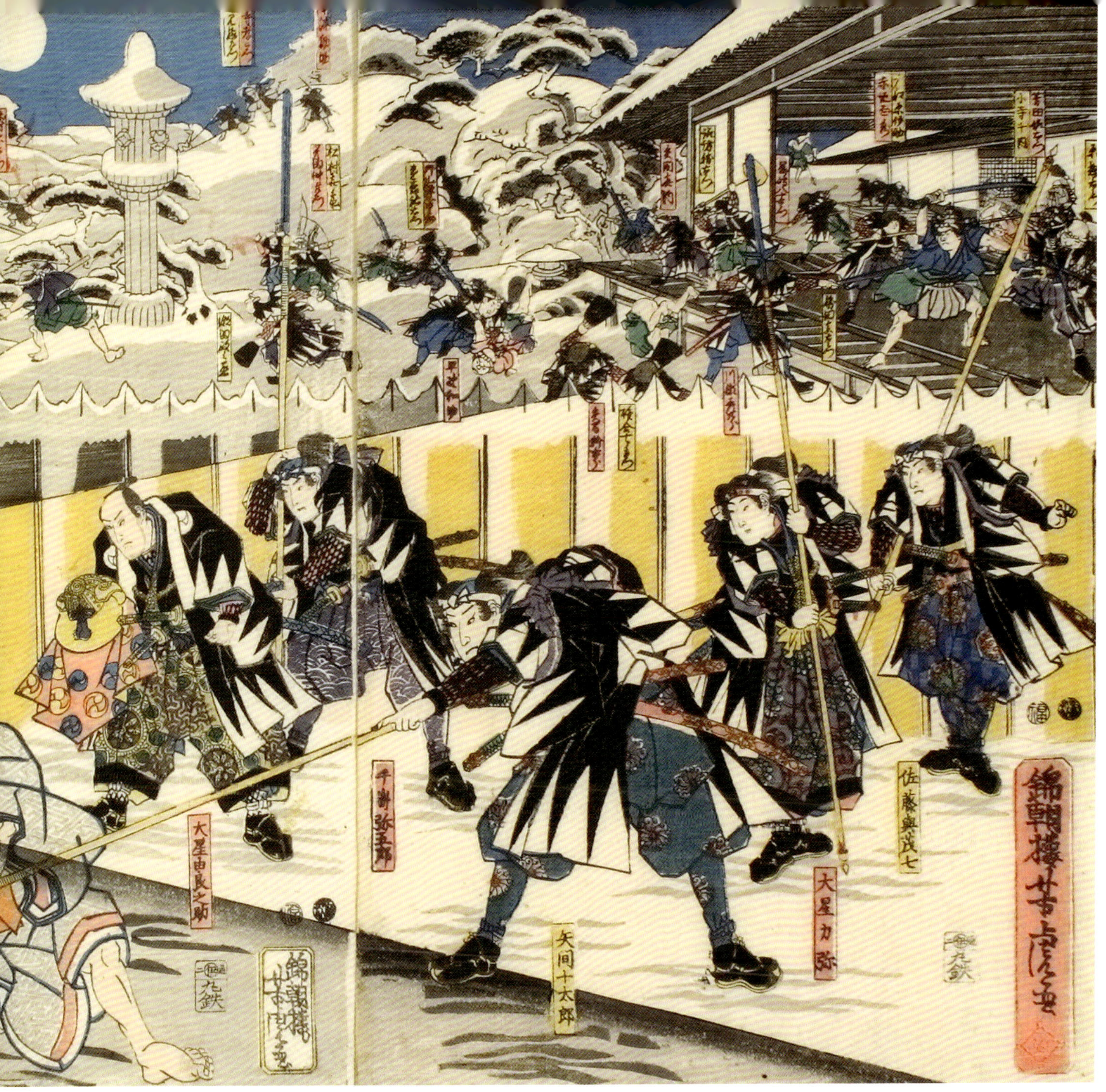

of the play, mixing fact and fiction in their efforts to create both single-sheet and horizontal multi-sheet works. Among the print artists were two of Kuniyoshi's best students—Utagawa Yoshitora (active ca. 1840–80) and Yoshitsuya Koko (1822–66). Yoshitora made several triptychs of historic battles and a number of series, including the *Biography of Royal Vassals*, inspired by Kuniyoshi's *Chushingura* series (**Fig. 185**), and *Sixty-odd Famous Generals of Japan*, about famous leaders and warriors. Yoshitsuya followed in his master's footsteps, specializing in woodblock prints of warriors and events from Japan's history and legends. His major series, *The Fifty-four Battle Stories of Hisago (Hideyoshi)*, shows events from the wars fought by Toyotomi Hideyoshi (1536–98), the second unifier of Japan. Yoshitsuya's designs are full of detail and action and are recognizable by their distinctive border pattern.

Another great source book of Japanese history and legend, *Heike monogatari (The Tale of the Heike)*, retells, along with several other similar chronicles, the complicated events surrounding the Gempei Wars (1180–85), the series of engagements between

FIG. 185
Utagawa YOSHITORA
芳虎 (active ca. 1840–80)
The Evening Attack on Kira's Mansion 忠臣蔵より　吉良邸の夜討
Triptych, 39 x 81 cm
Courtesy of Mita Arts Gallery

Historical warrior print triptychs typically depict the night attack or its aftermath and focus on group scenes. In this dramatic climax to a great epic, by one of Kuniyoshi's many pupils, we can observe the battle raging both inside Lord Kira Yoshinaka's mansion as well as outside its walls. The *samurai* in their dog's tooth patterned *kimono* wield all sorts of weapons. Yoshitora's *Biography of Royal Vassals* was inspired (some say copied) by Kuniyoshi's *Ronin* series.

the Minamoto (Genji) and Taira (Heike) clans for supremacy in Japan. The resulting Minamoto victory and the establishment of the Kamakura *shogunate* ended the hegemony of court culture and marked the rise of the warrior class. Stories of the rise and fall of the two families and their main protagonists, including Minamoto Yoshitsune, his faithful retainer Musashibo Benkei, and Toyotomi Hideyoshi, formed the basis of many exciting *ukiyo-e* interpretations by Kuniyoshi, his pupil Yoshitsuya, Yoshitoshi's pupil Nakazawa Toshiaki (1864–1921) and others (**Figs. 186–189**).

From the Edo period until modern time, ghost stories and legends inspired by Japanese literature were also a popular subject of woodblock prints. Some stemmed from a long tradition of telling ghost stories by the light of a hundred string wicks burning in an oil lamp. As each story was told, the wicks were extinguished one by one, leaving the gathering place darker and darker until, in the total darkness, a spirit appeared. Others drew upon the rich traditions of the fantastic, the occult and the supernatural found in China as well as in Buddhist lore. A rich variety of ghosts, demons, transformed creatures and mischievous beings in the guise of animals thus became part of the *ukiyo-e* woodblock print repertoire.

Among the *ukiyo-e* artists designing fantastical subjects, Tsukioka Yoshitoshi, discussed above in relation to warrior prints, was one of the foremost. Yoshitoshi strongly believed in the existence of ghosts and was convinced that he had personally seen supernatural apparitions. His print series *One Hundred Ghost Stories from China and Japan*, produced in 1865 when he was twenty-six, is based on supernatural themes.

It was Utagawa Kuniyoshi, however, whose warrior prints are also discussed above, who designed the largest number of prints portraying ghosts as well as other strange, unusual and fantastic creatures (**Figs. 190–192**). These new thematic prints satisfied a growing public interest in the exciting, the ghastly and the bizarre. They also allowed Kuniyoshi, in the face of increasingly strict censorship, to symbolically and humorously disguise his criticism of the social and political maladies of the day by having fantastic creatures appear as substitutes for real people, especially the ruling élite. His prints thus appealed enormously to the politically dissatisfied public. Stylistically, Kuniyoshi added impact to his colorful and lively triptychs by including overarching motifs that crossed all three blocks, something not previously attempted.

Two other artists deserve mention for the novelty of their works shown here. Utagawa Yoshiiku (1833–1904), one of Kuniyoshi's pupils and a great rival of Yoshitoshi, is best known for his *kabuki* actor prints as well as his series *A Set of Famous Murders* (1867), but he produced the occasional gem, such as the unusual cure for measles shown here (**Fig. 193**). Another specialist in theatrical prints, Utagawa Kunisada III (1848–1920), who studied under both Kunisada I and II, took a confusing number of names during his career, including Baido Hosai early on and, after 1889, Kochoro. He produced some innovative prints, the one here depicting skeleton puppets (**Fig. 194**).

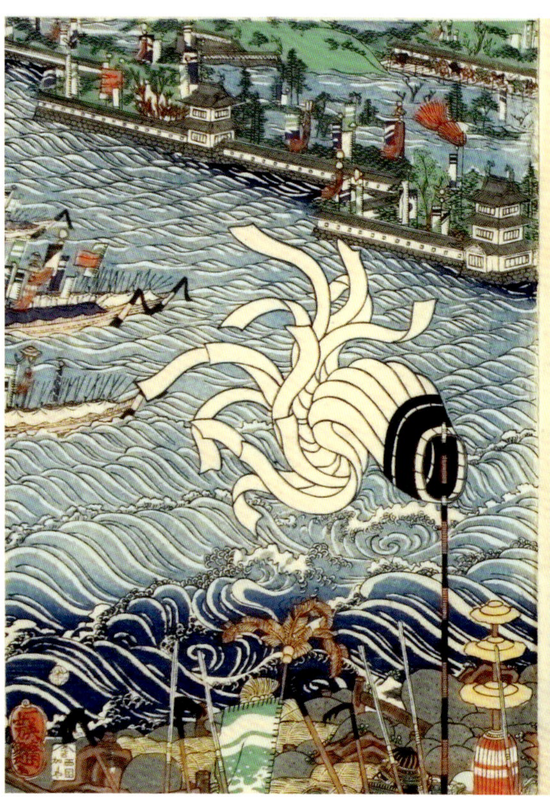

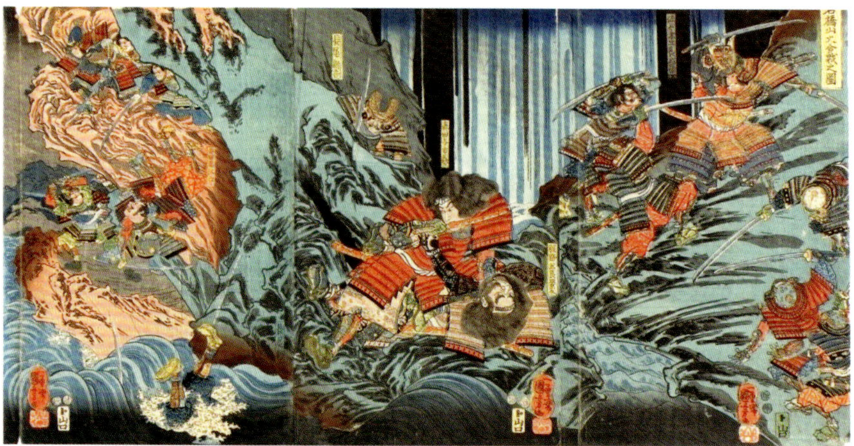

FIG. 187
Utagawa KUNIYOSHI
国芳 (1797–1861)
Battle of Ishibashiyama 石橋山の戦い (1850s)
Triptych, 39 x 27 cm
Courtesy of Mita Arts Gallery

This exciting image shows one of the first serious encounters between the Taira (Heike) and Minamoto (Genji) clans at the start of the Gempei Wars in 1180. Although the Minamoto general Minamoto Yoshitsune won the battle, he did not win the land. Kuniyoshi's depiction of men at war, their armor and their fierce demeanor, is superior to that of any other print artist.

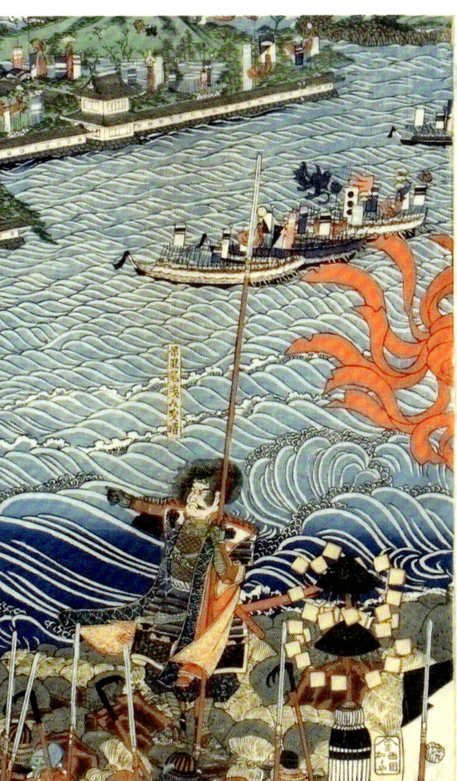

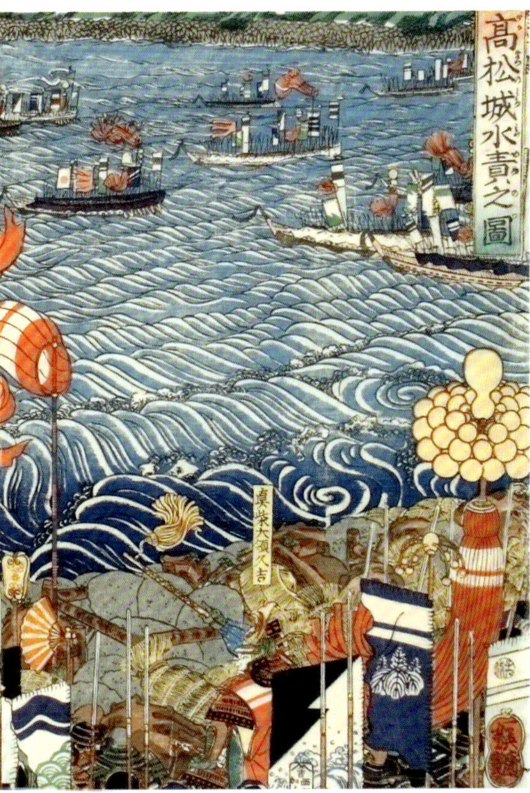

FIG. 186 (left)
YOSHITSUYA Koko
芳艶 (1822–66)
Naval Attack at Takamatsu Castle 高松城の海戦 (1860s)
Triptych, 39 x 81 cm
Courtesy of Mita Arts Gallery

Takamatsu Castle was built very close to sea level in Shikoku in the late sixteenth century. It was attacked in 1582. This scene shows one of Toyotomi Hideyoshi's generals, Ukita Hideie, in a dramatic battle scene. The print is full of wonderful details of battle flags and other decorative elements employed by warriors engaged in warfare.

FIG. 188 (below)
Utagawa KUNIYOSHI
国芳 (1797–1861)
Battle of Dannoura 壇の浦の戦い (1850s)
Triptych, 39 x 27 cm
Courtesy of Mita Arts Gallery

The major sea battle at Dannoura, in the Shimonoseki Strait, on 25 April 1185, signaled victory by the Minamoto (Genji) over the Taira (Heike) in the Gempei Wars. The tragic story of the drowning of the seven-year-old Emperor Antoku also set the scene for the beginning of the Minamoto *shogunate*, which ruled Japan from its new capital in Kamakura. The print shows the outnumbered Taira in the distance, who eventually all drowned in this important episode in Japanese history.

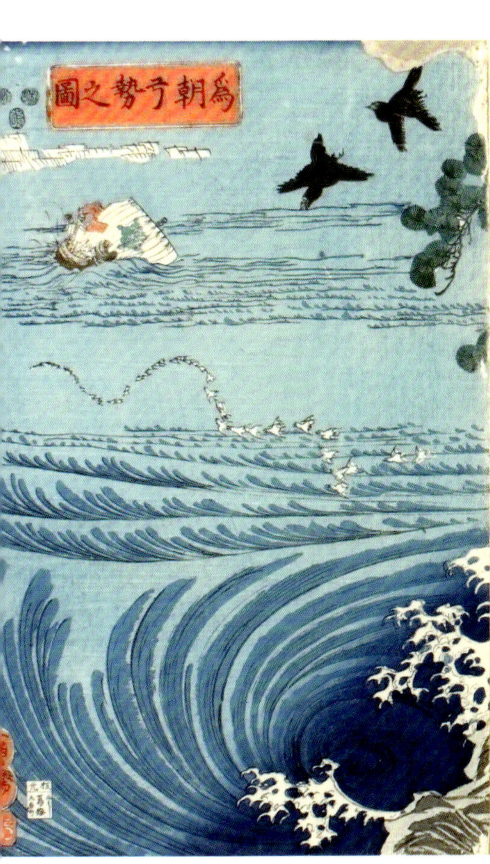

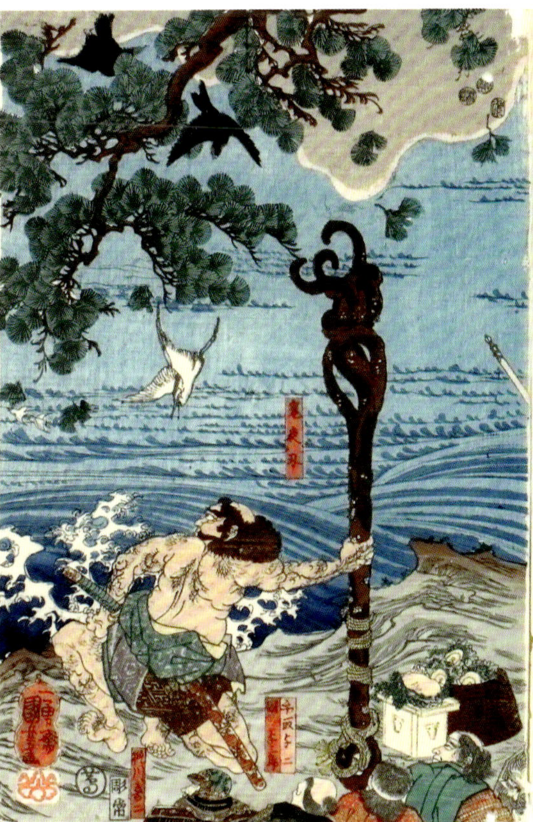

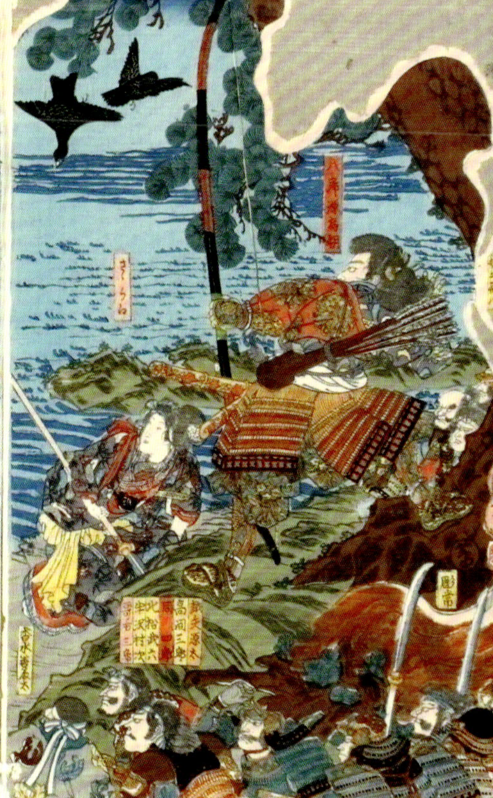

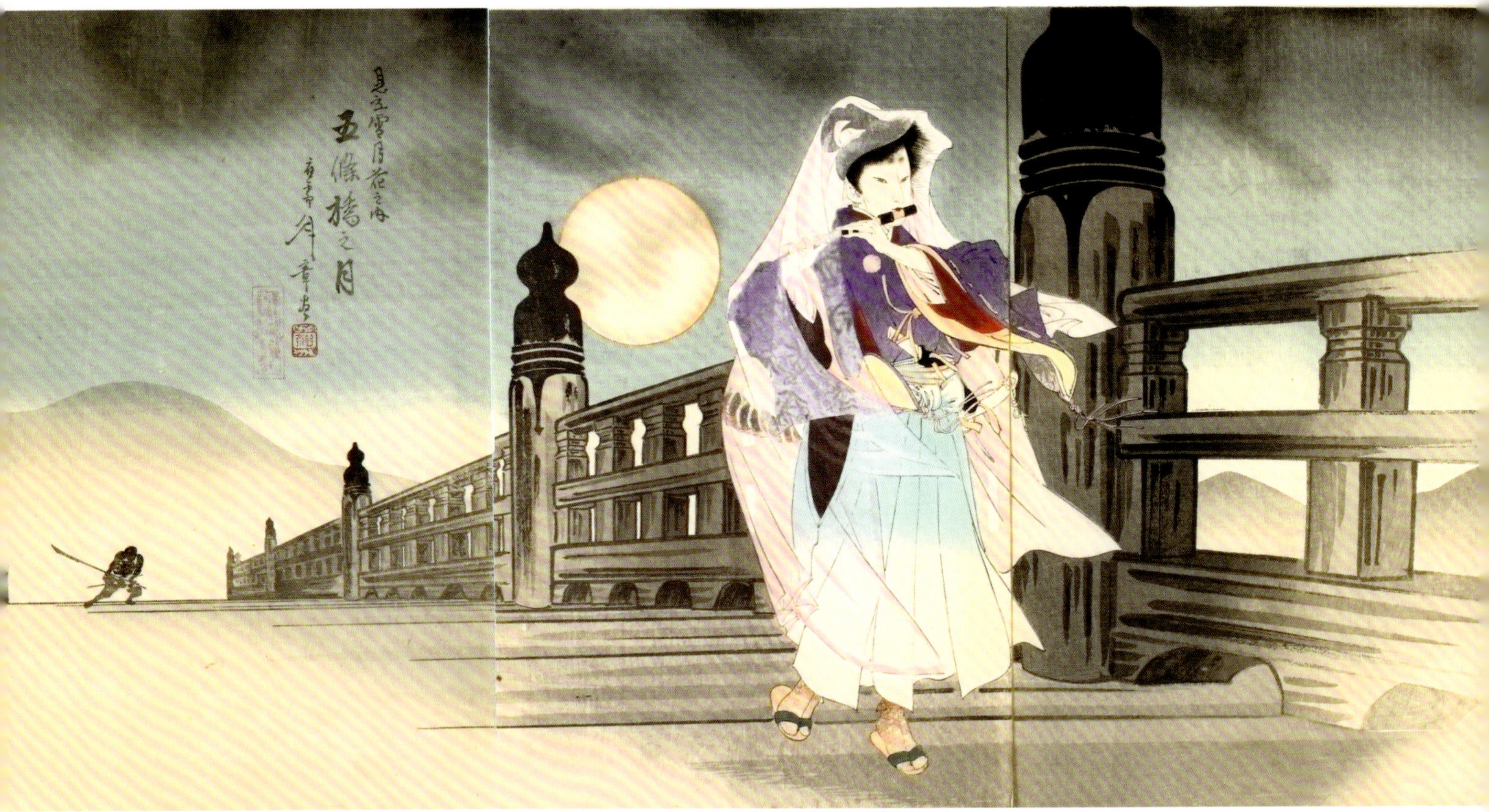

見立雪月花之内
五條橋之月

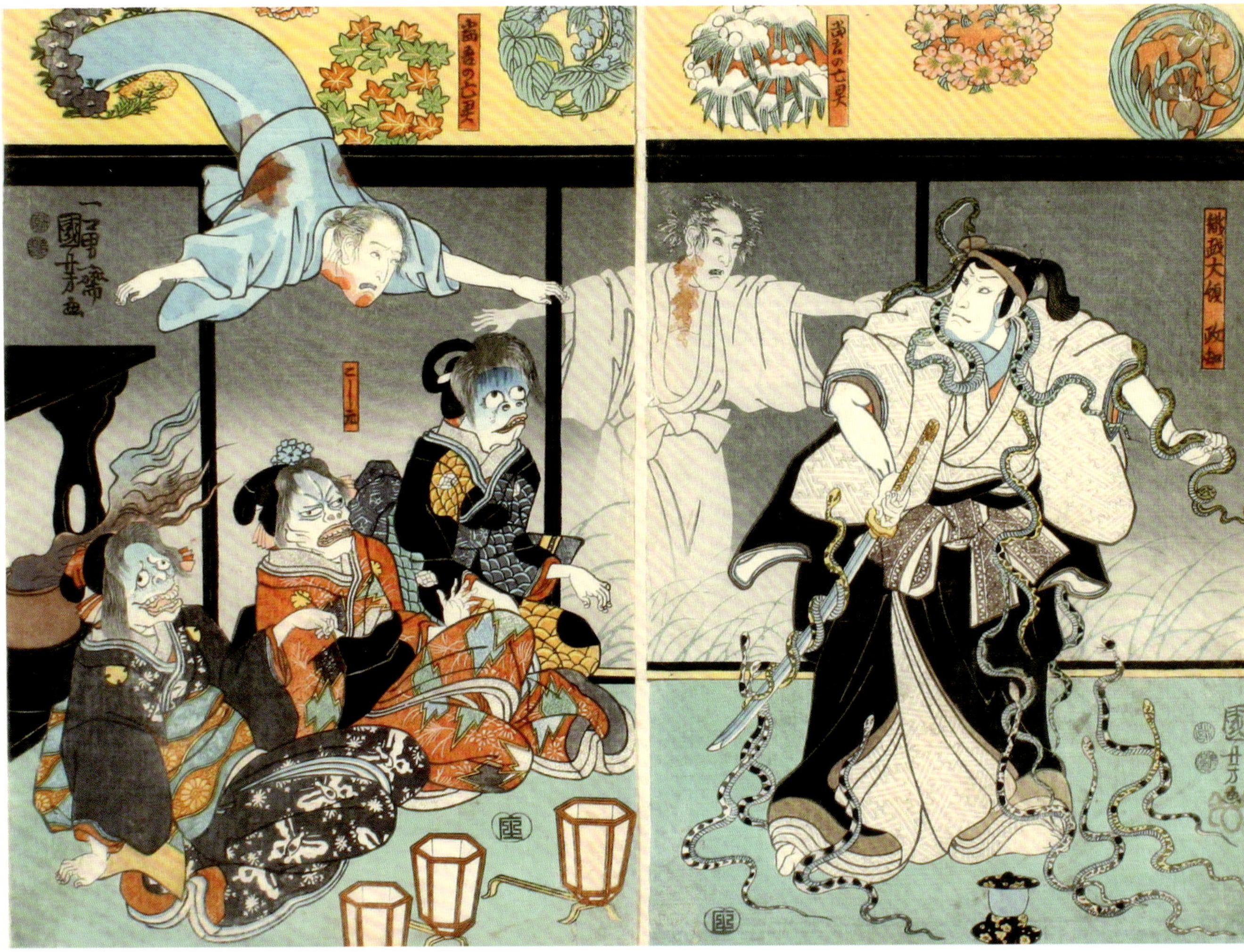

一勇齋國芳画

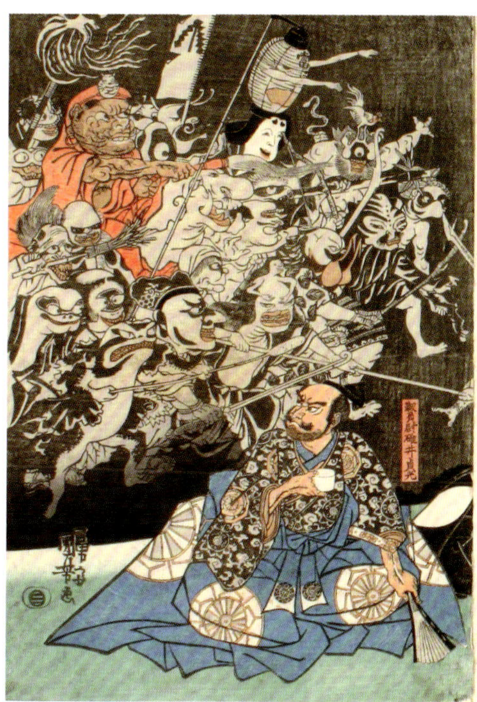
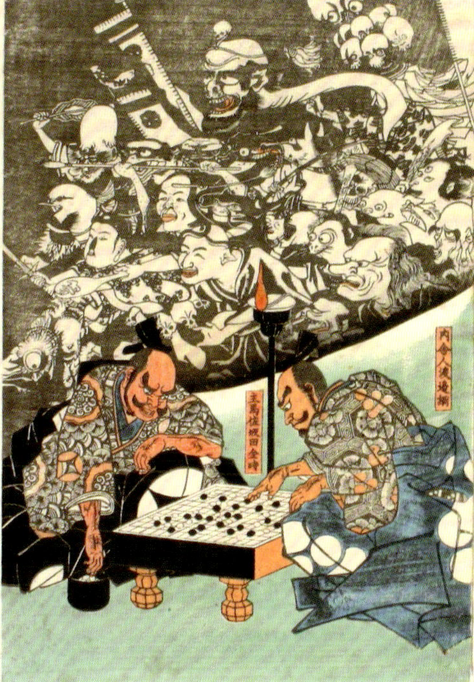
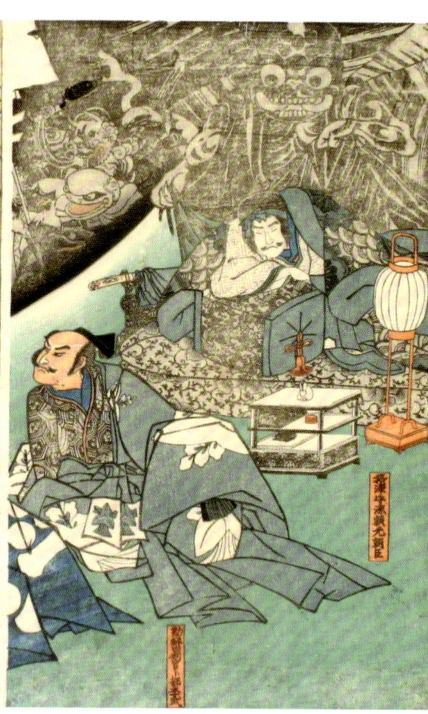

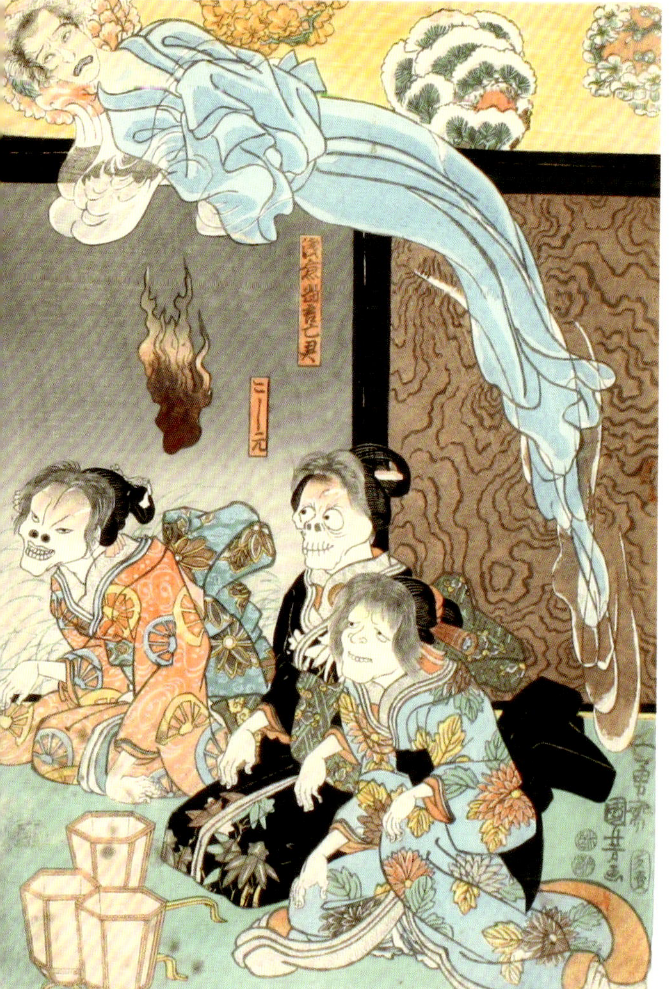

FIG. 189 (opposite above)
NAKAZAWA Toshiaki
年章 (1864–1921)
Full Moon at Gojo Bridge 五條橋の満月 (1897)
Triptych, 39 x 27 cm
Courtesy of Mita Arts Gallery

The combat between Minamoto Yoshitsune and the giant monk Musashibo Benkei on the Gojo Bridge in Kyoto is one of the most famous stories in Japanese history. Benkei, a famous swordsman, allowed no one to pass over the Gojo Bridge without challenging him to a fight. At last, after 999 victims, Benkei met his match in Yoshitsune, the younger brother of the Shogun Yoritomo, thanks to his training as a swordsman. Thereafter, Benkei becomes Yoshitsune's faithful vassal until both die in the closing stages of the Gempei Wars. This beautiful print shows Yoshitsune, unusually depicted in a rather feminine manner, playing his flute, unaware of the lurking monk in the background with his large spear or of the skirmishes that have taken part at the other end of the bridge. The drama of the situation is contrasted with the tranquility of the full moon.

FIG. 190 (opposite below)
Utagawa KUNIYOSHI
国芳 (1797–1861)
The Ghost of Asakura Togo Attacks Arikoshi Masatomo 朝倉當吾亡魂 (1857)
39 x 81 cm
Courtesy of Mita Arts Gallery

Asakura is seeking revenge on a lord, Masatomo, who inflicted severe hardship on the farmers of Sakura in the 1640s. As leader of a rebellion against Masatomo, he was tortured and crucified along with his family. Masatomo eventually goes mad and is shown here surrounded by ghosts and snakes. Even his court ladies have turned into demons. The story became a popular *kabuki* play, well known to the people of Edo.

FIG. 191 (above)
Utagawa KUNIYOSHI
国芳 (1797–1861)
The Earth Spider Manifesting Demons at the Mansion of Minamoto Yorimitsu
源 頼光公舘土蜘作妖怪図 (1843)
39 x 81 cm
Courtesy of Mita Arts Gallery

This print caused much controversy when it was published. It was intended to be a satire on the Shogun Ieyashu and his chief councilor Takakuni who were at odds over some of the reforms instituted by the *shogunate*. The print shows the warrior Minamoto Yorimitsu (944–1021) on his sick bed while two of his bodyguards play *go* (chess). Two other bodyguards on the left and right realize that the evil earth spider top right is creating a battle of two forces behind the dozing warrior. The demons symbolize various issues relating to the reforms. The publisher had to recall all the prints and plane down the blocks. He and some print sellers were fined and suffered severe penalties for this misadventure.

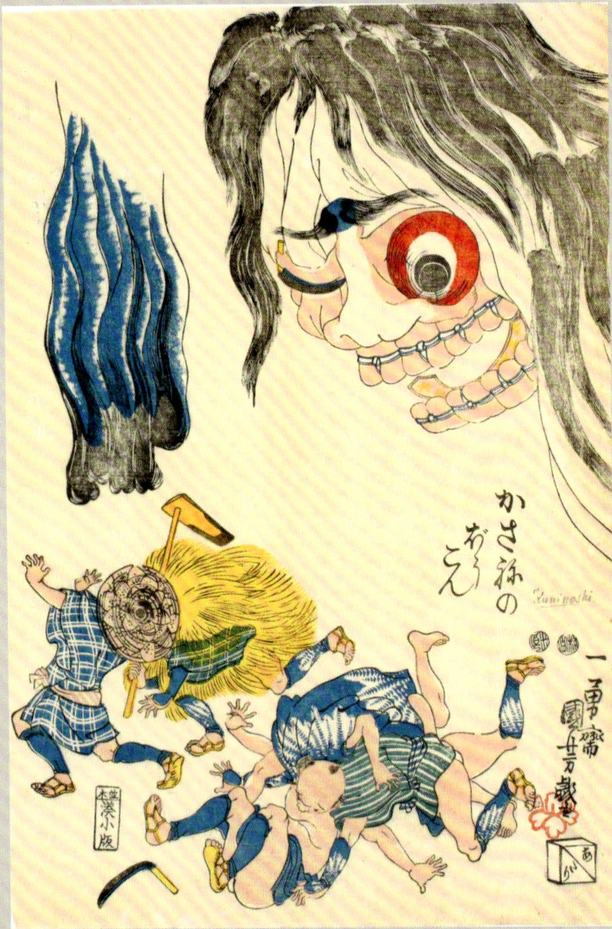

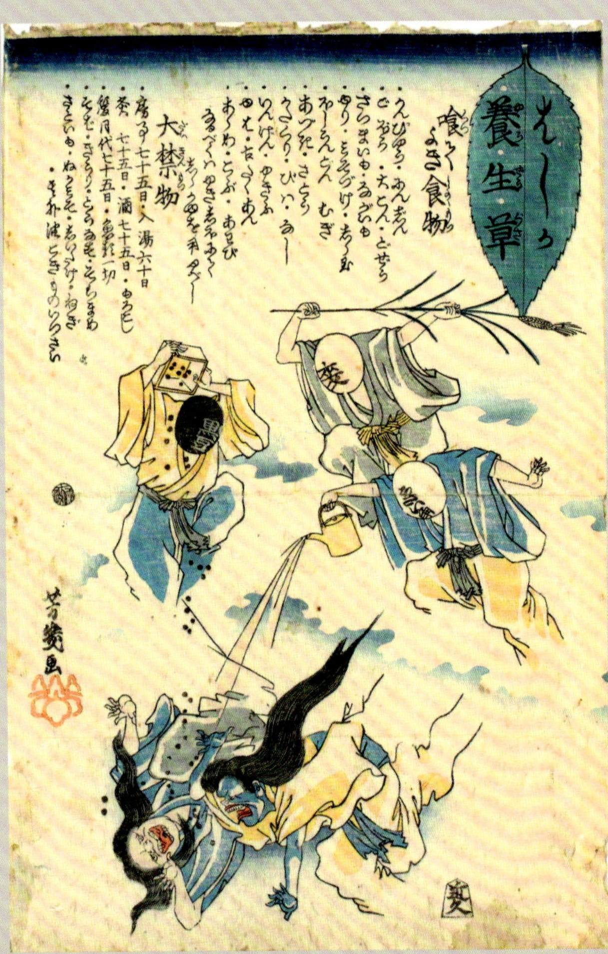

FIG. 192
Utagawa KUNIYOSHI
国芳 (1797–1861)
Humans Forming a Ghost かさねのぼうこん (1850s)
39 x 27 cm
Courtesy of Mita Arts Gallery

This is a humorous and rare print showing a ghost formed from a group of figures. Even the teeth are the rear end of men who are wearing *fundoshi* (underwear). The nose is a nude woman seen from the back with her legs stretched out. The ghost's hair is also formed of women's heads, their long hair flowing down her side. The ghost is scaring a group of farmers who have dropped their tools in terror. The flames on the left of the print are a typical symbol of ghosts. Even in movies when ghosts appear, they often take the form of small flames.

FIG. 193 (right)
Utagawa KUNIYOSHI
国芳 (1797–1861)
Men Forming a Textile Pattern
欠留人物更紗 (1840s)
27 x 39 cm
Courtesy of Mita Arts Gallery

Kuniyoshi created numerous prints showing the human form being used to create the shape of a person's head or other unrelated shapes. This unusual print shows a group of men entwined in an unbelievable number of positions, some of which border on the erotic. The subtitle of the print says "Using fourteen bodies to look like thirty-five." But there are more than fourteen. It is a parody on imported Indian textiles using complicated patterns as decorative designs.

FIG. 194
Utagawa YOSHIIKU
芳幾 (1833–1904)
Nutritional Food 養生草 (1880s)
36 x 24 cm
Author's Collection

This print has personal significance for me. About 1970 my wife was infected with the measles. Complaining to a print dealer friend about her condition, he gave me this print to pass to her as a cure. The print shows three human shapes in the form of medicine pulling out the measles in the shape of a demon. My wife was soon cured.

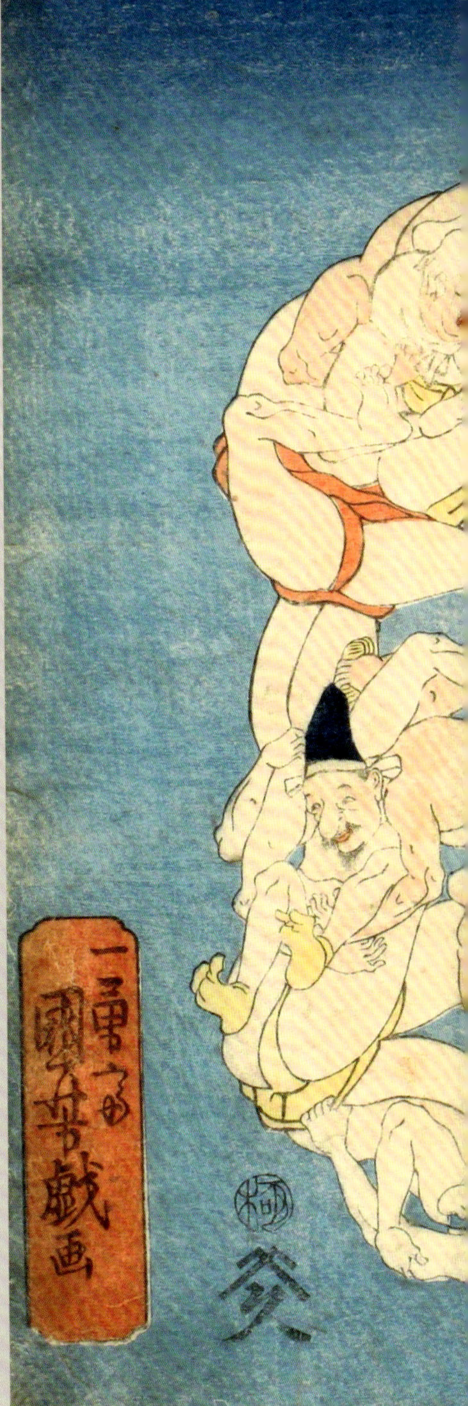

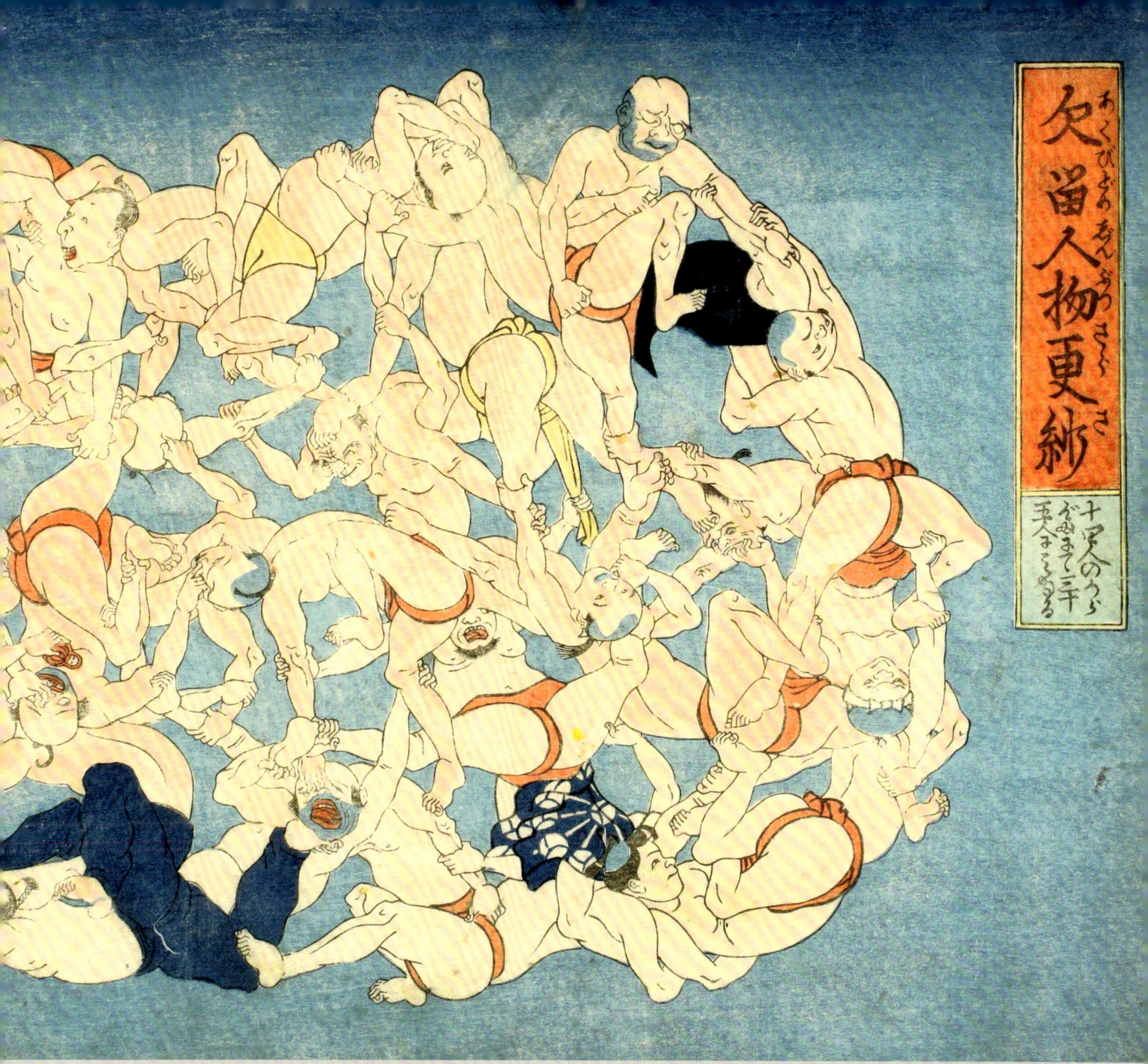

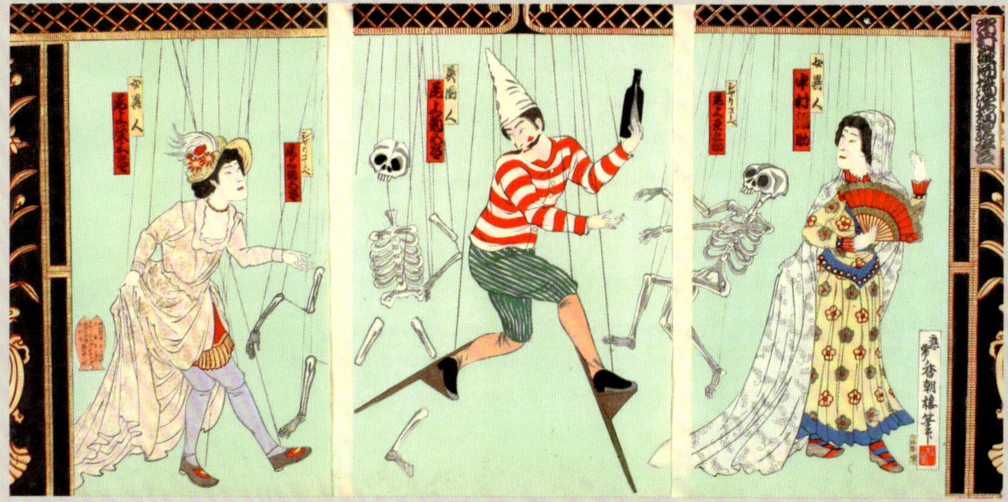

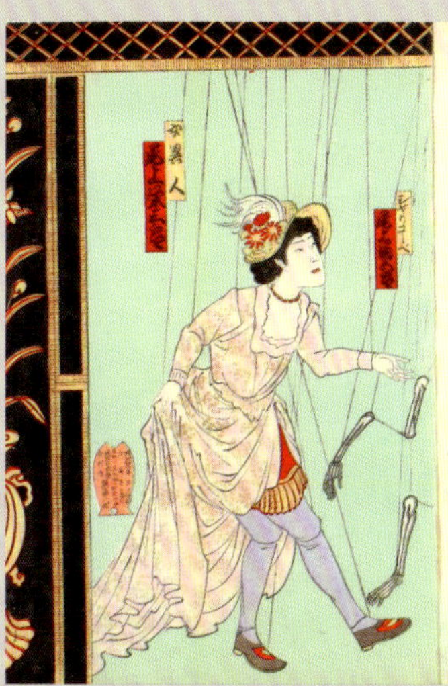

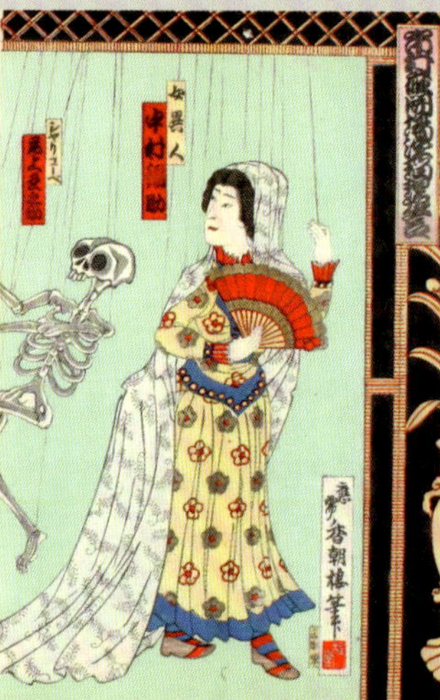

FIG. 195
KOCHORO (Utagawa Kunisada III)
香朝楼 (1848–1920)
Actors and Skeletons 市村座開場浄瑠璃狂言 (1880s)
39 x 81 cm
Courtesy of Mita Arts Gallery

It is difficult to tell if these actors are imitating puppets as they have strings attached to them or if they are part of a humorous play that included skeletons.

CHAPTER ELEVEN

Foreigners in Japan

FIG. 196
Utagawa SADAHIDE Gyokuransai
貞秀 (1807–73)
View of Yokohama 横濱風景 (1861)
6-panel print, 39 x 108 cm
Courtesy of Mita Arts Gallery

This large panoramic view of Yokohama, published in 1861, clearly depicts the rapid transformation of Yokohama from a fishing village in 1858 into a city in just three short years. Yokohama had the look of a substantial planned city from the very beginning. Row upon row of storehouses and residences radiate out from the Miyosaki entertainment quarter in the center of the painting, enclosed behind walls and surrounded by a moat. As yet, no national flags can be seen flying, but these would come as foreign legations were established.

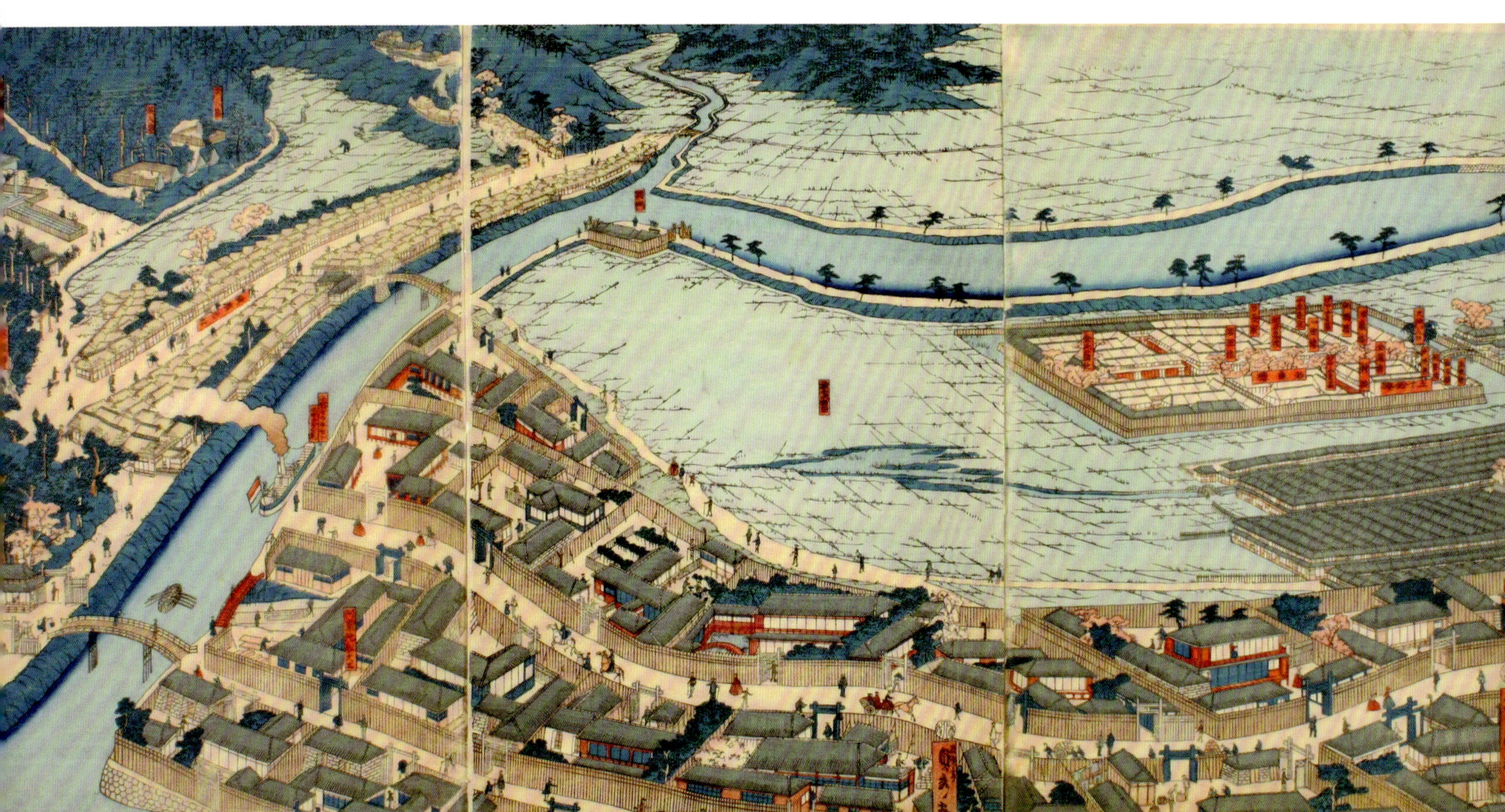

Japan's period of transition from historical isolation into a trading nation with diplomatic ties to the United States and the countries of Europe is vividly reflected in a small but distinctive sub-genre of *ukiyo-e* called "Yokohama prints" or *Yokohama-e*, woodblock prints depicting foreigners and scenes of Yokohama. During the rule of the Tokugawa, from the 1630s to the middle of the nineteenth century, Japan was almost completely isolated from the outside world. No Japanese were allowed to leave the country and no foreigners were allowed to enter. Trade with the outside was only permitted with the Dutch East India Company, which thus gained a monopoly on trade between Japan and the West. The Dutch, however, had to submit to very strict regulations. They were commanded, in 1641, to take up residence on Deshima, a small artificial island about half a square kilometer in size in Nagasaki harbor, on the southern island of Kyushu. Located at a safe distance from the Edo capital (Tokyo), Deshima was linked to the substantial town of Nagasaki on Kyushu by a single, narrow bridge. The few Chinese merchants permitted to remain were limited to a stretch of 180 square meters along the bay at Deshima.

The situation changed cataclysmically, however, when four US military vessels under the command of Mathew Calbraith Perry dropped anchor in the bay at Edo (Tokyo) in 1853 to persuade the Japanese, either by words or by force, to change its policy of isolation. The ensuing Treaty of Kanagawa, signed in 1854, allowed the Americans access to a limited number of ports. In 1858, England, France, Russia and Holland were granted the same trading rights as the Americans, and together they formed the five Treaty Nations. Their citizens were restricted to the area around the harbor of Yokohama, less than 20 miles south of Edo, and were forbidden to travel more than 25 miles outside the town.

The Perry expedition drastically altered the visual images Japanese people associated with foreigners. Pictures of foreigners had previously been confined largely to woodblock prints created at Nagasaki between 1750 and 1850. These prints, called *Nagasaki-e*, show the Dutch citizens and traders arriving at Nagasaki, the only port where they were allowed entry, the ships they came on and the exotic animals they brought with them, including camels, elephants and ostriches. Above all, the prints show the amazement with which the Japanese regarded the Dutch in Nagasaki: their physical appearance—pale, ugly, red-haired barbarians with large noses—clothing, customs and personal and household belongings. Chinese merchants were also depicted visiting temples. The prints were sold as cheap souvenirs to Japanese travelers who came from all over the country to visit Nagasaki, perhaps hoping to catch a glimpse of these strange-looking newcomers.

After 1859, Yokohama became Japan's international trading center and

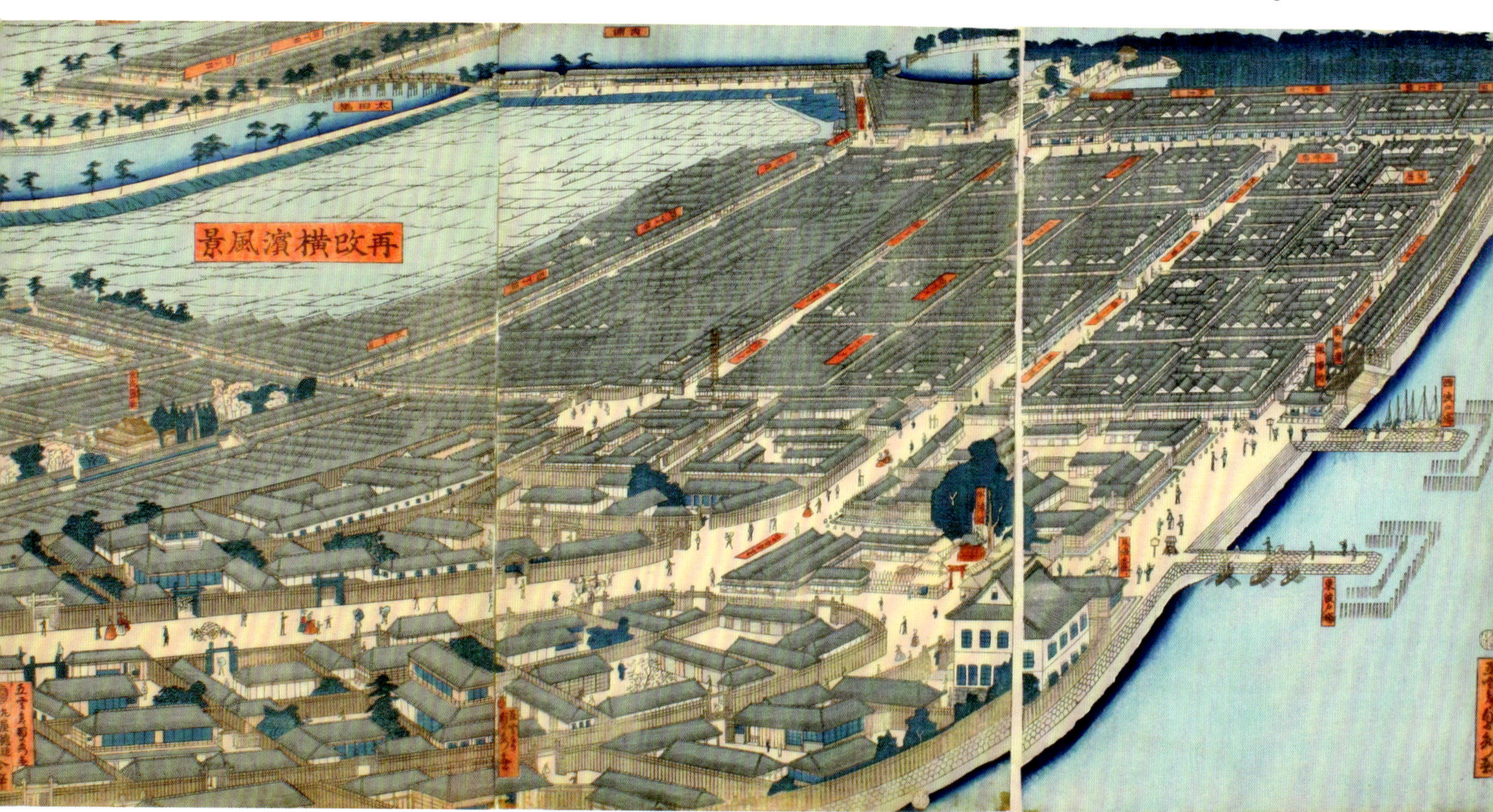

main foreign settlement. It was a thriving, bustling commercial port. Brick houses were built in the Western style to accommodate foreigners, with balconies, glass windows and hitching posts for horses. Foreigners often brought in servants from China and Southeast Asia. Commercial buildings were also constructed, as were hospitals and schools. Slaughterhouses were tolerated. The entire infrastructure of a new world descended on Tokugawa Japan in a very short time. By 1869 there were some 16,000 foreigners in Yokohama exporting raw silk and tea and importing almost everything else, including cotton and woolen fabrics, iron products, clocks and watches, glass and liquors. Holland was no longer the sole avenue for studying Western civilization. The Japanese discovered that England, France, Germany and America were the leading Western powers, and that English was the language of foreign studies. In the streets of Yokohama, the Japanese could learn about the clothing, the food, the homes and the customs of the West, stimulating a renewed interest in domestic tourism.

When the new young Emperor Meiji (1852–1912) was installed in 1868, active engagement with the outside world began in earnest. Delegations for all fields of science and technology were sent abroad and experts were brought in. There was a rapid increase in the number of foreigners employed by the Japanese government and in private enterprise. In 1875, less than twenty years after the first treaty, 520 foreigners were employed as engineers and educators as well as in government, and by 1897 760 foreigners, a record high. The English were the most numerous, while Americans dominated the private sector. In the 1870s, twenty foreigners, mostly British, were employed in the Mint. There were drastic needs in shipbuilding and communications. Western clothing, the solar calendar and Sunday holidays were adopted. Western dress became compulsory for government officials in 1872, and in 1876 frock coats were decreed business attire.

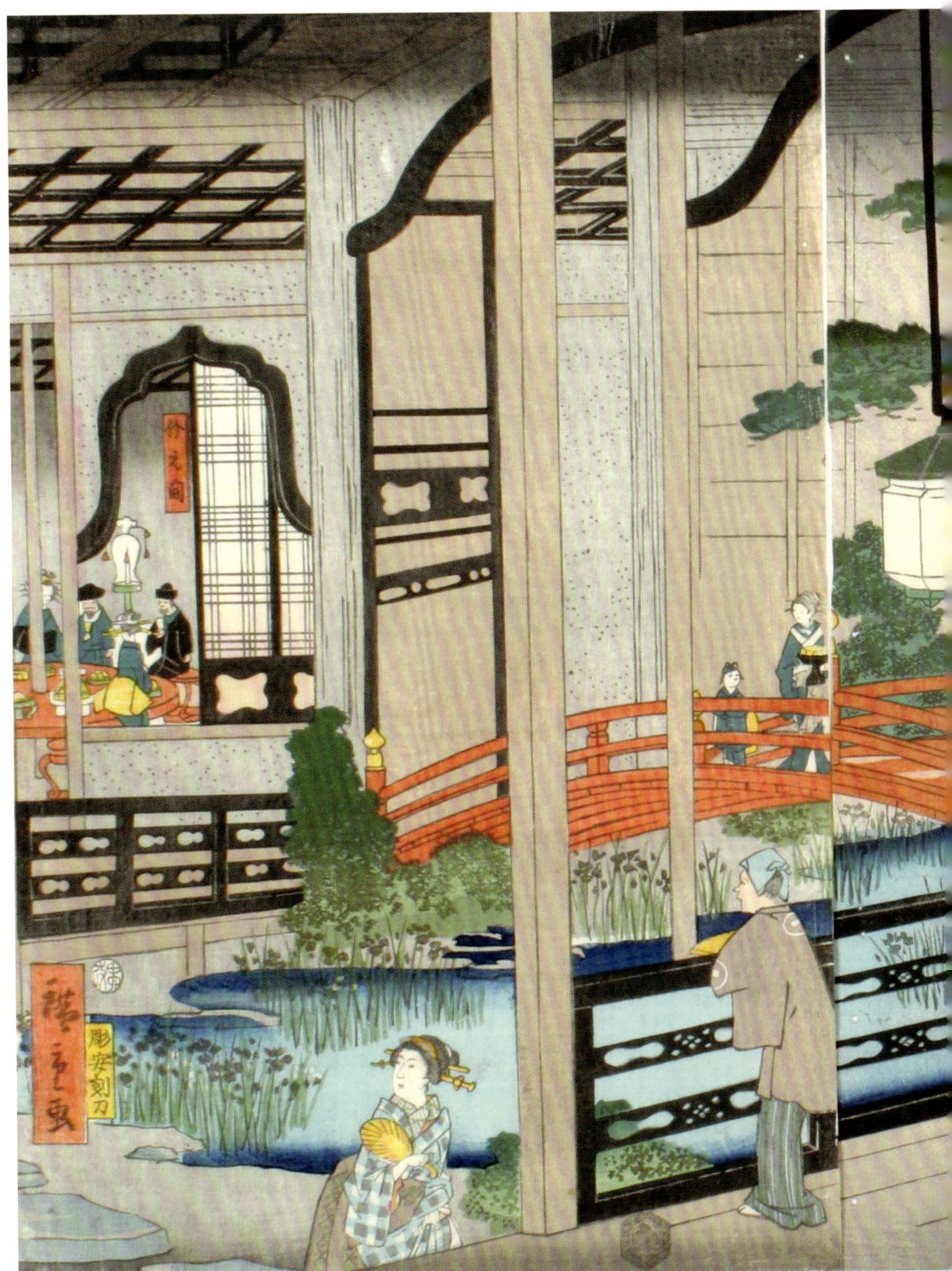

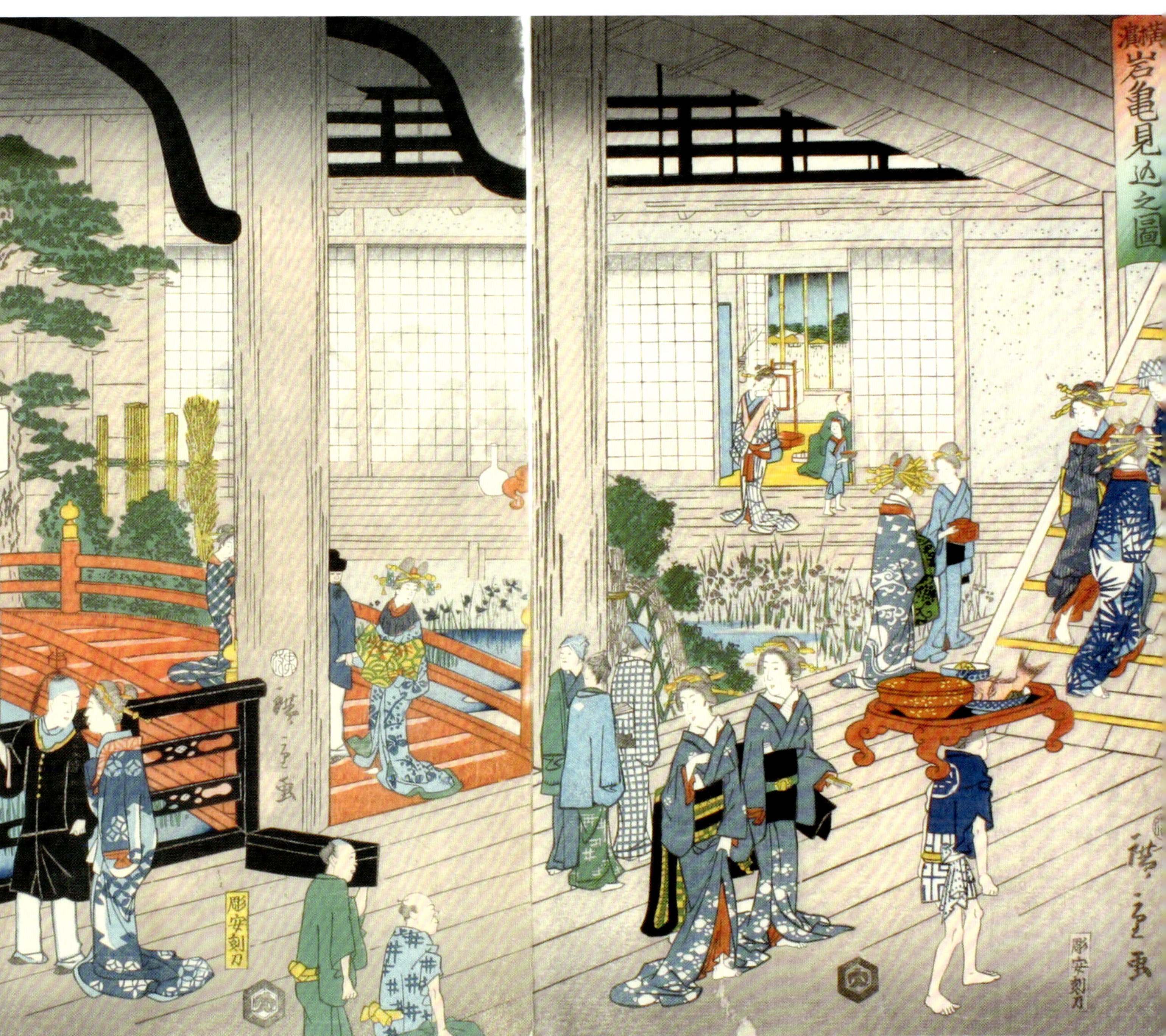

FIG. 197
Utagawa SHIGENOBU (Hiroshige II)
二代広重 (1826–69)
The Gankiro in Yokohama 横濱岩亀楼 (1860)
Triptych, 39 x 108 cm
Courtesy of Mita Arts Gallery

This triptych depicts foreigners (in the rear of the left side panel) being served food at the Gankiro Teahouse, a famous establishment in Yokohama. It was part of the moated pleasure quarter built by the government on reclaimed land behind the town to service newly arrived foreigners, who were usually bachelors, and to attract Japanese merchants. The architecture and interior decoration is an eclectic mix of styles. Japanese and Chinese servants serve the foreign'customers. One man carries a large table on his head, laden with food, toward the staircase where courtesans in *kimono* wait for clients before proceeding to the rooms upstairs.

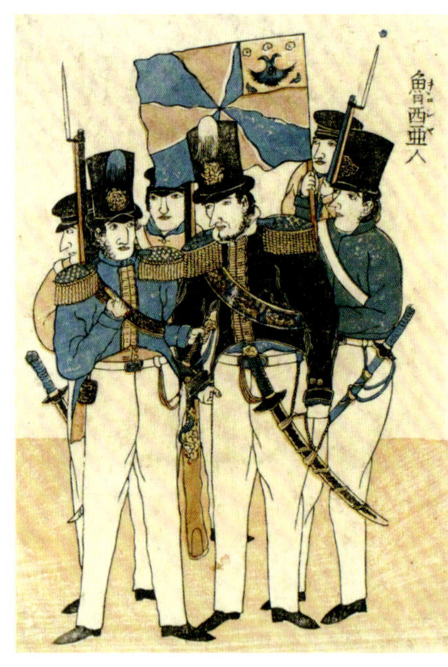

FIG. 198
Anonymous
作者不詳
Russian Soldiers 魯西亜人兵士 (1860s)
30.7 x 22.1 cm
Courtesy of Mita Arts Gallery

A fascination with foreign uniforms and weapons captivates this unknown artist. The soldiers' hooked or long, pointed noses, their wavy hair curling under top hats and their sideburns and beards were other novelties.

FIG. 199
Utagawa YOSHIKAZU
芳員 (active 1850s–70s)
Foreigners' Revelry at the Gankiro in Yokohama 横濱岩亀楼異人遊興の図
(1861)
Triptych, 39 x 108 cm
Courtesy of Mita Arts Gallery

In this view of the Gankiro Teahouse, we get a much better idea of the revelry that went on in this establishment. Seated on the floor, Japanese style, several foreign men enjoy food, *saké* served in ceramic bottles and the company of Japanese *geisha*. Two *geisha* play the *shamisen* while one of the foreigners performs a dance. At this time, before the Meiji Restoration, there were few foreign women in Japan and none are present here. There are also no *samurai* and no weapons.

All of the above presented a whole new source of inspiration for the artists who gravitated to the foreign enclave to seek new subject matter. In response to popular curiosity about the different way of life of the newest arrivals to Japan's shores, as well as their hitherto unknown technical inventions, *ukiyo-e* artists took up the challenge to satisfy this curiosity. Where foreigners came from and what they looked like, what clothes they wore, what food they ate, what games they played, all became the subject matter of *Yokohama-e*, as did their technological advancements, such as steamships, horse-drawn carriages, locomotives, and hot air balloons. Maps, aerial or bird's-eye views of the town, ceremonies, important events, commissioned portraits of individuals, couples and whole families, often with their servants and pets, and ordinary activities (people eating, drinking, smoking pipes, playing music, writing) were among the other subjects displayed in the prints.

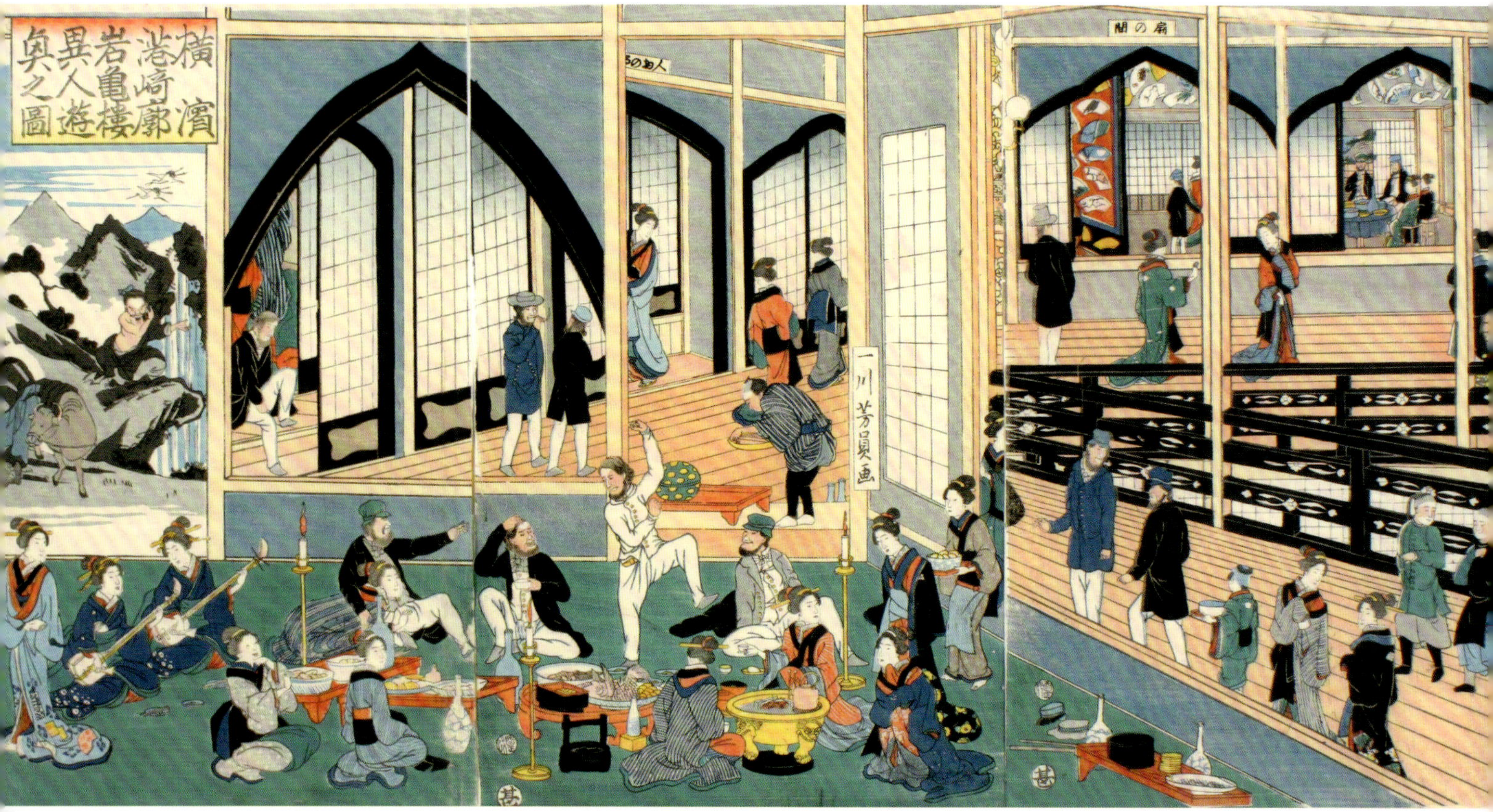

There were numerous problems facing the artists, in particular, how to make the foreigners look "foreign." The forms of their clothing were different. Initially, the artists did not know how to draw the garments without knowing how they were sewn. Looking at European books they realized that foreigners cast shadows. There is one interesting print of a street scene where the foreigners cast shadows but the Japanese do not. Foreign women, who were prohibited from living at Deshima but were allowed in Yokohama, are represented in many images. However, the details of their costumes, including fancy hats and lacy mantillas, are largely imaginary, as few artists seem to have had the opportunity to observe foreigners at first hand. Some imagery was borrowed from secondary sources, such as the earlier Nagasaki prints or wood engravings that appeared in the Western journals and newspapers that were beginning to arrive in Japan, such the *Illustrated London News* and *Frank Leslie's Illustrated Newspaper* from America. All sorts of anomalies and humorous representations are apparent in the prints, highlighting the lack of first-hand observation, but this only adds to their fascination.

Some thirty *ukiyo-e* artists produced more than 800 different woodblock prints of the town of Yokohama and its foreign inhabitants in the years 1858 to 1862, when they reached their peak. The prints, which were largely published in Edo, have a distinctive look. At first they seem crude compared with the traditional print subjects, partly because they were often produced rather quickly and with little care in an attempt to meet the high demand from the general public. Compositions were often copied from other works, with only minor changes made or with the simple addition of a title or explanatory note. But a closer examination shows them to be quite charming and unusual in showing how the Japanese interpreted this unique world that was so suddenly thrust upon them after centuries of independent cultural identity.

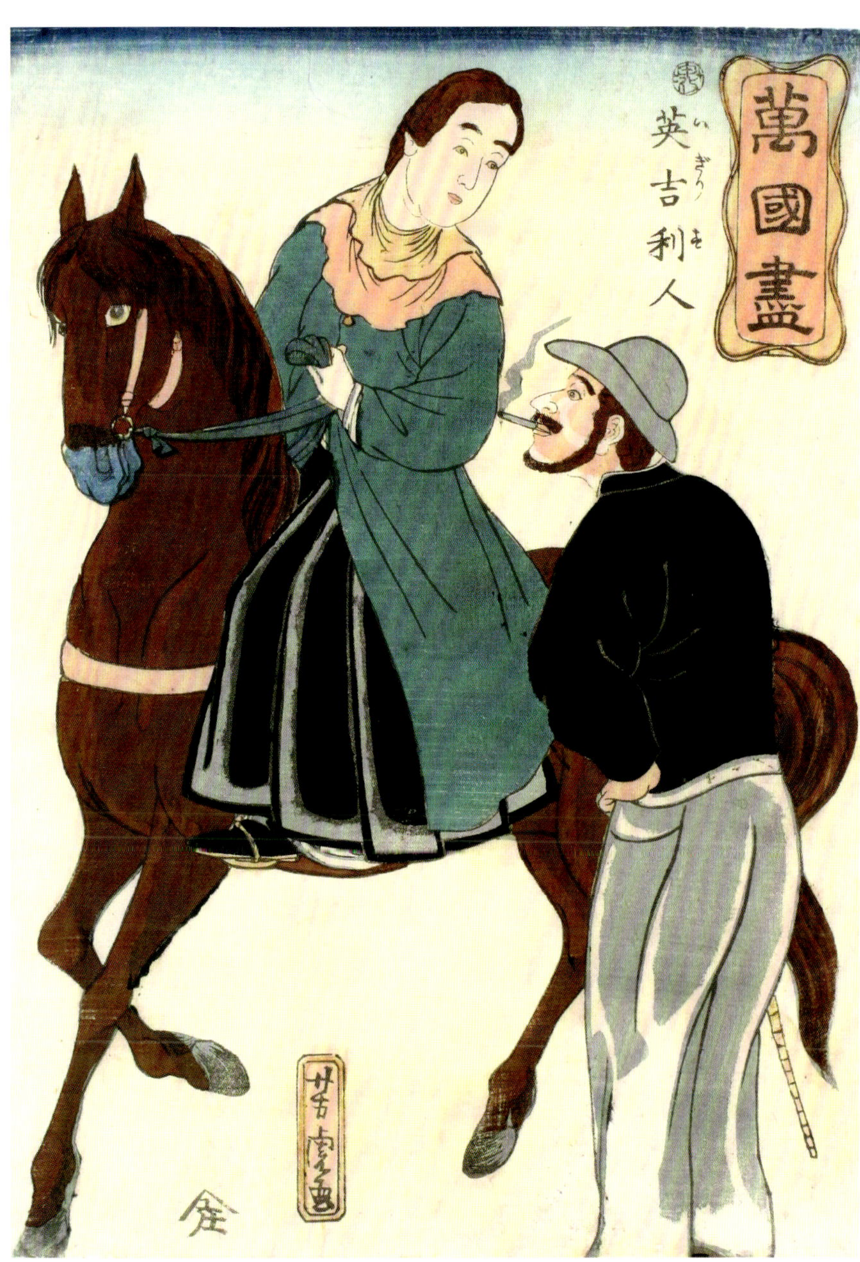

FIG. 200
Utagawa YOSHITORA
芳虎 (active ca. 1840–80)
An English Couple 英吉利人 (1860)
39 x 81 cm
Courtesy of Mita Arts Gallery

Yoshitora produced many pictures recording the novel appearance of various "types" of foreign men and women in Yokohama, very likely relying on illustrations and engravings from the West for inspiration. The Japanese characters in the title block top right indicate the subjects' nationality. Here, the dress of the English woman riding a horse and the man smoking a cigarette is largely imaginary, as artists themselves were seldom able to see the foreigners in real life. The folds of European clothing were not familiar to the Japanese artist, evidenced from the man's baggy trousers.

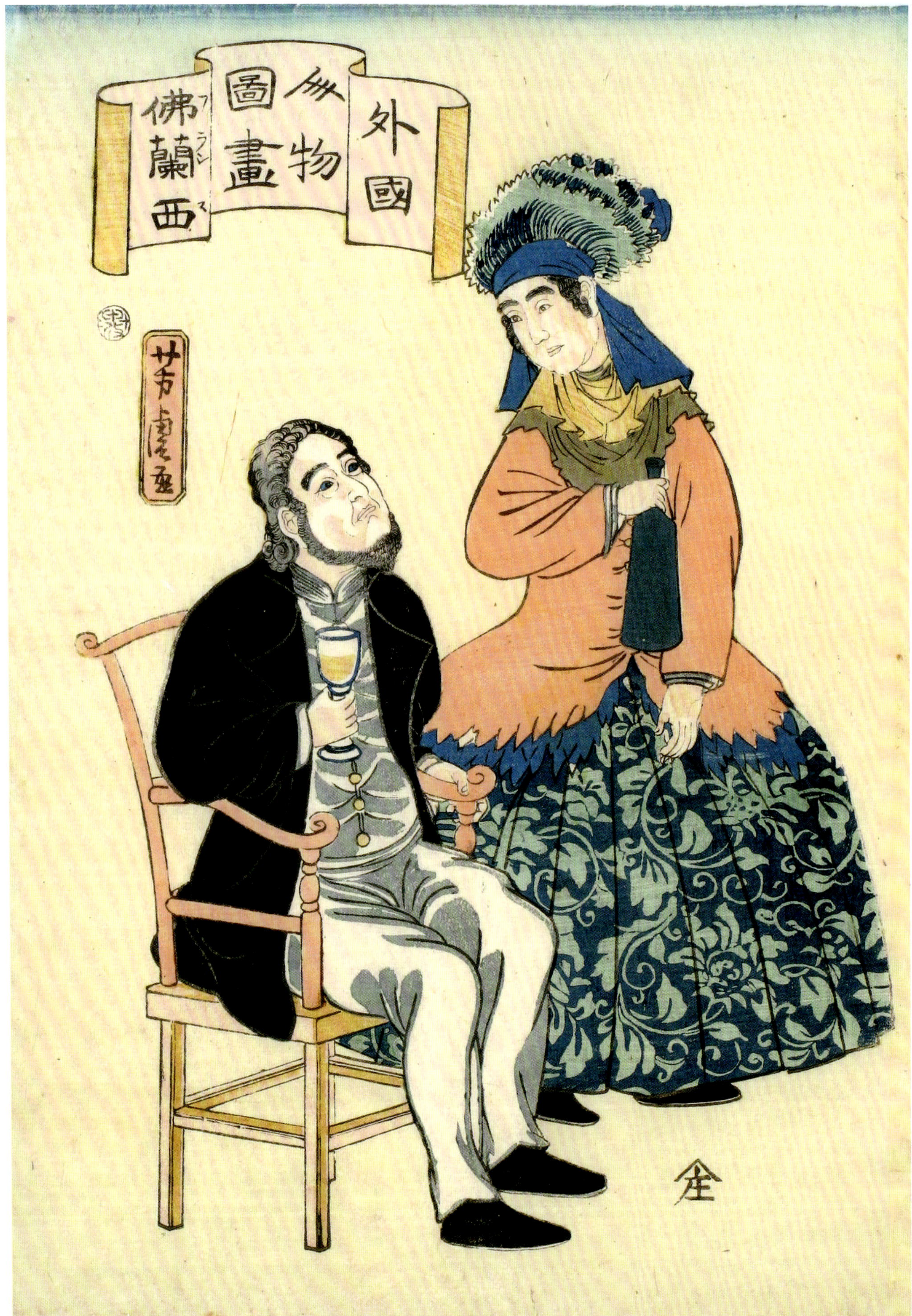
外國人物圖畫
佛蘭西
芳虎画

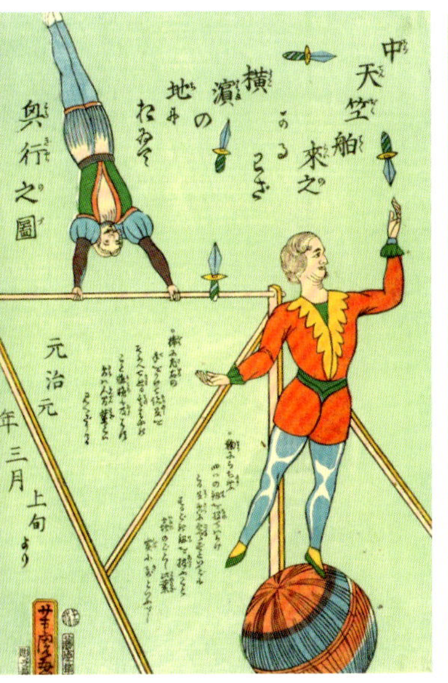

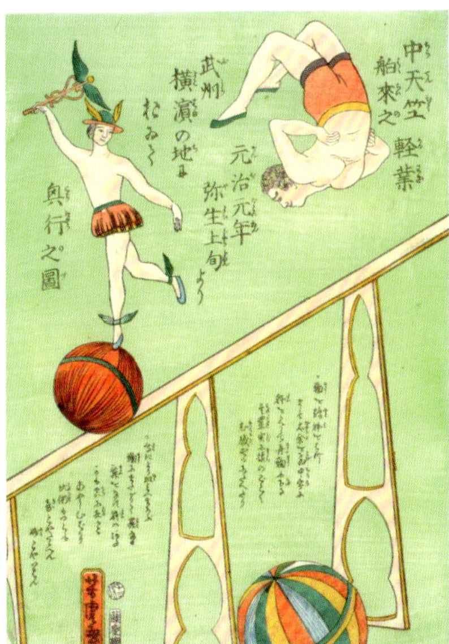

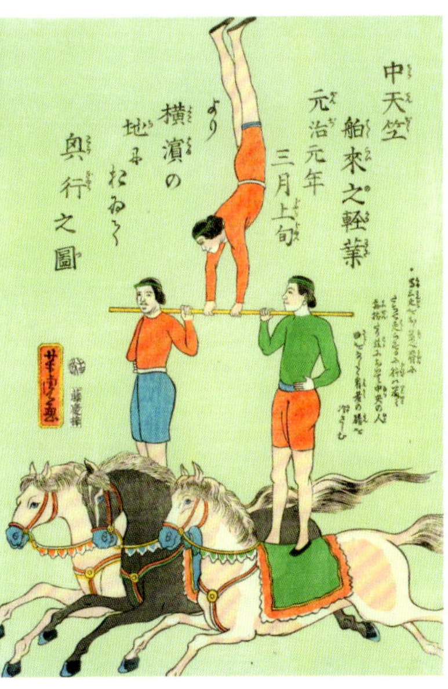

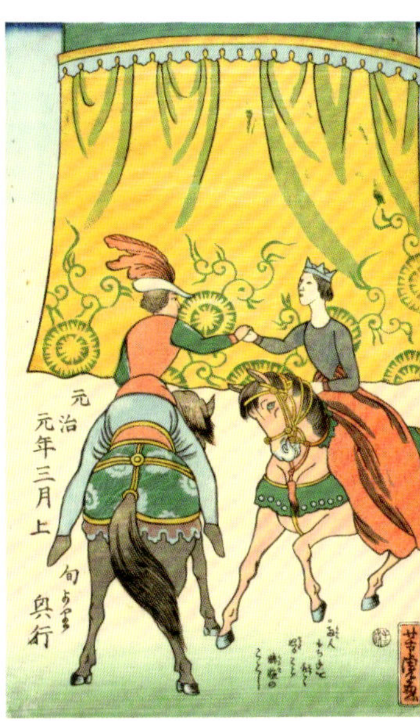

FIG. 201 (left)
Utagawa YOSHITORA
芳虎 (active ca. 1840–80)
A French Couple 佛蘭西人 (1860)
39 x 81 cm
Courtesy of Mita Arts Gallery

People of the five Treaty Nations were commonly portrayed in series of prints. In this portrait print, a French man is seated in a chair, something not seen in Japanese homes at that time, holding a wine goblet while his wife, standing beside him, holds a ceramic wine bottle. Her headgear and dress are somewhat bizarre.

FIG. 202 (above)
Utagawa YOSHITORA
芳虎 (active ca. 1840–80)
Circus in Yokohama 横濱のサーカス (1864)
4-panel print, 39 x 27cm
Courtesy of Mita Arts Gallery

This fascinating multi-panel print is, in fact, a flyer advertising the performance of a foreign circus in Yokohama in March/April 1865. One can imagine the interest a foreign circus would have aroused in Yokohama four years before the Meiji Restoration. It is not known where the circus was held or who attended.

Yokohama prints were sold in small bookshops, usually in series of five (representing the five Treaty Nations whose citizens were living in Japan), or in series of six, with the addition of China, which was allowed to trade in Japan despite having no official agreement. Initially, the main purchasers of *Yokohama-e* were Japanese tourists, who were clearly fascinated by the clothing, strange habits and occupations of the foreigners. But some prints were popular with the foreigners themselves and, as noted above, portraits were sometimes commissioned, particularly by diplomats.

The Yokohama prints published in Edo were primarily created by a small group of artists of the Utagawa school. Commercially the most successful lineage of artists in *ukiyo-e* history, these artists took advantage of the nature of the woodblock print as a commodity but were also adept at satisfying mass audiences of the times with their colorful, stylized prints. Among the most prominent *Yokohama-e* artists was Utagawa Sadahide Gyokuransai (1807–73), one of Utagawa Kunisada's best pupils. In his scenes of Yokohama and its foreign population, he used different perspectives, including bird's-eye or panoramic views, often adapting the perspective to

FIG. 203
Utagawa SADAHIDE Gyokuransai
貞秀 (1807–73)
Chinese and Indian
南京広東人と天竺暹羅図 (1861)
39 x 81 cm
Courtesy of Mita Arts Gallery

Two nationalities that accompanied Westerners to Yokohama were Chinese and South Indians, primarily men. The Chinese, identified by their distinctive gowns and long, braided queues, served as both domestic servants and mercantile assistants (compradors). The Indians, distinguished by their turbans and dark complexions, functioned mostly as servants to the British. The foreigners also brought with them hitherto unseen breeds of dogs.

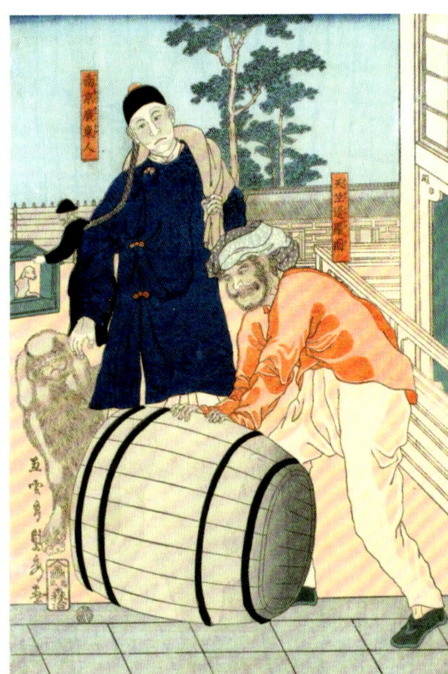

FIG. 204
Utagawa YOSHITORA
芳虎 (active ca. 1840–80)
Balloons (1872)
Triptych, 39 x 81 cm
Courtesy of Mita Arts Gallery

Four years after the Meiji Restoration, the new era of commerce had transformed Yokohama from a small fishing village into a bustling town with multistoried buildings. In this print, crowds of foreigners—probably the entire foreign community of Yokohama—and their servants have gathered to view the release of several hot air balloons. As yet, there was little engagement socially between the foreign community and local Japanese, so it comes as no surprise that no Japanese are shown among the spectators.

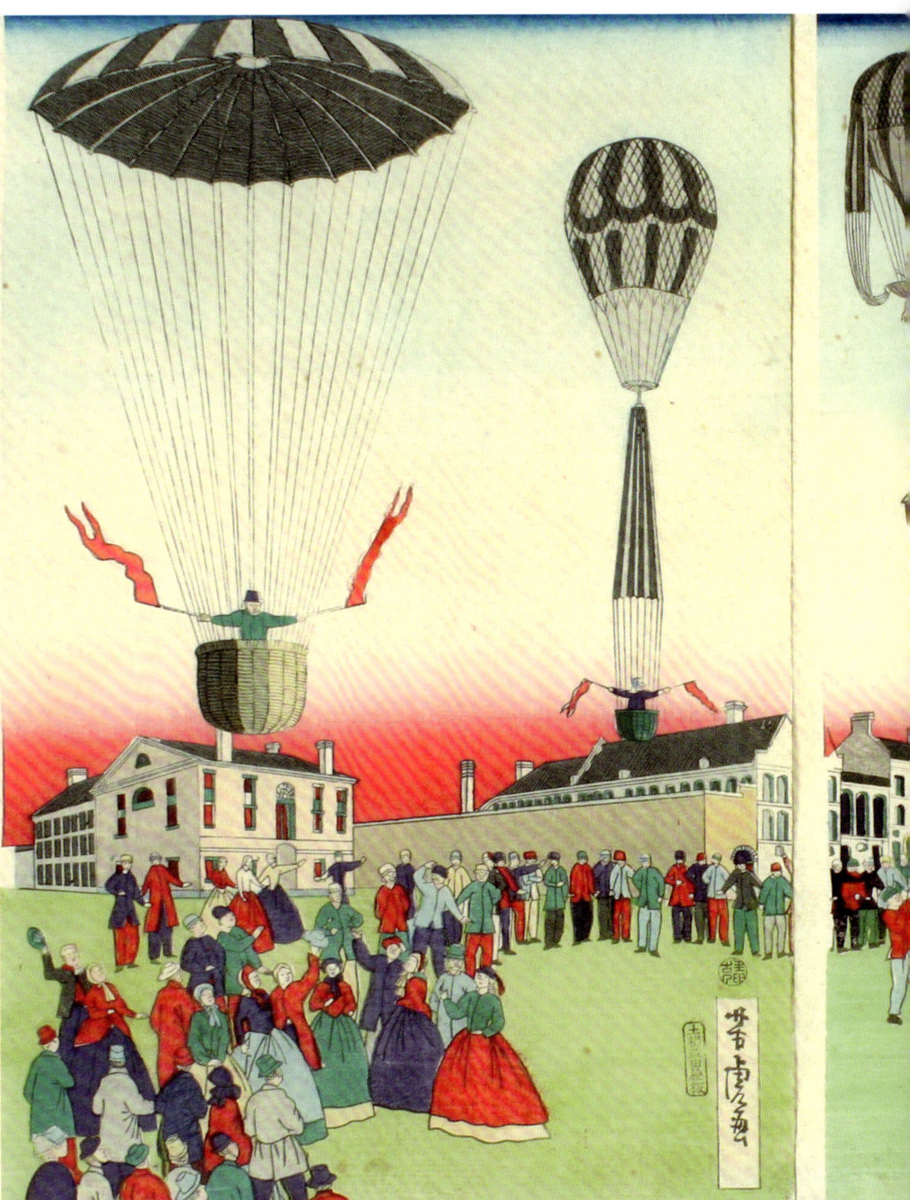

FIG. 205
Utagawa YOSHITORA
芳虎 (active ca. 1840–80)
Trial Balloon Launch at the Naval Academy Training Ground at Tsukiji 築地海軍省での軽気球試験 (1870)
Triptych, 39 x 81 cm
Courtesy of Mita Arts Gallery

In 1870, two years after the Meiji Restoration, a naval college was established at Tsukiji in Tokyo, where foreign teachers were employed. In this fascinating print, the Japanese navy department tests hot air balloons in front of the American consulate. American flags are displayed prominently. Two Japanese flags decorate the balloon, but there are no Japanese in the picture.

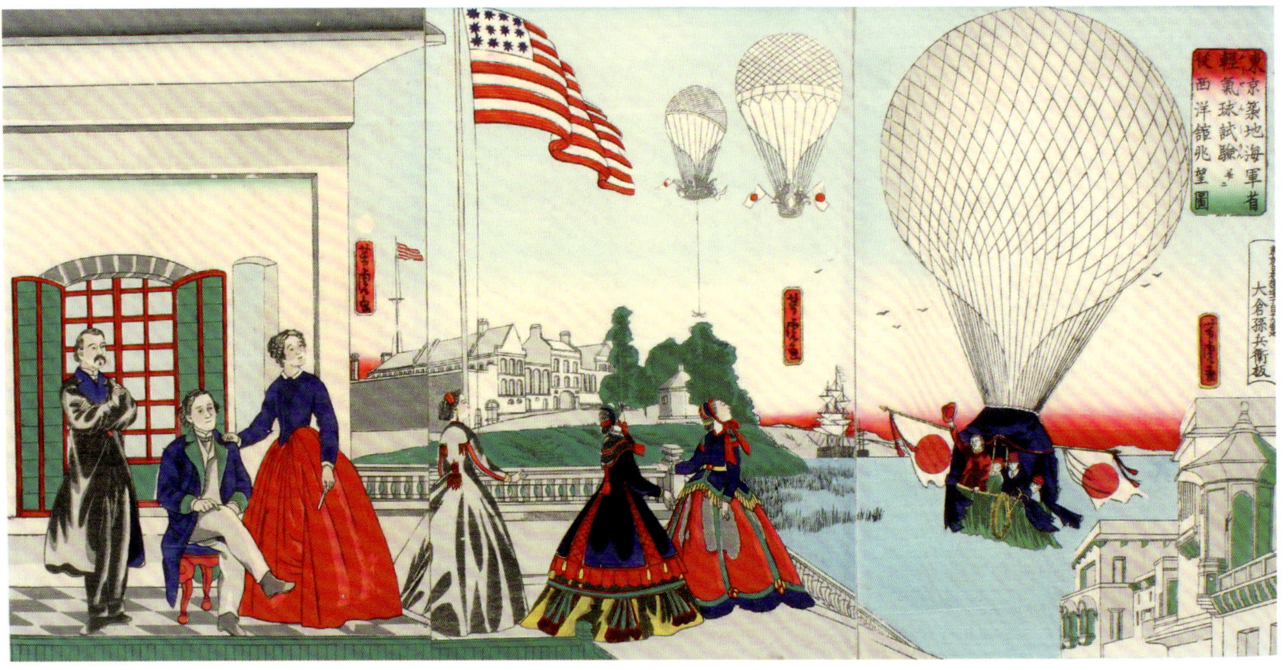

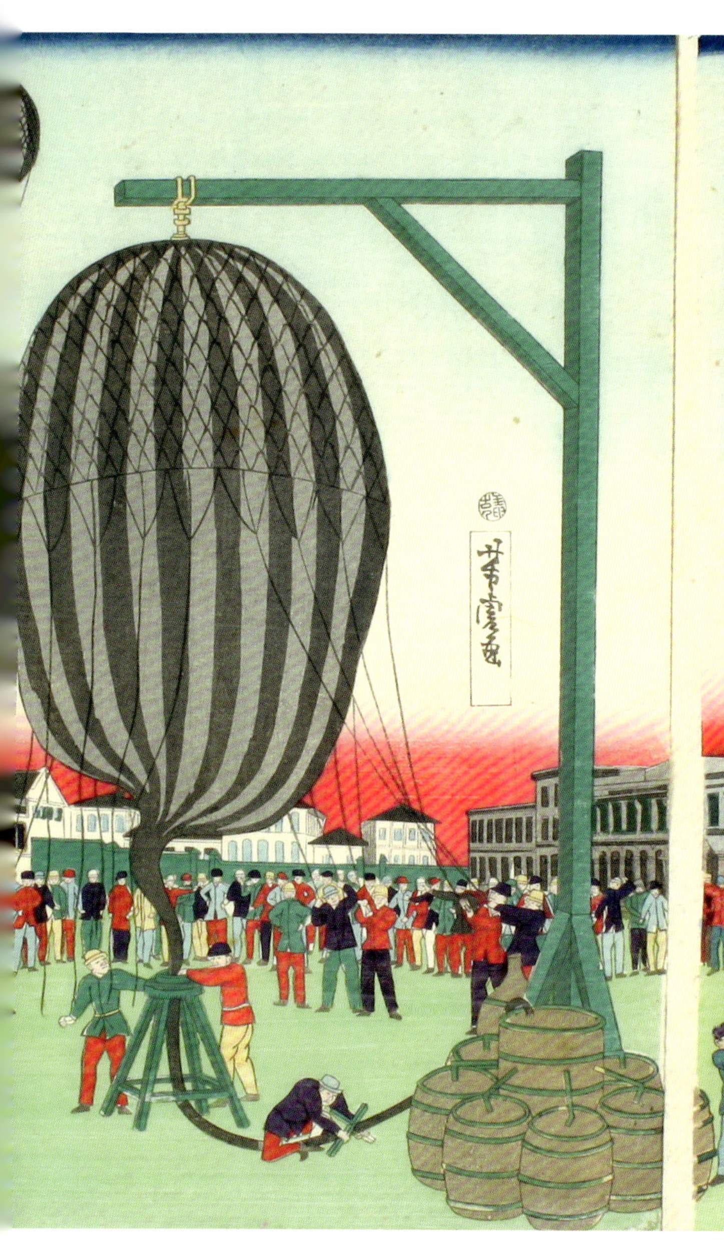

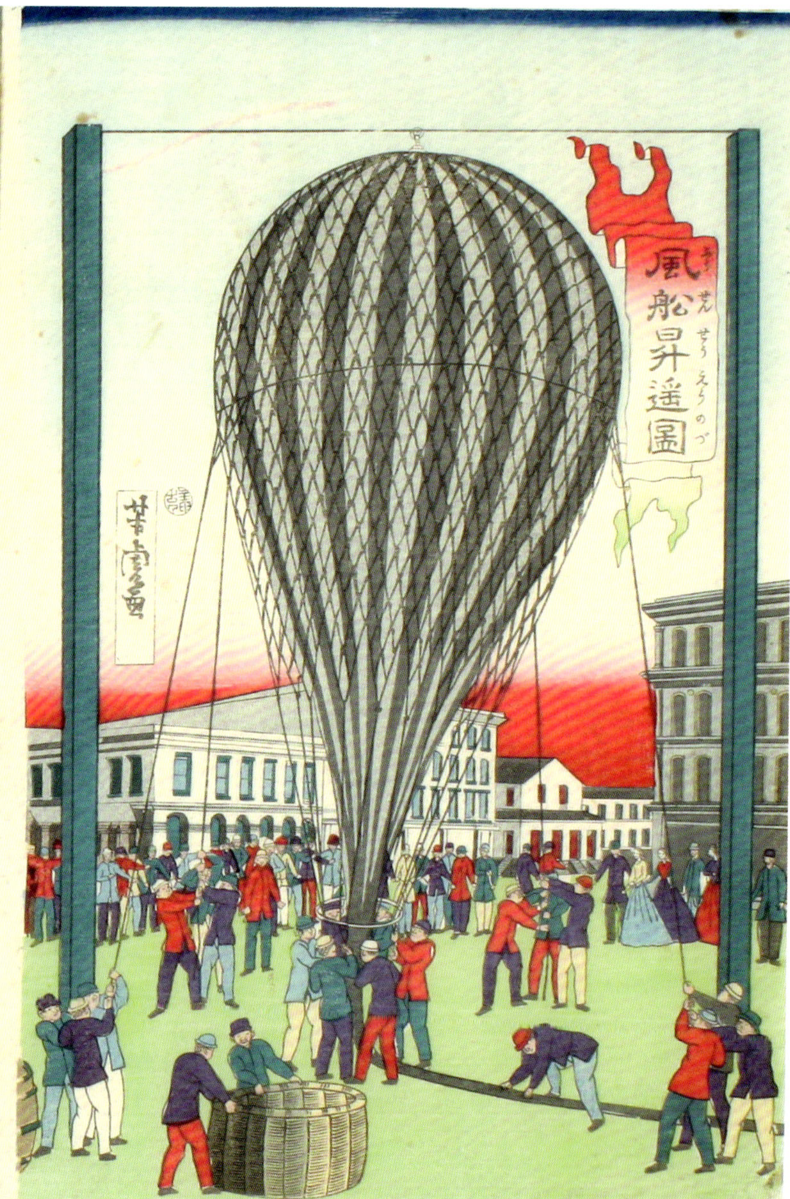

fit the necessary details into his paintings (**Fig. 196**).

One of the preferred formats of *Yokohama-e* was the triptych, and this was put to good effect by both Utagawa Shigenobu (Hiroshige II) (1826–69) (**Fig. 197**), pupil and adopted son of Hiroshige I and first husband of his daughter Otatsu, and Utagawa Shigemasa (Hiroshige III) (1843–94) (**Figs. 206, 208**), another Hiroshige protégé and Otatsu's second husband. Both worked in a style similar to their master. Shigenobu produced a number of print series, mostly views of places. His *One Hundred Views of Famous Places in Various Provinces* (1859–64) contains some first-rate images, including of Yokohama. Shigemasa is most known for his designs depicting the great changes during the Meiji period, featuring Western clothing, buildings, bridges, railroads, locomotives, etc.

Three pupils of Utagawa Kuniyoshi are also well known for their Yokohama prints. Utagawa Yoshitora (active ca. 1840–80) produced more *Yokohama-e* than any other artist of the time. The fact that many of his designs were made after illustrations in foreign newspapers and books is apparent from the costumes worn by some of his subjects (**Figs. 200, 201**). His four-panel work of a circus in Yokohama (**Fig. 202**) and triptychs of Western technical inventions (**Figs. 204, 205**) indicate the artist's fascination with things foreign. The favorite subjects of Utagawa Yoshikazu (active 1850s–70s) were foreigners and foreign manners, including their revelry in the pleasure quarters of Yokohama (**Figs. 199, 207**). Utagawa Yoshiiku (1833–1904), a popular newspaper illustrator, made both single-sheet works, among them his famous painting of a *sumo* wrestler tossing an upstart foreigner, and triptychs of foreign activities, which are full of fascinating detail (**Fig. 210**). Today, *Yokohama-e* are rather rare and therefore often expensive. They remain an excellent source for gaining insight into the first impressions of foreigners that were made available to ordinary Japanese.

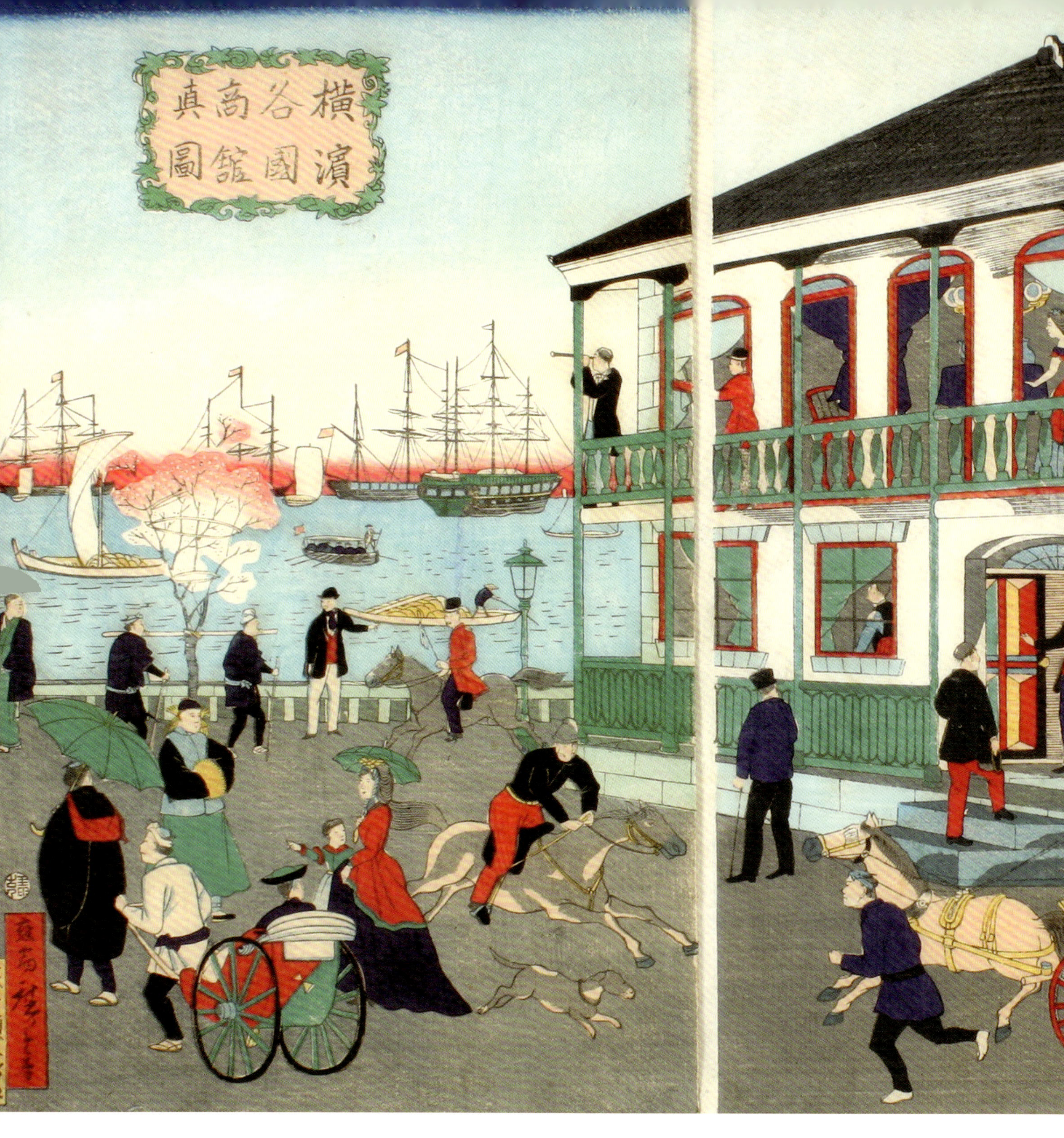
横濱各國商館真圖

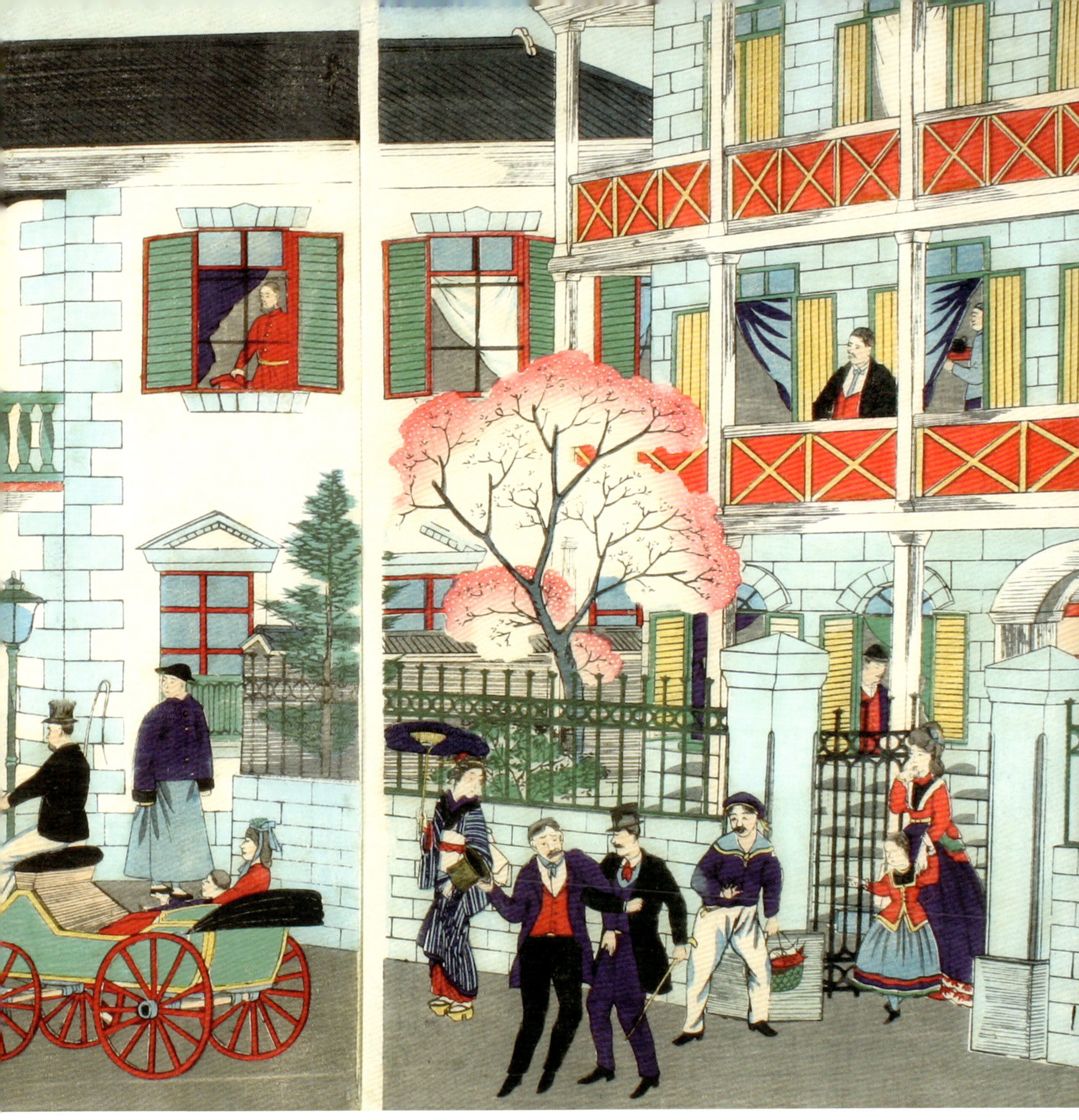

FIG. 206
Utagawa SHIGEMASA (Hiroshige III)
三代広重 (1843–94)
Mercantile Establishments in Yokohama 横濱各國商舘真図 (1872)
Triptych, 39 x 81 cm
Courtesy of Mita Arts Gallery

This is a perfect example of the hustle and bustle of the foreign settlement in Yokohama. Sailing ships, their national flags clearly displayed, and local craft can be seen in the harbor. Men, women and children are out in the streets, some walking or talking, others on horseback or in horse-drawn carriages and man-pulled rickshaws. The multistoried accommodations are built in a fusion of architectural styles, with balconies and numerous windows to allow for ventilation and views.

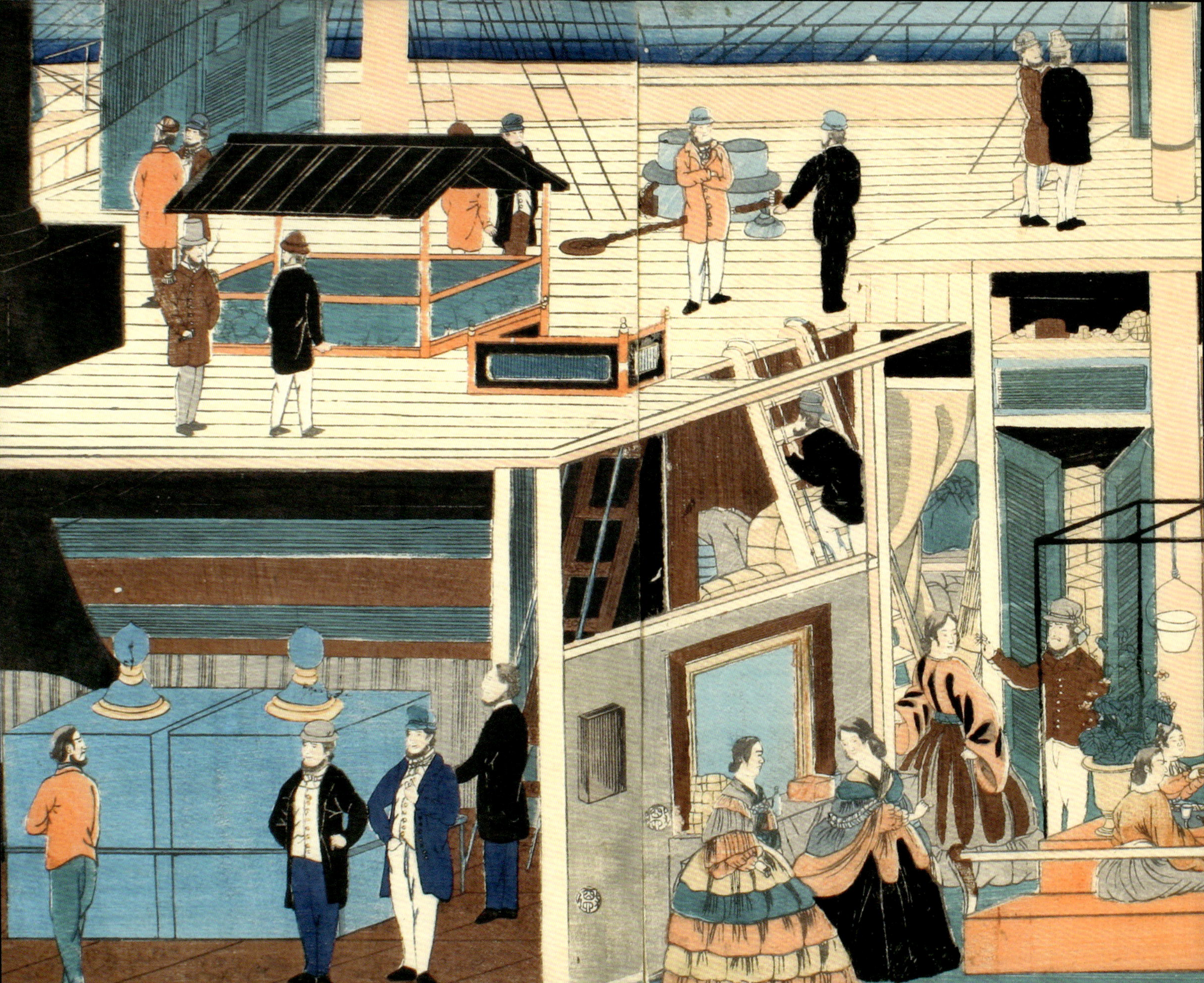

FIG. 207
Utagawa YOSHIKAZU
芳員 (active 1850s–70s)
Interior of an American Steamship 亜墨利加國蒸気船中之寫 (1861)
Triptych, 39 x 81 cm
Courtesy of Mita Arts Gallery

With the opening of the treaty ports in 1858, great numbers of foreign merchant ships, operating under both steam and sail, descended on Yokohama, opening up a new seafaring world for *ukiyo-e* artists. Here, the artist has cut away the partitions to allow a tantalizing view of life inside an American ship. Both foreign men and women sit down to dinner, but there is no sign of anyone serving the party. On the upper deck, a few merchants gaze at the distant port.

FIG. 208
Utagawa SHIGEMASA (Hiroshige III)
三代広重 (1843–94)
Steam Train from Yokohama 横濱からの蒸気車 (1872)
Triptych, 39 x 81 cm
Courtesy of Mita Arts Gallery

After the Meiji Restoration, woodblock prints became a means of illustrating events and news of interest to the public, including the astonishingly rapid developments in transportation. In this delightful scene, enhanced by Mount Fuji in the background, a steam locomotive crosses an iron railway bridge while a small boat goes under it. Parallel to the railway line, the Tokaido highway is featured with a trishaw and horse-drawn carriage. There are some amusing stories about people removing their shoes before boarding a train and expecting to retrieve them when they got off it.

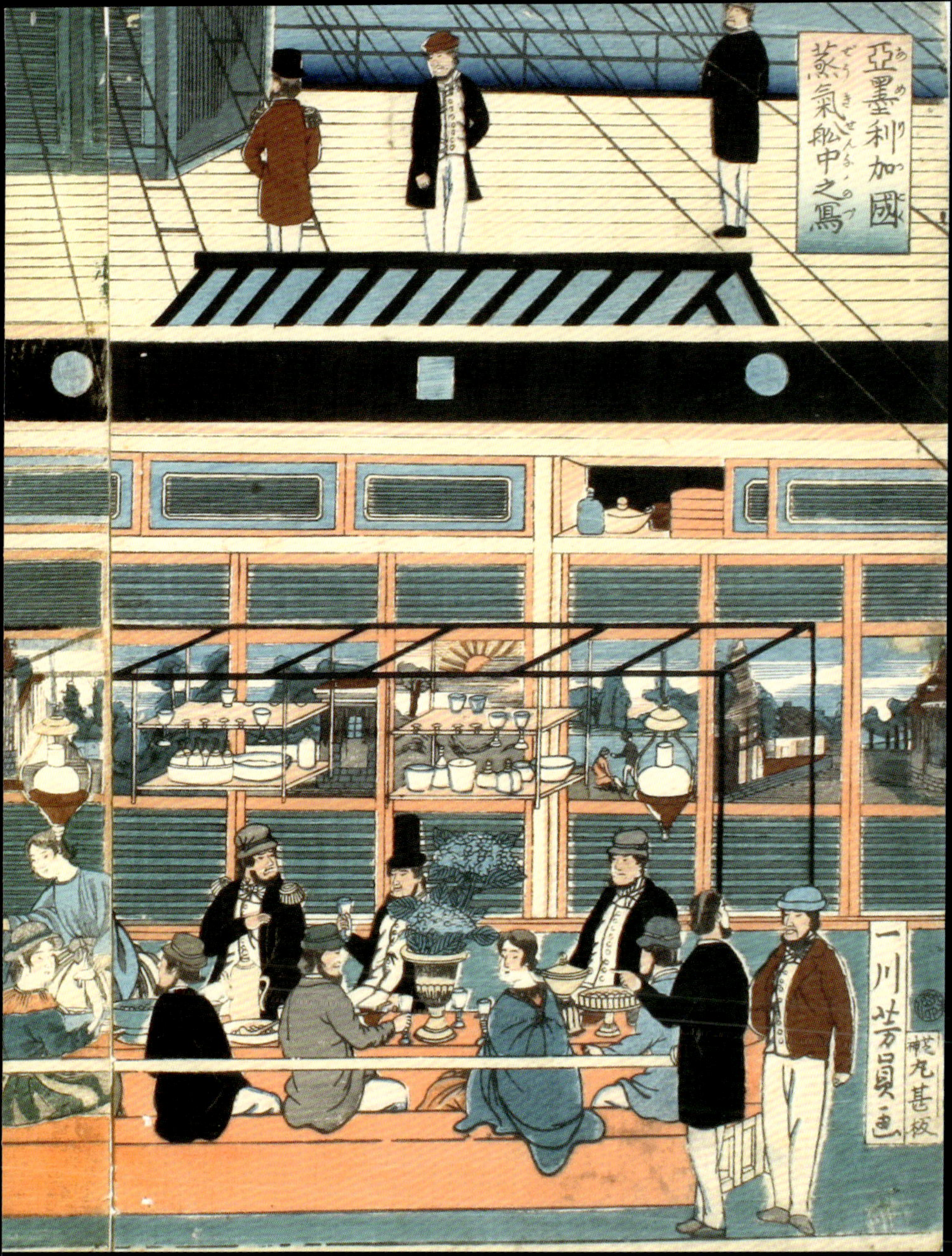

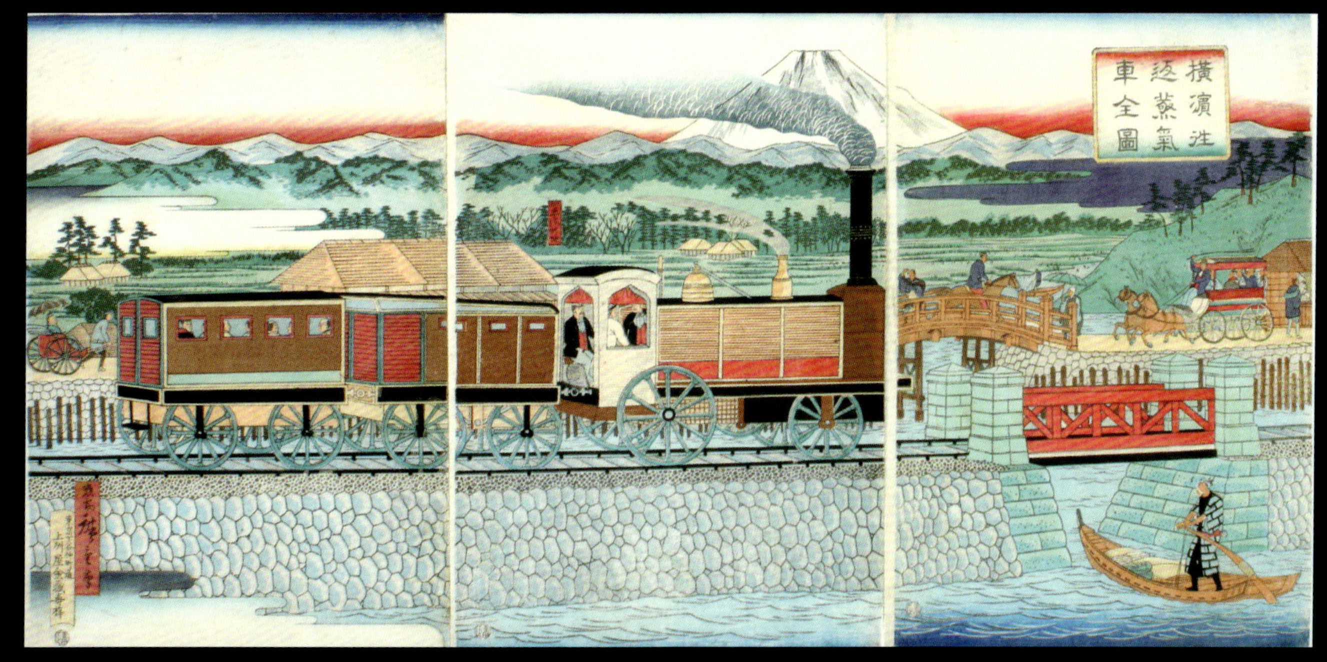
横濱往還蒸氣車全圖

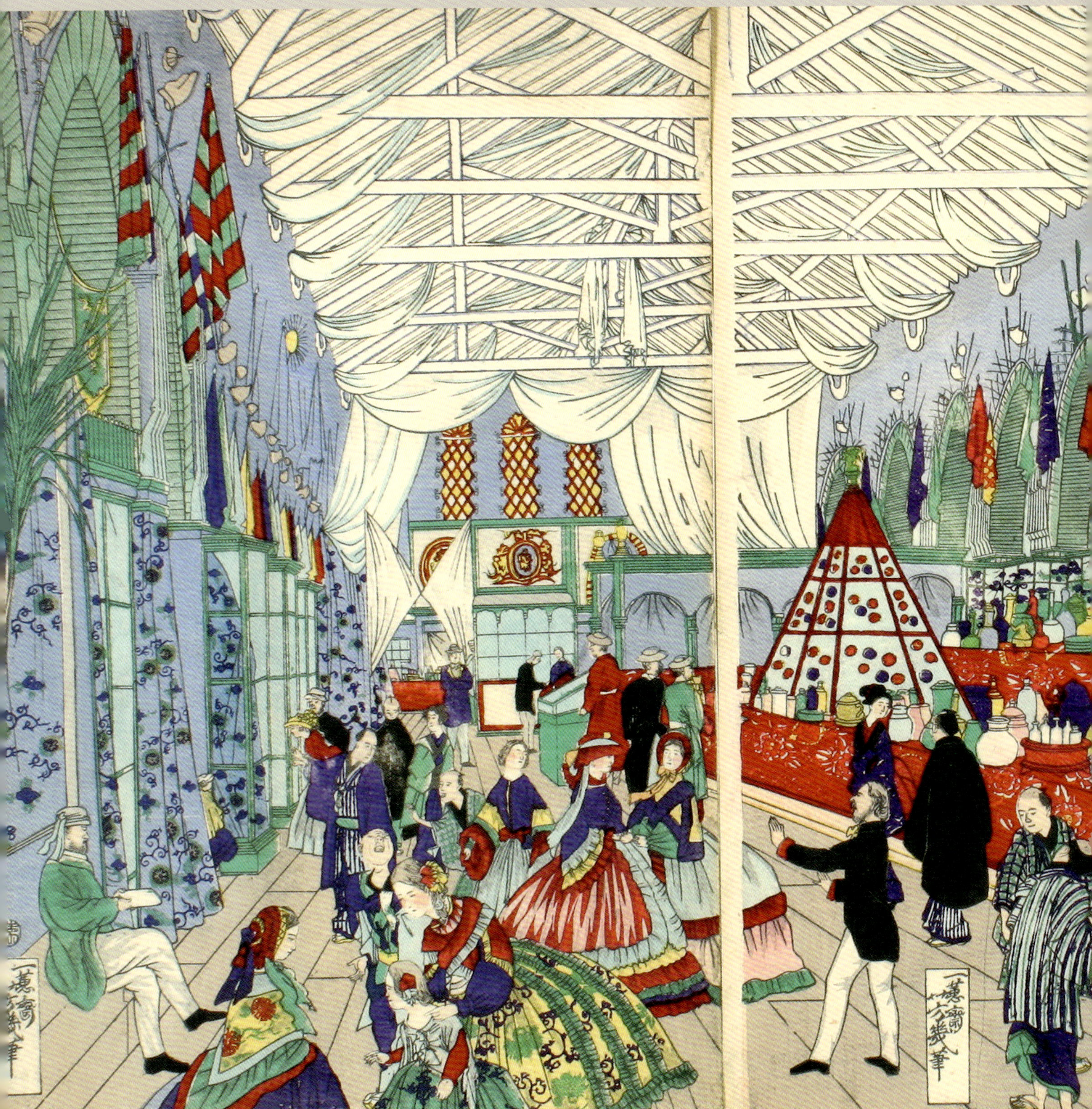

FIG. 209
Utagawa YOSHIIKU
芳幾 (1833–1904)
British Trade Fair at Their Chamber of Commerce 横濱英吉利西商館繁榮図 (1871)
Triptych, 39 x 81 cm
Courtesy of Mita Arts Gallery

This interesting picture shows the first efforts at trying to create a market in Japan for English products, such as porcelain and glassware, including lamps. Most of the people in the scene are foreigners, not Japanese, even though the sales target was Japanese. *Yokohama-e* like these were mostly bought by Japanese, not foreigners. The inclusion of a large group of foreigners in the picture was one of the attractions.

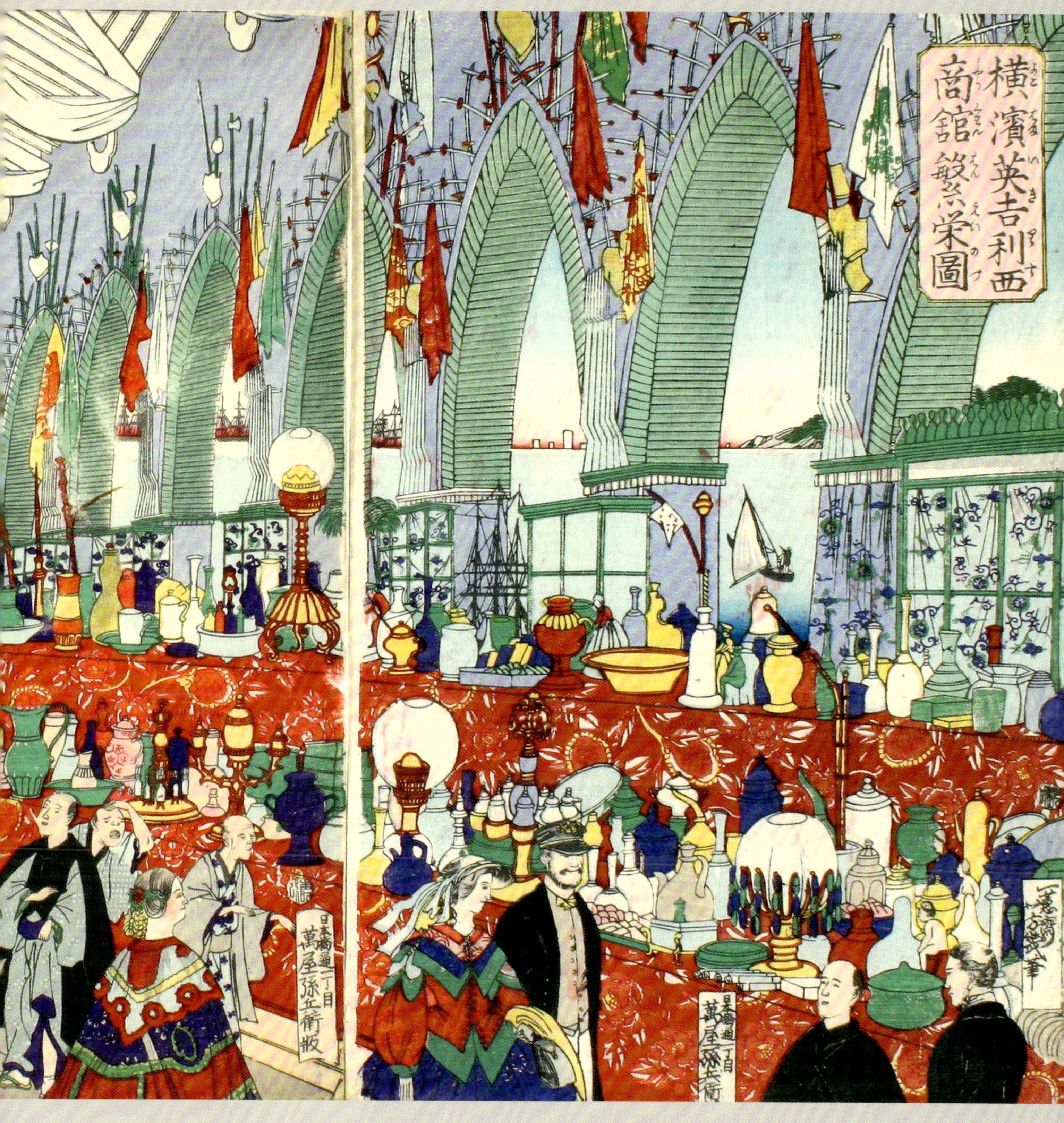
横濱英吉利西
商館繁栄圖
日本橋通一丁目
萬屋孫兵衛版
一恵斎芳幾筆

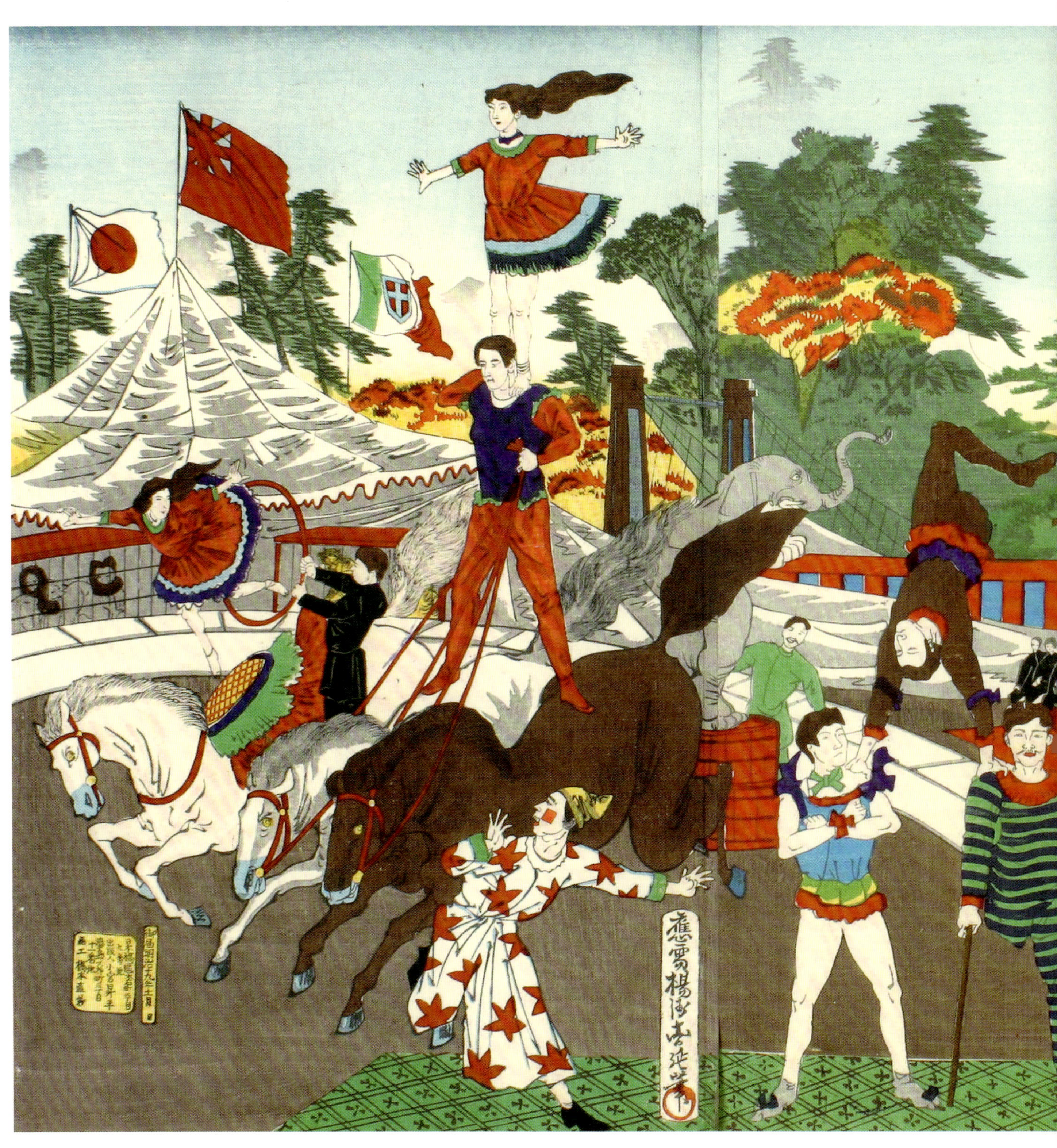
應需楊洲周延筆

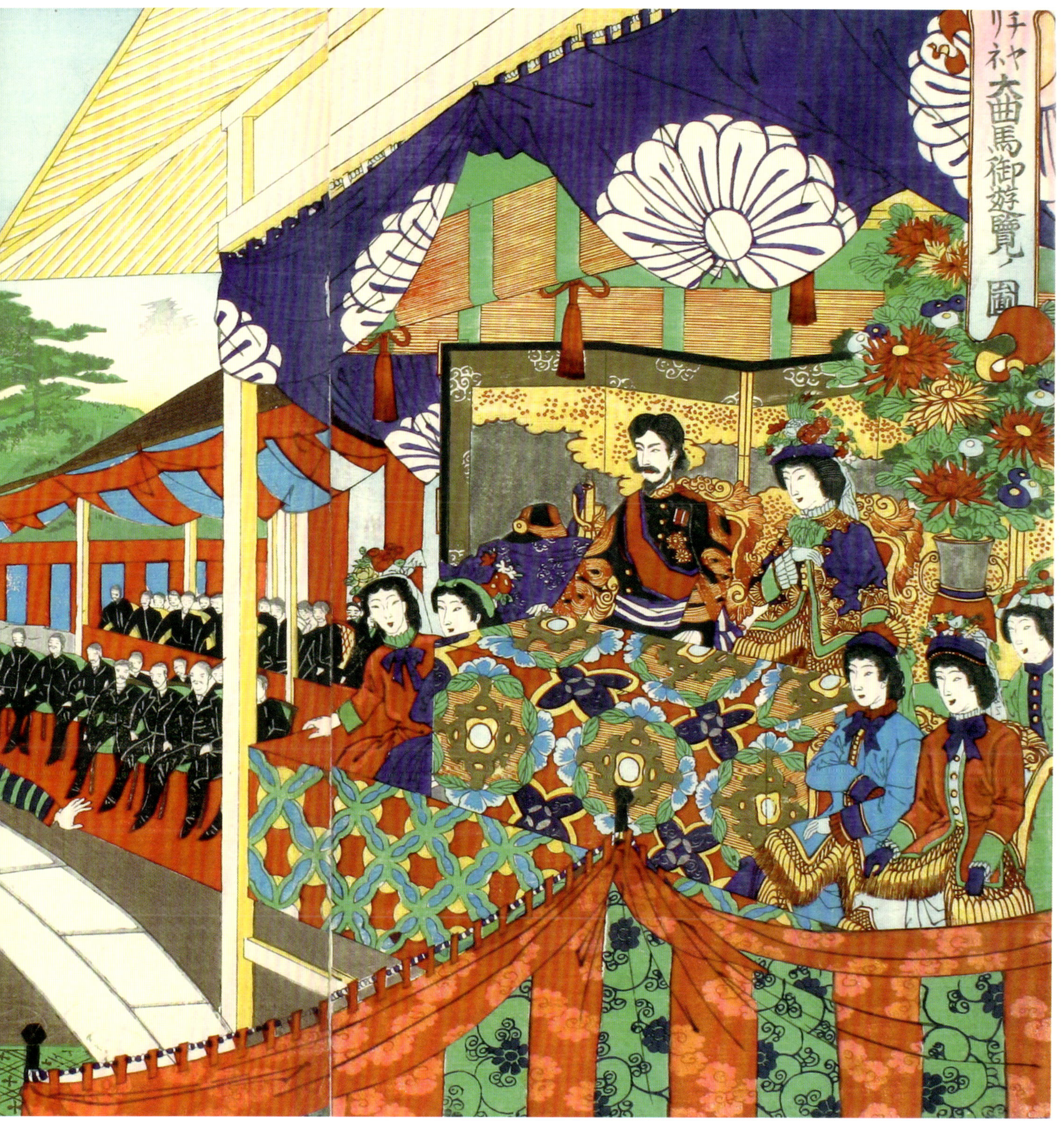

FIG. 210
Anonymous
作者不詳
The Imperial Family Enjoying a Circus チャリネ大曲馬御遊覧ノ図 (1886)
Triptych, 39 x 81 cm
Courtesy of Mita Arts Gallery

As Japan developed into a modern, industrialized world power, the Emperor and Empress Meiji acted as role models, adopting Western-style family customs and fashions. At this circus, where all the performers are foreigners, the Imperial family and their entourage are dressed in European fashion and the large mass of government officials in black European-style suits. The violet canopy over the viewing stand bears the chrysanthemum emblem, the exclusive mark of the Imperial family.

CHAPTER TWELVE

Collecting and Caring for Prints

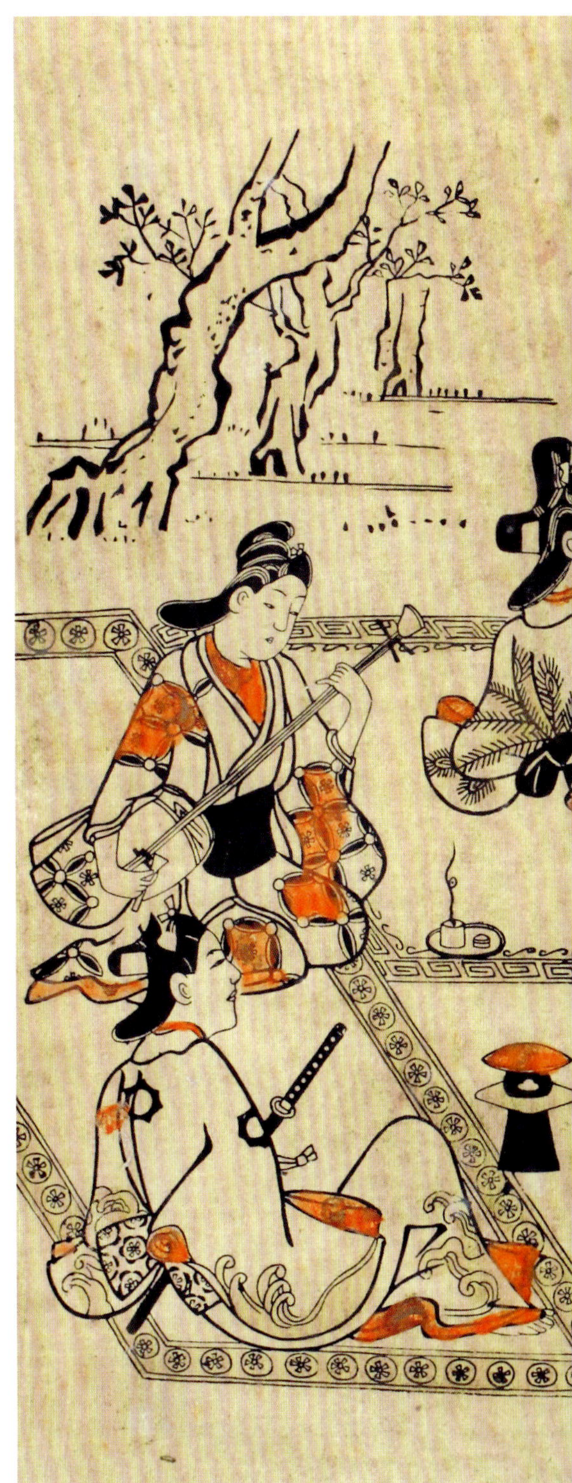

Japanese woodblock prints have captivated collectors, dealers and artists in the West since Commodore Perry's excursions and the opening of Japan to foreigners in the mid-nineteenth century. Like Perry himself, who brought back *ukiyo-e* prints to the United States, and many of the great painters of the day who collected them and assimilated elements from them into their own work, I felt the allure of these prints when first exposed to them at the Art Students League in New York City in 1950, courtesy of printmaker Martin Lewis. My service with the United States Army, as part of an international peacekeeping force during the Korean War (1950–3), took me to Korea and then to Japan where I settled down, learned much more about *ukiyo-e* and began assembling a portfolio.

When I first started collecting Japanese woodblock prints, the principal source was dealers in Japan, the country of their origin. Today, the Japanese woodblock print has become an international commodity. The ease of communication via the telephone, Internet and other technology has allowed prints to be purchased or traded at the mere push of a button or click of a mouse. Dealers have established themselves everywhere around the world. They trade with each other and eventually find a customer for a print in the home of a collector or in the collection of a museum. But this has not lessened the need for those aspiring to build up a collection of Japanese prints to first educate themselves on the art of *ukiyo-e*.

Although a number of art lovers and connoisseurs in Japan, Europe and the United States have amassed legendary collections of *ukiyo-e*, it is museums in these countries that have the largest holdings of Japanese prints and it is to these museums that aspiring collectors should head. Museums allow a broad audience to benefit from exhibitions and publications on offer. Visitors can enjoy—but only temporarily—the privilege of viewing a print. Owning a print and being able to view it at one's convenience is the privilege of the collector.

Therein lies the dilemma. Collectors of Japanese prints range from the beginner to the experienced, from the casual collector to the hardcore aficionado. Print collectors are often faced with a myriad of choices as to what to collect. Considerations such as aesthetics, collectability and cost may come into conflict. The fact that

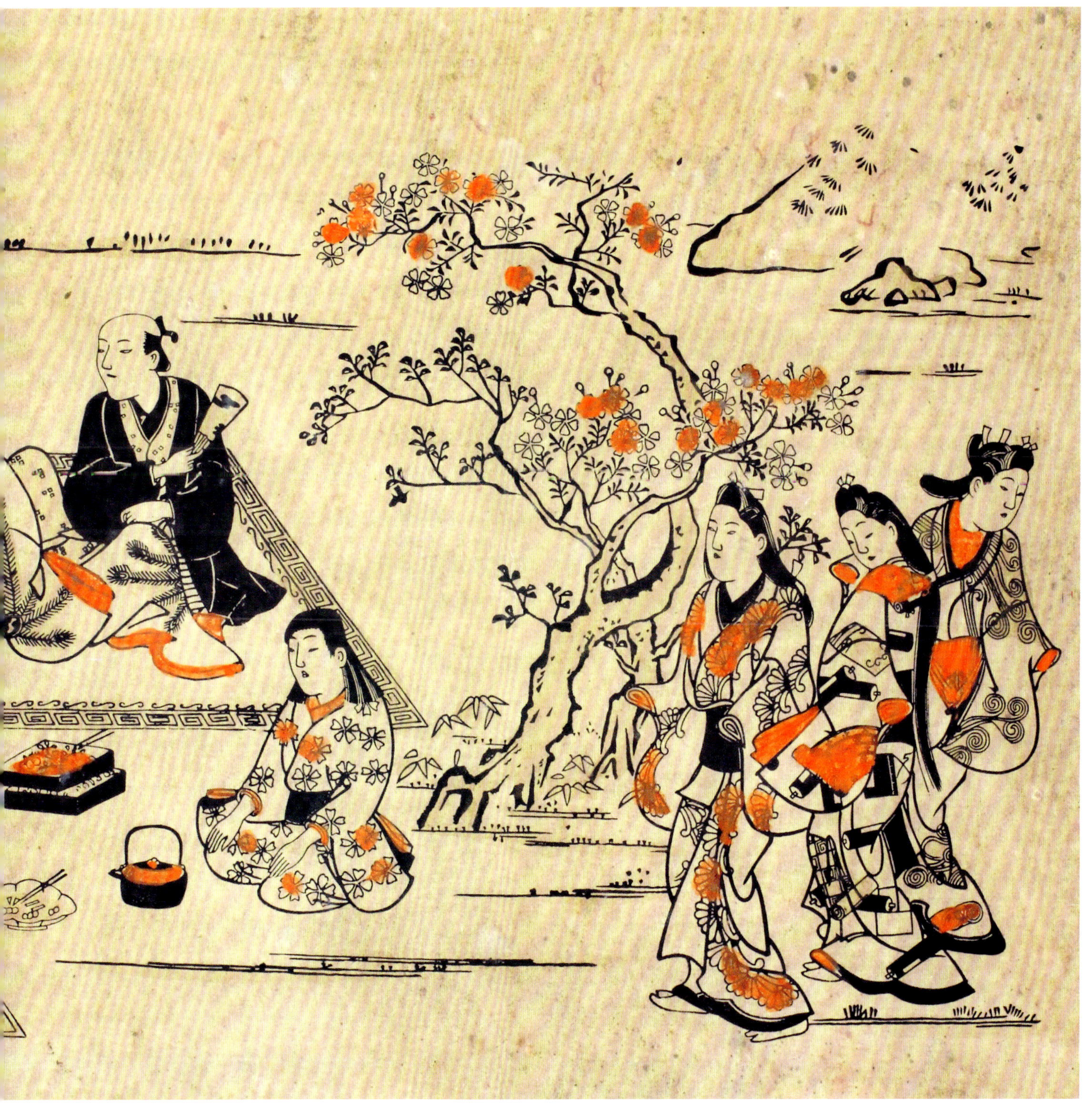

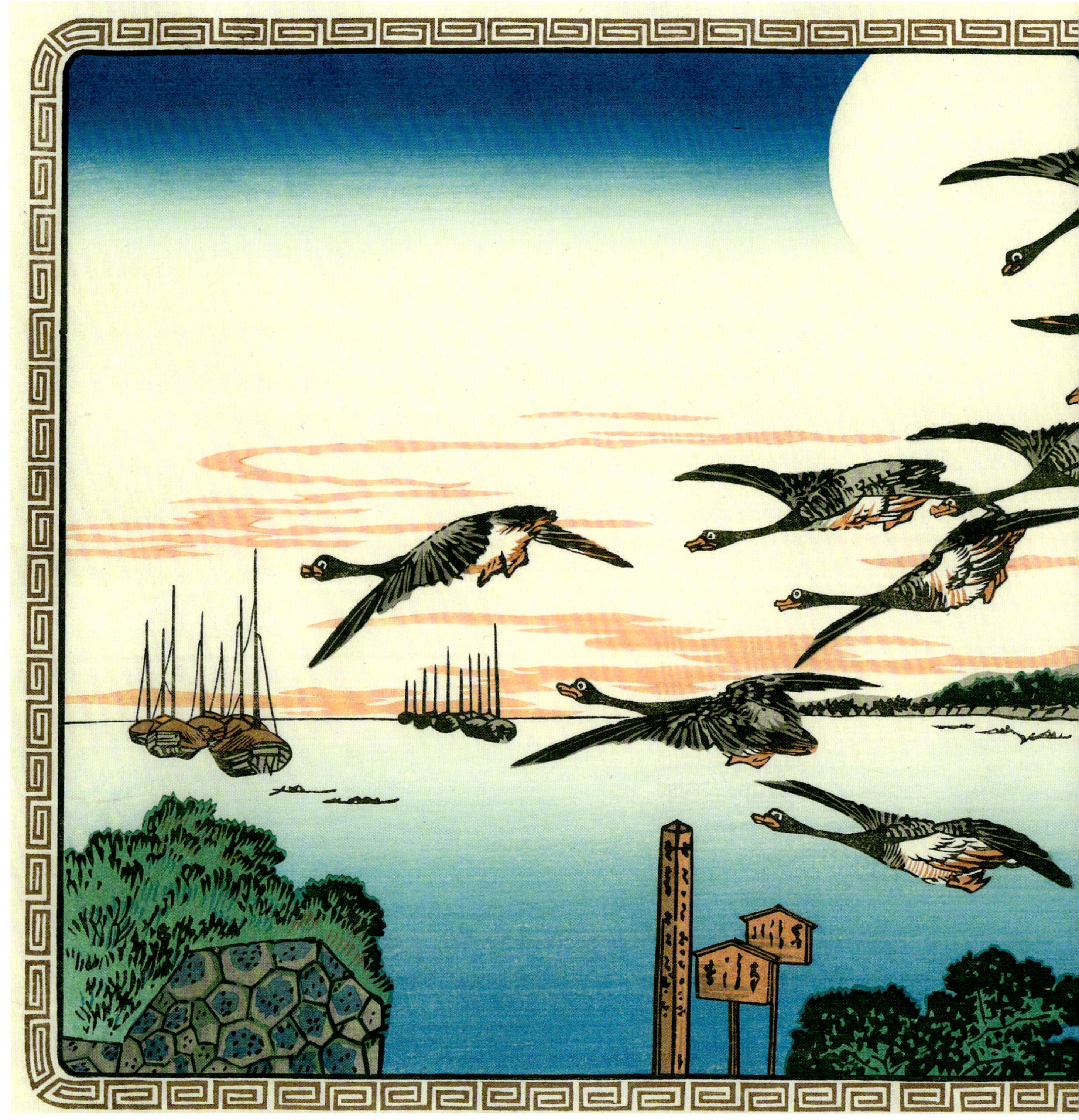

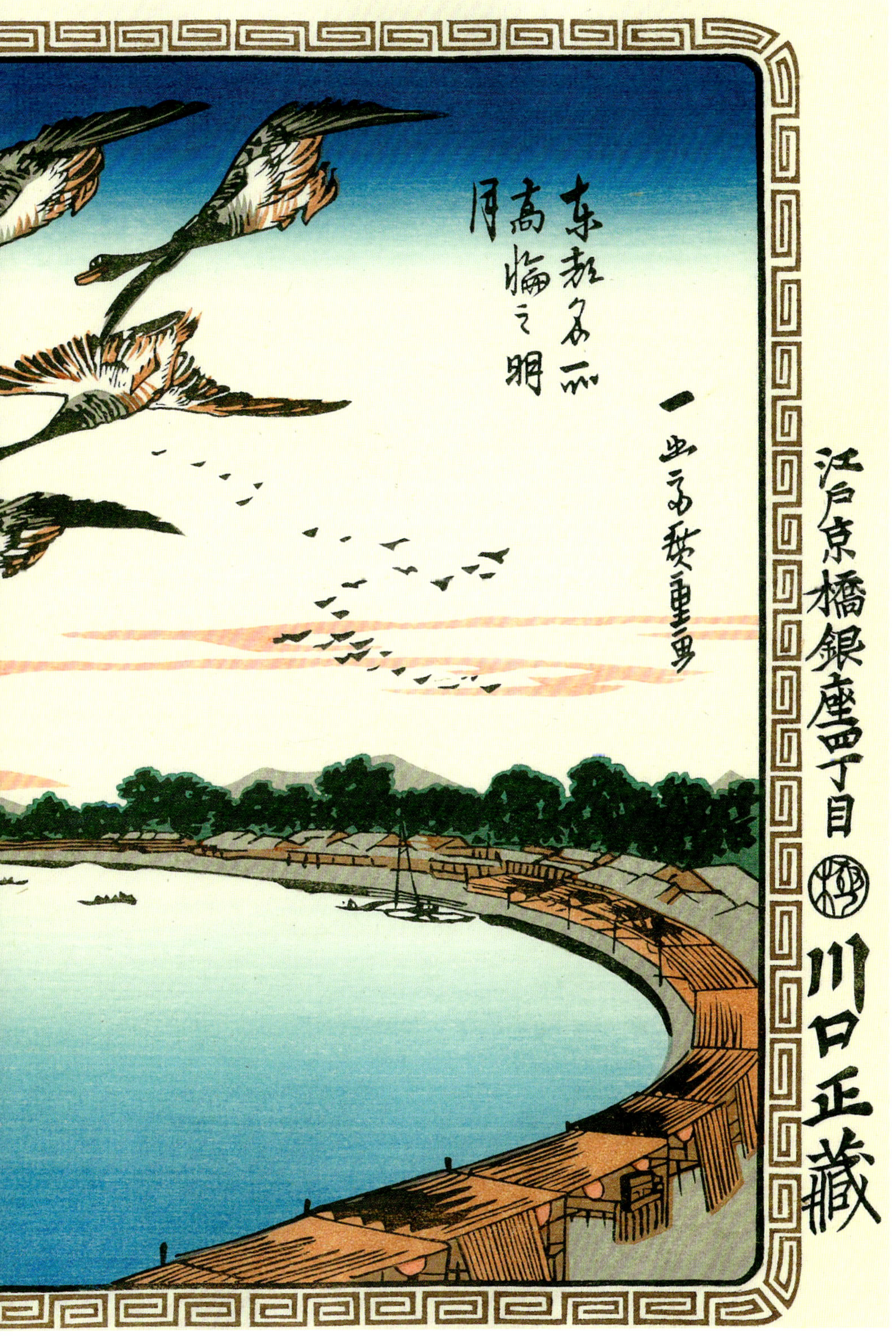

a print is one of numerous impressions also imposes considerations that are not applicable to a painting where there is only one image. In most cases, the vast majority of collectors—ordinary people like you and me—soon discover that collecting choices have to be made if they are to live within their budget while augmenting their collection of woodblock prints.

The market value of a woodblock print depends on a number of factors, including the reputation of the artist, the subject of the print, the condition of the print and how rare it is.

The following are those factors I consider most important when deciding whether or not to buy a print:

- The most important factor to me is the aesthetic quality of a print, the same criterion that most people would apply when buying any work of art. Some pictures are simply more beautiful than others. People's ideas of beauty do, of course, differ, but generally most people can spot a print that is truly beautiful.
- Having passed the test of appeal, a print needs next to be judged on its condition. Is it creased, folded or earmarked? Have the colors faded or run out or are they still fresh? Are there water stains, fox marks or signs of browning, yellowing or oxidation? Have the corners or margins worn down? Is there any sign of retouching? If possible, the reverse side of the print should be examined to check if it was previously laid down on a backing or glued at the corners. The print should be held up to a light to detect any repairs to worm holes or tears. Familiarity with the composition will determine if the print has been trimmed outside or within the margins.

- It is important also to try and determine the impression or edition of the print you are looking at. This is a very difficult task, especially with the landscape prints of Hiroshige. Because of the popularity of some designs, numerous prints were published more than once, with variations in details, colors and printing techniques. Sometimes additions or eliminations were made by carvers to large parts of a block, which changed the original composition.
- Rarity is another factor. If it is a unique print, is beautiful, and has survived the centuries intact, of course this has a bearing on its value.

Taking all the above into consideration, the most valuable print is clearly one that is in pristine condition, has not been cut or repaired, has not faded and is an early impression. On the other hand, it is important to realize that an original print that is, say, 100 or 150 years old, will never be in perfect condition. If it looks perfect, then it is likely to be a reproduction, especially if it is a print purportedly created by one of the more famous woodblock artists.

The best of prints can cost tens of thousands of dollars. Others can cost less than a hundred dollars. Market trends and fashions for particular artists or subjects naturally have a bearing on price. However, when contemplating a serious purchase, much depends on your personal impression. Do you like it and are you prepared to pay a particular amount for it?

Connoisseurship or simply education is a vital element in the decision process. Before the serious beginner contemplates buying a Japanese woodblock print, it is advisable to become familiar with the subject. Over time, by seeing as many high-quality Japanese prints as possible, you will develop your own eye. You will be able to discern the gradations of quality and be able to make more educated choices in developing your collection. Here are my suggestions for acquiring both knowledge and experience:

- Read as many books as you can on the subject. Learn about the history of *ukiyo-e* printing, for example the difference in technique between early one- or two-color prints and later multicolor prints, the subject areas of *ukiyo-e* and the most renowned artists in each field.
- Visit museums or galleries holding exhibitions on Japanese prints or which have collections available to the public for viewing in their print rooms. This will give you an opportunity to see the best original prints along with their descriptive captions. It will also allow you to discover artists and subjects that appeal to you and to compare and contrast styles of composition and technique.
- Visit dealers' shops to look, question and compare prints and costs. Try to build up a relationship with a reputable dealer so that you will receive good advice. Always ask for a reference or authentication before buying a print. A list of reputable dealers, who are accustomed to dealing with foreigners, is given on pages 186–7.
- Subscribe to the main auction house catalogs and follow the sales of the auctions, which are subsequently published. Many woodblock print dealers also list their sold inventory online with prices. If you are collecting for investment purposes, this will allow you to spot artists and subjects that are selling well.
- Be cautious of Internet auction sites. Some people who sell prints online know very little about them and may either deliberately or inadvertently sell a copy as an original. Only buy from sellers who offer references or authentication certificates.

Once you are the proud owner of your first print, you need to know how to care for it, especially how to store it or, if you prefer, frame and display it. Here are some tips on conserving prints:

- Never cut or trim a print.
- Never apply any glue or tape to the back of a print.
- If you decide to frame and display your print, use an acid-free window mat so that there is no direct contact between the glass and the print. Use ultraviolet filtering glass or perspex rather than normal glass. Hang the print on a wall away from direct sunlight. It is equally important to avoid strong artificial lighting. It is a good idea to rotate your framed prints from time to time to give them a rest.
- Use acid-free paper folders to store prints and place them flat in a cool, stable environment, preferably in a plan cabinet or a special non-acid collector's box. Interleave more than one print in a folder or box with acid-free tissue paper. Check prints regularly for signs of damage from insects or environmental conditions such as dampness and humidity.

Collecting Japanese woodblock prints can be a wonderful adventure, one that will enrich your life. Remember, there are many quality prints available at very little cost. Major purchases can be pursued after a little self-education.

My interest in *ukiyo-e* and my motivation for collecting these fascinating prints—and for writing this book—is best summed up by this quotation from the great print scholar/author and founder of the Japan Ukiyo-e Society, Narazaki Muneshige: "A great deal of the essence of the popular culture of Japan is conveyed in the prints, and I believe that it can be interpreted in larger terms—as an expression of some of the most significant character of the Japanese people—and perhaps in a still broader sense, as an expression of human values which prevail all over the world and at all times."

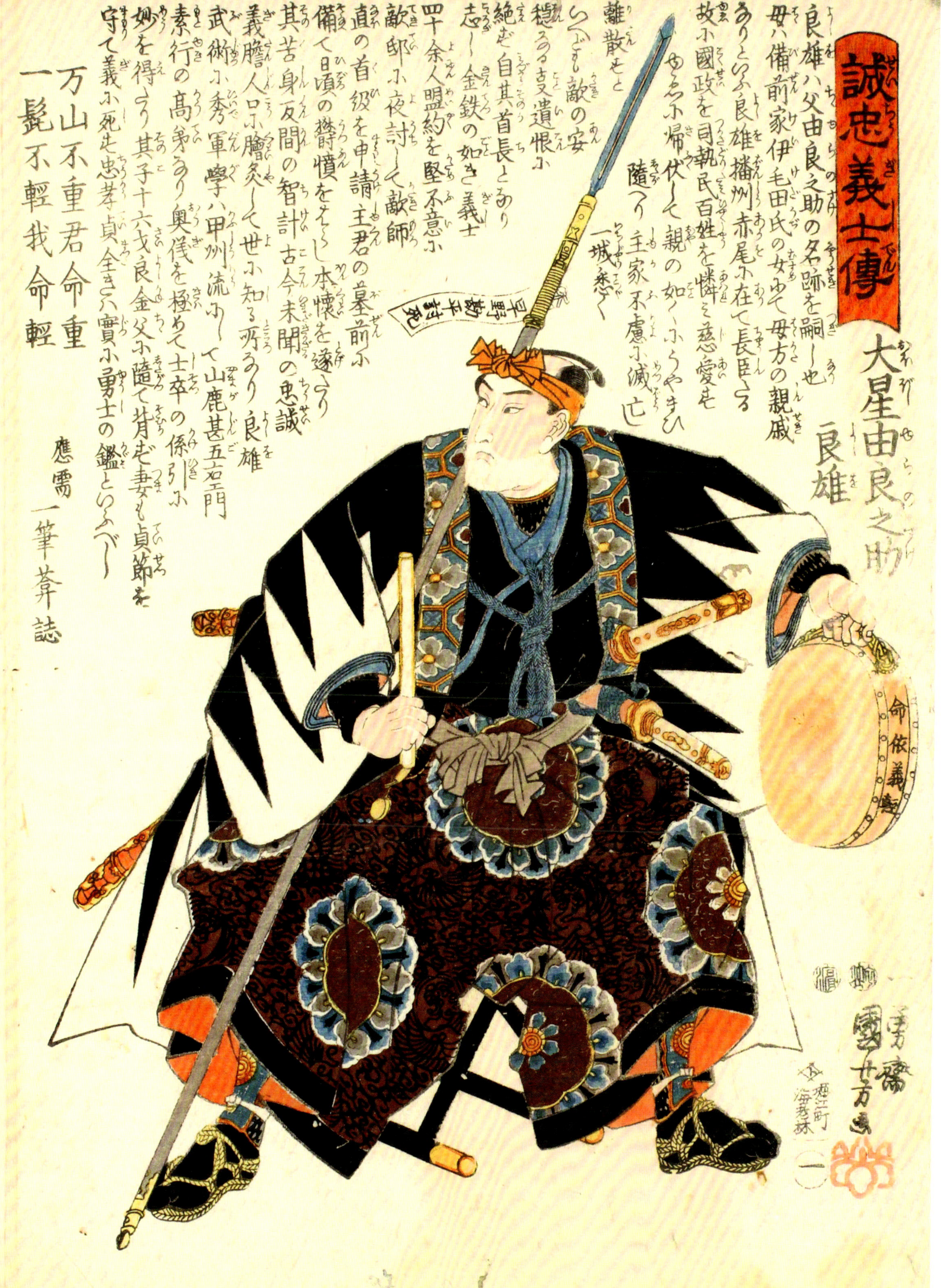
誠忠義士傳
大星由良之助
良雄
良雄ハ父由良之助の名跡を嗣し也
母ハ備前家伊毛田氏の女ゆて母方の親戚
なりとゆふ良雄播州赤尾ニ在て長臣たる
故ニ國政を司執民百姓を憐ミ慈愛を
なすゆ帰伏して親の如くふらやまひ
随ひ主家不慮ニ滅亡
一城悉く
離散せしと
いへとも敵の安
穏なるを遺恨ニ
絶ず自其首長となり
志し金鉄の如き義士
四十余人盟約を堅不意ニ
敵邸ニ夜討して敵師
直の首級を申請主君の墓前ニ
備て日頃の欝憤をそゝし本懐を遂たり
其苦身反間の智計古今未聞の忠誠
義膽人口ニ膾炙して世ニ知る所なり良雄
武術ニ秀軍學ハ甲州流ニして山鹿甚五左衛門
素行の高弟なり奥儀を極めて士卒の係引ニ
妙を得たり其子十六才良金父ニ随て背ず妻も貞節を
守て義ニ死せ忠孝貞全き實ニ勇士の鑑といふべし
万山不重君命重
一髪不輕我命輕
應需一筆菴誌
早野勘平討死
命依義輕
一勇斎國芳画
堀江町 海老林
一

CHAPTER THIRTEEN

Where to See and Buy Prints

Where To See Japanese Woodblock Prints

JAPAN

Edo-Tokyo Museum
1-4-1, Yokoami, Sumida-ku
Tokyo 130-0015
Tel: +81 03 3626 9974
www.edo-tokyo-museum.or.jp

Chiba City Museum of Art
3-10-8, Chuo, Chuo-ku
Chiba 260-8733
Tel: +81 43 221 2311
www.city.chiba.jp/art

Hokusai Museum
485 Obuse Town, Kamitakai
Nagano
Tel: +81 0262 47 5206
www.hokusai-kan.com

Japan Ukiyo-e Museum
2206-1, Shimadachi Koshiba
Matsumoto City, Nagano 390-0852
Tel: +81 0263 47 4440
www.ukiyo-e.co.jp

National Museum of Modern Art
3-1, Kitanomaru-koen, Chiyoda-ku
Toyo 102-0091
Tel: +81 03 3214 2561
www.momat.go.jp

Machida City Museum of Graphic Arts
4-28-1, Haramachida, Machida City
Tokyo 194-0013
Tel: +81 427 26 2771

Tokyo National Museum
13-9, Ueno Koen, Taito-ku
Tokyo 110-8712
Tel: +81 03 3822 1111
www.tnm.jp

USA

Brooklyn Museum of Art
200 Eastern Parkway, Brooklyn
New York 11238-6052
Tel: (718) 638 5000
www.brooklynmuseum.org

Metropolitan Museum of Art
1000 5th Avenue, New York
New York 10028
Tel: (212) 879 5500
www.metmuseum.org

Museum of Contemporary Art
220 East Chicago Avenue
Chicago, Illinois 60611
Tel: (312) 280 2660
www.mcachicago.org

Museum of Fine Arts, Boston
Avenue of the Arts
465 Huntington Avenue
Boston, Massachusetts 02115
Tel: (617) 267 9300
Tel: (617) 267 9300
www.mfa.org

Pacific Asia Museum
46 North Los Robles Avenue
Pasadena, California 91101
Tel: (626) 449 2742
www.pacificasiamuseum.org

UNITED KINGDOM

British Museum
Great Russell Street, London WC 1B
Tel: 020 7323 8838
www.britishmuseum.org

Victoria & Albert Museum
V&A South Kensington
Cromwell Road, London SW7 2RL
Tel: 020 7942 2000
www.vam.ac.uk

GERMANY

Museum für Ostasiatische Kunst
(Museum of East Asian Art, Cologne)
Universitätsstraße 100
D-50674 Köln
Tel: 0221 940518-0
www.museenkoeln.de

THE NETHERLANDS

Rijksmuseum Amsterdam
Stadhouderskade 42
1071 ZD Amsterdam
Tel: +31 (0)20 6747000
www.rijksmuseum.nl

Where To Buy Japanese Woodblock Prints

JAPAN

Hara Shobo
3, Kanda-jinbocho 2-chome
Chiyoda-ku, Tokyo 101-0051
Tel: +81 03 5212 7801
Fax: +81 03 3230 1158
E-mail: ukiyoe@harashobo.com
www.harashobo.com

Mita Arts Gallery
IVY Building, 4F
10-1, Kanda-jinbocho
Chiyoda-ku, Tokyo 101-0051
Tel: +81 03 3294 4554
Fax: +81 03 3294 4556
E-mail: ken@mita-arts.com
www.mita-arts.com

The Adachi Institute of Woodcut Prints
3-13-17, Shimoochiai
Shinjuku-ku, Tokyo 161-0033
Tel: +81 03 3951 2681
Fax: +81 03 3951 2137
adachi@adachi-hanga.com
www.adachi-hanga.com

Yamada Shoten
Yamada Building, 2F
8, Kanda-jinbocho 1-chome
Chiyoda-ku, Tokyo 101-0051
Tel: +81 03 3295 0252
Fax: +81 03 3295 0061
E-mail: yasushi@yamada-shoten.com
www.yamada-shoten.com

For a complete list of dealers, contact:
Ukiyo-e Dealers Association of Japan
San'ei Bldg. 5F, 11-4, Shinbashi 1-
Chome
Minato-ku, Tokyo 105-0004
Tel: +81 03 5568 3645
Fax: +81 03 5568 3646

USA
Arts and Designs of Japan
P.O. Box 22075
San Francisco, California 94122
Tel: (415) 759 6233
Fax: (415) 759 9017
E-mail: gilder@artsanddesignsjapan.com
www.artsanddesignsjapan.com

Carolyn Staley Fine Japanese Prints
2003 Western Avenue, Suite 107
Seattle WA 98121
Tel: (206) 621 1888
Fax: (206) 621 6493
E-mail: carolynstaleyprints.com
www.carolynstaleyprints.com

Castle Fine Arts
P.O. Box 725
Del Mar, California 92014
Tel: (858) 350 5810
Fax: (858) 350 9946
E-mail: info@castlefinearts.com
www.castlefinearts.com

East West Gallery
P.O. Box 414
Fairport, New York 14450
Tel: (585) 248 3261
E-mail: japaneseprints@gmail.com

Edo Prints Gallery
106 Spring Street
New York, New York 10012
Tel: (212) 226 0618
E-mail: edoprints@edoprints.com
www.edoprints.com

Egenolf Gallery
P.O. Box 4240
Burbank, California 91503
Tel: (818) 841 9551
Fax: (818) 8419553
E-mail: v_miller@earthlink.net
www.egenolfgallery.com

Floating World Gallery Ltd
858 West Armitage Avenue
Chicago, Illinois 60614
Tel: (312) 587 7800
www.floatingworld.com

Japan Gallery
P.O. Box 1273
New York, New York 10028
Tel: (212) 288 2241
Fax: (212) 794 9497
E-mail: japangallery.ny@gmail.com
www.japangalleryprints.com

Joan B. Mirviss Ltd
39 East 78th Street
New York, New York 10075
Tel: (212) 799 4021
E-mail: info@mirviss.com
www.mirviss.com

John Adams Japanese Woodblock Prints
2480 Incline Drive
Santa Rosa, California 95404
Tel: (707) 544 5231
E mail: hokuci@sonic.net
www.adamsjapaneseprints

Ronin Gallery
425 Madison Avenue, 10F
SE Corner of 49th Street
New York, New York 10017
Tel: (212) 688 0188
E-mail: roningallery@aol.com
www.roningallery.com

The Art of Japan
P.O. Box 2967
Issaquah, WA 98027
Tel: (425) 557 4775
E-mail: info@theartofjapan.com
www.theartofjapan.com

Tokugawa Gallery
1714 West Wescott Drive
Phoenix, Arizona 85027
Tel: (623) 516 1867
www.tokugawagallery.com

Verne Collection
2207 Murray Hill Road
Cleveland, Ohio 44106
Tel: (216) 231 8866
Fax: (216) 231 8877
E-mail: vernegallery@.att.net
www.vernegallery.com

UNITED KINGDOM
Japan Print Gallery
43 Pembridge Road, Notting Hill
London W11 3HG
Tel: +44 (0)20 7221 0927
www.japaneseprints.net

Japanese Gallery
23 Camden Passage
Angel, Islington
London N1 8EA
Tel: +44 (0)20 7226 3347
E-mail: info@japanesegallery.co.uk
www.japanesegallery.co.uk

Richard Kruml
1 Church Terrace
Richmond, TW 10 6SE
Tel: +44 (0)20 8940 2614
Fax: +44 (0)20 8940 0794
E-mail: info@japaneseprints-london.com
www.japaneseprints-london.com

GERMANY
Ukiyo-E-Gallery
An der Brunnenstube 8
72488 Sigmaringen
Tel: 07571 4773
www.ukiyo-e-gallery.de

THE NETHERLANDS
Hotei Japanese Prints
Rapenburg 19
2311 GE Leiden
Tel: +31 71 5143552
Fax: +31 71 5141488
E-mail: ukiyoe@xs4all.nl
www.hotei-japanese-prints.com

Bibliography

Baird, Merrily, *Symbols of Japan: Thematic Motifs in Art and Design*, New York: Rizzoli International Publications, 2001.

Binyon, Lawrence and Sexton, J. J. O'Brien, *Japanese Colour Prints*, London: Faber and Faber, 1960; first published 1923.

Brown, Louise Norton, *Block Printing and Book Illustration in Japan*, London: George Routledge and Sons, 1924.

The Cambridge History of Japan, 6 vols, Cambridge: Cambridge University Press, 1989–93.

Carpenter, John T. (ed.), *Hokusai and His Age*, Leiden: Hotei Publishing, 2005.

______, *Reading Surimono: The Interplay of Text and Image in Japanese Prints, With a Catalogue of the Marino Lusy Collection*, Leiden: Hotei Publishing, 2008.

Chibbett, David, *The History of Japanese Printing and Book Illustration*, Tokyo: Kodansha International, 1977.

Clark, Timothy, *Kuniyoshi,* London: Royal Academy Publications, 2009.

Evans, Tom and Evans, Mary Ann, *Shunga: The Art of Love in Japan*, 2nd edn, London: Paddington Press, 1975; first published 1949.

Gerstle, C. Andrew, with Timothy Clark and Akiko Yano, *Kabuki Heroes on the Osaka Stage 1780–1830*, London: British Museum Press, 2005.

Hillier, Jack, *The Art of the Japanese Book*, 2 vols, London: Sotheby's Publications, 1987.

______, *Hokusai: Paintings, Drawings and Woodcuts*, London: Phaidon Publishers, 1955.

______, *The Japanese Picture Book: A Selection from the Ravicz Collection*, New York: Harry N. Abrams, 1991.

Holloway, Owen E., *Graphic Art of Japan: The Classical School*, Tokyo: Charles E. Tuttle, 1971; first published London: Alec Tiranti, 1957.

Keyes, Roger S., *Ehon: The Artist and the Book in Japan*, New York: New York Public Library and University of Washington Press, 2006.

______, *Surimono: Privately Published Japanese Prints in the Spencer Museum of Art*, New York: Kodansha International, 1984.

Klompmakers, Inge, *Japanese Erotic Prints: Shunga by Harunobu and Koryusai,* Leiden: Hotei Publishing, 2008.

Merritt, Helen and Yamada, Nanako, *Guide to Modern Japanese Woodblock Prints 1900—1975*, Honolulu: University of Hawaii Press, 1992.

Michener, James A., *The Hokusai Sketch-Books: Selections from the Manga*, Tokyo and Rutland, Vermont: Charles E. Tuttle, 1958.

______ (with notes on the prints by Richard Lane), *Japanese Prints: From the Early Masters to the Modern*, Tokyo and Rutland, Vermont: Charles E. Tuttle, 1959.

Narazaki, Muneshige (English adaptation by C. H. Mitchell), *The Japanese Print: Its Evolution and Essence*, Tokyo: Kodansha International, 1966.

Roberts, Laurance P., *A Dictionary of Japanese Artists: Painting, Sculpture, Ceramics, Prints, Lacquer*, Tokyo: Weatherhill, 1976.

Salter, Rebecca, *Japanese Woodblock Printing*, London: A. C. Black and Honolulu: University of Hawaii Press, 2001.

Stephens, Amy Reigle (ed.), *The New Wave: Twentieth Century Japanese Prints from the Robert O. Muller Collection*, London: Bamboo Publishing, 1993.

Strange, Edward F., *The Color-Prints of Hiroshige*, London: Cassell and Company, 1925.

______, *Japanese Color Prints*, London: Wyman and Sons, 1908.

Uhlenbeck, Chris and Winkel, Margarita (eds), *Japanese Erotic Fantasies: Sexual Imagery of the Edo Period*, Leiden: Hotei Publishing, 2005.

Acknowledgments

In initial discussions with the publisher Eric Oey regarding the compilation of this book, he expressed concern over my inability to use a computer. I was not at all worried. I told him that Tolstoy had written *War and Peace* with a quill and I, at least, was in the possession of fountain pens. I also knew that there were people who would be able to help me produce the necessary computer disks from my handwritten manuscript.

My first assistant was Ms Nguyen Thi Diu in Hanoi, who has given me unstinting support throughout this whole project. Ms Michiko Yano, who took over from her, not only typed the text for me but also corrected any mis-takes in my translation and interpre-tation of the Japanese script on the prints. Finally, there was the enormous assistance of Ms Kayoko Shimokawa, who organized the compilation of the illustrations required for the text— and also managed me when I became confused over the sheer volume of illustrations we had to assemble for the book. I am most grateful for the wonderful assistance of these three women.

I also owe special thanks to David and Ken Caplan, father and son owners of Mita Arts Gallery, one of the world's leading dealers of Japanese woodblock prints. This book would never have come to fruition without their support. Their knowledge of prints and their willingness to loan me items from their collection to illustrate this book are very much appreciated. Ken Caplan answered my numerous questions almost daily and always with a smile.

I am also grateful to the Adachi Institute of Woodblock Prints who allowed me access to their reprints of *ukiyo-e* masterpieces and also provided the photographs of master woodblock craftsmen at work.

It was most fortunate that I was able to locate an original *Darani Sutra* in the collection of Mr Akira Yagi, who allowed it to be photographed and was most helpful in answering my questions. My old friend Mr Ryo Kami assisted me in photographing the scroll, as well as the original Kuniyoshi block from my collection.

A special thanks goes to Mr Masaki Kasuya, my colleague, who took time off from his busy schedule to photograph the numerous pages from the illustrated books (*e-hon*) in my personal collection.

The *Hokusai Manga* was loaned to me for photography purposes by Mr Hara Shobo, an established *ukiyo-e* dealer in Jinbo-cho, Tokyo, to whom I am also very grateful.

Finally, I owe a great deal of thanks to Mrs Noor Azlina Yunus who was not only my editor but advised me in putting this text into readable form.

If I have left anyone out, my sincere apologies. This book has been a great adventure in learning.

"Books to Span the East and West"

Tuttle Publishing was founded in 1832 in the small New England town of Rutland, Vermont [USA]. Our core values remain as strong today as they were then—to publish best-in-class books which bring people together one page at a time. In 1948, we established a publishing outpost in Japan—and Tuttle is now a leader in publishing English-language books about the arts, languages and cultures of Asia. The world has become a much smaller place today and Asia's economic and cultural influence has grown. Yet the need for meaningful dialogue and information about this diverse region has never been greater. Over the past seven decades, Tuttle has published thousands of books on subjects ranging from martial arts and paper crafts to language learning and literature—and our talented authors, illustrators, designers and photographers have won many prestigious awards. We welcome you to explore the wealth of information available on Asia at **www.tuttlepublishing.com.**

Index

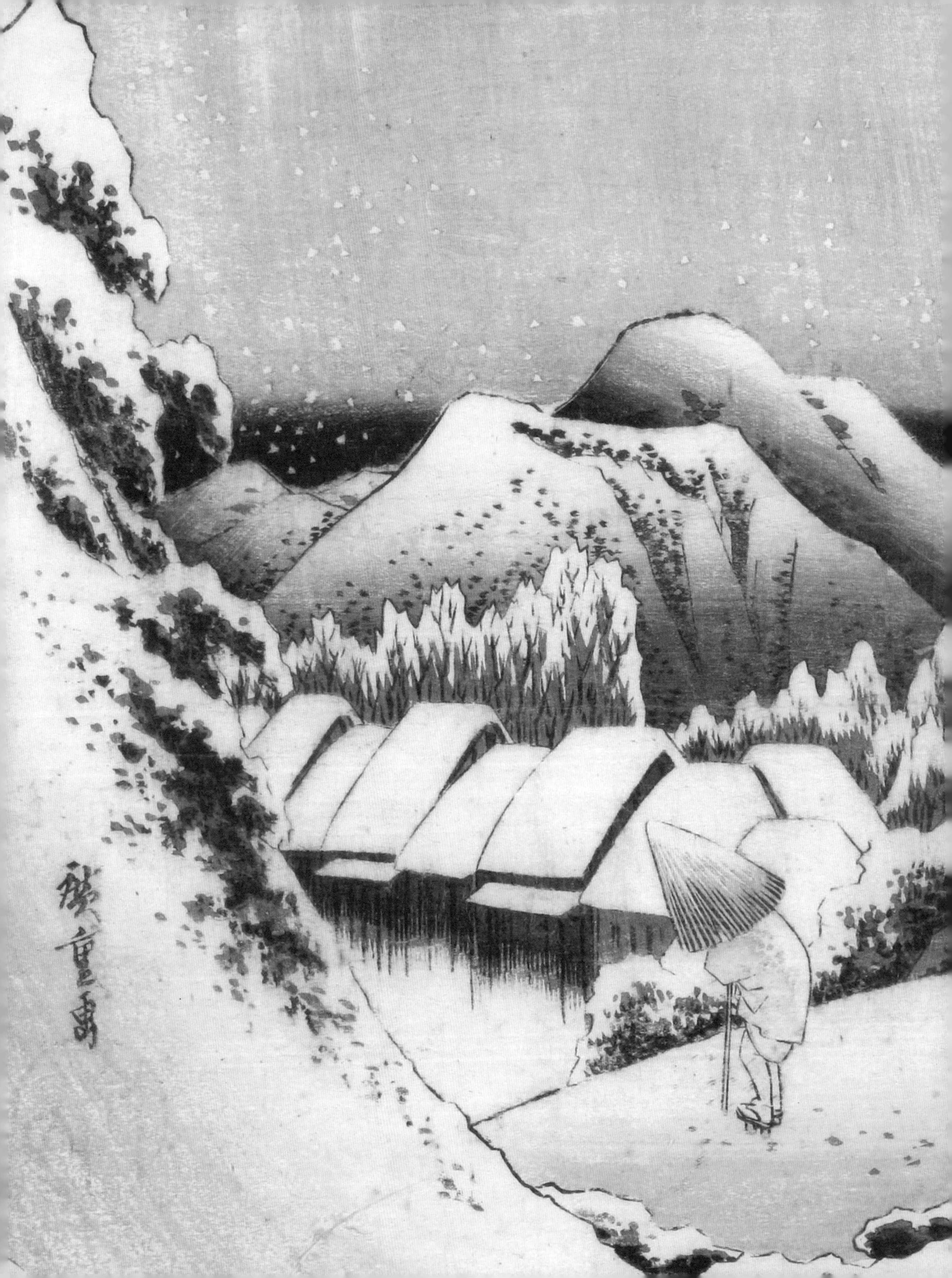
廣重画